ADVANCED COMPOSITION:

A Book of Models for Writing

HERITAGE EDITION

Complete Course

RELATED SERIES

English Grammar and Composition, First Course through
   Complete Course

Composition: Models and Exercises, First Course through
   Fifth Course

THE AUTHORS

John E. Warriner has taught English for 32 years in junior
and senior high schools and in college. He is chief author of
the *English Grammar and Composition* series, coauthor of the
English Workshop series, and general editor of the *Composition: Models and Exercises* series.

Richard M. Ludwig, who received his Ph.D. from Harvard
University, is Professor of English and Assistant University
Librarian for Rare Books and Special Collections at Princeton
University. His publications include *Aspects of American Poetry, Letters of Ford Madox Ford, Dr. Panofsky and Mr. Tarkington,* and *Literary History of the United States* (with Robert
E. Spiller and others).

Francis X. Connolly was, until his death, Professor of English
at Fordham University, where he received his Ph.D. Among
his publications are *Poetry: Its Power and Wisdom, A Rhetoric
Case Book, The Types of Literature, The Sentence in Context*
(with Donald Sears), *Harbrace College Handbook* (with John
Hodges), and the Classic Edition of *Adventures in Reading*
(coeditor).

ADVANCED COMPOSITION:

A Book of Models for Writing

Heritage Edition

Complete Course

JOHN E. WARRINER

RICHARD M. LUDWIG

FRANCIS X. CONNOLLY

HARCOURT BRACE JOVANOVICH

New York   Chicago   San Francisco   Atlanta   Dallas   *and*   London

ACKNOWLEDGMENTS:

For permission to reprint copyrighted material, grateful acknowledgment is made to the following sources:

American Association for the Advancement of Science: "Between Two Extremes" by Joseph Turner from *Science,* Vol. 131, p. 1013, 8 April 1960.

American Council of Nationalities Service: "Chee's Daughter" by Juanita Platero and Siyowan Miller from *Common Ground* 8, Winter, 1948.

The Atlantic Monthly: "Invisible Death" by Clark Van Fleet. Copyright © 1964, by The Atlantic Monthly Company, Boston, Mass.

Mr. James Baldwin: "The Creative Process" by James Baldwin.

Mr. John Ciardi and Saturday Review: "Robert Frost: The Way to the Poem" by John Ciardi, from *Saturday Review of Literature,* April 12, 1958.

Trustees of Columbia University in the City of New York: "Science and the Humanities," from *If You Don't Mind My Saying So* by Joseph Wood Krutch (New York, William Sloane Associates, 1964).

Curtis Brown, Ltd.: "R.M.S. *Titanic*" by Hanson Baldwin. Copyright © 1933 by Harper & Row, Publishers, Incorporated; © re-

CONTENTS

INTRODUCTION   1

PART ONE: DESCRIPTION   7

1. Primarily Subjective Experience   12

    John Updike, *Three Boys*   12
    Laurie Lee, *A Winter Treat*   23
    Thomas Sancton, *The Silver Horn*   34
    Ruth McKenney, *A Loud Sneer for Our
      Feathered Friends*   49
    Maya Angelou, FROM *I Know Why
      the Caged Bird Sings*   60
    James Thurber, *University Days*   70

2. Primarily Objective Experience   82

    John Steinbeck, *The Turtle*   82

Jane van Lawick-Goodall, *First
    Observations*   89
Edwin Way Teale, *Bird of Freedom*   100
James Ramsey Ullman, *Kilimanjaro!*   117
Hanson W. Baldwin, *R.M.S.* Titanic   135

PART TWO: EXPOSITION   157

3. Elementary Exposition: Definition   160

Two Dictionary Entries   161
An Encyclopedia Entry   163
An Entry in H. W. Fowler's Modern English
    Usage   164
Richard D. Altick, *Newspaperese*   168
Gerard H. Matthes, *Quicksand*   172

4. Elementary Exposition: Process   180

Margaret Mead, *Living with the Natives of
    Melanesia*   181
E. G. F. Sauer, *Celestial Navigation
    by Birds*   195

5. Reports and Analyses   208

McCandlish Phillips, *Lone Sailor Is Back, Recounts
    Perils*   210
Joseph Durso, *Aaron Hits 715th, Passes
    Babe Ruth*   215
Scott Carpenter, *The Great Secret*   219
William L. Laurence, *Dawn over Zero*   237
S. I. Hayakawa, *The Language of Reports*   250
Arthur C. Clarke, *The Secret of the Sun*   270
Alex Haley, *Search for an Ancestor*   283
Loren C. Eiseley, *The Bird and
    the Machine*   297

6. The Critical Essay: Society   310

Eric Sevareid, *The Dark of the Moon*   311
C. P. Snow, *The Future of Man*   316
Virginia Woolf, *Professions for Women*   327
James Baldwin, *The Creative Process*   336

7. The Critical Essay: Literature   345

J. B. Priestley, Macbeth: *An Afterword*   346
John Ciardi, *Robert Frost: The Way
   to the Poem*   357
Letty C. Pogrebin, *Girls' Liberation*   374
Cleanth Brooks and Robert Penn Warren,
   "Araby": An Interpretation   383

8. The Informal Essay   391

James Thurber, *How to Name a Dog*   392
E. B. White, *A Report in Spring*   401
Joyce Maynard, *"I Remember . . ."*   410
Joseph Campbell, *The Moon Walk*   417
William K. Zinsser, *Verel Modacrylic and
   Mr. Inside Floormat*   425

PART THREE: ARGUMENT AND
PERSUASION   437

9. Argument and Persuasion   438

Joseph Turner, *Between Two Extremes*   440
Philip Wylie, *Science Has Spoiled
   My Supper*   444
Jeffrey Schrank, *Mythology Today*   456
The New Yorker, Two Stories   473
Joseph Wood Krutch, *Science and the
   Humanities*   478

Richard L. Neuberger and Harley B. Markham,
   Outdoor Advertising: Two Points of View   492
Clark C. Van Fleet, *Invisible Death*   511

PART FOUR: NARRATION   525

10. Simple Narrative, First Person   530

James Joyce, *Araby*   530

11. Simple Narrative, Third Person   541

Eudora Welty, *A Worn Path*   541
Juanita Platero and Siyowin Miller,
   Chee's Daughter   555

12. Narrative and Characterization   575

Katherine Mansfield, *Miss Brill*   575

13. Narrative and Theme   586

Walter Van Tilburg Clark, *The Portable
   Phonograph*   586

GLOSSARY   601

STYLE SHEETS   606

INDEX   610

INTRODUCTION

How this book will help you to write better

The purpose of this book is to improve writing. We learn to write better in three ways: (1) by studying sentence structure, mechanics, and organization; (2) by reading widely; and (3) by writing and rewriting. This book provides you with many different types of good prose to examine and to use as models and suggests many techniques for you to imitate and topics for you to write about.

The essays and stories that follow are divided for your convenience into four parts: Description, Exposition, Argument and Persuasion, and Narration. As you come to each of the four parts, you will find first a general discussion of what is meant by "description" or "exposition" or "narration," and then, in the chapters that follow, a variety of models to illustrate the characteristics of the type of writing. As you read each model, examine it to see what the writer's purpose is, how the writer has handled the material, how the writer commands the reader's attention. The critical "Analysis," the "Questions on Technique," and the suggested "Techniques to Imitate" which follow most selections will guide you in your study.

You will find that most of the rhetorical terms used in the analyses are defined in context where they first occur. When a rhetorical term recurs, it is marked with a circle, thus: °, which directs you to the Glossary on page 601 for explanation. Here all rhetorical terms used in the text are listed in alphabetical order. They are defined in more detail than in the text itself and illustrated with additional examples. Difficult words, proper names, and allusions occurring in the models are also marked with a circle, referring you to a footnote which explains how the author is using the term or what the reference means. Words marked with an asterisk, thus: *, are suggested additions to your vocabulary. Look these words up in a dictionary and memorize their meanings. They, together with frequently used words marked with °, are repeated in a brief section called "Add to Your Vocabulary" after the model.

After you have carefully studied a model, you are ready to write. Suggestions for writing follow the questions on content and technique. Many of the models deal with topics about which you yourself have ideas, or they may remind you of experiences of your own. As you try your hand at an expository or a descriptive or a narrative or an argumentative piece, apply the technique you observed in the model. This does not mean that you should imitate slavishly the author whose piece you have studied. But every good writer, regardless of style, employs certain techniques which the models in this book exemplify, and which you too must master if you would learn to write well. These techniques are highlighted by the "Questions on Technique" and the "Techniques to Imitate."

Writing means planning

In undertaking any writing assignment, you will want to progress by several stages. You will not want to plunge into your subject at once, uncertain of where you are going. If you do this, your essay will be built on shifting ground, a house of words with a weak foundation. Suppose, for example, that your assignment is to describe a memorable personal experience. As a subject you have chosen your first journey alone away from home. As a working title you have chosen "Stranger on a Train." How shall you begin?

First, you will want to recall and make notes on *specific* details: how old were you, where were you going, why, how long was the journey, what happened? How did things in the train look, feel, smell, sound? Your title at first glance suggests *you* were the stranger, since it was your first journey by yourself; but you have, perhaps, someone else in mind: the man in the derby who asked to share your seat on the train. You will need to recall *more* specific details: who was he, what did he look like, what was he carrying, why were you suspicious of his behavior? Stage one, then, is the assembling of your material: who, when, what, where. These rough notes are a beginning.

Second, you will want to decide in what order you will use this material. You may organize it chronologically, progressing from your leaving home to your arrival at your destination. Or you may begin in the middle of the incident with the stranger walking toward you down the aisle. Or you may organize the composition not as a story, but as an essay, beginning with why this event was memorable and going on to describe the event and its effect on you. No matter which approach, which ordering of events you choose, a complete outline or plan is of great importance. You must have your conclusion clearly in mind before you begin writing.

Third, you need to decide where your main emphasis will lie. Although you are writing in the first person, is this a story about you, about the stranger, or about a journey? Let us suppose the man in the derby is the center of interest. You will want, therefore, to focus attention on him fairly soon. You cannot afford to waste words on unimportant details if your reader is to *see* this stranger, to *feel* your reaction to what happens after he sits down beside you and begins to talk. Following your outline will keep all details in the right order. You must also decide in advance which detail is to be the center of the composition.

Writing means thinking

All these steps involve clear thinking. In fact, good writing begins with clear thinking. It is impossible to separate the two processes. That is not to say that all writers elaborately outline their work before they put words on paper. Professional writers are able to organize their source material rapidly and concisely, sometimes out of sheer force of habit. But these professionals have had practice in establishing the primary ideas in their writing, in arranging their sentences for strongest emphasis, in cutting away all unnecessary words and phrases. Much of their outlining is done mentally. Clear thinking and deep concentration are habitual with them.

PART ONE

DESCRIPTION

Perhaps the simplest kind of writing we can attempt is descriptive writing. Description tells how something appears to a writer's senses. Description usually tells what something looks like. It may also tell what it sounds like, or even smells like. It may tell if something has taste and texture. Description may communicate a definite feeling that something is pleasant, or that it is repulsive. Descriptive writing does not tell a story or explain how to make vegetable soup: when writers use description, they are simply trying to communicate how they have perceived something through their senses. Description, of course, may be used as *part* of a story or of an explanation.

Careful observation

Good descriptive writing begins with careful observation of details. Putting these details into your writing does not mean a mere heaping up of adjectives. One precise adjective will serve far better than four carelessly chosen. In fact, nouns and verbs are more important to descriptive writing than adjectives and adverbs, and they, too, need to be selected carefully if we are to give the reader an accurate impression of what we see and hear. Our conversation is generally repetitive; our writing should not be. When our friends listen to a description of a mountain lake, they have the advantage of our gestures, inflections, and facial expressions to augment our words. They can *see* the log cabin, the rocky path down to the dock, the gold shimmer on the water at sunset because we have used more than words to describe them. When we come to write that description, in a letter or a diary, words alone must re-create the impression. They must *show* us as well as *tell* us.

Appeals to all senses

How do professional writers develop atmosphere and impressions through descriptive writing? How do they make us not only *see* but use our other senses as well?

Let us look at the opening paragraph of a novel. The English novelist Joseph Conrad begins *Lord Jim* with a primarily visual description of the hero.

> He was an inch, perhaps two, under six feet, power-fully built, and he advanced straight at you with a slight stoop of the shoulders, head forward and a fixed from-under stare, which made you think of a charging bull. His voice was deep, loud, and his manner displayed a kind of dogged self-assertion which had nothing aggressive in it. It seemed a necessity, and it was directed apparently as much at himself as at anybody else. He was spotlessly neat, appareled in immaculate white from shoes to hat, and in the various Eastern ports where he got his living as ship-chandler's water-clerk he was very popular.

Conrad uses common words to create an effective first impression. A "fixed from-under stare" is a simple but memorable way of indicating bullishness in a man. To have Jim's loud voice "directed apparently as much at himself as at anybody else" is the first subtle indication of character in an otherwise physical portrait. Conrad will have much more to say about Jim's psychological qualities as the story unravels. For the moment he wants simply to *show* us the man. Dressed "in immaculate white from shoes to hat" he is a great contrast to the hurly-burly of the docks on which he works.

But *seeing* is not the whole problem. Good descriptive writing uses all the senses, and it extends naturally to places, emotions, and experiences as well as to persons. In *A Walker in the City,* Alfred Kazin recalls his childhood in Brownsville, in east Brooklyn. As he describes his mother's kitchen, "the warm odor of a coffeecake baking in the oven" pervades his memory. It is the expected detail. But as he continues, another odor, more unusual, identifies another member of his family.

My great moment came at six, when my father returned from work, his overalls smelling faintly of turpentine and shellac, white drops of silver paint still gleaming on his chin. Hanging his overcoat in the long dark hall that led into our kitchen, he would leave in one pocket a loosely folded copy of the New York *World;* and then everything that beckoned to me from that other hemisphere of my brain beyond the East River would start up from the smell of fresh newsprint and the sight of the globe on the front page. It was a paper that carried special associations for me with Brooklyn Bridge. They published the *World* under the green dome on Park Row overlooking the bridge; the fresh salt air of New York harbor lingered for me in the smell of paint and damp newsprint in the hall. I felt that my father brought the outside straight into our house with each day's copy of the *World*.

The English novelist C. S. Forester writes that he was "brought up in the wrong part of London, the dull part where nothing ever happened," yet in his essay "Hornblower's London," he makes Peckham Road, in south London, sound like a feast for a small boy's senses.

Peckham Road in those days was a wonderful place (and I suppose still is to little boys not yet in their teens). It was incredibly noisy; the steel-tired wheels of the cart rumbled like thunder over the granite setts ° and macadam, and the trampling of the horses added to the din. The horses added considerably to the dirt as well; on a rainy day the vast hoofs of the dray horses, coming down ponderously into the puddles, would splash a loathsome mixture all about, sometimes as high as the upper windows. . . . But the horse trams disappeared quite early in the century—1905 would be my guess. . . . Thereafter electric trams sailed up and down the Peckham Road, singing what to a little boy were magnificent melodies as they boomed along; at night they were like great ships of light cleaving a way through the darkness.

setts: squared paving stones, usually granite.

From rumbling carts to singing trolley cars—Forester slips out of one era and into another through a simple auditory description.

Other examples of descriptive writing come to mind: the now famous opening paragraph of *Moby-Dick* in which Melville describes Ishmael's state of mind and why it leads him to sea again; the nineteenth chapter of *The Adventures of Huckleberry Finn* in which Mark Twain makes us see and hear the Mississippi River at dawn just as Huck saw it; the wooden jail with "rust on the ponderous ironwork of its oaken door" in the opening chapter of Hawthorne's *The Scarlet Letter*. But the list is unending. Every good writer uses description.

Dominant impression

In the selections which follow under the general heading of description, the writers wish to tell us what something looked like or how it felt or what it meant, what it was worth. They approach their material differently, and so it is convenient to divide them into two groups. The selections in Chapter 1 concern personal or subjective experience. The writers use the first person pronoun, as we would expect. It is natural to write about our childhood or adolescence in this way. The selections in Chapter 2 concern more nearly objective or impersonal experience, although complete objectivity is difficult to find outside the laboratory. Writers choose the pronouns, the vocabulary, and the style which best fit their intentions. Here again the division is not absolute. Just as narrative and descriptive techniques merge at times, so does subjectivity merge with objectivity. What is important for you to remember is not what category your writing falls into but what dominant impression you wish to create. Once you have chosen your subject and your approach, you are ready to arrange in some kind of order the significant details. All of the selections that follow are full of vivid, memorable impressions.

1

PRIMARILY SUBJECTIVE EXPERIENCE

JOHN UPDIKE

Three Boys

Novelist and poet John Updike remembers his home-town, Shillington, Pennsylvania, as a stable, healthy community for a young person to grow up in. "My boy-hood," he writes, "was spent in a world made tranquil by two invisible catastrophes: the Depression and World War II. Between 1932, when I was born, and 1945, when we moved away, the town of Shillington changed, as far as I could see, very little." When he came to write his popular novel *The Centaur* (1963), this town, its school buildings, its movie house and alleys and vacant lots formed the backdrop for his fiction.

In a long essay called "Boyhood in the 1940's," Up-dike describes in close detail his family, neighbors, class-mates, and friends. In the section of the essay printed here, three of these friends remain anonymous; but we soon realize that names are unimportant. How Updike reacted to his friends, as a child and later as an adult reminiscing, is the vital part of his description. We glimpse a fourth boy in this recollection: the author himself. As you read his reminiscence, do not lose sight of him.

1 A, *B,* and *C,* I'll say, in case
they care. *A* lived next door; he *loomed* next door, rather.
He seemed immense—a great wallowing fatso stuffed with
possessions; he was the son of a full-fashioned knitter.° He
seemed to have a beer-belly—solid, portentous,* proud.
After several generations beer-bellies may become congenital.* Also his face had no features; it was just a blank
ball on his shoulders. He used to call me "Ostrich," after
Disney's Ollie Ostrich. My neck was not very long; the
name seemed horribly unfair; it was its injustice that made
me cry. But nothing I could say, or scream, would make
him stop. And I still, now and then sometimes—in reading, say, a book review by one of the apple-cheeked
savants ° of the quarterlies or one of the pious gremlins
who manufacture puns for *Time*—get the old sensations:
my ears close up, my eyes go warm, my chest feels thin as
an eggshell, my voice churns silently in my stomach. From
A I received my first impression of the smug, chinkless,
irresistible *power* of stupidity; it is the most powerful force
on earth. It says "Ostrich" often enough, and the universe
crumbles.
2   *A* was more than a boy, he was a force-field ° that
could manifest itself in many forms, that could take the
wiry, disconsolate shape of wide-mouthed, tiny-eared boys
who would now and then beat me up on the way back from
school. I did not greatly mind being beaten up, though I
resisted it. For one thing, it firmly involved me, at least
during the beating, with the circumambient * humanity
that so often seemed evasive. Also, the boys who applied
the beating were misfits, periodic flunkers, who wore
knickers whose knees had lost the corduroy ribbing and
men's shirts with the top button buttoned—this last an
infallible * sign of deep poverty. So that I felt there was

full-fashioned knitter: a person who runs a knitting machine designed to produce articles of clothing, especially hosiery, that con-
form to the body lines of the wearer.
savants: learned people.
force-field: a region of space in which magnetic or electric
forces are operating.

some justice, some condonable * revenge, being applied
with their fists to this little teacher's son. And then there
was the delicious alarm of my mother and grandmother
when I returned home bloody, bruised, and torn. My father
took the attitude that it was making a boy of me, an
attitude I dimly shared. He and I both were afraid of me
becoming a sissy—he perhaps more afraid than I.
3   When I was eleven or so I met *B*. It was summer and
I was down at the playground. He was pushing a little
tank with moving rubber treads up and down the hills in
the sandbox. It was a beautiful little toy, mottled with
camouflage green; patriotic manufacturers produced
throughout the war millions of such authentic miniatures
which we maneuvered with authentic, if miniature, hate.
Drawn by the toy, I spoke to him; though taller and a
little older than I, he had my dull straight brown hair and
a look of being also alone. We became fast friends. He
lived up the street—toward the poorhouse, the east part
of the street, from which the little winds of tragedy blew.
He had just moved from the Midwest, and his mother was
a widow. Besides wage war, we did many things together.
We played marbles for days at a time, until one of us had
won the other's entire coffee-canful. With jigsaws we cut
out of plywood animals copied from comic books. We
made movies by tearing the pages out of Big Little Books
and coloring the drawings and pasting them in a strip,
and winding them on toilet-paper spools, and making a
cardboard carton a theater. We rigged up telephones, and
racing wagons, and miniature cities, using orange crates
and cigar boxes and peanut-butter jars and such potent
debris. We loved Smokey Stover ° and were always saying
"Foo." We had an intense spell of Monopoly.° He called
me "Uppy"—the only person who ever did so. I remember
once, knowing he was coming down that afternoon to my

Smokey Stover: a comic-strip character with a brash sense of
humor.
Monopoly: a board game in which the players buy and sell
real estate. The winner gains the monopoly by forcing his opponents into bankruptcy.

house to play Monopoly, in order to show my joy I set up the board elaborately, with the Chance and Community Chest cards fanned painstakingly, like spiral staircases. He came into the room, groaned, "Uppy, what are you doing?" and impatiently scrabbled the cards together in a sensible pile. The older we got, the more the year between us told, and the more my friendship embarrassed him. We fought. Once, to my horror, I heard myself taunting him with the fact that he had no father. The unmentionable, the unforgivable. I suppose we patched things up, children do, but nothing was quite right after that. He had a long, pale, serious face, with buck teeth, and is probably an electronics engineer somewhere now, doing secret government work.

4   So through *B* I first experienced the pattern of friendship. There are three stages. First, acquaintance: we are new to each other, make each other laugh in surprise, and demand nothing beyond politeness. The death of the one would startle the other, no more. It is a pleasant stage, a stable stage; on austere rations of exposure it can live a lifetime, and the two parties to it always feel a slight gratification upon meeting, will feel vaguely confirmed in their human state. Then comes intimacy; now we laugh before two words of the joke are out of the other's mouth, because we know what he will say. Our whole two beings seem marvelously joined, from our toes to our heads, along tingling points of agreement; everything we venture is right; everything we put forth lodges in a corresponding socket in the frame of the other. The death of the one would grieve the other. To be together is to enjoy a mounting excitement, a constant echo and amplification. It is an ecstatic and unstable stage, bound of its own agitation to tip into the third: revulsion. One or the other makes a misjudgment; presumes; puts forth that which does not meet agreement. Sometimes there is an explosion; more often the moment is swallowed in silence, and months pass before its nature dawns. Instead of dissolving, it grows. The mind, the throat, are clogged; forgiveness, forgetfulness, that have arrived so often, fail. Now everything jars and is distasteful; the betrayal, perhaps a tiny fraction in itself, has inverted the tingling column of agreement, made all pluses minuses. Everything about the other is hateful, despicable; yet he cannot be dismissed. We have confided in him too many minutes, too many words; he has those minutes and words as hostages, and his confidences are embedded in us where they cannot be scraped away, and even rivers of time cannot erode them completely, for there are indelible stains. Now—though the friends may continue to meet, and smile, as if they had never trespassed beyond acquaintance—the death of the one would please the other.

5   An unhappy pattern to which *C* is an exception. He was my friend before kindergarten, he is my friend still. I go to his home now, and he and his wife serve me and my wife with alcoholic drinks and slices of excellent cheese on crisp crackers, just as twenty years ago he served me with treats from his mother's refrigerator. He was a born host, and I a born guest. Also, he was intelligent. If my childhood's brain, when I look back at it, seems a primitive mammal, a lemur ° or shrew,° his brain was an angel whose visitation was widely hailed as wonderful. When in school he stood to recite, his cool rectangular forehead glowed. He tucked his right hand into his left armpit and with his left hand mechanically tapped a pencil against his thigh. His answers were always correct. He beat me at spelling bees and, in another sort of competition, when we both collected Big Little Books, he outbid me for my supreme find (in the attic of a third boy), the first Mickey Mouse. I can still see that book, I wanted it so badly, its paper tan with age and its drawings done in Disney's primitive style, when Mickey's black chest is naked like a child's and his eyes are two nicked oblongs. Losing it was perhaps a lucky blow; it began to wean me away from any hope of ever having possessions.

6   *C* was fearless. He deliberately set fields on fire; he engaged in rock-throwing duels with tough boys. One

---

lemur: a mammal allied to the monkey, with a muzzle like a fox, and woolly fur. It lives chiefly in Madagascar.

shrew: a molelike mammal, with a long sharp snout.

afternoon he persisted in playing quoits with me although —as the hospital discovered that night—his appendix was nearly bursting. He was enterprising. He peddled magazine subscriptions door-to-door; he mowed neighbors' lawns; he struck financial bargains with his father. He collected stamps so well his collection blossomed into a stamp company that filled his room with steel cabinets and mimeograph machinery. He collected money—every time I went over to his house he would get out a little tin box and count the money in it for me: $27.50 one week, $29.95 the next, $30.90 the next—all changed into new bills nicely folded together. It was a strange ritual, whose meaning for me was: since he was doing it, I didn't have to. His money made me richer. We read Ellery Queen ° and played chess and invented board games and discussed infinity together. In later adolescence, he collected records. He liked the Goodman ° quintets but loved Fats Waller.° Sitting there in that room so familar to me, where the machinery of the Shilco Stamp Company still crowded the walls and for that matter the tin box of money might still be hiding, while my pale friend grunted softly along with that dead dark angel on "You're Not the Only Oyster in the Stew," I felt, in the best sense, patronized.* The perfect guest of the perfect host. What made it perfect was that we had spent our entire lives in Shillington. . . .

ANALYSIS

John Updike is a careful stylist. He knows how to make words work for him, and in this brief essay he can indulge in vivid descriptive language, in carefully chosen verbs and adjectives which pin his subjects to the page. There is no problem of organization or emphasis here. He

Ellery Queen: pen name of Frederic Dannay (1905–   ) and Manfred B. Lee (1905–1971), but also the name of their fictional detective hero.

Goodman: Benny Goodman (1909–   ), jazz clarinetist and bandleader.

Fats Waller: Thomas ("Fats") Waller (1904–1943), jazz pianist.

simply devotes two paragraphs to each boy, first placing them in his past, then contemplating what these friendships mean to him now.

A, B, and *C* could hardly be more different: a bully, a congenial playmate, and an organizer. Updike's treatment of *A,* the bully, is succinct, sharp, even ominous. He not only lived next door, he *loomed.* The verb suggests distortion or exaggeration, and Updike pursues the idea with a barrage of adjectives: *immense, great, wallowing, stuffed, solid, portentous, proud.* But his slang hits the target even faster: *fatso, beer-belly.* We see the little monster at once. We even see that his face is "a blank ball on his shoulders"; there is something nightmarish about this featureless bully. For *A* is more than a caricature. When Updike shifts from the langauge of the playground ("fatso") to the language of the physics lab ("force-field"), the portrait enlarges considerably. We could call this intentional exaggeration. *A* was no mere boy, he was a whole field, suggesting magnetic or electrical charges. Now it is the adult Updike recalling not only the taunts of his childhood ("Ostrich") but the powerful forces of stupidity, forces that can make the universe crumble. We sense that Updike has met *A* several times over in the course of his life.

B serves another purpose in this reminiscence. He is the playmate who exhilarates the young Updike, who inspires him to invent new games, to build a fantasy world of pure childhood joy. Notice how, contrasted with "Ostrich," the new nickname, "Uppy," suggests intimacy rather than scorn. But the intimacy was also to be broken. Updike needs only a pronoun and a verb to evoke finality: "we fought." From *B,* Updike learns "the pattern of friendship": acquaintance, intimacy, revulsion; and he devotes paragraph 4 to wise generalizations. The language here is unusually acute: "austere rations" in stage one; "tingling points of agreement" in stage two; "the betrayal . . . made all pluses minuses" in stage three. The idea of death hovering over the whole concept of friendship suddenly intensifies the subject. Updike risks straying from the subject announced in his title.

The portrait of *C,* however, returns the essay to the descriptive method. *C* was fearless, enterprising, prosperous, a generous host, a lively mind. The accumulated detail once again serves Updike well. *C's* "brain was an angel," yet his enterprises were clearly earthbound: mowing lawns, collecting stamps, inventing board games. Updike reveled in these enterprises. The two boys complemented each other: born host and born guest. And, remarkably, the two men continue the same comfortable relationship, the kind which knows no stages of development; it just is. We feel we understand *C* and what makes him thrive. *A* and *B* were only phases of Updike's childhood, but *C* is a phase of his entire life.

Questions on Content

1. How does *A* represent "the smug, chinkless, irresistible *power* of stupidity"? Why does Updike italicize the word "power"?
2. Updike taunted *B* with the fact that he had no father. Why were the taunts "the unmentionable, the unforgivable"?
3. In paragraph 4, Updike speaks of "words and minutes" confided in a friend. Why should they become "hostages" and "indelible stains"? Is the third stage of friendship inevitable?
4. What specifically keeps the friendship of Updike and *C* as steadfast as it was in childhood? What does Updike imply in his last sentence: that they are still "small town" boys; that they shared a common experience, no more; that they both live partially in the past?
5. How would you describe Updike himself from what you infer in reading this essay?

Add to Your Vocabulary

portentous, congenital, circumambient, infallible, condonable, patronized.

Questions on Technique

1. Updike calls his friends *A, B,* and *C* "in case they care." We can assume he would not want to use their real names, but would he have made his friends more immediate if he had called them, for example, Walter, Billy, and Fred?
2. Describing *A* as a "force-field that could manifest itself in many forms" is inspired writing. What details does Updike go on to supply that explain this unusual metaphor?
3. The use of proper names like Smokey Stover, Monopoly, Goodman, and Fats Waller "date" this essay. Would the decade he is writing about have been just as clear if he had written, instead, "We loved the same books, the same games, the same jazz records"?
4. Could Updike have eliminated paragraph 4 without diminishing the force of his essay? Why do you think so?
5. Does the essay need a final paragraph, or would a summary dull the edge of these portraits?

Techniques to Imitate

1. *Careful word selection—verbs and adjectives*
2. *Inclusion of many details*

1. In our Analysis of "Three Boys," we called your attention to one of the most important characteristics of Updike's writing—the great care with which he chooses his words, especially in this selection, his verbs and adjectives. We can be sure that Updike is not a hasty or a casual writer. He is not satisfied with the first or second or third word that occurs to him. Undoubtedly he works at his vocabulary, searching always for the exact word, trying a number of different words until he finds one that says most clearly what he wishes to say. Note, for example, the precision of word choice in these examples: "the smug, chinkless, irresistible *power* of stupidity," "tingling points of agreement," "To be together is to

enjoy a mounting excitement, a constant echo and amplification," "my voice churns silently in my stomach." In your own descriptive writing, try to imitate Updike's painstaking concern for the best, the most exact, word.

2. Updike also demonstrates his grasp of a technique especially important in narrative and descriptive writing. This is the inclusion of a great many carefully chosen details. For example, note how much we learn about *A*'s bullying friends from these details: "the wiry, disconsolate shape of wide-mouthed, tiny-eared boys" who were "misfits, periodic flunkers, who wore knickers whose knees had lost the corduroy ribbing and men's shirts with the top button buttoned—this last an infallible sign of deep poverty."

Another example of Updike's skillful amassing of details is his account of the things he and *B* did together: "We played marbles for days at a time, until one of us had won the other's entire coffee-canful. With jigsaws we cut out of plywood animals copied from comic books. We made movies by tearing the pages out of Big Little Books and coloring the drawings and pasting them in a strip, and winding them on toilet-paper spools, and making a cardboard carton a theater. We rigged up telephones, and racing wagons, and miniature cities, using orange crates and cigar boxes and peanut-butter jars and such potent debris." The coffee can, the Big Little Books, the orange crates, cigar boxes and peanut-butter jars are details that help us to relive Updike's childhood experience.

In your own writing, recognize, as Updike does in his, the great importance of supplying a great many revealing details.

Suggestions for Writing

1. In 300 words, describe from your own viewpoint as a child your first friend. Give the impressions that he or she made on you then.

2. Write three paragraphs in which you describe three different people. Each paragraph will concentrate on a description of one person. Try to open each paragraph with a sentence that summarizes the personality or appearance of that person, and use the rest of the paragraph for details that support or clarify what you've said. The people do not have to be drawn from actual life. It's possible to describe three absolutely distinct characters from literature you've read recently or from films you have seen. In a fourth paragraph, try to define how these three people are connected in your memory; in other words, why did you select these three?

3. One of the interesting aspects of Updike's essay—especially to people who were children during the era he describes here—is his detailed listing of the games he played with these three boys. Write a paragraph, or several paragraphs, in which you describe the games you played as a child. Be as precise as you can in describing them, and in using the names they were known by. Were some games played only during certain seasons? Were some shared only with certain people and not with others? Did you despise some of these games and like others?

LAURIE LEE

A Winter Treat

Laurie Lee is an English poet and musician who was born in the Cotswolds, in Gloucestershire. In 1959, he published his recollections of his boyhood in the west of England (called *The Edge of Day* when it appeared in this country) in which he fondly describes his little village, the country school, the Squire's Big House, and especially his own family—an intrepid mother and seven children; the father had disappeared.

One of his chapters is devoted to outings and festivals, memorable times for all children. "The year," he writes, "revolved around the village, the festivals round the year, the church round the festivals, the Squire round the church, and the village round the Squire." He gets them all into this recollection of a post-Christmas party which begins with rehearsals and anticipation. Eileen Brown is a neighbor; Marjorie is Lee's eldest sister; the Squire is the town's chief citizen. Note how every detail is seen through a small boy's eyes.

1   The Parochial Church Tea and Annual Entertainment was the village's winter treat. It took place in the schoolroom, round about Twelfth Night, and cost us a shilling to go. The Tea was an orgy of communal gluttony, in which everyone took pains to eat more than his money's worth and the helpers ate more than the customers. The Entertainment which followed, home-produced and by lamplight, provided us with sufficient catch phrases for a year.

2 Regularly, for a few weeks before the night, one witnessed the same scenes in our kitchen, the sisters sitting in various corners of the room, muttering secretly to themselves, smiling, nodding, and making lah-di-dah gestures with a kind of intent and solitary madness. They were rehearsing their sketches for the Entertainment, which I found impossible not to learn, too, so that I would be haunted for days by three nightmare monologues full of one-sided unanswered questions.

3 On the morning of the feast we got the school ready. We built a stage out of trestles and planks. Mr. Robinson was in the cloakroom slicing boiled ham, where he'd been for the last three days, and three giggling helpers were now forking the meat and slapping it into sandwiches. Outside in the yard John Barraclough had arrived and set up his old field kitchen, had broken six hurdles across his knee and filled up the boiler with water. Laid out on the wall were thirty-five teapots, freshly washed and drying in the wind. The feast was preparing; and by carrying chairs, helping with the stage, and fetching water from the spring, Jack and I made ourselves sufficiently noticeable to earn a free ticket each.

4 Punctually at six, with big eating to be done, we returned to the lighted school. Villagers with lanterns streamed in from all quarters. We heard the bubbling of water in Barraclough's boiler, smelt the sweet woodsmoke from his fire, saw his red face lit like a turnip lamp ° as he crouched to stoke up the flames.

5 We lined up in the cold, not noticing the cold, waiting for the doors to open. When they did, it was chins and boots and elbows, no queues; we just fought our way in. Lamplight and decorations had transformed the schoolroom from a prison into a banqueting hall. The long trestle-tables were patterned with food: fly-cake, brown buns, ham sand-

turnip lamp: the hollow rind of a turnip employed as a lantern.

wiches. The two stoves were roaring, reeking of coke. The helpers had their teapots charged. We sat down stiffly and gazed at the food; fidgeted, coughed and waited. . . .

6 The stage curtains parted to reveal the Squire, wearing a cloak and a deer-stalking hat. He cast his dim, wet eyes round the crowded room, then sighed and turned to go. Somebody whispered from behind the curtain. "Bless me!" said the Squire, and came back.

7 "The Parochial Church Tea!" he began, then paused. "Is with us again . . . I suggest. And Entertainment. Another year! Another year comes round! . . . When I see you all gathered together here—once more—when I see— when I think . . . And here you all are! When I see you here—as I'm sure you all are—once again . . . It comes to me, friends!—how time—how you—how all of us here —as it were . . ." His moustache was quivering, tears ran down his face, he groped for the curtains and left.

8 His place was taken by the snow-haired Vicar, who beamed weakly upon us all.

9 "What is the smallest room in the world?" he asked.

10 "A mushroom!" we bawled, without hesitation.

11 "And the largest, may I ask?"

12 "ROOM FOR IMPROVEMENT!"

13 "You know it," he muttered crossly. Recovering himself, he folded his hands: "And now, O bountiful Father . . ."

14 We barked through grace and got our hands on the food and began to eat it in any old order. Cakes, buns, ham, it didn't matter at all, we just worked from one plate to the next. Folk by the fires fanned themselves with sandwiches, a joker fried ham on the stove, steaming brown teapots passed up and down, and we were so busy there was small conversation. Through the lighted windows we could see snow falling, huge feathers against the dark. "It's old Mother Hawkins a-plucking her geese!" cried someone; an excellent omen. Twelfth Night, and old Mother Hawkins at work, up in the sky with her birds; we loosened our belts and began to nod at each other; it was going to be a year of fat.

15 We had littered the tables with our messy leavings of cake crumbs and broken meat; some hands still went through the motions of eating, but clearly we'd had enough. The Vicar rose to his feet again, and again we thanked the Lord. "And now, my friends, comes the—er—feast for the soul. If you would care to—ah—take the air a moment, willing hands are waiting to clear the hall and prepare for the—um—Entertainment. . . ."

16 We crowded outside and huddled in the snow while the tables were taken away. Inside, behind curtains, the actors were making up—and my moment, too, was approaching. The snow whirled about me and I began to sweat; I wanted to run off home. Then the doors reopened and I crouched by the stove, shivering and chattering with nerves. The curtains parted and the Entertainment began, with a comic I neither saw nor heard. . . .

17 "For the next item, ladies and gentlemen, we have an instrumental duet, by Miss Brown and—er—young Laurie Lee."

18 Smirking with misery I walked to the stage. Eileen's face was as white as a minim.° She sat at the piano, placed the music crooked, I straightened it, it fell to the ground. I groped to retrieve it; we looked at one another with hatred; the audience was still as death. Eileen tried to give me an A, but struck B instead, and I tuned up like an ape threading needles. At last we were ready, I raised my fiddle; and Eileen was off like a bolting horse. I caught her up in the middle of the piece—which I believe was a lullaby —and after playing the repeats, only twice as fast, we just stopped, frozen motionless, spent.

19 Some hearty stamping and whistling followed, and a shout of "Give us another!" Eileen and I didn't exchange a glance, but we loved each other now. We found the music of "Danny Boy" and began to give it all our emotion, dawdling dreamily among the fruitier chords and scampering over the high bits; till the audience joined in, using their hymn-singing voices, which showed us the utmost re-

minim: a provincial expression for minnow, a tiny, silvery white fish.

spect. When it was over I returned to my seat by the stove, my body feeling smooth and beautiful. Eileen's mother was weeping into her hat, and so was mine, I think. . . .

20 Now I was free to become one of the audience, and the Entertainment burgeoned * before me. What had seemed to me earlier as the capering of demons now became a spectacle of human genius. Turn followed turn in variety and splendor. Mr. Crosby, the organist, told jokes and stories as though his very life depended on them, trembling, sweating, never pausing for a laugh, and rolling his eyes at the wings for rescue. We loved him, however, and wouldn't let him go, while he grew more and more hysterical, racing through monologues, gabbling songs about shrimps, skipping, mopping, and jumping up and down, as though humoring a tribe of savages.

21 Major Doveton came next, with his Indian banjo, which was even harder to tune than my fiddle. He straddled a chair and began wrestling with the keys, cursing us in English and Urdu.° Then all the strings broke, and he snarled off the stage and started kicking the banjo round the cloakroom. He was followed by a play in which Marjorie, as Cinderella, sat in a goose-feathered dress in a castle. While waiting for the pumpkin to turn into a coach, she sang "All alone by the telephone."

22 Two ballads came next, and Mrs. Pimbury, a widow, sang them both with astonishing spirit. The first invited us to go with her to Canada; the second was addressed to a mushroom:

> *Grow! Grow! Grow! Little mushroom, grow!*
> *Somebody wants you soon.*
> *I'll call again tomorrow morning—*
> *See!*
> *And if you've grown bigger you will just suit* ME!
> *So Grow! Grow! Grow! little mushroom—Grow!*

23 Though we'd not heard this before, it soon became part of our heritage, as did the song of a later lady. This

Urdu: official language of Pakistan.

last—the Baroness von Hodenburg—sealed our entertainment with almost professional distinction. She was a guest
star from Sheepscombe and her appearance was striking;
it enshrined all the mystery of art. She wore a loose green
gown like a hospital patient's, and her hair was red and
long. "She writes," whispered Mother. "Poems and book-
lets and that."

24   "I am going to sink you," announced this lady, "a
little ditty I convected myself. Bose vords und music, I
may say, is mine—und zey refer to ziss pleasant valleys."

25   With that she sat down, arched her beautiful back,
raised her bangled wrists over the keyboard, then ripped
off some startling runs and trills, and sang with a ringing
laugh:

> *Elfin volk come over the hill!*
> *Come und dance, just vere you vill!*
> *Brink your pipes, und brink your flutes,*
> *Brink your sveetly soundink notes!*
> *Come avay-hay! Life is gay-hay!*
> *Life—Is—Gay!*

26   We thought this song soppy, but we never forgot it.
From then on, whenever we saw the Baroness in the lanes
we used to bowl the song at her through the hedges. But
she would only stop, and cock her head, and smile dreamily
to herself. . . .

27   After these songs the night ended with slapstick; rough
stuff about babies, chaps dressed as women, broad Glouces-
ter exchanges between yokels and toffs,° with the yokels
coming off best. We ached with joy, and kicked at the
chairs; but we knew the end was coming. The Vicar got
up, proposed a vote of thanks, and said oranges would be
distributed at the gate. The National Anthem was romped
through, we all began coughing, then streamed outdoors
through the snow.

28   Back home our sisters discussed their performances

toffs: gentlemen (British slang).

till the tears dripped off their noses. But to us boys it was not over, not till tomorrow; there was still one squeeze left in the lemon. Tomorrow, very early, we'd go back to the schoolroom, find the baskets of broken food—half-eaten buns, ham coated with cake crumbs—and together we'd finish the lot.

ANALYSIS

Laurie Lee has a keen ear for dialogue. The Squire's fumbling speech is wondrous syntax (or rather lack of good sentence structure); the Vicar's is typically hesitant; the Baroness von Hodenburg's is unforgettable because we can hear her urge us to "brink your sveetly soundink notes." But good description does not depend upon dialogue. What Lee does here so successfully is to combine children's language with descriptive phrases a literate adult would use in recollecting a childhood party. His sisters made "lah-di-dah gestures"; three giggling helpers were "forking the meat and slapping it into sandwiches"; the Vicar said grace and "[we] got our hands on the food and began to eat in any old order"; Eileen and Laurie "found the music of 'Danny Boy' and began to give it all [their] emotion, dawdling dreamily among the fruitier chords and scampering over the high bits."

This is fine, colloquial (or informal, conversational) language. It brings a youthful zest to the description. And yet Lee can call the Tea "an orgy of communal gluttony," the long trestle-tables are "patterned with food," he "tunes up like an ape threading needles," Baroness von Hodenburg "sealed our entertainment with almost professional distinction"—clearly not a child's vocabulary. It is a measure of Lee's skill in writing that the two "vocabularies" do not jar. Quite clearly he is recollecting an occasion here, but we feel we are sitting with the young Laurie Lee *now*.

Even more important than Lee's vocabulary is his good sense of proportion. This story has a beginning, a middle, and an end. The author is always in control, and so we always know where we are. The first paragraph identifies the occasion, the second cites the preparation; together they make a simple introduction. The next three paragraphs start the festival. The Squire and the Vicar are, properly, the first to speak. Then comes food. Then the cleaning away of the food. Then entertainment. Note that Lee promised this order in his first sentence, when he gave us the name of the festival. We come quickly to Lee's part in the entertainment. Call it foreshortening of the description, if you wish; that is, he could well have described *all* the acts, but he chose, for emphasis on the first person narrative, to come quickly to his own. We race through the description just as Lee and Eileen raced through the music; the verbs are almost staccato, their impact swift. Then he writes that "now I was free to become one of the audience." The pace slackens, and we meander through the middle section of the story. Two paragraphs from the end Lee literally announces the end. We hear briefly of the slapstick comedy and are soon streaming "outdoors through the snow." As a coda he gives us the last squeeze of the lemon: the "half-eaten buns" and "ham coated with cake crumbs" will make a second feast tomorow. Lee has written of his festival so well we feel that we want to share the leftovers with these Cotswold boys in their schoolroom.

Questions on Content

1. Why do you suppose the entertainment takes place in the schoolroom and not in the church?
2. In what way is the time of year important to the atmosphere Lee creates?
3. What adjectives would you use to describe the humor of this story?

Add to Your Vocabulary

burgeoned. What is a trestle-table?

Questions on Technique

1. This story is written in the first person, yet Lee incorporates other "performers" and includes considerably detailed description of their contributions. Would

he have written a better story if he had described only himself and his part in the proceedings?

2. Find passages in which Lee makes effective use of sensory impressions other than those of sight. Show that they help us to experience the events fully.

3. Inspect the verbs in any of the longer paragraphs. Show that Lee achieves through the use of verbs what many writers try for adjectively. What other words might he have chosen?

4. Could we eliminate without loss the words to Mrs. Pimbury's and Baroness von Hodenburg's songs? Why do you think so?

5. If you were asked to state the dominant theme of this story, what would you say: how one boy reacted to a festival; how an English village entertains itself; how local talent performs on stage; how a small town can laugh?

Techniques to Imitate

1. *Inclusion of many details*
2. *Sensory impressions*

1. To be a competent writer of description, you must be a careful observer so that you can, like Updike and Lee, give the readers enough details to enable them to see what you saw. That Lee is a careful observer is evident from the abundance of details in his writing. In paragraph 3, for example, he includes the stage built of trestles and planks, Mr. Robinson slicing the ham, the three giggling helpers, the thirty-five teapots, the boys carrying chairs, helping with the stage, and fetching water. A less effective writer might have said simply, "Jack and I on the morning of the feast made ourselves sufficiently noticeable by helping with the preparations to earn a free ticket each," but such a general account gives no idea at all of what actually took place that morning. Note the details in his description of the duet he played with Eileen: "Smirking with misery I walked to the

stage. Eileen's face was as white as a minim. She sat at the piano, placed the music crooked, I straightened it, it fell to the ground. I groped to retrieve it; we looked at one another with hatred; the audience was still as death. Eileen tried to give me an A, but struck B instead, and I tuned up like an ape threading needles. At last we were ready, I raised my fiddle; and Eileen was off like a bolting horse. I caught her up in the middle of the piece —which I believe was a lullaby—and after playing the repeats, only twice as fast, we just stopped, frozen motionless, spent."

2. Lee's description is full of sensory impressions, and he appeals to more than one of our senses. Paragraph 4 is one example of this technique: "Punctually at six, with big eating to be done, we returned to the lighted school. Villagers with lanterns streamed in from all quarters. We heard the bubbling of water in Barraclough's boiler, smelt the sweet woodsmoke from his fire, saw his red face lit like a turnip lamp as he crouched to stoke up the flames." In paragraph 5 he writes, "The long trestle-tables were patterned with food: fly-cake, brown buns, ham sandwiches. The two stoves were roaring, reeking of coke. The helpers had their teapots charged. We sat down stiffly and gazed at the food; fidgeted, coughed and waited."

When you plan a description, take time to observe or to remember all the details in the scene and make a list of them, including even the smallest details. Then, when you have squeezed all the details from the scene, select from your list those you think will most effectively create the impression you wish to convey. Try also to make your descriptive writing effective by using sensory details that appeal to more than one of the senses. Your readers are as alert to sounds and smells as they are to visual images.

Suggestions for Writing

1. In 400 words, describe a single event that you remember well from your childhood. Do not just narrate the

action; recall the details "around" it. Try to give the impressions you had as a child.

2. When did you first "perform" before an audience? Do you remember the state of your nerves, the faces in the crowd, the response to the performance? Write a 400-word description about it.

3. There are many famous meals described in literature. One such description that you probably have read is in Washington Irving's story "The Legend of Sleepy Hollow." Perhaps you recall the meal that met the ravenous Ichabod Crane's eyes when he arrived for a party at the home of his beloved Katrina Van Tassel. Irving uses the technique that Lee uses here, the piling up of specific details about various foods spread out on the table. Write your own description of a meal—a community supper, a picnic, a barbeque. If you can't think of an actual meal, make one up. Pile up the names of the specific foods, and describe their smells, tastes, appearances, textures.

4. Laurie Lee is reveling in familiar sights and sounds, familiar to his village, that is. Describe briefly a visit you made to a *strange* place as a child and what your reactions were.

THOMAS SANCTON

The Silver Horn

Putting a Cotswold festival on stage, as it were, is somewhat more difficult than merely "turning back the pages" to recall "how it was then." Laurie Lee showed us a remarkably large number of his neighbors in a short space. Thomas Sancton, a newspaperman in his native city of New Orleans, turns this recollection of his youth into equally vivid prose even though his locale is simply a Boy Scout summer camp on a Louisiana bayou, his style is in a low key, his friends remain nameless. Sancton wants us to see and feel what he saw and felt as a young boy, but he does not parade his material as Lee does.

This is another sort of descriptive writing. We might call it descriptive reflection, for Sancton attempts to answer here, as he says, when and where it was that he "first began to believe what [he] now believe[s] about the Southern world." The temptation for most writers, on such an occasion, would be to moralize or to argue the reader into sharing a point of view, but Sancton avoids both. He is as relaxed in his writing as he was at the summer camp. When he does offer us a judgment, he does it tentatively. There is always a fine balance between the events and what they meant to him. "Little things that happened during these years," he writes, "seemed of great importance."

As you read this reminiscence, consider the tense of

the verb *seemed*. Could not Sancton also be suggesting, although indirectly, that even now, in his adult years, these little things *seem* important because he did his "first real thinking in this camp"? This descriptive essay is written in the first person. It begins as reminiscence. It quickly develops into more than that.

1   The scene is a Boy Scout summer camp, thickly grown with pines and cypress. There is a row of green clapboard cabins, with clean floors and neat double-decker bunks; there is an open field and a flag hanging still in the heavy air; and at the field's edge the land drops down a little to the dark water of a bayou. I spent five summers here, from the time I was twelve until I entered college. I did my first real living and my first real thinking in this camp.

2   And I think of it now. Like some reader of a long novel who turns back through the pages to find a forgotten part of the plot, and who comes with a flash of recognition across old scenes and dialogues, and characters who have gone out of the narrative but whose personalities and substance once filled pages and pages, I have gone turning back through the pages of my life. When was it and where was it—I have been asking—that I first began to believe what I now believe about the Southern world I left not many years ago, about Negroes, about democracy, about America, about life and death, about men and all their curious fates? This search has been long and turning. Often it has led me back to the years of my early teens and to the summers I spent in the camp.

3   I was born to the sidewalks and asphalt of the largest city and the widest street in the South. In New Orleans, broad Canal Street was never empty of speeding automobiles and streetcars, even late at night, and of people walking by, their footsteps echoing on the sidewalk. But here on the bayou another world existed. In the morning it was the strange, thin call of a bugle that broke into our sleep. Almost before we were awake we could smell the wet exercise field and the forest. Birds popped from tree to tree, plump and colorful, bluejays, mockingbirds, cardinals, flickers—Audubon had painted in these woods. Rabbits ran into the bushes. Snakes we had no fear of, long thick blue racers and speckled king snakes, slid through the weeds at our approach.

4 Standing in the wet grass, still yawning and sleepy, we took the morning exercises. Night chill was in the air, but behind our backs the sun was rising, and its warmth crept onto our shoulders. After the exercises we raced along a wagon road to the swimming pool, and as we ran up, shouting and excited, two or three startled frogs made tremendous leaps and plumped beneath the glassy surface of the water. After the swim we dried our skinny sunburned bodies and ran to the mess hall.

5 Most of us in the camp were poor boys, or boys who were almost poor. It was not a welfare camp, but the fees were low, less than a dollar a day for a camper. As a consequence it was filled with boys from modest New Orelans neighborhoods and also from the tough ones. There was always a smattering of the democratic rich: the son of the traction company president came every summer. So did his cousin from Texas, a wild, hard towhead with plenty of money and the soul of a true picaroon.° He fascinated and dominated the rest of us. He was the first colorful outlaw I ever knew. But most of the well-to-do families sent their boys to camps in the Maine woods or the North Carolina mountains. Our camp was only forty miles from the city. Department store clerks, streetcar motormen, little grocers could afford the fees.

6 We had no saddle horses, no golf course, and only a weed-grown tennis court which no one used. For diversion we fell back on nature. In the morning we performed a work detail, cutting a patch of weeds or hauling dirt in wheelbarrows to mend a road. After this we were free

picaroon: a rogue or pirate.

to swim, to paddle on the bayou in slender little Louisiana boats called pirogues, to fish for the boisterous black bass and yellow perch and fat blue catfish, and to work for our Boy Scout medals and merit badges, tracking through the grassy cut-over pine lands, cooking dough and bacon on sweet-gum spits, bandaging one another with first-aid splints.

7   These little medals and bits of colored ribbon meant a great deal to us. We wrote home enthusiastic letters about our progress, describing in detail how we had passed the tests, forwarding the comments of some eighteen-year-old camp officer as though it really mattered. Our parents, most of whom did not have very big events happening in their own lives, were just as eager and simple-hearted about these things, and one or two of the fathers were foolishly ambitious to have their sons win the highest number of merit badges in the area.

8   Little things that happened during these years seemed of great importance. I remember that in my first year at camp I wore an ill-fitting Boy Scout hat. One of the councilors, a boy five years my senior who seemed to me to belong already to the grown-up world of brilliance and authority, began, in a pleasant way, to tease me about the hat. Every morning for a week he led us to the abandoned logging road and clocked us as we walked and trotted a measured mile. My hat was anchored down by a heavy chin strap; it flopped and sailed about my head as I ran to the finish line. The boy began to laugh at me. He waved his arms and called out, "Come on, you rookie!" The other kids took it up and Rookie became my first nickname. I loved it. I tingled when someone called it out. I painted it on my belt, carved it in my packing case, inked it into my hatband, and began to sign it to my letters home. Years later when we were grown I knew this camp officer again. The gap between our ages had vanished and in real life now he seemed to me a rather colorless young lawyer. He did not remember about the hat.

9   At mealtime we ate ravenously in the mess hall. There were steaming platters of pork and beans and cabbage

and stew. As we walked to the long clapboard building
with our hair freshly combed and water glistening on our
faces, which we washed at the flowing pipe of a big artesian
well, we existed in a transport of driving hunger. In the
steamy fragrance of the mess hall we set up a clatter of
knives and forks and china, and afterward we went to our
cabins and flopped on the bunks in a state of drowsy
satisfaction. Somehow, fat never formed on our skinny
frames. We ran too much. We paddled in the boats. We
swam. We cut firewood and played softball after supper.
When there was nothing else to do we climbed in the
rafters of our cabins, trying to invent complicated monkey
swings that no one else could do. Every year some campers
broke their arms.

II

10   During those summers in camp a love grew up in me
for the rhythms of nature, for tropical rains that came
sweeping through the pines and oaks, for the fiery midday
sun, for long evenings, and the deep black nights. Great
campfires were lit beside the bayou and a rushing column
of luminous smoke and sparks ascended to the cypress
trees. Fire gleamed in the water where bass were sleeping
in the stumps. Campers wandered toward the meeting
place, their flashlights swinging in the woods. We sat about
the fire, singing, beating deep rumbling tom-toms made
of hollowed oak logs, performing an ageless repertoire of
skits and mimicry. And after these sessions one leader took
the Protestant boys and another the Catholics and, standing in the open fields, in our separate groups, we prayed
aloud.
11   My heart had strayed already from the formal, repeti-
tious praying. A towering pine tree at the field's edge made
a silhouette in the starry sky. I knew the constellations, the
Giant, the Dipper, the Bear. I looked for the two inseparable stars, Misar and Alcar, horse and rider, and sensed
the fact that Arabs named these stars a thousand years
before me, and even in my boy's ignorance I felt aware of

man's long and varied time upon the earth. I knew this night-filled wilderness had stretched beneath these stars for endless ages before Frenchmen had come in boats to build New Orleans. I thought of the Indians who had fished and hunted here, whose bones and broken pottery we sometimes found in grassy mounds. I felt worshipful of the earth, the pine tree, the night itself.

12 Sometimes we packed provisions and tents and mosquito bars and paddled down the bayou to the lake, ten miles away. The lake was a great inland finger of the Gulf of Mexico, twenty miles long, ten wide. Twenty miles below us, in prehistoric times, the mouth of the Mississippi River had built up new land, and these watery prairies had pinched off the small inland gulf and made a lake of it, but it connected still through a series of passes with the Mexican Gulf. The lake teemed with croakers, catfish, shrimp, and big blue-clawed crabs. At the northern end, where we camped, a network of tributary bayous emptied into the lake. For the last mile or so of their crooked lengths, where the brackish * water of the lake crept into the slow-moving bayous, fish and small life were abundant, bass fed in the rushes, and muskrats built their cities of the plains.

13 There was a relatively high, sandy point near the mouth of the bayou, where we camped. The sun went down red into the lake and left a long, clear twilight. A few stars came out. A salty wind blew in from the Mexican Gulf; it came out of the south every night. The breeze swept over the rushes and made small waves break on the sandy, grassy shore. There was a red beacon light on weather-beaten piles out in the lake and its long reflection shimmered in the water. We sprayed our mosquito netting with citronella ° and built up a driftwood fire and lay down on canvas bedrolls spread upon the thin, tough grass and sand. The trade wind blew through our tents throughout the night. We listened to the waves. A yellow moon came out of the gulf. Far down the lake we could see the

  citronella: a fragrant grass of southern Asia, used in making perfumes and insect repellent.

lights of a railroad bridge. We felt the beauty of this wilderness like a hunger.

14 After two days of fishing and swimming in the lake, our shoulders and faces darker from the sun, we paddled back up the winding bayou.

III

15 One summer when I was sixteen a party of us, paddling upstream to buy some candy at a crossroads store, came upon three young girls who were bathing in a sandy cove. There were four of us in the long pirogue, all of an age. For a long moment we were speechless. At last we said hello, and they answered in warm gay voices. We drifted the boat into the cove and began to speak to them. Two of the girls were sisters. The three of them had come to visit a relative who kept a fine summer lodge in the woods across the bayou from the camp. One of the sisters was fifteen and the others were seventeen. They were aglow with fresh and slender beauty, and their bathing suits were bright flags of color. Their impact upon us was overwhelming. We grew silly, tongue-tied, said foolish things we did not mean to say, shoved one another about in the boat, and finally overturned it. The loreleis ° laughed musical little laughs. They seemed unbearably beautiful. We had no idea what to do about it.

16 The girls had been at the lodge for a week. They missed their beaux in New Orleans, they missed the dating and the dancing and the music. It was a gay town in the summertime. The older girls looked upon us as children; but still—they must have reflected—we were not such children at that. The younger sister, a slender child with thick brown hair and heavily crimsoned lips, sat on the bank and regarded us with a happy open face.

17 At last we took courage and asked if we could call on them that night.

---

loreleis: In German legend, the Lorelei was a siren who lured sailors to destruction by singing from a rock on the Rhine River.

18 "Oh, yes!" they cried eagerly. Life at that moment was dazzling.

19 Making this rendevous was an impulsive thing to do, for it was midweek and we should have to steal away after taps and walk down a path without flashlights through a snake-infested lowland and—because the boats were counted and chained at nightfall—swim across the bayou, holding our clothes above our heads.

20 We crept from our cabins at ten o'clock that night and met in the pine woods. One of us intoned * a counting-out rhyme; the loser had to walk first down the path through the snake hole. He cut a long gum sapling and rattled it down the path ahead of us. We walked bunched tightly together, tense with fear, giggling at our own un-believable audacity, trembling in our eagerness. At the bayou's edge we slipped out of our shorts and shirts and sneakers and, holding them above our heads with one hand, we felt our way round the knees and along the sunken roots of a cypress tree, and pushed off into the bayou and began to swim.

21 The moon had not yet risen. We had only the sil-houettes of trees to guide us. We swam closely together, cautioning one another to silence, bursting into convulsive squeals as water lilies brushed against our bodies or when a fish broke the surface near us. We swam upstream from the camp, past two bends, and waded from the water in the cove where we had met the girls. Now we were laugh-ing with relief and excitement, and popping one another on the backsides. We scraped the glistening water from our bodies, dressed, and combed our wet hair and hurried off down the wagon path into the woods. Long ago the cove had been a landing stage for small schooners which came to load pine firewood for New Orleans.

22 The girls were waiting for us, dressed in bright print cotton dresses and wearing hair ribbons. The soft light gave age and mystery to their youthful shoulders, to their slender bodies; and, like nameless night-blooming vines in the woods about us, they bore a splendid fragrance all their own, a fragrance of youth and cleanliness and fresh cosmetics. They were playing a phonograph on the wide porch of the lodge. This was the summer of Maurice Chevalier's ° great success in American movies. The little sister sang his song, rolling her eyes, turning out her soft pink lip:

> *If ze night-ting gail*
> *Cood zing lak you . . .*

And she sang another:

> *. . . you make me feel so grand*
> *I want to hand the world to you.*
> *You seem to understand*
> *Each foolish little dream I'm dreaming, scheme I'm*
> *scheming . . .*

23 I was so in love with her I could hardly catch my breath. I was in love with the other sister too, and with their friend. All of the boys were in love with all of the girls; the girls—so they said—had crushes on each of us. Our hearts were afire.

24 We walked hand in hand down the wagon trail to the cove and built a bonfire. We stretched out on blankets, laughing, singing. We sang the songs that people always sing by rivers and campfires, "There's a Long, Long Trail A-Winding," "The Sweetheart of Sigma Chi," all the rest. We kissed the girls and they held fast to us. Before this night we had been only boys, holding hands with girls in movies, not quite sure why we pursued them and acted silly. Now, lying beneath the open sky, for the first time we understood the poignance * and the beauty of the human heritage.

25 Every night for two weeks we came to see them. And when they told us good-by the last kiss was as much a discovery as the first, and we knew that love was a thing that could never grow old. After they had gone we would steal from our cabins to sit on the back porch of

Maurice Chevalier: French-born singer and movie star.

the camp hospital, on a hill, where we could see the bayou and the cove and the woods where we had found them; and we sat there talking late into the night, like daemon lovers in the ballads of old. I never passed the cove again, even years later when I would paddle down the bayou fishing, without remembering our meetings with a suddenly racing heart. First love is unforgettable.

IV

26   I had no lessons to do in those summer months of camp life. There was plenty of time to think. I was living a communal life with other boys. Among us were embryonic bullies, scoundrels, cheats, promoters, Babbitts,° and stuffed shirts; and there were also the boys of good heart, the unselfish, the humorous, the courageous, boys who were the salt of the earth, but who, often in their later lives, would be misled and preyed upon and set against one another by the sharp ones. One and all we lived together, ate together, slept together. Our personalities clashed, fermented, or formed amalgams.° Sitting together at night in the lamplit cabins, with darkness and towering woods closing in upon us, we had our first grave talks about religion, about death, about sex. The future stretching before us was wide and fathomless. And all about us, in the grass, in the underbrush, in towering summer skies, we beheld the face of nature and the earth's wide harmonies as they had never been revealed in our city lives. At night we could stretch out upon the field, observe the stars, and grasp for the first time the fact that some were vastly deeper in space than others. In our star-study courses we heard phrases like "light years." It began to seep into the consciousness of many of us that a hundred years or the life of an individual had little meaning in the total universe; and from this point some of us began our first gropings after moral philosophy,

Babbitts: from Sinclair Lewis' novel, *Babbitt,* whose hero was an unimaginative "go-getting" businessman.
amalgams: compounds of different things.

gropings for a belief that could give the total universe a meaning in our own lives.

27   There was a bugler in our camp who was the first consummate * expert, in any field, that I had known. He had no other talent but this music. He was a good-natured, chubby, curly-headed Italian boy, rather lazy, and when he was not back in the woods practicing his cornet he walked round with a dreamy look, as though our own handicrafts could not possibly be of interest to him.

28   Paolo had a silver trumpet and he preferred it to the bugle. He wanted to be a great musician. He would take his horn and music back into a pine clearing a quarter of a mile from the camp and all day long we could hear him practicing the runs. He blew the trumpet with a clear, sweet tone. We had supreme confidence as we stood at attention on the parade grounds and the flag came down the creaking flagpole pulley in the late afternoon sunlight, and Paolo stood alone, with everyone watching, and bugled. We were proud of him when visitors came. He had that ability of experts to create a sense of possessiveness in others.

29   It was at bedtime that Paolo gathered up into his clear, thin music all the ineffable ° hungering of our awakening lives. At ten o'clock he climbed a high ladder to a life-guard platform we had nailed into the branches of a tall cypress tree beside the bayou. Paolo lived for this moment and, with the whole camp silent and listening below him in the darkness, he blew taps with a soft and ghostly beauty all his own. Somehow the music spoke for us, uttered the thing we knew but had no words for, set up a wailing in the pine trees of the brevity and splendor of human life. Lying in our bunks in the darkness of the cabin, some of us fell into sleep; but some lay in silence thinking longer, alive to the night, and I was one of these.

30   One night some ten years later I entered a smoke-filled tavern in another city where Paolo was playing in a band. By this time he had made a small reputation as a

ineffable: indescribable.

boy with a hot trumpet. I watched his now older face as he tore through the hot routines. He was tired. The silver horn made noise but, though I knew little about it, I could see that he was not a great jazz musician.

31 I did not go to see him any more. I wanted to remember Paolo before he had lost something, before any of us had lost it, a kind of innocence. I wanted to remember him in the land of our first discoveries, when he had climbed into a cypress tree to blow his horn, and there was a kind of Gothic ° night-drench in our lives.

ANALYSIS

Sancton divides his essay into four parts. The first might be subtitled "Cast of Characters." In a pleasantly indirect manner, he introduces us to his camp friends and their daily routine. Part two is more personal and the style is richer with descriptive adjectives. We could call it "Faces of Nature," keeping in mind that the author is telling us as much about himself as he is about camping on the bayou. Call the third part "Escapade," in both meanings of the word. Sancton narrates an incident here, but he also describes young love. It is a good example, as we said earlier, of how descriptive writing merges into narrative on occasion. In the last part, which we are not encouraged to sub-title since it gives the title to the whole essay, Sancton returns to his initial motive in recalling these days. He says, "There was plenty of time to think." Remember that he introduced this aspect of his essay in his topic sentence,° at the end of the first paragraph: "I did my first real living and my first real thinking in this camp." How is he to illustrate (rather than merely to enumerate) what he thought about? By describing the communal life of the camp? By talking of stargazing late at night in the open fields?

These serve, but he chooses Paolo—the only camper he feels it necessary to name—both as "the first consummate

Gothic: wild, unrestrained.
topic sentence: See Glossary.

expert, in any field, that [he] had known" and as a symbol of lost innocence. Through Paolo, Sancton is able to say many things: the early respect he had for skill, and devotion to that skill, the way music "spoke for" the boys at taps, the isolation of a young boy as he lay in his bunk, thinking, unable to sleep. But most of all, Paolo serves as a rude awakening and forceful conclusion, simultaneously. Sancton wishes to end this reminiscence in time present, as it began. We plunge, therefore, from taps at camp to a "smoke-filled tavern," from a "clear, thin music" to a "hot trumpet." If the contrast is not sharp enough, if you perchance miss his point, he spells it out in the final paragraph: "I did not go to see him anymore. . . . I wanted to remember him in the land of our first discoveries."

We might call this kind of organization discursive or rambling, quite different from Laurie Lee's; yet it suits Sancton's purpose. He does not wish to proceed from a fixed point in time through a single incident, building his description of people and places on a chronological pattern. He uses chronological flash-backs, it is true, but we could more accurately describe the structure of this essay as elaboration of topic paragraph or theme with variations. The incidents span five years, from the time Sancton was twelve until he entered college. The last variation, the concluding elaboration, is Paolo; and consciously or not we are led to agree with Sancton that the "clear, sweet tones" in a cypress bayou, and all they stood for, are gone with his youth. The carefully detailed descriptions all point toward this conclusion. The essay is discursive but never uncontrolled.

Questions on Content

1. Why does Sancton not name his camp, nor its location, nor his friends, except for Paolo? Does it make any difference to you, as reader? What details of location and daily routine do you remember?
2. How much of what Sancton writes about do you think is typical of only a Southern camp? Would you call this a regional essay?

3. Why should "Rookie" be such an apt nickname for this author?

4. Sancton concludes his third section with this sentence: "First love is unforgettable." What descriptive details bear out this conclusion? Near the end of this section, he writes: ". . . for the first time we understood the poignance and the beauty of the human heritage." What has this idea to do with first love?

Add to Your Vocabulary

brackish, intoned, poignance, consummate, ineffable.

Questions on Technique

1. The opening paragraph of this essay is a model of declarative statement and simple announcement of purpose. How do the second and third paragraphs develop Sancton's initial ideas?

2. How could the train of events in this essay have been organized in a different way? Would your suggested organization improve the essay?

3. What particular seasonal details does Sancton use to describe a summertime camp? What part do certain sounds play in creating the atmosphere the author wishes to share with us? What do the lyrics of popular songs add to the third section?

4. Sancton twice uses references to the stars, in the second and the fourth part. What more does he make of them than *mere* reference? What else is he trying to say? Does this technique—saying one thing in terms of another—apply to any other elements of the essay?

Techniques to Imitate

Selection of details to establish a mood or feeling

Like Updike and Lee, Sancton provides us with descriptive passages that are excellent models for imitation. His essay is subjective description at its best. He wants his reader to share his feelings as a boy at summer camp when he began to think seriously about life. Description here is used not primarily to create a word picture, but to help the reader to share the author's feelings and emotions— to create a mood. Yet it is through his masterful picturing of the setting that he is able to make us feel the mood that the surroundings inspired in him.

Reread paragraphs 3 and 4. Note how Sancton makes you feel the excitement of the boys in their new environment.

Reread paragraphs 10, 11, and 13 to see how clearly he portrays the boys' feelings of awe and wonder in the presence of nature. For example, in paragraph 10, he tells how the campfire, the towering pine tree, and the constellations stirred thoughts that made him feel "worshipful of the earth, the pine tree, the night itself." As you read, notice the careful selection of details and the sensory impressions and how they contribute to the mood.

Suggestions for Writing

1. It is your first day at camp or at a new school. In 400 words, record your impressions as you remember them.
2. In four or five paragraphs, describe a childhood friend who possessed a skill you much admired, such as dancing, horseback riding, diving, singing.
3. What childhood possession can you think of that was, now that you look back, a symbol of some strong feeling, that stood for something more than just another toy or gift or handmade object? Explain its meaning to you in three or four paragraphs.
4. What did the Boy Scouts or Girl Scouts (or any group with whom you went camping) mean to you as a child? Describe in 500 words one occasion which illustrates your feelings about these days.
5. Can you select from your childhood an experience which taught you an important lesson, perhaps about behavior or about life or about human beings? If you can recall such an experience, describe it in detail so that the reader will understand in what way it was important to you.

RUTH McKENNEY

A Loud Sneer for Our
Feathered Friends

As a humorist and reporter in the nineteen twenties
and thirties, Ruth McKenney was not widely known in
America. Her book *My Sister Eileen* first appeared in
1938. Years later, Leonard Bernstein and others made
a brilliant Broadway musical from it, called *Wonderful
Town*. The film was equally successful. Not all of the
chapters of the McKenney autobiography were utilized
on stage, however. Ruth and Eileen also went to camp.
They hated it. No pirogues on the bayou, no silver horns,
no speculation on the stars for them. In the reminiscence
that follows, we see the other side of "living with
nature." The girls hated camp councilors, Indian lore,
organized recreation, and particularly birds. Ruth Mc-
Kenney is not one to conceal her loathing. In fact, this
essay is a splendid mixture of satire ° and humor with
a description of an old-fashioned girls' camp. The language is colloquial,° the attitudes flippant.

1 From childhood, my sister
and I have had a well-grounded dislike for our friends
the birds. We came to hate them when she was ten and I

satire: See Glossary.
colloquial: See Glossary.

was eleven. We had been exiled by what we considered an unfeeling family to one of those loathsome girls' camps where Indian lore is rife and the management puts up neatly lettered signs reminding the clients to be Good Sports. From the moment Eileen and I arrived at dismal old Camp Hi-Wah, we were Bad Sports, and we liked it.

2   We refused to get out of bed when the bugle blew in the morning, we fought against scrubbing our teeth in public to music, we sneered when the flag was ceremoniously lowered at sunset, we avoided doing a good deed a day, we complained loudly about the food, which was terrible, and we bought some chalk once and wrote all over the Recreation Cabin, "We hate Camp Hi-Wah." It made a wonderful scandal, although unfortunately we were immediately accused of the crime. All the other little campers *loved* dear old Camp Hi-Wah, which shows you what kind of people they were.

3   The first two weeks Eileen and I were at Camp Hi-Wah, we sat in our cabin grinding our teeth at our councilor and writing letters to distant relatives. These letters were, if I say so myself, real masterpieces of double dealing and heartless chicanery.° In our childish and, we hoped, appealing scrawl, we explained to Great-Aunt Mary Farrel and Second Cousin Joe Murphy that we were having such fun at dear Camp Hi-Wah making Indian pocketbooks.

4   "We would simply L-O-V-E to make you a pocketbook, dear Aunt Mary," we wrote, "only the leather costs $1 for a small pocketbook or $1.67 for a large size pocketbook, which is much nicer because you can carry more things in it, and the rawhide you sew it up with, just exactly the way the Indians did, costs 40 cents more. We burn pictures on the leather but that doesn't cost anything. If we O-N-L-Y had $1 or $1.67 and 40 cents for the rawhide, we could make you the S-W-E-L-L-E-S-T pocketbook."

5   As soon as we had enough orders for Indian pocketbooks with pictures burnt on them, we planned to abscond * with the funds sent by our trusting relatives and run away to New York City, where, as we used to explain

chicanery: trickery.

dramatically to our cabin-mates, we intended to live a life of sin. After a few days, our exciting plans for our immediate future were bruited ° all over the camp, and admirers came from as far away as Cabin Minnehaha, which was way down at the end of Hiawatha Alley, just to hear us tell about New York and sin.

6   Fame had its price, however. One of the sweet little girls who lived in our cabin turned out to be such a Good Citizen ("Camp Hi-Wah Girls Learn to Be Good Citizens") that she told our dreadful secret to our councilor. Our mail was impounded * for weeks, and worst of all, we actually had to make several Indian pocketbooks with pictures burnt on them. My pictures were all supposed to be snakes, although they were pretty blurred. Eileen specialized in what she believed to be the likeness of a werewolf, ° but Cousin Joe, who had generously ordered three pocketbooks, wrote a nice letter thanking Eileen for his pretty pocketbooks with the pretty pictures of Abraham Lincoln on them. We were terribly disgusted by the whole thing.

7   It was in this mood that we turned to birds. The handicraft hour at Camp Hi-Wah, heralded by the ten-thirty A.M. bugle, competed for popularity with the bird walks at the same hour. You could, as Eileen had already somewhat precociously * learned how to say, name your own poison. After three weeks of burning pictures on leather, we were ready for anything, even our feathered friends.

8   So one hot morning in July, the two McKenney sisters, big and bad and fierce for their age, answered the bird-walk bugle call, leaving the Indian-pocketbook teacher to mourn her two most backward pupils. We were dressed, somewhat reluctantly, to be sure, in the required heavy stockings for poison ivy and brambles, and carried, each of us, in our dirty hands a copy of a guide to bird lore called *Bird Life for Children*.

9   *Bird Life for Children* was a volume that all the Good Citizens in Camp Hi-Wah pretended to find engrossing.

bruited: reported, rumored.
werewolf: a person transformed into a wolf.

Eileen and I thought it was stupefyingly dull. Our favorite literary character at the time was Dumas' Marguerite de Valois,° who took her decapitated lover's head home in a big handkerchief for old times' sake. Eileen, in those days, was always going to name her first girl child Marguerite de Valois.

10 *Bird Life for Children* was full of horrid pictures in full color of robins and pigeons and redbirds. Under each picture was a loathsomely whimsical paragraph describing how the bird in question spent his spare time, what he ate, and why children should love him. Eileen and I hated the book so, we were quite prepared to despise birds when we started off that morning on our first bird walk, but we had no idea of what we were going to suffer, that whole awful summer, because of our feathered friends. In the first place, since we had started off making leather pocketbooks, we were three weeks behind the rest of the Hi-Wah bird-lovers. They had been tramping through blackberry bushes for days and days and had already got the hang of the more ordinary bird life around camp, whereas the only bird I could identify at the time was the vulture. Cousin Joe took me to a zoo once, and there was a fine vulture there, a big, fat one. They fed him six live rats every day in lieu of * human flesh. I kept a sharp eye out for a vulture all summer, but one never turned up at Camp Hi-Wah. Nothing interesting ever happened around that place.

11 On that first bird walk, Eileen and I trotted anxiously along behind the little band of serious-minded bird-lovers, trying desperately to see, or at least hear, even one bird, even one robin. But alas, while other bird-walkers saw, or pretended to see—for Eileen and I never believed them for a moment—all kinds of hummingbirds and hawks and owls and whatnot, we never saw or heard a single, solitary feathered friend, not one.

12 By the time we staggered into camp for lunch, with stubbed toes, scratched faces, and tangled hair, Eileen and

Dumas' Marguerite de Valois: Alexandre Dumas, *père*, wrote *Marguerite de Valois*, a novel, in 1845. The real Marguerite de Valois was the wife of Henry IV of France.

I were soured for life on birds. Our bird logs, which we carried strapped to our belts along with the *Guide,* were still chaste and bare, while all the other little bird-lovers had fulsome * entries, such as "Saw and heard redbird at 10:37 A.M. Molting."

13 Still, for the next three days we stayed honest and suffered. For three terrible mornings we endured being dolts * among bird-walkers, the laughing-stock of Camp Hi-Wah. After six incredibly tiresome hours, our bird logs were still blank. Then we cracked under the strain. The fourth morning we got up feeling grim but determined. We sharpened our pencils before we started off on the now-familiar trail through the second-growth forest.

14 When we got well into the woods and Mary Mahoney, the premier bird-walker of Camp Hi-Wah, had already spotted and logged her first redbird of the morning, Eileen suddenly stopped dead in her tracks. "Hark!" she cried. She had read that somewhere in a book. "Quiet!" I echoed instantly.

15 The bird-walkers drew to a halt respectfully and stood in silence. They stood and stood. It was not good form even to whisper while fellow bird-walkers were logging a victim, but after quite a long time the Leader, whose feet were flat and often hurt her, whispered impatiently, "Haven't you got him logged yet?"

16 "You drove him away," Eileen replied sternly. "It was a yellow-billed cuckoo."

17 "A yellow-billed cuckoo?" cried the Leader incredulously.

18 "Well," Eileen said modestly, "at least *I* think it was." Then, with many a pretty hesitation and thoughtful pause, she recited the leading features of the yellow-billed cuckoo, as recorded in *Bird Life for Children.*

19 The Leader was terribly impressed. Later on that morning I logged a kingfisher, a red-headed woodpecker, and a yellow-bellied sapsucker, which was all I could remember at the moment. Each time, I kept the bird-walkers standing around for an interminable period, gaping into blank space and listening desperately to the rustle of the wind in the trees and the creak of their shoes as they went from one foot to another.

20 In a few days Eileen and I were the apple of our Leader's eye, the modest heroes of the Camp Hi-Wah bird walks. Naturally, there were base children around camp, former leading bird-walkers, who spread foul rumors up and down Hiawatha Alley that Eileen and I were frauds. We soon stopped this ugly talk, however. Eileen was the pitcher, and a very good one, too, of the Red Bird ball team and I was the first base. When Elouise Pritchard, the worst gossip in Cabin Sitting Bull, came up to bat, she got a pitched ball right in the stomach. Of course it was only a soft ball, but Eileen could throw it pretty hard. To vary this routine, I tagged Mary Mahoney, former head bird-walker, out at first base, and Mary had a bruise on her thigh for weeks. The rumors stopped abruptly.

21 We had begun to get pretty bored with logging rare birds when the game took on a new angle. Mary Mahoney and several other bird-walkers began to see the same birds we did on our morning jaunts into the forest. This made us pretty mad, but there wasn't much we could do about it. Next, Mary Mahoney began to see birds we weren't logging. The third week after we joined the Camp Hi-Wah Bird Study Circle, everybody except the poor, dumb Leader and a few backward but honest bird-lovers was logging the rarest birds seen around Camp Hi-Wah in twenty years. Bird walks developed into a race to see who could shout "Hark!" first and keep the rest of the little party in fidgety silence for the next five minutes.

22 The poor bird-walk Leader was in agony. Her reputation as a bird-lover was in shreds. Her talented pupils were seeing rare birds right and left, while the best she could log for herself would be a few crummy old redbirds and a robin or so. At last our Leader's morale collapsed. It was the day when nearly everybody in the study circle swore that she saw and heard a bona-fide nightingale.

23 "Where?" cried our Leader desperately, after the fourth nightingale had been triumphantly logged in the short space of five minutes. Heartless fingers pointed to a vague bush. The Leader strained her honest eyes. No notion of our duplicity * crossed her innocent, unworldly mind.

24 "I can't see any nightingale," our Leader cried, and burst into tears. Then, full of shame, she sped back to camp, leaving the Camp Hi-Wah bird-lovers to their nightingales and guilty thoughts.

25 Eileen and I ate a hearty lunch that noon because we thought we would need it. Then we strolled down Hiawatha Alley and hunted up Mary Mahoney.

26 "We will put the Iron Cross on you if you tell," Eileen started off, as soon as we found Mary.

27 "What's the Iron Cross?" Mary squeaked, startled out of her usual haughty poise.

28 "Never mind," I growled. "You'll find out if you tell."

29 We walked past Cabin Sitting Bull, past the flagpole, into the tall grass beyond the ball field.

30 "She'll tell," Eileen said finally.

31 "What'll we do?" I replied mournfully. "They'll try us at campfire tonight."

32 They did, too. It was terrible. We denied everything, but the Head of Camp, a mean old lady who wore middy blouses and pleated serge bloomers, sentenced us to no desserts and eight-o'clock bedtime for two weeks. We thought over what to do to Mary Mahoney for four whole days. Nothing seemed sufficiently frightful, but in the end we put the wart curse on her. The wart curse was simple but horrible. We dropped around to Cabin Sitting Bull one evening and in the presence of Mary and her allies we drew ourselves up to our full height and said solemnly in unison, "We put the wart curse on you, Mary Mahoney." Then we stalked away.

33 We didn't believe for a moment in the wart curse, but we hoped Mary would. At first she was openly contemptuous, but to our delight, on the fourth evening she developed a horrible sty in her eye. We told everybody a sty was a kind of a wart and that we had Mary in our power. The next day Mary broke down and came around

to our cabin and apologized in choked accents. She gave Eileen her best hair ribbon and me a little barrel that had a picture of Niagara Falls inside it, if you looked hard enough. We were satisfied.

ANALYSIS

Anyone who has seen *Wonderful Town* knows that explosiveness is one of its main ingredients. In a milder way, Ruth McKenney etches her reactions to Camp Hi-Wah. The essay bristles not with sensory images or carefully wrought physical description but with blunt opinionated judgments, usually negative. The tone, that is, the attitude of the writer toward her subject, is wholly consistent: "We were Bad Sports, and we liked it." The details of the essay are indirectly aimed at proving the thesis. But be assured that as Thomas Sancton permits his memory to color simple fact, so does Ruth McKenney. She knows how to embellish, to exaggerate, to undercut. Where Sancton recalls happy days, she remembers only gloom, and because the gloom is exaggerated we laugh easily at what she writes.

How she writes is our concern here. Let us, with this essay, inspect the language rather than the structure. Cast your eye over the first seven paragraphs. Note some of the verbs she uses; they rend the air: "we had been exiled by what we considered an unfeeling family"; "we refused . . . we fought . . . we sneered . . . we complained"; "we sat in our cabin grinding our teeth"; "we planned to abscond with the funds"; "our exciting plans . . . were bruited all over the camp"; "our mail was impounded for weeks"; "we turned to birds." These are not only vigorous verbs (*abscond, bruited, impounded* shape the exaggerated tone), they set the stage for the main incident of the reminiscence. Ruth and Eileen obviously turned to birds in desperation. Witness the title.

The adjectives she employs in the bird-watching episode work equally well for her in establishing a negative, disapproving attitude—the basis of good satire. Nothing would change their opinion of this camp: with "dirty" hands they read *Bird Life for Children,* full of "horrid" pictures; the descriptions of the birds were "loathsomely whimsical"; after their first bird-hike, they staggered into camp with "stubbed" toes, "scratched" faces, and "tangled" hair; on the fourth morning they got up feeling "grim but determined." These adjectives are unusually ordinary, but they are always apt and, compared with the verbs, unobtrusive. The temptation to overstress one's feelings with harsh adjectives is great here, but the author avoids it.

Much of the humor in this satirical story comes from the way the writer contrasts herself and her sister with their peers—those Good Sports and Good Citizens of Camp Hi-Wah. The other campers are described as innocents, where the McKenney sisters are described as near-outlaws who can expound on New York and sin. *Their* favorite bird is not the robin or the redbird, but the vulture, and *they* burn pictures of snakes and werewolves on their leather wallets. This distinction between the experienced McKenneys and the innocents of Camp Hi-Wah is well set forth in the descriptions of two books. The McKenneys' favorite novel is Dumas' story about Marguerite de Valois, who takes her lover's decapitated head home in a hankie. The Good Citizens, on the other hand, read *Bird Life for Children.*

Questions on Content

1. The camp, we are told, is loathsome. In what ways did it offend Ruth and Eileen?
2. Do we ever hear the other side of the story: what Camp Hi-Wah thought of the McKenney sisters? Why do you suppose the author sounds so biased?
3. What picture have you of the councilors of this camp?

Add to Your Vocabulary

abscond, chicanery, impounded, precociously, in lieu of, fulsome, dolts, duplicity.

Questions on Technique

1. This essay abounds in colloquialisms (informal or conversational language): "a few crummy old redbirds"; "a mean old lady"; "dismal old Camp Hi-Wah." Find more of them. Do they sometimes border on worn-out phrases, what we call clichés? Would you eliminate them if you were rewriting this essay?

2. Of what use are the digressions that McKenney uses: Dumas' Marguerite de Valois; the vulture Cousin Joe showed Ruth at the zoo?

3. Readers do not always laugh at the same things. Where do you think McKenney is writing most humorously?

4. "If we O-N-L-Y had $1" is an old stylistic device, that is, a way of emphasizing. Do you think it is apt here? Why?

5. Thomas Sancton's essay is for the most part devoid of names; Ruth McKenney's is rife with them. Has she chosen effective names (assuming that they are most likely substitutes for the real ones)?

6. What effect has the last paragraph, particularly the last sentence, on you as reader? How would you have ended the essay?

Techniques to Imitate

Tone

The tone of a piece of writing is the writer's attitude toward the subject. In his account of his experience at a Boy Scout camp, Sancton's tone is romantic, serious, philosophical. In Ruth McKenney's account of her camp experience, the tone is satirical; she is poking fun at Camp Hi-Wah. To a large degree, tone is established by a writer's choice of words. As we pointed out in the Analysis, Ruth McKenney selected her words carefully to reveal her attitude toward the camp. She also chose an informal, fast-moving, slangy style. Understatement ° and exaggeration help to produce the desired satirical tone.

understatement: See Glossary.

When you write, consider carefully the tone you wish to convey: satirical, sarcastic, bitter, angry, informal, formal, serious, flippant, and so on. Make clear in your first paragraph, as Ruth McKenney does, what your tone is to be.

Suggestions for Writing

1. In four or five paragraphs, describe a person or a place you know well, paying close attention to the adjectives you use. Then describe a simple incident involving a person or place (do not tell a story, only set a scene) in which you strive to select forceful verbs.
2. Write a short satiric essay on a sport you dislike, a camp you were forced to attend, a boring trip you took. Use understatement, exaggeration, or both.
3. In an essay, contradict from your own experiences what Ruth McKenney says about camping and bird study.
4. The title of this selection, of course, is mocking the commonly used phrase "a loud cheer for . . ." Write an essay with a title that mocks some familiar phrase or cliché. ("There's no place like somebody else's home," "Absence makes the heart grow colder," "Don't cross your bridges until they're burned," and so on.) Try in your essay to set up a humorous contrast between the expected and the reality.

MAYA ANGELOU

FROM I Know Why
the Caged Bird Sings

Maya Angelou was three years old and her brother Bailey was four when they arrived in the rural town of Stamps, Arkansas. The children had been sent alone across the continent, from California, to live with their grandmother. This matriarch, whom the children called Momma, owned a general merchandise store in the Black area of Stamps. Maya (Marguerite) was a lonely child. She was also certain she was homely.

Maya Angelou eventually moved, physically and psychologically, a long way from Stamps, Arkansas. She became a professional dancer, worked with Dr. Martin Luther King, Jr., and reported for newspapers in Cairo and Ghana. She also has written books.

This selection is from her autobiography *I Know Why the Caged Bird Sings*. The book's title is from "Sympathy" by Paul Laurence Dunbar, a poem in which the Black poet identifies with the imprisoned songbird. In this episode Maya is about ten years old, and has just returned to Arkansas from a visit in St. Louis with her mother.

1 For nearly a year, I sopped around the house, the Store, the school and the church, like an old biscuit, dirty and inedible. Then I met, or rather got to know, the lady who threw me my first life line.

2   Mrs. Bertha Flowers was the aristocrat of Black Stamps. She had the grace of control to appear warm in the coldest weather, and on the Arkansas summer days it seemed she had a private breeze which swirled around, cooling her. She was thin without the taut look of wiry people, and her printed voile dresses and flowered hats were as right for her as denim overalls for a farmer. She was our side's answer to the richest white woman in town.

3   Her skin was a rich black that would have peeled like a plum if snagged, but then no one would have thought of getting close enough to Mrs. Flowers to ruffle her dress, let alone snag her skin. She didn't encourage familiarity. She wore gloves too.

4   I don't think I ever saw Mrs. Flowers laugh, but she smiled often. A slow widening of her thin black lips to show even, small white teeth, then the slow effortless closing. When she chose to smile on me, I always wanted to thank her. The action was so graceful and inclusively benign.°

5   She was one of the few gentlewomen I have ever known, and has remained throughout my life the measure of what a human being can be.

6   Momma had a strange relationship with her. Most often when she passed on the road in front of the Store, she spoke to Momma in that soft yet carrying voice, "Good day, Mrs. Henderson." Momma responded with "How you, Sister Flowers?"

7   Mrs. Flowers didn't belong to our church, nor was she Momma's familiar. Why on earth did she insist on calling her Sister Flowers? Shame made me want to hide my face. Mrs. Flowers deserved better than to be called Sister. Then, Momma left out the verb. Why not ask, "How *are* you, *Mrs.* Flowers?" With the unbalanced passion of the young, I hated her for showing her ignorance to Mrs. Flowers. It didn't occur to me for many years that they were as alike as sisters, separated only by formal education.

benign: gentle, kind.

8   Although I was upset, neither of the women was in the least shaken by what I thought an unceremonious greeting. Mrs. Flowers would continue her easy gait up the hill to her little bungalow, and Momma kept on shelling peas or doing whatever had brought her to the front porch.

9   Occasionally, though, Mrs. Flowers would drift off the road and down to the Store and Momma would say to me, "Sister, you go on and play." As I left I would hear the beginning of an intimate conversation. Momma persistently using the wrong verb, or none at all.

10   "Brother and Sister Wilcox is sho'ly the meanest"— "Is," Momma? "Is"? Oh, please, not "is," Momma, for two or more. But they talked, and from the side of the building where I waited for the ground to open up and swallow me, I heard the soft-voiced Mrs. Flowers and the textured voice of my grandmother merging and melting. They were interrupted from time to time by giggles that must have come from Mrs. Flowers (Momma never giggled in her life). Then she was gone.

11   She appealed to me because she was like people I had never met personally. Like women in English novels who walked the moors (whatever they were) with their loyal dogs racing at a respectful distance. Like the women who sat in front of roaring fireplaces, drinking tea incessantly from silver trays full of scones and crumpets. Women who walked over the "heath" and read morocco-bound books and had two last names divided by a hyphen. It would be safe to say that she made me proud to be Negro, just by being herself.

12   She acted just as refined as whitefolks in the movies and books and she was more beautiful, for none of them could have come near that warm color without looking gray by comparison.

13   It was fortunate that I never saw her in the company of powhitefolks. For since they tend to think of their whiteness as an evenizer, I'm certain that I would have had to hear her spoken to commonly as Bertha, and my image of her would have been shattered like the unmendable Humpty-Dumpty.

14   One summer afternoon, sweet-milk fresh in my memory, she stopped at the Store to buy provisions. Another Negro woman of her health and age would have been expected to carry the paper sacks home in one hand, but Momma said, "Sister Flowers, I'll send Bailey up to your house with these things."

15   She smiled that slow dragging smile, "Thank you, Mrs. Henderson. I'd prefer Marguerite, though." My name was beautiful when she said it. "I've been meaning to talk to her, anyway." They gave each other age-group looks.

16   Momma said, "Well, that's all right then. Sister, go and change your dress. You going to Sister Flowers'."

17   The chifforobe was a maze. What on earth did one put on to go to Mrs. Flowers' house? I knew I shouldn't put on a Sunday dress. It might be sacrilegious. Certainly not a house dress, since I was already wearing a fresh one. I chose a school dress, naturally. It was formal without suggesting that going to Mrs. Flowers' house was equivalent to attending church.

18   I trusted myself back into the Store.

19   "Now, don't you look nice." I had chosen the right thing, for once.

20   "Mrs. Henderson, you make most of the children's clothes, don't you?"

21   "Yes, ma'am. Sure do. Store-bought clothes ain't hardly worth the thread it take to stitch them."

22   "I'll say you do a lovely job, though, so neat. That dress looks professional."

23   Momma was enjoying the seldom-received compliments. Since everyone we knew (except Mrs. Flowers, of course) could sew competently, praise was rarely handed out for the commonly practiced craft.

24   "I try, with the help of the Lord, Sister Flowers, to finish the inside just like I does the outside. Come here, Sister."

25   I had buttoned up the collar and tied the belt, apron-like, in back. Momma told me to turn around. With one hand she pulled the strings and the belt fell free at both sides of my waist. Then her large hands were at my neck, opening the button loops. I was terrified. What was happening?

26 "Take it off, Sister." She had her hands on the hem of the dress.

27 "I don't need to see the inside, Mrs. Henderson, I can tell . . ." But the dress was over my head and my arms were stuck in the sleeves. Momma said, "That'll do. See here, Sister Flowers, I French-seams around the armholes." Through the cloth film, I saw the shadow approach. "That makes it last longer. Children these days would bust out of sheet-metal clothes. They so rough."

28 "That is a very good job, Mrs. Henderson. You should be proud. You can put your dress back on, Marguerite."

29 "No ma'am. Pride is a sin. And 'cording to the Good Book, it goeth before a fall."

30 "That's right. So the Bible says. It's a good thing to keep in mind."

31 I wouldn't look at either of them. Momma hadn't thought that taking off my dress in front of Mrs. Flowers would kill me stone dead. If I had refused, she would have thought I was trying to be "womanish" . . . . Mrs. Flowers had known that I would be embarrassed and that was even worse. I picked up the groceries and went out to wait in the hot sunshine. It would be fitting if I got a sunstroke and died before they came outside. Just dropped dead on the slanting porch.

32 There was a little path beside the rocky road, and Mrs. Flowers walked in front swinging her arms and picking her way over the stones.

33 She said, without turning her head, to me, "I hear you're doing very good school work, Marguerite, but that it's all written. The teachers report that they have trouble getting you to talk in class." We passed the triangular farm on our left and the path widened to allow us to walk together. I hung back in the separate unasked and unanswerable questions.

34 "Come and walk along with me, Marguerite." I couldn't have refused even if I wanted to. She pronounced

my name so nicely. Or more correctly, she spoke each word with such clarity that I was certain a foreigner who didn't understand English could have understood her.

35   "Now no one is going to make you talk—possibly no one can. But bear in mind, language is man's way of communicating with his fellow man and it is language alone which separates him from the lower animals." That was a totally new idea to me, and I would need time to think about it.

36   "Your grandmother says you read a lot. Every chance you get. That's good, but not good enough. Words mean more than what is set down on paper. It takes the human voice to infuse them with the shades of deeper meaning."

37   I memorized the part about the human voice infusing words. It seemed so valid and poetic.

38   She said she was going to give me some books and that I not only must read them, I must read them aloud. She suggested that I try to make a sentence sound in as many different ways as possible.

39   "I'll accept no excuse if you return a book to me that has been badly handled." My imagination boggled at the punishment I would deserve if in fact I did abuse a book of Mrs. Flowers. Death would be too kind and brief.

40   The odors in the house surprised me. Somehow I had never connected Mrs. Flowers with food or eating or any other common experience of common people. There must have been an outhouse, too, but my mind never recorded it.

41   The sweet scent of vanilla had met us as she opened the door.

42   "I made tea cookies this morning. You see, I had planned to invite you for cookies and lemonade so we could have this little chat. The lemonade is in the icebox."

43   It followed that Mrs. Flowers would have ice on an ordinary day, when most families in our town bought ice late on Saturdays only a few times during the summer to be used in the wooden ice-cream freezers.

44   She took the bags from me and disappeared through the kitchen door. I looked around the room that I had never in my wildest fantasies imagined I would see.

Browned photographs leered or threatened from the walls and the white, freshly done curtains pushed against themselves and against the wind. I wanted to gobble up the room entire and take it to Bailey, who would help me analyze and enjoy it.

45 "Have a seat, Marguerite. Over there by the table." She carried a platter covered with a tea towel. Although she warned that she hadn't tried her hand at baking sweets for some time, I was certain that like everything else about her the cookies would be perfect.

46 They were flat round wafers, slightly browned on the edges and butter-yellow in the center. With the cold lemonade they were sufficient for childhood's lifelong diet. Remembering my manners, I took nice little lady-like bites off the edges. She said she had made them expressly for me and that she had a few in the kitchen that I could take home to my brother. So I jammed one whole cake in my mouth and the rough crumbs scratched the insides of my jaws, and if I hadn't had to swallow, it would have been a dream come true.

47 As I ate she began the first of what we later called "my lessons in living." She said that I must always be intolerant of ignorance but understanding of illiteracy. That some people, unable to go to school, were more educated and even more intelligent than college professors. She encouraged me to listen carefully to what country people called mother wit. That in those homely sayings was couched the collective wisdom of generations.

48 When I finished the cookies she brushed off the table and brought a thick, small book from the bookcase. I had read *A Tale of Two Cities* and found it up to my standards as a romantic novel. She opened the first page and I heard poetry for the first time in my life.

49 "It was the best of times and the worst of times . . ." Her voice slid in and curved down through and over the words. She was nearly singing. I wanted to look at the pages. Were they the same that I had read? Or were there notes, music, lined on the pages, as in a hymn book? Her sounds began cascading gently. I knew from listening to a thousand preachers that she was nearing the end of her reading, and I hadn't really heard, heard to understand, a single word.

50 "How do you like that?"

51 It occurred to me that she expected a response. The sweet vanilla flavor was still on my tongue and her reading was a wonder in my ears. I had to speak.

52 I said, "Yes, ma'am." It was the least I could do, but it was the most also.

53 "There's one more thing. Take this book of poems and memorize one for me. Next time you pay me a visit, I want you to recite."

54 I have tried often to search behind the sophistication of years for the enchantment I so easily found in those gifts. The essence escapes but its aura remains. To be allowed, no, invited, into the private lives of strangers, and to share their joys and fears, was a chance to exchange the Southern bitter wormwood for a cup of mead with Beowulf or a hot cup of tea and milk with Oliver Twist. When I said aloud, "It is a far, far better thing that I do, than I have ever done . . ." ° tears of love filled my eyes at my selflessness.

55 On that first day, I ran down the hill and into the road (few cars ever came along it) and had the good sense to stop running before I reached the Store.

56 I was liked, and what a difference it made. I was respected not as Mrs. Henderson's grandchild or Bailey's sister but for just being Marguerite Johnson.

57 Childhood's logic never asks to be proved (all conclusions are absolute). I didn't question why Mrs. Flowers had singled me out for attention, nor did it occur to me that Momma might have asked her to give me a little talking to. All I cared about was that she had made tea cookies for *me* and read to *me* from her favorite book. It was enough to prove that she liked me.

A speech from Dickens' novel *A Tale of Two Cities*. The narrator of that story imagines that the hero Sydney Carton speaks this as he goes to die on the guillotine so that another man can live.

ANALYSIS

This is a straightforward description of an event and, above all, of a person who had an important effect on the writer's life. The second sentence states the topic: "the lady who threw me my first life line."

The structure of the description is very easy to discern: Paragraphs 2–13 describe the lady. Paragraph 14 opens the description of the event that had the life-giving effect on the writer. The last two paragraphs act as a summary, in which the writer tries to explain why this person and her actions meant so much.

As many do who write from the point of view of a child, Angelou has chosen a style that at times is almost childlike itself. She is not afraid to write a simple sentence like "She wore gloves too." She does not try to create complex sentences and lengthy paragraphs. Just the opposite. She re-creates her character in words and phrases and rhythms that she is comfortable with. She does not even philosophize at length about the meaning of the event. She simply remarks, "I was liked, and what a difference it made."

Questions on Technique

1. In telling a story, a writer must be careful to reproduce dialogue accurately. Explain how the accurate reproduction of Momma's speech is necessary to support these statements in the story:
   "It didn't occur to me for many years that they [Momma and Mrs. Flowers] were as alike as sisters, separated only by formal education."
   "She [Mrs. Flowers] said that I must always be intolerant of ignorance but understanding of illiteracy."
2. Although she seems to write effortlessly, Angelou demonstrates her competence as a writer by her careful selection of words. Explain the effectiveness of the italicized words in these excerpts:
   "She smiled that slow *dragging* smile . . ."
   "They gave each other *age-group* looks."

"I *trusted* myself back into the Store."

"My imagination *boggled* at the punishment I would deserve if in fact I did abuse a book of Mrs. Flowers."

Techniques to Imitate

Use of figurative language ° *in description*

Good description is almost always figurative. Angelou here describes herself as having "sopped around" the house "like an old biscuit, dirty and inedible," but Mrs. Flowers is different. That "aristocrat of Black Stamps" "had a private breeze which swirled around, cooling her." Her skin "would have peeled like a plum if snagged." Her voice "slid in and curved down through and over the words" when she read, and her sounds were "cascading gently," as if they were a waterfall. Even the summer afternoon that Maya went to Mrs. Flowers' house is "sweet-milk fresh" in her memory. And the woman's name itself could be seen as a metaphor:° Mrs. *Flowers*.

Suggestions for Writing

1. Imitate the structure of this selection and write a description of a person who impressed you. Open, as Angelou does, with a statement of your topic. Then describe the appearance and appeal of the person, and tell a story or anecdote that supports your point.
2. In one of the striking similes° in this description, Mrs. Flowers' skin is compared to a plum. Make a list of metaphors or similes that you could use to describe skin textures, hair, eyes, teeth, gait. Avoid clichés.
3. Write a description of two people in which you proceed by a series of contrasts to let your reader know what each person is like. You might use figurative language that will help heighten the contrast, just as Angelou does here when she compares one character to an old biscuit and the other's skin to a rich black plum.

figurative language, metaphor, and similes: See Glossary.

JAMES THURBER

University Days

James Thurber believed "humor is a kind of emotional chaos told about calmly and quietly in retrospect." He practiced it with enormous success for over thirty years, mainly in the pages of the *New Yorker*. In 1945, he published *The Thurber Carnival*, a retrospective cross-section of his genius—short stories, fables, satirical essays, and his distinctive line drawings—beginning with excerpts from his first volume, *My World—and Welcome to It*.

The Thurber world is very special indeed. Though born in Columbus, Ohio, Thurber spent most of his life in New York and Connecticut writing of "the little perils of routine living." His habitat is the metropolis and the "secret life" we must develop (like Walter Mitty) to face the forces of mechanization. He knew the weakness of our civilization almost more acutely than he had a right to. He said of his drawings that they "sometimes seem to have reached completion by some other route than the common one of intent." Be assured that Thurber always knows where his writing is taking him, discursive though it may seem at first glance. His sense of form and style is unfaltering. Like excellence in most things, his descriptive ease in writing hides much hard work in "laying out" his subject and, one guesses, considerable rewriting to find the one perfect word or metaphor. ° Thurber

metaphor: See Glossary.

had poor eyesight: one eye was destroyed in a childhood accident. Even with perfect vision, he might not
have ever seen what he was supposed to see in this
microscope.

1   **I** passed all the other courses
that I took at my university, but I could never pass botany.
This was because all botany students had to spend several
hours a week in a laboratory looking through a microscope
at plant cells, and I could never see through a microscope.
I never once saw a cell through a microscope. This used to
enrage my instructor. He would wander around the laboratory pleased with the progress all the students were making
in drawing the involved and, so I am told, interesting structure of flower cells, until he came to me. I would just be
standing there. "I can't see anything," I would say. He
would begin patiently enough, explaining how anybody can
see through a microscope, but he would always end up in a
fury, claiming that I could *too* see through a microscope
but just pretended that I couldn't. "It takes away from the
beauty of flowers anyway," I used to tell him. "We are not
concerned with beauty in this course," he would say. "We
are concerned solely with what I may call the *mechanics* of
flars." "Well," I'd say, "I can't see anything." "Try it just
once again," he'd say, and I would put my eye to the microscope and see nothing at all, except now and again, a
nebulous * milky substance—a phenomenon of maladjust-
ment. You were supposed to see a vivid, restless clockwork
of sharply defined plant cells. "I see what looks like a lot
of milk," I would tell him. This, he claimed, was the result
of my not having adjusted the microscope properly; so he
would readjust it for me, or rather, for himself. And I
would look again and see milk.
2 I finally took a deferred pass, as they called it, and
waited a year and tried again. (You had to pass one of the
biological sciences or you couldn't graduate.) The professor had come back from vacation brown as a berry, bright-

eyed, and eager to explain cell structure again to his classes. "Well," he said to me, cheerily, when we met in the first laboratory hour of the semester, "we're going to see cells this time, aren't we?" "Yes, sir," I said. Students to right of me and to left of me and in front of me were seeing cells; what's more, they were quietly drawing pictures of them in their notebooks. Of course, I didn't see anything.

3   "We'll try it," the professor said to me, grimly, "with every adjustment of the microscope known to man. As God is my witness, I'll arrange this glass so that you see cells through it or I'll give up teaching. In twenty-two years of botany, I—" He cut off abruptly for he was beginning to quiver all over, like Lionel Barrymore,° and he genuinely wished to hold onto his temper; his scenes with me had taken a great deal out of him.

4   So we tried it with every adjustment of the microscope known to man. With only one of them did I see anything but blackness or the familiar lacteal opacity,* and that time I saw, to my pleasure and amazement, a variegated * constellation of flecks, specks, and dots. These I hastily drew. The instructor, noting my activity, came back from an adjoining desk, a smile on his lips and his eyebrows high in hope. He looked at my cell drawing. "What's that?" he demanded, with a hint of a squeal in his voice. "That's what I saw," I said. "You didn't, you didn't, you *did*n't!" he screamed, losing control of his temper instantly, and he bent over and squinted into the microscope. His head snapped up. "That's your eye!" he shouted. "You've fixed the lens so that it reflects! You've drawn your eye!"

5   Another course that I didn't like, but somehow managed to pass, was economics. I went to that class straight from the botany class, which didn't help me any in understanding either subject. I used to get them mixed up. But not as mixed up as another student in my economics class who came there direct from a physics laboratory. He was a tackle on the football team, named Bolenciecwcz. At that time Ohio State University had one of the best football

Lionel Barrymore: a Hollywood star (1878–1954) noted for playing irritable old men.

teams in the country, and Bolenciecwcz was one of its out-standing stars. In order to be eligible to play it was neces-sary for him to keep up in his studies, a very difficult matter, for while he was not dumber than an ox he was not any smarter. Most of his professors were lenient and helped him along. None gave him more hints, in answering ques-tions, or asked him simpler ones than the economics pro-fessor, a thin, timid man named Bassum. One day when we were on the subject of transportation and distribution, it came Bolenciecwcz's turn to answer a question. "Name one means of transportation," the professor said to him. No light came into the big tackle's eyes. "Just any means of transportation," said the professor. Bolenciecwcz sat staring at him. "That is," pursued the professor, "any medium, agency, or method of going from one place to another." Bolenciecwcz had the look of a man who is being led into a trap. "You may choose among steam, horse-drawn, or electrically propelled vehicles," said the instructor. "I might suggest the one which we commonly take in making long journeys across land." There was a profound silence in which everybody stirred uneasily, including Bolenciecwcz and Mr. Bassum. Mr. Bassum abruptly broke this silence in an amazing manner. "Choo-choo-choo," he said, in a low voice, and turned instantly scarlet. He glanced appeal-ingly around the room. All of us, of course, shared Mr. Bas-sum's desire that Bolenciecwcz should stay abreast of the class in economics, for the Illinois game, one of the hardest and most important of the season, was only a week off. "Toot, toot, too-toooooooot!" some student with a deep voice moaned, and we all looked encouragingly at Bolen-ciecwcz. Somebody else gave a fine imitation of a locomo-tive letting off steam. Mr. Bassum himself rounded off the little show. "Ding, dong, ding, dong," he said, hopefully. Bolenciecwcz was staring at the floor now, trying to think, his great brow furrowed, his huge hands rubbing together, his face red.

6 "How did you come to college this year, Mr. Bolen-ciecwcz?" asked the professor. "*Chuf*fa chuffa, *chuf*fa chuffa."

7 "M'father sent me," said the football player.

8 "What on?" asked Bassum.

9 "I git an 'lowance," said the tackle, in a low, husky voice, obviously embarrassed.

10 "No, no," said Bassum. "Name a means of transportation. What did you *ride* here on?"

11 "Train," said Bolenciecwcz.

12 "Quite right," said the professor. "Now, Mr. Nugent, will you tell us—"

13 If I went through anguish in botany and economics—for different reasons—gymnasium work was even worse. I don't even like to think about it. They wouldn't let you play games or join in the exercises with your glasses on and I couldn't see with mine off. I bumped into professors, horizontal bars, agricultural students, and swinging iron rings. Not being able to see, I could take it but I couldn't dish it out. Also, in order to pass gymnasium (and you had to pass it to graduate) you had to learn to swim if you didn't know how. I didn't like the swimming pool, I didn't like swimming, and I didn't like the swimming instructor, and after all these years I still don't. I never swam but I passed my gym work anyway, by having another student give my gymnasium number (978) and swim across the pool in my place. He was a quiet, amiable blond youth, number 473, and he would have seen through a microscope for me if we could have got away with it, but we couldn't get away with it. Another thing I didn't like about gymnasium work was that they made you strip the day you registered. It is impossible for me to be happy when I am stripped and being asked a lot of questions. Still, I did better than a lanky agricultural student who was cross-examined just before I was. They asked each student what college he was in—that is, whether Arts, Engineering, Commerce, or Agriculture. "What college are you in?" the instructor snapped at the youth in front of me. "Ohio State University," he said promptly.

14 It wasn't that agricultural student but it was another a whole lot like him who decided to take up journalism, possibly on the ground that when farming went to pot he could fall back on newspaper work. He didn't realize, of course, that that would be very much like falling back full-length on a kit of carpenter's tools. Haskins didn't seem cut out for journalism, being too embarrassed to talk to anybody and unable to use a typewriter, but the editor of the college paper assigned him to the cow barns, the sheep house, the horse pavilion, and the animal husbandry * department generally. This was a genuinely big "beat," for it took up five times as much ground and got ten times as great a legislative appropriation as the College of Liberal Arts. The agricultural student knew animals, but nevertheless his stories were dull and colorlessly written. He took all afternoon on each of them, because he had to hunt for each letter on the typewriter. Once in a while he had to ask somebody to help him hunt. "C" and "L," in particular, were hard letters for him to find. His editor finally got pretty much annoyed at the farmer-journalist because his pieces were so uninteresting. "See here, Haskins," he snapped at him one day, "why is it we never have anything hot from you on the horse pavilion? Here we have two hundred head of horses on this campus—more than any other university in the Western Conference except Purdue—and yet you never get any real lowdown on them. Now shoot over to the horse barns and dig up something lively." Haskins shambled out and came back in about an hour; he said he had something. "Well, start it off snappily," said the editor. "Something people will read." Haskins set to work and in a couple of hours brought a sheet of typewritten paper to the desk; it was a two-hundred-word story about some disease that had broken out among the horses. Its opening sentence was simple but arresting. It read: "Who has noticed the sores on the tops of the horses in the animal husbandry building?"

15 Ohio State was a land grant university and therefore two years of military drill was compulsory. We drilled with old Springfield rifles ° and studied the tactics of the Civil

Springfield rifles: officially designated *United States rifle, Model of 1903*. They were breech-loading magazine .30 caliber rifles of the bolt type.

War even though the World War was going on at the time. At 11 o'clock each morning thousands of freshmen and sophomores used to deploy over the campus, moodily creeping up on the old chemistry building. It was good training for the kind of warfare that was waged at Shiloh but it had no connection with what was going on in Europe. Some people used to think there was German money behind it, but they didn't dare say so or they would have been thrown in jail as German spies. It was a period of muddy thought and marked, I believe, the decline of higher education in the Middle West.

16 As a soldier I was never any good at all. Most of the cadets were glumly indifferent soldiers, but I was no good at all. Once General Littlefield, who was commandant of the cadet corps, popped up in front of me during regimental drill and snapped, "You are the main trouble with this university!" I think he meant that my type was the main trouble with the university but he may have meant me individually. I was mediocre at drill, certainly—that is, until my senior year. By that time I had drilled longer than anybody else in the Western Conference, having failed at military at the end of each preceding year so that I had to do it all over again. I was the only senior still in uniform. The uniform which, when new, had made me look like an interurban railway conductor, now that it had become faded and too tight, made me look like Bert Williams ° in his bellboy act. This had a definitely bad effect on my morale. Even so, I had become by sheer practice little short of wonderful at squad maneuvers.

17 One day General Littlefield picked our company out of the whole regiment and tried to get it mixed up by putting it through one movement after another as fast as we could execute them: squads right, squads left, squads on right into line, squads right about, squads left front into line, etc. In about three minutes one hundred and nine men were marching in one direction and I was marching away from them at an angle of forty-five degrees, all alone.

Bert Williams: a comedian, part of the Williams and Worker team.

"Company halt!" shouted General Littlefield. "That man is the only man who has it right!" I was made a corporal for my achievement.

18   The next day General Littlefield summoned me to his office. He was swatting flies when I went in. I was silent and he was silent too, for a long time. I don't think he remembered me or why he had sent for me, but he didn't want to admit it. He swatted some more flies, keeping his eyes on them narrowly before he let go with the swatter. "Button up your coat," he snapped. Looking back on it now I can see that he meant me although he was looking at a fly, but I just stood there. Another fly came to rest on a paper in front of the general and began rubbing its hind legs together. The general lifted the swatter cautiously. I moved restlessly and the fly flew away. "You startled him!" barked General Littlefield, looking at me severely. I said I was sorry. "That won't help the situation!" snapped the general, with cold military logic. I didn't see what I could do except to chase some more flies toward his desk, but I didn't say anything. He stared out the window at the faraway figures of co-eds crossing the campus toward the library. Finally, he told me I could go. So I went. He either didn't know which cadet I was or else he forget what he wanted to see me about. It may have been that he wished to apologize for having called me the main trouble with the university; or maybe he had decided to compliment me on my brilliant drilling of the day before and then at the last minute decided not to. I don't know. I don't think about it much any more.

ANALYSIS

Although this essay is built around disparate episodes in Thurber's college career, it easily divides into five sections. The first four paragraphs describe botany class; then he moves on to economics, gymnasium class, journalism, and military drill. It is not a survey of a college course nor is it meant to be. What holds the sections together is the first person pronoun, Thurber's delicious sense of humor, and above all his sense of timing. Note how each section ends with no waiting for a laugh, with an abrupt switch to another subject: "You've fixed the lens so that it reflects! You've drawn your eye!" or " 'What college are you in?' the instructor snapped at the youth in front of me. 'Ohio State University,' he said promptly." Thurber depends on our appreciating his own awkwardness or the comical forthrightness of his fellow students. The obvious is often the source of humor. He plays upon it here with a fine hand for building a climax, for describing an incident "just as it happened," for omitting any unnecessary editorial or explanatory comment. Some writers build up their essays from a thesis, through examples, to a conclusion. Thurber has no conclusion, just as he has, in effect, no introduction.

How, then, is this effective writing? First, the essay demonstrates a relaxed organization, well-fitted to writing *about* college days, rather than surveying a four-year course. Thurber wants to give us facets of life at Ohio State seen through *his* eyes. A personal view may be a distorted view (he says elsewhere that his badly focused, gold-rimmed glasses forever needed straightening so he saw not two of everything but one and a half) yet the author's personality lies in these very distortions.

Second, Thurber's style is based on skillful repetition of words. Notice in the opening sentence how the ear and eye pick up the last word, "botany." Thurber then repeats "botany" in the next sentence, and introduces two naturally allied words, "microscope," both in the middle and the end of the sentence, and "cell." Sentence three uses both words again—"I never once saw a cell through a microscope"— thereby firmly establishing in our minds what this first episode is about. Follow this technical device through the first four paragraphs and you will notice these words emphasized through repetition: "sea," "adjust," "milk," and the pronoun "we" (when the instructor, like the nurse who asks if we are ready to take our medicine, clearly means "you"). In each succeeding section he plays on a word or words: "transportation," "swim" and "swimming," "horses" and "horse barn," "drill," and "swatter." This repetition gives an almost painful obviousness to the point someone in the episode is trying to make, which is exactly the response Thurber desires.

Third, Thurber is not afraid of exaggeration. He does not exactly depart from what we might accept as credible, but he makes effective overstatement: "As God is my witness, I'll arrange this glass so that you see cells through it or I'll give up teaching," or "Once in a while he had to ask somebody to help him hunt. 'C' and 'L,' in particular, were hard letters for him to find," or "Some people used to think there was German money behind it. . . . It was a period of muddy thought and marked, I believe, the decline of higher education in the Middle West." Thurber knows we will not take him wholly seriously, and we know that he knows—an altogether happy relationship between author and reader. Were he to use ordinary hyperbole—such gross exaggeration as a million when he meant fifteen—he would lose all the humor implicit in these half-serious overstatements. Thurber's instincts are sound. He has the good taste to write it "straight" most of the time. Indeed his "straight" writing is the bulk of this essay. We finish with a feeling that Thurber enjoyed Ohio State University, in spite of microscopes and swimming and drill.

Questions on Content

1. Thurber writes of his botany instructor that "his scenes with me had taken a good deal out of him." How does he convince us this is true?
2. Of gymnasium work, he writes "I don't even like to think about it." Why doesn't he?
3. What is wrong with the agricultural student's basic approach to journalism?
4. In speaking of using a microscope, what does he mean by not seeing anything but "blackness or the familiar lacteal opacity"?

Add to Your Vocabulary

nebulous, opacity, variegated, husbandry.

Questions on Technique

1. For what reasons do you think Thurber sometimes uses dialogue in this descriptive essay? Why does he wish to combine anecdotes with descriptive writing?
2. What kind of humorous effect does he get from "Choo-choo-choo," "Toot, toot, too-toooooooot," and "*Chuf*fa chuffa, *chuf*fa chuffa"? from "the sores on the tops of the horses"? from Springfield rifles and Civil War tactics?
3. Thurber sees himself as a certain kind of character type (paragraph 16). How would you define this character type, and where else have you met him, or her?

Techniques to Imitate

The humor of overstatement and of the incongruous

Really humorous writing is very difficult to achieve. Yet awareness of some of the techniques writers use to make us laugh may be helpful to any writer who already has some talent for the humorous essay.

If skillfully used, overstatement, or exaggeration, can be very funny. Some examples from Thurber's essay are given in the Analysis. You can easily find others.

Another kind of humor Thurber uses is the humor of the incongruous. This kind of humor is based on the absurdity of a situation in which two things are inconsistently related or set side by side. For example, we find it hilarious that a normally dignified biology professor should be frustrated to the point of hysteria by a student who insists he can see only "milk" through his microscope. Equally incongruous is the absurd picture Thurber draws of a professor of economics hopefully saying, "choo-choo-choo" and "ding dong, ding dong" as though he were teaching a kindergarten class. Other examples of the incongruous are the journalism student who required an entire afternoon to write a story, largely because he could not find quickly enough the keys on his typewriter, and the military students who "studied the tactics of the Civil War even though the World War was going on at the time."

When you write a humorous essay, try your hand at overstating the subject and at describing incongruous details. Humor is obvious more often than it is subtle.

Suggestions for Writing

1. Describe in 400 words a single incident that illustrates your own attitude toward physical education, or some other aspect of your schooling.
2. Describe your most difficult course in high school and explain why you had difficulty.
3. Try your hand at humorous writing, keeping it descriptive but using yourself (as Thurber does) as the butt of the humor. Suggested subjects: learning to speak a new language, learning to play a musical instrument, your first date, your first public speech, an adult dinner party.
4. Organize an essay called "High School Days." What will you include or eliminate? Write the essay in 500 words.
5. Inspect several college humor magazines to determine the kind of article they print. Write a 500-word essay you could submit to one of them.

2

PRIMARILY OBJECTIVE EXPERIENCE

JOHN STEINBECK

The Turtle

The Grapes of Wrath was one of the most popular novels to be published in America in the 1930's. It appeared late in the decade, in 1939. Steinbeck had gone to live among the migrant farmers in their transient California tent camps in order to know their plight at first hand. The novel was an explosive indictment, and it was damned and banned as often as it was praised. The story of the Joad family sold widely in many countries. It reached millions more when John Ford made his remarkable film of Steinbeck's novel.

Steinbeck broke his novel into two kinds of chapters, alternately—first a chapter describing the countryside or the people or nature in general, then a chapter telling the story of the Joads. His general descriptions are full of commentary, frequently oblique, on the migrant labor problem or human nature under stress or the animal world. This brief essay, "The Turtle," is the third chapter of the novel. The highway could be Route 66, but the place does not matter. Steinbeck is writing for all time, all places.

1   The concrete highway was edged with a mat of tangled, broken, dry grass, and the grass heads were heavy with oat beards to catch on a dog's coat, and fox-tails to tangle in a horse's fetlocks, and clover burrs to fasten in sheep's wool; sleeping life waiting to be spread and dispersed, every seed armed with an appliance of dispersal, twisting darts and parachutes for the wind, little spears and balls of tiny thorns, and all waiting for animals and for the wind, for a man's trouser cuff or the hem of a woman's skirt, all passive but armed with appliances of activity, still, but each possessed of the anlage ° of movement.

2   The sun lay on the grass and warmed it, and in the shade under the grass the insects moved, ants and ant lions to set traps for them, grasshoppers to jump into the air and flick their yellow wings for a second, sow bugs like little armadillos,° plodding restlessly on many tender feet. And over the grass at the roadside a land turtle crawled, turning aside for nothing, dragging his high-domed shell over the grass. His hard legs and yellow-nailed feet threshed slowly through the grass, not really walking, but boosting and dragging his shell along. The barley beards slid off his shell, and the clover burrs fell on him and rolled to the ground. His horny beak was partly open, and his fierce, humorous eyes, under brows like fingernails, stared straight ahead. He came over the grass leaving a beaten trail behind him, and the hill, which was the highway embankment, reared up ahead of him. For a moment he stopped, his head held high. He blinked and looked up and down. At last he started to climb the embankment. Front clawed feet reached forward but did not touch. The hind feet kicked his shell along, and it scraped on the grass, and on the gravel. As the embankment grew steeper and steeper, the more frantic were the efforts of the land turtle. Pushing hind legs strained and slipped, boosting the shell along, and the horny head protruded as far as the neck could stretch. Little by little the shell slid up the embankment until at last a parapet ° cut straight across its line of

anlage: foundation or rudiment.
    armadillos: a variety of burrowing animals with bony plates covering their body.
    parapet: a protective wall or barrier.

march, the shoulder of the road, a concrete wall four inches high. As though they worked independently, the hind legs pushed the shell against the wall. The head upraised and peered over the wall to the broad smooth plain of cement. Now the hands, braced on top of the wall, strained and lifted, and the shell came slowly up and rested its front end on the wall. For a moment the turtle rested. A red ant ran into the shell, into the soft skin inside the shell, and suddenly head and legs snapped in, and the armored tail clamped in sideways. The red ant was crushed between body and legs. And one head of wild oats was clamped into the shell by a front leg. For a long moment the turtle lay still, and then the neck crept out and the old humorous frowning eyes looked about and the legs and tail came out. The back legs went to work, straining like elephant legs, and the shell tipped to an angle so that the front legs could not reach the level cement plain. But higher and higher the hind legs boosted it, until at last the center of balance was reached, the front tipped down, the front legs scratched at the pavement, and it was up. But the head of wild oats was held by its stem around the front legs.

3   Now the going was easy, and all the legs worked, and the shell boosted along, waggling from side to side. A sedan driven by a forty-year-old woman approached. She saw the turtle and swung to the right, off the highway, the wheels screamed and a cloud of dust boiled up. Two wheels lifted for a moment and then settled. The car skidded back onto the road, and went on, but more slowly. The turtle had jerked into its shell, but now it hurried on, for the highway was burning hot.

4   And now a light truck approached, and as it came near, the driver saw the turtle and swerved to hit it. His front wheel struck the edge of the shell, flipped the turtle like a tiddly-wink, spun it like a coin, and rolled it off the highway. The truck went back to its course along the right side. Lying on its back, the turtle was tight in its shell for a long time. But at last its legs waved in the air, reaching for something to pull it over. Its front foot caught a piece of quartz and little by little the shell pulled over and flopped

upright. The wild oat head fell out and three of the spear-head seeds stuck in the ground. And as the turtle crawled on down the embankment, its shell dragged dirt over the seeds. The turtle entered a dust road and jerked itself along, drawing a wavy shallow trench in the dust with its shell. The old humorous eyes looked ahead, and the horny beak opened a little. His yellow toe nails slipped a fraction in the dust.

ANALYSIS

This essay is as simple and direct as objective ° description can be. Steinbeck lets graphic visual images build the whole picture. He does not need to intrude as author. The first person pronoun has no place here.

He could easily begin this essay with a description of the turtle. Why introduce first seeds and their dissemination, then the smaller insects, before reaching the main subject? Perhaps he wishes to give a sense of continuity in the natural world: nothing exists in isolation. Perhaps he wants to tie his first paragraph to his last: the turtle unknowingly deposits the seeds on the other side of the road. The life process continues. Why introduce in so brief a description, we might also ask, not one but two motorists? Perhaps Steinbeck intends to comment obliquely, or indirectly, on human nature—the thoughtful and the thoughtless—and to make the turtle impervious to both, as it were. There is a splendid inevitability about the turtle's progress. It is painfully slow, but only in comparison with our clocks, not with nature's. The "old humorous eyes looked ahead" and the turtle moved on. Steinbeck comes to no conclusions. He only describes a simple daily event. If he has his own opinions about what this turtle might stand for—the common people?—he is not giving them.

Questions on Content

1. What particular attributes do the seeds described in the

objective: See Glossary.

first paragraph possess? How does he reuse them in the last paragraph?

2. How do the turtle's legs work: independently or in unison?

3. What does the red ant add to this description?

Questions on Technique

1. What differences do you note between the vocabulary of the first paragraph and the rest of the essay?

2. What effect does Steinbeck achieve with this idea: ". . . at last a parapet cut straight across its line of march, the shoulder of the road, a concrete wall four inches high." Why is "wall" the perfect word here?

3. Why bother to tell us the sedan is driven by a forty-year-old woman? Could not this paragraph be omitted?

4. Why repeat the description of the turtle's "humorous" eyes?

Techniques to Imitate

Close observation and the patient search for details

Steinbeck's completely objective description is a good model for you to imitate. Its success may be explained by his meticulous care for details. Steinbeck includes such a vast number of details because he knows that only by doing so can he make readers see, as in a motion picture, exactly what they would see if they were there beside the highway actually watching the turtle, the grass, the concrete "wall," the drivers, car and truck. In fact, the description is all detail.

This kind of writing may look easy, but it is not. Steinbeck had to know his subject thoroughly. He had to be a very close observer to collect so many details. The difference between a commonplace objective description and a masterful one rests on the difference between the abilities of the authors to seek out and describe a great many details.

Steinbeck uses a very simple vocabulary, but he makes it do for him exactly what he wants. Note the exactness of "his hard legs," "yellow-nailed feet," "horny beak," "fierce,

humorous eyes," "brows like fingernails." In his description
of the turtle's actions, he is equally detailed:

"As though they worked independently, the hind legs
pushed the shell against the wall. The head upraised and
peered over the wall to the broad smooth plain of cement.
Now the hands, braced on top of the wall, strained and
lifted, and the shell came slowly up and rested its front
end on the wall. For a moment the turtle rested. A red
ant ran into the shell, into the soft skin inside the shell,
and suddenly head and legs snapped in, and the armored
tail clamped in sideways. The red ant was crushed between
body and legs. And one head of wild oats was clamped
into the shell by a front leg. For a long moment the turtle
lay still, and then the neck crept out and the old humorous
frowning eyes looked about and the legs and tail came
out. The back legs went to work, straining like elephant
legs, and the shell tipped to an angle so that the front legs
could not reach the level cement plain. But higher and
higher the hind legs boosted it, until at last the center of
balance was reached, the front tipped down, the front legs
scratched at the pavement, and it was up. But the head of
wild oats was held by its stem around the front legs."

Writing like this requires time and patience: time to
observe (or imagine) and patience to select the exact word
to describe what is there to see. In preparing to write
a description, allow yourself plenty of time and be patient
in your search for the most effective words for your purpose.

Suggestions for Writing

1. Select an animal you know well from observation and
   describe it as graphically as you can, but limit the description to activity. For instance, describe a cat stalking (and perhaps capturing) a bird. Describe each
   movement that brings the cat close to the bird, the capture of the bird, or its escape, and so forth.
2. Write an essay wherein you compare the method in
   which a number of animals move. For example, the
   chipmunk, the bear, the cat, the snake, and the cow.

How closely related to the means of locomotion is the size of each animal?

3. Project Steinbeck's descriptive method to the sight of three small children trying to cross a busy city street.

4. Describe the driver of the light truck in terms of the rest of his trip down the highway. Write your description as if you are an objective observer of the truck's journey.

JANE VAN LAWICK–GOODALL

First Observations

Students of human behavior have long been interested in the behavior of chimpanzees. Of all creatures on Earth, none so closely resemble human beings as the chimpanzees do. But up until the 1960's, scientists believed it would be impossible to observe chimpanzees' behavior in their natural forest habitat for any extended period of time.

Then in the early 1960's reports began coming out of Tanganyika (now Tanzania) that a young Englishwoman named Jane Goodall was making a sustained effort at close-range observation. The famed paleontologist Louis B. Leakey had recommended that Goodall make a serious study of chimpanzees, despite the fact (or perhaps because of it) that she was trained neither in animal behavior nor in anthropology.

In 1971 Goodall published a book about her experiences called *In the Shadow of Man*. As this selection from that book opens, Goodall has been camped in the dense forest for a little over four months. The fever from her first malaria attack has been gone for one month. During this time she has found what she is looking for: a band of chimpanzees who seem to accept her presence in their midst.

1   **D**uring that month I really came to know the country well, for I often went on expeditions from the Peak, sometimes to examine nests, more frequently to collect specimens of the chimpanzees' food plants, which Bernard Verdcourt had kindly offered to identify for me. Soon I could find my way around the sheer ravines and up and down the steep slopes of three valleys—the home valley, the Pocket, and Mlinda Valley —as well as a taxi driver finds his way about in the main streets and byways of London. It is a period I remember vividly, not only because I was beginning to accomplish something at last, but also because of the delight I felt in being completely by myself. For those who love to be alone with nature I need add nothing further; for those who do not, no words of mine could ever convey, even in part, the almost mystical awareness of beauty and eternity that accompanies certain treasured moments. And, though the beauty was always there, those moments came upon me unaware: when I was watching the pale flush preceding dawn; or looking up through the rustling leaves of some giant forest tree into the greens and browns and black shadows that occasionally ensnared a bright fleck of the blue sky; or when I stood, as darkness fell, with one hand on the still-warm trunk of a tree and looked at the sparkling of an early moon on the never still, sighing water of the lake.

2   One day, when I was sitting by the trickle of water in Buffalo Wood, pausing for a moment in the coolness before returning from a scramble in Mlinda Valley, I saw a female bushbuck ° moving slowly along the nearly dry streambed. Occasionally she paused to pick off some plant and crunch it. I kept absolutely still, and she was not aware of my presence until she was little more than ten yards away. Suddenly she tensed and stood staring at me, one small forefoot raised. Because I did not move, she did not know what I was—only that my outline was somehow strange. I saw her velvet nostrils dilate as she sniffed the air, but I was downwind and her nose gave her no answer. Slowly she came closer, and closer—one step at a time, her neck craned forward—always poised for instant flight. I can still scarcely believe that her nose actually touched my

bushbuck: an African antelope.

knee; yet if I close my eyes I can feel again, in imagination, the warmth of her breath and the silken impact of her skin. Unexpectedly I blinked and she was gone in a flash, bounding away with loud barks of alarm until the vegetation hid her completely from my view.

3 It was rather different when, as I was sitting on the Peak, I saw a leopard coming toward me, his tail held up straight. He was at a slightly lower level than I, and obviously had no idea I was there. Ever since arrival in Africa I had had an ingrained, illogical fear of leopards. Already, while working at the Gombe,° I had several times nearly turned back when, crawling through some thick undergrowth, I had suddenly smelled the rank smell of cat. I had forced myself on, telling myself that my fear was foolish, that only wounded leopards charged humans with savage ferocity.

4 On this occasion, though, the leopard went out of sight as it started to climb up the hill—the hill on the peak of which I sat. I quickly hastened to climb a tree, but halfway there I realized that leopards can climb trees. So I uttered a sort of halfhearted squawk. The leopard, my logical mind told me, would be just as frightened of me if he knew I was there. Sure enough, there was a thudding of startled feet and then silence. I returned to the Peak, but the feeling of unseen eyes watching me was too much. I decided to watch for the chimps in Mlinda Valley. And, when I returned to the Peak several hours later, there, on the very rock which had been my seat, was a neat pile of leopard dung. He must have watched me go and then, very carefully, examined the place where such a frightening creature had been and tried to exterminate my alien scent with his own.

5 As the weeks went by the chimpanzees became less and less afraid. Quite often when I was on one of my food-collecting expeditions I came across chimpanzees unexpectedly, and after a time I found that some of them would

Gombe: the Gombe Stream Chimpanzee Reserve, the home of her chimp group.

tolerate my presence provided they were in fairly thick forest and I sat still and did not try to move closer than sixty to eighty yards. And so, during my second month of watching from the Peak, when I saw a group settle down to feed I sometimes moved closer and was thus able to make more detailed observations.

6   It was at this time that I began to recognize a number of different individuals. As soon as I was sure of knowing a chimpanzee if I saw it again, I named it. Some scientists feel that animals should be labeled by numbers—that to name them is anthropomorphic °—but I have always been interested in the *differences* between individuals, and a name is not only more individual than a number but also far easier to remember. Most names were simply those which, for some reason or other, seemed to suit the individuals to whom I attached them. A few chimps were named because some facial expression or mannerism reminded me of human acquaintances.

7   The easiest individual to recognize was old Mr. McGregor. The crown of his head, his neck, and his shoulders were almost entirely devoid of hair, but a slight frill remained around his head rather like a monk's tonsure. He was an old male—perhaps between thirty and forty years of age (the longevity record for a captive chimp is forty-seven years). During the early months of my acquaintance with him, Mr. McGregor was somewhat belligerent. If I accidentally came across him at close quarters he would threaten me with an upward and backward jerk of his head and a shaking of branches before climbing down and vanishing from my sight. He reminded me, for some reason, of Beatrix Potter's old gardener in *The Tale of Peter Rabbit*.

8   Ancient Flo with her deformed, bulbous nose and ragged ears was equally easy to recognize. Her youngest offspring at that time were two-year-old Fifi, who still rode everywhere on her mother's back, and her juvenile son,

anthropomorphic: ascribing human characteristics to nonhuman things.

Figan, who was always to be seen wandering around with his mother and little sister. He was then about six years old; it was approximately a year before he would attain puberty. Flo often traveled with another old mother, Olly. Olly's long face was also distinctive; the fluff of hair on the back of her head—though no other feature—reminded me of my aunt, Olwen. Olly, like Flo, was accompanied by two children, a daughter younger than Fifi, and an adolescent son about a year older than Figan.

9   Then there was William, who, I am certain, must have been Olly's blood brother. I never saw any special signs of friendship between them, but their faces were amazingly alike. They both had long upper lips that wobbled when they suddenly turned their heads. William had the added distinction of several thin, deeply etched scar marks running down his upper lip from his nose.

10   Two of the other chimpanzees I knew well by sight at that time were David Graybeard and Goliath. Like David and Goliath in the Bible, these two individuals were closely associated in my mind because they were very often together. Goliath, even in those days of his prime, was not a giant, but he had a splendid physique and the springy movements of an athlete. He probably weighed about one hundred pounds. David Graybeard was less afraid of me from the start than were any of the other chimps. I was always pleased when I picked out his handsome face and well-marked silvery beard in a chimpanzee group, for with David to calm the others, I had a better chance of approaching to observe them more closely.

11   Before the end of my trial period in the field I made two really exciting discoveries—discoveries that made the previous months of frustration well worth while. And for both of them I had David Graybeard to thank.

12   One day I arrived on the Peak and found a small group of chimps just below me in the upper branches of a thick tree. As I watched I saw that one of them was holding a pink-looking object from which he was from time to time pulling pieces with his teeth. There was a female and a youngster and they were both reaching out toward the

male, their hands actually touching his mouth. Presently the female picked up a piece of the pink thing and put it to her mouth: it was at this moment that I realized the chimps were eating meat.

13 After each bite of meat the male picked off some leaves with his lips and chewed them with the flesh. Often, when he had chewed for several minutes on this leafy wad, he spat out the remains into the waiting hands of the female. Suddenly he dropped a small piece of meat, and like a flash the youngster swung after it to the ground. Even as he reached to pick it up the undergrowth exploded and an adult bushpig charged toward him. Screaming, the juvenile leaped back into the tree. The pig remained in the open, snorting and moving backward and forward. Soon I made out the shapes of three small striped piglets. Obviously the chimps were eating a baby pig. The size was right and later, when I realized that the male was David Graybeard, I moved closer and saw that he was indeed eating piglet.

14 For three hours I watched the chimps feeding. David occasionally let the female bite pieces from the carcass and once he actually detached a small piece of flesh and placed it in her outstretched hand. When he finally climbed down there was still meat left on the carcass; he carried it away in one hand, followed by the others.

15 Of course I was not sure, then, that David Graybeard had caught the pig for himself, but even so, it was tremendously exciting to know that these chimpanzees actually ate meat. Previously scientists had believed that although these apes might occasionally supplement their diet with a few insects or small rodents and the like they were primarily vegetarians and fruit eaters. No one had suspected that they might hunt larger mammals.

16 It was within two weeks of this observation that I saw something that excited me even more. By then it was October and the short rains had begun. The blackened slopes were softened by feathery new grass shoots and in some places the ground was carpeted by a variety of flowers. The Chimpanzees' Spring, I called it. I had had a frustrating morning, tramping up and down three valleys with never a sign or sound of a chimpanzee. Hauling myself up the steep slope of Mlinda Valley I headed for the Peak, not only weary but soaking wet from crawling through dense undergrowth. Suddenly I stopped, for I saw a slight movement in the long grass about sixty yards away. Quickly focusing my binoculars I saw that it was a single chimpanzee, and just then he turned in my direction. I recognized David Graybeard.

17   Cautiously I moved around so that I could see what he was doing. He was squatting beside the red earth mound of a termite nest, and as I watched I saw him carefully push a long grass stem down into a hole in the mound. After a moment he withdrew it and picked something from the end with his mouth. I was too far away to make out what he was eating, but it was obvious that he was actually using a grass stem as a tool.

18   I knew that on two occasions casual observers in West Africa had seen chimpanzees using objects as tools: one had broken open palm-nut kernels by using a rock as a hammer, and a group of chimps had been observed pushing sticks into an underground bees' nest and licking off the honey. Somehow I had never dreamed of seeing anything so exciting myself.

19   For an hour David feasted at the termite mound and then he wandered slowly away. When I was sure he had gone I went over to examine the mound. I found a few crushed insects strewn about, and a swarm of worker termites sealing the entrances of the nest passages into which David had obviously been poking his stems. I picked up one of his discarded tools and carefully pushed it into a hole myself. Immediately I felt the pull of several termites as they seized the grass, and when I pulled it out there were a number of worker termites and a few soldiers, with big red heads, clinging on with their mandibles. There they remained, sticking out at right angles to the stem with their legs waving in the air.

20   Before I left I trampled down some of the tall dry grass and constructed a rough hide—just a few palm fronds leaned up against the low branch of a tree and tied together at the top. I planned to wait there the next day. But it was another week before I was able to watch a chimpanzee "fishing" for termites again. Twice chimps arrived, but each time they saw me and moved off immediately. Once a swarm of fertile winged termites—the princes and princesses, as they are called—flew off on their nuptial flight, their huge white wings fluttering frantically as they carried the insects higher and higher. Later I realized that it is at this time of year, during the short rains, when the worker termites extend the passages of the nest to the surface, preparing for these emigrations. Several such swarms emerge between October and January. It is principally during these months that the chimpanzees feed on termites.

21   On the eighth day of my watch David Graybeard arrived again, together with Goliath, and the pair worked there for two hours. I could see much better: I observed how they scratched open the sealed-over passage entrances with a thumb or forefinger. I watched how they bit the ends off their tools when they became bent, or used the other end, or discarded them in favor of new ones. Goliath once moved at least fifteen yards from the heap to select a firm-looking piece of vine, and both males often picked three or four stems while they were collecting tools, and put the spares beside them on the ground until they wanted them.

22   Most exciting of all, on several occasions they picked small leafy twigs and prepared them for use by stripping off the leaves. This was the first recorded example of a wild animal not merely *using* an object as a tool, but actually modifying an object and thus showing the crude beginnings of tool*making*.

23   Previously man had been regarded as the only toolmaking animal. Indeed, one of the clauses commonly accepted in the definition of man was that he was a creature who "made tools to a regular and set pattern." The chimpanzees, obviously, had not made tools to any set pattern. Nevertheless, my early observations of their primitive tool-

making abilities convinced a number of scientists that it was necessary to redefine man in a more complex manner than before. Or else, as Louis Leakey put it, we should by definition have to accept the chimpanzee as Man.

24 I sent telegrams to Louis about both of my new observations—the meat-eating and the toolmaking—and he was of course wildly enthusiastic. In fact, I believe that the news was helpful to him in his efforts to find further financial support for my work. It was not long afterward when he wrote to tell me that the National Geographic Society in the United States had agreed to grant funds for another year's research.

ANALYSIS

Goodall's main purpose is to describe her two "first observations." Paragraph 1 describes where she is and what her feelings are about her surroundings. Paragraphs 2–4 describe encounters with other animals: the bushbuck and the leopard. Paragraphs 5–10 describe some individuals in the group of chimpanzees she is observing. Paragraph 11 states that she made two "really exciting discoveries." Here is the major topic of this chapter of Goodall's, which is then developed in paragraphs 12–23.

Paragraph 24 concludes this chapter and points toward another topic: "another year's research."

There is certainly something of Jane Goodall herself in this account. Why, then, is this called "primarily *objective* experience"? Compare this selection with Sancton's description of his experience with another kind of forest. We discover much that is personal about Sancton: his family, his hopes, his disappointments. We learn little or nothing about how the camp is run, and we do not really care. But although Goodall describes her personal reactions to the forest in her opening paragraphs, she never invites us into her heart. Her purpose is entirely different from Sancton's: she wants us to know about two discoveries of immense importance, for she feels that these "first observations" will alter the way we define what it means to be human. Given this as a writer's purpose, excessive subjectivity would be out of place.

Questions on Content

1. What are the two exciting first observations?
2. Why are they of such immense importance?

Questions on Technique

1. In paragraph 1, Goodall tells where she is and what her feelings are about the setting. What does this personal revelation add to her account?
2. Why does she include the anecdotes about the two animals in paragraphs 2–4?
3. Goodall apologizes for naming the animals she is observing. What is the effect of this? Would you prefer the omission of names? Why?
4. How does Goodall's technique differ from Steinbeck's?

Techniques to Imitate

1. *Use of sensory impressions*
2. *Selection of precise details*

Goodall's description illustrates clearly two writing skills that we already called to your attention in preceding selections: the use of words that appeal to the senses, and the careful selection of precise details.

1. Even though she retains strict objectivity, Goodall writes as though she were answering the question: What was it like in the wild East African hills observing chimpanzees? To help us to share the experience and appreciate the observations she has made, she tells not only what she sees but also what she hears, feels, and smells.

> Sound: *trickle of water, crunch* of eating a plant, loud *barks* of alarm, halfhearted *squawk, thudding* of feet, *silence, screaming* and *snorting* pig

> Touch: *coolness, velvet* nostrils, *warmth* of breath,

silken impact of skin, the *pull* of termites

Smell: *rank* smell of cat

2. The selection abounds in examples of Goodall's care in selecting precise details to help us see exactly what she sees. For example, she says that the young chimpanzee "swung" to the ground. She might have used the verb "dropped," but "swung" describes much more precisely the chimpanzee's natural movement. Note these examples of precise descriptive words:

Adjectives: *sheer* ravines, *bulbous* nose, *ragged* hair, *springy* movements, *feathery* new grass shoots

Verbs: *crunch, tensed, craned, ensnared, wobbled*

Nouns: pale *flush* preceding dawn, *fleck* of blue sky, slight *frill* around his head

Finding words that describe sensory impressions and using precise descriptive details are two techniques to imitate in your descriptive writing.

Suggestions for Writing

1. Jane Goodall had no training in animal behavior but she had other qualifications: a real desire for knowledge and a sympathetic understanding of animals. Take as a subject some process or object you are very much interested in (for example: the behavior of animals, how children play, the ways homes are built or decorated, the kinds of food people eat, the ways we communicate). Describe as objectively as you can what you perceive about this subject: tell exactly what you see and, when possible, what you hear, smell, touch, taste.

2. Describe objectively the meals you had yesterday. Devote one paragraph to each meal. Provide as many sensory details as you think are suitable.

3. If possible, go to a place where you can be alone. Sit quietly there for a while and be alert to what you perceive through your senses. Then write a brief description of your observations.

EDWIN WAY TEALE

Bird of Freedom

John Steinbeck was primarily a novelist, but we need only look at his *Sea of Cortez* (written with Edward F. Ricketts, published in 1941) to discover that marine biology was one of his hobbies. Edwin Way Teale is primarily a roving naturalist, but he is also a dedicated writer and photographer. He has been awarded the John Burroughs Medal for distinguished nature writing and is a member of numerous scientific organizations, including the Explorers Club and the New York Entomological Society.

In "Bird of Freedom," which first appeared in the *Atlantic Monthly*, Teale describes the bald eagles, since 1782 the emblem of our nation. Few of us have seen at close range this remarkably majestic bird. We could not distinguish it easily from the more common golden eagle. Teale argues that "the spread of mechanized civilization, the growth of population, changing environment, the destruction of nesting sites," not to mention the bounty that used to be paid for each pair of talons, have been making the bald eagles almost extinct. Since Teale wrote this essay, the population of bald eagles has increased again. In the late 1960's the number of bald eagles in the U.S. (except Alaska) was estimated at just over five thousand. Alaska now has more than 90 percent of this country's bald eagles.

Yet it would be wrong to say that Teale is arguing a case here. The bald eagle's habits and virtues are the

subject he wishes to explore. He is deeply concerned
about the fate of the bird, but he first of all wants us
to learn its history from his essay. Teale's talent for
making us see and understand is enormous. He describes
with the eye of a photographer; he teaches us from his
rich background in natural history.

1 Since a late-June day in
Philadelphia, just a century and three quarters ago this
year, ° the bald eagle has been America's most celebrated
bird. On that day, June 20, 1782, the Continental Congress
selected it as the emblem of the nation. Its image since
then has appeared on United States currency, has formed
the central figure of the Great Seal, has been part of every
treaty and important document of state. During most of
these 175 years, however, the bird itself has been warred
upon and pushed along the road toward extirpation.* In all
the forty-eight states ° of the Union today probably fewer
than a thousand pairs of these great birds are still alive.
Revered in image and persecuted in life—that has been
the paradoxical * story of the American eagle.
2   Yet no other native bird, in repose or in the air, approaches it as a symbol of dignity and power and freedom.
Clinging to some lofty perch, it habitually sits erect, its
white head of impressive size held high, its yellow eyes
surveying with that piercing, concentrated gaze peculiar to
its kind the scene spread out below. In every line it imparts an impression of majesty, of unflinching independence. And this is the eagle quiescent.*
3   It is the eagle active, soaring in a wide, windy sky on
a day of brilliant sunshine, that becomes transcendently *
the symbol of our freedom. Many years have passed since
the day, but I remember vividly one such bird as it
mounted above my canoe floating on a forest lake in the
Adirondacks. With wings outspread, riding the updrafts in
effortless ascent, white head and tail gleaming in the sun,

   this year: 1957.
   forty-eight states: Teale published this essay before Alaska and
Hawaii became states.

it left the earth, the lake, the forest, the mountains behind. My paddle forgotten, I watched it recede into the
shining sky of that August day. It shrank to sparrow size,
this bird with a wingspan of nearly seven feet. As long as
I could see it, it turned endlessly in spirals and graceful
curves, writing its poetry of motion on a blue page of the
sky.

4   Above all other birds it is the soaring eagle, with its
size and weight, that gives the most abiding impression of
power and purpose in the air. It advances solidly like a
great ship cleaving the swells and thrusting aside the
smaller waves. It sails directly where lesser birds are
rocked and tilted by the air currents. A number of times
on the lichen-splotched rocks of Hawk Mountain, in Pennsylvania, I have held soaring eagles in my glasses as they
rode by. Sometimes they were level with my eyes, sometimes above, sometimes below. But always in passing they
presented the same appearance of stability, of superiority
to small disturbances, of moving ahead calmly poised in
an unstable element.

5   And so the eagle has moved across the sky above many
events in our history. It no doubt circled over Ponce de
León when he roamed Florida searching for the Fountain
of Youth. It no doubt met Henry Hudson when he sailed
into the river that bears his name. It looked down on the
Jamestown colonists and knew the rock-bound New England shore where the *Mayflower* came to anchor. It saw
Bunker Hill and Fort Ticonderoga. It watched the pioneers
roll west. It flew at Kitty Hawk before the Wright Brothers.
And it was patrolling the Potomac when Washington became the nation's capital.

6   Unlike the golden eagle, a cosmopolitan that embraces
virtually the full circle of the Northern Hemisphere, the
bald eagle is almost exclusively the bird of a single continent. On that long-ago June day when, unknown to itself,
it became the country's emblem, the American eagle inhabited all but the more arid interior portions of the land.
The decades since have marked a long retreat. The eagle
trees, with their immense nests of sticks, that were land-

marks of a former time are now, in numerous regions, but fading memories in the minds of older inhabitants. Two far-removed places, Alaska and Florida, today hold the bulk of the bald eagle population. The former is a reservoir of the northern subspecies, the latter of the southern subspecies.

7   On the Fourth of July, in 1831, a crowd gathered in what is now Cortland, New York, to witness a novel event. The local silversmith, an ardent admirer of Henry Clay,° had engraved on a metal clasp a greeting to his hero. This he attached to the leg of an American eagle. Shouts and musket fire started the bird in the general direction of Clay's Kentucky. Seven days later and 725 miles to the west, on a high bluff on the far bank of the Mississippi near Dubuque, Iowa, an Indian's bullet brought it down. The week's wandering of this pioneer banded bird supplied the earliest precise information on the wide-ranging character of an eagle's flight.

II

8   Knowledge of the life and ways of our national bird has been curiously slow in evolving. It was ninety years after the flight of the Cortland eagle, 140 after the action of the Continental Congress, before any serious scrutiny was made of the day-to-day home life of the bald eagle. In the 1920s, Francis H. Herrick, a professor at Western Reserve University, began recording in notes and photographs the activity at nests on the Lake Erie shore, near Vermilion, Ohio. He worked hidden in blinds at the top of towers erected beside the eyries.° One of these structures, anchored in concrete and containing four tons of steel, ascended to a height of ninety-six feet. The temperature within the khaki blind rose as high as 104 degrees and once, in a sudden storm, lightning struck a neighboring oak. Out of years of carefully amassed notes Herrick produced *The American Eagle*. Published in 1934, this book contributed greatly to a better understanding of the

Henry Clay: American statesman and orator (1777–1852).
eyries: nests; also spelled aeries.

habits and character and ecology ° of the "bird of freedom."

9   During more recent years a Canadian, a retired Winnipeg banker, Charles L. Broley, has been advancing this
knowledge still further. In retirement Broley turned to the
strenuous hobby of climbing trees and banding Florida
eagles. At seventy-eight he is still ascending lofty pines
and pulling himself among the upper branches of hundred-
foot cypresses. In January, 1939, he banded his first eaglet.
Since then the number has risen to more than 1200, with
150 banded in a single year, 1946.

10   Far out on the Kissimmee Prairie, north of Lake
Okeechobee,° I once accompanied this remarkable man
on one of his banding expeditions. He was then nearly
seventy, keen of eye, athletic and agile, arranging his rope
ladders and working his way nearly eighty feet up the trunk
of a long-dead pine and over the stick ramparts of the
nest to reach the eaglet on top. Some of the trees he
ascends are half eaten through by fire. Others are so old
they go down in the next storm. Several times in the back
country Broley has been mistaken for a revenue officer,
and on one occasion he nearly lost his automobile in a
grass fire set to drive him off. When he began banding
he was arrested as a suspicious character three times in
one month. One day on the Gulf coast, among dry pal-
mettos, he stepped back to look up at a nest and trod
squarely on a coiled diamondback, his heel, providentially,
pinning its head to the ground.

11   As the life of an eagle is long—some estimates place
its longevity at as much as a hundred years—the fruits of
Broley's activity may continue to be harvested for decades
to come. Hardly had this ex-banker taken up his hobby
before it yielded an important and wholly unknown fact
about Florida eagles. One of the first birds he banded was
killed, a few weeks after it left the nest, at Columbiaville,
New York, 1100 miles to the north. Later returns from

   ecology: the division of biology that deals with the relations
between organisms and their environment.
   Lake Okeechobee: a large lake in south central Florida.

Maine, from the Maritime Provinces, even from 200 miles above Broley's old home, Winnipeg, Canada, have confirmed the fact that Florida eagles wander far to the north, perhaps even into the Arctic, during summer months.

12 In the latter days of August and the early part of September each year, scores of bald eagles pass Hawk Mountain, moving south. Other migrating birds are leaving their nesting areas behind. But the eagles are heading home. In Florida they nest mainly in winter, from mid-November into April. The northern eagles, able to endure privation and cold, do not migrate; they merely shift slightly southward in times of special hardship. Around the Great Lakes nesting usually begins in March.

III

13 To most birds a nest is a comparatively flimsy, temporary affair, used but a few weeks and abandoned forever. But American eagles, mated for life, use the same nest year after year. It is the center of their existence. Few creatures evidence so great an attraction for home. During wartime years one pair stubbornly clung to its nesting tree even though it stood in the middle of a practice bombing range. The Great Eyrie, near Vermilion, Ohio, was occupied for thirty-six years without a break. In southern Georgia I was once told of an eagle tree on an island that had formed a landmark for three generations of natives in following the water trails that led into the heart of the Okefenokee Swamp.°

14 On rare occasions eagles have made their nests on the ground, on cliffs, even in the haymow of an abandoned barn. But normally they choose the top of a lofty tree, adding material each year, so the mass increases as the tree grows old. Herrick estimated that the Great Eyrie weighed about two tons when it crashed to the ground in a March storm in 1925. It was twelve feet high and eight and a half wide. An even larger nest, without doubt the

Okefenokee Swamp: 660-square-mile area in southeastern Georgia.

largest eagle nest in America, fills a treetop near St. Petersburg, Florida. This mass of sticks has been accumulating for forty years. It rises for twenty feet, ending in a flattened top nine and a half feet across.

15 It is at the time when the nests are repaired, the time of courtship and mating, that the aerial prowess of the American eagle comes into full display. Not content with picking sticks from the ground, it often hurls itself, with outstretched talons, against dry branches, snapping them from the trees. At other times it hovers above a treetop, closes its wings, plummets down, and let its weight and momentum break off the dead limb.

16 For the watching earth-bound man, however, the supreme thrill of these days is provided by the acrobatics of courtship—twisting climbs, inverted flight, thunderbolt dives with half-closed wings. At its climax the great birds grasp talons and plunge through space, turning over and over like a wheel in the sky as they fall. Two of my friends have witnessed this event. Their luck is associated in my mind with the confession of Izaak Walton: ° "I envy not him that eats better meat than I do, nor him that is richer, or wears better clothes than I do. I envy nobody but him and him only, that catches more fish than I do." As Walton felt about the more fortunate anglers, so I have felt about these more fortunate friends of mine.

17 Before the eggs are laid—usually two, sometimes one, rarely three—the eagles cover the sticks of the nest with a deep mattress of dry grass and dead vegetation. In harvesting this material they fly low, raking their talons across open fields. On rare occasions they utilize some source of supply already gathered together. In one instance an eagle flew off with a small haycock, in another with half of a muskrat house clutched in its talons. The males have a propensity for bringing home whatever oddity strikes their fancy. In Florida nests Broley has found electric light bulbs, clothespins, old shoes, gunny sacks,

Izaak Walton: English writer (1593–1683) whose most famous book, *The Compleat Angler,* is a classic essay on fishing.

a family photograph in a heavy frame, wax candles, air plants, magazines, and pieces of bright-colored cloth.

18　A songbird's brood is fledged and gone in a few weeks, but the eagle spends more than a third of a year raising its young. For five weeks the two birds take turns incubating the eggs. As parents they are among the most solicitous * in the world, tearing food into bites of just the right size for the growing eaglets, sheltering them from the sun with outspread wings, crouching low over them in storms, shielding them with their bodies from rain and hail. When smoke from a palmetto fire billowed up around an eagle tree, Broley once heard the mother bird keep up a continuous murmur as though reassuring her eaglet. Another occasion when these impressive, austere-looking birds revealed an almost human quality was when a pair returned to their Florida nest-tree after a summer in the north. They came back in the evening and a man living close by heard them "talking all night long" as though excited and delighted to be home again.

19　For the eaglet the flat top of the nest is a practice flying field. Here it waves its wings for minutes at a time, strengthening its muscles. Here it flaps a foot or two into the air. As its twelfth week approaches, and the white fuzz of its earliest days has been replaced through several juvenal molts ° with dark brown feathers, it lifts itself repeatedly several feet above the nest and hovers there like a helicopter. The time of its first flight is near at hand. This usually begins when one of the parents, a fish in its talons, swings close, screams, then veers away. In its hunger the young bird starts in pursuit and finds itself suddenly launched into full flight. So well have wing-waving and nest-hopping conditioned its muscles that this initial aerial journey may continue for a mile or more. When only a few days out of the nest it is able to mount to a great height in the sky.

20　At this time the young bald eagle is completely brown,

　juvenal molts: a bird's first feathers, also called juvenal plumage.

resembling the golden eagle except for its lower legs, which are bare instead of feathered. Three years pass before the fledgling reaches maturity and attains the white head and tail, the yellow bill and legs and eyes, of the adult. The head of a bald eagle is fully feathered, not bare. In its name the word "bald" is used with the older meaning of "white." Paradoxically, on the day the young bird leaves the nest it is larger than either parent. The contraction of bones and more strenuous exercise account for the later reduction. But during its first months of flight it may exceed its parents by as much as a pound in weight and a foot in wingspan. It is this fact that is believed to have deceived John James Audubon ° into describing what is now known to have been an immature northern bald eagle as a new species, his long-mystifying "Bird of Washington."

IV

21 Years ago I stood beside a cage at the Bronx Zoo and rashly tried to outstare an eagle. Its yellow eyes, with their untamable depths, never wavered. In the end that gaze, so fiercely concentrated, produced a curious illusion, the impression that there was weight and substance and penetration in its glance. Soaring in the sky, a bald eagle has been observed to detect, and head directly for, a fish floating on the surface of a lake three miles away. Its keenness of vision is one of its most important aids to hunting.

22 Ever since the earliest accounts of American natural history, the robbing of the osprey ° has been featured in every recital of the hunting habits of the bald eagle. The twisting attack, the dropping of the fish, the plunge of the eagle to snatch it from the air before it strikes the water— these have been told innumerable times. They have tended to obscure the fact that the American eagle is resourcefully varied in its own hunting for food. In plunging after a swimming fish it sometimes submerges entirely. An eagle can,

John James Audubon: American naturalist and painter of birds (1785–1851).

osprey: a large brown and white hawk.

although it rarely does, alight upon the water, ride the surface like a gull, then take off again with no great difficulty. Audubon tells of seeing an eagle wading in a shallow stream in Pennsylvania and striking at fish with its beak. During winter, northern birds have been observed waiting for fish beside holes in the ice. Each year, usually in February and March, they search for food along the Hudson River, riding on ice cakes as far south as New York City.

23   In their hunting, eagles have plucked flying fish from the air above warm southern waters and have swooped down to snatch up rodents plowed from fields by tractors. Beneath the eagle tree on the Kissimmee Prairie I noticed nearly a dozen empty turtle shells. Rabbits, squirrels, woodchucks, weasels, snakes, birds of various kinds, all find a place on the eagle's menu. But almost invariably the bulk of its diet consists of fish. Rarely does it build its nest far from water.

24   Dead as well as living fish and mammals are acceptable to the eagle. More than a century ago when immense numbers of gray squirrels left an area of overpopulation and many were drowned swimming the Ohio River near Wheeling, West Virginia, Alexander Wilson noted bald eagles for days afterwards feasting on their stranded bodies. There seems little doubt that many of the smaller farm animals brought to nests by eagles were already dead and discarded in the fields when found. Careful observations in Alaska, where the bald eagle has been under long and bitter attack by commercial fishing interests, indicate that most of the salmon taken are dead or exhausted after spawning —fish that already have come to the natural end of their lives.

25   No doubt the eagles of Alaska, the greatest concentration anywhere in the world, do feed on live salmon as the millions of fish swim upstream at spawning time. But so they had been doing for thousands of years while the salmon remained undiminished in numbers. Uncontrolled fishing, increasing canneries, illegal seining ° by man, not the infinitesimal fraction subtracted by the eagles, have

seining: fishing with nets called seines.

been the obvious causes of the dwindling supply. Benjamin Franklin condemned the bald eagle as "bad" because, he said, it did not hunt its own food. Alaskans condemned the bald eagle as "bad" because, they said, it did. Which reveals much about the absurdity of the homocentric ° viewpoint in evaluating the morals of wildlife.

v

26   Aloft in the sky the American eagle is a bird supreme. It is master of virtually every other creature that flies. But often it keeps its power in reserve. Confident in its strength, it seems slow to anger. With powerful wingbeats it will flap along in dignified aloofness surrounded by a flock of screaming, diving crows. It submits to the attack of kingbirds and even, as Herrick once observed, of the thumb-sized blue-gray gnatcatcher. Some, witnessing these events, have called the eagle a coward. But always, when aroused, it can whirl on any attacker, scattering a flock or annihilating an individual.

27   Man with his gun is the eagle's only potent enemy. Experience has taught it to be wary. While Broley ascended to the nest in the Kissimmee tree, I watched the parent birds circle beyond gunshot, uttering not the scream popularly associated with the eagle but a curiously small, rusty-hinge creaking call, their note of alarm. They made no effort to attack the man. This attitude, too, has been attributed to cowardice. It might just as fairly be called a sign of intelligence. The eagle learned quickly that the price of life and liberty was vigilance in remaining beyond the range of guns. This caution has played an important part in the survival of these birds at a time when many factors have combined to reduce their numbers.

28   As a small boy in the dune country of northern Indiana, soon after the turn of the century, I used to spend hours clinging to the roof of a low farmhouse watching eagles that passed high overhead toward the Lake Michigan shore. At that time there were eagle trees in the dunes.

homocentric: having a common center, but Teale uses the word here to mean seeing the world as if the human viewpoint were the only viewpoint.

Today no bald eagle nests in the region. The bird itself comes there only as a wandering or casual visitor.

29 As early as 1904, John Burroughs ° was writing in *Far and Near:* "I see fewer eagles along the Hudson River than I used to see fifteen years ago." Throughout the land the great birds have been shot for fun or to produce a stuffed trophy or in a self-righteous war on "vermin." Egg collectors have robbed their eyries. Farmers have chopped down their nesting trees. Game commissions have done little to provide protection. Everywhere the decrease of the eagle has been the handiwork of man. Only a small proportion of Americans today have ever seen the emblem of their country soaring high above them, wild and free.

30 From 1917 to 1952, a period of thirty-five years, every bald eagle in Alaska lived with a price on its head. Its destruction was rewarded with a bounty. For each pair of talons, the territorial government offered first fifty cents, then a dollar, finally two dollars. During these years more than $100,000 was paid out in such bounties. Before the slaughter ended, about 115,000 American eagles had been destroyed.

31 It was not until 1940, 158 years after it had been honored by the Continental Congress, that the eagle received legal protection in all of the forty-eight states. And 170 years had passed before, on July 1, 1952, protection was extended to the bird in Alaska. Federal statutes now provide for a fine up to $500 for harming an American eagle. Thus the long persecution of our national bird is over—officially. Nowhere now is a price set on its head. Everywhere under the Stars and Stripes the bird is protected by law.

32 But other factors, more difficult to control than bounties and firearms, still work against the eagle. The spread of mechanized civilization, the growth of population, changing environment, the destruction of nesting sites—these are producing a profound effect among the birds in some areas, particularly in Florida. In a recent letter Charles L. Broley

John Burroughs: American naturalist, essayist, and poet (1837–1921).

reports that along the coast between Tampa and Engle-
wood where, only a decade ago, he counted more than
eighty nests producing young, this year he could find but
two. In the past fifteen years, he estimates, the number of
active nests in Florida has dropped from about 450 to
fewer than 200. Immature birds have become relatively
scarce. In the early 1930s more than 50 per cent of all
American eagles passing Hawk Mountain in the fall were
immature birds. In recent years, however, this figure has
dropped to about 20 per cent. It is Broley's belief that well
over half the adult eagles in Florida today are too old to
reproduce.

33   From mid-December to mid-February, each winter,
concentrations of American eagles build up along the Mississippi in the Illinois-Iowa region. As many as fifty or a
hundred may congregate in one place. But these birds are
drawn from a vast nesting area to the north still relatively
unaffected by the spread of population. It is in the eastern
states, to some extent around Chesapeake Bay but most of
all in Florida, that the impact of human expansion is producing the most abrupt change in the status of the eagle.
As the wave of building has swept down the west coast of
Florida, felling many of the ancient nesting trees, there is
evidence that some of the birds have retreated to inland
cypress swamps. It may be that among stands of such trees
in sanctuaries like the Everglades National Park the Florida
eagles will find an undisturbed and permanent nesting place.

ANALYSIS

If we begin with the title of this essay, we have a clue to
the author's intentions. The American eagle has been a
symbol of independence for almost two hundred years,
but symbols grow out of reality. Teale is, frankly, in awe of
this giant bird's "dignity and power" as well as of its freedom. He wants us to know it, to see it as he has. In order
not to burden his reader with too many technical details
(he is writing for the general public, not for ornithologists),
he builds his essay in several stages.

The first seven paragraphs are a kind of historical introduction. He cites specific details to "place" the bird in our national history. Paragraph 8 begins a brief survey of how we came to know more about "the day-to-day home life of the bald eagle": Herrick's researches, which produced a valuable book; Broley's banding of Florida eagles; Teale's own observations. In paragraph 13, Teale settles down to describe in sharp detail two vital aspects of the eagle's life: nesting and feeding. In a sense, these paragraphs (13–25) are the heart of the essay, topics three and four, as it were. We are amazed to learn that the nests often measure nine feet across and weigh several tons, that the female seldom lays more than two eggs at a time, that eagles can see their prey as far as three miles away, that fish are their main diet. Only in paragraph 25 does Teale shift from his objective description to the problem of their survival, and this shift serves him well as a transition into what we could call his fifth and last topic: the eagle's enemies. Paragraphs 26–33 are a double-barreled conclusion to this descriptive essay. The main subject is still the eagle but we, the American people, past and present, are incorporated at once into the prose with the sentence "Man with his gun is the eagle's only potent enemy." It takes Teale only five paragraphs to convince us that our ignorance was to blame for the fate of this bird. Words like "robbed," "chopped," "self-righteous war," and "slaughter" color his prose. Not surprisingly, then, he approaches his final sentence in a somewhat discouraged mood. From Chesapeake Bay to Florida the inroads of an expanding population are driving the bald eagle from its natural home, the ancient nesting trees. Teale offers only the words "may be" when he speaks of the Everglades National Park as their permanent nesting place.

How do you react now to Teale's fifth sentence back in paragraph 1: "In all forty-eight states of the Union today [meaning 1957] probably fewer than a thousand pairs of these great birds are still alive"? Has his compelling prose made you not only aware of but concerned for the fate of the American eagle?

Questions on Content

1. Teale opens paragraph 2 with a statement of opinion. List the details he supplies in paragraphs 2, 3, and 4 to support and explain this statement.
2. What methods did Herrick and Broley use to observe the eagle closely?
3. Since bald eagles are not really "bald," what does the adjective mean?
4. Describe the eagle's method of caring for its young.
5. What do eagles eat?
6. Why do some people call eagles cowardly? What evidence does Teale give to demonstrate that these people, out of ignorance, are mistaken?

Add to Your Vocabulary

extirpation, paradoxical, quiescent, transcendently, solicitous.

Questions on Technique

1. How successful are Teale's first seven paragraphs as a general introduction? What do the Cortland, New York, details add to the opening?
2. What details has Teale assembled in paragraphs 13–20 to illustrate his statement that to American eagles the nest is the center of their existence? Why do you think he needs this quantity of detail to help you to *see* the bird?
3. In paragraph 22, notice the words chosen to discuss the eagle's hunting habits. Are they strong enough to suggest the power of this bird? What substitutes would you make?
4. How does Teale impress upon us the disappearance of a great number of bald eagles? Will facts alone arouse your interest? How important are the statistics as a means of supporting Teale's point?
5. Is the conclusion of this essay an anticlimax? Would you have written it differently? In what respects?

Techniques to Imitate

Knowing your subject thoroughly

The most impressive characteristic of Teale's essay is his obviously vast knowledge of his subject. Since the purpose of his essay is to inform, the more information he has at his disposal, the more effective his writing will be. In your own educational experience, you are frequently expected to write informatively, whether in a report prepared from your reading or in an essay answer to an examination question. From your reading of Teale's essay, you can easily recognize the importance of knowing your subject thoroughly and of using your knowledge to support fully your general statements or topic sentences.° When Teale wishes to impress upon us (in paragraph 13) that eagles have a great attraction to their nest, he cites three examples of their unusual steadfastness. When he opens paragraph 32 by saying that "other factors" still work against the eagle, he cites four of these factors and uses statistics to illustrate the resultant drop in eagle population.

In his account of the nest and the eagle's domestic life, Teale crams into eight paragraphs a vast amount of information, each paragraph richly adding to our knowledge of this unique bird. Many of the facts, such as those about the age and size of the nests, are, as isolated facts, interesting, even startling, in themselves, but it is only by the gradual accumulation of a great many of them that he gives weight to the overall impression he wishes to leave with the reader.

From Teale, then, we can learn the great importance of being fully informed about our subject, and for our own informative writing we know that we must be well prepared with enough facts to make our writing coninvncing. When critics characterize one of your paragraphs or one of your essays as "thin," they mean that you have not developed it fully enough.

topic sentence: See Glossary.

Suggestions for Writing

1. Those of us who are not naturalists would have great trouble describing an eagle in as much detail as Teale does. But we do have eyes to observe the natural world. Select a subject with which you are familiar—a reptile, an insect, a flower, an animal—and, in a descriptive paragraph or two, make your reader see some of its characteristics. You may want to weave into your observations some facts obtained from reference books. Telling an incident will add interest to your essay.

2. Describe the façade, or the front, of some building. Be as detailed as possible in telling your reader precisely what you see.

3. Conservation is a constant problem, a particularly vital one to the Department of the Interior. Choose a subject related to conservation of your own local resources, and write a descriptive essay of 400–500 words on how and why the natural resource is diminishing. If possible, be as specific as Teale is in paragraphs 29–32.

JAMES RAMSEY ULLMAN

Kilimanjaro!

The answer to the common question "Why climb mountains?" is the now-familiar "Because they are there." Jungfrau, Matterhorn, Annapurna, Everest—they have challenged climbers in the past; they will continue to entice adventurers to climb them. James Ramsey Ullman was a celebrated writer on the topic of mountains. His novel *The White Tower* (1945) deserved its great popularity because Ullman could not only tell a superb adventure story of six oddly assorted people and a Swiss mountain, but could also write out of personal experience. He fills the pages of *High Conquest: The Story of Mountaineering* and *The Other Side of the Mountain: An Escape to the Amazon* with his own exploits. It was only a matter of time before he would be tempted by Kilimanjaro, "the apex of Africa."

To divorce a description of this great mountain from the narration of his climbing is, for Ullman, impossible. "Kilimanjaro!" is a combination of portrait and story. Most readers will agree, however, that what remains after they have experienced this climb vicariously is the feeling not of the energy Ullman expended or the dangers involved but of Kilimanjaro's size and imperturbable dominance. "Raise our eyes, wherever we were," he writes, "and there *it* was. . . . Changeless above change unending, the white ghost in the sky." This is the mountain Ernest Hemingway immortalized in 1936 in his short story "The Snows of Kilimanjaro." In the intrigu-

117

ing epigraph to that story, Hemingway records that "its western summit is called the Masai 'Ngàje Ngài,' the House of God. Close to the western summit there is the dried and frozen carcass of a leopard. No one has explained what the leopard was seeking at that altitude."

Ullman and Thomas, his Wachagga guide, conquered Kilimanjaro in three and a half days. It is likely that our memories of this description will last far longer. We feel we are there, in the village of Marangu, at Pieter's Hut, at Mawenzi and Kibo. We can see the whole of Africa "lying clear and bright in crystal space."

1　　　　　　　　　　　**I**t has been called the House of God. It has been called the High One. The Cold One. The White One. On close acquaintance, by climbers, it has been called a variety of names rather less printable. But to the world at large it is Kilimanjaro, the apex of Africa and one of the great mountains of the earth.

2　For two weeks we had been on safari in southern Kenya and northern Tanganyika, and it was a realm of glorious variety. We moved from the red lands of Tsavo to the white lands of Amboseli; from prairie to parkland to forest to swamp to desert. We rode out from the towns of the settlers, through the villages of the Masai, into the domain of the lion, the rhino, and the elephant, and everywhere was something new and fresh and different from what we had seen before. Only one thing remained constant. Raise our eyes, wherever we were, and there *it* was. Above the giraffes' ears, above the baobab trees,° above the bright white cloud puffs in the African sunlight. Changeless above change unending, the white ghost in the sky.

3　Slowly we circled it, and the circle grew tighter. "They say it's one of the easiest big mountains in the world," I said to son Jim; and Jim nodded, but awkwardly, because his neck was craned back so far. "And it's only a mile higher than the Matterhorn," I added cheerfully.

baobab trees: broad-trunked African timber trees of the silk-cotton family; they bear a gourd-like fruit.

4 Our white hunter, to whom mountaineers were a stranger breed than albino zebras, kept pointing off in sundry directions across what he affectionately called MMBA. Translation: Miles and Miles of Bloody ° Africa. But by now we were incapable of focusing on anything except the center of our magic circle, the Miles and Miles of Bloody Kilimanjaro.

5 It is a thing of contradictions; a long-dead volcano built up from the plains in vast gentle slopes and known to expert cragsmen as a "nothing" mountain, an antagonist that calls for neither rope nor ax nor crampon nor any special climbing skills. It is, at the same time, an awful lot of nothing. The surrounding plains are at a mere 3000-foot elevation, its summit at 19,340—and Everest itself boasts no such three-mile leap from base to tip. A German scientist, Dr. Hans Meyer, first conquered Kilimanjaro in 1889, and since then it has been challenged by more climbers than any peak of its size on earth. Few have ever fallen from it, but well over half its challengers, through the years, have run out of gas on its upper flanks and had to turn back defeated.

6 Until a little more than a century ago the very existence of Kilimanjaro was unsuspected by the outside world. It was during the great European land grabs in Africa, when Kenya fell to the British and Tanganyika to the Germans, that it was discovered that the highest point of the continent stood flush on their borders. In a moment of generosity, Queen Victoria (who had plenty of mountains in her realm) presented a gift to her nephew the Kaiser (who had none) by authorizing a bulge in the boundary whereby the peak became all German. But the British got it back, with compound interest, in the first World War, and it has been theirs ever since. °

Bloody: British slang, difficult to approximate, but its meaning here is close to that of "extraordinary."

The mountain is now part of the republic of Tanzania, which was formed in 1964 by the union of Tanganyika and Zanzibar. This story was published in 1957.

II

7   Road's end was the village of Marangu, sprawled on the
mountain's southern flank at about the 5000-foot level.
There Jim and I bade temporary farewell to jeep and white
hunter (no neck-craner he), picked up our provisions and
equipment, and joined forces with our porters. These added
up to nine: a headman-guide, a cook, and seven rank-and-
file load bearers. All were men of the Wachagga tribe
(called Chaggas for short), and they ranged in age from a
sixteen-year-old boy, who was having his first go at the
mountain, to Thomas, the headman, who, at fifty-four,
would be making his uncounted-hundredth ascent. Of the
lot of them only Thomas had the job of going all the way
to the top—*if* his employers were able to follow him. We
also joined forces with a third *bwana:* ° Fred Hughes, an
official in the Tanganyika Forestry Service and secretary of
the local mountaineering club.

8   If we followed the usual schedule we would be gone
five days: three and a half up, one and a half down. "Got
your dark glasses for the snowfields?" Fred asked. And it
was a startling thought in that tropical world of black
Africa. We were in shorts and T shirts. We sweated. We
plodded. We hiked ten miles to climb the three thousand
feet of our first day's ascent.

9   During the first two hours we were in inhabited country—primitive but not squalid or poverty-stricken. On the
contrary, it had a bright multihued Land of Oz quality, a
mixture of sunshine and greenery and gay clothing and
chatter and laughter.

10   Then we entered the forest. This was pure jungleland:
a maze of black boles,° dense shrubbery, ferns, fronds °
and lianas.° Orchids and begonias winked on and off like
lights in the surrounding shadow. Birds cawed. Monkeys

bwana: boss. *Bwana* comes from Swahili, a language common
to Central and East Africa.
   boles: trunks or stems of trees.
   fronds: leaves, especially of palm trees.
   lianas: climbing plants that root in the ground.

jabbered. Jabbering right back at them, our long file wound its way between the great green-bearded trees.

11 By now we were strung out loosely, each going at his own pace, meaning that Fred and Jim were up ahead, well out of my ken, and I dead last in the procession. Well, next to dead last. Headman Thomas considered it his duty to stay with the feeblest of his *bwanas* and crept loyally behind me.

12 Unfortunately there was not much communication between us. Thomas' English was pretty well limited to his own name, presumably acquired in a mission house. And my mastery of the African tongues was somewhat less than that. Our major attempt at conversation came during a brief stop, when Thomas pointed at me and inquired, "Nairobi?"

13 "No, America," I told him.

14 "Ah," he said, "missionary."

15 And we let it go at that.

16 The lowest of Kilimanjaro's three huts, at about 9000 feet, is called the Bismarck. The head of our column took four hours to reach it. I needed about five.

17 The second day's trek, to Pieter's Hut, was another ten-odd miles, another 3000-plus feet higher. At first we were still in dense forest, but then the vegetation began to thin, we came out onto great moorlike slopes, and the surrounding world swung slowly into view. To the east, and the Indian Ocean, a cloud bank spread away beneath us into blue miles, gleaming white and frozen as a polar snow-field. To south and west, there was not white but brown, no cloud but only distance—an incredible sweep of MMBA stretching to horizons so distant that the eye faltered trying to reach them.

18 Then the eye turned. It looked north. It looked up. And there, again, was Kilimanjaro. It is not a single tapering peak but a huge and sprawling massif, almost a range in itself. To our right—the east—was the lesser of its two ultimate summits, called Mawenzi, an ancient volcanic core of red crumbling rock, raising its jagged towers to a height of some 17,000 feet. Then to the west, and directly above us, its walls leveled out into a long skyline saddle which swept on for some seven miles before beginning to rise again—this time into the slopes of Kibo. Kibo is *the* top of the mountain, and utterly unlike Mawenzi: a symmetrical truncated cone, perpetually snow-capped, and so vast it dwarfs its rival. This is the Kilimanjaro of the stories, the legends, the photographs: the fabulous white-topped pudding athwart the equatorial sky.

19 I have, in my day, described the great silences on certain mountains, but there were no silences that day on Kilimanjaro. The porters jabbered; they laughed; they told each other stories at a distance of a quarter of a mile. And though almost all were barefoot, they moved like chamois over rocks and gravel that were trying hard to tear my stout boots to ribbons. On their heads, nonchalantly, swayed their forty-pound loads of foodstuffs, utensils, and blankets. Two men, I noted, carried fine new capacious * knapsacks—presumably the gifts of previous employers—but even these went balanced atop their craniums.

20 And so up we went, now through long slanting meadows, with Alpine flowers bright around us, and by the time my private rear guard reached Pieter's Hut it was midafternoon. Here at 12,300 feet, it was cold even in the sunshine, and when night came we sat huddled in blankets long before turning into our bunks. Far below us, on the plains, we could see the pinprick lights of towns and villages, and in the emptiness beyond them the orange glow of bush fires. From the Chaggas' lean-to, bursting with smoke, came a low, slow sing-song that was half mission-house hymn and half ancient tribal chant.

21 In the morning the fires below were invisible. But there was fire above: the ice-white summit of Kibo ablaze in the rising sun. In the stainless clarity of air, it seemed close enough to reach out and touch, but there was still another full day's climb ahead of us before we would be even at the base of the final cone. Toward noon we reached our first major goal: the great 14,000-foot saddle between Kibo and Mawenzi. Seven miles long and almost as broad, it is utterly barren and flat as a ball field, and I had been told by previous climbers how terribly the wind could blow across its unprotected wastes. Our luck held, however. We had no wind. Only sun.

22 The trail came out close to the base of Mawenzi, and its tattered spires rose sheer above us. Then we turned our backs and slogged across the saddle. At this altitude, I knew all too well, a whole encyclopedia of ailments can afflict the climber, among them headache, nausea, sore throat, thumping heart. But so far I was all right; and even after we crossed the seven flat miles and began the ascent of Kibo's skirts, my anatomy continued to hold together. Right foot, left foot. Right, left. Perhaps a hundred steps—ten seconds' rest—a hundred more. Ahead, a slowly emerging speck on the scree ° slopes, was Kibo Hut—about 16,500 feet up, higher than the highest peak of the Alps.

23 Kibo Hut was tiny. It was dirty. It was freezing. Here there was neither water nor firewood, and all we had brought up was the minimal amount needed for drinking and cooking. Such problems, however, did not prevent our cook, Samuel, from dispensing a de luxe tea and supper, complete with serving cloth and napkins. And for the eighth time in eight meals he hopefully set out the prize item in his larder—a jar of ferocious-looking mustard pickles that, to his great distress, no one had yet deigned to touch.

24 "Jim, don't you think we owe it to Samuel—"

25 That was as far as I got. Suddenly I was conscious of something even yellower than the horrid pickles, and that something was Jim's face.

26 "Ex-cuse me," he mumbled weakly, and lurched from the hut.

27 It was the demon Altitude, striking without warning; and from then on Jim had no respite from nausea and racking headaches. We gave him aspirin. No effect. Sundry other pills. No effect. "A night's sleep will fix you up," we told him. But there was no sleep for poor Jim. When I awoke at 3:30—the grim hour of up-and-at-it—it was to find him miserably climbing back into his bunk after still another bout of sickness outside.

scree: a pebble; a stone; also a heap of stones or debris.

28 It was obvious that he could go no higher.

29 "Don't feel too bad about it," Fred comforted him. "Even George Mallory—the *Everest* Mallory—got sick up here at Kibo and had to go back."

30 This information didn't seem to cheer Jim greatly, but he was realist enough to know the score, and it was decided that at daylight he would go down to Pieter's. Fred, too, would be going no higher, but this was according to plan. He had already been up the mountain three times. So now it was I alone who bestirred myself, sloshing down the tea that Samuel brought me and pulling on my heavy clothing in the cold candlelit hut.

31 Then the door opened and Thomas stomped in, dressed now in heavy boots, woolen helmet, and a too-small British-army overcoat that must have dated from the Zulu Wars. And a moment later there were just we two—and Kilimanjaro.

32 It was still full night, but the stars and a late-waning moon gave light enough to see by, and above us Kibo's snow dome loomed like a great beacon lighted from within. There remained some 3500 vertical feet to go to the top— no more, to be sure, than we had climbed on each of the previous days, but now the angle of ascent steeped sharply. There was no solid rock, but only loose scree and crumbled lava in which one floundered and backslid maddeningly. And with each foot gained the lungs struggled harder and more futilely for breathable air.

33 Step—slip. Step—slip. Multiplied a hundred times, and then a thousand.

34 We followed a long shallow gully up to our left; then another to the right. My rests were no longer at hundred-step intervals but at fifty, and then thirty and then twenty. Yet, basically, there was no sign of *real* trouble. Heart, lungs, and legs, to be sure, were working overtime—but still working. My stomach behaved, and aspirin dissolved a gathering headache. Best of all, the mountain was keeping its sharpest claws sheathed, for there was neither wind nor bitter cold.

35 As we climbed on, the night thinned and the stars

faded. For perhaps half an hour we crept on in gray twilight, and then the grayness was shattered by the wildest, most savage sunrise I have ever seen. The whole eastern horizon was banded with crimson. Mawenzi, its summit already beneath us, flamed red as fire. And Kibo's snow-cap, above us, was suddenly no longer a mountaintop but a vast spectrum, itself a sun in the gleaming sky. I put on dark goggles, and so did Thomas. But even through their green film the light seemed too brilliant for mere human eyes.

36 We were at 17,000 feet—seventeen-five—eighteen. Kibo's walls now rose up smoothly. No gullies, no humps or ridges; only an endless hateful grind of scree and lava.

37 At the end of the endlessness, clamped into the sky above, were the rocks of Gillman's Point, lowest notch in the crater's rim, and through the minutes, and then the hours, it seemed to remain exactly the same distance above us.

38 Step—slip. Step—slip. I was half convinced we were not moving at all. But apparently we were, for around us there were changes. Red Mawenzi was remote below. To the left and right were snow slopes and glaciers. And to the right, too, and only a little below the rim, we could see the bulge in the mountainside known as Leopard Point. Kibo's famous leopard is no legend. He was not invented by Ernest Hemingway for "The Snows of Kilimanjaro," but was right there for years, a carcass frozen amid the ice and rock—with no one knowing how, or why, he had climbed to it. And the reason he is there no longer is that he was gradually hacked to bits by climbers and carried away as souvenirs.

39 Leopard Point is at 18,500 feet, and now it was below us. Gillman's is at 18,635, and at last it seemed closer. It was very close. We had almost reached it. We *had* reached it. We were standing, not on scree but on solid rock, and before us the mountain no longer climbed skyward but fell sharply away into its summit crater.

40 "Is O.K., *bwana*," said Thomas.

41 "Yes, O.K."

42 O.K.? It was marvelous. It was heaven. To be there, to stand there. To *sit down*.

43 Kilimanjaro's crater, like the rest of the mountain, is on the grand scale. More than a mile across and some three and a half in circumference, it is a double crater whose deepest point is about 900 feet lower than the highest summit. Gillman's Point, where we now were, is on the crater scarp.° Six hundred feet down steep walls is the crater floor, a piebald * sweep of black and white, lava and snow, almost perfectly level, except for a number of huge and fantastic ice masses that have been given such names as the Dome, the Battleship, and the Cathedral. At the center of this circle, like a bull's-eye in a target, is the inner crater, another 300 feet deep, complete with a second scarp, steep walls and, at the very bottom, the volcano's cold core, called the Ash Pit.

44 I would have liked to go down and see the Ash Pit, but there was something I wanted more—and that something was not down but up. In the rulebook of Kilimanjaro, Gillman's Point "counts"; if you reach it you have climbed the mountain. But it is not the top. *The* top is some 700 feet higher and a mile and a quarter distant to the south and west, along the ups and downs of the crater rim. It is still known by its old German name, the Kaiser Wilhelm Spitze, and it is only there that all of Africa is beneath you.

45 Par for the climb from Kibo Hut to Gillman's is five hours. It had taken me seven, and I was thoroughly conscious that I had not spent the morning in bed. In all honesty, I had not expected to get this far. I was surprised and delighted that I had, and decided the only sane course was to leave well enough alone. "Gillman's counts," I told myself. "It's enough, and we'll go down." Then Thomas looked at me inquiringly, and my hand, quite on its own, pointed up.

46 The hateful scree was below us. We were on blessed solid rock. For all of ten steps, that is. Then we came off

scarp: a line of cliffs.

the rock onto snow, the snow was soft and crustless in the midday sunshine, and we sank in to the knee, the thigh, the waist. I lurched. I floundered. In no time my mouth was open like a boated fish's, gasping for air, and my heart was pounding fit to crack my ribs.

47 Even Thomas was not quite superhuman. He sank in too. But sinking or not, he was able to keep going steadily, whereas my ratio of movement to rest was about one to three. On the downslopes of the ragged rim my gait was a stumbling crawl. On the upgrades, which of course predominated, the crawl seemed in comparison to have been a light-footed sprint.

48 We searched for snowless rock. But now there was snow everywhere. Ahead, on the endless hummocks ° of the rim; to the right, choking the crater; to the left, falling away endlessly in billowing waves of glacier. The snow gleamed. The snow glared. The billows were no longer static but undulating, and from their crests darted long white lances of light that struck blindingly into my eyes. I fumbled in a pocket for my goggles but didn't find them. I had them on. The whiteness beat against their green lenses as if it would crack them with its force.

49 In that frozen world it was not cold. It was warm, even hot. Sweat was trickling on my back and down my forehead, under the goggles, into my eyes. My eyes were bothering me even more now than legs, lungs, or heart. Sweat and snow seemed to mingle, forming patterns and images that wove before me. Soon the whole mountaintop was weaving. Crater and rim revolved slowly in space, like an enormous wheel.

50 I was terribly tired, and the snow was soft. It was a great pillow, a featherbed, all around me, and in the deep drifts, leaning against it, I closed my eyes. I had read, sometimes even written, of climbers overwhelmed by sleep at high altitudes, and now for the first time it was actually happening to me. With eyes closed, the awful glare was gone. Resting motionless in my featherbed, I felt breathing and heartbeat ease, and I sank gently, deliciously, into

hummocks: ridges of ice, as in an ice field.

a shadowed doze. Luckily the shadows never closed in entirely. My head jerked back. My eyes opened. I crept on again, willing myself to move, my eyes to stay open.

51 I had estimated an hour from Gillman's Point to the summit, but now, after twice that, we seemed to be nowhere at all. All recognizable features of rim and crater were gone. There were the endless humps, the snow, the sky; and now something was happening to the sky, too, for it was no longer blue but white. Like the mountain, it was covered with snow—or was it cloud? Yes, it was cloud, I decided. And then suddenly, through a rent in the cloud, I saw a sight that I thought was hallucination: a soaring plane. It was not silver, as a plane should be, but gleaming amber, and it moved high and still, like a specter, and then vanished in the gulfs of space.

52 It had not been illusion, I learned later; Thomas had seen the plane too. But then I didn't know. I couldn't even find Thomas. Like the spectral thing in the sky, he had disappeared, too, into the whiteness. And then a second hallucination: a black disk. The disk was not in the sky but on the rim before me. It grew larger as I approached. It was Thomas's face, and he had turned and was waiting.

53 Down—up. Up—down. Then up and more up. The cloud seemed to be gone, and there was only the rim and the crater spinning around me. Then they, too, dissolved, as I tripped and fell headlong into the snow. When I arose it was to see still another hallucination. In the whiteness ahead, there was something that was not white. On a hump of snow there was what seemed to be a pile of stones—a pile fashioned not by nature but by man—and rising from the stones two bamboo poles. I climbed another few steps and the pile didn't vanish. I reached out to touch it, and it was there. *We* were there. On the Kaiser Wilhelm Spitze, 19,340 feet high. I shook hands with Thomas and sat down. Or maybe I sat down first.

54 After a few minutes my head was clear, my breathing normal. I smoked a cigarette, and it was good. From beneath the stones I pulled a black metal box, took out the summit register and signed it; and that was good, too, except that I wished Jim were there to sign with me.

55 Then I looked slowly around. MMBK lay all below us. MMBA lay all around us. If I say I could see the Indian Ocean, Johannesburg, the Nile, the Congo, I am obviously lying. But I would not have thought so then, for it seemed to me I could see *everything*—the whole of Africa—lying clear and bright in crystal space. There are few men in the world as happy as the mountaineer atop his mountain, and for half an hour, on that magical summit, I savored my reward to the full.

56 Then—*"Bwana—"*

57 "Yes, Thomas."

58 He pointed at my wristwatch. There was still a full installment of the price to be paid: those Miles and Miles of Bloody Kilimanjaro in reverse.

III

59 I shall make it brief, which it wasn't. First there was the crater rim again: the humps, the whiteness, the ups, the downs; but now, at least, the downs predominated. There was our self-made trail to follow; and in half the time of our upward crawl we were back on the rocks of Gillman's Point. Here I was greeted by another hallucination. A figure was moving. A voice was speaking. Presently they turned into Fred Hughes, and Fred said, "Have some chocolate." Then he added, "I thought I'd amble up and see how you were doing."

60 "So the worst is over," I thought—and failed to hear the sound of off-stage laughter. But I heard it clearly enough during the hours that followed, as I crept and lurched and stumbled down the endless slopes of scree and lava. The proper way to descend a mountain like Kilimanjaro is on the double-quick—sliding, almost running, as gravity pulls you along. But for me gravity was no ally, for I had not the strength to brace against it. Every time I tried to advance at more than a crawl, my knees buckled, and I swayed and fell.

61 So a crawl it was. Down the miles. Through the hours.

Sometimes Fred and Thomas were with me; sometimes they were no more than specks far below. But always there were knees, calves, feet, toes. There were stones, stones, stones. There was an ache spreading upward that would have been almost unendurable if I had not been at least half asleep from fatigue.

62 Day was ending; Kibo Hut appeared. But this was not journey's end. Not only Jim but all the porters had gone on down to Pieter's, taking our food and blankets along.

63 "Can you keep going?" Fred asked me.

64 "I most certainly cannot," I assured him. But after an hour's rest, somehow, I did; and on through the night I went, hobbling into Pieter's Hut a little before midnight.

65 This time it was Jim who was the nurse and I the patient.

66 Then came the last day—the walk down to Marangu. "There's nothing to it," Fred and Jim reminded me cheerfully. But by now there was nothing much to me either. My face was round and swollen as a red balloon; my knees jerked and twitched like a puppet's; and my toes wore monstrous blisters.

67 Hobble, hobble, hobble. Sway, stumble, trip. I tried walking pigeon-toed; I tried walking duck-footed. No good. Nothing was any good. At every step the rocks in the path seemed to rise gleefully and kick me, and I kicked them savagely back, and groaned.

68 "Snows!" I thought. Mr. Hemingway could have his snows. What I would remember would be the *toes* of Kilimanjaro.

69 Still, all things have an end—even MMBK. And at five that afternoon our 1957 Kilimanjaro Expedition had passed into history. We were on the terrace of the hotel at Marangu. I was barefoot. I was pouring the third beer into my swollen face. I was swearing silently that in the rest of my life I would climb nothing higher than New York's Murray Hill.

70 Then our white hunter joined us.

71 "Well, how was it?" he asked.

72 "It was wonderful," I heard myself saying, and the darndest thing is that I was telling the truth.

ANALYSIS

Ullman faces two problems in writing this essay. Since his subject is the mountain as well as the climb, his reader deserves geographical and historical orientation. How can he best dispense it? And second, how can he keep his narrative (what happened) from dominating his description (what it looked like, how it felt)?

He solves the first problem handily. The mountain presides over the first six paragraphs. We learn its size, its history, its many names, its location (though it is in northern Tanganyika, it can be seen in Kenya). Ullman slowly intrudes himself and his friends into this general introduction. The transition to the climb itself is thus easily made.

The second problem (keeping the narrative from dominating the description) is more difficult. Ullman's solution is to describe, whenever possible, who was climbing, what equipment they carried, what conditions they met, what reactions they experienced. Never does the reader ask, "Are they going to make it?" Ullman underplays the climbers' role constantly. He stresses the fatigue not the difficulty. He describes the terrain, the altitude, the view and not the skill it takes to reach 19,000 feet. The accumulative effect is MMBK. Expert cragsmen may call it a "nothing" mountain, but from the terrace of the hotel at Marangu (where we end this essay) it looks huge and exhausting, tormenting and exhilarating. Ullman sums up his own reaction in an easy pun on Hemingway's title: "What I would remember would be the *toes* of Kilimanjaro."

Stylistically this account of an expedition has much to commend it, more than we can point out here. In the first paragraph Ullman introduces one of his most effective devices: staccato sentences or phrases. Note how successfully he uses them in paragraphs 10, 18, 23, 27, and especially 42, where he gains the reader's smile and respect through his honest anticlimax: "It was marvelous. It was heaven. To be there, to stand there. To *sit down*." When he comes to paragraph 59, he is ready to let the short sentence take over in order to make his descent brief. But like all good writers, Ullman knows the value of variety. Paragraph 60 breaks the staccato rhythm long enough to "slide" for a few sentences.

There are other devices he employs. For humor he uses MMBA, MMBK, and his conversations with Thomas; for verisimilitude, young Jim's sudden nausea on the ascent and Ullman's own twitching knees and swollen face on the descent; for contrast, paragraphs 46–53, the snow fields above the scree and crumbled lava; for a memorable conclusion, the expected reverse-twist—" 'It was wonderful,' I heard myself saying, and the darndest thing is that I was telling the truth." Professional writers have many such devices to bring variety and zest to their prose. What they learn early to avoid is overusing them.

Questions on Content

1. What vital statistics about Kilimanjaro do we learn from Ullman's essay?
2. What details do you recall of this group of twelve men as they set off for the ascent?
3. How does the summit Mawenzi differ from Kibo, *the* top of the mountain?
4. How does Ullman describe Kilimanjaro's crater and Gillman's Point?
5. What kind of man was Thomas, the guide?
6. What satisfaction and pleasures which Ullman experienced served to counteract the hardships?

Add to Your Vocabulary

capacious, piebald.

Questions on Technique

1. Ullman divides the essay into three parts. What is the function of each division?

2. What makes his description of Kibo Hut and what happened there (paragraphs 22–31) effective?
3. What senses are important in this description of mountain climbing? List several examples.
4. Why does he devote only one paragraph (55) to a description of the whole reason for the effort: the summit?

Techniques to Imitate

Figurative language—the simile and the metaphor°

Ullman is adept at comparisons and identifications—similes and metaphors. He thinks in terms of likenesses. Read and evaluate the effectiveness of the following examples:

Similes

Orchids and begonias winked on and off like lights in the surrounding shadow.

. . . a cloud bank spread away beneath us into blue miles, gleaming white and frozen as a polar snowfield.

[The porters] moved like chamois over rocks and gravel . . .

[The saddle] is utterly barren and flat as a ball field . . .

. . . Kibo's snow dome loomed like a great beacon lighted from within.

At the center of this circle, like a bull's-eye in a target, is the inner crater . . .

Metaphors

[Kilimanjaro:] the white ghost in the sky.

. . . our long file wound its way between the great green-bearded trees.

[Kilimanjaro:] the fabulous white-topped pudding athwart the equatorial sky.

It was the demon Altitude, striking without warning . . .

Best of all, the mountain was keeping its sharpest claws sheathed, for there was neither wind nor bitter cold.

figurative language, simile, and metaphor: See Glossary.

And Kibo's snowcap, above us, was no longer a mountaintop but a vast spectrum, itself a sun in the gleaming
sky.

. . . long white lances of light that struck blindingly
into my eyes.

[The snow] was a great pillow, a featherbed, all around
me . . .

Suggestions for Writing

1. Ullman uses striking similes and metaphors to describe an amazing natural wonder. In a paragraph, imitate this technique by using figurative language to
describe something in nature or some fantastic human
creation. Before you write, decide what other things
you want to compare or identify your subject to. Try
to select language that will help your reader to understand your own feelings about this "thing."
2. One of Ullman's techniques here is the use of the staccato style to describe aspects of the expedition: the
mountain, the climb, the hut, the sickness, the reactions
when they arrived. Write a description of some action
or of some place or person and use the staccato style
to make your description particularly forceful.
3. In paragraph 18 Ullman describes the mountain in
terms of its location: he tells what is to the right, to
the left, and what the eye sees as it looks up. Describe
something you can be looking at as you write. Tell
what surrounds it, and what is above it and below it. In
your description be sure to use words indicating location: words like *left, right, east, west, up, down, across,
surrounding,* and so on.
4. In paragraph 42, in a few short sentences, and in paragraphs 49 and 50, Ullman describes how he felt about
two experiences. Describe some experience you have
had and include details describing how you *felt* (emotionally) and about your physical sensations. Be as
objective as possible. You might also make up a situation and describe how you imagine a person might feel
in the midst of it.

HANSON W. BALDWIN

R.M.S. *Titanic*

The sinking of the *Titanic* off the Grand Banks of Newfoundland in April, 1912, is an event that has been told many times and in many media. Hanson W. Baldwin, since 1929 a member of the news staff of the *New York Times,* published this version in 1934. As a graduate of the U.S. Naval Academy, he possesses a knowledge of ships that is something more than amateur. As a reporter, he knows how to muster facts, how to build a story, where to place emphasis to hold his reader's attention. What is so remarkable about Baldwin's essay is the obvious fact of its not being an eye-witness report. Baldwin was only nine years old when the *Titanic* sank, yet he makes his research come alive, through a variety of techniques.

The *Titanic* left Southampton, England, on April 10, 1912. It sank at 2:20 A.M. on April 15, less than three hours after striking an iceberg. Of the 2,201 persons on board, almost 1,500 lost their lives. These are the facts Baldwin had to begin with. How he holds our attention to this descriptive account—suspense is obviously not one method—is worth close study. This essay is full of graphic details. As you read, try to distinguish their variety.

1   The White Star liner *Titanic,* largest ship the world had ever known, sailed from Southampton on her maiden voyage to New York on

April 10, 1912. The paint on her strakes ° was fair and bright; she was fresh from Harland and Wolff's Belfast yards, strong in the strength of her forty-six thousand tons of steel, bent, hammered, shaped, and riveted through the three years of her slow birth.

2   There was little fuss and fanfare at her sailing; her sister-ship, the *Olympic*—slightly smaller than the *Titanic* —had been in service for some months and to her had gone the thunder of the cheers.

3   But the *Titanic* needed no whistling steamers or shouting crowds to call attention to her superlative qualities. Her bulk dwarfed the ships near her as longshoremen singled up her mooring lines and cast off the turns of heavy rope from the dock bollards.° She was not only the largest ship afloat, but was believed to be the safest. Carlisle, her builder, had given her double bottoms and had divided her hull into sixteen water-tight compartments, which made her, men thought, unsinkable. She had been built to be and had been described as a gigantic lifeboat. Her designers' dreams of a triple-screw giant, a luxurious, floating hotel, which could speed to New York at twenty-three knots, had been carefully translated from blue prints and mold loft lines at the Belfast yards into a living reality.

4   The *Titanic's* sailing from Southampton, though quiet, was not wholly uneventful. As the liner moved slowly toward the end of her dock that April day, the surge of her passing sucked away from the quay the steamer *New York,* moored just to seaward of the *Titanic's* berth. There were sharp cracks as the manila mooring lines of the *New York* parted under the strain. The frayed ropes writhed and whistled through the air and snapped down among the waving crowd on the pier; the *New York* swung toward the *Titanic's* bow, was checked and dragged back to the dock barely in time to avert a collision. Seamen muttered, thought it an ominous start.

5   Past Spithead and the Isle of Wight the *Titanic* steamed.

strakes: the planking or plates on the sides or bottom of a vessel.
bollards: vertical posts on which mooring rope is tied.

She called at Cherbourg at dusk and then laid her course
for Queenstown. At 1:30 P.M., on Thursday, April 11,
she stood out of Queenstown harbor, screaming gulls soaring in her wake, with 2,201 persons—men, women and
children—aboard.

6 Occupying the Empire bedroom and Georgian suites
of the first-class accommodations were many well-known
men and women—Colonel John Jacob Astor and his young
bride; Major Archibald Butt, military aide to President
Taft, and his friend, Frank D. Millet, the painter; John
B. Thayer, vice-president of the Pennsylvania Railroad,
and Charles M. Hays, president of the Grand Trunk Railway of Canada; W. T. Stead, the English journalist;
Jacques Futrelle, French novelist; H. B. Harris, theatrical
manager, and Mrs. Harris; Mr. and Mrs. Isidor Straus; and
J. Bruce Ismay, chairman and managing director of the
White Star line.

7 Down in the plain wooden cabins of the steerage class
were 706 immigrants to the land of promise, and trimly
stowed in the great holds was a cargo valued at $420,000:
oak beams, sponges, wine, calabashes,° and an odd miscel-
lany of the common and the rare.

8 The *Titanic* took her departure on Fastnet Light and,
heading into the night, laid her course for New York.
She was due at Quarantine the following Wednesday morning.

9 Sunday dawned fair and clear. The *Titanic* steamed
smoothly toward the west, faint streamers of brownish
smoke trailing from her funnels. The purser held services
in the saloon ° in the morning; on the steerage deck aft
the immigrants were playing games and a Scotsman was
puffing "The Campbells Are Coming" on his bagpipes in
the midst of the uproar.

10 At 9 A.M. a message from the steamer *Caronia* sput-
tered into the wireless shack:

    calabashes: gourds, or bottles made from gourds.
    saloon: a large room for the common use of passengers on a
passenger vessel.

Captain, *Titanic*—Westbound steamers report bergs growlers and field ice in 42 degrees N. from 49 degrees to 51 degrees W. 12th April.

Compliments—
Barr

11 It was cold in the afternoon; the sun was brilliant, but the *Titanic,* her screws turning over at 75 revolutions per minute, was approaching the Banks.

12 In the Marconi cabin Second Operator Harold Bride, ear-phones clamped on his head, was figuring accounts; he did not stop to answer when he heard *MWL,* Continental Morse for the nearby Leyland liner, *Californian,* calling the *Titanic.* The *Californian* had some message about the icebergs; he didn't bother then to take it down. About 1:42 P.M. the rasping spark of those days spoke again across the water. It was the *Baltic,* calling the *Titanic,* warning her of ice on the steamer track. Bride took the message down and sent it up to the bridge. The officer-of-the-deck glanced at it; sent it to the bearded master of the *Titanic,* Captain E. C. Smith, a veteran of the White Star service. It was lunch time then; the Captain, walking along the promenade deck, saw Mr. Ismay, stopped, and handed him the message without comment. Ismay read it, stuffed it in his pocket, told two ladies about the icebergs, and resumed his walk. Later, about 7:15 P.M., the Captain requested the return of the message in order to post it in the chart room for the information of officers.

13 Dinner that night in the Jacobean dining room was gay. It was bitter on deck, but the night was calm and fine; the sky was moonless but studded with stars twinkling coldly in the clear air.

14 After dinner some of the second-class passengers gathered in the saloon, where the Reverend Mr. Carter conducted a "hymn sing-song." It was almost ten o'clock and the stewards were waiting with biscuits and coffee as the group sang:

> *O, hear us when we cry to Thee*
> *For those in peril on the sea.*

15 On the bridge Second Officer Lightoller—short, stocky, efficient—was relieved at ten o'clock by First Officer Murdoch. Lightoller had talked with other officers about the proximity of ice; at least five wireless ice warnings had reached the ship; lookouts had been cautioned to be alert; captains and officers expected to reach the field at any time after 9:30 P.M. At 22 knots, its speed unslackened, the *Titanic* plowed on through the night.

16 Lightoller left the darkened bridge to his relief and turned in. Captain Smith went to his cabin. The steerage was long since quiet; in the first and second cabins lights were going out; voices were growing still, people were asleep. Murdoch paced back and forth on the bridge, peering out over the dark water, glancing now and then at the compass in front of Quartermaster Hichens at the wheel.

17 In the crow's nest, Lookout Frederick Fleet and his partner, Leigh, gazed down at the water, still and unruffled in the dim, starlit darkness. Behind and below them the ship, a white shadow with here and there a last winking light; ahead of them a dark and silent and cold ocean.

18 There was a sudden clang. "Dong-dong. Dong-dong. Dong-dong. Dong!" The metal clapper of the great ship's bell struck out 11:30. Mindful of the warnings, Fleet strained his eyes, searching the darkness for the dreaded ice. But there were only the stars and the sea.

19 In the wireless room, where Phillips, first operator, had relieved Bride, the buzz of the *Californian's* set again crackled into the ear-phones:

> *Californian:* "Say, old man, we are stuck here, surrounded by ice."
> *Titanic:* "Shut up, shut up; keep out. I am talking to Cape Race; you are jamming my signals."

20 Then, a few minutes later—about 11:40 . . .

II

21 Out of the dark she came, a vast, dim, white, monstrous shape, directly in the *Titanic's* path. For a moment Fleet doubted his eyes. But she was a deadly reality, this ghastly *thing*. Frantically, Fleet struck three bells—*something dead ahead*. He snatched the telephone and called the bridge:

22 "Iceberg! Right ahead!"

23 The First Officer heard but did not stop to acknowledge the message.

24 "Hard-a-starboard!"

25 Hichens strained at the wheel; the bow swung slowly to port. The monster was almost upon them now.

26 Murdoch leaped to the engine-room telegraph. Bells clanged. Far below in the engine-room those bells struck the first warning. Danger! The indicators on the dial faces swung round to "Stop!" Then "Full speed astern!" Frantically the engineers turned great valve wheels; answered the bridge bells . . .

27 There was a slight shock, a brief scraping, a small list to port. Shell ice—slabs and chunks of it—fell on the foredeck. Slowly the *Titanic* stopped.

28 Captain Smith hurried out of his cabin.

29 "What has the ship struck?"

30 Murdoch answered, "An iceberg, sir. I hard-a-starboarded and reversed the engines, and I was going to hard-a-port around it, but she was too close. I could not do any more. I have closed the water-tight doors."

31 Fourth Officer Boxhall, other officers, the carpenter, came to the bridge. The Captain sent Boxhall and the carpenter below to ascertain the damage.

32 A few lights switched on in the first and second cabins; sleepy passengers peered through porthole glass; some casually asked the stewards:

33 "Why have we stopped?"

34 "I don't know, sir, but I don't suppose it is anything much."

35 In the smoking room a quorum of gamblers and their prey were still sitting around a poker table; the usual crowd of kibitzers looked on. They had felt the slight jar of the collision and had seen an eighty-foot ice mountain glide by the smoking room windows, but the night was

calm and clear, the *Titanic* was "unsinkable"; they hadn't bothered to go on deck.

36   But far below, in the warren of passages on the starboard side forward, in the forward holds and boiler rooms, men could see that the *Titanic's* hurt was mortal. In No. 6 boiler room, where the red glow from the furnaces lighted up the naked, sweaty chests of coal-blackened firemen, water was pouring through a great gash about two feet above the floor plates. This was no slow leak; the ship was open to the sea; in ten minutes there were eight feet of water in No. 6. Long before then the stokers had raked the flaming fires out of the furnaces and had scrambled through the water-tight doors into No. 5 or had climbed up the long steel ladders to safety. When Boxhall looked at the mailroom in No. 3 hold, twenty-four feet above the keel, the mailbags were already floating about in the slushing water. In No. 5 boiler room a stream of water spurted into an empty bunker. All six compartments forward of No. 4 were open to the sea; in ten seconds the iceberg's jagged claw had ripped a three-hundred-foot slash in the bottom of the great *Titanic*.

37   Reports came to the bridge; Ismay in dressing gown ran out on deck in the cold, still, starlit night, climbed up the bridge ladder.

38   "What has happened?"

39   Captain Smith: "We have struck ice."

40   "Do you think she is seriously damaged?"

41   Captain Smith: "I'm afraid she is."

42   Ismay went below and passed Chief Engineer William Bell fresh from an inspection of the damaged compartments. Bell corroborated the Captain's statement; hurried back down the glistening steel ladders to his duty. Man after man followed him—Thomas Andrews, one of the ship's designers, Archie Frost, the builder's chief engineer, and his twenty assistants—men who had no posts of duty in the engine room but whose traditions called them there.

43   On deck, in corridor and stateroom, life flowed again.

Men, women, and children awoke and questioned; orders were given to uncover the lifeboats; water rose into the firemen's quarters; half-dressed stokers streamed up on deck. But the passengers—most of them—did not know that the *Titanic* was sinking. The shock of the collision had been so slight that some were not awakened by it; the *Titanic* was so huge that she must be unsinkable; the night was too calm, too beautiful, to think of death at sea.

44 Captain Smith half ran to the door of the radio shack. Bride, partly dressed, eyes dulled with sleep, was standing behind Phillips, waiting.

45 "Send the call for assistance."

46 The blue spark danced: "CQD—CQD—CQD—CQ—"

47 Miles away Marconi men heard. Cape Race heard it, and the steamships *La Provence* and *Mt. Temple.*

48 The sea was surging into the *Titanic's* hold. At 12:20 the water burst into the seamen's quarters through a collapsed fore and aft wooden bulkhead. Pumps strained in the engine rooms—men and machinery making a futile fight against the sea. Steadily the water rose.

49 The boats were swung out—slowly; for the deckhands were late in reaching their stations, there had been no boat drill, and many of the crew did not know to what boats they were assigned. Orders were shouted; the safety valves had lifted, and steam was blowing off in a great rushing roar. In the chart house Fourth Officer Boxhall bent above a chart, working rapidly with pencil and dividers.

50 12:25 A.M. Boxhall's position is sent out to a fleet of vessels: "Come at once; we have struck a berg."

51 To the Cunarder *Carpathia* (Arthur Henry Rostron, Master, New York to Liverpool, fifty-eight miles away): "It's a CQD, old man. Position 41–46 N.; 50–14 W."

52 The blue spark dancing: "Sinking; cannot hear for noise of steam."

53 12:30 A.M. The word is passed: "Women and children in the boats." Stewards finish waking their passen-

gers below; life-preservers are tied on; some men smile at
the precaution. "The *Titanic* is unsinkable." The *Mt.
Temple* starts for the *Titanic;* the *Carpathia,* with a double-
watch in her stokeholds, radios, "Coming hard." The
CQD changes the course of many ships—but not of one;
the operator of the *Californian,* nearby, has just put down
his ear-phones and turned in.

54 The CQD flashes over land and sea from Cape Race
to New York; newspaper city rooms leap to life and
presses whir.

55 On the *Titanic,* water creeps over the bulkhead between Nos. 5 and 6 firerooms. She is going down by the
head; the engineers—fighting a losing battle—are forced
back foot by foot by the rising water. Down the promenade deck, Happy Jock Hume, the bandsman, runs with
his instrument.

56 12:45 A.M. Murdoch, in charge on the starboard side,
eyes tragic, but calm and cool, orders boat No. 7 lowered. The women hang back; they want no boat-ride on
an ice-strewn sea; the *Titanic* is unsinkable. The men encourage them, explain that this is just a precautionary
measure: "We'll see you again at breakfast." There is little
confusion; passengers stream slowly to the boat deck. In
the steerage the immigrants chatter excitedly.

57 A sudden sharp hiss—a streaked flare against the
night; Boxhall sends a rocket toward the sky. It explodes,
and a parachute of white stars lights up the icy sea. "God!
Rockets!" The band plays ragtime.

58 No. 8 is lowered, and No. 5. Ismay, still in dressing
gown, calls for women and children, handles lines, stumbles
in the way of an officer, is told to "get out of here." Third
Officer Pitman takes charge of No. 5; as he swings into the
boat Murdoch grasps his hand. "Good-by and good luck,
old man."

59 No. 6 goes over the side. There are only twenty-eight
people in a lifeboat with a capacity of sixty-five.

60 A light stabs from the bridge; Boxhall is calling in
Morse flashes, again and again, to a strange ship stopped
in the ice jam five to ten miles away. Another rocket drops

its shower of sparks above the ice-strewn sea and the dying ship.

61 1:00 A.M. Slowly the water creeps higher; the fore ports of the *Titanic* are dipping into the sea. Rope squeaks through blocks: lifeboats drop jerkily seaward. Through the shouting on the deck comes the sound of the band playing ragtime.

62 The "Millionaires' Special" leaves the ship—boat No. 1, with a capacity of forty people, carries only Sir Cosmo and Lady Duff Gordon and ten others. Aft, the frightened immigrants mill and jostle and rush for a boat. An officer's fist flies out; three shots are fired in the air, and the panic is quelled. . . . Four Chinese sneak unseen into a boat and hide in its bottom.

63 1:20 A.M. Water is coming into No. 4 boiler room. Stokers slice and shovel as water laps about their ankles —steam for the dynamos, steam for the dancing spark! As the water rises, great ash hoes rake the flaming coals from the furnaces. Safety valves pop; the stokers retreat aft, and the water-tight doors clang shut behind them.

64 The rockets fling their splendor toward the stars. The boats are more heavily loaded now, for the passengers know the *Titanic* is sinking. Women cling and sob. The great screws aft are rising clear of the sea. Half-filled boats are ordered to come alongside the cargo ports and take on more passengers, but the ports are never opened— and the boats are never filled. Others pull for the steamer's light miles away but never reach it; the lights disappear, the unknown ship steams off.

65 The water rises and the band plays ragtime.

66 1:30 A.M. Lightoller is getting the port boats off; Murdoch the starboard. As one boat is lowered into the sea a boat officer fires his gun along the ship's side to stop a rush from the lower decks. A woman tries to take her Great Dane into a boat with her; she is refused and steps out of the boat to die with her dog. Millet's "little smile which played on his lips all through the voyage" plays no more; his lips are grim, but he waves good-by and brings wraps for the women.

67 Benjamin Guggenheim, in evening clothes, smiles and says, "We've dressed up in our best and are prepared to go down like gentlemen."

68 1:40 A.M. Boat 14 is clear, and then 13, 16, 15 and C. The lights still shine, but the *Baltic* hears the blue spark say, "Engine-room getting flooded."

69 The *Olympic* signals, "Am lighting up all possible boilers as fast as can."

70 Major Butt helps women into the last boats and waves good-by to them. Mrs. Straus puts her foot on the gunwale of a lifeboat, then she draws back and goes to her husband: "We have been together many years; where you go I will go." Colonel John Jacob Astor puts his young wife in a lifeboat, steps back, taps cigarette on fingernail: "Good-by, dearie; I'll join you later."

71 1:45 A.M. The foredeck is under water, the fo'c'sle head almost awash; the great stern is lifted high toward the bright stars; and still the band plays. Mr. and Mrs. Harris approach a lifeboat arm in arm.

72 Officer: "Ladies first, please."

73 Harris bows, smiles, steps back: "Of course, certainly; ladies first."

74 Boxhall fires the last rocket, then leaves in charge of boat No. 2.

75 2:00 A.M. She is dying now; her bow goes deeper, her stern higher. But there must be steam. Below in the stokeholds the sweaty firemen keep steam up for the flaring lights and the dancing spark. The blowing coals slide and tumble over the slanted grate bars; the sea pounds behind that yielding bulkhead. But the spark dances on.

76 The *Asian* hears Phillips try the new signal—SOS.

77 Boat No. 4 has left now; boat D leaves ten minutes later. Jacques Futrelle clasps his wife: "For God's sake, go! It's your last chance; go!" Madame Futrelle is half-forced into the boat. It clears the side.

78 There are about 660 people in the boats, and 1,500 still on the sinking *Titanic*.

79 On top of the officers' quarters men work frantically to get the two collapsibles stowed there over the side.

Water is over the forward part of A deck now; it surges up the companionways toward the boat deck. In the radio shack, Bride has slipped a coat and lifejacket about Phillips as the first operator sits hunched over his key, sending— still sending—"41–46 N.; 50–14 W. CQD—CQD—SOS —SOS—"

80 The captain's tired white face appears at the radio-room door: "Men, you have done your full duty. You can do no more. Now, it's every man for himself." The captain disappears—back to his sinking bridge, where Painter, his personal steward, stands quietly waiting for orders. The spark dances on. Bride turns his back and goes into the inner cabin. As he does so, a stoker, grimed with coal, mad with fear, steals into the shack and reaches for the lifejacket on Phillips' back. Bride wheels about and brains him with a wrench.

81 2:10 A.M. Below decks the steam is still holding, though the pressure is falling—rapidly. In the gymnasium on the boat deck the athletic instructor watches quietly as two gentlemen ride the bicycles and another swings casually at the punching bag. Mail clerks stagger up the boat-deck stairways, dragging soaked mail sacks. The spark still dances. The band still plays—but not rag-time:

> *Nearer my God to Thee,*
> *Nearer to Thee* . . .

82 A few men take up the refrain; others kneel on the slanting decks to pray. Many run and scramble aft, where hundreds are clinging above the silent screws on the great uptilted stern. The spark still dances and the lights still flare; the engineers are on the job. The hymn comes to its close. Bandmaster Hartley, Yorkshireman violinist, taps his bow against a bulkhead, calls for "Autumn" as the water curls about his feet, and the eight musicians brace themselves against the ship's slant. People are leaping from the decks into the nearby water—the icy water. A woman cries, "Oh, save me, save me!" A man answers, "Good lady, save yourself. Only God can save you now." The band plays "Autumn":

> *God of Mercy and Compassion!*
> *Look with pity on my pain.* . . .

83   The water creeps over the bridge where the *Titanic's* master stands; heavily he steps out to meet it.

84   2:17 A.M. "CQ—" The *Virginian* hears a ragged, blurred CQ, then an abrupt stop. The blue spark dances no more. The lights flicker out; the engineers have lost their battle.

85   2:18 A.M. Men run about blackened decks; leap into the night; are swept into the sea by the curling wave which licks up the *Titanic's* length. Lightoller does not leave the ship; the ship leaves him; there are hundreds like him, but only a few who live to tell of it. The funnels still swim above the water, but the ship is climbing to the perpendicular; the bridge is under and most of the foremast; the great stern rises like a squat leviathan.° Men swim away from the sinking ship; others drop from the stern.

86   The band plays in the darkness, the water lapping upwards:

> *Hold me up in mighty waters,*
> *Keep my eyes on things above,*
> *Righteousness, divine atonement,*
> *Peace and everlas* . . .

87   The forward funnel snaps and crashes into the sea: its steel tons hammer out of existence swimmers struggling in the freezing water. Streams of sparks, of smoke and steam, burst from the after funnels. The ship upends to 50—to 60 degrees.

88   Down in the black abyss of the stokeholds, of the engine-rooms, where the dynamos have whirred at long last to a stop, the stokers and the engineers are reeling

leviathan: the biblical sea monster; any huge marine animal, such as a whale.

against hot metal, the rising water clutching at their knees.
The boilers, the engine cylinders, rip from their bed plates;
crash through bulkheads; rumble—steel against steel.

89   The *Titanic* stands on end, poised briefly for the
plunge. Slowly she slides to her grave—slowly at first, and
then more quickly—quickly—quickly.

90   2:20 A.M. The greatest ship in the world has sunk.
From the calm, dark waters, where the floating lifeboats
move, there goes up, in the white wake of her passing,
"one long continuous moan."

III

91   The boats that the *Titanic* had launched pulled safely
away from the slight suction of the sinking ship, pulled
away from the screams that came from the lips of the
freezing men and women in the water. The boats were
poorly manned and badly equipped, and they had been
unevenly loaded. Some carried so few seamen that women
bent to the oars. Mrs. Astor tugged at an oar handle; the
Countess of Rothes took a tiller. Shivering stokers in
sweaty, coal-blackened singlets and light trousers steered
in some boats; stewards in white coats rowed in others.
Ismay was in the last boat that left the ship from the starboard side; with Mr. Carter of Philadelphia and two seamen he tugged at the oars. In one of the lifeboats an Italian
with a broken wrist—disguised in a woman's shawl and
hat—huddled on the floor boards, ashamed now that fear
had left him. In another rode the only baggage saved from
the *Titanic*—the carry-all of Samuel L. Goldenberg, one
of the rescued passengers.

92   There were only a few boats that were heavily loaded;
most of those that were half empty made but perfunctory *
efforts to pick up the moaning swimmers, their officers and
crew fearing they would endanger the living if they pulled
back into the midst of the dying. Some boats beat off the
freezing victims; fear-crazed men and women struck with
oars at the heads of swimmers. One woman drove her fist
into the face of a half-dead man as he tried feebly to climb

over the gunwale. Two other women helped him in and
stanched the flow of blood from the ring-cuts on his face.
93   One of the collapsible boats, which had floated off the
top of the officers' quarters when the *Titanic* sank, was an
icy haven for thirty or forty men. The boat had capsized
as the ship sank; men swam to it, clung to it, climbed upon
its slippery bottom, stood knee-deep in water in the freezing
air. Chunks of ice swirled about their legs; their soaked
clothing clutched their bodies in icy folds. Colonel Archibald Gracie was cast up there, Gracie who had leaped from
the stern as the *Titanic* sank; young Thayer who had seen
his father die; Lightoller who had twice been sucked down
with the ship and twice blown to the surface by a belch of
air; Bride, the second operator, and Phillips, the first. There
were many stokers, half-naked; it was a shivering company. They stood there in the icy sea, under the far stars,
and sang and prayed—the Lord's Prayer. After a while
a lifeboat came and picked them off, but Phillips was dead
then or died soon afterward in the boat.
94   Only a few of the boats had lights; only one—No. 2—
had a light that was of any use to the *Carpathia,* twisting
through the ice-field to the rescue. Other ships were "coming hard" too; one, the *Californian,* was still dead to opportunity.
95   The blue sparks still danced, but not the *Titanic's.*
La Provence to *Celtic:* "Nobody has heard the *Titanic*
for about two hours."
96   It was 2:40 when the *Carpathia* first sighted the
green light from No. 2 boat; it was 4:10 when she picked
up the first boat and learned that the *Titanic* had foun-
dered. The last of the moaning cries had just died away
then.
97   Captain Rostron took the survivors aboard, boatload
by boatload. He was ready for them, but only a small
minority of them required much medical attention. Bride's
feet were twisted and frozen; others were suffering from
exposure; one died, and seven were dead when taken
from the boats, and were buried at sea.

98 It was then that the fleet of racing ships learned they were too late; the *Parisian* heard the weak signals of *MPA*, the *Carpathia,* report the death of the *Titanic*. It was then —or soon afterward, when her radio operator put on his ear-phones—that the *Californian,* the ship that had been within sight as the *Titanic* was sinking, first learned of the disaster.

99 And it was then, in all its white-green majesty, that the *Titanic's* survivors saw the iceberg, tinted with the sunrise, floating idly, pack-ice jammed about its base, other bergs heaving slowly nearby on the blue breast of the sea.

IV

100 But it was not until later that the world knew, for wireless then was not what wireless is today, and garbled messages had nourished a hope that all of the *Titanic's* company were safe. Not until Monday evening, when P. A. S. Franklin, Vice-President of the International Mercantile Marine Company, received relayed messages in New York that left little hope, did the full extent of the disaster begin to be known. Partial and garbled lists of the survivors; rumors of heroism and cowardice; stories spun out of newspaper imagination, based on a few bare facts and many false reports, misled the world, terrified and frightened it. It was not until Thursday night, when the *Carpathia* steamed into the North River, that the full truth was pieced together.

101 Flashlights flared on the black river when the *Carpathia* stood up to her dock. Tugs nosed about her; shunted her toward Pier 54. Thirty thousand people jammed the streets; ambulances and stretchers stood on the pier; coroners and physicians waited.

102 In mid-stream the Cunarder dropped over the *Titanic's* lifeboats; then she headed toward the dock. Beneath the customs letters on the pier stood relatives of the 711 survivors, relatives of the missing—hoping against hope. The *Carpathia* cast her lines ashore; stevedores looped them over bollards. The dense throngs stood quiet as the first survivor stepped down the gangway. The

woman half-staggered—led by customs guards—beneath
her letter. A "low wailing" moan came from the crowd;
fell, grew in volume, and dropped again.

103 Thus ended the maiden voyage of the *Titanic.* The
lifeboats brought to New York by the *Carpathia,* a few
deck chairs and gratings awash in the ice-field off the
Grand Banks 800 miles from shore, were all that was left
of the world's greatest ship.

v

104 The aftermath of weeping and regret, of recriminations and investigations, dragged on for weeks. Charges
and countercharges were hurled about; the White Star line
was bitterly criticized; Ismay was denounced on the floor
of the Senate as a coward, but was defended by those who
had been with him on the sinking *Titanic* and by the Board
of Trade investigation in England.

105 It was not until weeks later, when the hastily con-
vened Senate investigation in the United States and the
Board of Trade report in England had been completed,
that the whole story was told. The Senate investigating
committee, under the chairmanship of Senator Smith, who
was attacked in both the American and British press as a
"backwoods politician," brought out numerous pertinent *
facts, though its proceedings verged at times on the farcical.* Senator Smith was ridiculed for his lack of knowledge
of the sea when he asked witnesses, "Of what is an iceberg
composed?" and "Did any of the passengers take refuge
in the water-tight compartments?" The Senator seemed
particularly interested in the marital status of Fleet, the
lookout, who was saved. Fleet, puzzled, growled aside,
"Wot questions they're arskin' me!"

106 The report of Lord Mersey, Wreck Commissioner
in the British Board of Trade's investigation, was tersely
damning.

107 The *Titanic* had carried boats enough for 1,178
persons, only one-third of her capacity. Her sixteen boats
and four collapsibles had saved but 711 persons; 400
people had needlessly lost their lives. The boats had been

but partly loaded; officers in charge of launching them had been afraid the falls would break or the boats buckle under their rated loads; boat crews had been slow in reaching their stations; launching arrangements were confused because no boat drill had been held; passengers were loaded into the boats haphazardly because no boat assignments had been made.

108 But that was not all. Lord Mersey found that sufficient warnings of ice on the steamer track had reached the *Titanic,* that her speed of 22 knots was "excessive under the circumstances," that "in view of the high speed at which the vessel was running it is not considered that the lookout was sufficient," and that her master made "a very grievous mistake"—but should not be blamed for negligence. Captain Rostron of the *Carpathia* was highly praised. "He did the very best that could be done." The *Californian* was damned. The testimony of her master, officers, and crew showed that she was not, at the most, more than nineteen miles away from the sinking *Titanic* and probably no more than five to ten miles distant. She had seen the *Titanic's* lights; she had seen the rockets; she had not received the CQD calls because her radio operator was asleep. She had attempted to get in communication with the ship she had sighted by flashing a light, but vainly.

109 "The night was clear," reported Lord Mersey, "and the sea was smooth. When she first saw the rockets the *Californian* could have pushed through the ice to the open water without any serious risk and so have come to the assistance of the *Titanic*. Had she done so she might have saved many if not all of the lives that were lost.

110 "She made no attempt."

ANALYSIS

Baldwin must have decided early in organizing this essay that one of the hazards of reporting a past event, and especially one so sensational as this, is the mass of conflicting reports. What actually did happen? Can hearings and court testimony re-create an event? Very likely not, so Baldwin breaks his essay carefully.

He chooses the past tense for part one. He begins with the day of the maiden voyage, April 10, and takes this part up to 11:40 P.M., April 14. These facts are ascertainable: the ship's design, the passenger list, the course it set, the messages it sent and received, the warnings it should have heeded, and so forth. Baldwin is reporting fact.

The second part is mainly imaginative writing, or at best it is the piecing together of survivors' testimony added to Baldwin's knowledge of ships. How accurate are the details is a question Baldwin assumes we will not ask. At 12:25 A.M. he shifts into the present tense. He wants us to feel we are there, *as though* it happened this way.

Parts three, four, and five revert to the past tense: what happened in and around the twenty boats launched, how the *Carpathia* brought 711 survivors to New York harbor, what the aftermath of recriminations and investigations revealed.

This is a long essay. Its divisions help readers immeasurably to sift their impressions of Baldwin's description. But the organization of the essay is not the only one Baldwin could have used. He might have written it from the viewpoint of one survivor (J. Bruce Ismay, chairman and managing director of the White Star line, for example). He could have used the Board of Trade investigation in England as his point of departure. But Baldwin, like James Ramsey Ullman, chooses a chronological description. His subject is the *Titanic,* just as Ullman's is Kilimanjaro. Put the subject into action, make the description come alive, give the reader names, dates, places, build the description toward a climax, or at least a firm conclusion—these seem to be the principles by which both authors operate. The reader must decide their effectiveness.

Questions on Content

1. Why did the builders think the *Titanic* was unsinkable?
2. Why did the *Californian* not hear the *Titanic's* SOS? Had they been in communication earlier in the evening?

3. Who, according to Baldwin's account of the sinking, was to blame for this accident? Explain.
4. What significant facts come to light through the investigations which followed the sinking?

Add to Your Vocabulary

perfunctory, pertinent, farcical.

Questions on Technique

1. To what purpose does Baldwin list all the proper nouns in paragraph six? How do they add to the impact of the story? Does it help to know the names of the crew members, such as Bride, Phillips, Smith, and the others?
2. Explain the effectiveness of Baldwin's timed "reports" in part two. Why should time play such an important role here?
3. Part two is filled with dialogue, some of which Baldwin could only imagine. Does it sound credible to you? Would you have eliminated it entirely? parts of it?
4. Why quote the words of the hymns sung that night aboard the *Titanic?* Is there irony in the name of the ship as well?
5. Part three is relatively calm, well-ordered description. Why does Baldwin not try to heighten the action here as he does in part two?
6. The docking of the *Carpathia* could be an occasion for elaborate description. Why should Baldwin choose to be so concise in this section?
7. What effect does he seek, in part five, by singling out Senator Smith and Lord Mersey from among all the people involved in the charges and counter-charges after the disaster?
8. Discuss your reaction to Baldwin's last sentence (note that it is a one-sentence paragraph).

Techniques to Imitate

Adapting style to subject—the staccato style for rapid action

Part two of Baldwin's account of the *Titanic* disaster is not only the longest of the five parts, but also the most graphic. It is the part in which he describes the complex final moments of the great ship. The technique to be noted here is that for his description of many actions and a rapid succession of events, Baldwin uses short sentences and short paragraphs, even, at times, one-sentence paragraphs. This staccato, choppy style conveys the speed and urgency of the events he is portraying. Long and formal sentences could not have given an effective picture of the confused scene.

The following excerpts show what we mean by the staccato style:

> Murdoch leaped to the engine-room telegraph. Bells clanged. Far below in the engine-room those bells struck the first warning. Danger! The indicators on the dial faces swung round to "Stop!" Then "Full speed astern!" Frantically the engineers turned great valve wheels; answered the bridge bells . . .

> There was a slight shock, a brief scraping, a small list to port. Shell ice—slabs and chunks of it—fell on the foredeck. Slowly the *Titanic* stopped.
> Captain Smith hurried out of his cabin.

> A sudden sharp hiss—a streaked flare against the night; Boxhall sends a rocket toward the sky. It explodes, and a parachute of white stars lights up the icy sea. "God! Rockets!" The band plays ragtime.

Although there are five parts to this essay, part two contains nearly twice as many paragraphs as all the other parts combined. This kind of abrupt, straightforward writing is exactly right for the task Baldwin has assumed. Because he is describing events that happen rapidly, his style must move rapidly.

It would be interesting to rewrite these paragraphs to do away with the short, choppy sentences. Is the effect different? Is the excitement as great?

Ullman, in his essay on Kilimanjaro (pages 117–31), uses the same staccato style to describe particularly significant or tense moments. Writers—especially sportswriters—often use this style when describing rapid action; it tends to create tension and some excitement. It is interesting to note that Steinbeck, in the description of the turtle's movements across the highway on page 82, does not use short, choppy sentences, but leisurely and lengthy ones. If Steinbeck's description were rewritten in a staccato style, how would the effect be different? (Does staccato style fit a turtle's movements?)

Suggestions for Writing

1. Search your memory for a past occasion when you were involved in an experience that demanded quick thinking. Describe in five or six paragraphs the thoughts that passed through your mind as well as the situation itself. Try to imitate Baldwin's staccato style as you describe your thoughts and the action taking place. If nothing like this has ever happened to you, make up such an incident.
2. People react differently to an emergency. Describe an emergency in such a way that attention is centered on the different reactions of individuals to the same circumstances. You may have witnessed, for instance, a hurricane or tornado, a fire, an accident, an emergency plane landing. Describe the different reactions as objectively as you can. Again, if you have not had any personal experience of this sort of thing, invent a story.
3. In describing this event, Baldwin ticks off the hours and minutes, and frequently opens his paragraphs with a terse statement of the precise time. This technique, along with the short, rapid sentences, contributes to the excitement. Write about some event that happened in a clearly defined sequence (make up an event if you can't think of an actual one). Describe what happened by citing the hour and minute each phase occurred.

PART TWO

EXPOSITION

If you have studied Part One, you have seen through a variety of models that descriptive writing tells us what a person or a thing or an experience looks like, sounds like, feels like. Our senses become attuned to the writer's by means of word pictures. We share James Ramsey Ullman's exhilaration on Kilimanjaro, for example, because his descriptive prose tells us just how the mountain looks, what it reminds him of, how he feels during the climb, what the heat is like and what the cold is like. He tells how the altitude affects a human being, how the scree makes climbing difficult, what hazards one encounters in a snowfield. We *see* the eagles Edwin Way Teale describes because he tells us what they look like, how they behave, where they live, how they sound. He describes their habits and their anatomy. John Steinbeck makes us *feel* the slow pace and the dogged determination of a turtle crossing a highway by telling us in minute detail exactly what the turtle does as it moves its cumbersome body. Clear sensory impressions are at the base of successful descriptive writing.

Expository prose does not, by any definition, avoid description, not any more than description avoids incorporating the kind of writing we call narration. Ullman describes a mountain. His description is mainly concerned with the *what* of his subject. His narrating the events of the climb chronologically (*when* all this happened) is important too, but it is a secondary concern. Expository prose is primarily concerned with the *why* or *how* of things. Description and narration are used within exposition when needed to make the explanation clearer or more interesting.

Expository prose (as we use the term in this book) might define a word, explain a process, report an incident, analyze an idea, evaluate or judge an experience. You meet expository prose whenever you consult an editorial, an analysis of current events, a book review, a scientific article, or a political discussion.

The expository models that follow are arranged in six groups. Call these groups subdivisions of the larger term, if you wish. Call them methods of approach to the subject. But remember that the groupings are ours; the models could just as well be arranged in some other way. They are grouped this way here according to the writer's *primary* intention, as we see it. We begin with the most elementary forms of exposition, and move from there to reporting, analysis, criticism, and finally the informal or personal essay.

3

ELEMENTARY EXPOSITION: DEFINITION

The purest form of definition is a dictionary entry. We have chosen two different dictionaries to illustrate the variety that can be achieved even in so standard a form of writing. These entries are followed by an encyclopedia definition of the same word. You will notice how much more complete this longer definition can be. When we ask each other, in conversation, "What do you mean by that?" or "How are you using that word?" we frequently need to explain usage. We have included in this chapter, therefore, an entry from a special kind of word-book, a dictionary of usage, which describes fine distinctions in the English language. Finally, we come to two attempts to define words that benefit from more explanation than a dictionary or an encyclopedia normally gives us.

We will not deal with the models under this chapter as essays proper. They are all extracts from larger works and do not, therefore, interest us in terms of organization, style, and literary techniques. Definitions are, by their very nature, brief and utilitarian.

Let us pretend that you have never seen an opossum. How well does a dictionary do its job in showing us this animal through definition only?

Two Dictionary Entries

opos·sum \(ə-)¹päs-əm \ *n, pl* **opossums** *also* **opossum** [fr. *ǎpäsŭm,* lit., white animal (in some Algonquian language of Virginia)] **1** : any of various American marsupials (family Didelphidae); *esp* : a common omnivorous largely nocturnal and arboreal mammal (*Didelphis virginiana*) of the eastern U.S.

By permission. From *Webster's New Collegiate Dictionary* © 1976 by G. & C. Merriam Co., Publishers of the Merriam-Webster Dictionaries.

Opossum (ŏpρ·sŭm). 1610. [Amer. Indian name in Virginia.] **1.** General name of the small marsupial mammals of the American family *Didelphyidæ,* mostly arboreal, some (genus *Chironectes*) aquatic, of nocturnal habits, with an opposable thumb on the hind foot, and tail usu. prehensile; esp. *Didelphys virginiana,* the common opossum of the U.S. (Colloq. shortened to POSSUM, q.v.) **2.** Extended to various small or moderate-sized marsupials ; *esp.* the common name in Australia and Tasmania of those of the sub-family *Phalangistinæ,* more properly called Phalangers 1777.
   attrib. and *Comb.,* as **o.·mouse,** the Pygmy Flying Phalanger of Australia ; **·shrimp,** a shrimp of the genus *Mysis* or family *Mysidæ,* so called from the brood-pouch in which the female carries her eggs.

The *Shorter Oxford English Dictionary,* revised and edited by C. T. Onions. Reprinted by permission of the Oxford University Press, Oxford.

ANALYSIS

The first entry, from Webster's dictionary, tells us several things. First, we learn the pronunciation, by means of diacritical markings. We need only to turn to the guide in the front of the dictionary to learn that the first vowel is pronounced like the "a" in "abut," the second like the "o" in "cot," the third like the "u" in "abut." The accent is on the second syllable. The plural of the word is opossums, but sometimes opossum. The bracketed information gives us etymological history, that is, the origin or derivation of the word. Here we find that it is derived from the word *apasum,* which is from some Algonquian language of Virginia. So far we have no verbal picture of the animal.

In three lines, the opossum is classified. Alas, most readers will need the dictionary to define the defining words! We have here a model of conciseness. But is this definition genuinely helpful? Not until we inform ourselves that "marsupials" are animals which carry their young in a pouch, that "omnivorous" comes from the Latin *omnis* (all) plus *vorare* (to eat greedily) and means this animal will upset your garbage pail in search of food, that "nocturnal" means active by night, that "arboreal" means inhabiting trees, that "mammal" means that the female nourishes its young with its milk. Adequate and accurate though it is, the definition is not sufficient to *show* us fully what opossums are like. If we were not familiar with the phrase "playing possum," we would not learn of it here.

Turning to an historical dictionary, we learn more facts. Opossum first appeared in writing in 1610, most likely in accounts of the Virginian settlers. The colloquial usage has shortened it to possum. Following the suggestion "q.v."—an abbreviation for *quod vide,* meaning "which see"—we look up possum and learn what Webster did not tell us: "to play possum" means (in the United States) "to feign; to pretend illness." The *Oxford English Dictionary* also informs us there are Australian opossums which should be called, properly, phalangers, as they were named in 1777. And further, there are combined uses of the word in "opossum-mouse" and "opossum-shrimp." Your next door neighbor might say that these two definitions still do not sound like the animal shot in the truck garden. Dictionaries, we remind ourselves, identify and distinguish words.

For a fuller definition of this common noun, we turn to a multi-volumed encyclopedia.

An Encyclopedia Entry

OPOSSUM, *uh PAHS uhm,* is any member of a family of furry mammals that live in the Western Hemisphere. The female opossum carries its young in a pouch on its abdomen. Opossums, kangaroos, and other mammals that carry their young about in the mother's pouch after birth are called *marsupials.* Opossums are the only marsupials that are native to North America. They live from Ontario in Canada southward into South America.

There are many species of opossums, most of which live in Central and South America. Small, tree-dwelling *murine opossums* resemble mice. *Woolly opossums* have thick, soft fur. Another kind of opossum, the *yapok,* is the only marsupial that is adapted for living in water. Its webbed feet help make it a good swimmer.

The *common opossum* is the only kind of opossum found in the United States. This species grows about as big as a house cat. It has rough grayish-white hair, a long snout, dark eyes, and big hairless ears. This opossum has a long tail that does not have much hair on it. The animal can hang upside down by wrapping its tail around the branch of a tree. A common opossum has 50 teeth, more than any other North American mammal. Its teeth and claws are sharp. Opossum tracks are easy to recognize because the animal has long, widely separated toes.

Opossums are born in groups of from 5 to 20. At birth, an opossum is only about as big as a kidney bean. The female opossum carries its tiny babies in a pouch on the outer skin of its abdomen for about two months after birth. After leaving the pouch, the young stay near the mother for several more weeks. When they can take care of themselves, the young go off on their own.

Opossums hunt at night. They eat almost any kind of animal or vegetable food. When in danger, opossums lie motionless and appear to be dead. From this habit, we say a person is "playing possum" when he pretends to be injured.

Frank B. Golley

> **Scientific Classification:** Opossums make up the opossum family, *Didelphidae.* The common opossum is genus *Didelphis,* species *D. marsupialis.*

> See also ANIMAL (picture: Animals of the Temperate Forests); MARSUPIAL.

From *The World Book Encyclopedia,* copyright © 1976 Field Enterprises Educational Corporation. Reprinted by permission of the publishers.

ANALYSIS

An encyclopedia is generally not interested in word derivations, although this one does provide pronunciations. Some details from this entry illustrate the difference between the dictionary's definition which classifies, and the encyclopedia's definition which describes. For examples, the entry says that some opossums "resemble mice" and it compares another kind of opossum to a "house cat." The comparison of the new-born opossum to a "kidney bean" makes a strong impression. There are other unusual images: the opossum's nearly hairless tail which it uses to hang from a tree; its big hairless ears; its long snout; its night hunting; its instinct to lie motionless and appear to be dead when in danger. In other words, the descriptive definition is not a biological or etymological classification, but an illustrative embellishment.

A third kind of definition we might call comparative, or definitive in terms of usage. It is almost always confined to linguistic problems.

An Entry in H. W. Fowler's
MODERN ENGLISH USAGE

jargon is perhaps the most variously applied of a large number of words that are in different senses interchangeable, & under it the distinctions between them may be pointed out. The words are: *cant, dialect, gibberish, idiom, jargon, lingo, parlance, slang, vernacular.*

cant in current English means the insincere or parrotlike appeal to principles, religious, moral, political, or scientific, that the speaker does not believe in or act upon, or does not understand. It is best to restrict it to this definite use; but its earliest sense—special vocabulary of the disreputable—is still used by philologists & in etymological discussions; & it means sometimes what is now more often expressed by *jargon* or *slang,* the special vocabulary of an art, profession, etc.

dialect is essentially local*; a d.* is the variety of a language that prevails in a district, with local peculiarities of vocabulary, pronunciation, & phrase.

gibberish is the name for unintelligible stuff: applied by exaggeration to a language unknown to the hearer (for which, as a familiar term, *lingo* is better), & to anything either too learnedly worded, or on the other hand too rudely expressed, for him to make out its meaning.

idiom is the method of expression characteristic of or peculiar to the native speakers of a language; i.e., it is racy or unaffected or natural English (or French etc.), especially so far as that happens not to coincide with the method of expression prevalent in other languages; & *an i.* is a particular example of such speech. An earlier sense, the same as that of *dialect,* still occurs sometimes. See also *idiom.*

jargon is talk that is considered both ugly-sounding & hard to understand: applied especially to (1) the sectional vocabulary of a science, art, class, sect, trade, or profession, full of technical terms (cf. *cant, slang*); (2) hybrid speech of different languages; (3) the use of long words, circumlocution, & other clumsiness.

lingo is a contemptuous name for any foreign language. It is sometimes used instead of jargon (1) & (2).

parlance, which means manner of speaking, has the peculiarity of possessing no significance of its own & being never used by itself; you can say That is dialect, That is slang, etc., but not That is parlance; *parlance* is always accompanied by an adjective or defining word or phrase, & that adjective, not *parlance*, gives the point: *in golfing* or *nautical parlance, in the parlance of the literary critics,* etc.

slang is the diction that results from the favourite game among the young & lively of playing with words & renaming things & actions; some invent new words, or mutilate or misapply the old, for the pleasure of novelty, & others catch up such words for the pleasure of being in the fashion; many slang words & phrases perish, a few establish themselves; in either case, during probation they are accounted unfit for literary use. *S.* is also used in the sense of *jargon* (1), & with two distinctions: in general it expresses less dislike & imputation of ugliness than *jargon;* & it is naturally commoner about sporting vocabularies (*golf s.* etc.) than *jargon,* because many of the terms used in sports are slang in the main sense also.

vernacular describes the words that have been familiar to us as long as we can remember, the homely part of the language, in contrast with the terms that we have consciously acquired. *The vernacular* was formerly common, & is still occasional, for English as opposed to any foreign language; & by an unessential limitation, it is often applied specially to rustic speech & confused with *dialect.*

H. W. Fowler, *A Dictionary of Modern English Usage.* Reprinted by permission of the Oxford University Press, Oxford.

ANALYSIS

Is it legitimate to define one word in terms of another? When fine distinctions are what is sought, yes. Fowler's lexicon, published in England, has been an invaluable aid to writers for several decades. Margaret Nicholson's *Dictionary of American-English Usage* (Oxford Press, New York, 1957) is the American counterpart. Together they answer many questions on when a certain word is appropriate and when it is not. The words they choose to discuss are selective, of course. We cannot expect to find every word that troubles us in their pages.

The excerpt we have chosen may discuss several words new to your own vocabulary, like "parlance," "cant," or "vernacular." Several others—"jargon," "slang," "gibberish," "lingo"—are common to everyday speech. What Fowler is doing here is making distinctions that will help us to place these words in relation to each other and to choose exactly the right one when we are identifying speech we hear or read. Note that he does not give examples. This is a concise dictionary, as is Webster's *New Collegiate Dictionary*. Should he once begin illustration, there would be no end. He is trying, like Webster, to supply helpful explanations without wasting words. You will find it a challenge to apply illustrations of your own to these terms.

A fourth kind of definition is analytical or investigative. It searches *around* a subject. It offers tentative suggestions. It sometimes begins by eliminating what the word is not. It finds illustration helpful; and it often defines in terms of usage, or in terms of the author's particular viewpoint. The two following definitions—of newspaperese and quicksand —do not belong in a dictionary. They are explanations of what two words mean to these particular writers.

RICHARD D. ALTICK

Newspaperese

1   The jargon peculiar to newspapers is a combination of the cliché, deadwood, and the weak passive or impersonal construction. The great objection to it, as to all jargon, is that it is machine-made. It is written according to formula, and material written to formula inevitably loses much of its color and interest. Here is a short sampling of newspaper clichés together with their simpler equivalents:

The death toll rose to ten today in the wake of the disastrous fire . . . (*or:* Death today claimed four more victims . . .)	Four more people died as a result of the fire . . .
The mercury soared to a record high for the year (*or* plummeted to a new low) . . .	Today was the hottest (*or* coldest) day of the year . . .
At an early hour this morning the identity of the victim had not yet been established . . .	Early this morning the body was still unidentified . . .
Traffic was snarled (*or* paralyzed, *or* at a standstill, *or* moved at a snail's pace, *or* crept bumper to bumper) as snow blanketed the metropolitan area . . .	The snowfall slowed traffic . . .

State Police, aided by local law enforcement officers, today were combing the area adjacent to Center City in search of clues that might lead to the solution of the mystery of the murder-kidnaping . . .

State and local police were looking for clues to the man who kidnaped and murdered . . .

Three persons suffered injuries when the automobile in which they were riding figured in a collision with a large truck . . .

Three persons were hurt when their car hit a big truck . . .

As he completed his investigation, the coroner said it was his opinion that death was instantaneous . . .

The coroner thought the man had been killed instantly . . .

In addition, there are numerous single words, especially epithets ° and verbs, which are seemingly indispensable to newspaper reporting. Any better-than-ordinary fire or auto accident is *spectacular;* an accident that is more peculiar than disastrous is *freak;* when public men approve of something they *hail* it, when they disapprove of it they *attack* it, and when they want something they *urge* it; when two factions have a disagreement they *clash;* when anything is announced it is made *public;* and when men accuse others of wrongdoing they *allege.* (*Assert,* another newspaper war horse, has a slightly less negative connotation.)

2 The weak passive is used in newspaper writing for essentially the same reason it is used in governmental correspondence: to achieve the impersonal note, and thus, in many instances, to disclaim direct responsibility for statements that are based on hearsay. When newspapers send a reporter for an eyewitness story of a disaster or a court trial, or when they quote a press release or statements made during an interview, they can state positively that this and that are true. But much news cannot be treated in so open and confident a fashion—news based on private information picked up by reporters or on rumors circulating in the

epithets: See Glossary.

city hall or the stock exchange. Although the papers wish
to relay this news, they cannot do so on their own authority;
the man who gave the reporter his information refuses to
be quoted, and the public will be suspicious of anything
plainly labeled "rumor." The solution, then, is to use weak
passive or impersonal constructions which do not require
an agent: "It was revealed (*or* learned *or* reported)" (*not:*
the City Commissioner told our reporter but warned him
not to use his name); "indications increased" or "a survey
today showed" (*not:* our reporter asked several people,
and their replies, when put together, suggested). Another
device of passing on news without revealing its source (or,
it may be, without revealing that it has no source outside
the mind of an inventive reporter) is the use of those mysterious oracles, the *officials who asked that their names be
withheld, spokesmen, informed quarters, observers,* and
sources usually considered reliable. Judged from the viewpoint of clear, accurate communication, "newspaperese"
has as little to recommend it as does any other kind of
roundabout, machine-made language.

3   One particular brand of newspaper jargon, the language
of the sports page, deserves special study. Sports writers,
perhaps because they deal with lively, entertaining matters
that seldom have dead-serious implications, have greater
freedom, and indeed a greater necessity, than do other
reporters to invent new ways of saying things. Sports pages
are filled with metaphorical language. When first used,
such terms add a welcome novelty to the narration of what
are, after all, fairly routine events. (One baseball game
differs from another only in details, not in general pattern:
usually a game has nine innings, each inning is divided into
halves, a side is always retired after the third out.) But,
like all clichés, sports-page terms soon lose their vividness
through overuse. Reporters keep on employing them just
the same: *four-bagger* or *circuit clout* for *home run, coveted
pasteboards* for *hard-to-get tickets, grid classic* for *big
game, thin-clads* for *track team, signal-caller* for *quarter-
back, tankmen* for *swimmers, century* for *100-yard dash,
swivel-hipped pigskin toter* for *agile ball-carrier,* and so on.

ANALYSIS

Altick's definition of "newspaperese" is hardly an exhaustive treatment of the subject, nor is it meant to be. Yet his definitions go further than those in Fowler's dictionary. He first of all enlarges on Fowler's definition of "jargon" by defining in detail a particular kind of jargon, the kind found in newspapers. This consists of not merely specialized or ugly-sounding words but worn-out, stereotyped words (known as clichés) and elaborate circumlocutions which never say anything simply. Then he does what all definers frequently do—he gives us specific examples, in this case from daily papers: "death claimed four more victims" or "traffic was snarled as snow blanketed the metropolitan area" or "state police are combing the city." These tired phrases are so familiar that we no longer react to them, and that is exactly Altick's point. Jargon leads to prose without color or interest. Our conversations are frequently full of clichés because we speak faster than we think; but when we write, we are obligated to choose the most apt phrase, not merely the easy formula. "Freak" accidents might also be called "strange" or "unexpected," "capricious" or "whimsical," "peculiar" or "monstrous." But some reporters prefer machine-made prose. Altick hopes we will not follow their example.

Likewise he warns us against the weak passive: "It was revealed tonight that Senator Clark will not accept the nomination." Impersonality, he argues, leads to faceless prose. And a third habit is just as bad as clichés and the passive voice, namely elaborate circumlocutions. Any sports fan knows hundreds of them. "Coveted pasteboards" may have been a novel variant at one time, but it no longer holds our attention. It may even amuse us, as do phrases like "grid classic" and "the big fix." Altick is not showing us how to avoid writing "newspaperese." He merely defines by examples and analysis.

GERARD H. MATTHES

Quicksand

1   **Q**uicksand is not a word that
one hears often nowadays. The malevolent * phenomenon
figured prominently in the landscapes of 19th-century ro-
mances (where it was frequently a convenience to authors
needing to dispose of unwanted characters) and in the
pioneering of the U. S. West. In our day of the automobile
and paved roads few people ever encounter it. Yet quicksand is as prevalent as it ever was and may be the more
dangerous for being less familiar. As a scientific study it
offers many points of interest, not the least of which is the
correction of some of the romantic misconceptions about it.
2   I shall discuss here the most common form of quicksand, that found along the shores and in the beds of rivers.
It is simply sand supersaturated with water under pressure
from beneath, as from a spring. A model of it can be made
in a tub fitted with a water pipe leading into the bottom of
the tub. The water flowing into the sand permeates the
spaces between the sand grains and, by separating them
slightly, makes the sand's bulk swell. When the water pressure from below equals, or a little more than equals, the
weight of the sand, the sand becomes "quick." The grains,
being suspended and frictionless, will not support a weight,

and any object placed on the surface at once begins to sink. How fast it sinks will depend on its weight and the extent of its surface area, as well as on the kind of sand.

3 It was long believed that only sand composed of round, small, uniform grains could form quicksand, but this is not so. Any kind of sand, even with coarse, angular grains, can be quick when it is saturated with water under pressure from below. Sands composed of fine, rounded grains do, however, become quick more readily than coarser types, because the spaces between the grains are more uniform and slower to lose water to the surrounding mass of firm sand.

4 Quicksand is nearly always confined to a relatively small area where the underlying spring maintains pressure. In a sandy river bed the water drains away from the quicksand area through the surrounding sand. Extended quicksand areas are found only where spring water, under weak pressure, issues from a fissure in the side of a cliff extending for some distance parallel with the stream. Quicksand cannot exist where the water inflow is large in volume or under high pressure. In such cases the bed sand, instead of becoming "quick," is washed away and deep holes are formed in both the bed and the bank.

5 Quicksand is uncommon in flat country, where there is too little gradient ° to produce springs. It is also rare in rivers that run in gorges or canyons through hilly country. Deep cuts of that sort permit the ground water, which might otherwise collect in the rocks and build up spring pressure, to drain directly into the stream. Quicksand is likely to occur in hilly country, especially where the rocks are limestones and dolomites.° These formations harbor caverns and channels and are notorious producers of springs. Rivers cut through any rocks are apt to contain springs in their banks and beds. Quicksand will form along their courses in three situations: above water level along the

gradient: slope.
dolomites: rocks composed of various-colored carbonates of calcium and magnesium.

shores of streams of all sizes; under water, usually near a bank but occasionally in midstream; occasionally in the bed of an apparently dry river.

6 How does one detect quicksand? It cannot be done by the eye alone, for a sand which is to all appearances perfectly firm may suddenly collapse and trap anyone who ventures out on it. This is particularly true when the top sand has become dry and crusted in the sun. In such cases a fast walker can sometimes get across, but anyone following in his footsteps is almost certain to be caught. The only way to be sure is to test the sand before walking on it. Anyone who walks along the edge of a sandy lake or along a sandy river course where the sand may be quick should carry a pole or long stick (a cane is useless) for test probing. This precaution is especially important when a stream is to be forded, for one almost instinctively chooses a spot where a pleasantly smooth stretch of sand interrupts an otherwise rocky or muddy channel. Repeated stamping with the feet will help to determine the limits of the danger area, though this method may cause you to reject a route which is in fact safe. Any thoroughly wet sand, especially one composed of small, round grains, will quake a little when sufficiently stamped upon, but it may be perfectly fordable. It is not easy to distinguish such a sand from the quick variety. By far the most satisfactory method of detection, particularly when a more or less permanent path is being mapped, is to drive long stakes into the sand with a maul.° Pronounced quaking will identify it as quickened.

7 Certain clues are a help in doubtful cases. If there is clay in the sand, the footing will be safe. A clayey sand may mire a vehicle but can be crossed with impunity * by a pedestrian. Swiftly running water also is evidence that a stream bottom is sound. Here, however, the traveler may encounter a "near quicksand." When a layer of coarse sand overlies a layer of fine and thoroughly saturated silt, the spaces between the grains of sand sometimes fill with the

maul: a heavy hammer.

silt and form a crust. Anyone who walks on it will break through the crust and through the silt beneath. Although the sensation is alarming, the drop to firm bottom is rarely more than a foot, usually a matter of inches.

8 In true quicksand a trapped pedestrian soon sinks to the depth of his knees and will sink further if he stands still or struggles wildly. He must act promptly and with purpose. He should at once lie on his back and stretch out his arms. If a companion is at hand to help him out, his situation is not usually serious. Contrary to popular notion, quicksand does not suck objects down, and even at its worst it will support a great deal more weight than water alone.

9 Rescuers may build a platform on the sand from which to extricate * the victim. For this almost any material at hand will do: boards, fence rails, brush, branches, a large piece of canvas or a ladder. In arid regions sagebrush offers good support because of its sturdy branch system. The mired person must be pulled out slowly and gently, for the sand holds its prey tightly and he may be badly injured.

10 A solitary traveler who stumbles into quicksand is in a more awkward situation, but even his case is not desperate if he knows what to do. Attempts to force a way to shore will prove worse than useless; standing still and yelling will be fatal unless help arrives soon. The trapped man's first move must be to drop his pole behind him, if he is foresighted enough to have one, and fall back upon it, meanwhile stretching his arms out at right angles to his body. In this position he could float in water and he will certainly float on sand if he gets rid of any heavy object he may be carrying. He may now call out for help. If there is no prospect of help, the victim may begin to rescue himself. The first step in this operation is to get the pole at right angles to the body beneath the shoulders and then work it down until it is supporting the hips. It is difficult work, but once done the individual is in a position to pull his legs out of the mire, one at a time. He should do this slowly and with frequent rests. Once his feet are out, he looks about and selects the shortest route to solid ground.

He then begins rolling toward his goal. Rolling is the easiest—and indeed the only—way of getting off the soft area.
It can be done in short stages, but rests must be taken on
the back with arms outstretched or he will begin to sink
again. The pole is pulled along and used for support.

11   When the quicksand is under water, one can usually
swim to safety, provided the water is deep enough for
swimming. It is not too hard to pull the legs out of the
quicksand, because the water helps to loosen it. But when
the water is less than a foot deep, the victim is in virtually
the same position as if the quicksand were at the surface.

12   Animals caught in quicksand often do not get out
by themselves. A dog generally succeeds, but it must be
encouraged to work hard and not wait for its master's help.
A horse will usually fight its way to safety, making frantic,
rabbitlike jumps. The rider or driver must know where
to guide it, however, for it can soon become exhausted
and then rapidly sink in the sand. A loaded or harnessed
mule will lie down on its belly with its feet tucked under
as soon as the ground gives beneath it. In that position the
animal will not sink. The mule's hooves are so small and
narrow that it cannot struggle if it is at all weighted down.
Once freed of any equipment, it can usually be urged to
get itself out of the morass.° It is a good idea to station
a horse, preferably a mare, on the nearest firm land as a
guide and further inducement.

13   Cattle invariably panic in quicksand. The only sound
way of rescuing them is to tie a rope around their horns or
necks and pull them out, very gradually, with a steady
team or a tractor. Unlike horses or mules, which seem
grateful for assistance, cattle are apt to charge their rescuers as soon as they emerge. It is wise to have a knife
handy for cutting the tow rope. When animals are found
sunk to their necks and with their eyes bulging from the
pressure on their bodies, they are best put out of their
misery with a bullet. They cannot be saved, and the death
that awaits them is agonizing.

morass: marshy ground; a bog.

ANALYSIS

Gerard Matthes defines his subject from first-hand knowledge. Born in 1874 in Holland, he came to this country to study engineering at the Massachusetts Institute of Technology; and at the turn of the century he worked for the U.S. Geological Survey in the Far West. Before fording rivers with heavy equipment, he used to ride into them on horseback to test the weight the river bottoms could hold. He soon discovered how to recognize and avoid quicksand. Consequently what he gives us here is a definition with elaboration, more personal than an encyclopedia entry, far more imaginative than a dictionary. He offers clues to detection and corrects misconceptions at the same time that he defines his subject.

Paragraphs 1–5 tell us what quicksand is and where it is usually found. Paragraphs 6–7 explain how to detect it. Paragraphs 8–13 offer suggestions for survival should a person or animal be trapped in it. In short, Matthes "walks" around his subject, analyzing, investigating, answering questions before they are asked. He could easily have used anecdotes from past experience or from romantic fiction. He could have resorted to drawings or photographs to "show" us the hazards of quicksand. He prefers instead the simplest kind of writing, a utilitarian prose, with which he treats only the subject itself. This directness does not make for colorful writing, but it gives clarity and focus to his task. Matthes blends the formality of a reference book with the informality of a personal account.

Add to Your Vocabulary

malevolent, impunity, extricate, morass.

Techniques to Imitate

Adapting style to purpose

Matthes's article is an extended, or elaborated, definition of quicksand. His purpose is to give the facts about quicksand and, in so doing, to correct "some of the romantic misconceptions about it." Because this is his purpose, he uses a direct, simple, unadorned style. He is being instructive rather than entertaining. One can imagine a quite different description of quicksand—one filled with dramatic stories of victims caught and gradually drowned, replete with overelaborate descriptions and moments of suspense and horror. But for Matthes's quite different purpose, the simple, matter-of-fact style is right. His article is effective in achieving its goal because he has used a style of writing adapted to his purpose.

Whenever you write, consider the relationship between style and purpose. Use a style which will most effectively bring about the result you want.

Suggestions for Writing

1. Without referring to a dictionary, write a definition of three of these words, giving their basic meaning and their common present-day usage: drama, supermarket, comic strip, highbrow, egghead, skateboard, wrestling, watercolor, barbecue. Write the definition as if you are preparing an entry for a dictionary.

2. Write an essay on the problem of distinguishing between the words in one of the following groups:
   a. attraction, infatuation, love
   b. advertisement, commercial, propaganda
   c. insult, slander, libel
   d. compromise, appeasement, capitulation

3. Fowler defines "jargon" in terms of "slang," "dialect," "lingo," and other words. He does not mention "colloquialisms," "newspaperese," or "gobbledygook" (also called "officialese"). Define and explain how these three words are related to jargon.

4. Attempt in an essay of 300 words a more complex, analytical definition of one of these words: democracy, conservatism, geography, censorship, comedy, literature, emotion, knowledge, faith, economics.

5. Develop one of these topics by definition:
    a. the best use of leisure
    b. the need for learning
    c. the pleasures of reading
    d. the joy of listening to music
    e. the habit of watching television
    f. the hypnosis of watching a film
6. Write an article in which you define, in a way similar to that used by Matthes in "Quicksand," one of the catastrophes listed below. If you can, write from first-hand experience and use your experience to elaborate your definition.
    a. a blizzard
    b. a hurricane
    c. a flood
    d. a forest fire

4

ELEMENTARY EXPOSITION: PROCESS

A second, more complex type of definition might be called explanation of a process. Other words for "process" could be "structure" and "mechanism." Explanations of this type tell us in more detail, while using the method of definition, what is involved in a series of interrelated activities. As biology students, for example, we could seek a definition of "osmosis" or "chlorophyll," but would what we found answer the larger question of how plants grow? More than likely not. The concise definition of single terms is not sufficient if we are seeking the explanation of a larger structure or mechanism or process. We need illustrations by example or precedent or even by anecdote. To understand the process of plant growth we must know about problems of soil, fertilization, light, and seasonal change. "Process," "structure," and "mechanism" are not only scientific terms, of course. This kind of extended definition is also applied to oil painting, cooking, theories of language development, furniture manufacture, and dog training.

MARGARET MEAD

Living with the Natives
of Melanesia

Margaret Mead is perhaps the world's most famous anthropologist. In 1925, when it was unthinkable that a twenty-three-year-old woman would make such a distant field trip, Margaret Mead sailed from the United States to Samoa in the South Sea Islands. Her purpose was to study the adolescent girl, specifically to test the extent to which the troubles of adolescence depend on the attitudes of a particular culture, and the extent to which they are inherent in the development of all human beings. From this field trip came the now-classic study *Coming of Age in Samoa* (1928). Mead returned to the South Seas on other ethnological expeditions (expeditions set up to analyze and compare cultures). The article reprinted here explains the process of how she set up and carried out fieldwork among the Manus Island people of Melanesia.

The museum referred to here is the American Museum of Natural History in New York City, an institution that Margaret Mead has been associated with since 1926.

1   In the cases of the South Seas Hall of the American Museum hang many specimens, pieces of costumes, ceremonial staves, ornaments, weapons, canoe models, the outer and visible symbols of the civilizations which have been built up by the patient brown peoples of the Pacific Islands. To the hall in the Museum it is only possible to bring these physical things, the carved float and net, the kava ° bowl with its opalescent * tint testifying to the generations of kava drinkers which it has served, the child's grass skirt, tightly bound to preserve the carefully crinkled waves against the day when it was to be worn. But if these lifeless specimens are to be placed in their true setting, if we are to understand the uses to which they were put, the difficulties under which they were manufactured, the human needs which they satisfied, it is necessary to go to these island communities and learn meticulously those aspects of their lives which can never be enclosed within a wall case, nor caught more than superficially in a model. It becomes the task of Museum ethnologists to make expeditions into primitive communities just as those who are to prepare the great habitat groups of animals have to follow the elephant and the tiger into their native haunts.

2   We are accustomed to think of expeditions as large groups of scientists equipped to the teeth with scientific paraphernalia. Such expeditions carry preparators, cameramen, guides, shooters, beaters, in addition to the central quota of scientists. They march across deserts or into jungles, carrying their food and their tents with them, setting up a microscopic world of their own wherever they go. Such are the ideal conditions for an expedition in the natural sciences other than ethnology. But the ethnologist cannot march upon a native community like an invading army, for that community is going to be not only a source of labor and food, but also the very stuff of his investigation. He must slip in quietly, lower himself or herself as gently as possible into the placid waters of native life, make the unprecedented arrival of an inquiring white per-

kava: an alcoholic drink made from the root of a shrubby pepper plant.

son as inconspicuous as possible. For such an expedition there are no cameramen, no preparators, no army of carriers, not even servants, because to take servants from another community causes friction and upsets the nice balance of native life. An ethnological expedition is limited to one, unless it be that a husband and wife or father and daughter can go together and take their place in native society. Two members of the same sex would work against each other, vying for the attention of the same informants, and the natives would not be slow to play them off against each other. Upon our last field trip my husband and I went together, a felicitous * scientific arrangement, as there are such strong sex antagonisms in Melanesia that no member of one sex can hope thoroughly to win the confidence or understand the point of view of the other.

3 As one cannot take an army of helpers neither can one take too bulky an amount of equipment. Tents and pavilions would stand out too sharply on the native scene, tend to distinguish the investigator from the native at the very points at which the investigator wishes to blur the differences. We therefore took with us only a minimum amount of equipment, two stretchers, two tables, two chairs, a typewriter, camera, developing apparatus, and a shotgun. The rest of our luggage was packed with notepaper, drawing paper for the children—I took a thousand sheets and the supply ran out in the first month—baubles by the gross, beads, toys, balloons, paper flowers, etc., and large and bulky amounts of rice and tobacco. Everything had to be packed into cedarwood boxes with double locks, one of which sang when it was turned like a musical clock to warn the owner of the prowling thief, the other put on for safety, as there were many duplicate keys about. The tobacco had to be unpacked from the telltale crates in which it is shipped from Louisiana and repacked in ambiguous cedar boxes.

4 In Rabaul, the capital of the Mandated Territory, we had acquired a Manus boy from the village of Pere, who spoke excellent pidgin and would serve as an interpreter in his own village. As he was a government servant and therefore allowed by ordinance to wear a shirt, he was of no use whatsoever for any more menial tasks. In Lorengau, the seat of the Manus district government, we acquired a second boy from the village of Pere, and our insidious approach was by now well begun.

5 The next step was taken by the District Officer, who summoned Gizikuk, so-called headman of the South Coast Manus, because he was the one man who could make the ten independent little democracies cooperate to the extent of providing canoes when these were needed by the government. Gizikuk came, very proud and bedizened ° with beadwork, and was presented with preliminary "grease," no less than twenty sticks of tobacco. He looked over our luggage and decided that it would take nine canoes to transport it the day's journey to Pere. This proved to be just four and a half times as many canoes as would really have been needed. We agreed to pay five shillings a canoe, and Gizikuk went away to muster the fleet. Meanwhile, with the aid of Banyalo and Manawai, the two Manus boys, and through the medium of pidgin English, a start was made on the Manus language.

6 The fleet which Gizikuk had declared necessary arrived, and a box or so was allotted to each craft, slender dugouts built up with wide sidestrakes, the whole topped by a wide platform, upon which small dome-shaped houses are constructed. As it was impossible to foresee what the attitude of the natives would be concerning questions of food, whether they would expect us to share their meal, resent our eating in their presence, or tabu eating in mixed company altogether, we took no provisions but prepared to tighten our belts for the day. And so it proved, for with characteristic Melanesian manners, our boat's crew cooked messes of sago ° and coconut oil on the small fireplaces on the edge of the platform and feasted happily, completely ignoring our famished presence. Entrance into na-

bedizened: adorned.
sago: a kind of palm.

tive life is always accompanied by just such delicate situations, into which the average white trader or government official can step without trepidation, * making the native custom bend to his whim, but toward which the ethnologist has to act with the greatest circumspection.* A misstep at the start may result in weeks or even months of delay. So on a Polynesian island, to take one's own food instead of relying upon the hospitality of the natives, which is always tendered with the grand manner, would be to insult one's hosts irrevocably.

7   After traveling all day along the edges of the mangrove swamps, sometimes crossing the reef, more often poling our way through the shallow reef-bound lagoons, we arrived at about eight in the evening at Bunei, the village of Gizikuk. Here another situation arose. Gizikuk wished us to stay in his village; but Bunei was smaller than Pere— this had been ascertained from the census—and as I wanted particularly to study children, it was necessary for the village to be large. Furthermore, we had two boys from Pere who might be miserable in Bunei. But if Gizikuk were really a chief, as he claimed to be, to offend him by refusing to make his capital our headquarters would have been fatal. However, we bet on his authority being a mere matter of personality and government backing (a guess which subsequent experience proved to be correct), and we insisted, to his great disgruntlement, upon pushing ahead to Pere. At midnight the fleet of canoes, under full sail, swept into the moonlit lagoon village, between the rows of pile-built houses, up to the doors of the "House Kiap," the government barracks, where we took up our temporary abode.

8   The "House Kiap" is in the village, built by government order to accommodate traveling officials and other white men, but it is distinctly not of it. From its narrow walls, 14 by 12 feet, we again temporized,* learned more of the language, tried to get an accurate enough picture of the social scene so as to know whom to trust and whom it was dangerous to displease. Meanwhile, through our two boys, and another and then another who were speedily

added to our ménage,° we let it be known that we wished to learn the language and witness all the important events in the lives of the people. For one to understand the onslaught to which we were subjected by such an invitation it is necessary to remember that these people have had only one kind of contact with white people, as inferiors, either as work boys or merely as native British subjects dealing with the occasional government officials very much on their dignity. The house of a white man, any house in which a white man took up temporary quarters, was forbidden to the native, except in his servant capacity as cook or houseboy. Missionaries, who must use softer methods to entice the heathen into the fold, had never been among the Manus. Into this setting stepped ethnologists who could not work unless all these carefully constructed barriers for the peace of the white invader were summarily shattered. To the native it was as if we had hung up a shingle saying: "We want to be bothered. We aren't like other white people," and they responded to this chance of a lifetime with great vigor. All day the house was crowded and not until midnight was there any peace.

9   We set about having a native house built, and the clan of Pere proper courteously accorded us the privilege of building our house abutting on one of the two small bits of land which are used as village greens and dancing grounds. But obtaining a house site was not obtaining a house. The thatch had to be bought in lots of ten shingles each, from the land people. Payment had to be made in advance, then runners sent out to collect. It took two months before a large thatched structure on piles was almost ready to receive us. Before it was finished I came down with malaria, and within two days three of our boys were down also. In Manus, all sickness is due to the spirits, and an elder of the other end of the village, who was anxious to hasten our removal to his section, divined the cause of the illness as the malicious work of a dead police

ménage: domestic establishment.

boy, appropriately domiciled in the "House Kiap." Very solemn, he sat on the floor and explained that neither the boys nor I would recover until we moved into the new and uncompleted house. I balked for twenty-four hours, as the prospect of moving with half the household sick was not enticing; then a fourth boy came down with the fever, and we moved to a doorless, stepless dwelling, where the cookhouse had no floor. Such intimate participation in the religious and social life of the community is inconvenient and wearing, but it is the only way in which the necessary knowledge of native society can be obtained. And the way is full of pitfalls. I shall never forget the panic caused among a group of visitors, early in our stay, when my husband complied with one person's tentative request that he pronounce my name. Several people almost fell into the sea in their horrified retreat from such blasphemous behavior.

10   The endless tabus upon mentioning the names of any relative-in-law in a person's presence make it necessary to know the social organization of the village by heart, all the past marriages, the present marriages, the contemplated marriages. In addition it is necessary to know each person's three or four names. Even then one is continually trespassing, as when I inadvertently sneezed in the presence of a woman whose daughter was engaged to a youth named "Sneeze." There are relatives-in-law who may not look at each other, and it was necessary to construct a house with several exits, so that mothers-in-law could depart as sons-in-law entered, for it is always the women who have to do the running away. On one occasion, when I was alone in the village and had added to my household of six small boys and two girls, a man and his wife, there were so many complicated relationships that the only place where Ngaoli, my seventeen-year-old girl, could eat, without transgressing, was huddled in a corner behind the bed. And the linguistic confusion which resulted from getting a new cook boy who was the brother-in-law of three of the other boys was terrifying. One could not say his name in front of them but must refer to him grandiloquently as "the husband of Pondramet" (their sister); if he were also in the room, even this would not serve, as his wife's name could not be mentioned in his presence.

11 A large part of one's time in these remote villages is taken up with doctoring, as there is no doctor within a day's journey and often not one as near. Here again there are many dangers. To give medicine to someone who may die is to risk crippling one's fieldwork, as the natives may blame one for the resulting death. The children were continually fainting from malaria, a fact which was advertised to the entire village by the wails of the mother. The prescribed method of bringing the child around was for a hundred people to collect in the house, all the female relatives of the child gathering close about it, wailing, for which expression of affection they were subsequently paid, while some important man, or possibly two, stirred bowls of water with long sticks and invoked their guardian ghosts' aid in returning the child's purloined * soul stuff. It was a simple matter to thrust a bottle of aromatic spirits of ammonia under the children's noses, but the natives never admitted that this brought them to, insisting that the spitting and coughing were signs that the spirits disliked the horrid medicine.

12 Sometimes, however, my doctoring brought rich rewards. There was one tall, shaggy-headed sorcerer, with one injured eye and a bad case of ringworm, who sought my aid to cure his disfigured skin. Day after day he came to be treated, while I supervised the application by one of the small boys of a stronger lotion than the natives were allowed to have themselves. After about two months Pataliyan was cured and made me the confidant of his projected elopement with a widow. The wrath of the ghostly husband shook the village and killed an unfortunate woman go-between, and the whole village was thrown into confusion—which was priceless to the ethnologist—all from a steady application of ringworm medicine to make the lover beautiful and desirable to a much-wooed and most excellent maker of pots.

13 The children were my chief concern, as I was trying to add to our knowledge of child psychology at the same time that I worked on the general ethnological background of the people. By selecting the oldest boys of the adolescent group, youngsters of about fourteen, as house-boys, we were able to attract all the rest of the children to our little patch of backyard. Each fourteen-year-old had a ten-year-old slavey, who in turn delegated the disagreeable aspects of his task to a six-year-old. Dinner was often prepared by some dozen small hands, one small boy tending each pot, faithfully blowing up the twig fire underneath it. The little girls were enlisted to pluck the wild pigeons and to fetch the firewood. I was making a collection of drawings by these savage little youngsters who had never seen paper or pencil before, and this practically disrupted the household. Every available square inch of table, box, or trunk surface was pre-empted by children engaged in drawing. They would have drawn all night happily, had I permitted them, and they came to wake me before dawn with requests for "paypa." Getting meals prepared or floors cleaned in this general nursery-school atmosphere was often difficult and always accomplished in the midst of a terrific din of happy insistent voices.

14 Photography demanded more organizaion. In that climate films have to be developed at once; there is no packing them off to the darkroom of a commercial photographer. This meant working at night. Water had to be brought from the mainland almost a mile away, and the only water fit for photography came from a "place of blood" where some of the ancestors of the village had been slain. Such blood lingers and has a bad habit of entering the bodies of the descendants who are foolhardy enough to approach within its death-dealing atmosphere. So it took many sticks of tobacco to obtain a large enough supply of water for washing films. If the water ran out, there was no remedy, for no one would venture into that fearful place after dark. As there were many films to be washed, we trained a squad of native children as helpers, retaining two extra children, one to watch that no torchlit canoes came near the house and one to scratch the backs of the other children so that they wouldn't drop the films which they were washing.

15   By such devious means and amid such peculiar surroundings, we worked our way into native life, until our house was known generally as the "kamal" or clubhouse, because it was always so crowded. From the native children which I had assembled into a household, it was possible to reach out into their respective homes, and to follow the details of the ceremonies, quarrels, and reconciliations which went on within the thatched walls of other houses. By oneself assuming the tabus and duties, the privileges and obligations, of a native woman, as much as possible, one receives in return the confidence of the women and learns the carefully guarded secrets which have been hidden from twenty generations of husbands and fathers. The temper, the emphasis of native life, from the woman's point of view, gradually unfolds before one's eyes, as do the moods, the thought processes, the interests of the group of children who sleep on one's floor and eat one's rice day after day. The native language becomes more and more a familiar idiom. One learns to joke in it, perhaps even to pun a little (although I knew that I was never permitted to swear, as both of my parents are living and profanity is only permitted to the orphaned). One learns to shudder when tabus are violated, to meet the news of a misfortune with the immediate question "Which ghost is responsible?" The personalities of all these alien people who press about one all day long become as clearly realized as those of the members of a family.

16   Only a six-weekly or less frequent mail breaks this long detailed identification with native life, from which one finally emerges wearied with the continuous restraint, the continuous reevaluation of experience, but bearing, as a field trophy, a knowledge of the native customs and the native thought attainable in no other way.

ANALYSIS

The *Natural History Magazine,* for which this article was written in 1931, is published for a general readership. Mead probably was thinking of this audience when she opened her article with a description of some of the exhibits in the glass cases of the Museum of Natural History. It is a casual, interesting opening, and it leads naturally into the next paragraph and to her topic: how do ethnological expeditions "work"?

Some explanations can be dull beyond belief, though they are useful to certain interested people. An explanation of how an ethnological expedition works could bore anyone but an ethnologist, but this article is not a bore, any more than is another selection on another unlikely subject—Steinbeck's description of a turtle crossing the highway, on page 82. How can some people write about the most insignificant object or event and make it fascinating? How, on the contrary, can others write about the most fabulous events of human history and make them dull? Part of the answer lies in the writer's imagination, for that is what stimulates our own. Mead keeps us involved with her expedition, not only through her anecdotes (paragraphs 6, 9, 10, 12), but also through some unusual or humorous images. There is the image in paragraph 2 of the ethnologist as a deep-sea diver ("He must slip in quietly, lower himself or herself as gently as possible into the placid waters of native life . . ."). There is the image in the same paragraph of ethnologists marching upon a native community "like an invading army," and in paragraph 9 of the Manus "almost falling into the sea in their horrified retreat" from her husband's violation of a tabu.

Certainly, this article could be more thorough; Mead leaves questions unanswered. But she has succeeded in giving us a quick overview of how this kind of scientific expedition operates. Most important, she is enthusiastic, and she is articulate. Perhaps, for a start, those qualities can help any writer make any subject interesting.

Questions on Content

1. What is the purpose of an ethnological expedition into a community?
2. How is an ethnological expedition different from expeditions of natural scientists?
3. How did Mead set about studying the children?

Add to Your Vocabulary

opalescent, felicitous, trepidation, circumspection, temporized, purloined.

Questions on Technique

1. Mead delays mention of the purpose of her own expedition until paragraph 7, where she says, "I wanted particularly to study children." Explain why you think she chose not to begin her article with a statement of her purpose in going to Melanesia.
2. What other organization could Mead have given her explanation of how an ethnological expedition works?
3. What questions do you still have about the process of setting up a fieldwork project? Explain whether or not the article suffers because these questions are not dealt with.
4. From the words she uses to describe them, and from the anecdotes she tells, what would you say is Mead's attitude toward the people she is studying?
5. Explain Mead's use of the word *insidious* in paragraph 4.

Techniques to Imitate

Moving from the familiar to the unfamiliar

Mead knows that most of her readers will have little understanding of the nature of an ethnological expedition. She knows too that most of her readers do know something about other kinds of scientific expeditions. She therefore makes clear what an ethnological expedition is by contrasting it with the other kinds of scientific expeditions that are familiar to her readers. In other words, she proceeds in her explanation from the familiar to the unfamiliar. In this way she is able to lead her readers from what they already know to what she wants them to learn.

How does she do this? First, Mead assumes that her readers have visited a museum and are familiar with the displays in glass cases of objects brought from distant parts of the world. Therefore, she mentions first the glass cases of the South Seas Hall of the American Museum and their contents. These are "lifeless specimens," she says; the ethnologist wants to understand their uses, how they were made, and the human needs they satisfied.

Next, Mead mentions the scientific expeditions, the kind that she assumes we think of when we hear the word "expedition." She contrasts this kind of expedition with her own, and the difference, she tells us, is attributed to a difference in purpose: for the ethnologist, "that community is going to be not only a source of labor and food, but also the very stuff of his investigation."

Proceeding from the familiar to the unfamiliar has always been a sound technique in teaching. It is also a sound technique in expository writing which, after all, is a kind of teaching.

Suggestions for Writing

1. Write an explanation of some process that you are familiar with and interested in: setting up a camp, preparing for a holiday, training an animal, building something, cooking something. You might try to make your explanation interesting by including some personal anecdotes, or unusual images or comparisons.

2. Explain how you do the thing you can do well. (Everyone can do something well.) Imagine that you are explaining this process to someone who knows very little, if anything, about it. Compare this process to something

your reader will be familiar with. For example, if you want to explain the game of cricket, you might begin with a review of a game your readers are thoroughly familiar with—baseball. Then by drawing contrasts between the two sports, you can make the strange game of cricket familiar to your readers.

3. Imagine that an ethnological expedition from another planet is coming into your own society to study its structure and customs. Write an explanation of how such an expedition should be set up. Write from the viewpoint of one of the investigating scientists. Tell what tabus the scientists would be bound to learn about (every society has them); explain your society's attitudes toward meals and strangers; describe how the members of the expedition could obtain a "native house." You can follow the organization of Mead's article closely. You can open with a description of various objects from your society that might have already been placed in museum cases on the other planet, and so on.

E. G. F. SAUER

Celestial Navigation by Birds

The essay that follows is at once a definition, a report on experimental verification, and a hypothesis reached by inductive reasoning. For many years Professor Sauer had been interested in birds and their behavior patterns. As a student and teacher in Germany, he had made a systematic study of their migratory habits. In 1957–1958, he spent a year in South-West Africa studying European migratory birds within their winter quarters. Some of his observations are the basis for this brief account of one problem which had long fascinated him: how European warblers find their way from northern Europe to Africa and back again.

Sauer's prose is simple, direct, and nontechnical. The average reader can share his enthusiasm and his knowledge. As definition, the essay makes quite clear what celestial navigation entails. As a report on experimental verification, it lists three distinct sets of controls Sauer and his wife used to gather data. As a demonstration of a hypothesis, it sets out to show why Sauer's theory that the warbler flies by the stars is very likely true. As with all good scientists, Sauer is not insisting that we accept his point of view. There is less persuasion in

his voice than in Richard Neuberger's in an essay about
American highways (page 494); there is somewhat more
formality in his sentences than there is in Margaret
Mead's. But of what exposition needs above all—accuracy and clarity—there is plenty.

1 **I**n spring and summer the
songbirds known as the warblers are familiar residents in
the countries throughout Europe. City dwellers know
them well, for the small, gray birds find a home to their
liking in the shrubs and hedges of gardens and small parks.
During the spring breeding season the air is filled with
their loud, melodic singing as each male establishes a small
territory for himself in noisy battle with a rival. Once the
claims are decided, the truculence * and the songs subside;
the birds proceed to mate and to raise their young. In
late summer they feed amicably on elderberries and
blackberries and they flit about in peace among the bushes.
Then in August the birds begin to grow restless; their
migratory instinct stirs. Suddenly, in one night, the whole
resident population of one species is off and away. The
next morning the bushes are filled with a new lot of
warblers that have flown in from more northern areas;
they stay for a few days and then they too fly on to the
south. Through the weeks of September and October there
is a continuous coming and going of hordes of the migrating warblers. Gradually the number passing through diminishes. The species called the garden warblers disappears
first, then the whitethroats, after them the lesser whitethroats, and finally the blackcaps.

2 Where do they go? Ornithologists ° know exactly where
the warblers go, for they have banded these birds for many
years and followed them to their winter homes. With the
exception of some blackcaps, these warblers travel to vari-

ornithologists: zoologists who deal with birds.

ous parts of Africa. Some of them migrate as far as from Scandinavia to the southern part of Africa—a distance of seven thousand miles and more. In the spring the birds migrate back to the same place that they left in the fall.

3 Most remarkable of all is that each bird finds its own way to its destination! The warblers do not follow a leader or make the journey as a group; they navigate individually. And young birds making their first migration reach their goal as surely as the experienced travelers. Somehow, purely by instinct, the warblers know exactly how to set their course.

4 The navigation powers of birds have fascinated investigators for more than a century. By now there is a large literature of well-documented testimony to their amazing performances. The late Werner Rüppell of Germany, one of the leading experimenters on bird migration, found that starlings taken from their nests near Berlin and carried away to all points of the compass would find their way back to their nesting places from as far as 1,250 miles away. The Manx ° shearwater, a sea bird, has astonished investigators with still more spectacular feats; one shearwater, taken from the west coast of England by G. V. T. Matthews and flown by plane to Boston, was back in its English nest in 12 days, having winged its own way 3,067 miles across the unknown Atlantic. The North American golden plover migrates each fall from its breeding grounds along the west coast of Alaska to its winter home in the Hawaiian Islands. This bird, lacking webbed feet, cannot rest on the water as waterfowl do; it must fly on steadily for several weeks to reach its destination over thousands of miles of ocean. If it wandered only slightly off course, it would become lost and exhausted in the vast Pacific, but it finds its way unerringly to Hawaii.

5 Until recently attempts to explain the incredible navigation feats of birds were almost entirely a matter of speculation [see "The Navigation of Birds," by Donald R.

Manx: of the Isle of Man, in the Irish Sea off northwest England.

Griffin, *Scientific American,* December, 1948]. Various theorists proposed that the birds were guided by the earth's magnetic field, by the Coriolis force ° arising from the earth's rotation, by landmarks, and so on. But more and more ornithologists have been driven to the conclusion that birds must rely mainly on celestial navigation—the sun by day, the constellations by night.

6   The idea that birds are guided by the sun was suggested as long as half a century ago, but it was not taken seriously until the early 1950's, when experimenters began to turn up some interesting evidence. Gustav Kramer in Germany and G. V. T. Matthews in England discovered independently that homing pigeons and wild birds can use the sun as a compass and that they possess a "time sense" which allows them to take account of the sun's motion across the sky. Other zoologists have confirmed these findings. It has now been proved, in fact, that our warblers can orient * themselves by the sun.

7   But the warblers fly mainly at night. What sort of system do they use to steer their course in their nocturnal * migrations nearly halfway around the globe? Several years ago the author and his wife started a systematic laboratory study of this question by means of specially designed cages in our aviary ° at Freiburg.

8   We had already seen laboratory proof of the stirring of the migratory instinct in these small world-travelers and of a seasonal time sense that governed this urge. We had hatched and raised warblers in completely closed, sound-proof chambers where they lived in the illusion of eternal summer, year in and year out. Yet, although they seemed to have no outward cues of the yearly rhythm of nature, in

Coriolis force: named for the French engineer and mathematician G. C. Coriolis in 1835. "Because of the earth's rotation, an object moving horizontally relative to the earth's surface appears to be acted on by a force tending to deflect it to the right in the northern hemisphere, to the left in the southern hemisphere. The apparent, or inertia, force is known as the Coriolis force or as the deflecting or deviating force of the earth's rotation." [*Encyclopædia Britannica,* 1958, Vol. XV, p. 851.]

aviary: a house or enclosure in which birds are kept.

the autumn the birds would begin to flit restlessly from branch to branch or flutter continually over their perches, night after wakeful night. They kept this up for many weeks—about the length of time it would have taken them to fly to Africa. Then they went back to sleeping again at night. In the spring, about the time that warblers migrate back from Africa to their European homes, our birds again had a spell of restless, wakeful nights. It was as if they had an inner clock which told them when the time had come to take wing for distant parts.

9 To explore the orientation question we now placed warblers in a cage with a glass opening at the top, so that they could see part of the sky (but nothing else of their surroundings). At the season of migration the birds would begin to flutter and, peculiarly enough, each would take up a position pointing in a particular geographic direction, like the needle of a compass. Even when we tried to turn the birds away by rotating their ring-shaped perch, they stubbornly turned back to the preferred direction. The direction in each case was characteristic of the species: the garden warblers, the whitethroats, and the blackcaps all pointed toward the southwest, the lesser whitethroats toward the southeast (that is, in the fall; in the spring these directions were reversed). Now these are precisely the directions in which the respective species start their migrations from central Europe to Africa! The lesser whitethroats start southeastward, flying across the Balkans, and then turn south up the Nile Valley; the other species all take off southwestward and fly to Africa by way of Spain and Gibraltar.

10 Experienced or inexperienced, the birds invariably took up the appropriate direction of flight in the cage. How did they know the direction? Seemingly the only clue available to them was the starry night sky overhead. To explore this theory further we now put them through a series of tests. We found that when the stars were hidden by thick clouds, the birds became completely disoriented. They were likewise confused when only diffuse * and strongly polarized light came through their skylight. To adopt and

keep to a definite direction they needed a look at the starry sky. Indeed, the birds watched the sky so intently that shooting stars made them change their direction for a short time.

11   For still more rigidly controlled experiments we proceeded to test the birds in a cage placed in a planetarium: °
that is, with a dome showing an artificial replica of the natural starry sky. Again, when the dome was merely illuminated with diffuse light (showing no stars), the warblers were unable to choose a preferred direction. But when the planetarium sky matched the local night sky, the birds took up the proper direction just as if they were seeing the natural sky, but now adjusted to the artificial planetarium directions.

12   Now our artificial dome permitted us to shift the stars and constellations about. By changing the north-south declination (height) of the stars we could change the apparent geographical latitude, making the birds believe that they were farther south or north than they actually were. Similarly by shifting the sky in the east-west direction we might mislead the birds about their position in longitude. How would they behave under these circumstances?

13   To illustrate the results I shall describe some experiments with a lesser whitethroat warbler. Recall that the lesser whitethroat normally first travels southeastward across the Balkans and then turns due south, flying along the Nile to its winter home in the region of the Nile headwaters. In our experiments it turned out that as long as the planetarium sky was adjusted to the latitudes of 50 to 40 degrees north, this bird took up the expected flight position facing southeast. But as we shifted the sky, simulating *
more southerly latitudes, the bird tended to turn more and more toward the southern direction, until, at the latitude of 15 degrees, it set its course due south!

14   In other words, Johnny, a bird which had spent all its life in a cage and never traveled under a natu-

planetarium: an optical device which projects a representation of the heavens upon a dome through the use of many stereopticons in motion.

ral sky, let alone migrated to Africa, still displayed an inborn agility to use the guidance of the stars to follow the usual route of its species, adjusting its direction nicely at each given latitude. Earlier investigators had supposed that these birds used landmarks to find their route: for example, that the coastline at the eastern end of the Mediterranean was the cue which told them to turn south. But our experiments proved that the birds are able to do it only by the stars.

15 Now let us see what happened when we shifted the planetarium sky to change the longitude, or, corresponding to it, the time. One night, while the lesser whitethroat was flapping its wings and heading in the southeast direction, we suddenly presented the bird with a sky shifted to the configuration five hours and 10 minutes advanced to the local time; in other words, the apparent geographical position of the cage then corresponded to a point 77.5 degrees eastward in longitude at this particular time. The bird at once showed that it was deeply disturbed. It looked excitedly at the unfamiliar sky and for almost a full minute stood irresolutely. Then it suddenly turned and took wing in the westward direction. According to the sky, its position at the moment corresponded to a point near Lake Balkhash in Siberia; Johnny, to correct his displacement, was heading directly toward the usual migration starting point in Germany.

16 As we reduced its displacement, the bird shifted its heading more and more from due west toward the south. When the displacement was only an hour, corresponding to a position near Vienna, the lesser whitethroat headed south; when the canopy of stars was restored to the correct configuration at our locality for the season and time of night, the bird took up the normal heading toward the southeast.

17 Johnny's behavior, confirmed by experiments with other birds, leaves no doubt that the warblers have a remarkable hereditary mechanism for orienting themselves by the stars—a detailed image of the starry configuration of the sky coupled with a precise time sense which relates the heavenly canopy to the geography of the earth at every time and season. At their very first glimpse of the sky the birds automatically know the right direction. Without benefit of previous experience, with no cue except the stars, the birds are able to locate themselves in time and space and to find their way to their destined homes.

18 To be sure, the warblers do not have to rely solely on the constellations. In daytime they can guide themselves by the position of the sun. On cloudy nights they get some guidance from mountain ranges, coastlines, and river courses gleaming in the pale night shine. Only in almost total darkness, when thick clouds utterly hide the sky, are the birds in trouble: they circle helplessly and often are drawn to lighthouses.

19 We are going on to study the warblers' orientation system in more detail, systematically removing constellations or stars from our planetarium sky one by one to see if we can reduce the guidance cues to a basic pattern. One very interesting puzzle is the fact that the birds must somehow be able to make adjustments to astronomical evolution, for in the course of time the pattern of constellations in the sky is slowly but constantly changing. Even more difficult to explain is the mystery of how the birds ever came to rely on celestial navigation and to develop their skill in the first place. We know that the warblers are not the only creatures possessing this gift: other birds, insects, crabs, and spiders have been found by experiment to be capable of guiding themselves by the sun. But there are many other guidance mechanisms and signposts available on earth. What evolutionary process was it that endowed these animals with the highly sophisticated ability to read the stars?

20 Whatever the answer, we cannot help marveling at the wondrous celestial instinct of the warblers. When fall comes, the little garden warbler, weighing barely three quarters of an ounce, sets off one night on an unbelievable journey. All alone, never in the collective security of a flock, it wings its solitary way southwestward over Germany, France, and Spain, and then swings south to its distant goal in southern Africa. It flies on unerringly, covering a hundred miles and more in a single night, never once stopping in its course, certain of its goal. When drifted by heavy sidewinds, the bird navigates back to its primary course in the next calm night. In the spring it takes off again and northward retraces its path to its nesting place in a European thicket—there to give birth to a new generation of little warblers which will grow up, without being taught, with the selfsame capacity to follow the same route across the continents and oceans by the map of the stars.

ANALYSIS

Sauer's opening paragraph is a pleasantly oblique approach to his main subject—how birds navigate. He tells us here and in the next three paragraphs when they migrate, how far, and under what circumstances. In paragraph 5, he readily disposes of the old explanations of how they did it. Paragraph 6 is the actual beginning of his extended definition of celestial navigation. But "celestial" means "of the sky." Shall we learn about the birds' dependence on the sun as well as the stars? Paragraph 6 narrows the subject. Zoologists, we hear, have confirmed the "time sense" that allows birds "to take account of the sun's motion across the sky." The warblers, however, fly by night. They must possess a special sense to fly by the stars. With paragraph 8, Sauer begins his inductive reasoning. His experiments included completely closed chambers, glass-topped cages, and a planetarium with an artificial sky. The description of these experiments constitutes paragraphs 8–19, at which point Sauer stops short on a question he cannot answer: "What evolutionary process was it that endowed these animals with the highly sophisticated ability to read the stars?" The essay concludes gracefully with a paragraph that matches his opening. A bird weighing barely three quarters of an ounce sets off on an unbelievable journey. . . .

Sauer could have chosen several other ways of organizing his essay. He might have eliminated his general introduction and enlarged paragraph 5. Once the various theories were established, he could have set up his own to disprove them. Or he might have broken the essay into two parts: birds that orient themselves by the sun (Kramer's and Matthews' experiments) and the warblers' night flights (his own experiments). What does he gain by the organization as it stands? Far greater reader interest, surely. His essay is more than definition. It conveys much of the awe Sauer feels from his own discoveries. It is filled with specific fact, but it can also convey enthusiasm: "We are going on to study the warblers' orientation system in more detail"; "One very interesting puzzle"; "Even more difficult to explain . . ." Compared with Mead's, Sauer's essay is a more elaborate definition of a process.

Questions on Content

1. How do ornithologists keep track of bird flights?
2. What theories other than celestial navigation have been suggested to explain how birds fly from one continent to another?
3. How did Sauer employ a planetarium to test warblers?
4. Do warblers fly *only* by means of the stars? Explain.
5. What details about his "systematic laboratory study" does the author include? Would you have him tell us more about his aviary?

Add to Your Vocabulary

truculence, orient, nocturnal, diffuse, simulating.

Questions on Technique

1. Sauer cites other scientists—Rüppell, Matthews, Kramer —on the subject of navigation by birds. What does he add to his essay by doing so?
2. Paragraphs 15 and 16 may not be completely clear to some readers. How would you rewite them?
3. Sauer tells us nothing about the anatomy of the warbler, yet it is a bird that can fly thousands of miles in

migration. Why do you suppose Sauer never discusses the warbler itself?

Techniques to Imitate

Transitions between paragraphs

The successful expository writer keeps the trend of the essay constantly before the reader. The writer makes sure, in other words, that the reader is always able to follow the flow. One means of keeping the trend of thought clear to the reader is the use of transitional expressions to bridge the gaps between paragraphs.

Margaret Mead (page 181) uses this device frequently to help us follow her explanation of how an ethnologist's expedition functions. She opens paragraph 3 with the words "As one cannot take an army of helpers neither can one take . . . ," referring back to paragraph 2 which tells how she cannot have an army of helpers. She opens paragraph 5 with "The next step . . . ," referring back to paragraph 4 which talked about the beginning steps in their operation. She opens paragraph 12 with the words "Sometimes, however . . . ," referring back to a statement in paragraph 11. She opens paragraph 14 with the sentence "Photography demanded more organization," referring back to the topic of paragraph 13 with the comparative *more*. She opens paragraph 15 with the words "By such devious means," referring back to statements made in paragraph 14 with the word *such*.

Sauer also provides examples of this technique. To keep the progress of his essay clear to his reader, Sauer uses the technique of opening each paragraph (with some exceptions, of course) with a reference—direct or indirect—to the idea in the preceding paragraph. Compare the following paragraph endings and openings from his essay. The expressions that effect the transition are italicized.

End paragraph 1   ". . . The species called the garden warblers disappears first, then the whitethroats, after them the lesser whitethroats, and finally the blackcaps."

Opening paragraph 2   "Where do *they* go? . . ."

End paragraph 2   ". . . In the spring the birds migrate back [7,000 miles] to the same place that they left in the fall."

Opening paragraph 3   "*Most remarkable of all* is that each bird finds its own way to its destination! . . ."

End paragraph 3   ". . . Somehow, purely by instinct, the warblers know exactly how to set their course."

Opening paragraph 4   "*The navigation powers of birds* have fascinated investigators for more than a century . . ."

Explain how the following expressions, taken from other paragraph openings in Sauer's article, effect a transition from what has preceded to what is to follow:

Paragraph 7   But the warblers fly mainly at night. . . .

Paragraph 11   For still more rigidly controlled experiments . . .

Paragraph 13   To illustrate the results . . .

Paragraph 14   In other words . . .

Paragraph 15   Now let us see what happened . . . .

In your expository writing make use of transitional expressions to bridge the gap in thought between paragraphs.

Suggestions for Writing

1. Write at least four paragraphs explaining how something you are very familiar with "works," or "operates." It might be a plant, a child you know well, a dish-

washer, a car motor, a surfboard, a cat's stalking method, or the subway system. Open your essay with a question that states your topic. Use each paragraph to explain one distinct part of the whole process. (You do not have to explain mechanics necessarily; you can concentrate on what *you* have observed of the way in which this thing or system "works.")

2. Using Sauer's method of reaching a hypothesis (birds navigate by the stars) by inductive reasoning (the laboratory experiments), write an essay of about 500 words on a belief or theory you hold and the reasons for holding it.

3. Observe yourself, or someone else, and explain what your subject does from the time he or she eats breakfast in the morning until he or she eats dinner. (This also is a process.) Since you will be explaining a process that takes place in time, use transitional expressions that will help your reader move from one time to the next (expressions like *next, then, later, soon, a few hours after,* and so on).

5

REPORTS AND ANALYSES

When we pick up the morning paper just before breakfast, we want reports on the news and we want these reports to be concise. Reporters know that. When they file a story, they aim to tell us what happened, where, at what time, to whom. The first paragraph of a news report attracts our attention and gives us basic facts. "A young New Weston resident," we might read, "was slightly injured yesterday when his car plunged through a guard rail on the approach to the South Street Bridge and stopped just short of the Pennsylvania Railroad tracks. The accident occurred at 5:20 P.M. as Henry Burkhardt, 18, of 115 Elm Road, was returning from his bookkeeper's job at the New Weston Savings and Loan Association."

As the account continues (we have already decided whether we want to go on reading), the reporter will naturally fill in details: how Burkhardt sustained slight injuries, what caused the accident, who called the police, what hospital he was taken to. It is unlikely that he will pause to comment on youthful drivers, the epidemic of South Street traffic accidents, or the need for another railroad bridge. We might call this kind of writing "routine reporting," the prose we use to give the news. From the front page to the sports page, we expect concise coverage, with most of the important details recounted in the lead paragraphs.

Yesterday's news perishes quickly, however, and factual reports are not subtle compositions. They are not models we need to imitate unless we are students of journalism, serviceable though the prose may be. Yet this section of the book is labeled "Reports and Analyses," and the account of Mr. Burkhardt's accident is clearly expository prose. Are there perhaps various kinds of "reports"? Does the reporter ever have an opportunity to embellish a story, to write to make words "come alive" rather than just "service" the facts? Do some reports come close to being informative essays? Are some reports designed to inform us of certain facts ("report" on a situation or case study or committee meeting) and then to establish opinions, arrive at conclusions? The answer to all these questions is yes. Reports and analyses can be stimulating reading. They demand just as vibrant a vocabulary and careful an organization as descriptive essays do. The models that follow will demonstrate this kind of exposition.

We begin with two stories from the *New York Times* by two reporters who love words. They know how to make a vocabulary fit a situation, and they clearly have a sense of fitness, of when to give their readers factual details and when to intersperse the facts with direct quotations, descriptive asides, or general background information.

The first model is a human interest story. Watch how Phillips conveys all the basic facts, but in a somewhat leisurely order for so brief a report.

McCANDLISH PHILLIPS

Lone Sailor Is Back,
Recounts Perils

1   **W**illiam Willis, an aged
wanderer on trackless oceans, was back yesterday from
his latest agonizing adventure in solitude, looking like a
man who had spent a few days in Miami.
2   The 73-year-old mariner had lain almost helpless in
the bottom of a tiny cat-yawl, drifting back and forth in the
Atlantic, covering 1,750 miles in 60 days, alone against
the sea while a hernia stabbed his abdomen with knife-
twist pain.
3   He looked remarkably hale. "Well, plenty of fresh air,"
he shrugged. He is a lean man (5 feet 7½ inches and 138
pounds) with arms as tough as hawsers, eyes small and
sharp as an eagle's. He has wild, wiry eyebrows and a white
mustache with white beard on a bronze-red face.
4   He left New York June 22 in his 11½-foot yawl, the
size of a Central Park rowboat. He trusted the winds to
drive him to Plymouth, England, in 45 to 70 days.
5   He was 850 miles east-northeast of the city Monday
night when a Coast Guard Albatross seaplane brightened
the night with flares, and the cutter *Ingham* plucked him
from the ocean.
6   Back from the sea for rest and medical care, he re-

laxed in an armchair in his small suite in the Oliver Cromwell Hotel, just off Central Park West at 12 West 72nd Street.

7   Twelve years ago, when he was only 61, Mr. Willis drifted on a frail balsa raft from Peru to Pago Pago in Samoa with a cat and a parrot. The two-part, 9,800-mile Pacific voyage ended in September, 1964, at Tully, Australia.

8   It all began when he was only 4 years old at Hamburg, Germany, where he remembered "wandering down to the harbor, getting into the boats and being chased out."

9   The child was father of the man.

10   "Once I got out," he said, "and the harbor police caught me because I was drifting down the [Elbe] River, and my mother said to me, 'Ah! You were born with an angel on each shoulder.' "

11   Mr. Willis is a seafarer of few comforts, but one he cherished failed him:

12   "A transmitter was sent me from Marconi International—Lord Nelson himself sent it from London, a survival emergency transmitter," he said. "I had it lashed on deck and it never worked. It was absolutely dead." Lord Nelson, he reported, is chairman of the British Electric Company.

13   The loss of the transmitter was a critical one. When the hernia put him in "agony" after three weeks, he had no touch with human beings. His sextant allowed him to measure "the exact height of the stars, the planets, the moon and the sun—all the celestial bodies—above the horizon." That fixed his latitude and longtitude. A transistor radio brought in Government time signals "that give you the tick of the second 24 hours a day."

14   His rations had a John-the-Baptist-like severity. He lived on four teaspoonfuls of dry whole wheat flour three times a day. He packed the flour in small wax-lined paper bags obtained from the Kiehl pharmacy on the Lower East Side.

15   "There's no element for the human body that is not contained in this," he said, shaking a box of the flour. He

drank three medium tins of evaporated milk a day, but not with the flour. "If you mix it with liquid, you get very little good out of it," he said.

16 He also carried "a little honey and a little olive oil," his wife, Teddy, said. As on previous voyages, he took "no water—not a drop," Mr. Willis reported.

17 He carried a zippered kit that allowed him to take his "blood pressure, pulse, and urinalysis every day." He believed it was the first time anyone had ventured to cross the Atlantic in a boat without shelter.

18 As a 15-year-old, he went to sea "as a deck boy on a big, four-masted bark, a 3,000-ton sailing ship, one of the last of her kind, and we sailed from Hamburg to the Gulf of California in 168 days, with coke from the Ruhr for copper smelters."

19 He jumped ship at Galveston, Texas, when he was 18 and began loading ships, "carrying 300-pound sacks, the hardest labor on the face of the earth." He had 10 years of it and then he fell to wandering on land, "working in forests, woods, mines, harvest fields, oil fields—building oil derricks in Oklahoma, working only a day if I wanted to."

20 "It must be born in me to see other places, other people," he went on, "to seek solitude at times. I've lived an unimpeded life, never any constriction on me. I could quit any time I wanted."

21 In his days of pain, he "saw a few ships in the distance, but they didn't stop.

22 "By luck, the *Sapphire Gladys* came straight out of the mists, right at me, and still she passed by. I'd been waiting for weeks, and I knew I was really cooked. Then she swung round." The American freighter radioed the Coast Guard.

23 He said he would try again, with his wife's consent.

24 "I'm asserting myself," Mrs. Willis said quietly. "This last time it was too much to take," and Mr. Willis nodded and muttered something about it not being "worth breaking up my marriage."

ANALYSIS

Phillips has several facts to convey: who was rescued by whom; where and when the rescue took place; why Willis had to be rescued; what happened afterward. He could, it is true, tell us all this in one paragraph, but Phillips wants to expand the mere news report into a human interest "story." What we do not expect from a news report we happily find here: personality. William Willis, robust and craggy in appearance, is no ordinary sailor. He is dauntless in his ambitions, as independent a man as we could hope to meet. In the opening paragraph, Phillips calls him "an aged wanderer on trackless oceans" returned from "an adventure of solitude." He clearly wants us to see this man almost as a character out of Melville or Conrad. How does he do it?

First, he accumulates impressive details, although he does not try to impress us overtly with them. Willis is 73 years old, and he was suffering from abdominal pains when he was "plucked" from the ocean 850 miles east-northeast of New York City. He was drifting in a yawl only 11½ feet long. He had no shelter in his boat and only survival rations. Most important of all, his radio transmitter was dead. He was helpless. Phillips merely recounts these details; he does not comment on them.

Second, he lets Willis talk. His first comment is brief but nicely ironic. In answer to why he looks so remarkably hale after his near-disaster, Willis replies, "Well, plenty of fresh air." Later Willis tells us about his childhood in Germany, his youth in Texas, his theories on diet. And then Mrs. Willis speaks a few words. The intimacy of the interview is carefully recorded. We feel the strength of this man as well as his easy-going informality.

Third, Phillips shifts from present time to past and back to the present with surprising ease. Paragraphs 1–6 treat the rescue: what happened yesterday. Paragraphs 7–10 describe the distant past, his childhood. From paragraphs 11 through 17, we hear of the recent voyage. In paragraph

18, Phillips shifts to Willis' boyhood again, then to the immediate past in paragraphs 20–22. What better way to end this piece than with his last two paragraphs on the future. We almost hear Mrs. Willis' unspoken complaint: "At your age, William Willis. . . ."

Now it is apparent that Phillips could not treat all assignments this way. A meeting of the UN Assembly, a local election, a school board decision require a different approach. But as a good reporter, Phillips will make his prose work for him whenever he can. He will not merely *tell* us a fact (order the details, that is) when he can *show* us (that is, make us feel what is happening). When Phillips reported, on another occasion, the arrival of a political candidate at an airport, he wrote: "The eager Bostonians did everything but resolve themselves into formations to spell out 'WELCOME.' Four bands boomed out marches, usually in consecutive order, but sometimes in clashing coincidence." These details contribute graphic description to what might otherwise be routine facts. They form an image in our mind's eye and thus bring color to expository writing.

Reporter Joseph Durso was assigned to follow Hank Aaron in his quest for his 715th home run. Here is Durso's report of the event in Atlanta that not only made baseball history, but also made the front page of just about every daily newspaper in the country.

JOSEPH DURSO

Aaron Hits 715th,
Passes Babe Ruth

1   **H**enry Aaron ended the great
chase tonight and passed Babe Ruth as the leading home-
run hitter in baseball history when he hit number 715 before a national television audience and 53,775 persons in
Atlanta Stadium.

2   The 40-year-old outfielder for the Atlanta Braves broke
the record on his second time at bat, but on his first swing
of a clamorous evening. It was a soaring drive in the fourth
inning off Al Downing of the Los Angeles Dodgers, and it
cleared the fence in left-center field, 385 feet from home
plate.

3   Skyrockets arched over the jammed stadium in the
rain as the man from Mobile trotted around the bases for
the 715th time in a career that began a quarter of a
century ago.

4   It was 9:07 o'clock, 39 years after Ruth had hit his
714th and four days after Aaron had hit his 714th on his
first swing of the bat in the opening game of the season.

5   The history-making home run carried into the Atlanta
bull pen, where a relief pitcher named Tom House made
a dazzling one-handed catch against the auxiliary score-

board. He clutched it against the boards, far below the grandstand seats, where the customers in "Home-Run Alley" were massed, waiting to retrieve a cowhide ball that in recent days had been valued as high as $25,000 on the auction market. . . .

6 To many Atlantans, it was like the city's festive premiere of "Gone With the Wind" during the 1930's when Babe Ruth was still the hero of the New York Yankees and the titan of professional sports. All that was needed to complete the evening was home run number 715, and Aaron supplied that.

7 The first time he batted, leading off the second inning, Aaron never got the bat off his shoulder. Downing, a one-time pitcher for the Yankees, wearing number 44, threw a ball and a called strike and then three more balls. Aaron, wearing his own number 44, watched them all and then took first base while the crowd hooted and booed because their home-town hero had been walked.

8 A few moments later, Henry scored on a double by Dusty Baker and an error in left field, and even made a little history doing that.

9 It was the 2,063rd time he had crossed home plate in his 21-year career in the majors, breaking the National League record held by Willie Mays and placing Aaron behind Ty Cobb and Ruth, both American Leaguers.

10 Then came the fourth inning, with the Dodgers leading by 3-1 and the rain falling, with colored umbrellas raised in the stands and the crowd roaring every time Aaron appeared. Darrell Evans led off for Atlanta with a grounder behind second base that the shortstop, Bill Russell, juggled long enough for an error. And up came Henry for the eighth time this season and the second this evening.

11 Downing pitched ball one inside, and Aaron watched impassively. Then came the second pitch, and this time Henry took his first cut of the night. The ball rose high toward left-center as the crowd came to its feet shouting, and as it dropped over the inside fence separating the outfield from the bull-pen area, the skyrockets were fired and

the scoreboard lights flashed in six-foot numerals: "715."

12 Aaron, head slightly bowed and elbows turned out, slowly circled the bases as the uproar grew. At second base he received a handshake from Dave Lopes of the Dodgers, and between second and third from Russell.

13 By now two young men from the seats had joined Aaron, but did not interfere with his 360-foot trip around the bases into the record books.

14 As he neared home plate, the rest of the Atlanta team had already massed beyond it as a welcoming delegation. Aaron's 65-year old father, Herbert Aaron, Sr., had jumped out of the family's special field-level box and outraced everybody to the man who had broken Babe Ruth's record.

15 By then the entire Atlanta bull-pen corps had started to race in to join the fun with House leading them, the ball gripped tightly in his hand. He delivered it to Aaron who was besieged on the grass about 20 feet in front of the field boxes near the Braves' dugout.

16 Besides the ball, Henry received a plaque from the owner of the team, Bill Bartholomay, congratulations from Monte Irvin, the emissary from Commissioner Kuhn,° and a howling, standing ovation from the crowd.

17 The game was interrupted for 11 minutes during all the commotion, after which the Braves got back to work and went on to win their second straight, this time by 7-4. The Dodgers, apparently shaken by history, made six errors and lost their first game after three straight victories.

18 "It was a fastball, right down the middle of the upper part of the plate," Downing said later. "I was trying to get it down to him, but I didn't and he hit it good— as he would.

19 "When he first hit it, I didn't think it might be going. But like a great hitter, when he picks his pitch, chances are he's going to hit it pretty good."

20 Afterward the Braves locked their clubhouse for a time so that they could toast Aaron in champagne. Then

Commissioner Kuhn: Bowie Kuhn, the commissioner of baseball.

the new home-run king reflected on his feat and on some intimations that he had not been "trying" to break the record in Cincinnati.°

21 "I have never gone out on a ball field and given less than my level best," he said. "When I hit it tonight, all I thought about was that I wanted to touch all the bases."

Suggestions for Writing

1. Report on some event of interest to you—not something you have merely read about, but something you have actually observed. Tell *what* the event is all about, *who* is involved, *when* it happened, *where* it happened, and *how* it happened. Use chronological order. Try to add details that will give your readers some feeling for the atmosphere of the occasion, or for the personalities involved.

2. Make up a report on something that you imagine you are witnessing. Tell about the event as if you are in the press box. It might be a world series of some new sport in the year 2000, a chariot race in the Roman Empire, a duel between two ant armies.

3. Durso's is a report of a historic occasion, but ordinary events can be made interesting by a reporter who brings an appealing "twist" to the story. Write a report of an ordinary event, and give it some human interest. This can be done by the use of some unusual point of view: a football game as witnessed by the Manus people; a high school dance as seen by a visitor from Mongolia; a Halloween parade as seen through the eyes of a small child.

° Aaron's employers had wanted him to hit 715 in Atlanta, so had benched him on the alien soil of Cincinnati.

SCOTT CARPENTER

The Great Secret

McCandlish Phillips and Joseph Durso report their observations in the third person. Scott Carpenter has to use the first-person pronoun since the whole point of his report is the exhilaration of his discoveries and the real dangers he encountered that day in May, 1962, when he made his three-orbit space flight. Carpenter was no stranger to flight problems; he had flown Navy planes during the Korean War and had served on the aircraft carrier *U.S.S. Hornet* as air intelligence officer. But until he joined Project Mercury in 1959, he never imagined he would circle the earth three times in a little less than five hours at a maximum speed of 17,532 miles per hour.

Carpenter followed by just three months Lt. Col. John Glenn's historic space flight in the Mercury capsule *Friendship 7*. John Glenn had been the first astronaut to orbit the earth. Along with Carpenter's wife, Rene, and thousands of technicians, Glenn was waiting tensely for the re-entry of the *Aurora 7* through the atmosphere. For forty-five minutes everyone thought that Carpenter was lost because of a fuel shortage. When he did reappear, he overshot the landing point by 250 miles, and his capsule came to rest in the empty Atlantic Ocean. That perilous descent from a height of 167 miles is only part of the story. When the *Life* editors asked Carpenter to describe the flight, they must have known he could not resist telling it in his way, as it happened to one man, alone in space, observing the secrets of the universe. This report tells not only about escape from danger and imminent death, but also about awesome sights and surprising discoveries.

Note that Carpenter begins his report at the moment of return and then, in paragraph 4, shifts to "the days immediately before the launch." Journalists like McCandlish Phillips could never file a story for their papers that so intentionally shifted time and omitted vital facts. But this is a personal report, published two weeks after the event. Carpenter wants us to share the cramped space of the capsule with him, to see a sunset in space, to face some of the dangers. We are almost on a first-name basis. But let him tell it.

1   In between the time I fired the retro-rockets ° and the moment *Aurora 7* began its re-entry through the atmosphere, things were very tight indeed. My fuel supply was critically low and I was not at all sure that I had enough left to bring the capsule into the proper position. If we started the re-entry at the wrong angle and the fuel was exhausted, I would be unable to control the capsule during the descent. The chances that I would survive such an uncontrolled re-entry were not good. *2*   I have since heard recordings of my voice played at this tense time. In them I don't sound afraid or confused but oddly dejected. All the elation so audible in earlier portions of the flight is gone. The tone of my voice has dropped measurably and my sentences all end on a minor key. *3*   But at this low point I remember thinking, "This has been the greatest day of your life. You've got nobody to blame for being in this spot but yourself. If you do right, you may make it. If you don't do right, you're just going to

retro-rocket: auxiliary rocket on a space vehicle that decelerates it by producing thrust obliquely or directly opposite to the motion of the vehicle.

buy the farm." ° I decided I had to use more fuel to get into position for re-entry. It would have to last.

4 During the days immediately before the launch was first scheduled to go, I was tense and not at all at ease. I did not like the waiting, and I felt I needed more time to work on the flight plan and with the special equipment I would use. I was not convinced in my own mind that I would perform well under the stress of the flight, and one night I had real difficulty getting to sleep. I was not afraid of dying itself, but I hated the thought of losing the life of the father of my four children, and I regretted the many experiences I would miss. There were only a few people I really wanted to be with, and away from work itself I remained either alone or in the company of John Glenn and a few other close friends.

5 Then the flight was postponed, and things took a turn for the better. The scrub ° gave me the chance to practice more with the flight equipment and to study up on a few things I was worried about. I built up confidence and began thinking again the way I'd been thinking for three years—that on a successful flight I could make a valuable contribution and that it would be a great experience for me. I ate and slept well. As the new launch date approached I kept waiting for the tenseness to return, but it never did. I had reached the crest of the hill and become part of the machine.

6 If we had not had a 45-minute hold for weather the morning of the launch, I would not have called Rene from the capsule. The countdown had been moving along perfectly, and I had too much to do to take time out for a call. Rene and I had agreed that such a last-minute conversation might be upsetting for both of us. But during the brief delay I decided that I wanted to call and that I could handle it. She was having breakfast with the children in a house about 10 miles down the beach from where I lay in the capsule. I talked to all of them and it got through to me only once, briefly, and tears came to my eyes. But it passed.

to buy the farm: to die.
scrub: cancellation.

7 At work again I found myself amazed at my own calm. I felt a certain detachment, as if I could stand a little to one side and watch myself get ready. Perhaps this detachment is a defense against fear, much the way shock is a defense against pain, but I approached the moment the flight would begin with compelling curiosity. I remember from childhood that when my grandfather was dying of a stroke he said to his doctor, "At last I'll know the great secret." High on top of the Atlas ° I was confident that everything was going to be all right, but I felt that I, too, was going to be let in on a great secret, that this experience I had looked forward to for so long would soon be here.

8 The launch was a snap. We rose with very little vibration in the capsule. In fact, the whole period before I was placed in orbit was gentler than I'd anticipated. The engines made a big racket, but there was no violent trembling of the whole structure. I recall thinking to myself as I watched the altimeter needle wind up to 70,000, then 80,000, then 90,000 feet: "What an odd place to be—and going straight up!"

9 As we climbed I did notice a distinct swaying motion of the whole machine. John Glenn had reported this on his flight and had said it felt to him as if he were on the end of a springboard. It did not feel that way to me; it seemed rather that we swayed off to one side and stopped abruptly, then swayed back to the other side and stopped again. But the motion was not alarming.

10 When I reached orbit ° the first thing that impressed me was the silence. Almost immediately I knew the second great sensation, weightlessness. I could feel no pressure of my body against the couch, and the pressure suit, which is very constricting on the ground, became entirely comfortable. Though it was part of the planned routine to report this moment to the ground, it was so exhilarating that my report was really a spontaneous and joyful exclamation: "I

Atlas: the rocket which boosted the capsule off the launching pad with a thrust of 362,000 pounds.

reached orbit: left the earth's atmosphere and its gravitational force.

am weightless!" Now the supreme experience had really begun.

11 I turned the capsule around so that the blunt end would be heading along the track I would follow. On this maneuver I used the manual control system and it worked perfectly. I then checked out the system thoroughly and found that the capsule responded beautifully to my movements on the stick. As I moved it, small thrusters ° on the outside of the capsule pushed out their jets of hydrogen peroxide fuel and moved *Aurora 7* into whatever position I wanted. I checked the automatic control system and discovered that it did not seem to be working so well. As far as I could tell, this system, which operates on a separate fuel supply with its own thrusters, was not aligning the capsule properly. But there would be time to figure out that problem later in the flight. I had a lot of things to do, and a limited amount of time to get them all done.

12 As a matter of fact, it was in the extent of the things I had so carefully planned to do that my flight was different from John Glenn's. His was a real pioneer mission, and he had to concentrate on proving the reliability of the machine. Because he showed that a man can handle the machine under very difficult conditions, I was to have more freedom to measure, study, and observe events which were taking place *outside* the capsule. I had many sciences to serve.

13 I had looked out the window once briefly when the escape tower was jettisoned,* and I caught a glimpse of it right on the horizon, streaking away like a scalded cat. But in the early part of the first orbit I concentrated on the control systems and did not really look around. Now I did, and the sight was overwhelming. The window and the periscope were filled with beauty.

14 I could see black sky above me, clouds and sea below. I could look off for perhaps 1,000 miles in any direction, and everywhere I looked I found it difficult to tear my eyes away and go on to something else. Using the special camera

thrusters: rocket engines which develop a pushing or pulling force.

I carried, I took pictures as fast as I could, and as I raced toward night at 17,500 miles an hour, I saw the beginnings of the most fantastically beautiful view I've ever had—my first sunset in space.

15 Crossing Africa, I watched the earth blackening behind me, the sky above me, and I could see the sun actually dropping toward the western horizon. Right on the horizon as the sun fell, a band of color stretched away for hundreds of miles to the north and south. It was a glittering, iridescent * arc composed of strips of colors ranging from yellow-gold to reddish-brown, to green, to blue, then to a magnificent purplish-blue before it blended with the black of the sky. The colors glowed vigorously, alive with light, and I watched the band narrow until nothing was left but a rim of marvelous blue. I looked in the periscope soon after that and saw nothing but blackness ahead of me. I was on the dark side of the earth.

16 It was on this first dark-side pass that I used up a lot of fuel. The flight plan called for some flares to be set off on the ground in Australia and I was to observe them. Unfortunately Australia was mostly covered by clouds and I did not see the flares. But I maneuvered the capsule around a great deal to look for them, and this was a costly bit of travel. It is possible to change the capsule's attitude slowly by setting up a gentle movement with the controls and then waiting to arrive at the desired position. This is the economical way to do things; fuel is saved. But time is lost this way, and I was in a hurry to complete all the items on the flight plan. Because it is possible to kick the capsule around much faster by using more fuel, I did that. It was an expenditure that I would regret later in the flight.

17 At this time I also began my observations of the night sky. The stars were bright, and though I don't believe I saw as many through the window as I might have seen on earth on a clear night, I could track them easily. I found that I could hold the capsule in the proper attitude by fixing on a known star near the horizon. And as the sun rose ahead of me I got my first look at John Glenn's fireflies. As they drifted around the capsule near the window they looked

more like snowflakes to me, whitish in color and varying in size from one-sixteenth to one-half an inch in diameter.
18 I was already having some trouble with the suit temperature. I was now quite hot and uncomfortable and the sweat was pouring off my face and running into my eyes, making it difficult for me to see things properly. I tried various settings on the valve which controls suit temperature, and the ground control stations made other suggestions. Nothing seemed to work particularly well. The heat itself was not bad—the suit temperature never rose above 84 degrees—but the humidity was not being controlled as it should have been. In fact, I found that when I put up the visor on my helmet and exposed my face to the much hotter but far drier atmosphere of the cabin, I got the same sort of relief one would get if he stepped out of a stuffy room into the fresh air. All in all, it was a bothersome problem and took up more of my increasingly tightening schedule.
19 I crossed the United States in early morning light. In areas not covered by clouds I could see the ground remarkably well, note lakes and rivers, and as I passed over farm country in the southwest I could even see places where the south 40 ° was cultivated and the north 40 was lying fallow. At every new sight my elation was renewed. I could hardly wait to get to the next one.
20 As I passed over Cape Canaveral ° at the end of the first orbit, I checked the gauges and was appalled at the low state of my fuel. I had not much more than half my supply left for both the automatic and the manual control systems. I was warned that if I didn't conserve fuel, I would have to come down at the end of the second orbit. Cutting the flight short sounded like a terrible prospect to me. There was so much to be seen and done that I needed all the orbits I could get. I made up my mind to be very careful with the fuel.
21 The balloon experiment didn't go according to plan. I

south 40: colloquially, the south 40 acres of a farm.
Cape Canaveral: in East Florida near Banana River, the launching site of U.S. space exploration.

deployed the balloon, which was made of a combination of plastic film and aluminum foil, at the beginning of the second orbit. It was attached to the capsule by 100 feet of light nylon line, and the important objectives of the experiment were to measure the drag of the inflated balloon in the very thin atmosphere and to observe its behavior. It didn't inflate properly and took longer than expected to reach the end of its tether.° Whatever movements it made were entirely random and it was nearly impossible for me to make any drag measurements. Finally the switch that was supposed to release it did not operate and I continued to trail the balloon until retro-fire, like a tin can attached to the rear bumper of a car.

22 To save fuel I began to drift a great deal in flight, starting the capsule in a slight movement in one direction and just letting it continue to sweep around. I was able to make many observations this way, and I was impressed again and again with the wonder of weightlessness. A change of attitude means nothing in this state. Everything floats. Nothing rises or falls. "Up" loses all significance. You can assign your own "up" and put it anywhere— toward the ground, toward the horizon, or on a line drawn between two stars—and it is perfectly satisfactory. At one period I spent some time just playing with the camera, bouncing it off the fingertips of one hand and stopping it with the fingers of the other. Then I started it spinning slowly around in the air in front of me.

23 Midway through the second orbit the suit temperature problem got quite bad. The ground was reporting that my body temperature had risen to 102 degrees, and though I didn't think I was actually running a fever, I began to notice one of the first signs: I had trouble finding words to express myself in reports to the ground. I knew what I wanted to say but I couldn't say it with the same fluency I'd felt earlier in the flight. If this was caused by a rising body temperature, it was very important to get myself cooled off. Then, too, I expected a strong heat pulse

tether: a length of rope or chain by which an animal is fastened.

when I finally began the re-entry and I wanted to go into that with a cold soak.

24 I tried very hard to think the problem through and forced myself to back off and analyze it. Was I too hot or wasn't I? Was there really something wrong with the suit-cooling system? Which way should I adjust the valve? After studying it this way for a good while, I came to a couple of important conclusions. First, it takes longer than I expected for a change in the valve setting to affect the temperature of the suit. Second, if the face plate is open, the heat of the cabin gets into the suit and acts against any cooling efforts of the system. The latter seems ridiculously obvious, but the simple fact is that in all our preflight studies we had not taken account of this possibility. I closed the face plate and by trial and error managed to find a setting that finally made me comfortable. I was in good shape for the third orbit.

25 On the last time around I did a lot more drifting. Although I did make some efforts to figure out what was wrong with the automatic control system, I wasn't able to solve the problem. I found out later that the two horizon scanners, which seek out the horizon and give this information to the automatic control system, apparently were working inaccurately. But I did not know this at the time, and I used up a good bit of fuel trying to straighten things out. But I was involved in other matters, too: the earth and sky were waiting outside for me to investigate them.

26 The last hour before retro-fire passed quickly, just as all the rest of the time had passed. Flying through space, I felt a curious compression of time as if the speed at which I traveled had some effect on the length of moments and packed them too tight upon one another. I seemed always to be in a tremendous hurry as event upon event popped up like ducks in a shooting gallery. I photographed my last sunset, I tracked stars, I ate bite-sized chocolate bars and picked escaping cookie crumbs out of the air, I drank quantities of water, I was doing something all the time.

27 There was a lot going on at once when I came up on Hawaii on the final orbit. I was maneuvering the capsule

around to get pictures of the sunrise, trying to stow equipment in my ditty bag for the re-entry, talking to Hawaii about my retro-fire checklist. And then John's fireflies got going again. A particularly bright one came by the window, and I reached out to grab a light meter to take a reading on its intensity. In doing so I hit the cabin wall with my hand, and a whole cloud of particles flew off past the window. Fascinated with this surprise, I started thumping the wall all around me, and every time I hit it more fireflies or snowflakes or whatever they were popped away. Surely, I thought to myself, these particles were clinging like frost to the capsule and came from the capsule, not, as John had thought, from some other source. There wasn't time to think about it any longer. It was time to get ready for retro-fire and the long return to earth.

28   The flight plan called for me to use the automatic control system to get the capsule into position for the firing of the retro-rockets. They had to go off on time and the capsule had to be aligned correctly during their firing or I would not land in the right spot in the Atlantic more than 3,000 miles away.

29   I tried to line up the capsule with the automatic controls. The big thrusters spewed out precious quantities of fuel but still did not bring the capsule to the right attitude. I switched to fly-by-wire control, which is a system in which the Astronaut handles the capsule manually but uses the automatic fuel supply. My manual tanks were now very low. And here I made a mistake. When I went to fly-by-wire, I neglected to shut off the straight manual system. Thus every time I used the stick, I used fuel from both dwindling supplies.

30   At the time of retro-fire I believed that I had brought the capsule to the proper position, although there have been indications since that the alignment * was somewhat off. There was something else, too. The rockets were supposed to fire automatically, but they didn't. I watched the clock pass the right instant, then hit the retro-button myself a second later. They did not fire for about two more seconds. I noticed a puff of smoke in the cabin. It smelled like

burning metal and could have been caused by a short circuit. But I was mainly concerned about the delay. At my
speed this lapse of three seconds meant that I would be at
least 15 miles long ° in the recovery area.

31   The retro-fire itself felt comparatively gentle, and I
was able to control the movements of the capsule easily.
Now I found that though the manual tank still registered
7%, it was really empty, and I had only 15% left in the
other tank for the whole re-entry. I was dangerously short.

32   I maneuvered the capsule very gingerly, keeping the
horizon in view out the window, trying to use as little fuel
as possible. I held my position steady, and when I felt the
first welcome oscillations ° that meant I was entering the
atmosphere, I started the capsule rolling at a rate of 10°
per second. This was to help keep the capsule on course
on the way down, and now we were headed that way.

33   It was a beautiful re-entry. The ride most of the way
down was perfectly smooth, and we headed in at just the
right angle. The heat pulse never got into the cockpit,
although the temperature outside was 3,000 degrees. When
I glanced out of the window I saw an orange doughnut of
fiery particles from the heat shield stretching out like a
wake behind me.

34   Then I noticed a green, hazy glow building up around
the narrow end of the capsule. Since this is where the parachutes are kept, heat damage here could destroy my only
means of getting down safely. I spoke into the tape recorder
as I watched the glow. "I see a green glow from the small
end," I said. "It looks almost as if it is burning away.
Ooooooh, I hope not." As I spoke these words, I laughed
aloud. They are the words used in a comic record by a man
playing the part of a scared Astronaut. As we passed beyond the heat pulse, the glow faded away.

35   At about 100,000 feet the main part of the re-entry
was over. The G forces ° had tapered off, and the capsule

15 miles long: having overshot the recovery mark, that is.
oscillations: vibrations.

G forces: units of force equal to the forces exerted by gravity
on a body at rest.

and I were falling at about 600 miles an hour. My remaining fuel had lasted well on the way down, but now some violent swaying of the capsule began and almost immediately the last of the fuel was used up trying to control it.
36 The swaying built up rapidly. If it continued, it was entirely possible that the capsule would begin tumbling out of control. If that happened and the nose of the capsule pointed downward, the drogue chute ° might foul in the capsule when it came out. Or it might snap the capsule around so violently that the chute would be damaged.
37 I was not frightened. It was a tight situation and I was very alert. There isn't time in such a spot to get wide-eyed and say, "What'll I do now?" You don't clutch because you can't. That could be sudden death. You just have to keep interested in what's going on and work your way out of it. As the oscillations got worse, the capsule began to sway through a huge arc of about 270°—almost full circle. I punched the button to deploy the drogue. This was at 26,000 feet. The flight plan called for me to punch it at 21,000, but I needed it sooner to stop the oscillations. The six-foot drogue came out well and the descent steadied immediately. I was falling through clouds now. The altimeter swung toward 10,000 feet, the point at which the main chute is supposed to come out automatically. When it did not come out, I gave it 500 feet more before I pulled the ring. Out it came then, a glorious orange-and-white canopy, perfectly shaped and, supporting the capsule's weight, drawn as taut as sheet metal.
38 On the way down in the chute I picked up a transmission from Gus Grissom back at Cape Canaveral. He was transmitting blind but he advised me that I was probably long and that I should expect to wait for about an hour on the water before recovery. He also said that a plane with paramedics ° aboard was on its way to me. I tried several times to raise somebody with my own radio but was unable to get any reply. I was apparently out of range. I

---

drogue chute: a decelerating parachute, usually funnel-shaped.
paramedics: medical personnel trained to assist physicians.

was beneath the clouds now and I could see the water. I got ready for the landing.

39 We did not hit at all hard. The capsule went completely underwater and came up listing quite sharply to one side. There was a little water in the cockpit and, all things considered, I thought it would be sensible to get out. I took off my helmet and squeezed my way up past the instrument panel. I opened the hatch on the small end of the capsule. I put the camera in a safe place near the opening and dropped the small life raft into the water. I got into the raft, found it was upside down, got into the water and turned it over. Then I tied the raft to the capsule and turned on the Sarah beacon ° which would allow aircraft to home in on ° my position. I said a prayer, "Thank you, Lord," and relaxed for the wait. I have never felt better.

40 I sat for a long time just thinking about what I'd been through. It had been a tremendous experience, and though I couldn't really share it with anyone, I looked forward to telling others about it. I had made mistakes and some things had gone wrong, but other men could learn from my experiences. I felt that the flight was a success and was proud of that.

41 For a long time I looked at nothing but sky and sea. I saw a patch of sargasso weed.° Then I noticed a black fish about 18 inches long. Tame as a chicken, he was just floating in the water so close that I could have reached out and grabbed him. But I didn't because it might have hurt him, and at the time he was my only friend.

42 A little later I heard airplane engines and saw the first P2V approaching. I signaled him with a hand mirror and he began to orbit my position.

43 Not long after that it seemed to me that there were planes all around me, so many, in fact, that I did not notice

Sarah' beacon: a radio homing device originally used for personnel rescue. The word comes from Search And Rescue And Homing.

to home in on: to proceed toward a source of radiated energy used as a guide, such as radar.

sargasso weed: floating vegetation or gulfweed.

it when the first paramedic jumped. The first indication I had that he was around was when he swam up behind me, grabbed the raft and said hello. The second man came soon afterward and they got busy attaching a collar to the capsule which would keep it floating.

44 These divers probably saved the capsule from sinking, and they had no way of knowing that I did not need medical help. But in a funny way I resented their presence. That was my part of the ocean and I wanted to be there alone for a while longer and contemplate what had happened.

ANALYSIS

Carpenter had several choices to make when he came to record his flight. He could write for the space experts among the readers of *Life,* assuming they wanted technical data and mechanical problems analyzed. He could write biography; that is, he could tell how he happened to become America's second astronaut to orbit the earth, and he could describe the specialized training he was now putting to the test. Or he could combine these approaches and tell us, as he does here, the problems he encountered and how he, Scott Carpenter, surmounted them. The place of publication—a national weekly of huge circulation—also determined his style, but it could not wholly have determined the most engaging aspect of this report: its gross understatement. Carpenter was very close to losing his life, yet he ends the first paragraph with a matter-of-fact, unheroic statement: "The chances that I would survive such an uncontrolled re-entry were not good." Eight sentences later he is almost joking about it: "If you don't do right, you're just going to buy the farm." We know, of course, that he did not join the angels or he would not be writing this essay, yet suspense in low-keyed prose—suspense plus surprise—is his aim.

What details does he give his readers, knowing that they have never seen a space capsule and do not know a G force from a drogue chute? Paragraphs 4–7 are centered on frustration and delay: he thinks, naturally, he is not well enough prepared; he fears he might be depriving his four children of a father; the flight is postponed and he has more chance to prepare. Note that these facts, like the telephone call to his wife, are general facts. We can share his feelings with no difficulty. Paragraph 8 begins the launch. In no time he is in orbit, weightless, in complete silence: "Now the supreme experience had really begun." And at the same time technical problems take over. Note the casual way (paragraph 11) Carpenter first mentions the fuel supply and the balky automatic control system. He pushes it aside ("But there would be time to figure out that problem later in the flight") so that he can concentrate on beauty, not danger. We know, however, from paragraphs 1 and 2 what an immense problem a dwindling fuel supply was to become.

Beauty filled the periscope. He wants us to see it: "the sun actually dropping toward the western horizon," "the colors glowed vigorously, alive with light," "John Glenn's fireflies" looking like snowflakes. But technical problems keep intruding. He wastes fuel in maneuvering (paragraph 16); his suit temperature sends sweat running into his eyes (paragraph 18); the balloon experiment fails (paragraph 21); his body temperature rises to 102 degrees, and signs of serious disability appear: his speech begins to fail him (paragraph 23). Carpenter solves all the minor difficulties, but the nagging fuel problem remains. It becomes worse, in fact. At this point, he realizes his readers need more details to understand what alignment and retro-rockets mean to proper re-entry, not to mention that fuel supply! By the end of paragraph 31, Carpenter admits it "was dangerously short."

When he makes it back into the earth's atmosphere, we sigh with relief and observe the "orange doughnut of fiery particles" and "the green, hazy glow building up around the narrow end of the capsule," only to confront another, more serious problem: violent swaying of the capsule. Once more, Carpenter faces loss of control. Paragraphs 36–38 recount the dizzy descent, and for once Carpenter gives us the grim details: "the capsule began to sway through a huge

arc of about 270°—almost full circle." We can imagine
what it felt like in his cramped cabin. But Carpenter re-
assures us: "I was not frightened. It was a tight situation
and I was very alert." We believe him. He is not a man to
doubt; his honesty is evident in his simple prose.

That honesty makes the last six paragraphs the most delightful if not the most exciting part of the report. They
are full of simple details: a small life raft, the silence of
the sea around him, his brief prayer, a tame fish who at the
time was Carpenter's "only friend." And then the first paramedic arrives. Carpenter chooses to end his story here
rather than recount the rescue of the capsule and the return
to Cape Canaveral. For almost five hours he had had "a
supreme experience" and he "wanted to be there alone for
a while longer and contemplate what had happened." We
can only say that he made the right choice. He has given
us *his* report, personal, understated, disarming in its intimacy, heroic in spite of (or because of) his modesty.
Scott Carpenter's flight in the *Aurora 7* is almost a part of
our experience. This kind of reporting is rare.

Questions on Content

1. In paragraphs 8–9, Carpenter describes the actual
   launch. In what ways did the launching surprise him?
2. What first impressed him when he reached orbit? What
   other details of this "new state of being" are especially
   memorable?
3. How did Carpenter's flight differ from John Glenn's?
4. What was the balloon experiment supposed to show,
   and why did it fail?
5. How did Carpenter stop the swaying of the capsule after
   re-entering the earth's atmosphere?

Add to Your Vocabulary

jettison, iridescent, alignment, oscillations.

Questions on Technique

1. Why does Carpenter begin his report with the end of

the flight and then (in paragraph 4) shift to the days before the launch? What does this time-shift do to his story?

2. Would you have chosen to include the homely details of paragraph 6 in a description of so exciting a moment as a rocket launch? Why?

3. Does Carpenter describe specifically "the great secret" he first mentions in paragraph 7? Does he need to? Does he allude to it anywhere else in the report?

4. How often throughout this report does Carpenter quote himself, as in paragraph 3? How do these moments of speaking his thoughts help us to identify with Carpenter?

5. In paragraph 13, the escape tower of the rocket is seen streaking away "like a scalded cat." Search the article for other colloquial similes ° Carpenter uses in his prose. Are they effective figures of speech in this semi-technical report?

6. When Carpenter needs to use numbers he does not hesitate, as in paragraph 37. Should he have filled his report with even more statistics? Why?

7. Is the last paragraph of this report anticlimactic? Explain.

Techniques to Imitate

The colloquial style

Scott Carpenter's article is a report of a personal experience. Except for the opening paragraphs, it is written in chronological order, as most narratives are. In vocabulary and sentence structure, Carpenter's English is colloquial. It is the kind of informal English we use in conversation. Perhaps because he knows that the experience he is describing is in itself enough to hold the reader's interest, Carpenter does not try to "improve" it by using elaborate description or long, involved sentences. He writes as he would talk. "The launch," he says conversationally, "was a snap." "You don't clutch because you can't," he explains later. Both expressions are close to slang. His figures of speech are homely. The jettisoned escape tower streaked away

similes: See Glossary.

"like a scalded cat," and "I saw an orange doughnut of fiery particles from the heat shield stretching out like a wake behind me."

In the Analysis, we referred to Carpenter's habit of understatement. By using colloquial English and by understating the danger and excitement, he avoids the risk of letting his style get in the way of his story. The trip itself, not his way of telling about it, remains the principal interest.

When you write a report of one of your own exciting experiences, you may wish to imitate Carpenter's understated, colloquial style. This kind of writing may be no easier than a more elaborate and literary kind, though it is certainly easier to read. Since it permits complete concentration on what is said rather than on how it is said, it is a good style for this kind of narrative report.

Suggestions for Writing

1. Using Scott Carpenter's title, recount in 500 words an event in your own life that revealed to you a secret discovery, such as the moment when you first knew you could dance or swim or sing *well,* not just adequately. Keep your prose focused on your reactions to the event, giving your reader only as many details of the action as you think are necessary.

2. Using fairly technical language, write a 600-word report on an action that involved mechanical equipment, such as harvesting a crop, building a boat, setting up a laboratory experiment or a stage play. Make the event, not the mere description, the focus of your report.

3. You may have had an exciting experience that made you feel happy and perhaps relieved when you had completed it—climbed a mountain, broken a sports record, weathered a storm, effected a rescue, achieved a long-desired goal of any kind. Write an account of this experience through which your reader can share both the activity and your feelings.

WILLIAM L. LAURENCE

Dawn over Zero

Scott Carpenter reported personal experience from the heart of the action. He was in it and made it. In the report that follows, William L. Laurence recounts an equally memorable occasion, but from an observer's point of view. Where Carpenter could afford to embellish, Laurence has to restrain himself forcibly. He does not always succeed. The experience he witnessed transcends the power of words. Not that he was unprepared to do it justice. He had been science reporter for the *New York Times* since 1930. He was trained, therefore, to capture this occasion in words as well as to understand the scope of the undertaking. Scientist, lecturer, and journalist, Laurence has won two Pulitzer Prizes among other awards. In 1959 he published *Men and Atoms*. He was Official Reporter of the atomic bomb, and was named Science Editor Emeritus of the *New York Times*.

You will observe that Laurence incorporates both of these tasks—reporting and analyzing—in his prose. The journalist is relating all the facts; the scientist cannot resist commenting. But taken as a whole, this is a factual account. Paragraphs 6–27 are, in essence, a long countdown. We hear names, dates, places. We know what will take place at 5:30 A.M. It is not suspense he strives for. But the tension of waiting is there, nevertheless. Paragraphs 24–27 cannot move fast enough. Laurence has built his essay with this effect in mind. But he achieves other effects as well. First let us read this remarkable report.

1   The Atomic Age began at exactly 5:30 mountain war time on the morning of July 16, 1945, on a stretch of semi-desert land about fifty airline miles from Alamogordo, New Mexico, just a few minutes before the dawn of a new day on that part of the earth. At that great moment in history, ranking with the moment when man first put fire to work for him, the vast energy locked within the heart of the atoms of matter was released for the first time in a burst of flame such as had never before been seen on this planet, illuminating earth and sky, for a brief span that seemed eternal, with the light of many super-suns.

2   The elemental flame, first fire ever made on earth that did not have its origin in the sun, came from the explosion of the first atomic bomb. It was a full-dress rehearsal preparatory to dropping the bomb over Hiroshima and Nagasaki—and other Japanese military targets, had Japan refused to accept the Potsdam Declaration ° for her surrender.

3   The rehearsal marked the climax in the penultimate ° act of one of the greatest dramas in our history and the history of civilized man—a drama in which our scientists, under the direction of the Army Corps of Engineers, were working against time to create an atomic bomb ahead of our German enemy. The collapse of Germany marked the end of the first act of this drama. The successful completion of our task, in the greatest challenge by man to nature so far, brought down the curtain on the second act. The grand finale came three weeks afterward in the skies over Japan, with a swift descent of the curtain on the greatest war in history.

Potsdam Declaration: issued at Potsdam, Germany, July 26, 1945, outlining the terms under which Japan would be allowed to surrender to the Allied Forces.

penultimate: next to last.

4 The atomic flash in New Mexico came as a great affirmation to the prodigious * labors of our scientists during the past four years. It came as the affirmative answer to the until then unanswered question: "Will it work?"

5 With the flash came a delayed roll of mighty thunder, heard, just as the flash was seen, for hundreds of miles. The roar echoed and reverberated from the distant hills and the Sierra Oscuro range near by, sounding as though it came from some supramundane ° source as well as from the bowels of the earth. The hills said yes and the mountains chimed in yes. It was as if the earth had spoken and the suddenly iridescent * clouds and sky had joined in one affirmative answer. Atomic energy—yes. It was like the grand finale of a mighty symphony of the elements, fascinating and terrifying, uplifting and crushing, ominous, devastating, full of great promise and great forebodings.

6 I watched the birth of the era of atomic power from the slope of a hill in the desert land of New Mexico, on the northwestern corner of Alamogordo Air Base, about 125 miles southeast of Albuquerque. The hill, named Compania Hill for the occasion, was twenty miles to the northwest of Zero, the code name given to the spot chosen for the atomic bomb test. The area embracing Zero and Compania Hill, twenty-four miles long and eighteen miles wide, had the code name Trinity.

7 I joined a caravan of three buses, three automobiles, and a truck carrying radio equipment at 11 P.M. on Sunday, July 15, at Albuquerque. There were about ninety of us in that strange caravan, traveling silently and in the utmost secrecy through the night on probably as unusual an adventure as any in our day. With the exception of myself the caravan consisted of scientists from the highly secret atomic bomb research and development center in the mesas and canyons of New Mexico, twenty-five miles northwest of Santa Fe, where we solved the secret of translating the fabulous energy of the atom into the mightiest weapon ever made by man. It was from there that the caravan set out at

supramundane: above the earth.

5:30 that Sunday afternoon for its destination, 212 miles to the south.

8   The caravan wound its way slowly over the tortuous roads overlooking the precipitous canyons of northern New Mexico, passing through Espagnola, Santa Fe, and Bernalillo, arriving at Albuquerque at about 10 P.M. Here it was joined by Sir James Chadwick, who won the Nobel prize and knighthood for his discovery of the neutron, the key that unlocks the atom; Professor Ernest O. Lawrence of the University of California, master atom-smasher, who won the Nobel prize for his discovery of the cyclotron; Professor Edwin M. McMillan, also of the University of California, one of the discoverers of plutonium, the new atomic energy element; and several others from the atomic bomb center, who, like me, had arrived during the afternoon.

9   The night was dark with black clouds, and not a star could be seen. Occasionally a bolt of lightning would rend the sky and reveal for an instant the flat semi-desert landscape, rich with historic lore of past adventure. We rolled along on U. S. Highway 85, running between Albuquerque and El Paso, through sleeping ancient Spanish-American towns, their windows dark, their streets deserted—towns with music in their names, Los Lunas, Belen, Bernardo, Alamillo, Socorro, San Antonio. At San Antonio we turned east and crossed "the bridge on the Rio Grande with the detour in the middle of it." From there we traveled ten and one half miles eastward on U. S. Highway 380, and then turned south on a specially built dirt road, running for twenty-five miles to the base camp at Trinity.

10   The end of our trail was reached after we had covered about five and one fifth miles on the dirt road. Here we saw the first signs of life since leaving Albuquerque about three hours earlier, a line of silent men dressed in helmets. A little farther on, a detachment of military police examined our special credentials. We got out of the buses and looked around us. The night was still pitch-black save for an occasional flash of lightning in the eastern sky, outlining for a brief instant the Sierra Oscuro Range directly ahead of us. We were in the middle of the New Mexico desert,

miles away from nowhere, with hardly a sign of life, not even a blinking light on the distant horizon. This was to be our caravansary ° until the zero hour.

11 From a distance to the southeast the beam of a search-light probed the clouds. This gave us our first sense of orientation. The bomb-test site, Zero, was a little to the left of the searchlight beam, twenty miles away. With the darkness and the waiting in the chill of the desert, the tension became almost unendurable.

12 We gathered in a circle to listen to directions on what we were to do at the time of the test, directions read aloud by the light of a flashlight:

13 At a short signal of the siren at minus five minutes to zero, "all personnel whose duties did not specifically require otherwise" were to prepare "a suitable place to lie down on." At a long signal of the sirens at minus two minutes to zero, "all personnel whose duties did not specifically require otherwise" were to "lie prone on the ground immediately, the face and eyes directed toward the ground and with the head away from Zero." "Do not watch for the flash directly," the directions read, "but turn over after it has occurred and watch the cloud. Stay on the ground until the blast wave has passed (two minutes). At two short blasts of the siren, indicating the passing of all hazard from light and blast, all personnel will prepare to leave as soon as possible.

14 "The hazard from blast is reduced by lying down on the ground in such a manner that flying rocks, glass, and other objects do not intervene between the source of blast and the individual. Open all car windows.

15 "The hazard from light injury to eyes is reduced by shielding the closed eyes with the bended arms and lying face down on the ground. If the first flash is viewed, a 'blind spot' may prevent your seeing the rest of the show.

16 "The hazard from ultraviolet light injuries to the skin is best overcome by wearing long trousers and shirts with long sleeves."

caravansary: a kind of inn, in the Near East, where caravans rest at night.

17 David Dow, assistant to the scientific director of the Atomic Bomb Development Center, handed each of us a flat piece of colored glass such as is used by arc welders to shield their eyes. Dr. Edward Teller of George Washington University cautioned us against sunburn. Someone produced sunburn lotion and passed it around. It was an eerie sight to see a number of our highest-ranking scientists seriously rubbing sunburn lotion on their faces and hands in the pitch-blackness of the night, twenty miles away from the expected flash. These were the men who, more than anybody else, knew the potentialities of atomic energy on the loose. It gave one an inkling of their confidence in their handiwork.

18 The bomb was set on a structural steel tower one hundred feet high. Ten miles away to the southwest was the base camp. This was G.H.Q. for the scientific high command, of which Professor Kenneth T. Bainbridge of Harvard University was field commander. Here were erected barracks to serve as living-quarters for the scientists, a mess hall, a commissary, a post exchange, and other buildings. Here the vanguard of the atomists, headed by Professor J. R. Oppenheimer of the University of California, scientific director of the Atomic Bomb Project, lived like soldiers at the front, supervising the enormously complicated details involved in the epoch-making tests.

19 Here early that Sunday afternoon gathered Major General Leslie R. Groves, commander in chief of the Atomic Bomb Project; Brigadier General T. F. Farrell, hero of World War I, General Grove's deputy; Professor Enrico Fermi, Nobel prize winner and one of the leaders in the project; President James Bryant Conant of Harvard; Dr. Vannevar Bush, director of the Office of Scientific Research and Development; Dean Richard C. Tolman of the California Institute of Technology; Professor R. F. Bacher of Cornell; Colonel Stafford L. Warren, University of Rochester radiologist; and about a hundred and fifty other leaders in the atomic bomb program.

20 At the Base Camp was a dry, abandoned reservoir, about five hundred feet square, surrounded by a mound of earth about eight feet high. Within this mound bull-dozers dug a series of slit trenches, each about three feet deep, seven feet wide, and twenty-five feet long. At a command over the radio at zero minus one minute all observers at Base Camp lay down in their assigned trenches, "face and eyes directed toward the ground and with the head away from Zero." But most of us on Compania Hill remained on our feet.

21 Three other posts had been established, south, north, and west of Zero, each at a distance of 10,000 yards (5.7 miles). These were known, respectively, as South-10,000, North-10,000, and West-10,000, or S-10, N-10, and W-10. Here the shelters were much more elaborate—wooden structures, their walls reinforced by cement, buried under a massive layer of earth.

22 S-10 was the control center. Here Professor Oppenheimer, as scientific commander in chief, and his field commander, Professor Bainbridge, issued orders and synchronized the activities of the other sites. Here the signal was given and a complex of mechanisms was set in motion that resulted in the greatest burst of energy ever released by man on earth up to that time. No switch was pulled, no button pressed, to light this first cosmic fire on this planet.

23 At forty-five seconds to zero, set for 5:30 o'clock, young Dr. Joseph L. McKibben of the University of California, at a signal from Professor Bainbridge, activated a master robot that set off a series of other robots, until, at last, strategically spaced electrons moved to the proper place at the proper split second.

24 Forty-five seconds passed and the moment was zero.

25 Meanwhile at our observation post on Compania Hill the atmosphere had grown tenser as the zero hour approached. We had spent the first part of our stay eating an early morning picnic breakfast that we had taken along with us. It had grown cold in the desert, and many of us, lightly clad, shivered. Occasionally a drizzle came down, and the intermittent flashes of lightning made us turn apprehensive glances toward Zero. We had had some disturbing reports that the test might be called off because of the weather. The radio we had brought with us for communication with Base Camp kept going out of order, and when we had finally repaired it some blatant * band would drown out the news we wanted to hear. We knew there were two specially equipped B-29 Superfortresses high overhead to make observations and recordings in the upper atmosphere, but we could neither see nor hear them. We kept gazing through the blackness.

26 Suddenly, at 5:29.50, as we stood huddled around our radio, we heard a voice ringing through the darkness, sounding as though it had come from above the clouds: "Zero minus ten seconds!" A green flare flashed out through the clouds, descended slowly, opened, grew dim, and vanished into the darkness.

27 The voice from the clouds boomed out again: "Zero minus three seconds!" Another green flare came down. Silence reigned over the desert. We kept moving in small groups in the direction of Zero. From the east came the first faint signs of dawn.

28 And just at that instant there rose from the bowels of the earth a light not of this world, the light of many suns in one. It was a sunrise such as the world had never seen, a great green super-sun climbing in a fraction of a second to a height of more than eight thousand feet, rising ever higher until it touched the clouds, lighting up earth and sky all around with a dazzling luminosity.

29 Up it went, a great ball of fire about a mile in diameter, changing colors as it kept shooting upward, from deep purple to orange, expanding, growing bigger, rising as it expanded, an elemental force freed from its bonds after being chained for billions of years. For a fleeting instant the color was unearthly green, such as one sees only in the corona of the sun during a total eclipse. It was as though the earth had opened and the skies had split. One felt as though one were present at the moment of creation when God said: "Let there be light."

30 To another observer, Professor George B. Kistiakowsky of Harvard, the spectacle was "the nearest thing to

doomsday that one could possibly imagine." "I am sure," he said, "that at the end of the world—in the last milli-second of the earth's existence—the last man will see what we have just seen!"

31   A great cloud rose from the ground and followed the trail of the great sun. At first it was a giant column, which soon took the shape of a supramundane mushroom. For a fleeting instant it took the form of the Statue of Liberty magnified many times. Up it went, higher, higher, a giant mountain born in a few seconds instead of millions of years, quivering convulsively. It touched the multicolored clouds, pushed its summit through them, kept rising until it reached a height of 41,000 feet, 12,000 feet higher than the earth's highest mountain.

32   All through this very short but extremely long time-interval not a sound was heard. I could see the silhouettes of human forms motionless in little groups, like desert plants in the dark. The newborn mountain in the distance, a giant among the pygmies of the Sierra Oscuro Range, stood leaning at an angle against the clouds, a vibrant vol-cano spouting fire to the sky.

33   Then out of the great silence came a mighty thunder. For a brief interval the phenomena we had seen as light repeated themselves in terms of sound. It was the blast from thousands of blockbusters going off simultaneously at one spot. The thunder reverberated all through the desert, bounced back and forth from the Sierra Oscuro, echo upon echo. The ground trembled under our feet as in an earthquake. A wave of hot wind was felt by many of us just before the blast and warned us of its coming.

34   The big boom came about one hundred seconds after the great flash—the first cry of a newborn world. It brought the silent, motionless silhouettes to life, gave them a voice. A loud cry filled the air. The little groups that had hitherto stood rooted to the earth like desert plants broke into a dance—the rhythm of primitive man dancing at one of his fire festivals at the coming of spring. They clapped their hands as they leaped from the ground—earthbound man symbolizing the birth of a new force that for the first time gives man means to free himself from the gravitional pull of the earth that holds him down.

35 The dance of the primitive man lasted but a few seconds, during which an evolutionary period of about 10,000 years had been telescoped. Primitive man was metamorphosed * into modern man—shaking hands, slapping his fellow on the back, all laughing like happy children.

36 The sun was just rising above the horizon as our caravan started on its way back to Albuquerque and Los Alamos. We looked at it through our dark lenses to compare it with what we had seen.

37 "The sun can't hold a candle to it!" one of us remarked.

ANALYSIS

What problems faced Laurence when he came to assemble the facts and write this essay? He had observed history in the making. How was he to treat the event? First, the good reporter would tell us what happened (how foolish that question sounds here, but nonetheless we do want to know), where it happened, when, and who witnessed it. Laurence does all this conscientiously. He names the scientists and the military men; he identifies them; he locates Compania Hill and Zero; he keeps a chronological order; he gives us distances and heights in accurate numbers. Second, he *shows* us what he saw: the night of July 16 was "dark with black clouds," the desert was cold and the men shivered, a "green flare flashed out through the clouds." Then came the great explosion. Paragraphs 28–33 are pure description. Awesome it must have been. Laurence wants us to hear it as well as see it. Third, he feels he must comment on this monumental occasion, if only briefly. He begins his essay with these comments (paragraphs 1–4). He concludes with a few more (paragraphs 34–35). They round out his report.

A highly critical reader might suggest to Laurence that he mars this essay by what he writes in paragraph 5, and where he places it, as well. Let us look closely at the opening of the report. The topic sentence ° is almost a pronouncement, but considering the subject it is what we need and expect. The rest of this first paragraph is written in the same key. An historical event of prime importance took place on July 16, 1945. Laurence does not underrate it. Paragraph 4 ends with the question which American scientists must have asked hundreds of times in the months before this experiment: "Will it work?" Since the reader knows at this stage in the essay that it did, indeed, work, one wonders if paragraph 5 is not anticipating (even spoiling) Laurence's "climax" (paragraphs 28–29) and at the same time indulging in a kind of ornate prose which does not match the rest of the essay. This is a minor point, to be sure. It is one questionable paragraph in a memorable record. But place paragraph 5 next to paragraphs 28–29. Are not the latter two more forcefully written (the string of adjectives in paragraph 5 is particularly unconvincing)? Is not the "climax" (paragraphs 28–29) the point at which the reader is ready, even breathless, for a description of the mighty flash, the reverberating thunder? You will want to answer these questions for yourself.

Questions on Content

1. Where did this first atomic explosion take place? Describe the area.
2. What instructions were given to the witnesses?
3. Was the bomb *dropped?* What does Laurence say about its detonation?
4. What did the explosion look like? Describe what followed the flash.

Add to Your Vocabulary

penultimate, prodigious, iridescent, blatant, metamorphosed.

Questions on Technique

1. Why should Laurence want to give us the names of so

topic sentence: See Glossary.

many men associated with this experiment, paragraphs 8 and 19, for example?
2. Why does he devote four paragraphs to the directions on what the observers were to do at the time of the test?
3. This essay uses very little technical jargon such as Army talk or scientific terms. What does Laurence gain by avoiding it?
4. In paragraphs 34–35, Laurence compares his colleagues to primitive man dancing. Why is this comparison particularly apt here?
5. What effect does Laurence achieve with his last paragraph? Why is the cliché,° "can't hold a candle to it," so apt at this point in the essay?

Techniques to Imitate

The literary style

Laurence's report of the first atomic explosion affords, in the way it is told, a sharp contrast to Carpenter's report of an equally gripping experience. In the first place, Laurence is a professional writer, and his professionalism shows. He brings to his subject a much more sophisticated, a much less colloquial, style than Carpenter's. In the second place, Laurence is obsessed by the tremendous implications of the unleashing of atomic power, whereas Carpenter, although he surely knows the great implications of his earth-orbiting flight, is content to limit his account to what happened on the flight. Both reports are beautifully written, but one can imagine how differently the Carpenter report might have been written by Laurence, and the Laurence report by Carpenter. There is more than one effective way to describe an exciting event.

To vary your writing experience, you may wish in your next assignment to try to imitate Laurence's more formal literary style. Compared with the colloquial style, it is more emotional in tone and more elevated in vocabulary. In addition to straight reporting, Laurence discusses philosophical implications. If you choose to emulate his writing, you will

cliché: See Glossary.

have to use the full range of your vocabulary as well as your most sophisticated reflections on the event you describe.

To achieve a firm grasp of the Laurence style, reread analytically paragraphs 5, 28, 29, 34, and 35. You will observe that, unlike Carpenter, Laurence does not understate his observations or his reactions. Try to imitate his kind of stirring reportorial writing.

Suggestions for Writing

1. Read Laurence's essay carefully, then rewrite it in the third person in 600–800 words as though your report were going to be part of an objective historical article.
2. Using any of the details of the essay you wish, reorganize and rewrite Laurence's report in 700 words.
3. With a little research, write an essay of 600 words on what happened in Hiroshima, Japan, on August 6, 1945. John Hersey's essay "Hiroshima" (*New Yorker,* August 31, 1946, and subsequently in book form) is a moving reportorial account of that event.
4. From your own experience, choose an event of some consequence to you. Discuss the importance of what happened and then the details surrounding it, choosing details which will illustrate *why* this event was significant. For example, you wanted for several reasons to make a journey on your own. One day you finally boarded a train or bus for X city. Or, you always wanted to take part in a play because (a) you like the theater, (b) you admire actors, (c) you need self-assurance. Then came the day you were selected for a role in the school play.

S. I. HAYAKAWA

The Language of Reports

Few people in the United States are better qualified to discuss American English usage than S. I. Hayakawa. He has been writing on semantics and linguistic theories since 1929, when he arrived from Canada to take his doctoral degree at the Universtiy of Wisconsin. He was professor of English at California State University, San Francisco, from 1955 to 1968 and president of that school from 1969 to1973. He is the editor of *ETC.: A Review of General Semantics* and author of *The Use and Misuse of Language* and *Symbol, Status, and Personality*, among other books.

None of his publications, however, has been more popular than *Language in Action*, first printed in 1941, and revised, with a slight change in title, twice since then. As Hayakawa explains in the preface to the latest revision, he wants to approach the study of language through "the methods of modern semantics, that is, through an understanding in biological and functional terms of the role of language in human life, and through an understanding of the different uses of language: language to persuade and control behavior, language to transmit information, language to create and express social cohesion, and the language of poetry and the imagination. . . . To understand how language works, what pitfalls it conceals, what its possibilities are, is to understand what is central to the complicated business of living the life of a human being."

In the prose of Carpenter and Laurence, Phillips and
Durso, we have watched words "transmit information."
Now in this chapter from *Language in Thought and
Action,* Hayakawa wants to discuss some of the pitfalls
and possibilities of reports in order to make us aware of
differences in kinds of reporting. He insists we "increase
our linguistic awareness" by recognizing how inferences
and judgments enter into ordinary reporting and why
they do not belong there. In short, he discusses the art
of reporting and the allied art of reading reports. We
can do neither well if we are not alert to the way words
work. His essay is not itself a report, but it is designed
to give us hints and suggestions on report writing as well
as to explore the operation of inferences and judgments.

1 **F**or the purposes of the in-
terchange of information, the basic symbolic act is the
report of what we have seen, heard, or felt: "There is a
ditch on each side of the road." "You can get those at
Smith's hardware store for $2.75." "There aren't any fish
on that side of the lake, but there are on this side." Then
there are reports of reports: "The longest waterfall in the
world is Victoria Falls in Rhodesia." "The Battle of Hast-
ings took place in 1066." "The papers say that there was a
smash-up on Highway 41 near Evansville." Reports adhere
to the following rules: first, they are *capable of verification;* * second, they *exclude,* as far as possible, *inferences* *
and *judgments.* (These terms will be defined later.)

Verifiability

2 Reports are verifiable. We may not always be able to
verify them ourselves, since we cannot track down the evidence for every piece of history we know, nor can we all
go to Evansville to see the remains of the smash-up before
they are cleared away. But if we are roughly agreed on the
names of things, on what constitutes a "foot," "meter,"
"bushel," and so on, and on how to measure time, there is
relatively little danger of our misunderstanding each other.

Even in a world such as we have today, in which everybody seems to be quarreling with everybody else, *we still to a surprising degree trust each other's reports*. We ask directions of total strangers when we are traveling. We follow directions on road signs without being suspicious of the people who put them up. We read books of information about science, mathematics, automotive engineering, travel, geography, the history of costume, and other such factual matters, and we usually assume that the author is doing his best to tell us as truly as he can what he knows. And we are safe in so assuming most of the time. With the interest given today to the discussion of biased newspapers, propagandists, and the general untrustworthiness of many of the communications we receive, we are likely to forget that we still have an enormous amount of reliable information available and that deliberate misinformation, except in warfare, is still more the exception than the rule. The desire for self-preservation that compelled men to evolve means for the exchange of information also compels them to regard the giving of false information as profoundly reprehensible.*

3   At its highest development, the language of reports is the language of science. By "highest development" we mean greatest general usefulness. Presbyterian and Catholic, workingman and capitalist, East German and West German, *agree* on the meanings of such symbols as $2 \times 2 = 4$, $100°$ C., HNO_3, 3:35 A.M., *1940* A.D., *1000 kilowatts, Quercus agrifolia*,° and so on. But how, it may be asked, can there be agreement about even this much among people who disagree about political philosophies, ethical ideas, religious beliefs, and the survival of my business *versus* the survival of yours? The answer is that circumstances *compel men to agree,* whether they wish to or not. If, for example, there were a dozen different religious sects in the United States, each insisting on its own way of naming the time of the day and the days of the year, the mere necessity of having a dozen different calendars, a dozen different kinds of watches, and a dozen sets of schedules for business

Quercus agrifolia: a kind of oak tree, similar to the California live oak.

hours, trains, and television programs, to say nothing of the effort that would be required for translating terms from one nomenclature * to another, would make life as we know it impossible.[1]

4 The language of reports, then, including the more accurate reports of science, is "map" language, and because it gives us reasonably accurate representations of the "territory," it enables us to get work done. Such language may often be dull or uninteresting reading: one does not usually read logarithmic tables or telephone directories for entertainment. But we could not get along without it. There are numberless occasions in the talking and writing we do in everyday life that *require that we state things in such a way that everybody will be able to understand and agree with our formulation.*

Inferences

5 The reader will find that practice in writing reports is a quick means of increasing his linguistic awareness. It is an exercise which will constantly provide him with his own examples of the principles of language and interpretation under discussion. The reports should be about first-hand

[1] According to information supplied by the Association of American Railroads, "Before 1883 there were nearly 100 different time zones in the United States. It wasn't until November 18 of that year that . . . a system of standard time was adopted here and in Canada. Before then there was nothing but local or 'solar' time. . . . The Pennsylvania Railroad in the East used Philadelphia time, which was five minutes slower than New York time and five minutes faster than Baltimore time. The Baltimore & Ohio used Baltimore time for trains running out of Baltimore, Columbus time for Ohio, Vincennes (Indiana) time for those going out of Cincinnati. . . . When it was noon in Chicago, it was 12:31 in Pittsburgh; 12:24 in Cleveland; 12:17 in Toledo; 12:13 in Cincinnati; 12:09 in Louisville; 12:07 in Indianapolis; 11:50 in St. Louis; 11:48 in Dubuque; 11:39 in St. Paul; and 11:27 in Omaha. There were 27 local time zones in Michigan alone. . . . A person traveling from Eastport, Maine, to San Francisco, if he wanted always to have the right railroad time and get off at the right place, had to twist the hands of his watch 20 times en route." Chicago *Daily News* (September 29, 1948).

experience—scenes the reader has witnessed himself, meetings and social events he has taken part in, people he knows well. They should be of such a nature that they can be verified and agreed upon. For the purpose of this exercise, inferences will be excluded.

6 Not that inferences are not important—we rely in everyday life and in science as much on *inferences* as on reports—in some areas of thought, for example, geology, paleontology,° and nuclear physics, reports are the foundations, but inferences (and inferences upon inferences) are the main body of the science. An inference, as we shall use the term, is *a statement about the unknown made on the basis of the known*. We may *infer* from the material and cut of a woman's clothes her wealth or social position; we may *infer* from the character of the ruins the origin of the fire that destroyed the building; we may *infer* from a man's calloused hands the nature of his occupation; we may *infer* from a senator's vote on an armaments bill his attitude toward Russia; we may *infer* from the structure of the land the path of a prehistoric glacier; we may *infer* from a halo on an unexposed photographic plate that it has been in the vicinity of radioactive materials; we may *infer* from the sound of an engine the condition of its connecting rods. Inferences may be carelessly or carefully made. They may be made on the basis of a broad background of previous experience with the subject matter, or no experience at all. For example, the inferences a good mechanic can make about the internal condition of a motor by listening to it are often startlingly accurate, while the inferences made by an amateur (if he tries to make any) may be entirely wrong. But the common characteristic of inferences is that they are statements about matters which are not directly known, statements made on the basis of what has been observed.

7 The avoidance of inferences in our suggested practice in report-writing requires that we make no guesses as to what is going on in other people's minds. When we say, "He was angry," we are not reporting; we are making an

---

paleontology: the study of prehistoric geological periods as represented by fossil animals and plants.

inference from such observable facts as the following: "He pounded his fist on the table; he swore; he threw the telephone directory at his stenographer." In this particular example, the inference appears to be fairly safe; nevertheless, it is important to remember, especially for the purposes of training oneself, that it is an inference. Such expressions as "He thought a lot of himself," "He was scared of girls," "He has an inferiority complex," made on the basis of casual social observation, and "What Russia really wants to do is to establish a world communist dictatorship," made on the basis of casual newspaper reading, are highly inferential. We should keep in mind their inferential character and, in our suggested exercises, should substitute for them such statements as "He rarely spoke to subordinates in the plant," "I saw him at a party, and he never danced except when one of the girls asked him to," "He wouldn't apply for the scholarship although I believe he could have won it easily," and "The Russian delegation to the United Nations has asked for *A, B,* and *C.* Last year they voted against *M* and *N,* and voted for *X* and *Y.* On the basis of facts such as these, the newspaper I read makes the inference that what Russia really wants is to establish a world communist dictatorship. I agree."

8 In spite of the exercise of every caution in avoiding inferences and reporting only what is seen and experienced, we all remain prone to error, since the making of inferences is a quick, almost automatic process. We may watch a car weaving as it goes down the road and say, "Look at that *drunken driver,*" although what we *see* is only *the irregular motion of the car.* The writer once saw a man leave a one-dollar tip at a lunch counter and hurry out. Just as the writer was wondering why anyone should leave so generous a tip in so modest an establishment, the waitress came, picked up the dollar, put it in the cash register as she punched up ninety cents, and put a dime in her pocket. In other words, the writer's description to himself of the event, "a one-dollar tip," turned out to be not a report but an inference.

9 All this is not to say that we should never make inferences. The inability to make inferences is itself a sign of mental disorder. For example, the speech therapist Laura L. Lee writes, "The aphasic [brain-damaged] adult with whom I worked had great difficulty in making inferences about a picture I showed her. She could tell me what was happening at the moment in the picture, but could not tell me what might have happened just before the picture or just afterward." [2] Hence the question is not whether or not we make inferences; the question is whether or not we are aware of the inferences we make.

Judgments

10 In our suggested writing exercise, judgments are also to be excluded. By judgments, we shall mean *all expressions of the writer's approval or disapproval of the occurrences, persons, or objects he is describing.* For example, a report cannot say, "It was a wonderful car," but must say something like this: "It has been driven 50,000 miles and has never required any repairs." Again statements such as "Jack lied to us" must be suppressed in favor of the more verifiable statement, "Jack told us he didn't have the keys to his car with him. However, when he pulled a handkerchief out of his pocket a few minutes later, a bunch of car keys fell out." Also a report may not say, "The senator was stubborn, defiant, and uncooperative," or "The senator courageously stood by his principles"; it must say instead, "The senator's vote was the only one against the bill."

11 Many people regard statements such as the following as statements of "fact": "Jack *lied* to us," "Jerry is a *thief*," "Tommy is *clever*." As ordinarily employed, however, the word "lied" involves first an inference (that Jack knew otherwise and deliberately misstated the facts) and second a judgment (that the speaker disapproves of what he has inferred that Jack did). In the other two instances, we may substitute such expressions as, "Jerry was con-

[2] "Brain Damage and the Process of Abstracting: A Problem in Language Learning," *ETC.: A Review of General Semantics,* XVI (1959), 154–62.

victed of theft and served two years at Waupun," and "Tommy plays the violin, leads his class in school, and is captain of the debating team." After all, to say of a man that he is a "thief" is to say in effect, "He has stolen *and will steal again*"—which is more of a prediction than a report. Even to say, "He has stolen," is to make an inference (and simultaneously to pass a judgment) on an act about which there may be difference of opinion among those who have examined the evidence upon which the conviction was obtained. But to say that he was "convicted of theft" is to make a statement capable of being agreed upon through verification in court and prison records.

12 Scientific verifiability rests upon the external observation of facts, not upon the heaping up of judgments. If one person says, "Peter is a deadbeat," and another says, "I think so too," the statement has not been verified. In court cases, considerable trouble is sometimes caused by witnesses who cannot distinguish their judgments from the facts upon which those judgments are based. Cross-examinations under these circumstances go something like this:

WITNESS: That dirty double-crosser Jacobs ratted on me.

DEFENSE ATTORNEY: Your honor, I object.

JUDGE: Objection sustained. (Witness's remark is stricken from the record.) Now, try to tell the court exactly what happened.

WITNESS: He double-crossed me, the dirty, lying rat!

DEFENSE ATTORNEY: Your honor, I object!

JUDGE: Objection sustained. (Witness's remark is again stricken from the record.) Will the witness try to stick to the facts.

WITNESS: But I'm telling you the facts, your honor. He did double-cross me.

This can continue indefinitely unless the cross-examiner exercises some ingenuity in order to get at the facts behind the judgment. To the witness it is a "fact" that he was "double-crossed." Often patient questioning is required before the factual bases of the judgment are revealed.

13 Many words, of course, simultaneously convey a report and a judgment on the fact reported, as will be discussed more fully in a later chapter. For the purposes of a report as here defined, these should be avoided. Instead of "sneaked in," one might say "entered quietly"; instead of "politicians," "congressmen" or "aldermen" or "candidates for office"; instead of "bureaucrat," "public official"; instead of "tramp," "homeless unemployed"; instead of "dictatorial set-up," "centralized authority"; instead of "crackpots," "holders of nonconformist views." A newspaper reporter, for example, is not permitted to write, "A crowd of suckers came to listen to Senator Smith last evening in that rickety firetrap and ex-dive that disfigures the south edge of town." Instead he says, "Between seventy-five and a hundred people heard an address last evening by Senator Smith at the Evergreen Garden near the South Side city limits."

Snarl-Words and Purr-Words

14 Throughout this book, it is important to remember that we are not considering language as an isolated phenomenon. Our concern, instead, is with language in action—language in the full context of the nonlinguistic events which are its setting. The making of noises with the vocal organs is a muscular activity and, like other muscular activities, often involuntary. Our responses to powerful stimuli, such as to things that make us very angry, are a complex of muscular and physiological events: the contracting of fighting muscles, the increase of blood pressure, a change in body chemistry, clutching of our hair, *and* the making of noises, such as growls and snarls. We are a little too dignified, perhaps, to growl like dogs, but we do the next best thing and substitute series of words, such as "You dirty double-crosser!" "The filthy scum!" Similarly, if we are pleasurably agitated, we may, instead of purring or wagging the tail, say things like "She's the sweetest girl in all the world!"

15 Speeches such as these are, as direct expressions of

approval or disapproval, judgments in their simplest form. They may be said to be human equivalents of snarling and purring. "She's the sweetest girl in all the world" is not a statement about the girl; it is a purr. This seems to be a fairly obvious fact; nevertheless, it is surprising how often, when such a statement is made, both the speaker and the hearer feel that something has been said about the girl. This error is especially common in the interpretation of utterances of orators and editorialists in some of their more excited denunciations of "Reds," "greedy monopolists," "Wall Street," "radicals," "foreign ideologies," and in their more fulsome * dithyrambs ° about "our way of life." Constantly, because of the impressive sound of the words, the elaborate structure of the sentences, and the appearance of intellectual progression, we get the feeling that something is being said about something. On closer examination, however, we discover that these utterances merely say, "What I hate ('Reds,' 'Wall Street,' or whatever) I hate very, very much," and "What I like ('our way of life') I like very, very much." We may call such utterances "snarl-words" and "purr-words." They are not reports describing conditions in the extensional world in any way.

16 To call these judgments "snarl-words" and "purr-words" does not mean that we should simply shrug them off. It means that we should be careful to *allocate the meaning correctly*—placing such a statement as "She's the sweetest girl in the world" as a revelation of the speaker's state of mind, and not as a revelation of facts about the girl. If the "snarl-words" about "Reds" or "greedy monopolists" are accompanied by verifiable reports (which would also mean that we have previously agreed as to who, specifically, is meant by the terms "Reds" or "greedy monopolists"), we might find reason to be just as disturbed as the speaker. If the "purr-words" about the sweetest girl in the world are accompanied by verifiable reports about her appearance, manners, character, and so on, we might find reason to admire her too. But "snarl-words" and "purr-words" as such, unaccompanied by reports, offer nothing

dithyrambs: impassioned or exalted expressions.

further to discuss, except possibly the question, "Why do you feel as you do?"

17 It is usually fruitless to debate such questions as "Is the President a great statesman or merely a skillful politician?" "Is the music of Wagner the greatest music of all time, or is it merely hysterical screeching?" "Which is the finer sport, tennis or baseball?" "Could Joe Louis in his prime have licked Bob Fitzsimmons in his prime?" To take sides on such issues of conflicting judgments is to reduce oneself to the same level of stubborn imbecility as one's opponents. But to ask questions of the form, "Why do you like (or dislike) the President (or Wagner, or tennis, or Joe Louis)?" is to learn something about one's friends and neighbors. After listening to their opinions and their reasons for them, we may leave the discussion slightly wiser, slightly better informed, and perhaps slightly less one-sided than we were before the discussion began.

How Judgments Stop Thought

18 A judgment ("He is a fine boy," "It was a beautiful service," "Baseball is a healthful sport," "She is an awful bore") is a conclusion, summing up a large number of previously observed facts. The reader is probably familiar with the fact that students almost always have difficulty in writing themes of the required length because their ideas give out after a paragraph or two. The reason for this is that those early paragraphs contain so many judgments that there is little left to be said. When the conclusions are carefully excluded, however, and observed facts are given instead, there is never any trouble about the length of papers; in fact, they tend to become too long, since inexperienced writers, when told to give facts, often give far more than are necessary, because they lack discrimination * between the important and the trivial.

19 Still another consequence of judgments early in the course of a written exercise—and this applies also to hasty judgments in everyday thought—is the temporary blindness they induce. When, for example, a description starts with the words, "He was a real Madison Avenue executive," or "She was a typical sorority girl," if we continue writing at all, we must make all our later statements consistent with those judgments. The result is that all the individual characteristics of this particular "executive" or this particular "sorority girl" are lost sight of; and the rest of the account is likely to deal not with observed facts but with the writer's private notion (based on previously read stories, movies, pictures, and so forth) of what "Madison Avenue executives" or "typical sorority girls" are like. The premature judgment, that is, often prevents us from seeing what is directly in front of us, so that clichés take the place of fresh description. Therefore, even if the writer feels sure at the beginning of a written account that the man he is describing is a "real leatherneck" or that the scene he is describing is a "beautiful residential suburb," he will conscientiously keep such notions out of his head, lest his vision be obstructed. He is specifically warned against describing *anybody* as a "beatnik" —a term (originally applied to literary and artistic Bohemians) which was blown up by sensational journalism and movies into an almost completely fictional and misleading stereotype. If a writer applies the term to any actual living human being, he will have to spend so much energy thereafter explaining what he does *not* mean by it that he will save himself trouble by not bringing it up at all.

Slanting

20 In the course of writing reports of personal experiences, it will be found that in spite of all endeavors to keep judgments out, some will creep in. An account of a man, for example, may go like this: "He had apparently not shaved for several days, and his face and hands were covered with grime. His shoes were torn, and his coat, which was several sizes too small for him, was spotted with dried clay." Now, in spite of the fact that no judgment has been stated, a very obvious one is implied. Let us contrast this with another description of the same man. "Although his face was bearded and neglected, his eyes

were clear, and he looked straight ahead as he walked rapidly down the road. He seemed very tall; perhaps the fact that his coat was too small for him emphasized that impression. He was carrying a book under his left arm, and a small terrier ran at his heels." In this example, the impression about the same man is considerably changed, simply by the inclusion of new details and the subordination * of unfavorable ones. Even if explicit * judgments are kept out of one's writing, implied judgments will get in.

21 How, then, can we ever give an impartial report? The answer is, of course, that we cannot attain complete impartiality while we use the language of everyday life. Even with the very impersonal language of science, the task is sometimes difficult. Nevertheless, we can, by being aware of the favorable or unfavorable feelings that certain words and facts can arouse, attain enough impartiality for practical purposes. Such awareness enables us to balance the implied favorable and unfavorable judgments against each other. To learn to do this, it is a good idea to write two accounts of the same subject, both strict reports, to be read side by side: the first to contain facts and details likely to prejudice the reader in favor of the subject, the second to contain those likely to prejudice the reader against it. For example:

FOR	AGAINST
He had white teeth.	His teeth were uneven.
His eyes were blue, his hair blond and abundant.	He rarely looked people straight in the eye.
He had on a clean white shirt.	His shirt was frayed at the cuffs.
His speech was courteous.	He had a high-pitched voice.
His employer spoke highly of him.	His landlord said he was slow in paying his rent.
He liked dogs.	He disliked children.

22 This process of selecting details favorable or unfavorable to the subject being described may be termed *slanting*.

Slanting gives no explicit judgments, but it differs from reporting in that it deliberately makes certain judgments inescapable. Let us assume for a moment the truth of the statement "When Clyde was in New York last November he was seen having dinner with a show girl. . . ." The inferences that can be drawn from this statement are changed considerably when the following words are added: ". . . and her husband and their two children." Yet, if Clyde is a married man, his enemies could conceivably do him a great deal of harm by talking about his "dinner-date with a New York show girl." One-sided or biased slanting of this kind, not uncommon in private gossip and backbiting, and all too common in the "interpretative reporting" of newspapers and news magazines, can be described as a technique of lying without actually telling any lies.

Discovering One's Bias

23 Here, however, a caution is necessary. When, for example, a newspaper tells a story in a way that we dislike, leaving out facts we think important and playing up important facts in ways that we think unfair, we are tempted to say, "Look how unfairly they've slanted the story!" In making such a statement we are, of course, making an inference about the newspaper's editors. We are assuming that what seems important or unimportant to us seems equally important or unimportant to them, and on the basis of that assumption we infer that the editors "deliberately" gave the story a misleading emphasis. Is this necessarily the case? Can the reader, as an outsider, say whether a story assumes a given form because the editors "deliberately slanted it that way" or because that was the way the events appeared to them?

24 The point is that, by the process of selection and abstraction imposed on us by our own interests and background, experience comes to all of us (including newspaper editors) already "slanted." If you happen to be pro-labor, pro-Catholic, and a stock-car racing fan, your ideas of what is important or unimportant will of necessity be different from those of a man who happens to be indifferent to all three of your favorite interests. If, then, some newspapers often seem to side with the big businessman on public issues, the reason is less a matter of "deliberate" slanting than the fact that publishers are often, in enterprises as large as modern urban newspapers, big businessmen themselves, accustomed both in worth and in social life to associating with other big businessmen. Nevertheless, the best newspapers, whether owned by "big businessmen" or not, do try to tell us as accurately as possible what is going on in the world, because they are run by newspapermen who conceive it to be part of their professional responsibility to present fairly the conflicting points of view in controversial issues. Such newspapermen are *reporters* indeed.

25   The writer who is neither an advocate nor an opponent avoids slanting, except when he is seeking special literary effects. The avoidance of slanting is not only a matter of being fair and impartial; it is even more importantly a matter of making good maps of the territory of experience. The profoundly biased individual cannot make good maps because he can see an enemy *only* as an enemy and a friend *only* as a friend. The individual with genuine skill in writing—one who has imagination and insight—can look at the same subject from many points of view. The following examples may illustrate the fullness and solidity of descriptions thus written:

> Adam turned to look at him. It was, in a way, as though this were the first time he had laid eyes on him. He saw the strong, black shoulders under the red-check calico, the long arms lying loose, forward over the knees, the strong hands, seamed and calloused, holding the reins. He looked at the face. The thrust of the jawbone was strong, but the lips were heavy and low, with a piece of chewed straw hanging out one side of the mouth. The eyelids were pendulous, slightly swollen-looking, and the eyes bloodshot. Those eyes, Adam knew, could sharpen to a quick, penetrating, assessing

glance. But now, looking at that slack, somnolent face, he could scarcely believe that.
                    —ROBERT PENN WARREN, *Wilderness*

Soon after the little princess, there walked in a massively built, stout young man in spectacles, with a cropped head, light breeches in the mode of the day, with a high lace ruffle and a ginger-coloured coat. This stout young man [Pierre] was the illegitimate son of a celebrated dandy of the days of Catherine, Count Bezuhov, who was now dying in Moscow. He had not yet entered any branch of the service; he had only just returned from abroad, where he had been educated, and this was his first appearance in society. Anna Pavlovna greeted him with a nod reserved for persons of the very lowest hierarchy in her drawing-room. . . .

Pierre was clumsy, stout and uncommonly tall, with huge, red hands; he did not, as they say, know how to come into a drawing-room and still less how to get out of one, that is, how to say something particularly agreeable on going away. Moreover, he was dreamy. He stood up, and picking up a three-cornered hat with the plume of a general in it instead of his own, he kept hold of it, pulling the feather until the general asked him to restore it. But all his dreaminess and his inability to enter a drawing-room or talk properly in it were atoned for by his expression of good-nature, simplicity and modesty.   —COUNT LEO TOLSTOY, *War and Peace*
                    (Translated by Constance Garnett)

ANALYSIS

Hayakawa breaks his essay into seven brief sections in order to simplify what he wants to say. Although this procedure is not common in essay writing, it works well here because the chief purpose of the chapter is definition. We are dealing with terms, labels, rules. No matter what we call them, they help us distinguish kinds of reporting. Let us follow Hayakawa's example and comment briefly on some of these sections.

Verifiability: Most of us are so used to expecting accurate reports that we seldom question the reporter's evidence. What Hayakawa neglects to mention is the part which our opinion of the reporter plays in this trust. Who the reporter is and how often in the past we have had reason to believe the reporter affect our acceptance of the simplest facts, whether we are aware of it or not. Of course "circumstances compel men to agree," as Hayakawa claims, or else we would not get the world's work done. But when McCandlish Phillips reports that "William Willis, an aged wanderer on trackless oceans, was back yesterday from his latest agonizing adventure in solitude, looking like a man who had spent a few days in Miami," we take his word not because we are compelled to but because the *New York Times* has a reputation for accuracy, because Phillips has worked for that paper for many years, and because we ourselves are not able to observe at first hand most of what that notable paper publishes. The good reporter begins here, with verifiable, unadorned facts.

Inferences: The word may be new to you. In reporting for your school paper, you may never have had occasion to make "statements about matters which are not directly known," especially if you have been reporting firsthand experience, what you yourself have witnessed. But we slip into inferring so-called facts more easily than we realize. A good reporter tells us that Lakewood High School won its third basketball game of the season on Tuesday night, defeating Newton High School by 78–40. The reporter does not draw any inferences from this fact, such as that Newton's coach is second-rate, that Lakewood might have lost the game if Ann Diller had not played so well, that both teams will fail to reach the state championship tournament. These are not verifiable facts, only inferences. Too many inferences in any report will lead a reader to say the reporter is editorializing the news.

Judgments: Hayakawa defines the term and then illustrates it with remarkable clarity. Here again we are all guilty. How easily we use the worn-out adjectives "terrific" and "lousy" without adequate cause. We even write statements that pose as facts but are not. Generally these snap judgments are based on emotions or memories or partial information; but more than that, they lead to false impressions. Unless we are aware of making these hasty judgments ourselves, we will hardly be able to spot them in our reading.

Snarl-words and purr-words: Certain kinds of judgments lend themselves to strong expressions of approval and disapproval. Hayakawa's names for these expressions suggest the animal instincts from which they spring and imply emotional outbursts rather than rational thought. "They are not reports," he says, "describing conditions in the extensional world in any way." Yet we *accept* them as factual statements. How often are we aware that "beatnik," "Leftist," "Puritan," "slacker," are loaded words, words conveying overtones of meaning rather than defendable, factual opinions? He implies that choosing words carefully is one way of avoiding false reports.

Slanting: Total impartiality is impossible unless we are scientists using arbitary formulas and symbols. The chemist would hardly describe water as made up of two vibrant molecules of hydrogen and one sullen molecule of oxygen. As reporters, we are often likely to describe a local actress as "vibrant" and a young vandal who has been apprehended as "sullen." We need these adjectives, these selective judgments. But Hayakawa warns of the pitfalls "slanting" the news can create. If, as reporters, we are determined to inflate the performance of a play in order to flatter the actress or to sell more tickets, we can do it easily by choosing only the favorable judgments, and most readers will accept our report as factual. True, our report is not false, but it is partial, slanted, biased. It is not likely that we *write* such reports unconsciously, but we surely *read* them without constant attention to their bias.

Add to Your Vocabulary

verification, inferences, reprehensible, nomenclature, fulsome, discrimination, subordination, explicit.

Techniques to Imitate

Honesty and clarity in thinking and writing

Hayakawa's article is included here not as an example for you to imitate but rather as a piece of good advice for any writer. Having studied this analysis of the language of reports, you should now be aware of your own drawing of inferences and making of judgments and tendencies toward slanting. From now on you will know exactly what your teacher or your classmates mean when, in evaluating your writing, they make such comments as, "That seems like an unjustified inference," or "On what evidence is this judgment based?" or "Can this be verified?" or "These sound like snarl words," or "Aren't you slanting your report?"

Learning to write involves more than mastering the mechanics and developing an interesting style; it involves honesty and clear thinking, too.

Suggestions for Writing

1. A traffic accident has just occurred in front of your school, involving three cars and two pedestrians. Both pedestrians but none of the drivers are seriously injured. One of the cars was driven by a student who had been known in town as a careless driver. After inventing all the details you need, write:
   a. A report for the school paper, staying close to observable facts.
   b. A slanted account as it might be written by a news reporter who does not like eighteen-year-old drivers, but who also does not invent lies.
   c. A slanted report, to be delivered at a PTA meeting by a parent who has been arguing for driver training courses but who is also accustomed to making quick judgments.
2. Select a brief news report from today's paper and analyze it for bias, false judgments, withheld information. Obviously your selection has to be on a somewhat

controversial subject rather than a football game or a local card party.

3. Write a 300-word report about a new arrival in your school, a student who has transferred from another part of the country. Now rewrite the report, changing your slant to one wholly for or against this student, but keeping equally close to the true facts.

ARTHUR C. CLARKE

The Secret of the Sun

Arthur C. Clarke might be the colossus of science fiction, but he is also a scientist: he was trained in physics and mathematics and is past chairman of the British Interplanetary Society. Clarke has been writing on our solar system and space travel for many years, in both fiction and nonfiction, and he knows how to move from assembling facts (reporting) to projecting theories and interpretations (analysis) without indulging in what S. I. Hayakawa would call unfounded inferences and false judgments. Clarke is well known in his native England for an early book, *Interplanetary Flight* (1950), and in both England and America for, among other works, *Challenge of the Spaceship* (1959) and *Voices from the Sky* (1965). His science fiction includes *Childhood's End* (1953), *The City and the Stars* (1956), and (with Stanley Kubrick) the screenplay for *2001: A Space Odyssey*.

Clarke begins with elementary facts, explaining how we acquired our knowledge of the sun's composition and how much energy it produces. In paragraph 8, he pauses to ask two questions, not of his readers but of himself. The answers to these questions form the remainder of the essay. Paragraphs 9–25 discuss "where all the energy comes from" and some of the implications of the facts he produces. Paragraphs 26–32 consider,

less briefly, the vital question of how long this energy
will last.

This is expository writing that is both informative and
analytical. Clarke is writing for the intelligent general
reader who wants to learn "the secret of the sun" and
is willing to accept Clarke's analyses of the assembled
facts. Neither writer nor reader expects to debate the
issues involved.

1 If a hundred people were
asked the straightforward question, "What is the nearest
star?" ninety-five would say they didn't know, three would
name Alpha Centauri and the other two would say Proxima
Centauri. They would all be wrong, even the erudite *
two who knew that Proxima was a fraction of a light year
closer to earth than its companion Alpha. For the nearest
star is—the sun.

2 It took the human race quite a few thousand years
to discover this fact, for no objects could be more unlike
than the dazzling, burning sun and the coldly scintillating *
stars. But remove the sun to a million times its present
distance, and it would be an undistinguished though still
easily visible star. It is the sun's extreme closeness—a
trifling 93,000,000 miles—that makes it so overwhelmingly
important to us.

3 Indeed it was only about twenty years ago that astronomers began to have some idea of what makes it function.
Today, thanks to the patient detective work of generations
of scientists, we have not only learned the secret of the
sun but in the achievement of nuclear fusion we have
ignited its fires on earth, with awesome consequences for
the future of mankind.

4 To the ancients, the possibility of ever learning anything definite about the sun must have seemed not only
vain but presumptuous.

5 It is unwise to set limits to knowledge and discovery,
as proved by the example of the 18th century philosopher
who remarked: "If one thing is certain, it is that we shall

never know what the stars are made of." Today, because of the spectroscope, we know more about the composition of stars trillions of miles away than of the earth beneath our feet.

6   All atoms, when they are sufficiently heated, become tiny transmitting stations which broadcast light rather than radio waves. What is more, the wave length of that light is as characteristic of the particular atom as is his fingerprint of an individual man. The spectroscope can spread out the sun's light into a colored band yards in length—a band crossed with thousands of lines which show the sun's composition as clearly as if a sample of it could be put through chemical analysis. All the ordinary elements are present in the sun, but two of them—hydrogen and helium—are vastly more abundant than all the others put together. The composition of the sun, therefore, is different from that of the earth, which is mostly made of oxygen and silicon. This was a blow to the theory that the earth was once part of the sun.

7   As soon as fairly accurate measurements of the sun's distance and size (it is 864,000 miles in diameter, over a hundred times that of the earth) became available about three centuries ago, astronomers had a major problem on their hands, though they didn't realize just how major it was for another century. The amount of energy which the earth receives from the sun is enormous; it is roughly equivalent to a one-kilowatt electric heater on *every square yard* of our planet's surface. But the earth itself intercepts only a minute fraction of the sun's rays; most of the energy goes rushing past into space and, from our self-centered point of view, is completely wasted. The total waste, if you like nice round figures, is approximately half a million, million, million, million horsepower.

8   Where does all the energy come from? And even more important, how long is it going to last?

9   In the Victorian era, scientists began to ask these questions more and more insistently, and a splendid fight developed between the astronomers and the geologists. The problem was this: no source of energy known to science

could possibly keep the sun going for the periods of time the geologists demanded. If the sun were made of the best quality coal, for example, it would have burned itself out in a couple of thousand years. It was obvious, therefore, that chemical energy was quite insufficient to power the sun.

10   The astronomers racked their brains to think of an alternative, and at last they thought they had found one. The sun, they decided, obtained its energy from its slow contraction under gravity. But if the sun were contracting, it once must have been bigger, and it was not hard to calculate how long it had been since it had embraced the earth. The answer came to fifty million years, which obviously set a limit to the age of the earth.

11   Then the evidence of geology began to accumulate, and it was soon obvious that fifty, a hundred—even five hundred—million years was simply not long enough for all the changes our planet has seen. The geologists pointed to the mountains that had been worn away, the chalk beds miles thick that had been laid down on the beds of vanished seas, and told the astronomers to look for a few more zeros.

12   Not until the discovery of radioactivity was the paradox resolved. Then the astronomers realized that gigantic stores of energy were locked up in the atoms themselves, and that the sun was able to tap that energy, which was sufficient to keep it shining steadily for thousands of millions of years. That took care of the past—and of the future, too, as far ahead as anyone cared to look.

13   For several decades scientists speculated on the precise means by which the sun released the energy of matter. Some elements—radium, for example—are naturally unstable and continuously give out energy until they have decayed into less spendthrift substances such as lead. But even if the sun were made of radium—a highly unlikely assumption—that still could not account for such a vast generation of power over so long a period. The sun must have learned the secret of releasing energy from "ordinary" matter.

14 In the history of the world, there has been no more momentous quest than the search for that secret. The first major clue came in 1868, when the spectroscope revealed the lines of an element in the sun not yet discovered on earth. The new element was given the appropriate name "helium," and after an intensive search was found in our atmosphere in minute quantities.

15 Helium, though it aroused considerable interest because of the unusual way in which it was found, seemed no more than a scientific novelty. But it was a major milestone on the road which was to lead, eighty-four years later, to the hundred-mile-long H-bomb cloud above Eniwetok Atoll,° and to the promise of eternal power for all the machines that man would build.

16 We now know that helium is the ash left when hydrogen is burned in the atomic furnace of the sun. But the type of "burning" that takes place in the sun is infinitely fiercer than ordinary combustion; it is like the flame of a blow torch compared to the pale glow of a firefly. It is an atomic rather than a chemical process, and takes place at temperatures of millions instead of thousands of degrees. The sun's interior, in fact, is far too hot for fire as we know it to exist.

17 The solar transmutation of hydrogen to helium, with its enormous release of energy, is a complex process involving several intermediate stages, and is quite different from the reactions which took place in the H-bomb, although the final result is the same. The sun also operates on a slightly larger scale; every second about 4,000,000 tons of matter are converted into raw energy. We would have to explode 10,000,000,000 H-bombs *every second* if we wanted to equal the energy output of the sun.

18 Deep down in the solar core, under the influence of pressures and temperatures beyond imagination, the atoms of hydrogen are fused together to form helium, and the released energy batters its way up to the surface of the sun,

Eniwetok Atoll: in the northwestern part of the Marshall Islands, near New Guinea, in the Pacific Ocean. Atomic and hydrogen bomb tests were made here in 1947–1952.

hundreds of thousands of miles above. Then, in the form of light, heat and other radiations, the energy spreads out into space and is lost—apart from the tiny fraction that is intercepted by the earth and the other planets.

19 No man has ever seen the sun or ever will. Only a small part of its radiation—the narrow band of visible light—leaks down through the atmosphere, which acts as a filter eliminating the ultraviolet and X rays that would continually bombard us without its protection. When men leave the atmosphere and enter the direct solar rays, they will have to be shielded by the walls and windows of their space ships. An unprotected man out in space—even assuming that he could still breathe—would die in a few minutes from acute sunburn.

20 Much of the effort in the building of earth-satellite rockets is concerned with attempts to measure the sun's radiations before they enter the atmosphere, so that we can get a true picture of what the sun "looks like" when *all* its rays are taken into account. This work will have two immediate practical consequences. The solar rays absorbed in the upper atmosphere have a great, though still unknown, effect on the weather and on short-wave radio communication. There are times when the sun sends out sudden spurts of ultraviolet light that cause such intense electrification of the upper air that all long-distance radio circuits are disrupted.

21 It has also been discovered in the last few years that the sun is a powerful though erratic radio transmitter. Its outer layers are convulsed by great storms, often many times as large as our world, which are visible in telescopes as black areas on the sun's shining surface. Occasionally these areas, known as sunspots, are large enough to be seen by the naked eye, and for some still unknown reason they act as intense generators of radio waves. So also, on a smaller scale, does the sun's beautiful and mysterious envelope, the corona, which can be seen in its full glory only during the magical moments of a total eclipse.

22 If we could "see" the sun by its radio waves instead of its light waves we would not recognize it as the same object. It would appear much larger, and not even circular in shape. Normally it would be an irregular oval, slowly changing its shape from week to week. The brilliance of its surface would be very uneven; to the radio eye, the sunspots and corona would be the brightest portions, and the rest would be relatively dark. At rare intervals a tiny portion of the disc would erupt, for a few minutes at a time, in a blaze of radio brilliance so fierce that the sun might shine temporarily with hundreds of times its normal intensity. This outburst would be a "flare," one of the most spectacular phenomena of the sun's repertory.

23   In recent years it has been possible to make motion-picture films of events on the surface of the sun, and by speeding them up several hundred times to project on the screen the life story of cataclysmic * solar events which may occupy hours of time and quadrillions of cubic miles of space. Some of these films are awe-inspiring: they show immense fountains of flame spurting to heights of a hundred thousand miles from the sun's edge; bridges of fire, which could span a dozen earths, forming and crumbling; exact replicas of A-bomb bursts—but a thousand times as large—shooting up into space.

24   But some of the occurrences on the sun that have been filmed are not merely awe-inspiring, they are inexplicable.* Watching them, you are acutely aware of seeing the action of forces completely beyond our understanding. A slanting jet of incandescent * gas, for example, will shoot out on a long, flat trajectory, reach its apex, *and then whip back along its original path*—just as if a shell at the peak of its flight decided to return to the gun. And sometimes, thousands of miles above the sun's surface, cascades of glowing matter will pour down from no apparent source, as if they were created high in the solar atmosphere.

25   Since the sun is purely gaseous, it is surprising that its surface is so sharply defined, except in the areas disturbed by sunspots or sporadic * eruptions. Seen through the telescope, the edge of the sun is such a perfect circle that it is easier to imagine it composed of liquid than gas. One reason for the "flatness" of the sun's surface is its

intense gravity, twenty-eight times that of the earth's. On the sun a 160-pound man would weigh almost two tons.

26 Although many stars wax and wane in brilliance, the sun's output of heat and light has changed very little during the course of human history. (The theory that solar changes were responsible for the Ice Ages is not very popular today.) The sunlight which warms us has not altered its intensity since the first man walked the earth.

27 Yet in the early days of earth's history, the light that reached the surface of our planet was a fierce, searing flood of radiation that would have been fatal to all the life forms of our age. The atmospheric filters which protect us now had not yet formed, and the raw sunlight could pour down almost unhindered.

28 And what of the future? Despite its size and the inconceivable stores of hydrogen still untapped within it, the sun cannot maintain its present output forever, although it is still good for many billion years. What will happen when the sun starts to run out of fuel around the year A.D. 10,000,000,000, give or take a few billion? The obvious assumption is that the sun will gradually cool down to a dull red and finally gutter out into extinction; the wonderful closing chapter of H. G. Wells' masterpiece, *The Time Machine,* gives a description of the dying sun based on this hypothesis. But as is so often the case in science, the obvious assumption is not the correct one. The sun is not cooling down; it is warming up.

29 The effect on the weather will not be noticeable for about ten thousand million years, but then things will happen in a hurry. As the sun uses up its hydrogen fuel and the helium "ash" accumulates around its core, the solar furnace will burn hotter and hotter. It may seem strange that this should happen as the sun runs out of fuel, but the thickening blanket of helium will increase the rate of burning. So like a gambler who bets more and more frantically as he approaches the end of his resources, the sun will go out in a final blaze of glory. Within a span of a mere five million years it will increase its brilliance a hundredfold, melting down the earth and the inner planets

into balls of glowing lava. Then it will collapse swiftly to a tiny star only a few thousand miles in diameter, becoming one of the fantastically dense "white dwarfs" in which the mass of an entire sun is packed into the volume of a planet.

30 It will still be bright, but it will give little more heat to the earth than the full moon does today. The minute star which finally gutters to extinction amid the corpses of the planets will not be anything which we would recognize as the sun.

31 So, at least, runs the current theory of solar evolution, but to claim that this is an accurate description of what *must* happen to the sun would be rash indeed. With new knowledge our picture of the sun continually becomes more complicated. And even when we have attained a complete understanding of the processes taking place inside the sun, we cannot be sure that external factors—clouds of interstellar dust into which it may run, for example—may not write new and unexpected chapters in its history.

32 A lot may happen to the sun, and to the earth, in the millions of centuries that lie ahead. Certainly we need not worry about the sun blowing up, or going out, for the next few thousand years. And after that, if our sun starts to misbehave, we'll find another one.

ANALYSIS

Clarke does not waste space on introductory remarks. With the first paragraph, we plunge into a direct question which, he tells us, does not often elicit a correct answer. The technique—direct involvement of the reader—is an old one, but Clarke uses it to give us obliquely several vital facts: the sun is a star; it is 93,000,000 miles from the earth; the source of its energy is the "big secret" we are about to learn. He then elaborates on these facts before raising other questions.

Elaboration is at the heart of analysis. Let us look, for example, at the way in which Clarke handles the first question he asks in paragraph 8. If he were interested only

in assembling factual information about the sun's energy,
he could answer this question in a few sentences. But he
wishes instead to examine all aspects of his question, to
break down the subject for close scrutiny, to look critically
at the evidence he has to work with, using comparisons and
analogies ° for our keener comprehension. He begins historically: since the nineteenth century, astronomers and
geologists have disagreed on the source of the sun's energy,
but the discovery of radioactivity and the invention of the
spectroscope brought us new knowledge. By paragraph 14
we are introduced to the element helium, part of the answer
to Clarke's primary question. But if helium is "the ash left
when hydrogen is burned in the atomic furnace of the
sun," mere identification does not explain *how* the sun
transmutes one into the other.

Paragraphs 17–18 try to describe what happens within
the sun's core, and this leads Clarke to consider radiation,
one aspect of solar energy, one in fact very close to our
own experience since we know what "acute sunburn" is and
how difficult it is to "see" the sun. From radiation (paragraphs 19–20), Clarke moves to sunspots (paragraph 21),
flares (paragraph 22), and sporadic eruptions (paragraphs
23–25), defining these terms with descriptions that the
non-scientist can absorb. "Fountains of flame" and "bridges
of fire" mean more to the general reader than "quadrillions
of cubic miles of space."

Note that Clarke does *not* expect us to ask him for
charts and calculations. He could supply them, doubtlessly,
but this analytical essay is not the place to impress the
reader with figures. When he does use them, it is only to
emphasize a comparison: "We would have to explode
10,000,000,000 H-bombs *every second* if we wanted to
equal the energy output of the sun." We are impressed,
of course, but no more than by his description of how "a
slanting jet of incandescent gas, for example, will shoot
out on a long, flat trajectory, reach its apex, *and then
whip back along its original path*—just as if a shell at the
peak of its flight decided to return to the gun." Clarke's

analogies: See Glossary.

method is a combination of graphic description, simple analogies, elaboration, and concise definitions. Had he had more space, he might have posited more complex theories. As the essay stands, it is a simple analysis, an introduction to the subject, just what Clarke intended.

Questions on Content

1. How does the spectroscope aid in determining the composition of the sun?
2. How large is the sun and how far is it from the earth?
3. What evidence did the geologists accumulate about the earth's age?
4. Why has "no man ever seen the sun or ever will"?
5. What do motion picture films tell us about the sun?
6. How do scientists explain the "flatness" of the sun's surface, considering that it is purely gaseous?
7. What does Clarke say about the future of the sun's energy? Will it burn out?

Add to Your Vocabulary

erudite, scintillating, cataclysmic, inexplicable, incandescent, sporadic.

Questions on Technique

1. How effective is Clarke's opening paragraph? Does he arouse your interest or curiosity with his question?
2. Clarke uses memorable comparisons throughout this essay. In paragraph 7, for example, he compares the energy we receive from the sun with a "one-kilowatt electric heater on *every square yard* of our planet's surface." How effective are his other comparisons in paragraphs 6, 16, 17, 24, and 29?
3. How does Clarke explain (paragraph 19) why "no man has ever seen the sun or ever will"? What complications (paragraphs 20–23) does he encounter in explaining this phenomenon? Could he have made these paragraphs simpler by eliminating any of the details?
4. What part do statistics play in Clarke's prose? Would

you want him to use more figures or diagrams and a less descriptive prose? Why?

Techniques to Imitate

1. *Using the startling fact to arouse interest*
2. *Explaining difficult concepts in "everyday" terms*

1. Purely informational writing, which is necessarily full of facts, can make dull reading. One of Clarke's virtues is that he makes his reports exciting, and one way he does this is by recognizing the high interest value of the startling fact. Since few people have ever thought of the sun as a star, the fact that it is a star is startling, and Clarke makes effective use of this information to arouse the reader's interest at the very beginning of his article. He uses this technique again and again. "It is the sun's extreme closeness—a trifling 93,000,000 miles —that makes it so overwhelmingly important to us," he says, perhaps with tongue in cheek. "The total waste [of the sun's energy], if you like round figures, is approximately half a million, million, million, million horsepower." "No man has ever seen the sun or ever will." "The sun is not cooling down; it is warming up."

2. In addition to interspersing his factual account with the most startling facts and figures, Clarke displays also the ability to express such facts in "everyday" terms, terms that help the average reader to comprehend better. "Today," he says, "because of the spectroscope, we know more about the composition of stars trillions of miles away than of the earth beneath our feet." He refers to a "one-kilowatt electric heater on every square yard of our planet's surface." Compared to ordinary combustion, the burning that takes place in the sun is "like the flame of a blowtorch compared to the pale glow of a firefly." "On the sun a 160-pound man would weigh almost two tons." "So like a gambler who bets more and more frantically as he approaches the end of his resources, the sun will go out in a final blaze of glory."

Two techniques Clarke teaches us to use in our informational writing: (1) recognize the value of the startling fact as a means of arousing and holding your reader's interest; (2) try to make difficult concepts understandable by expressing them in "everyday" terms that the average reader can understand.

Suggestions for Writing

1. Select an activity, a phenomenon, or a mechanism that you are very familiar with and in about 600 words explain it by comparing it (or parts of it) to common, everyday processes or objects. Your goal will be to make the activity, phenomenon, or mechanism understandable to someone who has had no experience with it. You might choose from the following: the workings of a computer, the making of batiks, sailing a boat or flying a plane, the effects of advertising, snow.

2. Using the resources of a library, gather some facts about one of the areas of twentieth-century technology or culture that has grown up or changed rapidly. Examples are the art of filmmaking, air travel, telecommunications, mass higher education. In an essay of about 500 words, summarize the history of the area you choose, paying particular attention to startling facts that will hold your reader's attention. An alternative report might be on the history of your neighborhood or school. You might interview some people to find the information you need for such a report. Again, look for and highlight startling facts.

3. Clarke says, "It is unwise to set limits to knowledge and discovery, . . ." This remark can apply to each of us on a personal level. In a 500-word essay, analyze how you came to acquire some knowledge or skill that at one time you might have thought beyond your reach. Involve your readers directly by making it clear that you're going to share your discovery with them. Use as much detail as possible.

ALEX HALEY

Search for an Ancestor

There is no need to provide background information on Alex Haley, although you might like to know that he assisted Malcolm X in writing his autobiography. No information is necessary because "Alex Haley" is what this remarkable report is all about.

1　　　　　　　　　　**I** grew up in a little town called Henning, Tennessee, about fifty miles west of Memphis, and I lived there in the home of my grandmother, my mother's mother. Every summer my grandmother would have visitors come to our home. They would be older women of the family, her nieces, aunts and cousins, and every single evening that I can remember, they would sit out on the front porch in rocking-chairs, and I would sit behind my grandmother's rocking-chair and listen to them talking. They would tell about things that had happened to the family when they had been slaves, and they went back and back and back. The furthest-back person they would ever talk about was someone they described as "the African," and they would tell how this African had been brought on a ship to a place they pronounced as "Napalis." They told how he had been bought off that ship by a man whose name was John Waller, who had a plantation in a

place called Spotsylvania County, Virginia, and they told
how the African had kept trying to escape. The first three
times he escaped he was caught, brought back, given a
worse beating each time, and then, the fourth time he
escaped, he had the misfortune to be caught by a professional slave-catcher. . . .

[As punishment, the man had his foot chopped off.]

. . . When this particular slave managed to survive and
then to convalesce, he posed an economic question to his
master: slavery, after all, was an economic matter. Although he was crippled and hobbled around, he could do
limited work around the house and yard area of the plantation, so the master decided he would be worth more
kept to do this limited work than he would be just sold
away for less than one dollar in cash. And so he was kept
on one plantation for what turned out to be quite a long
period of time.

2   On that plantation, this slave met another slave. My
grandmother and the others said that she was named Belle,
the Big House cook, and of that union was born a little
girl, who was given the name Kissy. When Kissy got to be
four or five, and could begin to understand things, this
African, whenever he got a chance, would take her by the
hand (he knew her to be his daughter, she knew him to
be her father—an unusual thing in slavery at that point)
and lead her round the plantation. He would point out to
her various natural objects and tell her the names for them
in his native tongue: some sounds for *tree, rock, cow.* In
the slave-cabin area, he would point out a banjo or a
guitar and he would say one syllable, *ko,* and in time the
little girl came to associate the sound *ko* with a banjo or a
guitar. On the outer edges of the plantation there was a
small river, and when they were out in that area, he would
say to her something like *Kamby-Bolongo,* and the little
girl came to know that this sound meant river.

3   All the Africans who were brought to the United States
as slaves gradually learned a word here, a phrase there, of
the new language, English. As this began to happen with

this particular African, he would tell his daughter more involved things, little anecdotes about himself. He seemed to have a passion for trying to communicate to her a sense of his past. For instance, he would tell her how he had been captured. He told her he had not been far away from his village, chopping wood, when he had been set upon by four men, kidnapped, and taken into slavery. The first thing that happened to slaves when they got to a plantation was that they were given an Anglicized name: that was the first step in the psychic dehumanization of an individual—the removal from that individual of the name he had carried all his life, with which went, as it goes for us today, the sense of who we are. The master had given this African the name of "Toby" but, whenever any of the other slaves used the word "Toby," he would strenuously reject it and tell them his name was Kin-Tay.

4 Kissy stayed directly exposed to her father from Africa until she was sixteen years old. She had quite a considerable repertoire of knowledge about him, when she herself was sold away to a man named Tom Lea who had a much smaller plantation in North Carolina. It was on that plantation that Tom Lea became the father of Kissy's first child, a boy who was given the name of George. When George got to be about four or five, Kissy began to tell him the things she had learned from her father. Among the other slave children, his peers, he began to run into the common phenomenon that slave children rarely knew who their fathers were. He had something that made him singular: he had direct knowledge of a grandfather. The boy grew up and, when he got into his teens, became a gamecock fighter: that was a great sport in the Antebellum South. When he was about seventeen, he gained the nickname that he would take to his grave—"Chicken George."

5 When he was about eighteen, Chicken George met another slave, whose name was Matilda, and in time Matilda gave birth to seven children. On another plantation, a generation later, in another section of North Carolina, Chicken George would tell his children the story which had come down from his mother Kissy. Those children grew up and had children. One of them was named Tom. He became an apprentice blacksmith and was sold to a man named Murray who had a tobacco plantation in Alamance County, North Carolina. He met a slave whose name was Irene, the weaver on the plantation, and she bore him seven children. Tom the blacksmith would tell his seven children about something virtually unique among the slaves: direct knowledge of a great-great-grandfather. The youngest of his seven children was a little girl whose name was Cynthia, and Cynthia was to become my maternal grandmother. That was how it happened that I grew up in my grandmother's home in Tennessee, hearing from her that story which had passed down the family about all the rest of the family going back to that African who said his name was Kin-Tay, who called the river *Kamby-Bolongo,* and the guitar *ko,* and who said he had been chopping wood when he was captured. By the time I was in my mid-teens, I knew this story pretty well, having heard it for fully a decade.

6   I went to school briefly at small Black land-grant colleges around the South where my father was teaching, and when World War II came along I went into the U.S. Coast Guard. It was the time when if you were Black and you went into one of the Naval Services in the United States, you went into the Stewards' Department. You were messboy, you cleaned up the state rooms, waited on tables, washed the dishes, and, if you did well, advanced to cook. I became cook on a ship in the southwest Pacific during the war. It was boring. We would be put to sea for two or three months at a time before we would get ashore in Australia or New Zealand. My most precious possession was a portable typewriter. I had learned to type when I was in high school, and I would write letters to everybody I could think of: I would get thirty or forty letters at a time, simply because I wrote so much. Then I began trying to write marine dramas, sea stories. They didn't sell for a long time, but I kept writing for eight years, until finally a small magazine began to buy some of my stories. I stayed on in the Service, began to write for somewhat larger mag-

azines, and finally, when I was thirty-seven, I retired from the Coast Guard with twenty years service. At that time, something happened that seems to me to have been the first of a series of miracles that were to make it possible to pull together a document, a book ° of which I am now at the finishing stages, having to do in an unusual way with Black history, Black culture, Black pride, relating to the whole area of Blackness in Africa and the United States and the continuities.

7 The first thing that happened could scarcely have seemed to have less to do with Blackness. *Playboy* asked me if I would fly over to London to do an interview with a film actress, Julie Christie. There were long gaps when I couldn't get to see her. One morning I was in the British Museum, and I came upon the Rosetta Stone. I had read how the French scholar, Champollion, had matched the unknown characters on the stone with the Greek, and had finally been able to prove that the demotic ° and the hieroglyphics had the same text as the Greek. That fascinated me: I would go round in London doing other things, but I would find my mind going back to that Rosetta Stone.

8 I was on a plane going back to the United States when an idea hit me. What Jean Champollion really did was to match the unknown with the known, and so find the meaning of what hitherto had been unknown. In that story always told in our family there had been a language: the sounds that this African always said when he pointed to different objects. Obviously, many sounds would have been lost in the transmission down the generations, but I could see that the sounds which had survived tended to be hard, angular sounds of the sort that would survive: like *ko, Kin-Tay, Kamby-Bolongo*. They had to be fragments of some native tongue. Could I possibly find out where these sounds had come from? My research assistant, George Simms, came up with a list of people who were very knowledgeable in the field of African linguistics. One of them

book: Haley's book, *Roots,* was published in 1976 by Doubleday.
demotic: a simplified or colloquial form of a language; here, of ancient Egyptian.

was at the University of Wisconsin. His name was Doctor Jan Vansina. He had been trained in his native Belgium, and then at the University of London's Oriental and African Studies department. He had worked in Africa, living in African villages, and had written a book called *The Oral Tradition*. In the Vansinas' living room that evening, I told Dr. Vansina everything I could remember from the time I was a little boy: every bit of the stories, the sounds, the names of the people, the chronology of the family. As an oral historian, he was particularly interested in the physical transmission of the story from one generation to another. The following morning, Dr. Vansina came down with a very serious expression on his face. I learned that he had already been on the phone to knowledgeable colleagues of his. He said that they felt that the greatest possibility was that the sounds represented the Mandinka dialect. I had never heard of such a thing as Mandinka. From his knowledge of it, he began to guess-translate what those sounds had meant. There was a sound that probably meant the *baobab tree,* generic * in West Africa; there was a sound that probably meant *cow*. I heard about something that could be said to look like a banjo, an instrument called the *kora,* well-known where Mandinka was spoken. Finally, we came to *Kamby-Bolongo*: I heard that in Mandinka *bolongo* would mean *river* or *stream.* Preceded by *Kamby,* very probably it would mean *Gambia River*. I tend to be, if something hits me just right, very impulsive. It was Thursday morning when I heard the words *Gambia River*. On Monday morning I was in Africa. 9   On the Friday morning, I had looked among the names of African students in the United States. From that small country, the Gambia, the one I found who was physically closest to where I was was a fellow called Ebon Manga, attending Hamilton College at Clinton, New York. I hit that campus around 3:30, Friday afternoon, and practically snatched Ebon Manga out of an economics class. We got onto a Pan American that night and flew to Dakar. From there we got a light plane and flew over to Yanda, near Bathurst. We took a van into Bathurst. Ebon and his father helped to assemble a group of about eight members of the Gambian Government, mature men who met me in the patio of the Hotel Atlantic in Bathurst. There I sat with them, telling them the stories that had been passed down. It gives me the quivers sometimes when I reflect how tissue-thin have been the hinges upon which this whole adventure has swung at one time or another. What these men in the Gambia reacted to most was a sound which I had no idea had any particular meaning. They said: "There may be great significance in the fact that your fore-father said his name was Kin-Tay. In our country, our older villages are often named from the families which founded those villages centuries ago." And they showed me a little map, with names of villages like Kinte-Kundah Janneh-Ya. They also told me about men of whom I had never heard called *griots,* who were like walking, living archives. A line of *griots* would know the history of one village, they told me, or of one large family clan. They told me that they would look about to see what *griot* might be able to help me.

10 I went back to the United States. About six weeks later, a letter came to me from the Gambia saying that when I was able it might be worthwhile for me to return— as casually as that. In about a week I was back in Bathurst. The same men with whom I had talked at the Atlantic Hotel told me that the word had been put out in the back-country, and a *griot* knowledgeable about the history of the Kinte clan had been found. "Where is he?" I asked. I would have figured, from my experience as an American magazine writer, that the Government should have had him there with a public relations man for me to talk to. They said: "He's in his village." In order to see this man, I had to get together a total of fourteen people, three of whom were interpreters, and four musicians—they told me that, in the back-country, the *griots* wouldn't talk without music in the background.

11 Mud walls, conical-roofed huts, thatched roofs: there were only about seventy people in the village. As soon as I saw a man, I knew somehow that he was the man we had come to see. Small of build with a pillbox hat and off-white robe: I was later to learn that his name was Kebba Kanga Fofana. The interpreter with me went straight to him. Meanwhile I had stepped into a succession of events that were almost traumatic in their emotional effect upon me. First, the people, about seventy of them, crowded very closely around me. I began to notice how they were staring at me. Their brows were forward and the intensity of the eyes was just raking. It was as if they wanted to know me in corpuscular ° detail. I dropped my eyes: I had this sensation of looking at my own hands, my own complexion, and I had a tremendous feeling within me, like a gale-force wind. I was looking at a crowd of people and, for the first time in my life, everybody in the crowd was jet-black in color. That just hit me like a sledgehammer. And then, I had this second sledgehammer-type feeling: a kind of guilt, a feeling of being hybrid, of being impure among pure. Then the old man, Kebba Kanga Fofana, began to tell me, through the interpreters, the history of the Kinte clan.

12 *Griots* can talk for hours on end, telling the stories they have learned. Every now and then when the *griot* was spilling out lineage details of who married whom, who had what children and in what order, a couple of centuries ago, he would stop: a translation would come of some little detail about an individual—for example, that in the year of the Big Water he slew a water buffalo. Kebba Kanga Fofana said that the Kinte clan had begun in the country called Old Mali, and a branch of the clan had moved into Mauretania. In Old Mali, the clan had been characterized by the men being blacksmiths as a rule; the women were habitually potters and weavers. There had come out of Mauretania a son of the clan whose name was Kairaba Kunta Kinte. He came from Mauretania to the country of the Gambia. He stopped first in a village called Pakali N'Ding. He went next to a village called Jiffarong,

corpuscular: cellular (a corpuscle is a cell or a minute particle of the body).

and then to a village called Juffure. It was in Juffure that he took his first wife, a Mandinka maiden whose name was Sireng. By her he begot two sons whose names were Janneh and Saloum. Then he took (Moslem men, plural marriages) a second wife. Her name was Yaisa, and by Yaisa he begot a son whose name was Omoro.

13 The three sons grew up in the village of Juffure, and when they came of age the older two, Janneh and Saloum, went away and founded a new village called to this day Kinte-Kundah Janneh-Ya. The youngest son, Omoro, stayed there until he had thirty-nine rains; and at the age of thirty rains he took a wife whose name was Binta Kebba. Between 1750 and 1760, there were born four sons to Omoro and Binta Kebba: Kunta, Lamin, Suwadu and Madi. When he named those four brothers, the old man stopped and the interpreter said: "about the time the King's soldiers came." That was one of the time-fixing references which *griots* use. Later, in London, I found the British Parliamentary records, because I had to know the date. He was talking about a group called Colonel O'Hare's Forces, which had been sent from London to the Gambia River to guard the then-British-held fort, James Slave Fort, and the date was right on.

14 Then Kebba Kanga Fofana said: "About the time the King's soldier came, the eldest of these four sons, Kunta, went away from this village to chop wood, and he was never seen again." I sat there with goose pimples the size of lemons popping over me. He had no way of knowing that what he had told me meshed with what I had heard as a little boy on the front porch of my grandmother's home in Tennessee.

15 I suddenly became aware that the people of the village had formed a circle and were moving counterclockwise around me. They were chanting: up, down, loud, soft. I had been sitting on a chair, and I popped up as if I had been full of helium. All I could do was stand up. Then there came the music that was always in the background. I remember my ears slowly becoming aware that I was hearing sounds I had to recognize from a *kora* player, who was singing. I was hearing in a way I could understand. I could distinguish the words "Alex Haley." I could understand Kinte. I didn't know then that, in the way of *griots,* my having come to that village, my having been found to be a descendant of that village, was there and then being recorded as part of the village's history. They carried me into the mosque, and there was a prayer. It was translated as: "Praise be to Allah for one lost long from us whom God has returned."

16 We finally had to go back. I had to return to America and, on the road going out, I was full of the emotion of it. We got to the first village, and I saw people lined up on either side of the road. The people in this village already knew what had happened in the village of Juffure. As we came close with the Land Rover, the driver slowed down, and I was looking down at these people standing on either side waving, a great cacophony * of sound coming out of them, from wizened elders to little naked youngsters. I thought it was nothing but caprice: they were there, never having left Africa, and I, symbolizing to them all of us in America, happened to be standing up in there simply because of the caprice—which of our forefathers had been taken out. That was the only thing which had made the difference. Then I gradually became aware what the sound was they were crying out: "Mr. Kin-Tay, Mr. Kin-Tay." I'm a man, but a sob rolled up from foot level, and I just flung up my hands and cried as I never had in my life. It seemed to me that if you knew the story of how the Black people in America had come there, taken as slaves from all those countries, and you knew the continuity of us as a people, then, whatever else you might do, you really needed to start by weeping, because there were no words and no actions which could ever assuage what had happened in that terrible time in the history of both countries.

17 That's the saga of the Black people in America, and I had to write it. I had to know everything I could to put into this book. I wanted to find, if I could, the symbolic boat that, it is said, brought 1,500,000 of our forefathers to the U.S.A. To be the proper ship, it had to be the one that brought Kunta-Kinte out of the Gambia River. I knew now about the time "the King's soldiers had come," and I had found that Colonel O'Hare's Forces were his reference. I knew that it had happened in mid-1767. I went to Lloyds of London and I got help from them with the marine records of the 1700's. I searched for seven weeks. One afternoon in the Public Records Office, I was on the 123rd set of slave-ship records when I found a sheet with thirty ships' movements on it. Number 18 was moving out of Gambia River, James Fort. Number 18 was a ship that had stated her destination as Annapolis, Maryland. I knew that Kunta-Kinte had been taken to Annapolis.

18 In the next ten days I crossed the Atlantic Ocean three times, patching together little things I had to find out about that ship. I found she was called the *Lord Ligonier,* named after a British field marshal. She had been built in 1765 in the New England colonies. She set sail in 1766, with a cargo of rum, as a new slave ship to Gravesend. There she sold the rum. The profits were used to buy a cargo, the slaving hardware—the chains, the shackles, the other restraining objects to put on the extra crew—and the extra foodstuffs she would need, and she started sailing to Africa, to the source of what was called the "black gold" of Africa. I was able to follow the ship from the records along the Channel, and it became almost like running along the Channel, watching her. I knew her timbers, I knew her planking was loblolly pine and hackmatack cedar. I knew she had red oak timbers. I knew that the flax in her sails was out of New Jersey. I knew the kind of nails that held her together, how the black lopes were held together with a wedge of oak: I could almost read the captain's mind as he was driving to get to the African coast.

19 She went southerly across the Bay of Biscay, down past the Canaries, the Cape Virgins, into the mouth of the Gambia River. She was to spend the next ten months in the Gambia River, slaving. In the course of that ten months she got a cargo of 3,265 elephant tusks, 3,700 pounds of beeswax, 800 pounds of rough raw Gambian cotton, 32 ounces of Gambian gold and 140 slaves. She set sail on Sunday, July 5, 1767, headed directly for Annapolis. Her crossing voyage of about 5,000 miles took two months, three weeks and two days. She arrived in Annapolis, Maryland, on the morning of September 29, 1767.

20 September 29, 1967: I was standing on a pier in Annapolis looking seaward, drenched in tears. It was two hundred years to the day since my forebear had come to that city, and there in Annapolis I went into the tax records to find out what she had come in with. I found she came in with a cargo. She declared the same cargo she had leaving James Fort, Gambia River, except that her original 140 slaves had become 98. Forty-two had died on the crossing, which was about average for the ships making that trip in that period. I knew that when slaves were brought in they were always advertised, and I went down to the microfilm records of the Annapolis media of the time, the *Maryland Gazette,* and in the issue of October 1, 1767, on page three, was the ad of the agents of the ship, saying that the *Lord Ligonier* had just arrived under Captain Davies from the River Gambia, with a cargo of fresh choice, healthy slaves for sale, to be sold the following Wednesday at Meg's Wharf. Among them was Kunta-Kinte, who had come from the village of Juffure.

21 One thing remained to complete it. I knew that my grandmother and the others had always said that he had been named Toby by his master, and I knew that every kind of deal involving slaves was a matter of legal records. I went to Richmond, Virginia, and went into the legal deeds of the transactions of the 1760's. I found a deed dated September 5, 1768, between two brothers, John and William Waller, transferring goods between them: on the second page were the words "and also one Negro man slave, named Toby."

Questions on Content

1. What two major clues helped Haley locate his furthest-back ancestor's native country?
2. Describe three of the "tissue-thin hinges," besides the two major clues, upon which this adventure swung.
3. Haley says twice in this report that he wept. What realizations brought on this strong emotion?

Add to Your Vocabulary

generic, cacophony.

Questions on Technique

1. Haley uses almost straightforward chronology in making his report. What is the effect of this technique?
2. How would the effect have differed if Haley had opened with a statement of the "problem" (now in paragraph 8), or with the detailed story of Kinte's background, of how he was captured and brought to America (the material now in paragraphs 12–14)?
3. Haley includes several descriptions of personal reactions to his findings in this otherwise straightforward report (see paragraphs 8, 9, 11, 14, 16, 20). What is their effect on this report?

Techniques to Imitate

The plain style for straightforward reporting

Students sometimes get the impression from their study of literature that good writing is fancy writing: big words, rhetorical flourishes, elaborate description, complex sentences. As your study of writing techniques has shown, good writers do often write that way. But not always. Haley's account of how he searched for an ancestor is a good example of the plain style, which is ideal for straight factual reporting.

Haley has an involved, complicated story to tell, and he wants to give all the facts necessary to make it clear. He tells it straight out, as though he were talking to us face to face. Sentences tend to be simple or compound. Many of them are short. Only at a few highly emotional moments near the end does he change from the plain style.

The first paragraph of the report is an excellent example of this plain style. Haley tells us: "I grew up in a little town called . . . I lived there in the home of . . . my grandmother would have visitors . . . they would be older women . . . they would sit on the front porch . . . I would sit behind my grandmother's chair . . . they would tell . . . they went back and back . . . the furthest-back person was . . ."

When you are reporting a series of related incidents, which is what Haley is doing, your first obligation is to be clear. Know what you want to say. Many techniques are then open to you, but you will be doing well if you can reproduce the straightforward, plain style used here so effectively by Haley.

Suggestions for Writing

1. Write a report telling as much as you know about a family's history, your own or someone's else's. Go backward—in reverse chronological order. Start with yourself, or with people of a family living today, and then go back to the previous generation, and so on. Tell where you are in time, as Haley does, so your readers can follow clearly.

2. Write a report about a series of events that you are very familiar with (how someone spends a typical day, what people do on Saturdays where you live, how someone came to be born where he or she was born, how you solved a mystery). Report on these events in a straightforward style.

3. Watch a film or TV show carefully. Take notes if possible. Then write a report telling what happened, in chronological order. Use a straightforward, plain style.

LOREN C. EISELEY

The Bird and the Machine

Loren Eiseley is by training an anthropologist and by inclination a poet and philosopher. He has written many books about expeditions "into the earth" in search of its secrets. This essay comes from *The Immense Journey*.

1   **I** suppose their little bones have years ago been lost among the stones and winds of those high glacial pastures. I suppose their feathers blew eventually into the piles of tumbleweed beneath the straggling cattle fences and rotted there in the mountain snows, along with dead steers and all the other things that drift to an end in the corners of the wire. I do not quite know why I should be thinking of birds over the *New York Times* at breakfast, particularly of the birds of my youth half a continent away. It is a funny thing what the brain will do with memories and how it will treasure them and finally bring them into odd juxtapositions * with other things, as though it wanted to make a design, or get some meaning out of them, whether you want it or not, or even see it.

2 It used to seem marvelous to me, but I read now that there are machines that can do these things in a small way, machines that can crawl about like animals, and that it may not be long now until they do more things— maybe even make themselves—I saw that piece in the *Times* just now and then they will, maybe—well, who knows—but you read about it more and more with no one making any protest, and already they can add better

297

than we and reach up and hear things through the dark
and finger the guns over the night sky.

3   This is the new world that I read about at breakfast.
This is the world that confronts me in my biological books
and journals, until there are times when I sit quietly in
my chair and try to hear the little purr of the cogs in my
head and the tubes flaring and dying as the messages go
through them and the circuits snap shut or open. This is
the great age, make no mistake about it; the robot has
been born somewhat appropriately along with the atom
bomb, and the brain they say now is just another type of
more complicated feedback system. The engineers have
its basic principles worked out; it's mechanical, you know;
nothing to get superstitious about; and man can always
improve on nature once he gets the idea. Well, he's got it
all right and that's why, I guess, that I sit here in my chair,
with the article crunched in my hand, remembering those
two birds and that blue mountain sunlight. There is another
magazine article on my desk that reads "Machines Are
Getting Smarter Every Day." I don't deny it, but I'll still
stick with the birds. It's life I believe in, not machines.

4   Maybe you don't believe there is any difference. A
skeleton is all joints and pulleys, I'll admit. And when man
was in his simpler stages of machine building in the eight-
eenth century, he quickly saw the resemblances. "What,"
wrote Hobbes,° "is the heart but a spring, and the nerves
so many strings, and the joints but so many wheels, giving
motion to the whole body?" Tinkering about in their shops
it was inevitable in the end that men would see the world
as a huge machine "subdivided into an infinite number of
lesser machines."

5   The idea took on with a vengeance. Little automatons
toured the country—dolls controlled by clockwork. Clocks
described as little worlds were taken on tours by their designers. They were made up of moving figures, shifting
scenes, and other remarkable devices. The life of the cell
was unknown. Man, whether he was conceived as possessing a soul or not, moved and jerked about like these

Hobbes: Thomas Hobbes (1588–1679), British philosopher.

tiny puppets. A human being thought of himself in terms of his own tools and implements. He had been fashioned like the puppets he produced and was only a more clever model made by a greater designer.

6   Then in the nineteenth century, the cell was discovered, and the single machine in its turn was found to be the product of millions of infinitesimal machines—the cells. Now, finally, the cell itself dissolves away into an abstract chemical machine—and that into some intangible, inexpressible flow of energy. The secret seems to lurk all about, the wheels get smaller and smaller, and they turn more rapidly, but when you try to seize it the life is gone—and so, by popular definition, some would say that life was never there in the first place. The wheels and the cogs are the secret and we can make them better in time—machines that will run faster and more accurately than real mice to real cheese.

7   I have no doubt it can be done, though a mouse harvesting seeds on an autumn thistle is to me a fine sight and more complicated, I think, in his multiform activity, than a machine "mouse" running a maze. Also, I like to think of the possible shape of the future brooding in mice, just as it brooded once in a rather ordinary mousy insectivore ° who became a man. It leaves a nice fine indeterminate sense of wonder that even an electronic brain hasn't got, because you know perfectly well that if the electronic brain changes it will be because of something man has done to it. But what man will do to himself he doesn't really know. A certain scale of time and a ghostly intangible thing called change are ticking in him. Powers and potentialities like the oak in the seed, or a red and awful ruin. Either way, it's impressive; and the mouse has it, too. Or those birds, I'll never forget those birds—yet before I measured their significance, I learned the lesson of time first of all. I was young then and left alone in a great desert—part of an expedition that had scattered its men over several hundred miles in order to carry on research more effectively. I learned there that time is a

insectivore: any animal or plant that feeds on insects.

series of planes existing superficially in the same universe. The tempo is a human illusion, a subjective clock ticking in our kind of protoplasm.

8 As the long months passed, I began to live on the slower planes and to observe more readily what passed for life there. I sauntered, I passed more and more slowly up and down the canyons in the dry baking heat of mid-summer. I slumbered for long hours in the shade of huge brown boulders that had gathered in tilted companies out on the flats. I had forgotten the world of men and the world had forgotten me. Now and then I found a skull in the canyons, and those justified my remaining there. I took a serene cold interest in these discoveries. I had come, like many a naturalist before me, to view life with a wary and subdued attention. I had grown to take pleasure in the divested * bone.

9 I sat once on a high ridge that fell away before me into a waste of sand dunes. I sat through hours of a long afternoon. Finally, as I glanced beside my boot an indistinct configuration caught my eye. It was a coiled rattlesnake, a big one. How long he had sat with me I do not know. I had not frightened him. We were both locked in the sleep-walking tempo of the earlier world, baking in the same high air and sunshine. Perhaps he had been there when I came. He slept on as I left, his coils, so ill discerned by me, dissolving once more among the stones and gravel from which I had barely made him out.

10 Another time I got on a higher ridge, among some tough little wind-warped pines half covered over with sand in a basin-like depression that caught everything carried by the air up to those heights. There were a few thin bones of birds, some cracked shells of indeterminable age, and the knotty fingers of pine roots bulged out of shape from their long and agonizing grasp upon the crevices of the rock. I lay under the pines in the sparse shade and went to sleep once more.

11 It grew cold finally, for autumn was in the air by then, and the few things that lived thereabouts were sinking down into an even chillier scale of time. In the moments between sleeping and waking I saw the roots about me and slowly, slowly, a foot in what seemed many centuries, I moved by sleep-stiffened hands over the scaling bark and lifted my numbed face after the vanishing sun. I was a great awkward thing of knots and aching limbs, trapped up there in some long, patient endurance that involved the necessity of putting living fingers into rock and by slow, aching expansion bursting those rocks asunder. I suppose, so thin and slow was the time of my pulse by then, that I might have stayed on to drift still deeper into the lower cadences of the frost, or the crystalline life that glisters in pebbles or shines in a snow flake, or dreams in the meteoric iron between the worlds.

12 It was a dim descent, but time was present in it. Somewhere far down in that scale the notion struck me that one might come the other way. Not many months thereafter I joined some colleagues heading higher into a remote windy tableland where huge bones were reputed to protrude like boulders from the turf. I had drowsed with reptiles and moved with the century-long pulse of trees; now, lethargically, I was climbing back up some invisible ladder of quickening hours. There had been talk of birds in connection with my duties. Birds are intense, fast-living creatures—reptiles, I suppose one might say, that have escaped out of the heavy sleep of time, transformed fairy creatures dancing over sunlit meadows. It is a youthful fancy, no doubt, but because of something that happened up there among the escarpments * of that range, it remains with me a life-long impression. I can never bear to see a bird imprisoned.

13 We came into that valley through the trailing mists of a spring night. It was a place that looked as though it might never have known the foot of man, but our scouts had been ahead of us and we knew all about the abandoned cabin of stone that lay far up on one hillside. It had been built in the land rush of the last century and then lost to the cattlemen again as the marginal soils failed to take to the plow.

14 There were spots like this all over that country. Lost

graves marked by unlettered stones and old corroding rim-fire cartridge cases lying where somebody had made a stand among the boulders that rimmed the valley. They are all that remain of the range wars; the men are under the stones now. I could see our cavalcade winding in and out through the mist below us: torches, the reflection of the truck lights on our collecting tins, and the far-off bumping of a loose dinosaur thigh bone in the bottom of a trailer. I stood on a rock a moment looking down and thinking what it cost in money and equipment to capture the past.

15   We had, in addition, instructions to lay hands on the present. The word had come through to get them alive—birds, reptiles, anything. A zoo somewhere abroad needed restocking. It was one of those reciprocal * matters in which science involves itself. Maybe our museum needed a stray ostrich egg and this was the payoff. Anyhow, my job was to help capture some birds and that was why I was there before the trucks.

16   The cabin had not been occupied for years. We intended to clean it out and live in it, but there were holes in the roof and the birds had come in and were roosting in the rafters. You could depend on it in a place like this where everything blew away and even a bird needed some place out of the weather and away from coyotes. A cabin going back to nature in a wild place draws them till they come in, listening at the eaves, I imagine, pecking softly among the shingles till they find a hole and then suddenly the place is theirs and man is forgotten.

17   Sometimes of late years I find myself thinking the most beautiful sight in the world might be the birds taking over New York after the last man has run away to the hills. I will never live to see it, of course, but I know just how it will sound because I've lived up high and I know the sort of watch birds keep on us. I've listened to sparrows tapping tentatively on the outside of air conditioners when they thought no one was listening, and I know how other birds test the vibrations that come up to them through the television aerials.

18 "Is he gone?" they ask, and the vibrations come up from below, "Not yet, not yet."

19 Well, to come back, I got the door open softly and I had the spotlight all ready to turn on and blind whatever birds there were so they couldn't see to get out through the roof. I had a short piece of ladder to put against the far wall where there was a shelf on which I expected to make the biggest haul. I had all the information I needed just like any skilled assassin. I pushed the door open, the hinges squeaking only a little. A bird or two stirred—I could hear them—but nothing flew and there was a faint starlight through the hole in the roof.

20 I padded across the floor, got the ladder up, and the light ready, and slithered up the ladder till my head and arms were over the shelf. Everything was dark as pitch except for the starlight at a little place back of the shelf near the eaves. With the light to blind them, they'd never make it. I had them. I reached my arm carefully over in order to be ready to seize whatever was there and I put the flash on the edge of the shelf where it would stand by itself when I turned it on. That way I'd be able to use both hands.

21 Everything worked perfectly except for one detail—I didn't know what kind of birds were there. I never thought about it at all and it wouldn't have mattered if I had. My orders were to get something interesting. I snapped on the flash and sure enough there was a great beating and feathers flying, but instead of my having them, they, or rather he, had me. He had my hand, that is, and for a small hawk not much bigger than my fist he was doing all right. I heard him give one short metallic cry when the light went on and my hand descended on the bird beside him; after that he was busy with his claws and his beak was sunk in my thumb. In the struggle I knocked the lamp over on the shelf and his mate got her sight back and whisked neatly through the hole in the roof and off among the stars outside. It all happened in fifteen seconds and you might think I would have fallen down the ladder, but no, I had a professional assassin's reputation to keep up, and the bird, of course, made the mistake of thinking the hand was the enemy and not the eyes behind it. He chewed my thumb up pretty effectively and lacerated my hand with his claws, but in the end I got him, having two hands to work with.

22   He was a sparrow hawk and a fine young male in the prime of life. I was sorry not to catch the pair of them, but as I dripped blood and folded his wings carefully, holding him by the back so that he couldn't strike again, I had to admit the two of them might have been more than I could have handled under the circumstances. The little fellow had saved his mate by diverting me, and that was that. He was born into it, and made no outcry now, resting in my hand hopelessly, but peering toward me in the shadows behind the lamp with a fierce, almost indifferent glance. He neither gave nor expected mercy and something out of the high air passed from him to me, stirring a faint embarrassment.

23   I quit looking into that eye and managed to get my huge carcass with its fist full of prey back down the ladder. I put the bird in a box too small to allow him to injure himself by struggle and walked out to welcome the arriving trucks. It had been a long day, and camp was still to make in the darkness. In the morning that bird would be just another episode. He would go back with the bones in the truck to a small cage in a city where he would spend the rest of his life. And a good thing, too. I sucked my aching thumb and spat out some blood. An assassin has to get used to these things. I had a professional reputation to keep up.

24   In the morning, with the change that comes on suddenly in that high country, the mist that had hovered below us in the valley was gone. The sky was a deep blue, and one could see for miles over the high outcroppings of stone. I was up early and brought the box in which the little hawk was imprisoned out onto the grass where I was building a cage. A wind as cool as a mountain spring ran over the grass and stirred my hair. It was a fine day to be alive. I looked up and all around and at the hole in the cabin roof

out of which the other little hawk had fled. There was no sign of her anywhere that I could see.

25   "Probably in the next county by now," I thought cynically, but before beginning work I decided I'd have a look at my last night's capture.

26   Secretively, I looked again all around the camp and up and down and opened the box. I got him right out in my hand with his wings folded properly and I was careful not to startle him. He lay limp in my grasp and I could feel his heart pound under the feathers but he only looked beyond me and up.

27   I saw him look that last look away beyond me into a sky so full of light that I could not follow his gaze. The little breeze flowed over me again, and nearby a mountain aspen shook all its tiny leaves. I suppose I must have had an idea then of what I was going to do, but I never let it come up into consciousness. I just reached over and laid the hawk on the grass.

28   He lay there a long minute without hope, unmoving, his eyes still fixed on that blue vault above him. It must have been that he was already so far away in heart that he never felt the release from my hand. He never even stood. He just lay with his breast against the grass.

29   In the next second after that long minute he was gone. Like a flicker of light, he had vanished with my eyes full on him, but without actually seeing even a premonitory ° wing beat. He was gone straight into that towering emptiness of light and crystal that my eyes could scarcely bear to penetrate. For another long moment there was silence. I could not see him. The light was too intense. Then from far up somewhere a cry came ringing down.

30   I was young then and had seen little of the world, but when I heard that cry my heart turned over. It was not the cry of the hawk I had captured; for, by shifting my position against the sun, I was now seeing further up. Straight out of the sun's eye, where she must have been soaring restlessly above us for untold hours, hurtled his mate. And from far up, ringing from peak to peak of the

premonitory: giving warning in advance.

summits over us, came a cry of such unutterable and ecstatic joy that it sounds down across the years and tingles among the cups on my quiet breakfast table.

31   I saw them both now. He was rising fast to meet her. They met in a great soaring gyre ° that turned to a whirling circle and a dance of wings. Once more, just once, their two voices, joined in a harsh mild medley of question and response, struck and echoed against the pinnacles of the valley. Then they were gone forever somewhere into those upper regions beyond the eyes of men.

32   I am older now, and sleep less, and have seen most of what there is to see and am not very much impressed any more, I suppose, by anything. "What Next in the Attributes of Machines?" my morning headline runs. "It Might Be the Power to Reproduce Themselves."

33   I lay the paper down and across my mind a phrase floats insinuatingly *: "It does not seem that there is anything in the construction, constituents, or behavior of the human being which it is essentially impossible for science to duplicate and synthesize. On the other hand . . ."

34   All over the city the cogs in the hard, bright mechanisms have begun to turn. Figures move through computers, names are spelled out, a thoughtful machine selects the fingerprints of a wanted criminal from an array of thousands. In the laboratory an electronic mouse runs swiftly through a maze toward the cheese it can neither taste nor enjoy. On the second run it does better than a living mouse.

35   "On the other hand . . ." Ah, my mind takes up, on the other hand the machine does not bleed, ache, hang for hours in the empty sky in a torment of hope to learn the fate of another machine, nor does it cry out with joy nor dance in the air with the fierce passion of a bird. Far off, over a distance greater than space, that remote cry from the heart of heaven makes a faint buzzing among my breakfast dishes and passes on and away.

gyre: a circular or spiral motion.

ANALYSIS

Eiseley's technique in writing this "report" is as different from Alex Haley's as it could be. The techniques differ because the writers' intentions differ. Where Haley is straightforward and methodical because he wants to relate as clearly as possible the events of a complex story, Eiseley is oblique. Eiseley's story is very simple, but his idea is not, and he is concerned more with the idea than he is with the experience.

In his opening paragraphs, Eiseley is musing. We do not even know what the pronoun *their* refers to until the third sentence. In paragraph 2 Eiseley doesn't mention the birds at all; instead he introduces something else: machines. Given the title of the report, we can figure that he is eventually going to make connections between the birds and the machines. But not until the conclusion of paragraph 3 does he state his theme: "I'll still stick with the birds. It's life I believe in, not machines."

Eiseley knows what he is doing. The philosophical frame he begins building around his bird-report in paragraph 1, the frame which consists of musings about life versus machines, is picked up again in paragraph 32 and is finished off by paragraph 35. We have here, then, a report on an anthropologist's experience, which is framed by philosophical speculation on its meaning. By the end of this small masterpiece, Eiseley has returned us to his breakfast table, exactly where he began in paragraph 1.

Questions on Content

1. Why did Eiseley set the bird free?
2. What is significant about the fact that what Eiseley hears over the years is a cry of "unutterable and ecstatic *joy*"?
3. What does Eiseley mean by saying that the cry came from "the heart of heaven"?

4. According to Eiseley, what is the difference between life and a machine?

Add to Your Vocabulary

juxtaposition, divested, escarpment, reciprocal, insinuatingly.

Questions on Technique

1. Does the title help to clarify the theme of this report, or can you think of another title you would prefer?
2. Why does Eiseley insert the anecdotes about the snake and the climb (paragraphs 8–12)? What connection do these anecdotes have with his report?

Techniques to Imitate

Narration in exposition

The subject matter of exposition is ideas. Pure exposition, however, would not only be hard to write, but it would also make difficult, even dull, reading. This is why writers of exposition frequently illustrate their ideas by telling brief stories. They know that narrative is easier to understand and more interesting to read than is pure exposition.

Eiseley uses narration effectively. In his effort to make clear the differences between living things and machines, he narrates a personal experience—the story of the birds he found in a remote mountain cabin. Nearly one-half of his article is devoted to this story. The effect of the incident is hinted at in paragraph 12, but the story begins at paragraph 13: "We came into that valley through the trailing mists of a spring night." It ends with paragraph 31. In his final paragraphs, Eiseley summarizes the idea which is illustrated by his story. It is likely that his readers will remember the story and, Eiseley hopes, by remembering the story, they will remember also the ideas it illustrates.

Note that paragraphs 8–12 are also narrative. In them, Eiseley narrates several experiences which taught him the concept that "time is a series of planes existing superficially in the same universe. The tempo is a human illusion, a subjective clock ticking in our kind of protoplasm."

In your own expository writing, you can make ideas clear and interesting by relating anecdotes or stories that illustrate them.

Suggestions for Writing

1. Write a report on some experience you have had, or which someone else has had. Frame your narration of this experience with paragraphs that tell why this experience is so important or interesting. In other words, first tell why you happened to think of this experience. Then narrate it. Finally, tell what the experience taught you, and why it is part of your memory.
2. Eiseley's method here is, in part, one of contrast: he sets up contrasts between birds and machines (see paragraphs 33–35). Write a report using this technique of contrast (there are many possibilities: urban versus country life; youth versus age; imagination versus logic). Like Eiseley, make clear which of the things being contrasted has won your favor or support.
3. Select a story from the newspaper and write an essay giving your opinion of it, or telling what it reminds you of, or why you were glad you'd read it, or why you wished you'd never read it. Perhaps you can narrate some experience that will illuminate your feelings about the newspaper article.

6

THE CRITICAL ESSAY: SOCIETY

After inspecting three groups of exposition under the familiar rhetorical headings—definition, process, and report—we turn now to a somewhat freer form of expository writing: the essay. Like other expository forms, essays also observe, judge, and review. They are as much concerned with *why* and *how* as definitions, explanations, reports, and analyses are. However, essays are more personal and often less objective than most other writings in Part Two have been.

Writers of essays, as we shall discover, rarely adhere to an explicit pattern of logic. They do not always report events in chronological order. They do not always set forth arguments in series, though they may hold firmly to debatable points of view. Writers of essays feel freer to talk "around" a subject. That is not to suggest that essays are disorganized. Instead of analyzing a subject, an essay will illuminate a subject. In place of propounding ideas, it will explore ideas.

A critical essay, in particular, can give us new insight into a work of art or a problem in linguistics or a political issue. It can set us to thinking by raising questions, citing parallels, recalling history. A critical essay is a kind of exploration, an intellectual exercise. Its ends are sometimes persuasive, but more often a critical essay provides a perceptive judgment and a tentative conclusion.

We have limited the critical essays here to those about society and literature.

ERIC SEVAREID

The Dark of the Moon

Eric Sevareid's essay is a good introduction to social criticism. For years he worked for the Minneapolis *Star,* the Paris *Herald-Tribune,* and the United Press in Paris. He is now known internationally as CBS correspondent and reporter of world affairs. In print and on the air he has been commenting on history in the making. Here he discusses our advances toward putting a person on the moon——an event that took place eleven years after this essay appeared in the April 17, 1958, issue of *The Reporter* magazine. Note that what Sevareid has to say has no resemblance to a news report. He is not dealing in facts, figures, dates, or places. He uses no statistics, proves nothing. Yet he takes as his subject "front-page talk" in the year 1958. One aspect of social criticism is just this method of discussing an issue in general terms. Even though we have actually put human beings on the moon, the issues Sevareid raises are still very much with us.

1   This, thank goodness, is the first warm and balmy night of the year in these parts; the first frogs are singing. Altogether this is hardly the night for whispering sweet sentiments about the reciprocal trade act, the extension thereof. But since we are confined, by tradition, to the contemplation of public themes and issues, let us contemplate the moon. The lovely and luminous moon has become a public issue. For quite a few thousand years it was a private issue; it figured in purely bilateral negotiations between lovers, in the incantations of jungle witch doctors and Indian corn planters. Poets from attic windows issued the statements about the moon, and they made better reading than the mimeographed handouts now being issued by assistant secretaries of defense.

2   The moon was always measured in terms of hope and reassurance and the heart pangs of youth on such a night as this; it is now measured in terms of mileage and foot-pounds of rocket thrust. Children sent sharp, sweet wishes to the moon; now they dream of blunt-nosed missiles.

3   There must come a time, in every generation, when those who are older secretly get off the train of progress, willing to walk back to where they came from, if they can find the way. We're afraid we're getting off now. Cheer, if you wish, the first general or Ph.D. who splatters something ° on the kindly face of the moon. We shall grieve for him, for ourself, for the young lovers and poets and dreamers to come, because the ancient moon will never be the same again. Therefore, we suspect, the heart of man will never be the same.

4   We find it very easy to wait for the first photographs of the other side of the moon, for we have not yet seen the other side of Lake Louise or the Blue Ridge peak that shows through the cabin window.

5   We find ourself quite undisturbed about the front-page talk of "controlling the earth from the moon," because we do not believe it. If neither men nor gadgets nor both combined can control the earth from the earth, we fail to see how they will do so from the moon.

6   It is exciting talk, indeed, the talk of man's advance toward space. But one little step in man's advance toward man—that, we think, would be truly exciting. Let those who wish try to discover the composition of a lunar crater;

splatters something: the Russian multistage rocket Lunik II was the first to hit the moon, on September 13, 1959.

we would settle for discovering the true mind of a Russian commissar or the inner heart of a delinquent child.

7 There is, after all, another side—a dark side—to the human spirit, too. Men have hardly begun to explore these regions; and it is going to be a very great pity if we advance upon the bright side of the moon with the dark side of ourselves, if the cargo in the first rockets to reach there consists of fear and chauvinism and suspicion. Surely we ought to have our credentials in order, our hands very clean, and perhaps a prayer for forgiveness on our lips as we prepare to open the ancient vault of the shining moon.

ANALYSIS

In spite of his lighthearted opening paragraph, Sevareid is wholly serious. Not frightened, not pessimistic, he is nevertheless wary. He expresses this caution with a simple image. "We're afraid we're getting off [the train of progress] now," he says, using the editorial "we." Shall we take him at his word? Is Sevareid turning his back on the future? Would he like to call off all exploration of outer space, bring back the satellites we have put in orbit, close down Cape Canaveral—all to keep the "lovely and luminous moon" a "private issue" for lovers and poets? No, not exactly that. We will still have a luminous moon on "the first warm and balmy night" of every year. But Sevareid is troubled.

The dark side of the human spirit troubles him far more than the dark side of the moon entices our scientists. Consider his simple statement (paragraph 7): "Men have hardly begun to explore these [dark] regions." How many past attempts that implies! Sophocles, Shakespeare, Melville, Dickinson, to name only creative artists; the prophets of the Bible, and the founders of modern psychiatry; lawmakers and judges of every century; philosophers and scientists—all of this combined knowledge, some of it 3,000 years old, has only begun to answer the ancient question: who are we? If we were wholly rational creatures, we would need no disarmament conferences, we could disband the United Nations, we should have no fear of "fear and chauvinism and suspicion." But we have always been victims of our own emotions, singly, in groups, in nations. We might ask Sevareid: Must we wait until we become perfect before we take another giant step in science? Have we not always tried the impossible and called it progress? Shall we stop now? Sevareid does not write idly. He would undoubtedly have answers to these questions. Perhaps we ourselves know the answers even as we ask the questions.

Questions on Content

1. What does Sevareid mean when he says, "We find ourself quite undisturbed about the front-page talk of 'controlling the earth from the moon,' because we do not believe it"?
2. Explain what Sevareid means by his comparison between discovering the composition of a lunar crater and discovering the inner heart of a delinquent child.
3. What does Sevareid mean by saying we should "have a prayer or forgiveness on our lips" as we "open the ancient vault" of the moon?

Questions on Technique

1. Why is the phrase "purely bilateral negotiations between lovers" so apt where it is used (paragraph 1)?
2. What use does Sevareid make of Lake Louise, a Blue Ridge peak, a Russian commissar, and a delinquent child in this essay? What have they to do with space exploration?

Techniques to Imitate

Structure: beginning, middle, end

A news commentary is an essay, and Sevareid's is a model for all commentators and essayists. Because it is brief, its virtues are immediately apparent.

The beginning is clever and graceful. Radio and television commentators know they can be turned off or easily ignored; if they are to be listened to, they must somehow get the attention of their listeners. Sevareid's introduction is so interesting and so charmingly expressed that it must surely attract a listener's attention and arouse his curiosity.

The middle of the essay consists of a series of reflections given in ascending order of seriousness. Sevareid leads the reader step by step toward his conclusion, which, like the climax at the end of a short story, is forcefully expressed in the final paragraph. "Surely we ought to have our credentials in order, our hands very clean, and perhaps a prayer for forgiveness on our lips as we prepare to open the ancient vault of the shining moon."

Suggestions for Writing

1. Answer Sevareid's essay from an opposing point of view. A possible title might be "The Light of the Moon."
2. Write a brief essay on a "public issue" that concerns you right now. Open your remarks with a personal reflection on *why* you are writing on this particular theme. For your "middle," tell what others think and what *you* think of their ideas. For the "end," ask your readers a "summing-up" question.

C. P. SNOW

The Future of Man

Eric Sevareid's essay is an easy bridge to C. P. Snow's. Snow, too, is concerned about the future, how science is molding it, how we are facing it. As social critic, he writes from a more academic background than Sevareid. He is both a scientist and a novelist. Since the early 1930's, he has been writing in England a series of novels under the general title *Strangers and Brothers*. *The Masters* (1951) and *The Affair* (1960) have sold widely in the United States. Snow has also written much on the effect of organized science on our culture, what new problems future growth will bring, where moral responsibility lies. His little book *The Two Cultures and the Scientific Revolution* (1960) is compulsory reading for anyone concerned with the lack of communication in our society between literary and scientific intellectuals.

When this essay appeared in *Nation* in 1958, it was followed by an equally forceful article called "The Man of the Future," written by Philip Siekevitz, a biochemist. *Nation* gave the two essays the joint title "Science and Hope." Snow's contribution is all of that: hope in face of overwhelming scientific discoveries, in face of the devastating destruction of the past. He talks here about our fate, as individuals, as nations, as a race.

Since 1958 much has changed in the world. Snow's remarks on China (page 320), for example, are dated now. His frequent use of the words *man* and *mankind* to refer generically to the human race might strike us as awkward today. However, the force of Snow's argument does not rest on these particulars. This essay will probably be read and be found pertinent fifty years from now.

1   **A**uschwitz and Hiroshima.°
We have seen all that; in some of it we have acquiesced * or helped. No wonder we are morally guilty. Men like ourselves have done such things—and at the same time men like ourselves, sometimes the same men who have taken a hand in the horrors, have been showing more concern for the unlucky round them than has ever been shown by a large society in human history. That is the moral paradox in which we have to live.

2   It is wrong to try to domesticate the horrors. The mass slaughter of the concentration camps was both the most awful and the most degrading set of actions that men have done so far. This set of actions was ordered and controlled by abnormally wicked men, if you like, but down the line the orders were carried out by thousands of people like the rest of us, civil servants, soldiers, engineers, all brought up in an advanced Western and Christian society. While it was people not like the rest of us but a great deal better, people who for imagination and morality, not to speak of intellect, stand among the finest of our race, people like Einstein, Niels Bohr, and Franck,° who got caught up in

Auschwitz and Hiroshima: In World War II, the Germans maintained a concentration camp in Auschwitz, in southern Poland. Approximately 4,000,000 people, mostly Jews, were put to death here. Auschwitz is the German spelling for the Polish name, Oswiecim. On August 6, 1945, an atomic bomb was dropped on the city of Hiroshima, Japan, killing directly or indirectly 75,000–80,000 persons and destroying approximately 70,000 buildings. The second military use of an atomic bomb was over Nagasaki, Japan, on August 9, 1945.

Einstein, Niels Bohr, and Franck: Albert Einstein (1879–1955), German-born American physicist and mathematician; Niels Bohr (1885–1962), Danish physicist; James Franck (1882–1964), German-born American physical chemist.

the tangle of events which led to Hiroshima and Nagasaki . . .

3   At the same time we ought not to forget what there is
to our credit. Some kinds of optimism about man's nature
are dangerous—but so are some kinds of pessimism. Think
of the care the Swedes and the Danes are taking of their
old and poor, or of prisoners, or of social misfits. Nothing
like that has been done at any period or in any place until
our lifetime. We can congratulate ourselves in Britain,
too. The Scandinavians have not made anything like a
perfect society. In some ways we have not got as near to
it as they have. But we have both made a better shot at it
than anyone before us.

4   Britain is a much fairer and a much kinder society
than the one I was born into in 1905. It may seem sentimental to have consciences troubled about capital punishment, about removing one life when Western man has
recently eliminated twenty million: yet it is a sign of moral
sensitivity. So is the attempt, however grudging, to treat
women as though they were equal human beings. So is the
feeling behind the Wolfenden Report.° So is the conviction
—so urgent in the United States—that children have a
special right to happiness.

5   Some of these feelings may lead to practical follies (I
believe that the American one is making a mess of their
education), but that is not the point. They are signs of a
development of something very rare in the world up to
now, which one might call moral kindness. I have no doubt
that in Scandinavia, England, some, though not all, of the
United States, and perhaps three or four other countries
in the West, the amount of fairness, tolerance, and effective
kindness within the society would seem astonishing to any
nineteenth-century man.

6   It would also seem astonishing to any nineteenth-
century man how much we know. There is probably no

Wolfenden Report: Sir John Wolfenden, Vice-Chancellor of
Reading University, England, headed a committee which prepared a report for Parliament in 1957 on public law and private
morals.

one now alive as clever as Clerk Maxwell or Gauss; °
but thousands of people know more than Clerk Maxwell
or Gauss, and understand more of those parts of the world
that they spent their lives trying to understand. Put those
two down, or even greater men, such as Newton and
Archimedes,° in front of what is now understood—and
they would think it wonderful. So it is, and we can take
pride and joy in it. It will go on; the search to understand
is one of the most human things about us. Compared with
our ancestors, there are some trivial physical differences.
We are a good deal taller and heavier, we live much longer.
But above all, we know more.

7   All this it would be reasonable to call progress, so
long as we don't expect of progress more than it can give.
In each of our individual lives there is, of course, something beyond human help. Each of us has to live part of
his life alone: and he has to die alone. That part of our
experience is right outside of time and history, and progress
has no meaning there. In this sense, the individual condition is tragic. But that is no excuse for not doing our best
with the social condition.

8   To think otherwise, to take refuge in facile * despair,
has been the characteristic intellectual treachery of our
day. It is shoddy. We have to face the individual condition:
for good and evil, for pettiness and the occasional dash
of grandeur, we have to know what men are capable of:
and then we can't contract out. For we are part, not only
of the privileged North European–British-American enclave * of progress, but of another progress which is alter-
ing the whole world.

9   I mean something brutally simple. Most people in Asia
still haven't enough to eat: but they have a bit more than

Maxwell or Gauss: James Clerk Maxwell (1831–1879), British
physicist; Karl Friedrich Gauss (1777–1855), German mathematician.

Newton and Archimedes: Sir Isaac Newton (1642–1727), British
scientist who formulated the law of gravity; Archimedes (287?–
212 B.C.), Greek mathematician who discovered the principles of
specific gravity and of the lever.

before. Most people in Asia are still dying before their time (on the average, Indians live less than half as long as Englishmen): but they are living longer than before. Is *that* progress? This is not a subject to be superior or refined or ingenious about, and the answer is: *of course it is.*

10   It is because Western man has grown too far away from that elemental progress that we can't get on terms with most of the human race. Through luck we got in first with the scientific-industrial revolution; as a result, our lives became, on the average, healthier, longer, more comfortable to an extent that had never been imagined; it doesn't become us to tell our Chinese and Indian friends that that kind of progress is not worth having.

11   We know what it is like to live among the shops, the cars, the radios, of Leicester and Orebro ° and Des Moines. We know what it is like to ask the point of it all, and to feel the Swedish sadness or the American disappointment or the English Welfare State ° discontent. But the Chinese and Indians would like the chance of being well-fed enough to ask what is the point of it all. They are in search of what Leicester, Orebro and Des Moines take for granted: food, extra years of life, modest comforts. When they have got these things, they are willing to put up with a dash of the Swedish sadness or American disappointment. And their determination to get them is likely in the next thirty years to prove the strongest social force on earth. °

12   Will they get them? Will the social conditions everywhere reach within foreseeable time something like the standard of the privileged Western enclave? There is no technical reason why not. If it does, the level of moral kindness will go up in parallel. These ought to be realistic hopes. There seems only one fatality that might destroy

Leicester and Orebro: cities in England and Sweden, respectively.

English Welfare State: the term applied to the English social revolution which, since 1948, has brought such reforms as tight central governmental controls, nationalized railroads and health service, social security measures, and the like.

By the early 1970's the People's Republic of China was considered a superpower, one of the three most influential nations in the world.

them. That is, it goes without saying, an H-bomb war.

13 No one can pretend that it is not possible. For myself, I think that it won't happen even though we have seen how good and conscientious men have become responsible for horrors, even though two atomic bombs have been dropped already . . . But I still think, partly as a guess, partly as a calculation, that we shall escape the H-bomb war—just as I think we shall escape the longer-term danger of Malthusian ° overpopulation.

14 It may easily be that I am letting hope run away with me about the H-bomb war. Some of the wisest disagree with me. Let us imagine that they are right and that the H-bombs go off. Is that going to be the end? I find it difficult to believe. In England a lot of us would be dead, our children with us. A lot of Americans and Russians would also be killed outright. No one knows how many would die afterwards through effects of radiation. But I don't believe that men have at present the resources to destroy the race.

15 If that is so, and if after an H-bomb war a **viable** * fraction of the world population were left untouched (my guess is that it would be a large fraction, at least two-thirds), then we should all be amazed how soon hope of progress took possession again. The human species is biologically a very tough one, and tough in a sense no animal species can be, through its intelligence, its organization of knowledge, the capacity of its members not to be totally bound within the rapacious * self. After the most hideous H-bomb war, the inhabitants of Africa and India and South America would have the strength of those qualities to build on. The material and scientific gap, left through the devastation of the West and Russia, would be filled up at a speed not flattering to Western or Russian self-esteem. What would the moral scar be?

16 I think we can already answer that question, for we

Malthusian: Thomas Malthus (1766–1834), British political economist, contended that population, since it increased faster than the means of subsistence, should be checked by social and moral restraints.

too have, as I said at the beginning, witnessed horrors and assisted at them. Most of us don't live constantly in the presence of Hiroshima and Auschwitz: the memory doesn't prevent us getting morally concerned about the fate of one murderer or cross because a lonely and impoverished old man doesn't have enough calls from the District Visitor.°

17   It would be just the same if the Northern hemisphere became more or less destroyed. Men elsewhere would not live under that shadow; they would be busy with their own societies. If those societies were less fair and morally sensitive than ours is now, they would soon catch up. Within a bizarrely short interval, after hundreds of millions of people had been incinerated by H-bombs, men in countries unaffected would be passionately debating capital punishment. It sounds mad, but it is the kind of madness which makes human beings as tough as they are, and as capable of behaving better than they have so far behaved.

18   So there remains a sort of difficult hope. As long as men continue to be men, individual man will perceive the same darkness about his solitary condition as any of us does now. But he will also feel occasional intimations * that his own life is not the only one. In the midst of his egotisms, pettiness, power-seekings, and perhaps the horrors these may cause, he will intermittently * stretch a little beyond himself. That little, added to the intelligence and growing knowledge of the species, will be enough to make his societies more decent, to use the social forces for what, in the long sight of history, are good ends.

19   None of it will be easy. As individuals, each of us is almost untouched by this progress. It is no comfort to remember how short human history is. As individuals, that seems just an irony. But as a race, we have scarcely begun to live.

ANALYSIS

Snow discusses several major aspects of human nature

District Visitor: in England, a person who does social work in a district under the clergy's direction.

in this essay, and he does it with sufficient elaboration to let us digest what is on his mind. It might help us to list his main points:

1. We have shown to our fellow humans extreme cruelty at one moment in history and great kindness at another. This is the moral paradox or contradiction we must face (paragraphs 1–5).
2. We have extended our knowledge greatly in the last several centuries (paragraph 6).
3. The individual condition (a single life) is tragic and fleeting, but the social condition (the race as a whole) is improving (paragraphs 7–11).

Up to this point, you may feel that Snow is unusually optimistic about the future. As a scientist, he can foresee the day when we will have enough food for all people, though it may take several decades. He recognizes what we call "progress" in our modest comforts, our extra years of life. But the shadow is always there. He defines it in his fourth point.

4. We have also invented the means of blowing ourselves up, namely the H-bomb (paragraph 12).

The rest of his essay is devoted to two questions which naturally arise when the H-bomb is mentioned: Will we use it, and if we do, will people survive in sufficient numbers to propagate the race? The burden of his reply to both questions is as optimistic as the first half of this essay. Are we surprised? Not if we caught the conviction of his seventh paragraph. The individual person is weak, Snow admits, but collectively we are indestructible. He restates this feeling in paragraphs 17–19, calling it "a sort of difficult hope." Do you agree?

Questions on Content

1. What does Snow mean by "the privileged North Euro-

pean–British-American enclave of progress" (paragraph 8)?
2. How do Leicester, Orebro, and Des Moines differ from towns in India (paragraph 11)?
3. When Snow says (paragraph 14), "I don't believe that men have at present the resources to destroy the race," does he offer proof?

Add to Your Vocabulary

acquiesced, facile, enclave, viable, rapacious, intimations, intermittently.

Questions on Technique

1. Why are Auschwitz and Hiroshima effective words with which to open this essay?
2. What effect does Snow achieve with his many references to proper names: Einstein, Bohr, Franck, Newton, and so forth? Does he lose some of that effect if we do not know his local references, such as the Wolfenden Report and the District Visitor?
3. How does he substantiate his theory that we will survive even an H-bomb war?

Techniques to Imitate

Facing opposing views directly

Snow's article illustrates a technique commonly used by a skillful writer when planning to support one side of a controversial question. The technique is to admit the merits of the opposing view, indeed to seem at first, as Snow does, to be arguing that view. Then, having made clear exactly what it is that will be disagreed with, the writer proceeds to set forth in one-two-three order the reasons for disagreeing. The writer knows it will be more convincing to show a full understanding and appreciation of the opposing beliefs.

Snow begins by admitting the evil that accompanies the good in us—the moral paradox. He admits the damaging

evidence offered by those who cite Auschwitz and Hiroshima to prove that the so-called progress of humans is
a myth. Having made these admissions, Snow presents his
side of the argument, beginning with the third paragraph:
"At the same time we ought not to forget what there is
to our credit." He continues to use this technique in the
rest of his essay, facing up to other contrary evidence,
such as the unchanging tragedies of the individual life and
the great social menace of the H-bomb. By making clear
that he understands the views of those who disagree with
him, he impresses us with his fairness and strengthens our
faith in his beliefs.

When you are writing a comment on or a criticism of
society, and you know that there are many who disagree
with you, you will do well to use the technique Snow
illustrates—facing opposing views directly.

Suggestions for Writing

1. If you have read Eric Sevareid's essay, "The Dark of
   the Moon," reread Snow's paragraph 18. Does Snow
   unknowingly answer Sevareid's statement (in his last
   paragraph) that "it is going to be a very great pity if
   we advance upon the bright side of the moon with the
   dark side of ourselves"? Write a 500-word essay on
   these two authors' use of "individual man" and "mankind." Incorporate as many of your own opinions as
   you wish.

2. Write an essay of 400–600 words on the subject "The
   World I [We] Face." Do not write a simple description
   or a projection of your plans. Talk of the problems you
   know you will have to face and how you expect to sur-
   mount them.

3. Write a brief essay in which you explore your own ideas
   on the concept of progress. As part of your essay, face
   up to some definition of progress that you disagree with
   (perhaps you disagree with Snow's). Clarify for your
   reader exactly what the opposition's view *is*, and why
   you disagree with it.

4. On page 308 we discussed how a writer often uses nar-

ration within an expository essay. In that case, a narrative (or story) was used by the writer, Loren Eiseley, to illuminate the main idea of his essay. You might use this technique in writing an essay in which you explain your own views on the capability of human beings to behave better than they have sometimes behaved in the past (see Snow's paragraph 17).

5. Write a comparison between Snow's attitude toward science and Eric Sevareid's.

VIRGINIA WOOLF

Professions for Women

This speech was delivered in the 1930's to an organization called the Women's Service League, by British novelist and essayist Virginia Woolf. Virginia Woolf was born in 1882 into a brilliant and beautiful family, and she grew up amid all the comforts and advantages of wealth. As an adult, she moved in the company of the most articulate and creative writers, critics, and artists of her time. Above all else, Virginia Woolf considered herself a writer. She worked obsessively on her art, striving for the exact word and the exact impression. A long essay about her problems as a writer who is a woman is called "A Room of One's Own" (1929). She refers to this image in the speech that follows.

1   When your secretary invited me to come here, she told me that your Society is concerned with the employment of women and she suggested that I might tell you something about my own professional experience. It is true I am a woman; it is true I am employed; but what professional experiences have I had? It is difficult to say. My profession is literature; and in that profession there are fewer experiences for women than in any other, with the exception of the stage—fewer, I mean, that are peculiar to women. For the road was cut many years ago—by Fanny Burney, by Aphra Behn, by Harriet Martineau, by Jane Austen, by George Eliot—many famous women, and many more unknown and forgotten, have been before me, making the path smooth, and regulating my steps. Thus, when I came to write, there were very few material obstacles in my way. Writing was a reputable and harmless occupation. The family peace was not broken by the scratching of a pen. No demand was made upon the family purse. For ten and sixpence one can buy paper enough to write all the plays of Shakespeare—if one has a mind that way. Pianos and models, Paris, Vienna, and Berlin, masters and mistresses, are not needed by a writer. The cheapness of writing paper is, of course, the reason why women have succeeded as writers before they have succeeded in the other professions.

2   But to tell you my story—it is a simple one. You have only got to figure to yourselves a girl in a bedroom with a pen in her hand. She had only to move that pen from left to right—from ten o'clock to one. Then it occurred to her to do what is simple and cheap enough after all—to slip a few of those pages into an envelope, fix a penny stamp in the corner, and drop the envelope into the red box at the corner. It was thus that I became a journalist; and my effort was rewarded on the first day of the following month —a very glorious day it was for me—by a letter from an editor containing a check for one pound ten shillings and sixpence. But to show you how little I deserve to be called a professional woman, how little I know of the struggles and difficulties of such lives, I have to admit that instead of spending that sum upon bread and butter, rent, shoes and stockings, or butcher's bills, I went out and bought a cat—a beautiful cat, a Persian cat, which very soon involved me in bitter disputes with my neighbors.

3   What could be easier than to write articles and to buy Persian cats with the profits? But wait a moment. Articles have to be about something. Mine, I seem to remember, was about a novel by a famous man. And while I was writing this review, I discovered that if I were going to review books I should need to do battle with a certain phantom. And the phantom was a woman, and when I came to know her better I called her after the heroine of a famous poem, the Angel in the House. It was she who used to come

between me and my paper when I was writing reviews. It was she who bothered me and wasted my time and so tormented me that at last I killed her. You who come of a younger and happier generation may not have heard of her—you may not know what I mean by the Angel in the House. I will describe her as shortly as I can. She was intensely sympathetic. She was immensely charming. She was utterly unselfish. She excelled in the difficult arts of family life. She sacrificed herself daily. If there was chicken, she took the leg; if there was a draft she sat in it—in short she was so constituted that she never had a mind or a wish of her own, but preferred to sympathize always with the minds and wishes of others. Above all—I need not say it —she was pure. Her purity was supposed to be her chief beauty—her blushes, her great grace. In those days— the last of Queen Victoria—every house had its Angel. And when I came to write I encountered her with the very first words. The shadow of her wings fell on my page; I heard the rustling of her skirts in the room. Directly, that is to say, I took my pen in hand to review that novel by a famous man, she slipped behind me and whispered: "My dear, you are a young woman. You are writing about a book that has been written by a man. Be sympathetic; be tender; flatter; deceive; use all the arts and wiles of our sex. Never let anybody guess that you have a mind of your own. Above all, be pure." And she made as if to guide my pen. I now record the one act for which I take some credit to myself, though the credit rightly belongs to some excellent ancestors of mine who left me a certain sum of money—shall we say five hundred pounds a year?—so that it was not necessary for me to depend solely on charm for my living. I turned upon her and caught her by the throat. I did my best to kill her. My excuse, if I were to be had up in a court of law, would be that I acted in self-defense. Had I not killed her she would have killed me. She would have plucked the heart out of my writing. For, as I found, directly I put pen to paper, you cannot review even a novel without having a mind of your own, without expressing what you think to be the truth about human relations, morality, sex. And all these questions, according to the Angel of the House, cannot be dealt with freely and openly by women; they must charm, they must conciliate, * they must —to put it bluntly—tell lies if they are to succeed. Thus, whenever I felt the shadow of her wing or the radiance of her halo upon my page, I took up the inkpot and flung it at her. She died hard. Her fictitious nature was of great assistance to her. It is far harder to kill a phantom than a reality. She was always creeping back when I thought I had dispatched her. Though I flatter myself that I killed her in the end, the struggle was severe; it took much time that had better have been spent upon learning Greek grammar, or in roaming the world in search of adventures. But it was a real experience; it was an experience that was bound to befall all women writers at that time. Killing the Angel in the House was part of the occupation of a woman writer.

4   But to continue my story. The Angel was dead; what then remained? You may say that what remained was a simple and common object—a young woman in a bedroom with an inkpot. In other words, now that she had rid herself of falsehood, that young woman had only to be herself. Ah, but what is "herself"? I mean, what is a woman? I assure you, I do not know. I do not believe that you know. I do not believe that anybody can know until she has expressed herself in all the arts and professions open to human skill. That indeed is one of the reasons why I have come here—out of respect for you, who are in process of showing us by your experiments what a woman is, who are in process of providing us, by your failures and successes, with that extremely important piece of information.

5   But to continue the story of my professional experiences. I made one pound ten and six by my first review; and I bought a Persian cat with the proceeds. Then I grew ambitious. A Persian cat is all very well, I said; but a Persian cat is not enough. I must have a motorcar. And it was thus that I became a novelist—for it is a very strange thing that people will give you a motorcar if you will tell them a story. It is a still stranger thing that there is nothing

so delightful in the world as telling stories. It is far pleasanter than writing reviews of famous novels. And yet, if I am to obey your secretary and tell you my professional experiences as a novelist, I must tell you about a very strange experience that befell me as a novelist. And to understand it you must try first to imagine a novelist's state of mind. I hope I am not giving away professional secrets if I say that a novelist's chief desire is to be as unconscious as possible. He has to induce in himself a state of perpetual lethargy.* He wants life to proceed with the utmost quiet and regularity. He wants to see the same faces, to read the same books, to do the same things day after day, month after month, while he is writing, so that nothing may break the illusion in which he is living—so that nothing may disturb or disquiet the mysterious nosings about, feelings round, darts, dashes, and sudden discoveries of that very shy and illusive spirit, the imagination. I suspect that this state is the same both for men and women. Be that as it may, I want you to imagine me writing a novel in a state of trance. I want you to figure to yourselves a girl sitting with a pen in her hand, which for minutes, and indeed for hours, she never dips into the inkpot. The image that comes to my mind when I think of this girl is the image of a fisherman lying sunk in dreams on the verge of a deep lake with a rod held out over the water. She was letting her imagination sweep unchecked round every rock and cranny of the world that lies submerged in the depths of our unconscious being. Now came the experience that I believe to be far commoner with women writers than with men. The line raced through the girl's fingers. Her imagination had rushed away. It had sought the pools, the depths, the dark places where the largest fish slumber. And then there was a smash. There was an explosion. There was foam and confusion. The imagination had dashed itself against something hard. The girl was roused from her dream. She was indeed in a state of the most acute and difficult distress. To speak without figure, ° she had thought of something, something about the

figure: See Figurative Language in the Glossary.

body, about the passions which it was unfitting for her as a woman to say. Men, her reason told her, would be shocked. The consciousness of what men will say of a woman who speaks the truth about her passions had roused her from her artist's state of unconsciousness. She could write no more. The trance was over. Her imagination could work no longer. This I believe to be a very common experience with women writers—they are impeded by the extreme conventionality of the other sex. For though men sensibly allow themselves great freedom in these respects, I doubt that they realize or can control the extreme severity with which they condemn such freedom in women.

6   These then were two very genuine experiences of my own. These were two of the adventures of my professional life. The first—killing the Angel in the House—I think I solved. She died. But the second, telling the truth about my own experiences as a body, I do not think I solved. I doubt that any woman has solved it yet. The obstacles against her are still immensely powerful—and yet they are very difficult to define. Outwardly, what is simpler than to write books? Outwardly, what obstacles are there for a woman rather than for a man? Inwardly, I think, the case is very different; she has still many ghosts to fight, many prejudices to overcome. Indeed it will be a long time still, I think, before a woman can sit down to write a book without finding a phantom to be slain, a rock to be dashed against. And if this is so in literature, the freest of all professions for women, how is it in the new professions which you are for the first time entering?

7   Those are the questions that I should like, had I time, to ask you. And indeed, if I have laid stress upon these professional experiences of mine, it is because I believe that they are, though in different forms, yours also. Even when the path is nominally open—when there is nothing to prevent a woman from being a doctor, a lawyer, a civil servant—there are many phantoms and obstacles, as I believe, looming in her way. To discuss and define them is I think of great value and importance; for thus only can the labor be shared, the difficulties be solved. But besides this, it is necessary also to discuss the ends and the aims

for which we are fighting, for which we are doing battle with these formidable obstacles. Those aims cannot be taken for granted; they must be perpetually questioned and examined. The whole position, as I see it—here in this hall surrounded by women practicing for the first time in history I know not how many different professions—is one of extraordinary interest and importance. You have won rooms of your own in the house hitherto exclusively owned by men. You are able, though not without great labor and effort, to pay the rent. You are earning your five hundred pounds a year. But this freedom is only a beginning; the room is your own, but it is still bare. It has to be furnished; it has to be decorated; it has to be shared. How are you going to furnish it, how are you going to decorate it? With whom are you going to share it, and upon what terms? These, I think are questions of the utmost importance and interest. For the first time in history you are able to ask them; for the first time you are able to decide for yourselves what the answers should be. Willingly would I stay and discuss those questions and answers—but not tonight. My time is up; and I must cease.

ANALYSIS

The three metaphors ° around which this essay is organized are most remarkable. The first metaphor is introduced in paragraph 3. It is called the Angel in the House. The second metaphor is presented in paragraph 5. It presents the woman writer as a fisher whose imagination has rushed away to "the depths, the dark places where the largest fish slumber." The third metaphor concludes the essay. It is the metaphor of the "room of one's own"—a room which, as Woolf eloquently reminds her audience, is as yet unfurnished, undecorated, and unshared.

Woolf says that this room represents a freedom that is just a beginning. And this is where she leaves her audience: in the empty room, with several important questions that they must now begin to answer as they start to furnish it.

metaphors: See Glossary.

Questions on Content

1. How would the Angel in the House have "killed" Woolf as a writer, had she not killed the phantom first?
2. When Woolf describes her second experience, she says that women writers are impeded by the "extreme conventionality of the other sex." What does she mean?
3. Which problem has she not solved?

Add to Your Vocabulary

conciliate, lethargy.

Questions on Technique

1. How would this speech have differed if the writer had spoken literally, without metaphor at all? Do you think it would have been less effective or more effective without the metaphors? Explain.
2. Woolf uses effectively the rhetorical device of asking a question and then answering it. For example, she asks, "What could be easier than to write articles and to buy Persian cats with the profits?" After describing how she killed the Angel, she says, "The Angel was dead; what then remained?" What is your evaluation of this question-answer technique, particularly in an essay that was delivered as a speech?

Techniques to Imitate

Clarifying the train of thought for the reader

One important writing technique you can learn from Woolf's essay is how to help your reader, or listener, follow you. The plan of your composition may be clear to you, but this does not mean it will always be clear to your readers unless you keep them continually aware of it. You will see later in this book (page 372) how another writer, John Ciardi, helps readers to follow his train of thought in an article on Robert Frost.

In her first sentence, Woolf announces her subject. After some general comments on writing as a profession for women, she is ready to tell about her experiences and lets the reader know this by beginning her second paragraph with the guiding words, "But to tell you my story—it is a simple one." When she has told about her first important experience, killing the Angel in the House, she notifies the reader that she is continuing on to other experiences; she opens paragraph 4 with "But to continue my story." Digressing briefly from her story in paragraph 4, she leads the reader back once again to her topic at the beginning of her fifth paragraph: "But to continue the story of my professional experiences." In the ninth sentence of this paragraph, she reminds the reader of the purpose she had announced at the beginning of the essay. Even at the conclusion of the essay, she summarizes where she has taken her audience: "These then were two very genuine experiences of my own. These were two of the adventures of my professional life."

Suggestions for Writing

1. Write a brief essay in answer to this speech. Or, write a speech that could be delivered today on the topic of professions for women. Remember to let your audience know what your topic is.
2. In paragraph 3 Woolf develops the metaphor of the Angel in the House. A similar metaphor could be developed about the socially accepted view of the ideal man. First think of this "ideal" in terms of a metaphor. Express the metaphor in your opening sentences. Then, as Woolf does here in paragraph 3, develop the metaphor. (Here are two: a Charles Atlas, a Superman.)
3. Perhaps you feel that the Angel should not be exterminated. If so, write an essay in her defense. Face the opposing view, as set forth by Virginia Woolf, directly; make it clear exactly what you are going to disagree with (see page 324).

JAMES BALDWIN

The Creative Process

James Baldwin was born in Harlem, in New York City, in 1924. After graduation from high school, he took various jobs, though his major interest was writing. While he was working on a novel, he met the famous writer Richard Wright. Wright encouraged Baldwin, who subsequently won two literary awards which helped him move to Paris. There Baldwin lived and worked on his writing for ten years. He was there in 1952 when his first book (*Go Tell It on the Mountain*) was published in the United States. A collection of essays appeared next (*Nobody Knows My Name*, 1955), and then on November 17, 1962, an essay in the *New Yorker* magazine brought Baldwin's name before thousands of people who had never heard of him. This essay was later published as a book called *The Fire Next Time*, and it quickly became a best seller. Not since Richard Wright's own books (*Native Son* and *Black Boy*) had appeared in the 1940's had a Black man or woman given such eloquent and compassionate voice to the Black experience in the United States.

Baldwin's stay in Paris made him acutely aware of his identity as an American. In the essay that follows, in which he describes the creative process and its social uses, he also talks specifically about the role of the American artist.

1   **P**erhaps the primary distinction of the artist is that he must actively cultivate that state which most men, necessarily, must avoid: the state of being alone. That all men *are,* when the chips are down, alone, is a banality °—a banality because it is very frequently stated, but very rarely, on the evidence, believed. Most of us are not compelled to linger with the knowledge of our aloneness, for it is a knowledge that can paralyze all action in this world. There are, forever, swamps to be drained, cities to be created, mines to be exploited, children to be fed. None of these things can be done alone. But the conquest of the physical world is not man's only duty. He is also enjoined to conquer the great wilderness of himself. The precise role of the artist, then, is to illuminate that darkness, blaze roads through that vast forest, so that we will not, in all our doing, lose sight of its purpose, which is, after all, to make the world a more human dwelling place.

2   The state of being alone is not meant to bring to mind merely a rustic musing beside some silver lake. The aloneness of which I speak is much more like the aloneness of birth or death. It is like the fearful aloneness that one sees in the eyes of someone who is suffering, whom we cannot help. Or it is like the aloneness of love, the force and mystery that so many have extolled and so many have cursed, but which no one has ever understood or ever really been able to control. I put the matter this way, not out of any desire to create pity for the artist—God forbid!—but to suggest how nearly, after all, is his state the state of everyone, and in an attempt to make vivid his endeavor. The states of birth, suffering, love, and death are extreme states—extreme, universal, and inescapable. We all know this, but we would rather not know it. The artist is present to correct the delusions to which we fall prey in our attempts to avoid this knowledge.

3   It is for this reason that all societies have battled with

banality: an observation that has been expressed so frequently that it has become trite and commonplace.

that incorrigible ° disturber of the peace—the artist. I doubt that future societies will get on with him any better. The entire purpose of society is to create a bulwark ° against the inner and the outer chaos, in order to make life bearable and to keep the human race alive. And it is absolutely inevitable that when a tradition has been evolved, whatever the tradition is, the people, in general, will suppose it to have existed from before the beginning of time and will be most unwilling and indeed unable to conceive of any changes in it. They do not know how they will live without those traditions that have given them their identity. Their reaction, when it is suggested that they can or that they must, is panic. And we see this panic, I think, everywhere in the world today, from the streets of New Orleans to the grisly battleground of Algeria.° And a higher level of consciousness among the people is the only hope we have, now or in the future, of minimizing human damage.

4   The artist is distinguished from all other responsible actors in society—the politicians, legislators, educators, and scientists—by the fact that he is his own test tube, his own laboratory, working according to very rigorous rules, however unstated these may be, and cannot allow any consideration to supersede his responsibility to reveal all that he can possibly discover concerning the mystery of the human being. Society must accept some things as real; but he must always know that visible reality hides a deeper one, and that all our action and achievement rests on things unseen. A society must assume that it is stable, but the artist must know, and he must let us know, that there is nothing stable under heaven. One cannot possibly build a school, teach a child, or drive a car without taking some things for granted. The artist cannot and must not take anything for granted, but must drive to the

incorrigible: unreformable, unmanageable.
bulwark: a protection, a structure raised in defense (such as a seawall or rampart).
Algeria: a reference to Algeria's fierce struggle for independence from France.

heart of every answer and expose the question the answer hides.

5 I seem to be making extremely grandiloquent ° claims for a breed of men and women historically despised while living and acclaimed when safely dead. But, in a way, the belated honor that all societies tender their artists proves the reality of the point I am trying to make. I am really trying to make clear the nature of the artist's responsibility to his society. The peculiar nature of this responsibility is that he must never cease warring with it, for its sake and for his own. For the truth, in spite of appearances and all our hopes, is that everything is always changing and the measure of our maturity as nations and as men is how well prepared we are to meet these changes and, further, to use them for our health.

6 Now, anyone who has ever been compelled to think about it—anyone, for example, who has ever been in love —knows that the one face that one can never see is one's own face. One's lover—or one's brother, or one's enemy —sees the face you wear, and this face can elicit the most extraordinary reactions. We do the things we do and feel what we feel essentially because we must—we are responsible for our actions, but we rarely understand them. It goes without saying, I believe, that if we understood ourselves better, we would damage ourselves less. But the barrier between oneself and one's knowledge of oneself is high indeed. There are so many things one would rather not know! We become social creatures because we cannot live any other way. But in order to become social, there are a great many other things that we must not become, and we are frightened, all of us, of those forces within us that perpetually menace our precarious security. Yet the forces are there; we cannot will them away. All we can do is learn to live with them. And we cannot learn this unless we are willing to tell the truth about ourselves, and the truth about us is always at variance with what we wish to be. The human effort is to bring these two realities into a relationship resembling reconciliation. The human

grandiloquent: lofty.

beings whom we respect the most, after all—and sometimes fear the most—are those who are most deeply involved in this delicate and strenuous effort, for they have
the unshakable authority that comes only from having
looked on and endured and survived the worst. That nation is healthiest which has the least necessity to distrust
or ostracize ° or victimize these people—whom, as I say,
we honor, once they are gone, because somewhere in our
hearts we know that we cannot live without them.

7   The dangers of being an American artist are not greater
than those of being an artist anywhere else in the world,
but they are very particular. These dangers are produced
by our history. They rest on the fact that in order to conquer this continent, the particular aloneness of which I
speak—the aloneness in which one discovers that life is
tragic, and therefore unutterably beautiful—could not be
permitted. And that this prohibition is typical of all emer-
gent nations will be proved, I have no doubt, in many ways
during the next fifty years. This continent now is conquered, but our habits and our fears remain. And, in the
same way that to become a social human being one modifies
and suppresses and, ultimately, without great courage, lies
to oneself about all one's interior, uncharted chaos, so have
we, as a nation, modified and suppressed and lied about
all the darker forces in our history. We know, in the case
of the person, that whoever cannot tell himself the truth
about his past is trapped in it, is immobilized in the
prison of his undiscovered self. This is also true of nations. We know how a person, in such a paralysis, is unable to assess either his weaknesses or his strengths, and
how frequently indeed he mistakes the one for the other.
And this, I think, we do. We are the strongest nation in
the Western world, but this is not for the reasons that we
think. It is because we have an opportunity that no other
nation has of moving beyond the Old World concepts of
race and class and caste,° to create, finally, what we must

ostracize: exile or exclude.
   caste: a system of rigid social classification, based on birth,
wealth, occupation, etc.

have had in mind when we first began speaking of the New World. But the price of this is a long look backward whence we came and an unflinching assessment of the record. For an artist, the record of that journey is most clearly revealed in the personalities of the people the journey produced. Societies never know it, but the war of an artist with his society is a lover's war, and he does, at his best, what lovers do, which is to reveal the beloved to himself and, with that revelation, to make freedom real.

ANALYSIS

This lucid essay could well be used as the cornerstone of this section, "The Critical Essay: Society." What Baldwin is trying to make us understand here is the relationship of the artist to society, and the responsibility society must feel for its artists. If you think that other writers in this book have been too critical of society, Baldwin's essay might give you a new perspective on them.

The image of the artist as a gadfly, an insect that stings society to rouse it from its stupor, has been used for centuries. Socrates was called the gadfly of Athens, and American poet Robert Frost, using a more favorable image, wished to be known as one who waged a lover's quarrel with the world. Frost's image is the one used by Baldwin here. It is, ultimately, the image of a "questioner." As Baldwin says, the artists must drive to the heart of every answer, as one answer might disguise another question. It is interesting to note that most of the critical essays in this section, in fact, end with questions: Sevareid asks about the dark side of the human spirit, Snow asks if we will use the means we have to destroy ourselves, and Woolf asks her audience of women what they will now do with the empty room that is finally theirs.

If Baldwin's essay has appealed to you, you might be asking questions about some of his answers. What does he mean in paragraph 1 by saying that the purpose of art is to make the world "a more human dwelling place"? (How do we know what "human" is?) What does he mean by saying that nothing is "stable" under heaven? Are even the revelations of artists "unstable"? Where do artists get their authority to be the questioners of society?

Questions on Content

1. According to Baldwin in paragraph 1, what is the precise role of the artist in society?
2. Why have societies traditionally battled with their artists?
3. How, according to Baldwin, is the artist different from other "responsible actors" in society?
4. What is the "peculiar nature" of the artist's responsibility to society (paragraph 5)?
5. What, according to Baldwin, are the particular dangers of being an American artist?

Add to Your Vocabulary

banality, incorrigible, bulwark, grandiloquent, ostracize.

Questions on Technique

1. Like most imaginative writers, Baldwin uses a great deal of figurative language ° in this essay. What does he mean by "the great wilderness" in paragraph 1? Tell whether you feel that this is an effective description, or an ineffective one.
2. In the last sentence of paragraph 1, what does the pronoun "its" refer to? In your opinion, is this reference clear enough?
3. The concept of "aloneness" is crucial to this essay. The aloneness in paragraph 7 refers back to the aloneness described in paragraph 1. Does Baldwin tell in paragraph 1, or anywhere else, *why* we discover in our

figurative language: See Glossary.

aloneness that life is tragic? Do you think his essay would be more forceful if he had explained this further?

4. Why, if life is "tragic," is it "unutterably beautiful"? Why do you think Baldwin chooses not to explain this at length?

5. In the final sentence in paragraph 7, Baldwin refers to the "lover's war." What details in paragraph 6 does that final sentence refer back to?

Techniques to Imitate

Using an analogy to explain or clarify an idea

A common way to explain or clarify an idea is to draw an analogy, an extended comparison. For example, a teacher may explain the construction of a sentence by comparing writers to masons. Masons use stone or cement block; writers use words. By arranging blocks in a certain way, masons build the thing they have in mind. By arranging words in a certain way, writers express the ideas they have in mind.

To make clear the nature of the artist's responsibility to society, Baldwin draws an analogy between the artist and a lover. The artist's responsibility, he says, is to show society its true nature—"if we understood ourselves better, we would damage ourselves less." Baldwin then compares the artist to a lover who, out of love, shows the loved one his or her own true nature. Like a lover, the artist tries to help the thing that is loved. The artist loves society and tries to help society by revealing it to itself. In his final sentence, Baldwin summarizes his analogy. "Societies never know it, but the war of an artist with his society is a lover's war, and he does, at his best, what lovers do, which is to reveal the beloved to himself and, with that revelation, to make freedom real."

If, when you are writing an expository essay about a complex subject, you feel that a comparison would be helpful, imitate Baldwin's technique. Keep your analogy simple. Remember that it should be used to clarify your ideas, not to make your essay more complex.

Suggestions for Writing

1. Using Baldwin's idea that the artist wages a "lover's battle with society," write a brief essay in which you explain how everyone has this basic relationship to society. Perhaps you can think of a different comparison to express this relationship: we pointed out that Socrates was compared to a gadfly. You might try comparing society to a field of wheat and its critics to those who must sort out the wheat from the chaff. Or, you might compare society to a garden and its critics to those who attack the weeds.

2. If you agree with Baldwin's view of the artist's role, write an essay in which you explain specifically how one writer has attempted to reveal to society something about itself. (Some possibilities are Thoreau, Crane, Shakespeare, Frost.) In your essay, tell which of the author's works you will be discussing, summarize what this piece of writing is about, and then tell what it "reveals" to society about itself.

3. Write a 500-word essay in which you explain how in this essay Baldwin himself is speaking as an "artist" who has a battle with society. Explain what he is revealing to society in the last paragraph.

7

THE CRITICAL ESSAY: LITERATURE

For centuries, writers have used expository prose to discuss other writers' creative products. The shelves of commentaries on Shakespeare's work, for example, would astound the average theatergoer who simply enjoys the plays on stage, to say nothing of how they would affect Shakespeare were he to return today. We call this kind of exposition literary criticism.

You have been engaged in writing literary criticism longer than you think. Its simplest form is the book review. Perhaps you first reported on a book orally, telling the class what you read and how the story "turned out." When you came to writing reports, you realized that summarizing the plot was not enough if you wished to give your own views of the work. Good newspaper critics, especially in the Sunday supplements, also do more than summarize. They describe the contents of a new work and tell us *how* it succeeds or fails. A competent and well-read critic will also describe how the work relates to other writings that it has structural or thematic connections with. Some reviewers also tell us if something is "good" or "bad," value judgments which in general one should be wary of.

We include one book review among the four models of literary criticism here. The other three critical essays do more than review the first appearance of a book or survey the contents in a general way. Like the social critics Eric Sevareid, C. P. Snow, Virginia Woolf, and James Baldwin, these writers talk "around" their subject. They illuminate and explore.

J. B. PRIESTLEY

Macbeth: An Afterword

Literary criticism is never a substitute for the work of art itself. You might argue that neither is reading *Macbeth* a substitute for seeing it produced. True, but we must make a concession somewhere to the few opportunities many of us have to hear Shakespeare's poetry on the stage. Priestley assumes, in this essay, that we have at least read the play. He does not discuss the plot. He does not identify Duncan or Banquo. He never mentions Macduff. He speaks of the witches as though we all were aware of their prophecies. Priestley makes these assumptions in order to get at what he thinks is the heart of the play: ambition leading to violence. This essay, which has been reprinted widely in textbooks, was written well before we began to realize that some of our views of male and female behavior are stereotyped. Read carefully, then, as Priestley analyzes the roles given to Macbeth and to his queen.

In 1960 Priestley published a lengthy critical study called *Literature and Western Man.* The *New York Times* reviewer commented above all on the gusto with which Priestley wrote, the "sense of personal engagement with great books" which one feels in his presence. Since Priestley is a novelist and playwright as well as a critic, one is not surprised to find him bringing us close to the imaginative power that pervades a work of art. He is clearly in awe of this creature Macbeth. Watch how he transmits that feeling of wonder, and then of terror.

1   Like *Hamlet, King Lear,* and *Othello, Macbeth* was produced during what is generally called the third or tragic period of Shakespeare's life as a dramatist. It was a time when his stupendous powers were at their height, but when some inward conflict made him intensely aware of the contrast in our life between good and evil, light and dark, reasonable and peaceful order and chaotic violence. Some division in himself enabled him to give the fullest expression to these contrasts in hundreds of lines that haunt the mind like great tragic music. The world we discover in these tragedies is a terrible one.

2   Indeed, we might say that in *Macbeth,* a tragedy of tremendous power, Hell is let loose. Notice how much of it seems to take place at night, to be intimately concerned with darkness: it is a drama in black, edged with the crimson of spilled blood. Our old actors were very superstitious, and one of their superstitions, which I can remember myself, was that it was very unlucky to produce *Macbeth,* as if the presence of the play attracted to the theater various accidents and misfortunes. This is probably only another tribute to its astonishing power as a piece of literature.

3   To this day, after knowing the play for fifty years, some of its speeches make me feel my hair is standing on end. Macbeth himself is one of the great poets among Shakespeare's characters, for in line after line, speech after speech, he says wonderful things. And the fact that Shakespeare gives him such things to say, of a power and insight and poetry unmatched by any other character in the drama, proves definitely, to my mind, that Shakespeare saw it as Macbeth's play and nobody else's, not even Lady Macbeth's. The play is about what happens to Macbeth when ambition and the promptings of evil (represented by the witches) overcome the reluctance of an imaginative man— and Macbeth is essentially an imaginative man—to embark on a course of violent and criminal actions.

4   Many criminals, especially murderers, are people without imagination. They commit murder because other people, their victims, do not seem to them to be real persons like themselves but mere obstacles to be got out of the way. They are so unimaginative and strongly self-centered that they, alone, really exist in a world of robots, dummies, shadows. Strictly speaking, such criminals are so far removed from ordinary personal and social relationships that they are mad. They do not defy their consciences because they have no consciences to defy.

5   But Macbeth is not one of these dreamy criminal lunatics. He is an imaginative man, of unusual courage and ability, as Shakespeare makes us realize when Macbeth is first discussed, in Scene 2, Act I. (These opening scenes are always very informative and important in Shakespeare.) But there is some weakness, some fatal flaw, in his character. We are made to realize this as soon as he enters and speaks his very first line: "So foul and fair a day I have not seen." This revealing line is spoken within hearing of the witches, who are aware of this flaw in his character. It suggests that already, in the hour of his triumph as a victorious general, there is in him some strange and dangerous confusion, bringing together and mingling what is "foul" and what is "fair." And notice that in this scene Banquo, a straightforward man, merely expresses a natural disgust for the witches, whereas Macbeth is fascinated by their prophecies, urging them to tell him more. There is more than impatient ambition here—though there is that too, and Shakespeare is always suspicious of such ambition—for behind it there is this fatal flaw, this inability to keep a strict watch along the border between good and evil, a weakness of the central and all-important conscience.

6   We do not know, however, how far Macbeth would have gone (for we soon discover that he cannot help recoiling in disgust and horror from criminal acts) if it had not been for his wife. It is she who encourages him by every feminine device, from wifely sympathy to artful scorn of what she calls his cowardice. Had his wife been an ordinary tenderhearted woman, instead of being so ambitious, ruthless, callous, * then we feel that his career of crime— and that is what it is—would probably have been checked at the outset. But instead of pulling him out of it, she thrusts him further into it. Yet she is not really stronger than he is, for when he has reaped the full and terrible harvest of his crimes, she is no longer his partner, steeling his will, but a mere wreck of a woman, out of her mind.

7   What are we to make of this? It is all very difficult. My own view is that Shakespeare, beginning with the witches, felt so strongly impelled to hurry us into this atmosphere of darkness, evil, and doom, that he had to omit a scene that we need very badly. This scene, which would have had to be chiefly played between Macbeth and his wife, would have shown us what kind of relationship existed between them before any crime was committed or even considered. Lacking such a scene, and with it any knowledge of what their normal relationship was, we cannot help being puzzled by the character of Lady Macbeth. Why did she urge him on so relentlessly? And why, having shown herself to be far more ruthless than he was, does she break down so soon, leaving him alone to face the consequences of his actions?

8   This bewilderment explains something that always happens when this play is produced. In spite of the fact that she breaks down and then disappears from the play before it is over, the part of Lady Macbeth, with its many powerful speeches and highly dramatic situations, is always assumed by actresses, producers, directors, and critics, to be a very fine part, a magnificent gift from Shakespeare to any leading actress able to play tragedy. Yet it is my experience that whenever the part is actually played, no matter how gifted the particular actress may be, the more intelligent drama critics always express some disappointment, as if something in the part had escaped the actress. But in my view it is Shakespeare and not the actresses who must be blamed. The part is, in fact, not a fine part, the character of Lady Macbeth not having been solidly established and

not having been soundly welded into the action of the play. She is indeed its chief weakness.

9   We can only guess at what Shakespeare had in mind. Certainly he needed some character, entirely in Macbeth's confidence and determined to egg him on, in order to show us that he was not all criminal, that he had scruples * and terrible doubts, that he was very much a divided man. A wife would seem to be the best possible person to play this character. She could talk to Macbeth as nobody else could, playing confidently upon his feelings. And it is true that a very feminine woman devoted to her husband and his career and ruthlessly ambitious both for herself and him, might overcome his doubts and scruples better than anybody else could. (There is a bad tradition in the theater that Lady Macbeth should be played as a commanding and rather masculine type of woman, but it is much better, truer to life, if she is seen to be a rather small, dainty, very feminine type, as pretty and soft but as cunning and ruthless as a cat.) But that he should have such a wife, instead of the more usual kind ready to protect him from his worse self, is simply bad luck for Macbeth, and true tragedy should be outside mere bad luck. Unless, of course, one argues that it is the fatal flaw in Macbeth that led him to fall in love with and then marry a woman like Lady Macbeth, a woman who, when the time came, would strengthen his darker, criminal side.

10   To be as utterly ruthless and callous as she appears to be at first, when she is ready to do things her husband shrinks from doing, means that Lady Macbeth has had to suppress all her natural womanly feelings. But she can only do this up to a point, and when one crime follows another and there is no end to the bloodshed and horror, the suppressed half of her takes its revenge by striking at her very sanity, finally taking her out of reality altogether. And by this time, as we discover, Macbeth has almost ceased to care whether she is mad or sane, living or dead, for no personal relationship means anything to him any longer, existing as he does in a kind of Hell where there are no such relationships, where nothing now has any real meaning.

11   Macbeth's great speech, one of the greatest in all dramatic literature, which follows the news of the Queen's death, offers us the key to the whole tragedy:

> She should have died hereafter;
> There would have been a time for such a word.
> Tomorrow, and tomorrow, and tomorrow,
> Creeps in this petty pace from day to day
> To the last syllable of recorded time,
> And all our yesterdays have lighted fools
> The way to dusty death. Out, out, brief candle!
> Life's but a walking shadow, a poor player
> That struts and frets his hour upon the stage
> And then is heard no more. It is a tale
> Told by an idiot, full of sound and fury,
> Signifying nothing.

Now much earlier, in Scene 3, Act II, after Duncan's death has been discovered and Macbeth is pretending to be as astonished and as much shaken as the others, we can find in Macbeth's speech on his re-entrance a curious foretaste of his final despair:

> Had I but died an hour before this chance,
> I had lived a blessed time; for, from this instant,
> There's nothing serious in mortality.
> All is but toys; renown and grace is dead;
> The wine of life is drawn, and the mere lees *
> Is left this vault to brag of.

He is largely pretending, yet there is something in him, some defeated goodness, that is already beginning to feel that "the wine of life is drawn."

12   Nor is Macbeth alone in this, for a little later in the play, at the beginning of Scene 2, Act III, Lady Macbeth, left alone for a moment, speaks to herself in this vein:

> Naught's had, all's spent,
> Where our desire is got without content.
> 'Tis safer to be that which we destroy
> Than by destruction dwell in doubtful joy.

And very soon she will begin destroying herself, losing her wits in the attempt to lose a world no longer endurable.

13 As these two destroy life in others, they also destroy the life in themselves. Macbeth the murderer is slowly murdering Macbeth. And being an imaginative man, not without some goodness in him, he knows this, and has known it from the moment he committed his first crime. Whatever is good, cherishing life, expands it, adds form and rich color to it, gives it bloom and flavor. But evil, despising and hating life, contracts it, diminishes and bleaches it, makes it formless and meaningless in the end. Macbeth's famous speech shows us the defeat of goodness, the triumph of evil, in its terrible vision of a dusty nothingness and an endless idiocy.

14 We must not imagine that these ideas of good and evil only apply to life in Scotland in the eleventh century or in England early in the seventeenth century. They apply with equal force to our life here and now. Indeed, when reading about the more murderous types of American gangsters, I have often felt that their kind of life lacked precisely those qualities that stupid people imagined it to have: namely, excitement, zest, enthusiasm. They seemed to live in that stale, dead atmosphere which we find in Macbeth's last despairing vision of existence. The evil to which they had given themselves had cut them off from everything that expands and enhances, colors and flavors life.

15 "Methought I heard a voice cry 'Sleep no more. Macbeth does murder sleep.' " Yes, and soon, before he has done, he has murdered honor and friendship, murdered all possibility of innocent pleasure and joy, murdered love and all satisfying human relationships. And his tragedy is that from first to last he is terribly aware of what he is losing, for he is neither a madman nor a dumb brute, as so many murderers are, but a man who might have been great and good but for that fatal flaw in his nature. Through that crack in his conscience, as the witches perceived, the destructive forces of evil would invade his soul, giving him a crown that no longer meant anything, in a darkening ruin of a life on which the sun would never rise again.

ANALYSIS

Priestley has three theories about this tragedy. First, it is "Macbeth's play and nobody else's." Second, Lady Macbeth is its chief weakness. Third, "as these two [characters] destroy life in others, they also destroy the life in themselves." This "defeated goodness" is seen early in the play and comes to its climax in Macbeth's famous "Tomorrow, and tomorrow" speech in Act V. Priestley does not debate or argue these theories. He merely expounds them as a means of getting closer to the power of the play. He feels his theory on Lady Macbeth might help to illuminate a difficult role. He feels, also, that if we take Macbeth's "To-morrow, and tomorrow" speech as "the key to the whole tragedy" we will see more clearly "the triumph of evil" as Shakespeare wanted us to see it. This is what we mean by talking "around" a subject. Priestley calls his essay an "afterword." We might call it "thoughts on the nature of evil."

Readers will react to Priestley's criticism according to their own knowledge of and enthusiasm for the play. It is hard for critics to strike a common ground; they must adhere to their own ideas and hope they will fall among sympathetic readers. Lady Macbeth is one of the cruxes, or perplexing difficulties, of this play. Priestley's explanation of the problem is intriguing. Is her role badly written? Is playing her on stage a trap, not a gift, for a fine actress? Should she be soft but cunning rather than brash and commanding? If your answer to these questions is yes, have you then a better understanding of the complexity of this role?

We might say to Priestley that Lady Macbeth is a foil for Macbeth; that is to say, she is "sacrificed" early in the play to give Macbeth a warning of "which way madness lies." When Shakespeare takes her "out of reality altogether," is not Macbeth's insensitivity (if we can call it that) to her death a frightening aspect of the hero and of what is to follow? In paragraph 13, Priestley writes that "evil . . . makes [life] formless and meaningless in the end." To Macbeth, his wife's death is meaningless. In time, his own will seem the same. Had Shakespeare enlarged the role of Lady Macbeth, she might have dominated too much of the play. She might have been harder to "sacrifice." One is reminded of Mercutio (in *Romeo and Juliet*) and Julius Caesar in somewhat the same positions; they dominated the stage when they were on it. If this is "Macbeth's play and nobody else's" might not Shakespeare have been unwilling to run the risk of Macbeth's losing it?

These counter-arguments are only another way of talking "around" this perplexing but fascinating subject. Literary criticism is not so much interested in settling an issue as in raising intelligent questions. Interpretation is often tentative. What is your reaction to the play? to what Priestley writes? to this example of critical method?

Questions on Content

1. In paragraphs 6, 9, and 10, Priestley comments on Lady Macbeth's nature as a woman and on the nature of women in general. Do you agree with these opinions of Priestley's? If you do not, discuss whether they weaken his argument about Lady Macbeth as a character. Is there a subtle attitude here that is not fair to men? That is, is it fair to see ruthlessness and callousness as only male traits, "unnatural" in a woman?
2. What does Priestley have to say about criminals and imagination? How does Macbeth, through his work or deeds, show that he is an "imaginative man"?
3. What does Priestley mean when he says (paragraph 13) "Macbeth the murderer is slowly murdering Macbeth?"

Add to Your Vocabulary

callous, scruples, lees.

Questions on Technique

1. Priestley could easily have begun this essay with a consideration of the chronological order of events in this play. Why do you suppose he chose not to?

2. How does Priestley develop the "foul and fair" aspect of Macbeth's character after first discussing it in paragraph 5?

3. Interpret Lady Macbeth's lines: " 'Tis safer to be that which we destroy/Than by destruction dwell in doubtful joy." How does Priestley relate these lines to Macbeth's lines in the "Tomorrow, and tomorrow" speech?

4. Priestley gives his essay a neat introduction (two paragraphs) and conclusion (two paragraphs). How does he divide the remaining paragraphs; that is, what chief subjects does he discuss? Could you suggest a better balance?

Techniques to Imitate

1. *Being thoroughly acquainted with the subject*
2. *Supporting a view by specific references and quotations*

Priestley's critical essay suggests two important pieces of advice for a young critic: first, know thoroughly the literary selection you are writing about; second, give ample evidence from the selection to support your critical opinions.

1. A critical essay like Priestley's, which examines one or two limited features of a literary work, makes quite different demands of a critic from the demands made by the general book or play review found in newspapers and magazines. The newspaper review is necessarily based on first impressions following a brief acquaintance —one reading of a book or viewing of a play. Literary criticism, on the other hand, should be based on thorough acquaintance with the work, the result of many readings and much thoughtful reflection. Priestley says he has known *Macbeth* for fifty years, a kind of acquaintance few critics can imitate, but the point can still be made that truly meaningful criticism cannot be written abruptly "off the top of one's head." It can be written only after extensive study and hours of careful thought.

2. Priestley must, of course, comment on life as well as on

literature, but he never moves very far from *Macbeth*. He concentrates on the play, and to support his views he supplies evidence in the form of specific references to the play and quotations from it. A critic, then, must be thoroughly familiar with the literature being criticized, and must support the criticism with abundant specific evidence from the literature itself.

Suggestions for Writing

1. In a 400-word essay, defend Lady Macbeth's role as one which is soundly welded to the action of the whole play.
2. Write a 500-word essay on the witches and their contribution to the sense of horror in this play.
3. Choose another Shakespeare play with which you are familiar. Discuss in 400 words the hero's or heroine's role. Is it the dominant one of the play or are there other main roles? Is any role in the play difficult to cast?
4. If you disagree with Priestley on any of the points of his argument, write a "Reply to Priestley" giving reasons for your disagreement.
5. Write a critical essay on a serious film or play you have seen recently or a good novel you have read. Discuss in 500 words the major theme in this work of art—that is, the "point" or the "meaning" of the film or novel (such as the theme of *Macbeth* being ambition leading to violence and death).

JOHN CIARDI

Robert Frost:
The Way to the Poem

John Ciardi is an editor of *Saturday Review* magazine. He has been director of the Bread Loaf (Vermont)
Writers' Conference and a popular lecturer to college
audiences around the country. But his creative energies
go into his poetry. *Homeward to America* (1940) was his
first volume to be published. In the last thirty-five years
he has continued to write distinguished poetry for adults
and for children. As teacher and lecturer, Ciardi has
long been sharing with his students the pleasures of
poetry, the zest that goes into writing it and that can,
equally, go into reading it. "Creative reading" we
could call it.

In the essay that follows, Ciardi demonstrates what
we mean by a close reading of a poem. He takes Frost's
quatrains apart, but he also puts them back together
again so that we are left with a poem analyzed, not a
mere prose paraphrase. Ciardi believes that if we do
no more than "message hunt" (that is, turn the poetry
into a prose statement that makes a convenient moral or
a final examination answer), we close our eyes and ears
to beauty. The intelligent reading of a poem illuminates
all its facets: the rhythm, the rhyme scheme, the words,
the meaning.

In discussing the words of Frost's poem, Ciardi uses

three terms which may need definition: simile, metaphor, and symbol. A simile compares a thing or character, using the words *like* or *as,* to something of a different kind or character; for example, she was as happy as a lark, or, my love is like a red, red rose, or, his smile is like a dagger in my heart. A metaphor identifies one thing or character, without the words *like* or *as,* with another, generally of dissimilar kind or character; for example, a mighty fortress is our God, or, death is but one more tomorrow. A symbol, on the other hand, is the object, character, or quality which is a sign of, or which stands for, or suggests, something other than itself by reason of relationship, convention, or association; for example, the fox is a symbol of craftiness, purple is the symbol of rank or authority, a white flag is the symbol of surrender.

Stopping by Woods on a Snowy Evening
by Robert Frost

Whose woods these are I think I know.
His house is in the village, though;
He will not see me stopping here
To watch his woods fill up with snow.

My little horse must think it queer
To stop without a farmhouse near
Between the woods and frozen lake
The darkest evening of the year.

He gives his harness bells a shake
To ask if there is some mistake.
The only other sound's the sweep
Of easy wind and downy flake.

The woods are lovely, dark, and deep,
But I have promises to keep,
And miles to go before I sleep,
And miles to go before I sleep.

1   **T**he School System has much
to say these days of the virtue of reading widely, and not
enough about the virtues of reading less but in depth. There
are any number of reading lists for poetry, but there is not
enough talk about individual poems. Poetry, finally, is one
poem at a time. To read any one poem carefully is the
ideal preparation for reading another. Only a poem can
illustrate how poetry works.

2 Above, therefore, is a poem—one of the master lyrics
of the English language, and almost certainly the best-
known poem by an American poet. What happens in it?—
which is to say, not *what* does it mean, but *how* does it
mean? How does it go about being a human reenactment
of a human experience? The author—perhaps the thou-
sandth reader would need to be told—is Robert Frost.

3 Even the TV audience can see that this poem begins
as a seemingly-simple narration of a seemingly-simple incident but ends by suggesting meanings far beyond anything specifically referred to in the narrative. And even
readers with only the most casual interest in poetry might
be made to note the additional fact that, though the poem
suggests those larger meanings, it is very careful never to
abandon its pretense to being simple narration. There is
duplicity ° at work. The poet pretends to be talking about
one thing, and all the while he is talking about many others.

4 Many readers are forever unable to accept the poet's
essential duplicity. It is almost safe to say that a poem is
never about what it seems to be about. As much could be
said of the proverb. The bird in the hand, the rolling stone,
the stitch in time never (except by an artful double-decep-
tion) intend any sort of statement about birds, stones, or
sewing. The incident of this poem, one must conclude, is
at root a metaphor.

5 Duplicity aside, this poem's movement from the specific to the general illustrates one of the basic formulas of

---

   duplicity: deception, pretending to be or do one thing when
actually being or doing another.

all poetry. Such a grand poem as Arnold's "Dover Beach" and such lesser, though unfortunately better known poems as Longfellow's "The Village Blacksmith" and Holmes's "The Chambered Nautilus" are built on the same progression. In these three poems, however, the generalization is markedly set apart from the specific narration, and even seems additional to the telling rather than intrinsic ° to it. It is this sense of division one has in mind in speaking of "a tacked-on moral."

6   There is nothing wrong-in-itself with a tacked-on moral. Frost, in fact, makes excellent use of the device at times. In this poem, however, Frost is careful to let the whatever-the-moral-is grow out of the poem itself. When the action ends the poem ends. There is no epilogue and no explanation. Everything pretends to be about the narrated incident. And that pretense sets the basic tone of the poem's performance of itself.

7   The dramatic force of that performance is best observable, I believe, as a progression in three scenes.

8   In scene one, which coincides with stanza one, a man —a New England man—is driving his sleigh somewhere at night. It is snowing, and as the man passes a dark patch of woods he stops to watch the snow descend into the darkness. We know, moreover, that the man is familiar with these parts (he knows who owns the woods and where the owner lives), and we know that no one has seen him stop. As scene one forms itself in the theater of the mind's-eye, therefore, it serves to establish some as yet unspecified relation between the man and the woods.

9   It is necessary, however, to stop here for a long parenthesis: Even so simple an opening statement raises any number of questions. It is impossible to address all the questions that rise from the poem stanza by stanza, but two that arise from stanza one illustrate the sort of thing one might well ask of the poem detail by detail.

10   Why, for example, does the man not say what errand he is on? What is the force of leaving the errand generalized? He might just as well have told us that he was going

intrinsic: belonging to a thing by its very nature.

to the general store, or returning from it with a jug of molasses he had promised to bring Aunt Harriet and two suits of long underwear he had promised to bring the hired man. Frost, moreover, can handle homely detail to great effect. He preferred to leave his motive generalized. Why?

11 And why, on the other hand, does he say so much about knowing the absent owner of the woods and where he lives? Is it simply that one set of details happened-in whereas another did not? To speak of things "happening-in" is to assault the integrity * of a poem. Poetry cannot be discussed meaningfully unless one can assume that everything in the poem—every last comma and variant spelling —is in it by the poet's specific act of choice. Only bad poets allow into their poems what is haphazard or cheaply chosen.

12 The errand, I will venture a bit brashly for lack of space, is left generalized in order the more aptly to suggest *any* errand in life and, therefore, life itself. The owner is there because he is one of the forces of the poem. Let it do to say that the force he represents is the village of mankind (that village at the edge of winter) from which the poet finds himself separated (has separated himself?) in his moment by the woods (and to which, he recalls finally, he has promises to keep). The owner is he-who-lives-in-his-village-house, thereby locked away from the poet's awareness of the-time-the-snow-tells as it engulfs and obliterates the world the village man allows himself to believe he "owns." Thus, the owner is a representative of an order of reality from which the the poet has divided himself for the moment, though to a certain extent he ends by reuniting with it. Scene one, therefore, establishes not only a relation between the man and the woods, but the fact that the man's relation begins with his separation (though momentarily) from mankind.

13 End parenthesis one, begin parenthesis two.

14 Still considering the first scene as a kind of dramatic performance of forces, one must note that the poet has meticulously * matched the simplicity of his language to the pretended simplicity of the narrative. Clearly, the man stopped because the beauty of the scene moved him, but he neither tells us that the scene is beautiful nor that he is moved. A bad writer, always ready to overdo, might have written: "The vastness gripped me, filling my spirit with the slow steady sinking of the snow's crystalline perfection into the glimmerless profundities of the hushed primeval wood." Frost's avoidance of such a spate ° illustrates two principles of good writing. The first, he has stated himself in "The Mowing": "Anything *more* than the truth would have seemed too weak" (italics mine). Understatement ° is one of the basic sources of power in English poetry. The second principle is to let the action speak for itself. A good novelist does not tell us that a given character is good or bad (at least not since the passing of the Dickens tradition): he shows us the character in action and then, watching him, we know. Poetry, too, has fictional obligations: even when the characters are ideas and metaphors rather than people, they must be *characterized in action*. A poem does not *talk about* ideas; it *enacts* them. The force of the poem's performance, in fact, is precisely to act out (and thereby to make us act out emphatically, that is, to *feel out,* that is, to *identify with*) the speaker and why he stopped. The man is the principal actor in this little "drama of why" and in scene one he is the only character, though as noted, he is somehow related to the absent power.

15   End second parenthesis.

16   In scene two (stanzas two and three) a *foil* is introduced. In fiction and drama, a foil is a character who "plays against" a more important character. By presenting a different point of view or an opposed set of motives, the foil moves the more important character to react in ways that might not have found expression without such opposition. The more important character is thus more fully revealed —to the reader and to himself. The foil here is the horse.

17   The horse forces the question. Why did the man stop? Until it occurs to him that his "little horse must think it

---

spate: an excessive quantity.
understatement: See Glossary.

queer" he had not asked himself for reasons. He had simply stopped. But the man finds himself faced with the question he imagines the horse to be asking: what *is* there to stop for out there in the cold, away from bin and stall (house and village and mankind?) and all that any self-respecting beast could value on such a night? In sensing that other view, the man is forced to examine his own more deeply.

18 In stanza two the question arises only as a feeling within the man. In stanza three, however (still scene two), the horse acts. He gives his harness bells a shake. "What's wrong?" he seems to say. "What are we waiting for?"

19 By now, obviously, the horse—without losing its identity as horse—has also become a symbol. A symbol is something that stands for something else. Whatever that something else may be, it certainly begins as that order of life that does not understand why a man stops in the wintry middle of nowhere to watch the snow come down. (Can one fail to sense by now that the dark and the snow-fall symbolize a death-wish, however momentary, *i.e.,* that hunger for final rest and surrender that a man may feel, but not a beast?)

20 So by the end of scene two the performance has given dramatic force to three elements that work upon the man. There is his relation to the world of the owner. There is his relation to the brute world of the horse. And there is that third presence of the unownable world, the movement of the all-engulfing snow across all the orders of life, the man's, the owner's, and the horse's—with the difference that the man knows of that second dark-within-the-dark of which the horse cannot, and the owner will not, know.

21 The man ends scene two with all these forces working upon him simultaneously. He feels himself moved to a decision. And he feels a last call from the darkness: "the sweep/Of easy wind and downy flake." It would be so easy and so downy to go into the woods and let himself be covered over.

22 But scene three (stanza four) produces a fourth

force. This fourth force can be given many names. It is certaintly better, in fact, to give it many names than to attempt to limit it to one. It is social obligation, or personal commitment,* or duty, or just the realization that a man cannot indulge a mood forever. All of these and more. But, finally, he has a simple decision to make. He may go into the woods and let the darkness and the snow swallow him from the world of beast and man. Or he must move on. And unless he is going to stop here forever, it is time to remember that he has a long way to go and that he had best be getting there. (So there is something to be said for the horse, too.)

23   Then and only then, his question driven more and more deeply into himself by these cross-forces, does the man venture a comment on what attracted him: "The woods are lovely, dark and deep." His mood lingers over the thought of that lovely dark-and-deep (as do the very syllables in which he phrases the thought), but the final decision is to put off the mood and move on. He has his man's way to go and his man's obligations to tend to before he can yield. He has miles to go before his sleep. He repeats that thought and the performance ends.

24   But why the repetition? The first time Frost says "And miles to go before I sleep," there can be little doubt that the primary meaning is: "I have a long way to go before I get to bed tonight." The second time he says it, however, "miles to go" and "sleep" are suddenly transformed into symbols. What are those "something-elses" the symbols stand for? Hundreds of people have tried to ask Mr. Frost that question and he has always turned it away. He has turned it away *because he cannot answer it*. He could answer some part of it. But some part is not enough.

25   For a symbol is like a rock dropped into a pool: it sends out ripples in all directions, and the ripples are in motion. Who can say where the last ripple disappears? One may have a sense that he knows the approximate center point of the ripples, the point at which the stone struck the water. Yet

even then he has trouble marking it surely. How does one make a mark on water? Oh very well—the center point of that second "miles to go" is probably approximately in the neighborhood of being close to meaning, perhaps, "the road of life"; and the second "before I sleep" is maybe that close to meaning "before I take my final rest," the rest in darkness that seemed so temptingly dark-and-deep for the moment of the mood. But the ripples continue to move and the light to change on the water, and the longer one watches the more changes he sees. Such shifting-and-being-at-the-same-instant is of the very sparkle and life of poetry. One experiences it as one experiences life, for everytime he looks at an experience he sees something new, and he sees it change as he watches it. And that sense of continuity in fluidity is one of the primary kinds of knowledge, one of man's basic ways of knowing, and one that only the arts can teach, poetry foremost among them.

26 Frost himself certainly did not ask what that repeated last line meant. It came to him and he received it. He "felt right" about it. And what he "felt right" about was in no sense a "meaning" that, say, an essay could apprehend,* but an act of experience that could be fully presented only by the dramatic enactment of forces which is the performance of the poem.

27 Now look at the poem in another way. Did Frost know what he was going to do when he began? Considering the poem simply as an act of skill, as a piece of juggling, one cannot fail to respond to the magnificent turn at the end where, with one flip, seven of the simplest words in the language suddenly dazzle full of never-ending waves of thought and feeling. Or, more precisely, of felt-thought. Certainly an equivalent stunt by a juggler—could there be an equivalent—would bring the house down. Was it to cap his performance with that grand stunt that Frost wrote the poem?

28 Far from it. The obvious fact is that *Frost could not have known he was going to write those lines until he*

wrote them. Then a second fact must be registered: *he wrote them because, for the fun of it, he had got himself into trouble.*

29 Frost, like every good poet, began by playing a game with himself. The most usual way of writing a four line stanza with four feet to the line is to rhyme the third line with the first, and the fourth line with the second. Even that much rhyme is so difficult in English that many poets and almost all of the anonymous ballad makers do not bother to rhyme the first and third lines at all, settling for two rhymes in four lines as good enough. For English is a rhyme-poor language. In Italian and in French, for example, so many words end with the same sounds that rhyming is relatively easy—so easy that many modern French and Italian poets do not bother to rhyme at all. English, being a more agglomerate ° language, has far more final sounds, hence fewer of them rhyme. When an Italian poet writes a line ending with "vita" (life) he has literally hundreds of rhyme choices available. When an English poet writes "life" at the end of a line he can summon "strife, wife, knife, fife, rife," and then he is in trouble. Now "life-strife" and "life-rife" and "life-wife" seem to offer a combination of possible ideas that can be related by more than just the rhyme. Inevitably, therefore, the poets have had to work and rework these combinations until the sparkle has gone out of them. The reader is normally tired of such rhyme-led associations. When he encounters "life-strife" he is certainly entitled to suspect that the poet did not really want to say "strife"—that had there been in English such a word as, say, "hife," meaning "infinite peace and harmony," the poet would as gladly have used that word instead of "strife." Thus, the reader feels that the writing is haphazard, that the rhyme is making the poet say things he does not really feel, and which, therefore, the reader does not feel except as boredom. One likes to see the rhymes fall into place, but he must end with the belief that it is the poet who is deciding what is

   agglomerate: literally, collected into a cluster or mass. As Ciardi uses the word, it means mixed or blended.

said and not the rhyme scheme that is forcing the saying.

30 So rhyme is a kind of game, and an especially difficult one in English. As in every game, the fun of the rhyme is to set one's difficulties high and then to meet them skillfully. As Frost himself once defined freedom, it consists of "moving easy in harness."

31 In "Stopping by Woods on a Snowy Evening" Frost took a long chance. He decided to rhyme not two lines in each stanza, but three. Not even Frost could have sustained that much rhyme in a long poem (as Dante,° for example, with the advantage of writing in Italian, sustained triple rhyme for thousands of lines in "The Divine Comedy"). Frost would have known instantly, therefore, when he took the original chance, that he was going to write a short poem. He would have had that much foretaste of it.

32 So the first stanza emerged rhymed a-a-b-a. And with the sure sense that this was to be a short poem, Frost decided to take an additional chance and to redouble: in English three rhymes in four lines is more than enough; there is no need to rhyme the fourth line. For the fun of it, however, Frost set himself to pick up that loose rhyme and to weave it into the pattern, thereby accepting the all but impossible burden of quadruple rhyme.

33 The miracle is that it worked. Despite the enormous freight of rhyme, the poem not only came out as a neat pattern, but managed to do so with no sense of strain. Every word and every rhyme falls into place as naturally and as inevitably as if there were no rhyme restricting the poet's choices.

34 That ease-in-difficulty is certainly inseparable from the success of the poem's performance. One watches the skill-man juggle three balls, then four, then five, and every addition makes the trick more wonderful. But unless he makes the hard trick seem as easy as an easy trick, then all is lost.

35 The real point, however, is not only that Frost took on a hard rhyme-trick and made it seem easy. It is rather

Dante: Dante Alighieri (1265–1321), Italian poet.

as if the juggler, carried away, had tossed up one more ball than he could really handle, and then amazed himself by actually handling it. So with the real triumph of this poem. Frost could not have known what a stunning effect his repetition of the last line was going to produce. He could not even know he was going to repeat the line. He simply found himself up against a difficulty he almost certainly had not foreseen and he had to improvise to meet it. For in picking up the rhyme from the third line of stanza one and carrying it over into stanza two, he had created an endless chain-link form within which each stanza left a hook sticking out for the next stanza to hang on. So by stanza four, feeling the poem rounding to its end, Frost had to do something about that extra rhyme.

36   He might have tucked it back into a third line rhyming with the *know-though-snow* of stanza one. He could thus have rounded the poem out to the mathematical symmetry ° of using each rhyme four times. But though such a device might be defensible in theory, a rhyme repeated after eleven lines is so far from its original rhyme sound that its feeling as rhyme must certainly be lost. And what good is theory if the reader is not moved by the writing?

37   It must have been in some such quandary ° that the final repetition suggested itself—a suggestion born of the very difficulties the poet had let himself in for. So there is that point beyond mere ease in handling a hard thing, the point at which the very difficulty offers the poet the opportunity to do better than he knew he could. What, aside from having that happen to oneself, could be more self-delighting than to participate in its happening by one's reader-identification with the poem?

38   And by now a further point will have suggested itself: that the human-insight of the poem and the technicalities of its poetic artifice ° are inseparable. Each feeds the other. That interplay is the poem's meaning, a matter

---

symmetry: regularity of form or arrangement.
quandary: a state of perplexity or doubt.
artifice: workmanship, construction.

not of WHAT DOES IT MEAN, for no one can ever say entirely what a good poem means, but of HOW DOES IT MEAN, a process one can come much closer to discussing.
39 There is a necessary epilogue. Mr. Frost has often discussed this poem on the platform, or more usually in the course of a long-evening-after a talk. Time and again I have heard him say that he just wrote it off, that it just came to him, and that he set it down as it came.
40 Once at Bread Loaf,° however, I heard him add one very essential piece to the discussion of how it "just came." One night, he said, he had sat down after supper to work at a long piece of blank verse. The piece never worked out, but Mr. Frost found himself so absorbed in it that, when next he looked up, dawn was at his window. He rose, crossed to the window, stood looking out for a few minutes, and *then* it was that "Stopping by Woods" suddenly "just came," so that all he had to do was cross the room and write it down.
41 Robert Frost is the sort of artist who hides his traces. I know of no Frost worksheets anywhere. If someone has raided his wastebasket in secret, it is possible that such worksheets exist somewhere, but Frost would not willingly allow anything but the finished product to leave him. Almost certainly, therefore, no one will ever know what was in that piece of unsuccessful blank verse he had been working at with such concentration, but I for one would stake my life that could that worksheet be uncovered, it would be found to contain the germinal * stuff of "Stopping by Woods"; that what was a-simmer in him all night without finding its proper form, suddenly, when he let his still-occupied mind look away, came at him from a different direction, offered itself in a different form, and that finding that form exactly right the impulse proceeded to marry itself to the new shape in one of the most miraculous performances of English lyricism.
42 And that, too—whether or not one can accept so

Bread Loaf: a small community on Bread Loaf Mountain near Middlebury, Vermont, where classes are held for writers each summer.

hypothetical a discussion—is part of HOW the poem means. It means that marriage to the perfect form, the poem's shapen declaration of itself, its moment's monument fixed beyond all possibility of change. And thus, finally, in every truly good poem, "How does it mean?" must always be answered "triumphantly." Whatever the poem "is about," *how* it means is always how Genesis means: the word become a form, and the form become a thing, and—when the becoming is true—the thing become a part of the knowledge and experience of the race forever.

ANALYSIS

In his critical essay on *Macbeth,* J. B. Priestley discusses only one aspect of the play, the main characters. Ciardi moves carefully, line by line, through the whole of Frost's poem. The poem's brevity allows this close reading, and it would be both presumptuous and unnecessary to go over the ground Ciardi covers so well. But we might outline the essay in order to see how a critic uses a single poem to say something pertinent about the nature of poetry.

In rough outline form, "Robert Frost: The Way to the Poem" might look something like this:

    I. The obvious meaning and the larger meaning (paragraphs 2–7)
   II. Reading line by line
      A. "Scene one" (paragraph 8)
        1. Questions to be answered (paragraphs 9–13)
        2. Notes to be made (paragraphs 14–15)
      B. "Scene two" (paragraphs 16–22)
      C. "Scene three" (paragraphs 23–26)
  III. Looking at the poem in another way (paragraphs 27–37)
  IV. The nature of poetry in general (paragraph 38)
   V. Frost's writing of this poem (paragraphs 39–41)
  VI. How a poem means (paragraph 42)

There are doubtless other ways of outlining this essay, but what is likely to be evident in any outline is Ciardi's steady moving forward toward an explanation of his basic distinction (announced in paragraph 38): not WHAT DOES A POEM MEAN? but HOW DOES A POEM MEAN? Ciardi could have called his essay "The Way into *a* Poem," for what he is trying to do is show us how to read, creatively, imaginatively, how to allow the *suggested* meanings of a poetic line to take flight, as it were.

He does not use the words "denotation" and "connotation" here, but he might have. Words first of all *denote* a meaning, that is, mark plainly or point out as distinctly as possible what the word stands for. For example, the *denotation* of the word "dog" is "a carnivorous domesticated mammal." But the word "dog" also *connotes* meanings, that is, suggests, implies, leads you further on to associated meanings. For example, *connotations* of the word "dog" are friendliness or watchfulness, rascality or ostentation or worry. Ciardi explains throughout this essay that poetry makes constant use of connotations, the meanings "around" a word.

This, then, is another kind of literary criticism. Ciardi takes a particular poem to show us poetic form in action. He does not relate the poem to the body of Frost's work. We feel he could, however, easily go on from here to demonstrate with other poems *how* a poem means.

Questions on Content

1. How does Ciardi distinguish between a "tacked-on" moral and the "whatever-the-moral-is" growing out of the poem itself?
2. What is meant by a "foil," and how does Frost use one in this poem?
3. In what way did Frost get himself into trouble with the rhyme scheme of this poem? Why is the English language rhyme-poor in comparison with French and Italian?
4. In what way does Ciardi compare the juggler with the poet?
5. In paragraph 39, Ciardi says, "There is a necessary

epilogue." What does the epilogue add to our knowledge of how a poet works?

Add to Your Vocabulary

intrinsic, integrity, meticulously, spate, commitment, apprehend, quandary, artifice, germinal.

Questions on Technique

1. This essay develops around one poem. Why do you think Ciardi chose to give us a specific example rather than talk in general terms about "how a poem means"?
2. Paragraphs 9–15 use the parenthetical technique, that is, interrupt the main argument to digress for a moment. Do you find this a good writing method? Why?
3. Why is Ciardi's discussion of Italian and French rhyming (paragraph 29) a good introduction to what he has to say in the next eight paragraphs?

Techniques to Imitate

Helping the reader to follow the train of thought

That Ciardi writes from a highly disciplined mind is indicated by the orderliness of his thinking and the logical, step-by-step way in which he takes the reader along with him. His essay is like a college lecture in which the professor is always careful to make clear to his students exactly where he is going and how each part of his lecture is related to the central idea—in this instance, to how the poem means. In other words, Ciardi never forgets his reader; in fact, he goes out of his way to help his reader follow the train of thought.

To be sure that the reader is able to follow him at all times, Ciardi frequently states what he is doing. He announces what he is going to do next, and later, before announcing the next step, he summarizes what he has done. For example, notice the following excerpts—guideposts for the reader—which reveal how he does this.

"The dramatic form of that performance is best observable, I believe, as a progression in three scenes." (paragraph 7)

"In scene one . . ." (paragraph 8)

"It is necessary, however, to stop here for a long parenthesis . . ." (paragraph 9)

"End parenthesis one, begin parenthesis two." (paragraph 13)

"End second parenthesis." (paragraph 15)

"In scene two . . ." (paragraph 16)

"So by the end of scene two . . ." (paragraph 20)

"The man ends scene two . . ." (paragraph 21)

"But scene three (stanza four) produces a fourth force." (paragraph 22)

"Now look at the poem in another way." (paragraph 27)

The Ciardi writing technique you may wish to imitate, then, is the occasional use in the course of an essay of sentences like those listed above, which help the reader to follow the progress of your thought. Naturally, you cannot do this unless your essay is well organized to begin with.

Suggestions for Writing

1. Imitate Ciardi's poetic criticism in 500 words. Choose one poem you have studied and show how the words, the rhyme, and the rhythm combine to delight the reader.

2. Write a 500-word critical essay on Robert Frost's poetry in more general terms: his homely subject matter or his use of dialogue or his attitude toward nature. You may choose another poet if you wish.

3. Write an analysis of one of your own poems, explaining how you happened to write it, why you chose the words and figures of speech you did.

4. Write an essay, in 600 words, discussing why the short story is more rewarding an art form for you than the short poem. Or reverse this argument.

5. If you like poetry and enjoy reading it, write an essay (500 words) explaining why you like it. If you dislike poetry, write an essay telling why you dislike it.

LETTY C. POGREBIN

Girls' Liberation

This critical essay is from the *New York Times Book Review*, which is a supplement to the Sunday edition. This essay covers many books, not one, and the reviewer has a personal opinion to express, which it is important to locate. In all reviews, it is also important to identify the reviewer: this writer is an editor of *Ms.* magazine. Her opening statement prepares us for a certain viewpoint. Whether or not she will convince us will depend on her skill in summoning proof for her argument.

1   **W**here sexism ° is concerned, certain children's books can be said to offend with fair warning.

2 I'm prepared for the male eye of perception in the magical, marvelous worlds of Roald Dahl, Maurice Sendak or E. B. White. With the fairy tales, Babar, Christopher Robin and Pooh, the Little Prince or Paddington, I know in advance that there will be precious few female characters with whom my daughters can make positive identification.

3   While I regret this deeply, as a feminist and a parent I try to overlook male bias in books that are overwhelmingly literate and durable. Instead of banishing "Peter

sexism: prejudice or discrimination against a person on the basis of gender.

Pan" from the shelves because Wendy flies back to Neverland every year to do Peter's spring cleaning, it seems more constructive to engage my daughters in some bedtime consciousness-raising. That way, a literary classic survives while the stereotype of the domestic female doesn't filter into their dreams unchallenged.

4   On the other side of the spectrum from the "good" books are all those bland, undistinguished volumes one can live without on several grounds—including, but not limited to, their sexist content. Here again, we have fair warning. It's no surprise to find sex-typed occupations (male doctors and police; female nurses and teachers) or sex-role rigidity (ferocious daddy tigers; gentle mommy pussycats) in books that are altogether ordinary and conformist to begin with.

5   In this vast category the Peter Pan principle doesn't hold. There's no cause for compromise unless one gets quality. What's to be gained from a visit to Richard Scarry's unimaginative animal community, where aproned mother bears are forever dishing up breakfast treats and pushing shopping carts? In the vapid ° career guidance series, such as the "I Want To Be Books" (Children's Press) it's only "natural" for a little girl to have to chart her future from such limited offerings as waitress, airplane hostess, beauty operator, homemaker or secretary. We're not shocked to discover that virtually every book about cars, trucks or trains shows only men at the wheel. Conventional concepts reflect conventional myopia.

6   And, with few exceptions—like Joe Lasker's attractive "Mothers Can Do Anything" (Whitman) and Eve Merriam's lovely perennial "Mommies at Work" (Knopf)— it is only predictable that books about mothers are set in the kitchen, oblivious to the truth of everyday life for six million preschool children whose mommies work outside the home.

7   Most of these instances of sexism in children's books no longer surprise me.

vapid: lacking liveliness, or force; insipid.

8 What I do find both amazing and appalling are the scores of books that at first description seem to be responsive to the sex-role revolution ° but, once read, reveal themselves as standard fare. Lately I have been deceived by too many books that sound promising or safe, enlightened or at least innocuous *—but turn out to harbor a hidden punch.

9 Take simple science. Only a paranoid ° could anticipate sexism in the Random House Step-Up Book, "Animals Do the Strangest Things" by Leonora and Arthur Hornblow. The blurb guarantees "little known facts about some well known animals." As my 4-year-old son and I begin reading we learn that camels' eyelashes keep out the desert sand; that lions fear a campfire; and that otters sleep in the sea. Then suddenly, on page 20, in the chapter on little brown bats, we read: 'Sometimes women are afraid of bats. They are afraid that bats will fly into their hair."

10 Aside from the "little known fact" that few *men* are relaxed about the prospect of bats in *their* hair, the authors' comment does not contribute to my son's body of knowledge about little brown bats. But it does have something invidious ° to say about women. It reinforces stock myths about the "fearful female." Because such gratuitous ° statements are so typical, we cannot excuse them as trivial. For when we allow trivia to accumulate in layer after layer of literary and cultural reference we end up with girls who believe fearfulness is "feminine" and boys who disdain "hysterical" women.

11 Beware of trivia in datebooks too. I gave up on Macmillan's "Calendar for Children" after living with author Ruthven Tremain's version of a recent year. Marginalia accompanying her January calendar page included

sex-role revolution: a change in the assumption that certain human behavior patterns are "masculine" and certain others are "feminine."

paranoid: someone excessively suspicious, who is always feeling persecuted.

invidious: objectionable, likely to cause harm or resentment.

gratuitous: uncalled for, unjustified.

a time capsule sequence in which a boy was shown flying an airplane in the 1930's and walking on the moon in the future. The girl, on the other hand, was pictured wearing a cloth dress in the old days and a paper dress in the future. What progress!

12 With the more than 50 famous and obscure men honored in the datebook there were three women, all portrayed in reference to men: Queen Elizabeth I (shown knighting Sir Frances Drake), ballerina Maria Tallchief (identified as a descendant of Chief Peter Big Heart) and Katie Weeks, whose brother is said to have "invented" the potato chip when *Katie* dropped a sliver of potato into hot fat.

13 Ranking high in the category of unfulfilled promises are books about fathers. Each time one is announced I vainly hope that the shadowy "other parent" in a child's life will be given some kind of solid participatory presence. It seems a futile wish.

14 "The Daddy Book" by Robert Stewart (American Heritage) boasts several progressive assets: Don Madden's pictures are refreshingly interracial, fathers' clothes run from high hat to hippy, a few daddies' jobs are not your average Golden Books he-man occupations (there's a poet and hairdresser here), and the fathers are shown warmly involved with their kids. However, the underlying structure assumes that, no matter how diverse the daddies' lifestyles, all mommies stay home all day.

15 When Daddy comes home from work it's a special event. He sits in his big chair, eats dinner, uses his tools. Still, the hackles don't rise until I reach the disclaimer: "Daddy often does what Mommy does." That's how Stewart introduces the idea of a man who changes diapers, cooks dinner, washes dishes, bathes children, dresses them and tucks them in. As soon as Daddy becomes involved in the domestic (not the fun-and-games part of parenting), his activities are characterized as someone else's job.

16 "The Day Daddy Stayed Home" by Ethel and Leonard Kessler (Doubleday) sounded all right. Would Daddy take over the house, kids and all the chores? Did Daddy stay home that day because Mommy went out on job interviews? Or because his child was sick and Mommy couldn't take a day off from harnessing the atom in her lab? Perish the thought. Pop's only stuck at home because of a major snowstorm, and he starts his day down in the kitchen, where Mom serves him breakfast. Later, father and adoring son spend the time shoveling snow and watching the snowplow while Mom observes the happy scene from a window in the house, where she is undoubtedly ironing socks or peeling Daddy's camembert.°

17   Often in the struggle against stereotypes, one looks for nonsexist stories about bravery and heroism. The problem here is that courage is usually tested within the context of violence or amorality. "Molly and the Giant" by Kurt Werth and Mabel Watts (Parents') proves that little girls can be daring against great odds, but in the process of outwitting the giant, Molly must be a sneak thief. And, not incidentally, the rewards are still measured in husbands.

18   "The Practical Princess" by Jay Williams (Parents') is a charmingly told tale about a sensible, well-educated princess with a mind of her own. One can object that she decimates ° a dragon with gunpowder and deceit, thereby emulating macho ° tests of valor. However, lacking a time-tested formula for "proving one's womanhood" outside of the nursery, it would seem that girls are damned if they're active and dulled if they're not.

19   A few more not-so-rhetorical questions for this Sunday morning:

20   Why do so many assertive, independent female protagonists have to be given neuter or "boyish" names—as though a girl with such qualities must have a little maleness in her?

21   Why are so many of the gracefully written books not feminist and why are most of the books with a feminist

---

camembert: a kind of cheese.
decimates: destroys.
macho: aggressively "masculine" (*macho* is Spanish for "male").

consciousness not particularly well written? There must be a way of enlightening good writers to the virtues of open options and nonsexist characters. And there must come a time when feminist writers will express to young readers the rage, vision and frustration of the female experience without proselytism ° weighing down their prose.

22   And, finally, can we inspire our children through books that come out of good intentions but not out of reality? While "Firegirl" by Gibson Rich (The Feminist Press) is an admirable effort, not every little girl can stowaway on a fire truck; and there aren't any real-life women in boots and slickers to serve as models for a little girl's aspirations. It's not enough to have Norma Klein's "Girls Can Be Anything" (Dutton) or "What To Be?" by Meredith Powell and Gail Yokubinas (Children's Press) as long as women cannot really be space pilots and Presidents in our society.

23   I don't think it's that easy to soothe our consciences or fool our children. We shouldn't be replacing old myths with new fairy tales about everyday life. Make-believe space pilots and Presidents can wait. What we need now are airtight truths and well-supported challenges to the status quo; stories about strong, endearing females and tender, companionable males; and maybe even a picture book about a terrific woman driver.

ANALYSIS

In her opening paragraph this reviewer gives us a fairly good idea of what her topic will be: certain books for children are sexist. Because Pogrebin is a careful writer, she goes on in her following paragraphs to cite titles of children's books that she claims are sexist and she gives specific details showing why they are.

But first, and probably wisely, she wants to win over those slightly hostile readers who might already be mum-

---

proselytism: attempts at making converts.

bling under their breath, by admitting readily that she would not reject the "magical, marvelous worlds" of the classics simply because they have no female characters with whom her daughters can make positive identification. She is, for the most part, going to deal with more recent books.

In paragraph 4 she says further that she is also not going to waste time with poor quality books that are ordinary and conformist to begin with.

Not until paragraph 8 does she get into one of her main points: scores of books *seem* responsive to the sex-role revolution but are really standard fare or harbor a "hidden punch." In paragraphs 9–16 she cites four publications that specifically illustrate and support this point.

In paragraph 17 she says she is, furthermore, disappointed in her search for nonsexist stories about girls whose bravery and heroism are tested. This paragraph and the next offer two examples of books that have girls as their main characters, but their courage is tested within what she calls the "macho" tradition of violence and amorality.

Paragraphs 19–23, in a rush, list further problems which the reviewer notes about the current selection of children's books.

This review invites discussion, for the issue is controversial. A major discussion might spring from further analysis of paragraph 23, where Pogrebin says that we need "stories about strong, endearing females and tender, companionable males." From this statement, would you say that a better title for this review might have been "Human Liberation"?

Questions on Content

1. In paragraph 10 the reviewer mentions "stock myths." What is a "stock myth"? Try to name some, about both men and women. (Which "stock myth" is referred to in paragraph 23, last sentence?)
2. What complaint does Pogrebin level against children's books in regard to their portrayal of the father's role?

3. What does she mean when she says in paragraph 18 that "girls are damned if they're active and dulled if they're not"? What does she mean (in paragraph 21) by the "rage, vision and frustration of the female experience"?
4. What is your answer to the question posed in paragraph 21?

Add to Your Vocabulary

vapid, innocuous, invidious, gratuitous, decimates, proselytism.

Questions on Technique

1. In paragraph 16, Pogrebin mocks a book by saying that "undoubtedly" Mom is ironing socks or peeling Daddy's camembert. What is the effect of this and of other humorous or sarcastic statements? Are they effective, or do they diminish the force of the review? Explain.
2. At the end of the review, the writer states that she thinks we need stories about "strong, endearing females" and "tender, companionable" males. What is your opinion of her adjectives here? Would the review have been more forceful if she had stated this at the opening?
3. Pogrebin praises in part some of those books that she ultimately condemns. Find examples of this. What does she gain by this technique of praising certain aspects of materials which she later condemns on other grounds?

Suggestions for Writing

1. Perhaps you are familiar with children's books—either from the books you knew as a child or from your own reading to children. If so, write a book review in answer to this one. You might agree with this analysis of offerings in children's literature, or you might dissent. Whichever you do, support your opinions with references to specific books. (See "Techniques to Imitate," page 355.)

2. Suppose this review appeared in your Sunday newspaper. Write a letter to the editor commenting on it. You may dissent or agree, but state your views clearly and support them with specific references to the review itself.

3. Write a review of at least three fairy tales that you know very well. In your review, analyze the roles given to the male and female characters. Tell what the roles would suggest to children about what men and women must do to be happy in life.

4. Using some of the selections in this book, or others that you are familiar with, analyze the roles given to males and females. Are any of the women "strong and endearing"? Are any of the men "tender and companionable"?

CLEANTH BROOKS and
ROBERT PENN WARREN

"Araby":
An Interpretation

This essay comes from a textbook called *Understanding Fiction*. The textbook is comprised of a group of stories which are accompanied by commentaries, and its purpose is to introduce students to the craft of fiction.

The short story that the critics analyze here is by the Irish writer James Joyce. Before reading the essay, of course, you will have to know the story. It appears on page 530 of this book.

1   On what may be called the simplest level this is a story of a boy's disappointment. A great part of the story, however, does not directly concern itself with the boy's love affair, but with the world in which he lives—the description of his street, the information about the dead priest and the priest's abandoned belongings, the relations with the aunt and uncle. These matters seem to come very naturally into the story; that is, they may be justified individually in the story on realistic grounds. But if such elements *merely* serve as "setting" or as mere atmosphere, then the story is obviously overloaded with nonfunctional material. Obviously, for any reader except the most casual, these items do have a function. If we find in what way these apparently irrelevant items in

"Araby" are related to each other and to the disappointment of the boy, we shall have defined the theme of the story.

2   What, then, is the relation of the boy's disappointment to such matters as the belongings of the dead priest, the fact that he stands apart talking to the girl while his friends are quarreling over the cap, the gossip over the tea table, the uncle's lateness, and so on? One thing that is immediately suggested by the mention of these things is the boy's growing sense of isolation, the lack of sympathy between him and his friends, teachers, and family. He says, "I imagined that I bore my chalice safely through a throng of foes." For instance, when the uncle is standing in the hall, the boy could not go into the front parlor and lie at the window; or at school his ordinary occupations began to seem "ugly monotonous child's play." But this sense of isolation has, also, moments which are almost triumphant, as, for example, is implied when the porters at the station wave the crowds back, "saying that it was a special train for the bazaar" and was not for them. The boy is left alone in the bare carriage, but he is going to "Araby," moving triumphantly toward some romantic and exotic fulfillment. The metaphor ° of the chalice implies the same kind of precious secret triumph. It is not only the ordinary surrounding world, however, from which he is cruelly or triumphantly isolated. He is also isolated from the girl herself. He talks to her only once, and then is so confused that he does not know how to answer her. But the present which he hopes to bring her from Araby would somehow serve as a means of communicating his feelings to her, a symbol for their relationship in the midst of the inimical ° world.

3   In the last scene at the bazaar, there is a systematic, though subtle, preparation for the final realization on the part of the boy. There is the "improvised wooden platform" in contrast with the "magical name" displayed

metaphor: See Glossary.
inimical: hostile, unfriendly.

above the building. Inside, most of the stalls are closed. The young lady and young men who talk together are important in the preparation. They pay the boy no mind, except in so far as the young lady is compelled by her position as clerk to ask him what he wants. But her tone is not "encouraging." She, too, belongs to the inimical world. But she, also, belongs to a world into which he is trying to penetrate: she and her admirers are on terms of easy intimacy—an intimacy in contrast to his relation to Mangan's sister. It is an exotic, rich world into which he cannot penetrate: he can only look "humbly at the great jars that stood like eastern guards at either side of the dark entrance to the stall. . . ." But, ironically, the young lady and her admirers, far from realizing that they are on holy, guarded ground, indulge in a trivial, easy banter, which seems to defile and cheapen the secret world from which the boy is barred. How do we know this? It is not stated, but the contrast between the conversation of the young lady and her admirers, and the tone of the sentence quoted just above indicates such an interpretation.

4 This scene, then, helps to point up and particularize the general sense of isolation suggested by the earlier descriptive materials, and thereby to prepare for the last sentence of the story, in which, under the sudden darkness of the cheap and barnlike bazaar, the boy sees himself as "a creature driven and derided ° by vanity," while his eyes burn with anguish and anger.

5 We have seen how the apparently casual incidents and items of description do function in the story to build up the boy's sense of intolerable isolation. But this is only part of the function of this material. The careful reader will have noticed how many references, direct or indirect, there are to religion and the ritual of the church. We have the dead priest, the Christian Brothers' School, the aunt's hope that the bazaar is not "some Freemason affair," her remark when the uncle has been delayed, to "this night of Our Lord." At one level, these references merely indicate

derided: ridiculed.

the type of community in which the impressionable boy is growing up. But there are other, less obvious, references, which relate more intimately to the boy's experience. Even the cries of the shop boys for him are "shrill litanies." He imagines that he bears a "chalice safely through a throng of foes." When he is alone the name of Mangan's sister springs to his lips "in strange prayers and praises." For this reason, when he speaks of his "confused adoration," we see that the love of the girl takes on, for him, something of the nature of a mystic, religious experience. The use of the very word *confused* hints of the fact that romantic love and religious love are mixed up in his mind.

6   It has been said that the boy is isolated from a world which seems ignorant of, and even hostile to, his love. In a sense he knows that his aunt and uncle are good and kind, but they do not understand him. He had once found satisfaction in the society of his companions and in his school work, but he has become impatient with both. But there is also a sense in which he accepts his isolation and is even proud of it. The world not only does not understand his secret but would cheapen and contaminate it. The metaphor of the chalice borne through a throng of foes, supported as it is by the body of the story, suggests a sort of consecration like that of the religious devotee. The implications of the references to religion, then, help define the boy's attitude and indicate why, for him, so much is staked upon the journey to the bazaar. It is interesting to note, therefore, that the first overt indication of his disillusionment and disappointment is expressed in a metaphor involving a church: "Nearly all the stalls were closed and the greater part of the hall was in darkness. I recognized a silence like that which pervades a church after a service. . . . Two men were counting money on a salver.° I listened to the fall of the coins." So, it would seem, here we have the idea that the contamination of the world has invaded the very temple of love—there are, as it were, money-changers in the very temple. (The question may arise as to whether this is not reading too much into the

salver: plate.

passage. Perhaps it is. But whatever interpretation is to be made of the particular incident, it is by just such suggestion and implication that closely wrought stories, such as this one, are controlled by the author and embody their fundamental meaning.)

7 Is this a sentimental story? It is about an adolescent love affair, about "calf love," a subject which usually is not to be taken seriously and is often an occasion for amusement. The boy of the story is obviously investing casual incidents with a meaning which they do not deserve; and himself admits, in the end, that he has fallen into self-deception. How does the author avoid the charge that he has taken the matter over-seriously?

8 The answer to this question would involve a consideration of the point of view from which the story is told. It is told by the hero himself, but after a long lapse of time, after he had reached maturity. This fact, it is true, is not stated in the story, but the style itself is not that of an adolescent boy. It is a formal and complicated style, rich, as has already been observed, in subtle implications. In other words, the man is looking back upon the boy, detached and judicial.° For instance, the boy, in the throes ° of the experience, would never have said of himself: "I had never spoken to her, except for a few casual words, and yet her name was like a summons to all my foolish blood." The man knows, as it were, that the behavior of the boy was, in a sense, foolish. The emotions of the boy are confused, but the person telling the story, the boy grown up, is not confused. He has unraveled the confusion long after, knows that it existed and why it existed.

9 If the man has unraveled the confusions of the boy, why is the event still significant to him? Is he merely dwelling on the pathos ° of adolescent experience? It seems, rather, that he sees in the event, as he looks back on it, a kind of parable ° of a problem which has run through later

judicial: judgmental.
throes: painful struggle.
pathos: pitifulness.
parable: a short, simple story from which a moral can be drawn.

experience. The discrepancy between the real and the ideal scarcely exists for the child, but it is a constant problem, in all sorts of terms, for the adult. This story is about a boy's first confrontation of that problem—that is, about his growing up. The man may have made adjustments to this problem, and may have worked out certain provisional solutions, but, looking back, he still recognizes it as a problem, and an important one. The sense of isolation and disillusion which, in the boy's experience, may seem to spring from a trivial situation, becomes not less, but more aggravated and fundamental in the adult's experience. So, the story is not merely an account of a stage in the process of growing up—it does not merely represent a clinical interest in the psychology of growing up—but is a symbolic rendering of a central conflict in mature experience.

ANALYSIS

To analyze an "analysis" might seem absurd. But criticism is itself a kind of literature. As such, it can also be analyzed.

Unlike Priestley's lengthy essay on *Macbeth* and Ciardi's essay on the Frost poem, this article is brief, business-like, and to the point. Brooks and Warren have narrowed their concern to a few basic questions about this story; they could have written about many other topics also. They could have related this story to the body of Joyce's other work, for example, or they could have analyzed Joyce's style, or they could have related the story to Joyce's own life. Instead their focus is narrowed. In some ways, their analysis is like a detective story: a puzzle is presented at the opening of the essay (in paragraphs 1–2). The authors say that if they can solve this puzzle, they will have defined the theme of the story. In methodical, sleuth-like fashion, they proceed to amass evidence to convince us that their solutions to this puzzle deserve our attention.

Questions on Content

1. According to the critics, what is this story about on the simplest level?

2. The critics state a "problem" in the last sentence in paragraph 1. How do they eventually answer it?
3. Why do the critics believe that this story is not sentimental?
4. Why do they believe this event is still of significance to the adult narrator?
5. What *is* the "central conflict in mature experience" which the critics refer to in paragraph 9?

Add to Your Vocabulary

inimical, derided, judicial, throes, pathos.

Questions on Technique

1. In every paragraph, the critics have placed a key sentence. Find these key statements or questions. What details are used to support or answer them?
2. Find the sentence in the final paragraph that summarizes what these critics see as the story's major theme.
3. In paragraph 6 the critics say that some people might think they are "reading too much" into the details relating to church ritual. How do they answer this objection? What is your opinion of their answer?

Techniques to Imitate

Presenting your ideas as answers to questions

Brooks and Warren make effective use of a writing technique you might find useful in your own expository writing. This is the technique of asking a key question and then answering it in detail. The answer itself consists of the development of a major point in the essay.

These critics begin with the statement of what the story is about on the simplest level. They then go on to point out that a great part of the story concerns something else, and they assert that this description of "something else" has an important function. They lead into their explanation of its function by asking a question at the beginning of the second paragraph: "What, then," they ask, "is the relation of the boy's disappointment to such matters as the belongings of the dead priest, the fact that he stands apart talking to the girl while his friends are quarreling over the cap, the gossip over the tea table, the uncle's lateness, and so on?"

After they answer this question at length, the critics raise other questions and proceed to answer them. In paragraph 7 they ask two questions: "Is this a sentimental story?" and "How does the author avoid the charge that he has taken the matter over-seriously?"

Paragraph 9 begins with two questions: "If the man has unraveled the confusions of the boy, why is the event still significant to him? Is he merely dwelling on the pathos of adolescent experience?"

You have probably had the experience of wanting to ask questions of the writer while you are reading an article. You are interested and satisfied when the author asks the same questions and gives you answers. (If you disagree with the answers, your reactions are somewhat different.)

Suggestions for Writing

1. Write an interpretation of a story that, in your opinion, needs interpretation. Organize your interpretation around certain key questions. Here are some questions that might be asked about almost any narrative: What do the characters want? Why do they do what they do? What is the point, or theme, of the story? (Why did the writer want to tell this story?)
2. A useful technique in literary criticism is the use of specific quotations. (For a good example, see paragraph 5.) Choose a story and make a general statement about it. Support what you say with direct quotations from the story itself. (For example, if you want to write about the story by Angelou on page 60, you could use this topic statement: "Mrs. Flowers is described in words that suggest an ideal person.")

8
THE INFORMAL ESSAY

Two centuries ago, Dr. Samuel Johnson, the British author and lexicographer, defined the informal essay as "a loose sally of the mind; an irregular indigested piece; not a regular and orderly composition." The word "sally" is especially apt in this definition. It is a word with three distinct meanings: a rushing or bursting forth, as a raid of the besieged upon the besiegers; an excursion off the usual track, a jaunt; and a flight of wit or fancy.

You will find no "sortie of troops upon the besiegers" in the five selections we have chosen for this last division of expository prose, though William Zinsser's essay could be described as an outburst of resentment. Flights of wit and excursions off the beaten track you will find. All five essays demonstrate quite clearly that informal essayists follow no rigid set of rules. They might begin with one subject and digress into others at will. They might indulge in irony and satire.° Their humor is usually good-natured, sometimes eccentric. In a relaxed, almost conversational style they will invite us to listen; they establish a kind of friendship in a few dozen lines. Their argument, if there is one, is never forced. The issues might be crucial, but there will be no sermon, no clarion call for change. To hold us against our will, to preach at us, is the antithesis of the informal essayist's technique.

Some of the other selections in this book could be called "informal essays." Certainly, James Thurber's "University Days" has some of the relaxed digressive quality of the informal essay. Sevareid's "The Dark of the Moon" could also be here, despite the fact that he tentatively explores a disturbing topic. "Informality" is the important word: it is a word that certainly could not, for example, be applied to Hayakawa's thorough analysis of the language of reports on page 250.

irony and satire: See Glossary.

JAMES THURBER

How to Name a Dog

If you have read James Thurber's "University Days" on page 70 of this book, you will need no introduction to the wonderful world of whimsy he inhabited. The titles of his books alone tell us much about this great humorist: *The Middle-Aged Man on the Flying Trapeze, My Life and Hard Times, The Seal in the Bedroom, Let Your Mind Alone.* The essay that follows is taken from a collection called *The Beast in Me and Other Animals.* Thurber loved dogs. "Probably no one man should have as many dogs in his life as I have had," he once wrote, "but there was more pleasure than distress in them for me." There is also pleasure for us in Thurber's informal essay on how, or perhaps it is how *not,* to name a dog.

1   Every few months somebody writes me and asks if I will give him a name for his dog. Several of these correspondents in the past year have wanted to know if I would mind the use of my own name for their spaniels. Spaniel owners seem to have the notion that a person could sue for invasion of privacy or defamation * of character if his name is applied to a cocker without written permission, and one gentleman even insisted that we conduct our correspondence in the matter through a notary public. I have a way of letting communications of this sort fall behind my roll-top desk, but it has recently occurred to me that this is an act of evasion, if not, indeed, of plain cowardice. I have therefore decided to come straight out with the simple truth that it is as hard for me to think up a name for a dog as it is for anybody else. The idea that I was an expert in the business is probably the outcome of a piece I wrote several years ago, incautiously revealing the fact that I have owned forty or more dogs in my life. This is true, but it is also deceptive. All but five or six of my dogs were disposed of when they were puppies, and I had not gone to the trouble of giving to these impermanent residents of my house any names at all except Hey, You! and Cut That Out! and Let Go!

2   Names of dogs end up in 176th place in the list of things that amaze and fascinate me. Canine cognomens ° should be designed to impinge * on the ears of the dogs and not to amuse neighbors, tradespeople, and casual visitors. I remember a few dogs from the past with a faint but lingering pleasure: a farm hound named Rain, a roving Airedale named Marco Polo, a female bull terrier known as Stephanie Brody because she liked to jump from moving motor cars and second-story windows, and a Peke called Darien; ° but that's about all. The only animals whose naming demands concentration, hard work, and ingenuity are the seeing-eye dogs. They have to be given unusual names because passers-by like to call to seeing-eyers— "Here, Sport" or "Yuh, Rags" or "Don't take any wooden nickels, Rin Tin Tin." A blind man's dog with an ordinary name would continually be distracted from its work. A tyro ° at naming these dogs might make the mistake of

cognomens: names.

Peke called Darien: When we read this pun, Thurber expects us to recall a line from Keats' "On First Looking into Chapman's Homer": "Silent, upon a peak in Darien." The Isthmus of Panama was formerly called the Isthmus of Darien.

tyro: a beginner or novice.

picking Durocher or Teeftallow. The former is too much
like Rover and the latter could easily sound like "Here,
fellow" to a dog.

3 Speaking of puppies, as I was a while back, I feel that
I should warn inexperienced dog owners who have discovered to their surprise and dismay a dozen puppies in
a hall closet or under the floors of the barn, not to give
them away. Sell them or keep them, but don't give them
away. Sixty per cent of persons who are given a dog for
nothing bring him back sooner or later and plump him
into the reluctant and unprepared lap of his former owner.
The people say that they are going to Florida and can't
take the dog, or that he doesn't want to go; or they point
out that he eats first editions or lace curtains or spinets, or
that he doesn't see eye to eye with them in the matter of
housebreaking, or that he makes disparaging remarks under
his breath about their friends. Anyway, they bring him
back and you are stuck with him—and maybe six others.
But if you charge ten or even five dollars for pups, the new
owners don't dare return them. They are afraid to ask for
their money back because they believe you might think
they are hard up and need the five or ten dollars. Furthermore, when a mischievous puppy is returned to its former
owner it invariably behaves beautifully, and the person who
brought it back is likely to be regarded as an imbecile or a
dog hater or both.

4 Names of dogs, to get back to our subject, have a range
almost as wide as that of the violin. They run from such
plain and simple names as Spot, Sport, Rex, Brownie, and
Rover—all originated by small boys—to such effete and
fancy appellations as Prince Rudolph Hertenberg Gratz-
heim of Darndorf-Putzelhorst, and Darling Mist o' Love III
of Heather-Light-Holyrood—names originated by adults,
all of whom in every other way, I am told, have made a
normal adjustment to life. In addition to the plain and the
fancy categories, there are the Cynical and the Coy.* Cynical names are given by people who do not like dogs too
much. The most popular cynical names during the war

were Mussolini, Tojo, and Adolf.° I never have been able to get very far in my exploration of the minds of people who call their dogs Mussolini, Tojo, and Adolf, and I suspect the reason is that I am unable to associate with them long enough to examine what goes on in their heads. I nod, and I tell them the time of day, if they ask, and that is all. I never vote for them or ask them to have a drink. The great Coy category is perhaps the largest. The Coy people call their pets Bubbles and Boggles and Sparkles and Twinkles and Doodles and Puffy and Lovums and Sweetums and Itsy-Bitsy and Betsy-Bye-Bye and Sugarkins. I pass these dog owners at a dogtrot, wearing a horrible fixed grin.

5   There is a special subdivision of the Coys that is not quite so awful, but awful enough. These people, whom we will call the Wits, own two dogs, which they name Pitter and Patter, Willy and Nilly, Helter and Skelter, Namby and Pamby, Hugger and Mugger, Hokery and Pokery, and even Wishy and Washy, Ups and Daisy, Fitz and Startz, Fetch and Carrie, and Pro and Connie. Then there is the Cryptic * category. These people select names for some private reason or for no reason at all—except perhaps to arouse the visitor's curiosity, so that he will exclaim, "Why in the world do you call your dog *that?*" The Cryptics name their dogs October, Bennett's Aunt, Three Fifteen, Doc Knows, Tuesday, Home Fried, Opus 38, Ask Leslie, and Thanks for the Home Run, Emil. I make it a point simply to pat these unfortunate dogs on the head, ask no questions of their owners, and go about my business.

6   This article has degenerated into a piece that properly should be entitled "How Not to Name a Dog." I was afraid it would. It seems only fair to make up for this by confessing a few of the names I have given my own dogs, with the considerable help, if not, indeed, the insistence, of their mistress. Most of my dogs have been females, and they

----

Mussolini, Tojo, and Adolf: during World War II, the leaders of Italy, Japan, and Germany, respectively: Benito Mussolini, Hideki Tojo, and Adolf Hitler.

have answered, with apparent gladness, to such names as Jeannie, Tessa, Julie and Sophie. Sophie is a black French poodle whose kennel name was Christabel, but she never answered to Christabel, which she considers as foolish a name for a dog as Pamela, Jennifer, Clarissa, Jacqueline, Guinevere, and Shelmerdene. Sophie is opposed, and I am also, to Ida, Cora, Blanche, and Myrtle.

7   About six years ago, when I was looking for a house to buy in Connecticut, I knocked on the front door of an attractive home whose owner, my real estate agent had told me, wanted to sell it and go back to Iowa to live. The lady agent who escorted me around had informed me that the owner of this place was a man named Strong, but a few minutes after arriving at the house, I was having a drink in the living room with Phil Stong,° for it was he. We went out into the yard after a while and I saw Mr. Stong's spaniel. I called to the dog and snapped my fingers but he seemed curiously embarrassed, like his master. "What's his name?" I asked the latter. He was cornered and there was no way out of it. "Thurber," he said, in a small frightened voice. Thurber and I shook hands, and he didn't seem to me any more depressed than any other spaniel I have met. He had, however, the expression of a bachelor on his way to a party he has tried in vain to get out of, and I think it must have been this cast of countenance that had reminded Mr. Stong of the dog I draw. The dog I draw is, to be sure, much larger than a spaniel and not so shaggy, but I confess, though I am not a spaniel man, that there are certain basic resemblances between my dog and all other dogs with long ears and troubled eyes.

8   The late Hendrik Van Loon ° was privy to the secret that the dog of my drawings was originally intended to look more like a bloodhound than anything else, but that he turned up by accident with legs too short to be an authentic

Phil Stong: American journalist and novelist (1899–1957), known for his novels dealing with life in rural Iowa, especially *State Fair* (1932).

Hendrik Van Loon: Dutch-born American journalist (1882–1945), author of numerous popular books on history and science.

member of this breed. This flaw was brought about by the fact that the dog was first drawn on a telephone memo pad which was not large enough to accommodate him. Mr. Van Loon labored under the unfortunate delusion that an actual bloodhound would fit as unobtrusively into the Van Loon living room as the drawn dog does in the pictures. He learned his mistake in a few weeks. He discovered that an actual bloodhound regards a residence as a series of men's rooms and that it is interested only in tracing things. Once, when Mr. Van Loon had been wandering around his yard for an hour or more, he called to his bloodhound and was dismayed when, instead of coming directly to him, the dog proceeded to follow every crisscross of the maze its master had made in wandering about. "That dog didn't care a darn about where I was," Mr. Van Loon told me. "All he was interested in was how I got there."

9   Perhaps I should suggest at least one name for a dog, if only to justify the title of this piece. All right, then, what's the matter with Stong? It's a good name for a dog, short, firm, and effective. I recommend it to all those who have written to me for suggestions and to all those who may be at this very moment turning over in their minds the idea of asking my advice in this difficult and perplexing field of nomenclature.*

ANALYSIS

One has the feeling, after reading Thurber, that this author could write an essay on almost anything, given enough time and a reasonable subject. His style is the epitome of unpretentious eloquence. It is simple, direct, and exact. His criticisms of society, in his collected essays, are quietly penetrating; but they are seldom harsh. His drawings are expert caricature; ° but the original still shows beneath the exaggeration.

In these nine paragraphs, Thurber covers a surprising amount of territory. He does not do it by following a logical structure: beginning, middle, and end. In fact, for at

caricature: See Glossary.

least one-third of this essay he does not stay close to his subject—how to name a dog—though all he writes here is about dogs. Is the willful digression, you might ask, a part of the informal essayist's technique? Certainly it is part of Thurber's. Paragraphs 3 and 8, and much of paragraph 7, could easily be removed. The disposal of a litter of puppies, Phil Stong's spaniel, and Hendrik Van Loon's bloodhound are not *directly* connected with his title. But they enrich this essay by virtue of being digressions. This is unhurried writing. It aims at entertaining rather than informing you. And besides, Thurber warns us that "it is as hard for [him] to think up a name for a dog as it is for anybody else," that "names of dogs end up in 176th place in the list of things that amaze and fascinate [him]."

But could Thurber be making a more subtle use of these digressions than trying to avoid writing on a subject which, so he says, and we do not believe him, he is ill-prepared to discuss? With paragraph 3, he might wish to divert our attention from dogs' names, for a moment, but he also might wish to let us know that he has learned from long experience about puppies' behavior. No matter what he says about naming dogs he is not a tyro at raising them. Paragraph 8 tells us, if we do not know it already, that Thurber has been drawing dogs with something less than accuracy but with great imagination. Paragraph 7 is an obvious foretaste of his delightful conclusion. The informal essayist can teach us new techniques, such as these digressions, if we look closely enough.

And what of the humor in this piece, you ask? It permeates every paragraph. You need no help in finding it.

Questions on Content

1. Why should Thurber have the reputation of being an expert at naming dogs?
2. How does he distinguish among names that are Coy, Cynical, and Cryptic?
3. What did Hendrik Van Loon learn, to his sorrow, about bloodhounds?

Add to Your Vocabulary

defamation, cognomen, impinge, tyro, coy, cryptic, nomenclature.

Questions on Technique

1. Paragraph 1 is written in a simple vocabulary. Paragraph 2 opens with an exaggerated statement, for humorous effect. What effect does Thurber seek with the next sentence: "Canine cognomens should be designed to impinge on the ears of the dogs. . . ."? Why does he not say, "Dogs should hear their names easily"?
2. Speaking of exaggeration, consider paragraph 4. Is Thurber's wild imagination at work here or does he wish his reader to take him literally?
3. What is your reaction to the first three sentences of paragraph 6? Do you think Thurber planned his essay with this "confession" in mind?
4. Note that paragraph 7 is an anecdote, a short narrative used to make a point. This use of narrative is common in informal essays. How does this narrative arouse interest?
5. How are paragraphs 7 and 8 related to each other? Notice the transition sentences.

Techniques to Imitate

The entertaining digression

Writers of serious expository prose are advised not to get off the subject, not to digress from the central idea of their essay. Writers of the informal essay, however, are often most entertaining when they do digress. Since the purpose of an informal essay is usually to entertain the reader, entertaining digressions are not only permissible but desirable.

After sticking to dog names and dog-naming in his first two paragraphs, Thurber spends paragraph 3 on a complete digression in which he warns owners of a litter of puppies not to give the puppies away. At the beginning of paragraph 4, quite aware that he has digressed, he says, "Names of dogs, *to get back to our subject,* have a range almost as wide as that of the violin." He proceeds to make fun of the names people give to dogs and then (paragraph 6) admits that, "This article has degenerated into a piece that properly should be entitled, "How Not to Name a Dog," the opposite of the title with which he began. Paragraph 8, in which he explains his drawings of dogs and tells of Van Loon's experience with a bloodhound, is another digression.

When you are writing an informal essay and an amusing thought suddenly occurs to you that has little close relevance to the main point of your essay, don't stifle the impulse to write about it. The digression may prove to be the most entertaining part of the essay. Remember, however, that since a digression is a digression *from* something, your essay must have a basic structure or central idea from which to digress.

Suggestions for Writing

1. Try your hand at the same subject, but call your essay "Dogs [Cats, Birds] I Have Known."
2. Most families have had a pet of some kind at some time. Write a 500-word essay on your family's pet or pets. Do not only describe the animals.
3. Write a 400-word essay on "What's in a Name?"
4. Informal essayists express their ideas and opinions on a great variety of subjects and frequently without much basic research. Try writing a 400-word essay on "I Hate Gardening," "I'm Glad to See Summer End," "On Baby-Sitting," "Telephone Calls," or "On Studying for Examinations."

E. B. WHITE

A Report in Spring

James Thurber once referred to E. B. White's work as "those silver and crystal sentences which have a ring like nobody else's sentences in the world." In a review of White's *The Second Tree from the Corner* (1954), Irwin Edman, the late Columbia University philosopher, said "It is high time to declare roundly that E. B. White is the finest essayist in the United States." This kind of praise, from two highly qualified peers, White richly deserves.

After graduating from Cornell, E. B. White worked for the *Seattle Times* and then took a job as a contributing editor of the *New Yorker*. In 1937 he and his family moved to Maine. For the five years following, he wrote a column for *Harper's* magazine under the title "One Man's Meat." A book of the same name appeared in 1941, a collection of his pieces about Maine farms and farmers, about children, animals, war, and politics. More political commentary was gathered in *The Wild Flag* (1946). When, in 1960, he received the gold medal for essays and criticism from the American Academy of Arts and Letters, he said in reply: "A glance at the shelf of my published works leaves me wondering whether I am not simply a man of indecision. . . . My shelf begins with a thin volume of poems . . . and ends with a thin book of rules. In between are two works of fiction addressed to children who, as you know, will put up with almost anything. As for my essays, what is an essayist but a man who is too impatient to write a novel?''

White is modest in the extreme. An essayist of his caliber is not a thwarted novelist. He is a master of exposition and of the art of brevity. White can make four pages more memorable than most writers make forty. His admirers are not looking for a novel from his workshop, only for more of his eloquent essays.

Turtle Bay, May 10, 1957

1   I bought a puppy last week in the outskirts of Boston and drove him to Maine in a rented Ford that looked like a sculpin.° There had been talk in our family of getting a "sensible" dog this time, and my wife and I had gone over the list of sensible dogs, and had even ventured once or twice into the company of sensible dogs. A friend had a litter of Labradors, and there were other opportunities. But after a period of uncertainty and waste motion my wife suddenly exclaimed one evening, "Oh, let's just get a dachshund!" She had had a glass of wine, and I could see that the truth was coming out. Her tone was one of exasperation laced with affection. So I engaged a black male without further ado.

2   For the long ordeal of owning another dachshund we prepared ourselves by putting up for a night at the Boston Ritz in a room overlooking the Public Garden, where from our window we could gaze, perhaps for the last time, on a world of order and peace. I say "for the last time" because it occurred to me early in the proceedings that this was our first adoption case in which there was a strong likelihood that the dog would survive the man. It had always been the other way around. The Garden had never seemed so beautiful. We were both up early the next morning for a final look at the fresh, untroubled scene; then we checked out hastily, sped to the kennel, and claimed our prize, who is

sculpin: a broad-mouthed fish with a large spiny head.

the grandson of an animal named Direct Stretch of the Walls. He turned out to be a good traveller, and except for an interruption caused by my wife's falling out of the car in Gardiner, the journey went very well. At present, I am a sojourner in the city again, but here in the green warmth of Turtle Bay I see only the countenance of spring in the country. No matter what changes take place in the world, or in me, nothing ever seems to disturb the face of spring.

3 The smelts are running in the brooks. We had a mess for Monday lunch, brought to us by our son, who was fishing at two in the morning. At this season, a smelt brook is the night club of the town, and when the tide is a late one, smelting is for the young, who like small hours and late society.

4 No rain has fallen in several weeks. The gardens are dry, the road to the shore is dusty. The ditches, which in May are usually swollen to bursting, are no more than a summer trickle. Trout fishermen are not allowed on the streams; pond fishing from a boat is still permissible. The landscape is lovely to behold, but the hot, dry wind carries the smell of trouble. The other day we saw the smoke of a fire over in the direction of the mountain.

5 Mice have eaten the crowns of the Canterbury bells, my white-faced steer has warts on his neck (I'm told it's a virus, like everything else these days), and the dwarf pear has bark trouble. My puppy has no bark trouble. He arises at three, for tennis. The puppy's health, in fact, is exceptionally good. When my wife and I took him from the kennel, a week ago today, his mother kissed all three of us good-bye, and the lady who ran the establishment presented me with complete feeding instructions, which included a mineral supplement called Pervinal and some vitamin drops called Vi-syneral. But I knew that as soon as the puppy reached home and got his sea legs he would switch to the supplement *du jour*—a flake of well-rotted cow manure from my boot, a dead crocus bulb from the lawn, a shingle from the kindling box, a bloody feather from the execution block behind the barn. Time has borne me out; the puppy was not long discovering the delicious supplements of the farm, and he now knows where every vitamin hides, under its stone, under its loose board. I even introduced him to the tonic smell of coon.

6   On Tuesday, in broad daylight, the coon arrived, heavy with young, to take possession of the hole in the tree, but she found another coon in possession, and there was a grim fight high in the branches. The new tenant won, or so it appeared to me, and our old coon came down the tree in defeat and hustled off into the woods to examine her wounds and make other plans for her confinement. I was sorry for her, as I am for any who are evicted from their haunts by the younger and stronger—always a sad occasion for man or beast.

7   The stalks of rhubarb show red, the asparagus has broken through. Peas and potatoes are in, but it is not much use putting seeds in the ground the way things are. The bittern spent a day at the pond, creeping slowly around the shores like a little round-shouldered peddler. A setting of goose eggs has arrived by parcel post from Vermont, my goose having been taken by the fox last fall. I carried the package into the barn and sat down to unpack the eggs. They came out of the box in perfect condition, each one wrapped in a page torn from the *New England Homestead*. Clustered around me on the floor, they looked as though I had been hard at it. There is no one to sit on them but me, and I had to return to New York, so I ordered a trio of Muscovies from a man in New Hampshire, in the hope of persuading a Muscovy duck to give me a Toulouse gosling. (The theme of my life is complexity-through-joy.) In reply to my order, the duck-farm man wrote saying there would be a slight delay in the shipment of Muscovies, as he was "in the midst of a forest-fire scare." I did not know from this whether he was too scared to drive to the post office with a duck or too worried to fit a duck into a crate.

8   By day the goldfinches dip in yellow flight, by night the frogs sing the song that never goes out of favor. We opened the lower sash of the window in the barn loft, and

the swallows are already building, but mud for their nests
is not so easy to come by as in most springtimes. One afternoon, I found my wife kneeling at the edge of her perennial
border on the north side, trying to disengage Achillea-the-
Pearl from Coral Bell. "If I could afford it," she said
bitterly, "I would take every damn bit of Achillea out of
this border." She is a woman in comfortable circumstances,
arrived at through her own hard labor, and this sudden
burst of poverty, and her inability to indulge herself in a
horticultural purge, startled me. I was so moved by her
plight and her unhappiness that I went to the barn and returned with an edger, and we spent a fine, peaceable hour
in the pretty twilight, rapping Achillea over the knuckles
and saving Coral Bell.

9   One never knows what images one is going to hold in
memory, returning to the city after a brief orgy in the
country. I find this morning that what I most vividly and
longingly recall is the sight of my grandson and his little
sunburnt sister returning to their kitchen door from an excursion, with trophies of the meadow clutched in their
hands—she with a couple of violets, and smiling, he serious and holding dandelions, strangling them in a responsible grip. Children hold spring so tightly in their brown
fists—just as grownups, who are less sure of it, hold it in
their hearts.

ANALYSIS

The topic sentence of this delightful essay is where we
least expect it, in the conclusion to the second paragraph:
"At present, I am a sojourner in the city again, but here
in the green warmth of Turtle Bay I see only the countenance of spring in the country." Not that it matters, but
Turtle Bay is a division of New York City. It is the piece of
land along the East River in the Forties on which the
United Nations and vast apartment houses have been built.
What does matter is the method White uses to make this
essay as easy and informal as possible. As though he were

writing a letter, he gives us the place and date. Then he opens with the purchase of a puppy and a drive via Boston to Maine, only to switch back to Turtle Bay, New York. To what purpose? He wants this essay to be a report written in New York of what spring is like in his second home. If we wonder why he does not simply describe the Maine farm country and forget about New York City, we must reread the last paragraph, where he makes his point clearly. As White begins the essay, he is not telling.

How is he to make us feel and touch and smell "the countenance of spring in the country"? First, by using the present tense as often as possible, even though he is recalling what happened *last* week during his visit to Maine. In paragraph 4, he tells us "we *had* a mess [of smelts] for Monday lunch," yet the dominant tense is the present: "the smelts *are* running in the brooks" and "at this season, a smelt brook *is* the night club of the town." Likewise in paragraph 5, where the puppy "*arises* at three" and in paragraph 7, where "the stalks of rhubarb *show* red." We realize White is remembering these images of what happened last week (past tense), but at the same time we participate in them now (present tense). The method is tricky, but he pulls it off.

Second, he fills his reminiscence with sensory details— visual, auditory, olfactory. The hot, dry wind brings with it a threat of forest fires. The puppy discovers the tonic smell of coon. A setting of goose eggs arrives via the mails. Goldfinches and frogs and bitterns fill the air with bright color and familiar song.

Third, he chooses his words with great care and an easy sense of humor. Katharine White speaks of dachshunds in a tone of "exasperation laced with affection." The puppy, a "grandson of an animal named Direct Stretch of the Walls," wakes at three in the morning "for tennis." His "vitamin supplement" gives White a chance to poke fun at patent medicines. Patent medicines on a Maine farm! And the battle between Achillea-the-Pearl and Coral Bell is treated with mock seriousness, the same gentle exaggeration that leads him to call this week in Maine "a brief orgy."

Finally, he closes his essay as gracefully as he opens it. Buying a puppy is a notoriously successful way to start wooing the reader. Two young children holding wild flowers in tight fists are equally irresistible images, particularly since White wants to comment on the so-called wiser adults who know how quickly beauty vanishes.

Questions on Content

1. What meanings does White give to the word "sensible" in paragraph 1?
2. Why did the arrival of the goose eggs cause an unusual problem in the household?
3. What "brief images" other than those mentioned in the analysis above provided the Whites with signs of spring?

Questions on Technique

1. White could easily have begun this report with a description of Turtle Bay from his study window. Why do you think he chose to introduce the puppy first?
2. In paragraph 2, White tells us that the puppy "turned out to be a good traveller, and except for an interruption caused by my wife's falling out of the car in Gardiner, the journey went very well." A stage comedian would call this a "throwaway line," a funny incident treated so casually that we almost ignore it. What effect do you think White wanted here? Does he get it again in paragraph 5 when he says the puppy "arises at three, for tennis" and in paragraph 8 with the phrase "rapping Achillea over the knuckles and saving Coral Bell"? Does he run the risk of being "cute"?
3. Consider the last sentence in paragraphs 6 and 9. Does White's style suggest anything about the nature of the author himself? Does he strive, in these sentences, for something more than "a report in spring"?
4. An alert style centers on fresh description such as "a smelt brook is the night club of the town" and "as soon as the puppy reached home and got his sea legs." Find other phrases in this essay which hold the reader's attention.

Techniques to Imitate

Anecdotes in the informal essay

An experienced and expert essayist, White knows the high interest value of an incident, a brief story. Everyone likes a story. Although the purpose of an informal essay is to express the opinions of the writer, the best informal essays contain some narration. The expert essayist intersperses opinions with anecdotes that support or illuminate ideas.

It may have been White's awareness of the interest value of a story that led him to begin his essay with the account of his getting a dog, rather than with a description of the "countenance of spring," which is really his subject. He includes other incidents in his essay: the incident involving the raccoon, the one about the goose eggs, and the story of his wife's efforts to weed the Achillea out of the "perennial border on the north side."

When you write an informal essay, keep in mind the interest value of a story. If possible, include a few incidents that will support the opinions you are expressing.

Suggestions for Writing

1. White recalls a trip to Maine in spring. Using his title but your own part of the country for the details, write a 500-word essay similar to White's.
2. Have you ever lived or spent a vacation on a farm? Write an essay of 500 words called "Country Life," emphasizing the sensuous impressions the countryside made on you.
3. White is writing about a recurrent event—the appearance of spring—but he makes it seem fresh, even unique. Part of the reason for his success is his inclusion of incidents peculiar to the spring that is taking place as he writes. In an essay of about 500 words, write about an occurrence you've often experienced—for example, the beginning of a school year, a family holiday, a medical check-up. Convey the general feeling that this event always produces. But include incidents

specific to one particular school opening, holiday, check-up, etc. You might begin the essay with a humorous or remarkable incident that took place one year and then go on to discuss the recurring event in general.
4. Discovering a new city or country has its own delights. Keeping your language as fresh as White's, write an essay in which you share with your reader a first visit. Make your viewpoint as subjective as possible. Avoid sounding like a chamber of commerce advertisement.

JOYCE MAYNARD

"I Remember . . ."

It is ironic that an essay called "I Remember . . ."
should be narrated by the youngest voice in this book.
Joyce Maynard was twenty-one when this article was
published in *TV Guide* magazine.

A key experience in Maynard's youth—television—
is an experience that none of the writers in Part One
of this text (writers who also describe their childhoods)
could possibly have shared. Joyce Maynard does not,
like Thomas Sancton and Maya Angelou, describe memories rooted in the land or in people. Her memories are
dominated by the great product of modern technology:
the TV set.

1   We got our TV set in 1959,
when I was five. So I can barely remember life without television. I have spent 20,000 hours of my life in front of
the set. Not all of my contemporaries watched so much,
but many did, and what's more, we watched the same programs, heard the same commercials, were exposed to the
same end-of-show lessons. So there is, among this generation of television children, a shared history, a tremendous
fund of common experience. These massive doses of TV
have not affected all of us in an identical way, and it would
be risky to draw broad conclusions. But if a sociologist

were—rashly—to try to uncover some single most important influence on this generation, which has produced Patty
Hearst ° and Alice Cooper ° and the Jesus movement °
and the peace movement; if he were searching for the roots
of 1960's psychedelia and 1970's apathy,* he would do
well to look first at television.

2 My own motives are less ambitious. I know, simply,
that a rerun of *I Love Lucy* or *Father Knows Best,* the
theme music from *Dr. Kildare* or the sad, whistling refrain
from *Lassie* can make me stand, frozen, before the set. It
is as if I, and not Timmy Martin, had been stuck in an
abandoned mine shaft during a thunderstorm, as if I, and
not Lucy Ricardo, had dropped a diamond ring somewhere in the batter of a seven-layer cake. I didn't so much
watch those shows when I was little; I let them wash over
me. Now I study them like a psychiatrist on his own couch,
looking hungrily for some clue inside the TV set to explain the person I have become.

3 I was not a dull or energyless child, or neglected by
my parents. Our house was full of books and paints, and
sometimes I did choose to draw or ride my bike. But the
picture of my childhood that comes to mind is one of a
dimly lit room in a small New Hampshire town and a girl
listening, leaden-eyed, to some talk-show rendition of "I
Left My Heart in San Francisco." It is a picture of myself
at age eight, wise to the ways of "Vegas," the timing of
stand-up comics, the marriages of Zsa Zsa Gabor, the advertising slogans of Bufferin and Fab.

4 And what did all this television watching teach me?
Well, I rarely swallowed the little pellets of end-of-show
morals presented in the television shows I watched (that
crime does not pay, that one must always obey one's
parents). But I observed something of the way the world

Patty Hearst: young heiress kidnapped in 1974 by the revolutionary Symbionese Liberation Army.

Alice Cooper: performer of rock music.

Jesus movement: general term used to describe movement of
many people back to fundamental religious sects, or to charismatic
religious groups.

works: that life is easier if one fits in with the established conventions; that everything is easier if one has a pretty face.

5 And in the process of acquiring those melancholy truths I picked up an embarrassingly large fund of knowledge that is totally unusable (except, perhaps, ironically, on some television game show). I can hum Perry Mason's theme song or give the name of the actress who played Donna Reed's best friend. I would happily trade that knowledge for the facility with piano or ballet I might have if I'd spent those television hours practicing music and dance instead. But something else I gained from television should be less lightly dismissed. I guess it is a sense of knowing America, not simply its vulgarities but its strengths as well: the rubber face of Lucille Ball, the lovableness of Americans on *Candid Camera,* an athlete's slow-motion grace in an instant replay on *Monday Night Football.*

6 So many hours of television I watched—hundreds of bank robberies, touch-and-go operations and barroom fights, millions of dollars' worth of refrigerators awarded to thousands of housewives who kissed dozens of game-show moderators—and yet the list of individual programs I remember is very short. One is the Beatles' appearance, the winter I was ten, on *The Ed Sullivan Show.* I remember the on-camera shooting of Lee Oswald, and the face of Jacqueline Kennedy at her husband's funeral. A few particularly marvelous episodes of the old *Dick Van Dyke Show* stand out: Laura Petrie getting her toe stuck in the bathroom faucet; Rob imagining that he's going bald. One or two *I Love Lucy* shows, Andy Griffith shows, a Miss America contestant who sang a number from *The Sound of Music*—dressed like a nun—and then whipped off her habit to reveal a spangled bathing suit. I remember a special five-part *Dr. Kildare* segment in which a team of doctors had to choose five patients for a lifesaving kidney machine out of eight candidates. I remember getting up at midnight to watch Neil Armstrong land on the moon—expecting to be awed, but falling asleep instead.

7   My strongest memories are of one series and one character. Not the best, but the one that formed me more than any other, that haunts me still, and left its mark on a good-sized part of a generation: *Leave It to Beaver*. I watched that show every day after school (fresh from my own failures) and studied it, like homework, because the Cleaver family was so steady and normal—and my own was not—and because the boys had so many friends, played basketball, drank sodas, *fit in*. Watching that series and other family situation comedies was almost like taking a course in how to be an American.

8   I loved my father, but I longed secretly for a "Dad" like Ward Cleaver, who puttered in a work shed, building bookcases and oiling hinges, one who spent his Saturday afternoons playing golf or mowing the lawn or dipping his finger into cake batter whipped up by a mother in a frilly apron who spent her time going to PTA meetings and playing bridge with "the girls." Wally Cleaver, the older brother, was one of those boys destined to be captain of every team he plays on. But Beaver had his problems— often he was uncoordinated, gullible, less than perfectly honest, tricked by his older brother's friends, made fun of. He lost library books and haircut money. Once he sent away for a "free" accordion and suddenly found himself wildly in debt. Of course he got caught—he always did. I remember him so clearly, as familiar to me as a brother.

9   Occasionally I go to college campuses. Some student in the audience always mentions Beaver Cleaver, and when the name is spoken, a satisfied murmur can be heard in the crowd. Somebody—a stranger in his twenties now—wrote to say he watches *Beaver* reruns every morning. He just wanted to share memories of the show with me and recall favorite episodes. We were not readers, after all, this stranger and I. We have no great literary tradition behind us. Our heritage is television. Wally and Beaver Cleaver were our Tom Sawyer and Huck Finn.

10   There's something terribly sad about this need to reminisce, and the lack of real stories, true experiences, to reminisce about. Partly it is that we grew up in the 1960's,

when life was soft, and partly that we grew up with television, which made life softer. We had Vietnam, of course, and civil-rights battles, and a brief threat of nuclear attack that led neighbors, down the block, to talk of building a fallout shelter. But I remember the large events, like the Kennedy and King assassinations, the space launches and the war, as I experienced them through television. I watched it all from a goose-down-filled easy chair with a plate of oatmeal cookies on my lap—on television.

11 We grew up to be observers, not participants, to respond to action, not initiate it. And I think, finally, it was this lack of real hardship (when we lacked for nothing else) that was our greatest hardship and that led so many among this television generation to seek out some kind of artificial pain. Some of us, for a time at least, gave up matching skirt-and-sweater sets for saffron-colored Hare Krishna robes; some gave up parents and clean-cut fiancés for the romance of poverty and the excitement of crime. Rebellion like that is not so much inspired by television violence as it is brought about by television banality: it is a response not to *The Man from U.N.C.L.E.* but to *Father Knows Best*. One hears it said that hatred of an idea is closer to love than to indifference. Large and angry rejections of the bourgeois, the conventional—the Beaver Cleaver life— aren't so surprising, coming from a generation that grew up admiring those things so much.

12 Television smartened us up, expanded our minds, and then proceeded to fill them with the only kinds of knowledge it had to offer: names of Las Vegas nightclubs, brands of detergent, players of bit parts. And knowledge— accurate or not—about life: marriage as we learned about it from Ozzie and Harriet. Justice as practiced by Matt Dillon. Politics as revealed to us on the six o'clock news.

13 Anguished, frustrated and enraged by a decade of war in Vietnam as we saw it on the news, we became part of the news ourselves—with peace marches, rallies in the streets. But only briefly; we were easily discouraged, quick to abandon hope for change and to lose interest. That, also, comes from a television-watching childhood, I think: a short attention span, and a limpness, and inertia,* acquired from too many hours spent in the easy chair, never getting up except to change the channels.

Questions on Content

1. What effects did all the television watching ultimately have on this writer?
2. If watching *Leave It to Beaver* was almost like "taking a course in how to be an American," what did the "course" teach this writer?
3. Why, according to Maynard, did so many of her generation seek out some kind of "artificial pain"?

Add to Your Vocabulary

apathy, inertia.

Questions on Technique

1. In paragraph 2, Maynard states in a single sentence the topic of this essay. What is that sentence?
2. In paragraph 5, the writer says that she gained something else from television that should not be lightly dismissed: a sense of knowing America, "not simply its vulgarities but its strengths as well." Do you think that the specific details used to support and clarify this statement are well-chosen? Explain.
3. Maynard says in paragraph 9 that her generation has "no great literary tradition" behind them. Does she explain the significance of this? How would a generation *with* a literary tradition be different from hers?
4. In paragraph 11, Maynard says that rebellion is brought about not so much by TV violence as by TV banality. What details does she use to explain this? Is the statement clarified sufficiently? Explain.

Techniques to Imitate

Using the list, or series, to present many examples

Maynard covers a lot of ground—a decade of TV viewing—in a small space. Her article gains force from the many examples of TV shows that she believes affected the lives of her generation. As she looks back over her TV life, the hundreds of programs she has watched come flooding into her mind. Her problem is to get them all into a brief article, and she solves this problem by a writing technique worth noting. This is the skillful use of the list, or series, which enables her to cover a great many items quickly. Note the following examples of the effectively used list:

> "I know, simply, that a rerun of *I Love Lucy* or *Father Knows Best,* the theme music from *Dr. Kildare* or the sad, whistling refrain from *Lassie* can make me stand, frozen, before the set."
>
> "It is a picture of myself at age eight, wise to the ways of 'Vegas,' the timing of stand-up comics, the marriages of Zsa Zsa Gabor, the advertising slogans of Bufferin and Fab."

Suggestions for Writing

1. Just about everyone today has opinions and thoughts about television. Write a short personal essay describing your own reactions to a few specific television shows. Cite titles of specific shows and list the details about them that you want to talk about. Imitate Maynard's technique in paragraphs 2, 5, and 6.

2. Write an informal, conversational "essay" about a major influence on the childhood of your own generation: for example, a great event, changes in education, changes in life styles, etc. Do not write an analysis or use statistical data, but make your essay personal and reflective. If there are many memories of a specific kind that you want to note, cite them in lists or in a series.

3. The title of this essay is seductive. It invites us to join in a reminiscence; it also prods our own memories. Write an essay also entitled "I Remember . . ." Make it about anything in your memory that interests you: something in the past, or something that happened only last week but which won't happen again.

JOSEPH CAMPBELL

The Moon Walk

Myths, rituals, dreams, Buffalo-Gods, Quetzalcoatls, and Buddahs—all of these have been associated with the name Joseph Campbell since the 1930's. Campbell's best-known book is *The Hero with a Thousand Faces* (1949). In that book, Campbell proposes that the myths of the world, despite their infinite variety, offer a limited number of creative responses to the riddle of life.

The following selections are from a chapter in *Myths to Live By* (1972), a book which developed from lectures that Campbell delivered at the Cooper Union Forum in New York City. Unlike his other books, this is not a scholarly text but a personal work. Its tone is that of a person sharing ideas and speculations with a group of friends.

Joyce Maynard remembers that she fell asleep while watching Neil Armstrong walking on the moon. Joseph Campbell was also watching television on that summer night in 1969, but he remembers a totally different experience.

1   **I** remember when I was a very small boy my uncle one evening brought me down to Riverside Drive ° to see "a man," as he told me, "flying in

---

Riverside Drive: a road that runs alongside a park by the Hudson River, on the West Side of Manhattan.

an aeroplane [as they called them in those days] from Albany to New York." That was Glenn Curtis, 1910, in a sort of motorized box-kite he had built. There were people lined along the low wall at the westward margin of the city, watching, waiting, facing into the sunset. All the nearby rooftops, too, were crowded. Twilight fell. And then suddenly everybody was pointing, shouting, "There he comes!" And what I saw was like the shadow of a dark bird, soaring in the fading light some hundred feet above the river. Seventeen years later, the year I left Columbia, Lindbergh flew the Atlantic. And this year, on our television sets, we have seen two landings on the moon.

2   I want this chapter to be a celebration of the fabulous age in which we are living; also, of this country in which we are living; and of our incredible human race, which in the years just past broke free of its earth, to fly forth to the opening of the greatest adventure of the ages.

3   When I listen to some of my academic colleagues talk of their indifference to this epochal ° adventure, I am reminded of the anecdote of the little old lady who, when offered an opportunity to look at the moon through a telescope, commented, when she had done so, "Give me the moon as *God* made it!" The only really adequate public comment on the occasion of the first moon walk that I have found reported in the world press was the exclamation of an Italian poet, Giuseppe Ungaretti, published in the picture magazine *Epoca.* In its vivid issue of July 27, 1969, we see a photo of this white-haired old gentleman pointing in rapture to his television screen, and in the caption beneath are his thrilling words: *Questa è una notte diversa da ogni altra notte del mondo.*

4   For indeed that *was* "a different night from all other nights of the world"! Who will ever in his days forget the spell of the incredible hour, July 20, 1969, when our television sets brought directly into our living rooms the image of that strange craft up there and Neil Armstrong's booted foot coming down, feeling cautiously its way—to leave on

epochal: epoch-making, that is, highly significant. An epoch is a period of time marked by some memorable or distinctive event.

the soil of that soaring satellite of earth the first impress ever of life? And then, as though immediately at home there, two astronauts in their space suits were to be seen moving about in a dream-landscape, performing their assigned tasks, setting up the American flag, assembling pieces of equipment, loping strangely but easily back and forth: their pictures brought to us, by the way, through two hundred and thirty-eight thousand miles of empty space by that other modern miracle (also now being taken for granted), the television set in our living room. "All humanity," Buckminster Fuller once said, in prophecy of these transforming forces working now upon our senses, "is about to be born in an entirely new relationship to the universe."

5 From the point of view of a student of mythology, the most important consequences of what Copernicus wrote of the universe in 1543 followed from his presentation there of an image controverting and refuting the obvious "facts" that everybody everywhere could see.° All mankind's theological as well as cosmological thinking, up to that time, had been based on concepts of the universe visually confirmed from the point of view of earth. Also, man's notion of himself and of nature, his poetry and his whole feeling system, were derived from the sight of his earthbound eyes. The sun rose eastward, passed above, leaning southward, and set blazing in the west. The Polynesian hero Maui had snared that sun to slow it down, so that his mother could have time to finish her cooking. Joshua stopped both the sun and the moon, to have time to finish off a slaughter, while God, to assist, flung down from heaven a hail of prodigious ° stones: "and there was no day like that before it or after it, when Jehovah hearkened to the voice of a man."

6 The moon was in ancient times regarded, and in parts of the world still is regarded, as the Mansion of the

Copernicus denied the then-accepted theory that the earth was the center of the universe. He articulated the so-called Copernican theory that the earth and other planets revolve about the sun.

prodigious: enormous.

Fathers, the residence of the souls of those who have passed away and are there waiting to return for rebirth. For the moon itself, as we see it, dies and is resurrected. Shedding its shadow, it is renewed, as life sheds generations to be renewed in those to come. Whereas against all this, which had been confirmed and reconfirmed in the scriptures, poetry, feelings, and visions of all ages, what Copernicus proposed was a universe no eye could see but only the mind imagine: a mathematical, totally invisible construction, of interest only to astronomers, unbeheld, unfelt by any others of this human race, whose sight and feelings were locked still to earth.

7   However, now, in our own day, four and one-quarter centuries later, with those pictures coming down to us from the point of view of the moon, we have all seen—and not only seen, but felt—that our visible world and the abstract construction of Copernicus correspond. That fabulous color photograph of our good earth rising as a glorious planet above a silent lunar landscape is something not to forget. Giuseppe Ungaretti published in that issue of *Epoca* the first verse of a new-world poetry in celebration of this moon-born revelation:

> *Che fai tu, Terra, in ciel?*
> *Dimmi, che fai, Silenziosa Terra?*

> What are you doing, Earth, in heaven?
> Tell me, what are you doing, Silent Earth?

8   All the old bindings are broken. Cosmological centers ° now are any- and everywhere. The earth is a heavenly body, most beautiful of all, and all poetry now is archaic that fails to match the wonder of this view.

· · ·

9   To predict what the imagery of the poetry of man's future is to be, is today, of course, impossible. However, those same three astronauts,° when coming down, gave

cosmological centers: centers of the universe.
Here Campbell refers to the three astronauts who made the first manned flight around the moon, Christmas Eve, 1968.

voice to a couple of suggestions. Having soared beyond
thought into boundless space, circled many times the arid
moon, and begun their long return: how welcome a sight,
they said, was the beauty of their goal, this planet Earth,
"like an oasis in the desert of infinite space!" Now *there*
is a telling image: this earth, the one oasis in all space,
an extraordinary kind of sacred grove, as it were, set apart
for the rituals of life; and not simply one part or section
of this earth, but the entire globe now a sanctuary, a set-
apart Blessed Place. Moreover, we have all now seen for
ourselves how very small is our heaven-born earth, and
how perilous our position on the surface of its whirling,
luminously beautiful orb.

10   A second thought that the astronauts, coming down,
expressed was in reply to a question from Ground Control
asking who was then doing the navigating. Their immediate
answer was, "Newton!" Think of that! They were riding
back securely on the mathematics of the miracle of Isaac
Newton's brain.

11   This stunning answer brought to my mind the essential problem of knowledge considered by Immanuel Kant. °
How is it, he asks, that, standing in this place here, we
can make mathematical calculations that we know will be
valid in that place over there? Nobody knew how deep
the dust on the surface of the moon was going to be, but
the mathematicians knew exactly how to calculate the
laws of the space through which the astronauts would fly,
not only around our familiar earth, but also around the
moon and through all those miles of unexplored space between. How is it, asked Kant, that mathematical judgments
can be made *a priori* ° about space, and about relationships in space?

12   When you walk past a rippling mirror, you cannot
predict what the dimensions of your passing reflection are
going to be. Not so, however, in space. Through the whole
of space there are no such transformations of the mathe-

Immanuel Kant: German philosopher (1724–1804).

a priori: presumptively, that is, without having had actual experience with space.

matics of dimensions. When we saw on our television screens that parachuting spacecraft of the second moon flight descending from the sky to the very spot in the sea that had been programed for its splashdown, we all became eyewitness to the fact that, although the moon is over two hundred thousand miles away from us, a knowledge of the laws of the space through which it moves was already in our minds (or at least in Newton's mind) centuries before we got there. Also known beforehand was the fact that speeds out there could be timed according to earthly measure: that the distance covered in a minute out there would be the same as in a minute here. Which is to say, we had prior knowledge of those matters. And we know, also, that the same laws will apply when our spaceships get to Mars, to Jupiter, to Saturn, and even out beyond.

13   Space and time, as Kant already recognized, are the *"a priori* forms of sensibility," the antecedent ° preconditions of all experience and action whatsoever, implicitly known to our body and senses even before birth, as the field in which we are to function. They are not simply "out there," as the planets are, to be learned about analytically, through separate observations. We carry their laws within us, and so have already wrapped our minds around the universe. "The world," wrote the poet Rilke, "is large, but in us it is deep as the sea." We carry the laws within us by which it is held in order. And we ourselves are no less mysterious. In searching out its wonders, we are learning simultaneously the wonder of ourselves. That moon flight as an outward journey was outward into ourselves. And I do not mean this poetically, but factually, historically. I mean that the actual fact of the making and the visual broadcasting of that trip has transformed, deepened, and extended human consciousness to a degree and in a manner that amount to the opening of a new spiritual era.

14   The first step of that booted foot onto the moon was very, very cautious. The second astronaut descended, and for a time the two moved about carefully, testing their own

---

antecedent: logically prior to.

balances, the weights of their gear in the new environment. But then—by golly!—they were both suddenly jumping, hopping, loping about like kangaroos; and the two moon-walkers of the following voyage were giggling, laughing, enjoying themselves like a pair of lunatic kids—moon-struck! And I thought, "Well now, that lovely satellite has been out there circling our earth for some four billion years like a beautiful but lonesome woman trying to catch earth's eye. She has now at last caught it, and has caught thereby ourselves. And as always happens when a temptation of that kind has been responded to, a new life has opened, richer, more exciting and fulfilling, for both of us than was known, or even thought of or imagined, before." There are youngsters among us, even now, who will be *living* on that moon; others who will visit Mars. And their sons? What voyages are to be theirs?

Questions on Content

1. Why does Campbell believe that the night of the moon walk was different from all other nights?
2. What examples of sun and moon mythologizing support Campbell's statement that our notion of ourselves and of the world is derived from what we *see?*
3. How did Copernicus change all this?
4. What new image of the earth does Campbell think is a "telling" image (paragraph 9)?

Add to Your Vocabulary

epochal, cosmological, prodigious, *a priori,* antecedent.

Questions on Technique

1. What sentences in paragraphs 4 and 13 state major themes of this essay?
2. Campbell often uses metaphor.° What does he mean in paragraph 8 by saying, "All the old bindings are broken. Cosmological centers now are any- and every-where"?

metaphor: See Glossary.

Techniques to Imitate

Quoting from other writers

Drawing upon one's reading is a useful technique in writing. Very often, we find that another person can express our own feelings more clearly or more beautifully than we could ever do ourselves. For this reason, we sometimes memorize a passage; if we are like Campbell, we can later pull it out of our memory and use it to illustrate or support ideas of our own.

Most of us do not have as broad a literary background as Joseph Campbell has, but anyone who reads and studies does have an imaginative "word horde." You should use yours in your writing. Use your readings to make connections. A well-chosen quotation will often help you make something clear to your reader. A quotation from authority, of course, gives support to an argument.

Suggestions for Writing

1. Robert Frost's poem "Stopping by Woods on a Snowy Evening" (page 358) has often been used by orators and writers. Perhaps there is a line from this poem, or from another selection in this book, which expresses some feeling of your own, or some experience you have had. If so, try writing an informal essay around this quotation.

2. Maya Angelou (page 60) uses quotations in relating a childhood experience. Perhaps you recall some words or book or song that meant something to you as a child or that calls something from the past to your mind whenever you hear it today. If so, write an informal essay explaining what it meant to you then or the experience it reminds you of now.

3. In paragraph 14 Campbell describes an exciting scene on television and relates his personal thoughts about it. He is informal, saying things like "by golly" and "well now." If you have taken part in an exciting event that made an impression on you, describe the event and then tell, in a relaxed conversational way, what your thoughts and reactions were.

WILLIAM K. ZINSSER

Verel Modacrylic and
Mr. Inside Floormat

Social criticism need *not* be objective and statistical,
as Maynard has shown us, nor need it be wholly serious,
as William Zinsser is about to demonstrate in this informal "attack" on one of the follies of our society,
namely the gadget craze. Zinsser is clever enough to
keep us laughing as he concentrates his essay on useless
objects. But the wise reader will see that laughter and satire ° are cousins, and Zinsser is talking about "the follies
of modern America," not only floormats and guest rooms.

As an observer of social mores, Zinsser by now has a
wide reputation. Right after World War II, he began
working for the *New York Herald Tribune,* first as a feature writer, then as drama editor, film critic, and editorial
writer. During these twelve years he developed "the
Zinsser touch": sharp pokes at human behavior, delivered not with cruelty or even sarcasm but with the kind
of finesse that makes our pretensions look silly rather
than wrong. Since 1959, he has been a free-lance writer,
publishing his essays in a variety of magazines and then
collecting them in such volumes as *Seen Any Good
Movies Lately?* (1958) and *Weekend Guests* (1963). His
volume *Pop Goes America* (1966) dissects the super-

satire: See Glossary.

ficialities of our culture with Zinsser's usual vigor and hilarity. He is not just a man with a gripe.

The humorist who aims also at being a satirist must possess a faultless style. As you read this essay, pay close attention to *how* Zinsser hits his mark as well as to the gadgets he deplores. Deftness of style is one sign of talent in a writer, and Zinsser, like Thurber, is a model stylist.

1   **W**riters who ponder the follies of modern America—and the journalistic woods have never been so full of folly-ponderers—love to imagine an archaeologist of the future coming upon our ruins. "What would he make of *that?*" they ask, citing some arti- fact ° like a jukebox, and there they rest their case, certain that the archaeologist would be stumped. My only com- plaint with this approach is that it is projected too far ahead. America is full of objects that I don't understand right now.

2   They are objects which I never knew existed and which serve functions that I never dreamed were necessary. See- ing them in advertisements, I am as bewildered in 1964 as any archaeologist will be in 2964. To some extent my trouble is linguistic, for the idiom that describes these items is as strange as the items themselves. It is a language shorn of syntax and strewn with words like "leatherette," which make me uneasy, for I have no idea what they mean and have no way of finding out.

3   "Leatherette" at least contains one genuine noun, and that's a help. But some words don't even offer that com- fort. Consider the word "superette." It consists of a prefix meaning "big" and a suffix meaning "small"—and nothing else. Try that one on your Rosetta Stone,° Mr. Future Archaeologist. If there's anyone in the present audience who doesn't know what a superette is, it's a little super-

artifact: an object made by human work.
Rosetta Stone: found in 1799, it furnished the first clue to deciphering Egyptian hieroglyphics.

market. And if you wonder how a market that's big can also be small, you're beginning to understand my problem and are ready for the main course.

4 The main course has as its textbook the catalogue of Hammacher Schlemmer, a housewares store in Manhattan which took a two-page ad in the "New York Times" for its custom-fitted bomb shelter, complete with $249 TV set. Within this one catalogue, which arrives periodically, I find compressed almost everything that baffles me, both in merchandise and terminology, about the society that I allegedly live in. So profuse are the examples that I hardly know where to begin, but I'll start with the "Select-a-Rest," a $439 couch which "electrically raises legs or back in varying degrees at touch of button; for personal support."

5 The Select-a-Rest typifies the emphasis on ease that is the catalogue's pervading theme. These are, on the whole, objects designed to soften tasks that are not arduous * in the first place: an electric pencil sharpener for $29.95 ("just insert pencil"), a cordless electric carving set for $19.95, a push-button shine for $29.95 ("tap button with toe; place shoe against bonnet"), an egg scissors for $5.95 to open a boiled egg. I'm no student of the economy, least of all my own, but if that many people are willing to shell out thirty clams ° for an electric pencil sharpener ("simply shell out clams")—so many that a manufacturer finds it worthwhile to make them—there is either nothing wrong with the economy or something wrong with the people.

6 As for the $439 to get "personal support" from Select-a-Rest, that's a lot of personal support. Which brings up another linguistic riddle: what is personal support? Does it differ from impersonal support? Does it mean that if I buy Select-a-Rest it will support me personally but not my friends? Perhaps it will support my personal friends—a breed so often mentioned in the phrase "he's a personal friend of mine"—but not my animal friends.

7 This is one of modern America's most puzzling words —and not merely because it has spawned the peculiar subadjective "personalized." I often notice that an actress,

thirty clams: slang for $30.00.

stricken during the run of a play, has called in her "personal physician." What other kind is there? If the medical schools ever turn out an impersonal physician, one who will keep his hands off the patient and look away during an examination, he will be the most sought-after doctor in the land.

8 Speaking of personal friends, you can get a "guest closet kit" at Hammacher Schlemmer for $175. This doesn't seem to include the guest, but it does include twenty-seven squares of Plushtile and many "color coordinated materials." Plushtile is described as "55% Acrilan Acrylic, 45% Verel Modacrylic on an interlocking back; can be lifted out to change pattern, clean, even move with you. Colorfast, long-wearing, non-matting, non-allergenic.° In 20 decorator colors."

9 Curiously, I don't happen to know what Acrilan Acrylic and Verel Modacrylic are, but I don't doubt for a minute that they can move with me. If I ever left them behind in the guest closet, they would probably come running out and jump in the car. I do know, however, what the twenty decorator colors are. They are the colors that decorators come in: ruddy, flushed, wine red, Fire Island tan, sun lamp, sunburn pink, Noxzema, pancake, talc, office yellow, ashen, white, ulcer gray, subway green, soot, toast, English muffin, five o'clock shadow, midnight and winter blue. I have met decorators in all these colors, though not many of them were long-wearing and some weren't even colorfast.

10 This is another construction—the noun-adjective like "decorator"—that will vex the archaeologists. Tricky as Linear B,° it leaves the scholar to guess the meaning out of various possibilities, none of them plausible. A bathroom scale in the Hammacher Schlemmer catalogue, for example, is "doctor-type for no stooping." Does this mean that the scale looks like a doctor or is somehow shaped

non-allergenic: not having properties relating to allergens (substances inducing allergy).

Linear B: an ancient system of writing a very early form of Greek.

like a doctor? Does it mean that doctors don't stoop? I could swear that I've seen doctors stoop.

11   Then again I couldn't really swear to anything. The catalogue addles * me. I see an item like "wood snack table set" and my head spins. Is it a table for eating wood snacks? What about the D-Frost Master which "ends hand defrosting"? But I haven't *been* defrosting my hands. Ought I to pay $79.95 for a "floor hair dryer," which presumably dries hair that has fallen on the floor? What is a "hostess towel tree"—a towel tree hung with hostesses? How can I rest easy on the $219 Barcalounger ("for relaxation, comfort, TV viewing") when I see that its pillow back is made of Premier Naugahyde? Surely Premier Naugahyde was defenestrated ° in the Bosnian coup of 1912?

12   Confronted with such an abstract language, I lose my grip on reality. And language is only part of the problem. Equally unreal are the concepts that it expresses, such as this one: "Waterford Cut Plexiglas has old world charm but in virtually unbreakable Plexiglas; a practical version of crystal."

13   The sentence is positively electrical in its balance of positive and negative currents. Every clause carries its immediate cancellation. The whole point of Waterford glass is that it is not Plexiglas; old world charm derives from the fact that an object is both old and breakable; and part of the enjoyment of crystal is the awareness that it is not practical.

14   A more perfect conundrum * could hardly be posed by a wizard in Wonderland or Oz. And yet it is no isolated case. Modern America loves authentic names but hates the authentic flaws that accompany them, so it labors to root them out. "Mr. Inside Floormat," for instance, is available at Hammacher Schlemmer in "green striped nylon tweed." This material is rather hard to picture, as it can't be both nylon and tweed.

15   Obviously tweed is in the floormat only as an idea. Everybody likes tweed coats; therefore they would like a tweed floormat. But tweed gets dirty and wears out and

defenestrated: thrown out of a window.

shouldn't be wet. So the solution is to make the tweed of nylon, and everyone is happy—everyone, that is, except the archaeologists of the future and a few thousand crofters ° in the Scottish Highlands.

16 A similar paradox lies in a stove described in the catalogue as follows: "Radiant Broiling with Quartz Foil gives charcoal flavor without charcoal ($69.95)." Here we see a circle so fully turned that it swallows itself. Charcoal flavor began as a by-product of early outdoor stoves. Nobody really wanted his steak to taste like charcoal, but as this was unavoidable we were told that it was a great flavor and to enjoy it. Now that outdoor ranges have improved and steaks can taste like steaks again, they don't seem authentic. Hence this broiler that adds a tinge of charcoal. In fact, it doesn't go far enough. The next model should char the steaks on the outside and fill the patio with smoke.

17 No thought is spared in Hammacher Schlemmer to make the living easy and beautiful. It's not merely that the crystal doesn't break because it isn't crystal. The air is good ("Dynamic Ionaire Mark VII provides negative ions ° to reduce dry, staleair effects; restores natural ion balance of air. $149.50"). The floors are clean ("Disposable boots of polyethelene film are for bad weather, avoiding dirt"). The lights don't have to be turned on or off (Homelighter does it automatically, "according to sunlight"; Time-All does, too—"and does it indefinitely until you change the cycle; misleads burglars").

18 No more need you eat leftovers ("Party Grill makes leftovers into bite-sized toasted sandwiches"). No more need you rest on a plain old-fashioned pillow ("Comfort Aid," an object that looks like a pillow but costs $29.95, is "for either head or foot elevation; use for relaxation, tension and pressure relief"). You don't even have to hold the telephone; simply fit your "executive phone stand"

crofters: British tenant farmers.
negative ions: ions carrying negative charges, also called anions.

($39.95) with a "transistorized ° phone amplifier ($34.95)
for hands-free conference calls."

19   Comforts don't cease when you go for a drive. Your
car can be a home-away-from-home if you get the Head-
rest that "attaches to auto seat for rests, naps." I had supposed that this nap-inducing cushion was meant only for
passengers, but in an adjacent photograph the driver is also
resting his head on one and is presumably well on his way
to bye-bye land, if not eternity.

20   Another trait that the future archaeologist will note is
our mania for decoration. As any dime-store browser
knows, no object in America is too cheap to be embellished * with some sort of pattern, usually floral, and anyone foolish enough to want a plain object must search far
and pay more.

21   This point is also amply documented in Hammacher
Schlemmer's catalogue, especially in its bathroom, which
has a "poppy" shower curtain in Glo-chintz (the chintz
that isn't); a "poppy" tissue-box on "jade-white Plexiglas"
(since when has jade been white?); a "poppy" hamper,
"poppy" basket and "poppy" brush holder; four "poppy"
bath bottles; a hand-decorated "poppy" toilet seat; and a
"poppy" decorated scale. Now there's a bathroom with
poppies. The scale also comes in an undecorated model,
but that doesn't mean it is intended to stay undecorated, if
I understand correctly—and there's no reason why I should
—this sentence that describes it: "Slip own wallpaper, paint
color, curtain fabric sample under see-thru lid to match
decor."

22   Outside the bathroom there is also much to be embellished. You can get a "decorated toast cover with hand-
painted red bud roses," or a "decorated phone stand, floral
on white, which holds 2 books, all phones." (It's odd that
anyone would want all phones on one phone stand—the
upstairs phone, downstairs phone and kitchen phone—but
that's what decoration will do.) There are bottle stoppers
"imprinted with our gnomes"—maybe *that's* who writes

transistorized: equipped with a circuit employing transistors.

the catalogue—and there is a "guest terry robe with choice of any 2-toned colored name or 3-letter monogram."

23   Thus even the guest must be decorated, perhaps to help find him when he strays into the color-coordinated guest closet. Of course this means inviting the same guest again and again, or inviting guests who happen to have the same name or initials. The worst thing would be for a guest to drop in unexpectedly. He would be doomed to wear an undecorated terry robe and would probably spend most of the weekend, out of sheer insecurity, behind the poppy shower curtain.

24   And now if you'll excuse me, I'm going to put my head on my 6-Way Prop Pillow of lightweight polyfoam (if I can think of six ways to do it), take a drink from my Marbleized Rack Set (chairside size), put some wax-tipped Airfoam Nods in my ears and Sleep Shade on my eyes, clear the room of negative ions with dynamic * Mark VII, turn on the Time-All to mislead burglars, and drop off for a few minutes. If the doorbell rings, it's probably the "Home Massager" that I ordered from Hammacher Schlemmer. As described in the catalogue, "Oster Stimulax, Jr., imparts the rotating, patting motions of Swedish massage." I understand that young Oster studied with his dad in Stockholm—old man Stimulax was an eminent masseur— and for my money ($32.95) I personally think he's going to give me a lot of personal relief. He's doctor-type.

ANALYSIS

Zinsser's essay has much in common with Philip Wylie's diatribe on American food (p. 444); but whereas Wylie concentrates on reasoned argument, Zinsser laughs at his subject, or at least on the surface he finds the advertiser's world too bewildering and unsettling to cope with. When he tells us, in paragraph 12, that all this abstract language makes him lose his grip on reality, we know he is exaggerating. The informal essayist takes this stance quite naturally, aiming to amuse us as well as inform us. Such a writer inflates a subject intentionally, for dramatic effects.

In sum, the informal essayist will often use exaggeration as a device to make readers see matters in a new and arresting way.

What "follies of modern America" upset Zinsser to the point of despair? His choice is wide, so he settles on "objects which [he] never knew existed and which serve functions that [he] never dreamed were necessary," using the Hammacher Schlemmer catalogue as sourcebook. The first half of the essay deplores the abstract language one finds in these catalogues; the second half bewails the concepts expressed by the advertising writers. Both language and concepts lead Zinsser to despair, or perhaps we should say ostensibly to despair, for anyone with Zinsser's sense of humor cannot be wholly defeated by an ad writer. If his aim, then, is mock-seriousness, he needs a special tone in his own prose to convey exaggerated concern. Let us look at Zinsser's prose style rather than the organization of this essay, with an eye to learning how a writer molds audience reaction.

Zinsser wants us to share his bewilderment, so he concentrates on the ridiculous. "Leatherette" and "superette" are bad enough, but the "Select-a-Rest" couch is worse. Watch how Zinsser, in paragraphs 6 and 7, manipulates the word "personal" and its variants to make the innocuous phrase "personal support" sound meaningless. Again in paragraph 9, he pokes fun at patented names like Verel Modacrylic—an easy target—and at the confusion a phrase like "decorator colors" can create. With a straight face, he invents the colors decorators come in, a spectrum no painter has ever seen. Two paragraphs later, with an even straighter face, he defines Premier Naugahyde. Can we ever again look at the label on a vinyl chair without thinking of the suicide of a Middle European dictator? This is what we mean by mock-seriousness.

Ridiculous concepts are even funnier: an inside floormat made of tweed that is really nylon; Waterford Cut Plexiglas which is neither made in Waterford nor resembles crystal; Quartz Foil which gives charcoal flavor without charcoal. In this illusory world of ours we are surrounded by comforts we do not need and concepts we cannot understand. Zinsser mocks them by quoting directly from the catalogue blurbs ("Party Grill makes leftovers into bite-sized sandwiches") or resorting to flippant suggestions ("The next model should char the steaks on the outside and fill the patio with smoke"). He seldom resorts to sheer exasperation, as in paragraph 21: "Now there's a bathroom with poppies." Yet exasperation is part of his technique. He piles one ridiculous object on another in the poppy "explosion" of paragraph 21, and then tops it with the fantasy of an undecorated guest who spends the weekend "behind the poppy shower curtain."

How is Zinsser to end such a *tour de force?* By running the whole gamut in one wild assemblage of useless luxuries. Paragraph 24 is a rehearsal of all the abstract language and unreal concepts that constitute the rest of the essay. It will be a dull reader indeed who misses the satire, the personal satire, comic-type.

Questions on Content

1. Why does Zinsser incorporate archaeologists of the future into his opening paragraphs?
2. How do you answer his questions in paragraph 10?
3. What does he mean by "authentic flaws" in paragraph 14?
4. How would you describe Hammacher Schlemmer's aids to "make the living easy and beautiful," as enumerated in paragraphs 17–19?

Add to Your Vocabulary

arduous, addles, conundrum, embellished, dynamic.

Questions on Technique

1. Would you have organized the details of this essay in any other fashion, beginning, for example, with more outrageous luxury items from the catalogue or breaking down the illustrations into male, female, domestic, automotive, and athletic categories rather than Zinsser's

divisions: abstract language and unreal concepts? What advantages would the reorganization give you?

2. Does this essay need even more satiric comment or is his method of quoting from the catalogue adequate built-in criticism? What would sarcasm do to Zinsser's intent?

3. The comic writer must avoid the feeble joke and the tired wisecrack. Does Zinsser come perilously close, in any paragraph, to spoiling his effects?

Techniques to Imitate

The mild satire of the informal essayist

The informal essayist belongs among the "folly-ponderers" to whom Zinsser refers in his opening sentence. Zinsser's entire essay, in fact, is an example of folly-pondering. The tone of his essay is satirical. He is holding up to ridicule the follies of modern America, but the satire of the informal essayist is not the bitter or angry satire of the serious satirist. It is not meant to hurt. Rather, it is mild and good-natured.

Usually, informal essayists look upon the world as amused observers. They do not choose to write about human weaknessess of earth-shaking importance. They write indulgently about relatively unimportant peculiarities of human behavior which strike them as silly. They poke fun, but smile as they do so. In their bewilderment, they sometimes seem to be saying with Puck in *A Midsummer Night's Dream,* "Lord, what fools these mortals be!"

The amused-observer atttiude is a characteristic trait of the informal essayist. If you ponder the little follies of your fellow students, your teachers, parents, friends, and other groups, with amusement rather than with malice or bitterness, you will be able to imitate the informal essayist's mild and entertaining satire.

Suggestions for Writing

1. Write an essay on Zinsser's essay. Discuss in 500 words

the effect advertising in general has had on you and your family. Be specific.

2. Imitate Zinsser's subject matter. Using an issue of a commercial magazine (*Good Housekeeping, Better Homes and Gardens,* for example), or several television commercials you are familiar with, discuss the claims a variety of advertisements make and the ambiguous language of these claims.

3. Reverse Zinsser's technique and defend our mechanical civilization by citing in detail the advantages of gadgets and our hidden needs for them.

4. Choose a mechanism with which you are familiar, such as an automobile, a quadraphonic sound system, or a musical instrument, and write a 400-word advertisement designed to sell it.

5. Write an essay on "the spoiled moderns" or "the affluent absurd" or "gadgets in modern life," furthering Zinsser's argument with examples of your own.

PART THREE

ARGUMENT
AND PERSUASION

9

ARGUMENT AND PERSUASION

Part Two of this book tried to delineate varieties of expository prose, the kind of writing that is concerned with the *why* or the *how* of things. Gerard Matthes defined quicksand; E. G. F. Sauer explained how birds navigate; Scott Carpenter reported what space travel means; C. P. Snow urged us to think about the future. These essays are meant to inform us, primarily; entertain us, if possible; and describe processes or methods or events as the subject demands. As we said earlier, exposition is chiefly concerned with explaining something, with setting forth ideas.

We are confronted daily with another kind of expository writing. In letters, newspapers, magazines, brochures, we are urged to share this opinion or believe that viewpoint. Radio and television commercials coax us to try the large economy size. Political speeches urge us to vote for the "only qualified candidate." Organized propaganda aims at spreading biased information. We call this kind of writing argument and persuasion. Loosely defined, it is the type of prose which communicates opinions with the desire to convince the reader to accept them as just and true.

A finer distinction may be made between the two terms. Argument is the kind of writing which seeks to win assent to a belief or opinion. Philip Wylie will try to convince you in his essay that American food is deteriorating and science is to blame. Persuasion goes one step further and enlists arguments in order to accomplish some proposed action. Clark Van Fleet, for example, wants each one of us to agree that only by passing rigid laws against the manufacture, sale, and use of insecticides can we prevent further pollution of our natural resources. You will understand that it is not always easy to distinguish these two types of prose

438

because they are so closely allied. You have seen how reports and analyses merge on occasion. You will also discover in the seven models which follow that once the arguments are established, action is implied or anticipated if not directly sought.

Perhaps the simplest statement of argument is in the editorial, and so we begin there with a brief model. In *Science,* a weekly magazine published by the American Association for the Advancement of Science, Joseph Turner clearly and concisely demonstrates how good expository argument presents propositions, in this case three. We call these statements propositions because they are what the writer *proposes* to prove. They are not fact; they are debatable opinions. Two of these propositions could be called "extremes." The first argues that scientists should discover technical facts, and no more, since they are not responsible for "decisions of public policy." The second proposition says "scientists should consider the possible consequences of any piece of research before it is begun." Turner seeks to convince us of the validity of calling the third proposition an intelligent mean, or middle ground.

JOSEPH TURNER

Between Two Extremes

1   **W**ith science supporting an
ever-expanding military technology, many people in this
country are wondering to what extent American scientists
should assume responsibility for the uses to which the government puts their discoveries and talents. It has always
been possible, of course, to speak of pure research, just as
it has always been possible, we suppose, to speak of the
pure act of sitting down to a meal and consuming it with
impeccable table manners. But any piece of behavior can
acquire moral properties, given the appropriate circumstances—even eating one's fill, as when the roast is small
and the company large.
2   One view of the scientist's responsibility for the social
consequences of scientific truths is that this responsibility
ends with the scientist's willingness to do work directly or
indirectly for the government, including work on weapons.
According to this view, being a good scientist no more
gives one special privileges in determining national policy
than being a good information clerk at an airport entitles
one to select destinations for travelers. The area of special
competence of scientists lies in the discovery of technical
facts; decisions of public policy rest with elected or appointed public officials.
3   An opposite opinion concerning the obligations of sci-

entists holds that scientists should consider the possible consequences of any piece of research before it is begun, and if the research is judged more a threat to the country, or humanity at large, than a benefit, they should refuse their services. A man cannot delegate to a superior the responsibility for the moral consequences of his acts, the second view claims. To be sure, to predict future applications of new discoveries calls more for the talents of a prophet than for those of a scientist. No one now knows to what uses, or abuses, the fall of parity ° in physics may some day prove amenable.* But somewhere along the line, basic research becomes applied research, and forecasts about the uses of discoveries become something more than anybody's guess.

4 Between the two opposing positions lies a third position which holds that at least some scientists, although they fear the dangers posed by a further increase in military power, have the duty to work on projects that the government deems necessary, but that scientists also have the duty to state their opinions on matters lying outside science. If this is the age of specialization, so this argument runs, it is also the age of specialists working together on teams. Public officials should have the final word, but any attempt to understand the full range of consequences—military, political, economic, and moral—of new advances in research, requires the views of the men who understand those advances best.

5 It is this third position that expresses our own convictions, and that seems to express the convictions of most of

fall of parity: In 1957, Professor Tsung Dao Lee of Columbia University and Chen Nin Yang of the Institute for Advanced Study at Princeton received the Nobel prize in physics for "their penetrating investigation of the so-called parity laws which has led to important discoveries regarding elementary particles." Their contribution to physical research destroyed for all time what had long been called the "Principles of Conservation of Parity" according to which "space possessed a well-balanced quality of symmetry in which every existing object was balanced by a corresponding mirror image that had to respond to the same law of nature." (See the *New York Times,* November 1, 1957.)

the persons in this country who are presently concerned with these problems—although, admittedly, agreement on general principles does not necessarily imply agreement on particular cases. The first position errs because, pushed to its conclusion, it turns the citizen's obligations to the state into despotism; while the second position errs because, if pushed, it turns the moral integrity * of the individual into anarchy. The third position seeks the mean ° between the scientist's assuming too little responsibility for the consequences of his research and his assuming too much responsibility.

ANALYSIS

We should keep in mind that Turner's audience, in this magazine editorial, is composed chiefly of practicing scientists. He does not need to fill in details. In fact, most editorials assume that the reader is informed, alert, and ready to hear the argument. Space is limited.

Turner states his case concisely. Paragraph 1 announces the question: to what extent should American scientists assume responsibility for governmental use of their talents and discoveries? He gives us no elaborating instances; he cites no agencies, projects, or scientists by name. His editorial is concerned with principle only. Three points of view are presented in three succeeding paragraphs: (a) scientists are responsible only for the discovery of technical facts, not for decisions of public policy; (b) scientists are responsible for the moral consequences of an applied use of their technical discoveries; they should refuse their services if they foresee a threat; and (c) at least some scientists have the duty both to work on governmental projects and to share in understanding the full range of consequences. In brief, Turner has the scientist face no responsibility, full responsibility, or a shared responsibility with public officials. In paragraph 5 he tells us—convinces us?—why the third or mean position is the wisest solution.

This editorial is a bare outline of an argument, yet it

the mean: midway between two extremes.

illustrates neatly the presentation of propositions and the manner in which argument takes a decided stand, a specific point of view when alternatives are offered. There is no opportunity here to adduce facts or the opinion of authorities, as we shall observe in other models. Turner is not so much *proving* here as he is stating basic reasoning. The reasoning, he would wish us to believe, is sound.

Add to Your Vocabulary

amenable, integrity.

Suggestions for Writing

1. Turner's editorial suggests a major problem facing the world today, that of coping intelligently with the great and dangerous scientific advances now irretrievably part of our civilization. While we advance scientifically, we remain morally and psychologically the same confused human beings we have always been. For example, at a time when science has made it impossible for any nation to survive a major war, many nations are vigorously strengthening their military forces. In an essay of 500 words, state your opinion of what we must do to save ourselves from the possible dangers of scientific advancement.

2. Choose another subject and imitate in 400 words Turner's structure paragraph by paragraph: statement of subject, three propositions, your opinion on which of the three is wisest. You might choose to write about College Board examinations, learning foreign languages, summer work, or a topic of your own choice.

3. Write a 350-word editorial for your school paper on a current school issue of general interest to all students. Take a firm stand in stating your beliefs.

4. In a 400-word essay, criticize an editorial you have clipped from a recent newspaper. Discuss the method of organization, its language, power of convincing you (or not convincing you, as the case may be). How would you improve the writer's argument?

PHILIP WYLIE

Science Has Spoiled
My Supper

Unlike Turner's editorial, in which three propositions
are considered, Philip Wylie's essay deals with one main
argument. He announces it boldly in his title. He restates it in his second paragraph. He makes us feel the
subject has long been simmering and that now it has
come to a boil. Anyone who has read Wylie's *Generation
of Vipers* (1942) knows how relentlessly he can pursue
an argument, how severely he can complain of the
weaknesses he finds in American manners and morals.
This essay is out of that same mold.

Wylie, who died in 1971, had a varied writing career,
on the staff of the *New Yorker,* in Hollywood, on newspapers, and in publishing houses. He was so well known
for frank expression of his negative opinions that his
method came to be called, jestingly, veneration of
gripers. And an effective method it is, specific in its attack, full of bite, uncompromising in its conclusions. By
the time you finish reading Wylie's argument, you will
probably have developed some strong opinions of your
own.

1   **I** am a fan for Science. My
education is scientific and I have, in one field, contributed

444

a monograph to a scientific journal. Science, to my mind, is applied honesty, the one reliable means we have to find out truth. That is why, when error is committed in the name of Science, I feel the way a man would if his favorite uncle had taken to drink.

2 Over the years, I have come to feel that way about what science has done to food. I agree that America can set as good a table as any nation in the world. I agree that our food is nutritious and that the diet of most of us is well-balanced. What America eats is handsomely packaged; it is usually clean and pure; it is excellently preserved. The only trouble with it is this: year by year it grows less good to eat. It appeals increasingly to the eye. But who eats with his eyes? Almost everything used to taste better when I was a kid. For quite a long time I thought that observation was merely another index of advancing age. But some years ago I married a girl whose mother is an expert cook of the kind called "old-fashioned." This gifted woman's daughter (my wife) was taught her mother's venerable skills. The mother lives in the country and still plants an old-fashioned garden. She still buys dairy products from the neighbors and, in so far as possible, she uses the same materials her mother and grandmother did—to prepare meals that are superior. They are just as good, in this Year of Grace, as I recall them from my courtship. After eating for a while at the table of my mother-in-law, it is sad to go back to eating with my friends—even the alleged "good cooks" among them. And it is a gruesome experience to have meals at the best big-city restaurants.

3 Take cheese, for instance. Here and there, in big cities, small stores and delicatessens specialize in cheese. At such places, one can buy at least some of the first-rate cheeses that we used to eat—such as those we had with pie and in macaroni. The latter were sharp but not too sharp. They were a little crumbly. We called them American cheeses, or even rat cheese; actually, they were Cheddars.° Long ago, this cheese began to be supplanted by a material called

Cheddars: smooth-textured cheeses originally made at Cheddar, England, but now made extensively in the United States as well.

"cheese foods." Some cheese foods and "processed" cheese are fairly edible; but not one comes within miles of the old kinds—for flavor.

4 A grocer used to be very fussy about his cheese. Cheddar was made and sold by hundreds of little factories. Representatives of the factories had particular customers, and cheese was prepared by hand to suit the grocers, who knew precisely what their patrons wanted in rat cheese, pie cheese, American, and other cheeses. Some liked them sharper, some liked them yellower; some liked anise seeds in cheese, or caraway.

5 What happened? Science—or what is called science—stepped in. The old-fashioned cheeses didn't ship well enough. They crumbled, became moldy, dried out. "Scientific" tests disclosed that a great majority of the people will buy a less-good-tasting cheese if that's all they can get. "Scientific marketing" then took effect. Its motto is "Give the people the least quality they'll stand for." In food, as in many other things, the "scientific marketers" regard quality as secondary so long as they can sell most persons anyhow; what they are after is "durability" or "shippability."

6 It is not possible to make the very best cheese in vast quantities at a low average cost. "Scientific sampling" got in its statistically nasty work. It was found that the largest number of people will buy something that is bland and rather tasteless. Those who prefer a product of a pronounced and individualistic flavor have a variety of preferences. Nobody is altogether pleased by bland foodstuff, in other words; but nobody is very violently put off. The result is that a "reason" has been found for turning out zillions of packages of something that will "do" for nearly all and isn't even imagined to be superlatively good by a single soul!

7 Economics entered. It is possible to turn out in quantity a bland, impersonal, practically imperishable substance more or less resembling, say, cheese—at lower cost than cheese. Chain groceries shut out the independent stores and "standardization" became a principal means of cutting costs.

8 Imitations also came into the cheese business. There are American duplications of most of the celebrated European cheeses, mass-produced and cheaper by far than the imports. They would cause European food-lovers to gag or guffaw—but generally the imitations are all that's available in the supermarkets. People buy them and eat them.

9 Perhaps you don't like cheese—so the fact that decent cheese is hardly ever served in America any more, or used in cooking, doesn't matter to you. Well, take bread. There has been (and still is) something of a hullabaloo about bread. In fact, in the last few years, a few big bakeries have taken to making a fairly good imitation of real bread. It costs much more than what is nowadays called bread, but it is edible. Most persons, however, now eat as "bread" a substance so full of chemicals and so barren of cereals that it approaches a synthetic.*

10 Most bakers are interested mainly in how a loaf of bread looks. They are concerned with how little stuff they can put in it—to get how much money. They are deeply interested in using chemicals that will keep bread from molding, make it seem "fresh" for the longest possible time, and so render it marketable and shippable. They have been at this monkeyshine for a generation. Today a loaf of "bread" looks deceptively real; but it is made from heaven knows what and it resembles, as food, a solidified bubble bath. Some months ago I bought a loaf of the stuff and, experimentally, began pressing it together, like an accordion. With a little effort, I squeezed the whole loaf to a length of about one inch!

11 Yesterday, at the home of my mother-in-law, I ate with country-churned butter and home-canned wild strawberry jam several slices of actual bread, the same thing we used to have every day at home. People who have eaten actual bread will know what I mean. They will know that the material commonly called bread is not even related to real bread, except in name.

12 For years, I couldn't figure out what had happened to vegetables. I knew, of course, that most vegetables, to be enjoyed in their full deliciousness, must be picked fresh and cooked at once. I knew that vegetables cannot be over-cooked and remain even edible, in the best sense. They cannot stand on the stove. That set of facts makes it impossible, of course, for any American restaurant—or, indeed, any city-dweller separated from supply by more than a few hours—to have decent fresh vegetables. The Parisians manage by getting their vegetables picked at dawn and rushed in farmers' carts to market, where no middleman or marketman delays produce on its way to the pot.

13   Our vegetables, however, come to us through a long chain of command. There are merchants of several sorts—wholesalers before the retailers, commission men, and so on—with the result that what were once edible products become, in transit, mere wilted leaves and withered tubers.*

14   Homes and restaurants do what they can with this stuff—which my mother-in-law would discard on the spot. I have long thought that the famed blindfold test for cigarettes should be applied to city vegetables. For I am sure that if you puréed * them and ate them blindfolded, you couldn't tell the beans from the peas, the turnips from the squash, the Brussels sprouts from the broccoli.

15   It is only lately that I have found how much science has had to do with this reduction of noble victuals to pottage. Here the science of genetics ° is involved. Agronomists and the like have taken to breeding all sorts of vegetables and fruits—changing their original nature. This sounds wonderful and often is insane. For the scientists have not as a rule taken any interest whatsoever in the taste of the things they've tampered with!

16   What they've done is to develop "improved" strains of things for every purpose but eating. They work out, say, peas that will ripen all at once. The farmer can then harvest his peas and thresh them and be done with them. It is extremely profitable because it is efficient. What matter if such peas taste like boiled paper wads?

17   Geneticists have gone crazy over such "opportunities."

    genetics: the branch of biology dealing with heredity and variation among related organisms. As an applied science it deals with the fundamentals of plant and animal breeding.

They've developed string beans that are straight instead of curved, and all one length. This makes them easier to pack in cans, even if, when eating them, you can't tell them from tender string. Ripening time and identity of size and shape are, nowadays, more important in carrots than the fact that they taste like carrots. Personally, I don't care if they hybridize ° onions till they are as big as your head and come up through the snow; but, in doing so, they are producing onions that only vaguely and feebly remind you of onions. We are getting some varieties, in fact, that have less flavor than the water off last week's leeks.* Yet, if people don't eat onions because they taste like onions, what in the name of Luther Burbank ° do they eat them for?

18 The women's magazines are about one third dedicated to clothes, one third to mild comment on sex, and the other third to recipes and pictures of handsome salads, desserts, and main courses. "Institutes" exist to experiment and tell housewives how to cook attractive meals and how to turn leftovers into works of art. The food thus pictured looks like famous paintings of still life. The only trouble is it's tasteless. It leaves appetite unquenched and merely serves to stave off famine.

19 I wonder if this blandness of our diet doesn't explain why so many of us are overweight and even dangerously so. When things had flavor, we knew what we were eating all the while—and it satisfied us. A teaspoonful of my mother-in-law's wild strawberry jam will not just provide a gastronome's ° ecstasy: it will entirely satisfy your jam desire. But, of the average tinned or glass-packed strawberry jam, you need half a cupful to get the idea of what you're eating. A slice of my mother-in-law's apple pie will satiate * you far better than a whole bakery pie.

20 That thought is worthy of investigation—of genuine scientific investigation. It is merely a hypothesis,° so far,

hybridize: to interbreed.
Luther Burbank: United States naturalist (1849–1926) who produced a number of new species of plants.
gastronome: an epicure, one who knows and enjoys good food.
hypothesis: a proposition assumed as a premise in an argument.

and my own. But people—and their ancestors—have been eating according to flavor for upwards of a billion years. The need to satisfy the sense of taste may be innate * and important. When food is merely a pretty cascade of viands, with the texture of boiled cardboard and the flavor of library paste, it may be the instinct of *genus homo* ° to go on eating in the unconscious hope of finally satisfying the ageless craving of the frustrated taste buds. In the days when good-tasting food was the rule in the American home, obesity * wasn't such a national curse.

21 How can you feel you've eaten if you haven't tasted, and fully enjoyed tasting? Why (since science is ever so ready to answer the beck and call of mankind) don't people who want to reduce merely give up eating and get the nourishment they must have in measured doses shot into their arms at hospitals? One ready answer to that question suggests that my theory of overeating is sound: people like to taste! In eating, they try to satisfy that like. The scientific war against deliciousness has been stepped up enormously in the last decade. Some infernal * genius found a way to make biscuit batter keep. Housewives began to buy this premixed stuff. It saved work, of course. But any normally intelligent person can learn, in a short period, how to prepare superb baking powder biscuits. I can make better biscuits, myself, than can be made from patent batters. Yet soon after this fiasco * became an American staple, it was discovered that a half-baked substitute for all sorts of breads, pastries, rolls, and the like could be mass-manufactured, frozen—and sold for polishing off in the home oven. None of these two-stage creations is as good as even a fair sample of the thing it imitates. A man of taste, who had eaten one of my wife's cinnamon buns, might use the premixed sort to throw at starlings—but not to eat! Cake mixes, too, come ready-prepared—like cement and not much better-tasting compared with true cake.

22 It is, however, "deep-freezing" that has really rung down the curtain on American cookery. Nothing is im-

genus homo: anthropologically speaking, a person is genus *Homo,* family *Hominidae,* class *Mammalia.*

proved by the process. I have yet to taste a deep-frozen victual that measures up, in flavor, to the fresh, unfrosted original. And most foods, cooked or uncooked, are destroyed in the deep freeze for all people of sense and sensibility. Vegetables with crisp and crackling texture emerge as mush, slippery and stringy as hair nets simmered in Vaseline. The essential oils that make peas peas—and cabbage cabbage—must undergo fission and fusion in freezers. Anyhow, they vanish. Some meats turn to leather. Others to wood pulp. Everything, pretty much, tastes like the mosses of tundra,° dug up in midwinter. Even the appearance changes, often-times. Handsome comestibles you put down in the summer come out looking very much like the corpses of woolly mammoths ° recovered from the last Ice Age.

23 Of course, all this scientific "food handling" tends to save money. It certainly preserves food longer. It reduces work at home. But these facts, and especially the last, imply that the first purpose of living is to avoid work—at home, anyhow.

24 Without thinking, we are making an important confession about ourselves as a nation. We are abandoning quality—even, to some extent, the quality of people. The "best" is becoming too good for us. We are suckling ourselves on machine-made mediocrity. It is bad for our souls, our minds, and our digestion. It is the way our wiser and calmer forebears fed, not people, but hogs: as much as possible and as fast as possible, with no standard of quality.

25 The Germans say, *"Mann ist was er isst*—Man is what he eats." If this be true, the people of the U.S.A. are well on their way to becoming a faceless mob of mediocrities, of robots. And if we apply to other attributes the criteria we apply these days to appetite, that is what would happen! We would not want bright children any more; we'd merely want them to look bright—and get through

tundra: one of the vast, nearly level treeless plains of the arctic regions of Europe, Asia, and North America.

mammoths: large, extinct species of elephant.

school fast. We wouldn't be interested in beautiful women —just a good paint job. And we'd be opposed to the most precious quality of man: his individuality, his differentness from the mob.

26   There are some people—sociologists and psychologists among them—who say that is exactly what we Americans are doing, are becoming. Mass man, they say, is on the increase. Conformity, standardization, similarity—all on a cheap and vulgar level—are replacing the great American ideas of colorful liberty and dignified individualism. If this is so, the process may well begin, like most human behavior, in the home—in those homes where a good meal has been replaced by something-to-eat-in-a-hurry. By something not very good to eat, prepared by a mother without very much to do, for a family that doesn't feel it amounts to much anyhow.

27   I call, here, for rebellion.

ANALYSIS

American food is losing its flavor—this is Wylie's argument. How does he set out to "prove" his proposition? He uses three examples: cheese, bread, vegetables. And wisely he speaks of each from personal experience. He does not settle for principles alone. He has specific objections. Using his mother-in-law's table as the ideal standard, he employs strong contrasts. On one side are properly-aged cheeses, home-baked bread, freshly-picked vegetables. He admires equally his mother-in-law's country-churned butter and home-canned wild strawberry jam. On the other side are "improved processes," "scientific marketing," "greater shippability," and "premixed or deep-frozen products." The results, he assures us, are devastating: cheeses that strike him as bland and tasteless, bread that is mostly air, vegetables that resemble cooked cardboard. He makes few concessions to geneticists and cooking institutes. Why, he asks, must we continue to eat this tasteless fare?

With this main argument "proved," Wylie moves (paragraph 19) to a corollary argument, that is, an additional inference from his chief proposition. Are we, he asks, over-eating because we cannot taste what we eat? Has food become fodder, stuffing, pre-mixed, ready-prepared substitutes? Does deep-freezing lead directly to dieting? He is quite serious when he says (paragraph 20) that this theory is worthy of genuine scientific investigation.

Wylie suggests a second corollary (paragraph 25): if we are what we eat, we are well on our way "to becoming a faceless mob of mediocrities, of robots." Science has not only ruined our suppers and our waistlines, it has made mediocrity the standard. If we accept the "commonest low denominator" in foodstuffs, something-to-eat-in-a-hurry, we will, in time, accept mediocrity throughout our civilization. By paragraph 26, Wylie is almost ready to begin another essay on mobocracy, mass rule, and assembly-line thinking. His main argument has gathered momentum. His last, one-sentence paragraph cuts it off. He is not ready to propose, or at least not here, how the rebellion shall begin. His essay is a fine model of argument. He does not, in the rhetorical sense, directly relate his proofs to a proposed action. Argument stops short of persuasion.

Questions on Content

1. What are the differences Wylie cites between old-fashioned Cheddars and the modern processed cheese foods?
2. What does Wylie mean by the terms "scientific marketing" and "scientific sampling"? Be specific.
3. Why can we not find fresh vegetables in our markets?
4. What "opportunities" have geneticists taken "advantage" of?
5. What are Wylie's specific complaints about deep freezing?

Add to Your Vocabulary

synthetic, tubers, puréed, genetics, hybridize, leeks, satiate, hypothesis, innate, obesity, infernal, fiasco.

Questions on Technique

1. Wylie sees women's magazines (paragraph 18) and mothers "without very much to do" (paragraph 26) as contributing to a trend toward good-looking but tasteless food. Keep in mind that Wylie wrote this piece in the 1950's, before many people came to understand the complex roles of women, especially those women who work both in and out of the home. Nevertheless, does Wylie sacrifice his reader's sympathy because of his remarks about women? If so, what does this point out about how writers should treat their readers when they are trying to get them to accept their argument?

2. Wylie's mother-in-law plays a significant role in this essay. How would you describe it?

3. What experiment did Wylie try with a loaf of bread? Why is this a visually effective detail of his argument?

4. In paragraph 16, he says peas today taste like "boiled paper wads." This is an apt simile.° What other similes can you find in this essay?

Techniques to Imitate

The vigorous style

You can learn something about forceful writing by noting the vigorous, picturesque way in which Wylie describes the food he doesn't like.

> "Today a loaf of 'bread' . . . resembles, as food, a solidified bubble bath."
> "Peas taste like boiled paper wads."
> "When eating them [string beans] you can't tell them from tender string."
> "Vegetables with crisp and crackling texture emerge as mush, slippery and stringy as hairnets simmered in Vaseline."

Even when he is not describing the taste of the food, Wylie expresses himself with characteristic vigor.

> "Scientific sampling got in its statistically nasty work."
> "the scientific war against deliciousness"
> "It is the way our wiser and calmer forebears fed,

simile: See Glossary.

not people, but hogs: as much as possible and as fast as possible, with no standard of quality."

Lively phrasing of this kind, revealing the heat of Wylie's indignation, is the product of a natural talent. You, too, can, by making an effort, add color and force to your writing. By trying to imitate Wylie's all-out, no-punches-drawn style, you may at first produce expressions that are overdone, overelaborate, too picturesque, but the risk is worth taking. The effort to find more graphic phrasing will improve your style. There is always a great deal of satisfaction in producing, after several tries, a sentence that says exactly what you want it to say and in such a striking way as to reflect your true feeling.

Suggestions for Writing

1. Take Wylie's last paragraph as a springboard for a 500-word essay. Tell us how *you* would conduct the rebellion against tasteless food. Perhaps you wish to call your essay "It Won't Happen in My House."
2. Write an essay in which you reverse all of Wylie's arguments. Call it "Science Has Improved My Supper."
3. Let us imagine that Wylie wished to end his essay with paragraph 18, but he needed more proof to "fatten" his argument. What could you add? Homogenized milk, oleomargarine, dried potatoes, TV dinners, frozen soups, heat-'n-serve everything? Write a 500-word letter to Wylie describing these examples or others.
4. Write an essay of about 500 words called "We Don't Have Time for It Anymore." Use as your subject one or two of these aspects of modern civilization: Shakespeare's plays as cut for television, superhighways that avoid the countryside, condensed novels, and so forth.
5. In addition to being critical of prepared food, Wylie might also be subtly critical of women. He admires his mother-in-law, but in paragraph 26 he describes other women as "without very much to do." If you have opinions of Wylie's statements here, write a 500-word essay in which you present forceful arguments for your point of view.

JEFFREY SCHRANK

Mythology Today

Media & Methods, which published this article, is a monthly professional magazine. Its subscribers are chiefly elementary- and secondary-school teachers. Like many magazine articles which seem merely expository, this one definitely presents a point of view, and the author hopes to persuade his audience of something.

Suppose you are on the other side of the classroom desk. If you were a teacher of mythology, would you give consideration to the approaches suggested by Schrank?

1   Every few years various professional journals for teachers publish articles about teaching mythology. If any attempt is made to relate the world of ancient myth to modern life, the suggestions seem invariably to be directed at having students find as many products as they can which bear names derived from ancient myths. This little bit of kitsch-seeking ° is a harmless and sometimes enlightening pastime. But I have found that most of the teaching suggestions and units which result fail to communicate to students the omnipresence and vitality of myth today.

kitsch-seeking: kitsch is art or writing that attracts popular attention even though it is shallow or unimportant.

456

Mythology Today 457

2   Mythology units traditionally are concerned with a limited number of Greek and Roman stories, and at their conclusion students are tested on who did what and who was related to whom. Rarely are students taught either to recognize or to develop their own ability to create myths— to become mythopoets. And rarely are they taught to cultivate in themselves the sensibility or mindset that prompted the Greeks and Romans to look into the night sky and see all of history written in its light. Nor are they anywhere taught the creation of myths as a process which takes place all the time. Myths are usually disposed of in the category of things-people-did-long-ago-before-they-knew-any-better.

3   The most common use of the word "myth" these days is to describe something in opposition to reality. Book titles such as *Foreign Policy: The Myth and the Reality* tend to perpetuate a false distinction. The concept of myth as fiction is an inheritance from Victorian times when the rational was erected as the absolute good. Now we are beginning to appreciate the fact that rational thought and scientific method allow only very limited access to "reality." We have recently rediscovered the irrational, the mystical, and—the mythological.

4   Motivated by a belief that students today are receptive to the mythic mindset, I present here five different teaching approaches for dealing with mythic elements at work in modern American culture.

The Mythic World of the Commercial: Deus Ex Machina °

5   Nowhere is the mythic mind harder at work today than in the world of advertising. The less creative admen simply borrow names from mythology to lend an aura of the divine to plebeian ° products. A glance through a listing of trademarks reads like an index to Larousse's *Encyclopedia of Mythology*. But borrowing names is only the most

   deus ex machina: a person or thing which appears suddenly in fiction or in drama and produces a contrived solution to an apparently insoluble situation.
   plebeian: common.

obvious of modern advertising's use of mythological resources. There is one particular mythical theme and structure that Madison Avenue uses often and effectively: an
instant solution to a problem performed by magical means,
usually by a character with superhuman powers or by a
potion with magic powers. The organizational structure
of such a commercial is (1) the presentation of the problem, and (2) the quasi-magical ° resolution.

6   Television critics pick on these ads as prime examples
of mindless advertising and the treatment of the housewife (their usual target) as a third grader. But such criticisms fail to recognize the underlying profundity of these
seemingly senseless ads. The ads in fact depend for their
appeal on the remnants of the age-old desire to be a witch,
an alchemist or a sorcerer—a wish the ads represent as
attainable through the use of certain products.

7   Sometimes these mini-myths borrow a character directly from ancient mythology. The name is changed, no
doubt to protect the original god from embarrassment.
The White Knight of the Ajax commercials is an obvious
steal from medieval myth; Mr. Clean comes straight from
the *Arabian Nights,* the Jolly Green Giant from European
folklore where he is the benevolent patron saint of pea
pickers. Add to these the White Tornado, the Man from
Glad, Wally the Janitor, Mother Nature and others of more
recent creation and you have a pantheon * of divinities
with powers sufficient to cause envy amid an Olympian °
gathering of ages past.

8   The problem these modern gods face usually involves
a damsel in distress battling the presence of evil in one
of its many guises: odors, pain, a dissatisfied husband,
spotted dishes, or any of the hundreds of life situations
that pass as tragedy in the ad world. The mythic hero
pops out of air to the rescue. The prince charming–knight
can be a real character like the Man from Glad, or the
product itself come to life. The product solves the prob-

quasi-magical: quasi- means resembling, seeming to be.
Olympian: pertaining to the gods of ancient Greece who dwelt on
Mt. Olympus.

lem in an instant, transforms the distressed damsel back into a princess and, the commercial implies, the happy ending means that the housewife will be able to fight germs and dried out sandwiches on her own with the help of the magic potion. In fact, according to the commercials, the housewife is herself a hero of sorts, an alchemist who turns dirty floors, dishes and clothes into shiny new ones with the aid of her solutions. To the degree that they are successful, these commercials turn housework into a task with mythic dimensions.

9   The myth of the housewife heroine with special powers acquired from the gods is paralleled by the ad pitches for products in the area of personal hygiene. Here the ordinary mortal is presented as a menace to society, exuding noxious * odors from various parts of the body, trailing flaky dandruff, possessing bulges in the wrong places or not enough in the right places. In general the commercials using a mythic approach present the victim as untouchable. Girls ignore him, or the guys never look twice. But the Fairy Godmother and Prince Charming haven't died; they've simply gone into television advertising. A new deodorant, soap, perfume or hair spray will turn the ugly duckling into a ravishing beauty!

10   In commercials for personal care products it is the element of miraculous conversion that is mythic. The miracle is the difference between the before and after; the ordinary mortal achieves a new status through use of the products, and the 30- to 60-second length of the TV spot reinforces the impact of the instant metamorphosis.

11   The use of mythic devices like the *deus ex machina* solution and the Magic Metamorphosis is not mere coincidence, nor is its description the stretching of an overworked literary imagination. The magic solution and magic conversion are common facets of myth for exactly the same reason they are common in TV commercials. Who doesn't want to be able to wish away travail in some areas of life, or magically to perform plastic surgery upon oneself? Myths have always embodied these desires—commercials capitalize on them.

12 During childhood our imaginations are fed on stories of giants and strange magic creatures. In fact, to a three-foot-tall child the whole world of adults conforms nicely to a mystical conception. A child begins in a world of magic and gradually grows out of it, but the belief in miracles and benevolent or evil super creatures hangs on. This remnant of belief is pampered by commercials. If science can invent "instant" coffee, tea and Angel Food Cake, why not instant popularity, status and complete power? To ask, "But does anyone really believe those dumb commercials?" is certainly to miss their deep appeal.

13 Since the world of sport is still a mythic one, it is only to be expected that those who excel in this world will also be used by Madison Avenue to lend some of their god-like aura to good old corporate products. Sports' pantheon is enshrined in various halls of fame. Its heroes and gods are described by sportscasters in superhuman terms. So Joe Namath, Pete Maravich, O. J. Simpson, Wilt Chamberlain, Mark Spitz and dozens of others are likely to appear on television using various products. The idea behind these ads is not to convince the viewer that because Mark Spitz uses Schick he should too, or that if you use a Schick, kid, you will someday be a famous and wealthy gold-medal winner (although they work on this level at times with fans and children who identify closely enough with the athlete). They are intended to say simply that the product endorsed belongs in a superhuman world.

14 The force behind hero endorsements is something like the ancient belief that whatever is touched by a god receives some mana (power) from the contact. Religions still preserve the ritual importance of the touch or the laying on of hands as a remnant of this belief. The sometimes frantic desire for a relic, either of a religious saint or secular hero, is another sign that people still believe that whatever a "great one" touches is itself elevated to a new level. The old person in the back of a church worshipping a bone fragment of some long-dead saint and the ecstatic teeny bopper who has just torn the shirt off a pop hero both believe in this magic transfer of power.

The Confined World of Sports: Zeus Throws a No-Hitter

15 One who enters the world of organized play and sport indeed enters a mythical world. Inside this world exploits become superhuman and combat is a ritual re-enactment of the gods played before throngs of ordinary mortals. In this world, ordinary time/space and the rules of society are suspended and replaced with ritual elements. The world of the game proceeds within its own boundaries, according to its own fixed rules.

16 All sports events are enacted within a play*ground,* carefully marked off and set aside from the real world. The arena, gymnasium, game board, track, field, court, or even the stage or movie set are carefully marked by boundaries which set off the space inside as special, belonging to another world.

17 Inside this play world order reigns supreme, even though outside chaos rules. Only occasionally, such as during the tragedy at the Munich Olympics,° do the two collide. Players from the imperfect world enter the play territory and all agree to follow strict rules even though in the real world these same players may flaunt law and order. Referees, umpires and judges preserve order here, and constitute a tribunal from which there is rarely any appeal. They are tiny unarmed men and yet rule those nearly twice their size, and can even eject them from the game world without fear of reprisal. There are no criminals or constant rule breakers. A basketball player who refuses to dribble or a chess player who insists his pawns can move at random simply cannot survive. Those who do break rules are punished swiftly and justice rules supreme.

18 There are no revolutionaries in this play world either. A revolutionary athlete might question the basic assumptions of capitalism outside the playing field, but once he steps across the boundary he does not theorize if, for example, placing a ball through a hoop is a valid basis for basketball. Since Knute Rockne "invented" the forward

---

At the Munich Olympics in 1972, Palestinian terrorists invaded the Olympic compound and killed a group of Israeli athletes.

pass (an event much mythologized in the literature of sport) there have been few radical changes in American games.

19   Ordinary time is suspended on the playground. A special clock, a timer or some other system of keeping time is used. Often, as in football and basketball, time moves forward only when play is in progress, much unlike the non-play world where time never stops. The temporal boundaries provided by the umpire's call, the starting buzzer or ending gun strictly define the creation and demise of the play world.

20   Sport is a ritual, an acting out of a myth or series of myths. A sport which can be considered a national pastime can be expected to reflect national values and wishes. Sports which capture our national fancy are ritualistic enactments of the American Dream. Baseball is still called our national pastime, but is rapidly being replaced by American football.

21   We might speculate that football reflects the American character in a number of ways. It reflects our values and the dominant life style, for example, in its specialist functions (offense, defense, specialty teams, positions), its concern with the gain and loss of territory, its strict time regimentation and the design of the playing field, with each yard carefully measured to the nearest inch. The players in football are popular heroes, but the shots are really called by coaches and owners, so the players are more those who are played than those who play. In European football, in contrast, all space except the magical box defended by the goalie is nearly equal and neutral. In soccer a score is an instant event that can come at almost any time, while in football (except for exceptional events) a score is obtained by a well-executed strategy and gained on the installment plan, bit by bit. American football is far more precise and regulated than European football and therein, I think, lies an important clue to our values. The American use of statistics as almost a replacement for the game itself is another accurate indication of national character.

Entertainment: Heroes Today Come at About $25,000 a Minute

22   The heroic figure comes to us straight from mythology, and in spite of talk about the death of the hero, he is alive and well in contemporary life. Mythologists have studied hero stories from nearly every culture which can be shown to fit a very definite pattern. The recurrent pattern is of a superhuman or divine being who courageously sets out into the land of evil to battle the enemy—dragon, beasts, magical creatures or other gods. The heroic character is threatened and tested severely and faces seemingly impossible tasks. But he struggles and wins, defeats the enemy and often gains some valuable possession which he brings back to the forces of good. Superman fits this pattern as well as Hercules.

23   Take almost any film or TV series involving a hero and apply the mythic formula. In the *Mission Impossible* series, for example, the hero is a team. The evil forces are usually villains of the underworld. (Our word "underworld" is an interesting choice—perhaps a direct link to ancient myth.) The I M force represents goodness and battles the underworld exactly as in ancient myth. In reality the I M force seems to be patterned loosely after agents of the quasi-legal CIA. (The series has been banned in some countries because of its negative image of foreign governments, so this season I M troops stay more on American soil to battle the gangster underworld.) Whoever they are supposed to be, the I M force has no supernatural powers, but does use technological gimmickry to achieve miraculous effects. They battle the evil ones, are invariably victorious, take considerable risks and survive an assortment of improbable narrow escapes while remaining virtuous and seemingly indestructible.

24   The mythic heroes in ancient times were Samson, Hercules, Zeus, Atlas, etc. Today we have Captain Kirk, Perry Mason, Ironside, James Bond and Shaft. Each of these figures has extraordinary abilities, and all risk their lives to battle evil forces and bestow favors on mankind.

One current trend, as in *Mission Impossible,* is for heroes to rely less on their individuality and more on team membership. This is culturally consonant,° since most socially valued work is now done in teams, panels, groups or task forces. It is also fashionable to endow the hero with the quasi-magical trappings of science.

25 We all identify to some extent with a person we view as heroic. The hero evokes that part of us that would like to be brave, a symbol of goodness, powerful, worshipped, popular. Thus Superman is a perfect hero type. The mild-mannered Clark Kent is more like what we are in reality. But underneath this tame exterior is the mighty Super-being. Clark Kent is what we know we are; Superman is what we dream we can become. Because Superman reflects a wish fulfillment of our culture, he has remained a popular hero.

26 In fact, every hero, real or fictional, mirrors the time and place in which he lives. The hero is a public reflection of men's innermost hopes and beliefs. This helps explain why certain public figures become heroes of mythic proportions while others, just as capable and perhaps even more effective, are relegated to the public doghouse or at best to neglect.

27 In Lord Raglan's classic 1936 work *The Hero: A Study in Tradition, Myth and Drama,* Raglan names 22 elements that seem part of the heroic saga. Heroes like Oedipus, Theseus, Moses and King Arthur are rooted more in their sharing of the heroic saga than in their historical records. Marshall Fishwick in *The Hero: American Style* applies Raglan's theory to the former American President, John F. Kennedy, to show how his now-mythic fame fits the ancient structure:

His father was called to a royal court (as Ambassador to the Court of Saint James) and the son was educated by (presumably) wise men (at Harvard). Then he went off to fight an evil dragon (the Japanese Navy) and after a bloody fracas (PT 109) triumphed and returned to marry

consonant: in agreement, in accord.

the beautiful princess (Jackie). Having inherited his father's kingdom (politics), he fought and defeated a second contender (Nixon) before taking over as ruler (President). For a time he reigned smoothly and prescribed laws. Then he suddenly lost favor (Bay of Pigs), tried to rally his people, and died a sudden and mysterious death (Did Oswald really shoot Kennedy?). Amid great mourning (the first worldwide television funeral), he was buried on a sacred hillside (Arlington). Now he has many shrines (cultural center, airport, library, highway).

In the world of popular entertainment we have replaced the sentimental hero of Victorian times with heroes more suited to survive in our mechanized society—Billy the Kid, James Bond. But for society at large, heroes do seem to have fallen on bad times since Kennedy. But every culture needs heroes even if their creation takes a little bending of history, so from the age of the antihero certainly will rise a new pack of real heroes and gods. They are probably around right now merely awaiting elevation.

The Remnants

28   It is difficult to realize that the world of myth was the real world for the majority of people in past ages. For ancient man, myth filled the role we now allow science to take, and myth, history and religion were virtually indistinguishable. Such a dominant force doesn't vanish in a couple of hundred or even a couple of thousand years. The remnants of our mythic past still remain and are worth exploring.

29   We preserve ancient mythical beliefs and practices usually without awareness of their origins. At weddings, funerals, religious services, in dress and etiquette, in our architecture, superstitions and customs, we preserve bits and pieces of old myths.

30   In wedding ceremonies the preservation of past mythical elements are easily identified. There have been about thirty billion brides and grooms since we first appeared on

this planet, and each one has been married in a way that serves to link them to myths of the past. The wedding cake in our ceremony, for example, can be linked to the idea of sympathetic magic. Originally guests brought spiced buns to the celebration. These were piled into an enormous heap and the bride and groom danced on them to act out their anticipated affluence. The plastic statue of the bride and groom atop a towering cake is very likely a remnant of this belief in sympathetic magic.

31   June weddings date back to Roman times, when June was named for Juno, the wife of Jupiter, patroness of the young and goddess of marriage. The Romans believed that prosperity came to the man and woman who married in the latter part of Juno's month. There are still more marriages in June than in any other month. The bridal veil originally was used to ward off the evil eye; tying shoes to the rear of a couple's auto goes back at least to the English custom of throwing shoes after anyone starting on a long trip; carrying the bride across the threshold was to avoid the influence of the evil spirits who lurked near entrances; the honeymoon has obscure origins, but is somehow related to the mythical properties of the moon.

32   The moon, of course, has accumulated a wealth of mythic attributes and still plays a large symbolic role in literature, art and film. Its constant change of shape and cyclic movement early became associated with human irregularity. The word "lunatic" attests to the once-believed power of the moon to influence human affairs.

33   Our method of determining Easter by the first Sunday following the full moon after the vernal equinox ° is a myth-filled designation.

34   Almost any natural object (sea, sky, sun, moon, wind, rock) has a rich mythic past that still survives today in some fashion, usually among the people who are most primitive or most sensitive. The artistic mind thrives on

vernal equinox: the time in spring when the sun crosses the celestial equator, and day and night are of equal length on Earth; usually around March 21.

seeing in objects not only their present condition but also their history. A poet who uses the word "moon" is seldom referring to a lifeless hunk of rock with a few American flags stuck in it. He is calling to mind the beliefs of man over the ages; he is talking to the collective mythic mind that lives somewhere in each person.

35 It is difficult to understand how anyone not aware of myth can fully appreciate poetry, literature, painting or even contemporary film. And knowledge of myth means not only the classic Roman and Greek stories but also the richness of even more primitive myths.

Myth and Personality: Living Your Myth

36 It is tempting to speculate that ancient myths have survived only because they are perpetuated by formal schooling. Yet there must be a better reason to explain how stories can evade obscurity for thousands of years. The myths that have survived have done so because they manage to capture some universal truth, some part of human nature that is valid for each of the hundreds of generations that have followed the original mythmaker.

37 Psychologist Eric Berne believes that the Greek myths contain so much psychological truth that each person can be compared to some figure from mythology. The classic myths express contemporary life styles. As Joseph Campbell observes in *The Hero with a Thousand Faces,* "The latest incarnation of Oedipus, the continued romance of Beauty and the Beast, stands this afternoon on the corner of Forty-second Street and Fifth Avenue, waiting for the traffic light to change."

38 People do not consciously model themselves on the Greek myths, but the resemblances are amazing. Consider the two brothers Atlas and Prometheus and their many twentieth-century imitators. Both fought against the authority of Zeus, the chief god, and were punished for their rebellion. Atlas was sentenced to carry the weight of the world on his shoulders. Hercules, stronger than Atlas, offered to carry the load if Atlas would risk his life to pick the famed golden apples of Hesperides. Atlas agreed, but instead of having his burden relieved, he was conned by Hercules into again assuming the weight of the world.

39 Modern day Atlases come in many roles and guises: the teacher, housewife or worker who frequently complains about being overworked, about never having enough time. People who feel they must carry the whole load, or must assume the burdens of others, are reliving the Atlas type.

40 The brother of Atlas was Prometheus. He stole fire from the sun and gave this gift to man so that humans would be superior to animals. For his daring theft Prometheus was punished by being chained to a rock in perpetual torture for thirteen generations. To this day Prometheus is symbolic of heroic endurance, of undeserved suffering and strong will in resisting oppression. A modern Prometheus is one who fights for the underdog, the poor, the oppressed, and often imagines himself a savior of society or of mankind. He suffers in the process but endures the suffering since it is part of his mission in life.

41 In Greek and Roman myths the little nymph Echo was doomed to have no thoughts of her own. All she could do was repeat what others had already said. Many imitate her example. And there are many like Narcissus, so in love with themselves that they remain blind to the rest of the world.

42 Berne of course is not the first or only psychologist to utilize ancient myth in a system of personality analysis. Freud borrowed heavily from mythology as did Jung,° who believed myths to be part of man's collective unconscious. A tragic mistake in teaching mythology is to treat myth as if it were about things "out there and back then." The enchanted forest and the land of the dragons are part of the geography of the self. It is this relationship between myth and the inner life which helps keep myth alive and makes it important for classroom discussion.

Freud . . . Jung: Sigmund Freud (1856–1939), Austrian neurologist, father of psychoanalysis; Carl Jung (1875–1961), Swiss psychologist and psychiatrist.

ANALYSIS

If this article is convincing, its persuasiveness is due in part to two facts: Schrank states his theories clearly, and he supports each of his statements with many examples.

For example, when in paragraph 5 he says that the mythic mind is at work today in advertising, he uses ten paragraphs (5–14) to tell how commercials illustrate this. When he states that the world of sport is a mythic one, he uses seven paragraphs (15–21) to show how this is so. When he says in paragraph 23 that the mythic formula can be applied to almost any hero from film and TV, he names seven examples (paragraphs 23–25). When he says that the mythic formula can be applied to public figures, he cites how the "mythic fame" of former President John F. Kennedy applies. When he says that remnants of our mythic past remain, he uses eight paragraphs to itemize where they can be found (28–35). When he says that myths represent some parts of human nature (paragraph 36), he gives examples of four mythic characters who resemble people today (paragraphs 38–41).

According to Maynard (page 410), TV shortened attention spans and produced inertia. If TV uses mythic materials that have such deep human appeal, why did it have such a dulling effect on Joyce Maynard? Has Schrank omitted something from his argument? Does he distinguish between the use of mythic themes and characters on TV and their use in genuine literature? What is the difference between the use of the mythic formula in *Mission Impossible* and its use in Melville's *Moby-Dick?*

As is true with any argument, this article invites discussion and reply.

Questions on Content

1. In Schrank's opinion, why do advertisers use sports heroes to endorse products?
2. How is the world of sport a "mythic world"?
3. How does football reflect the American character?
4. What is the mythic formula for the typical hero?

5. Why, according to this writer, is Superman/Clark Kent a perfect hero type?
6. In what ways do remnants of the mythic past remain?
7. According to Schrank, why do the ancient myths survive?

Add to Your Vocabulary

plebian, quasi-, pantheon, noxious, consonant.

Questions on Technique

1. A sentence in paragraph 2 states that students should be taught that the creation of myths is "a process which takes place all the time." Is this idea developed sufficiently? Explain.
2. In paragraphs 2 and 3, Schrank tells what myth is *not*. Where does he say what myth *is*? Do you think he should have defined myth in his opening paragraphs?
3. How effective is the opening paragraph? If this article were to be reprinted in a general-interest magazine, how would you suggest the opening be revised?

Techniques to Imitate

Organization: using short essays within a long essay

The writer who has learned how to organize has mastered an important and often difficult technique. Schrank's article shows that he is such a writer. To argue that students should be taught "the omnipresence and vitality of myth today," he presents "five different teaching approaches for dealing with mythic elements at work in modern American culture." You might think of these five approaches as the five main topics in an outline. Each one is developed as a separate essay within the article, so that what Schrank gives is, in effect, five brief essays within one long essay.

That each brief essay is indeed a separate entity can be seen by studying its structure. As an example, take his first essay, "The Mythic World of the Commercial." Schrank begins with an introductory paragraph (5) in which he presents the general idea that advertisers use a particular mythical theme and structure often and effectively—an instant solution to a problem through magical powers. The following paragraphs (6–14) then develop this idea by offering a great many convincing examples. Readers find it easy to follow such careful organization.

When you are writing a long composition, you will do well to imitate Schrank's kind of organization. Use your major topics as subjects for mini-essays within the longer essay. If possible, give to each mini-essay the traditional essay structure—beginning, middle, and end.

Suggestions for Writing

1. In paragraph 22, Schrank outlines briefly the recurrent pattern of hero stories. In paragraphs 23–27 he applies this pattern to the life stories of some fictional and actual heroes. Imitating the structure of these paragraphs, write a brief essay in which you show how the mythic pattern applies to an actual or a fictional hero.

2. In paragraph 42, Schrank says that the enchanted forest and the land of dragons are "part of the geography of the self." If you agree with this, write an essay explaining how each pattern can "exist" within a person. Divide your longer essay into two shorter essays, one devoted to each of these patterns.

3. In paragraphs 5–14, Schrank tries to show the reader, by examples, how the mythic mind is at work in advertising. Choose at least three TV commercials and show how they use one or more of these mythic themes: a magic metamorphosis, a godlike figure who can perform wonders, the hero endorsement.

4. Perhaps you have opinions on how some subject should be taught in school. Write a brief essay giving your opinion. First state what you think the purpose of the subject is, and then tell how you think the subject should be presented to students. A possible topic would be the way something is taught to young children: art, music, reading.

5. Schrank tells us how he thinks football reflects the

American character (paragraph 21). Perhaps you have a different opinion on this. If so, write a response to Schrank. If you wish, write as if you are addressing a letter to the editor of *Media & Methods* magazine.

6. Schrank tells how remnants of our mythic past are in evidence today. Try to expand on this, and add to the examples he gives (paragraphs 29–35). Consider the naming of sports teams, the calendar, the Olympics, New Year's Eve.

7. If you know a bit of mythology, write an essay built around additional examples of mythic characters who can be recognized in people today (paragraphs 38–41). Some ideas: Phaethon, Icarus, Midas, Orpheus, Antigone.

THE NEW YORKER

Two Stories

This essay appeared in the *New Yorker* magazine on October 28, 1974. It was the lead article in that weekly magazine's section called "The Talk of the Town." As is often the case with articles in the *New Yorker*, this anonymous reporter is not "talking" about just the town of New York, but about a much larger community.

1 As we looked over the news from around the world last week, two stories—one from Monaco and one from India—arrested our attention. The story from Monaco, which appeared in *Time,* was about three men who are suffering from an excess of riches. They are three Saudi Arabian princes, including the Minister of the Interior, Mr. Fahd ibn Abdul Aziz, and they had come to Monaco to gamble. Such was their wealth and such was their jadedness ° in regard to ordinary winnings and losses that they had the usual maximum value of four hundred dollars for one chip raised to sixteen hundred dollars, and insisted that the Casino stay open all night so that they might go on gambling. When they were done, they had lost more than six million dollars. The story

---

jadedness: dissipation, a kind of dullness of morals caused by overindulgence.

from India, which appeared in the Washington *Post,* was about many thousands of people who are suffering from scarcity. In fact, they are starving. The problem in the afflicted district is not that food is unavailable; it is that "the poor have no money to buy it." One thousand people have starved to death within the past two months. For some, "a daily plate of gruel, which cannot be digested by starving children or adults," is supposed to be available. But "only people with cards issued by the village authorities can get even this." And "those without cards are forcibly turned away, and leave, moaning or weeping, to die." The *Post* reporter goes on to relate, "Across the road from a distribution van, a woman collapsed on the roadway, motionless except for her tongue moving in and out." And the reporter met "a young man" who "walked away, unfed, from a gruel kitchen, carrying an emaciated baby obviously close to death." The young man "burst into tears saying his wife had left him and his gruel entitlement card had been stolen."

2   In one place on our planet a few weeks ago, there were people staying up all night because they were unable to throw away enough money in the daytime, and in another place there were people starving within sight of food for lack of a few cents. In every age, the makings of juxtapositions like this one have been plentiful. In every age, too, there have been voices bearing witness to these injustices—voices saying that every injustice diminishes everyone. But in our time there is a difference. It is as though moral precepts that once existed on the level of abstractions or as imperatives had, through world developments that no one planned or anticipated, acquired practical force, and had lodged themselves concretely in our affairs. The oneness with the members of our species which men of moral imagination once urged us to feel is now an accomplished fact. The *Post* story, for instance, went on to point out that a shortage of fertilizer (which derives, in part, from the oil that made the Saudi gamblers rich) is likely to worsen the famine in India, and that the worldwide shortage of grain will also worsen it. These two

shortages, of course, are directly influenced in one way or another not only by the Saudi princes but by just about everyone, including, preëminently, ourselves. The word "humanity," which was once an all but abstract idea, now refers to something highly specific, much as the word "Canada" or "Venezuela" does. Humanity exists in a new way because ships, wires, pipelines, exchange rates, and airwaves bind its parts together, but it also exists in a new way because in a time of global scarcity we all draw on the same reserves. We all line up at the same breadline and sit down at the same table; and if three Saudi princes —or three Americans, or three Russians—take up a thousand extra seats, somewhere in India or Africa the gruel is going to run out and a thousand people will die.

Questions on Content

1. What are the two "stories" that this reporter juxtaposes and then comments on?
2. According to this writer, what makes this particular juxtaposition different from others that have been plentiful in every age?
3. Why does humanity now exist in a "new way"?

Questions on Technique

1. This anonymous writer uses the first-person plural pronouns in two ways. In the opening sentence it is used as the editorial "we." The subsequent usage of the first-person pronouns has a different purpose. What do *our, us, ourselves, we* refer to in paragraph 2? What is the effect? What would the effect be, on the other hand, if the reporter had used the words *the, this, people's, people,* etc., instead?
2. This writer uses figurative language ° in the concluding sentence. What image of humanity is created there? Do you think this is an effective way of concluding this essay? Explain.

figurative language: See Glossary.

Suggestions for Writing

1. Imitating this writer's opening sentence, write a two-part essay in which you comment on two news stories. In your first part, briefly summarize the content of the two stories. In the second part, tell why, of the many news stories you read, you have noted these two in particular. Is there a "moral lesson" you want to bring out?

2. Another approach for an essay based on a contrast is suggested by the opening sentence in paragraph 2. Write a two-part essay in which you juxtapose two dramatically different events that are taking place simultaneously on our planet. Is there a point you wish to make about the contrast?

3. Possibilities for comparisons and contrasts are found everywhere. You can find many in the articles in this book. For example, you could compare the three perilous journeys described in Ullman's "Kilimanjaro!," Phillips' "Lone Sailor Is Back," and Carpenter's "The Great Secret." Write a composition in which you compare (or contrast) these articles, or choose one of the following suggestions:

   Welty's "The Worn Path" and Steinbeck's "The Turtle" (two "small" journeys)

   Mansfield's "Miss Brill" and Welty's "The Worn Path" (images of two women)

   Joyce's "Araby" and Sancton's "The Silver Horn" (the coming of age of two boys)

   Joyce's "Araby" and Angelou's "I Know Why the Caged Bird Sings" (two quests for love)

   Essays by McKenney, Teale, Sauer, and Eiseley (four views of birds)

   Laurence's "Dawn over Zero"; the *New Yorker*'s "Two Stories"; Van Fleet's "Invisible Death"; Walter Van Tilburg Clark's "The Portable Phonograph" (four images of doomsday)

4. You may have strong opinions, one way or the other, about this essay. Write a 500-word essay of your own expressing these opinions. Whether you express admiration or dissent, support your views with examples and make them as clear and convincing as you can. (See page 324 for a technique you could imitate.)

5. Write an essay of about 500 words in which you present your arguments for the best use of the world's "bread." State the problem and its dimensions as you see them in your first paragraph. In the following paragraphs, give two or three ways that you believe the problem should be met.

JOSEPH WOOD KRUTCH

Science and the Humanities

Worldwide expansion of educational opportunities is a complex phenomenon, creating new problems at the same time as it solves many old ones. Joseph Wood Krutch approached one of these problems—how to reconcile the scientist and the humanist—from wide experience in journalism as well as in academia. He began his teaching career in 1917 as an instructor at Columbia University and retired from there as Brander Matthews Professor of Dramatic Literature in 1952. During the intervening years he lectured at the Polytechnic Institute of Brooklyn, Vassar College, and the New School for Social Research, and for more than two decades served as drama critic and associate editor of the *Nation,* a post to which he brought great distinction. Before his retirement, he published widely in literary criticism and biography, notably a volume called *The American Drama Since 1918* and lives of Henry David Thoreau and Edgar Allan Poe.

After he left New York City, he settled in Tucson, Arizona, to begin a second career as naturalist, social critic, and free-lance writer. *The Measure of Man* won him the National Book Award in 1954. It was followed the next year by his equally popular *The Voice of the Desert* and, in 1957, by *The Great Chain of Life.* Krutch, therefore, could talk from both worlds, the scientist's and the humanist's, though he would have been the first to admit that his laboratory experience was limited and he had long been, by nature, more an observer of scientific investigation than an experimenter. As a scientist, he was chiefly interested in the characteristics of living organisms, human beings included. As a humanist, he devoted years to the study of religion, philosophy, and literature.

For many years, Krutch was a contributing editor of *The American Scholar*. He called his column "If You Don't Mind My Saying So," and he used it to think aloud, as it were, on a great variety of subjects. "Science and the Humanities" was one of his columns (we have re-titled it in reprinting), but more than just thinking aloud it is a reasoned argument for a point of view which you may or may not share. Read it carefully and read it through before you pass judgment.

1 **W**hat used to be called the War between Science and Religion was a hot war. That now in progress between Science and the Humanities is a cold one. It is being fought somewhat more chivalrously and with many protestations of respect on both sides. The scientist doesn't want to exterminate literature, and the humanist certainly doesn't want to abolish science. "Co-existence" * is the catchword. But as in the case of the other cold war, the real question is, "On whose terms?" From both sides one gets something rather like the attitude of the Catholic priest who is said to have remarked to his Protestant opposite number: "After all, we are both trying to do God's work; you in your way and I—in His." There seems to be a good deal of question-begging and so many polite concessions that the terms are not usually clearly defined and the issues not squarely met.

2 C. P. Snow °—a champion *sans peur* and *sans reproche* °—seems to rest his case not so much on the su-

---

C. P. Snow: See page 316.
sans peur and *sans reproche*: without fear and without reproach.

periority of science over the humanities as upon the alleged fact that scientists are better guys. There is, he argues, more good will among them, a larger common ground on which to operate and more willingness to make common cause. Probably this is true as long as they stay on this common ground. But scientists not infrequently are also patriots, adherents to this or that social philosophy and even, sometimes, loyal sons of some church. Those who are scientists and nothing else may be a bit *too* neutral—as, for instance, a famous rocket expert who appears to have been so little interested in anything except rockets that he was perfectly willing to make them for either side even in the middle of what less "objective" people regarded as Armageddon.°

3   As William James ° said, "We may philosophize well or ill, but philosophize we must." Those who say they do not philosophize at all have usually answered philosophical questions arbitrarily and without thought. And for all the claims made that science itself can become an adequate philosophy, it seems to an unregenerate * humanist like myself that such philosophy provides no answer to questions that have to be answered either thoughtfully or, as the scientist often tends to answer them, arbitrarily. We may, says a distinguished American professor of experimental psychology, take it for granted that all ultimate questions can be reduced to one—namely, what is most likely to lead to survival? But who are the "we" who take this for granted? The better-red-than-dead ° boys apparently do. On the other hand, there is what some regard as good authority for "He who loseth his life shall gain it." Probably there is no way of arbitrating between the two attitudes. But there is certainly no purely scientific solution, and the humanist is at least more acutely aware of the problem.

4   I must repeat the familiar charge that science can tell us how to do a bewildering (indeed, an alarming) number

Armageddon: the last and completely destructive battle. See Revelations 16:14–16.

William James: American psychologist and philosopher (1842–1910), brother of Henry James, the novelist.

better-red-than-dead: better Communist than annihilated.

of things, but not which of them ought to be done; and I repeat it because I have never heard a satisfactory reply, and because it is perfectly evident that scientists themselves do not always agree in such decisions when called upon to make them. Of the medical practitioner it is sometimes said that medicine itself supplies him with an ethic. But take, for example, the case of the German doctors who used human beings as laboratory animals. They had learned the same medical science as those of their European and American fellows who found their experiments morally and even criminally shocking. At a medical congress both groups would have met on that common ground that Sir Charles ° regards as so important—so long as the discussion was confined to science. At a clinic they would have agreed on both diagnosis and treatment. Whatever the origin of their moral differences, it certainly did not lie in the field of the scientific knowledge that both had mastered. Their science gave them no guidance in the making of an ethical decision.

5   To this objection, which seems to me incontrovertible, either of two answers is usually given. One is that science, properly understood, *would* give an answer if properly attended to. The other is that "ought" implies a concept that corresponds to nothing outside the human mind and exists there only subjectively, induced by the conditioning effect of social custom; and that, therefore, we should be content to say merely that what we ought to do must be left to whatever society evolves as a result of the wise determination to devote ourselves exclusively to scientific knowledge.

6   Pushed into a corner those who maintain that only science is anything more than nonsense are likely to throw the question back into the face of the humanist. "Just how much progress have philosophy, metaphysics, religion and poetry ever made toward establishing 'oughts' conclusively demonstrated or widely agreed upon for long? You blame us for our failures. What are your successes?" This *tu quoque* ° is, to put it mildly, embarrassing—so embarrass-

Sir Charles: C. P. Snow.
tu quoque: literally, thou too; a countercharge of guilt.

ing, in fact, that I would rather drop the subject for the moment and come back to it (if I must) a little later in this discussion.

7   What seems to me necessary (and lacking) to clarify any general discussion of the "case for the humanities" is some clear definition of science on the one hand and, on the other, of the subject matter that the humanist believes he alone can deal with and of the methods he uses.

8   Originally, of course, science meant simply knowledge of any kind, and the humanities meant merely secular learning—knowledge about human affairs as contrasted with the divine, or, more simply still, the kind of thing one found in the writings of the Greeks and Romans before the Christian revelation made knowledge of the divine possible. But the meaning of the first term narrowed, and the meaning of the second grew more vague. Science came to mean a special kind of knowledge that can be acquired by certain techniques while the humanities came to mean, well, whatever is left over. What actually is left over came to seem to many less and less important if, indeed, it was important at all.

9   Suppose we say that science (and the definition would certainly have been accepted at a time when scientists were more modest) deals with whatever is measurable and subject to experimental verification. I cannot think of any scientific inquiry that has gone beyond that without ceasing to be completely scientific. Accept that definition, add that the subject matter of the humanities is whatever cannot be measured or verified experimentally, and it is obvious that what is left over is extensive and important.

10   Take, for example, the question of contentment, happiness and joy. Pope called the second "our beings' end and aim." At least some scientists would agree that it is as fundamental as survival since, if science can tell us how to survive but not how to be happy, it is wasting its time. Yet happiness cannot be measured and the assumption that this man is happier than that cannot be experimentally verified. The difficulty may not be quite as thorny as that which

involves the "ought," but it is thorny enough and important enough. Hedonists ° may say that what we ought to do is what will make us as individuals in our society most happy, but that still leaves happiness as one of the things that can neither be measured nor experimented with. And it is one of the things with which the literature of humanism is concerned in its own way.

11 The humanist does at least recognize the importance of happiness, and he does not brush it aside like the scientist whose logic is likely to run more or less thus: happiness cannot be measured, therefore it cannot be the subject of science; but since the methods of science are the only useful ones, we will just have to assume that happiness is directly proportional to something that can be measured— say, income, standard of living or even horsepower available per unit of population. That this is a monstrous assumption is made abundantly clear by the introspection and direct observation dealt with in humanistic literature. And if we are not even further than we are now down the road to radical discontent and alienation * in the midst of abundance, it is largely because humane letters still affect us.

12 So much for the kind of subject with which the humanities can and science cannot deal. What methods does the humanist, who can neither measure nor experiment, rely upon? He cannot, of course, prove anything. All that he can do is to carry conviction. He can, for example, draw a picture of a happy man and tell a story that seems to account for that man's happiness. There is no objective test for the truth or falsity of his assumptions. For his success or failure he depends upon one thing only—the extent to which he can carry conviction, and he convinces just to the extent that our own experience confirms his. Hence my own definition of the humanities would be simply this: they are that branch of inquiry concerned with the unmeasurable and the undemonstrable and dealing with it in such a way that although nothing is proved, something is, nevertheless, believed. The truths of the humanities are, in other words,

hedonists: believers in pleasure or happiness as the highest good.

those that cannot be demonstrated but can be recognized.
13 Thomas De Quincey's ° famous definition of humane
literature as the literature of power, as distinguished from
the literature of knowledge, is sound although sometimes
misunderstood. The literature of knowledge is that which
confers power; humane literature, that which *is* powerful.
The half-sciences of psychology, sociology and history
necessarily fall between two stools, and they would be both
more useful and less dangerous if they always recognized
the fact. So long as they deal only with what can be measured and experimentally verified, they rarely throw very
much light upon the most important subjects. When, as all
too often happens, they pretend to have proved something
that their facts do not really prove, they can be disastrously
misleading. They are most effective when they, like the
novelist, carry conviction by statements whose truths we
seem to recognize.
14 Sir Charles himself, when he expresses the opinion
that scientists are better guys than humanists, is indulging
in exactly the kind of loose, unsupported generalization
often cited as reproachable in the man of letters. He may
give random examples, but he presents no hard statistics.
We may agree or not, and whether we do agree will depend upon our own experience. He is speaking as a humanist, not as a scientist.
15 Freud ° offers a more striking case in point. He was
so far from establishing a science that there are by now
almost as many incompatible * schools of psychoanalysis °
as there are Christian sects. Competent physicists could not
possibly disagree among themselves on fundamentals as
psychoanalysts disagree. But Freud probably had as much
effect upon our mental climate as any man who lived during his time, because when we read what he had to say, we

Thomas De Quincey: English essayist (1785–1859).
Freud: Sigmund Freud (1856–1939), Austrian neurologist,
founder of psychoanalysis.
psychoanalysis: a method of treating neuroses by analyzing re-
pressed desires, the symbolic value of dreams, and the nature of
unconscious mental processes.

experienced "the shock of recognition." ° What he had
not actually demonstrated was recognized. We believed
because our past experience had prepared us to do so.

16 *The Lonely Crowd* ° is, I suppose, the most widely
read sociological work written in the United States during
the past twenty years. Yet, as sociologists with a narrower
conception of their quasi-science ° were quick to point out,
it didn't actually prove anything. There were no measurements and no experiments weighty enough to be taken
seriously. The examples of "inner-directed" and "other-
directed" personalities were not selected by any controlled
process of sampling but were treated merely as illustrations,
much as a literary essayist might have treated them. Yet,
most readers did experience the shock of recognition. *The
Lonely Crowd* is a contribution to "the humanities."

17 Scientists fear (not without reason) the power that
literature has to keep alive and to propagate all sorts of
notions, including the pernicious.* It can decline into mere
rhetorical oratory and sometimes make the worse appear
the better reason. Poets, said the American novelist and
paragrapher Ed Howe,° are the only prophets who are
always wrong. Exasperated by Alexander Pope, Bernard
Shaw exclaimed that "you can't make a lie true by putting
it into an heroic couplet." ° But the unfortunate fact is that
you can go a long way toward making it seem so. Said
Mark Twain, "The history of the human race is strewn
thick with evidence that a truth is not hard to kill; but that
a lie, well told, is immortal." "Well told" is the operative

"the shock of recognition": that is, conscious acceptance of what
unconsciously we already knew. Herman Melville first used the
phrase: "For genius, all over the world, stands hand in hand, and
one shock of recognition runs the whole circle round."

The Lonely Crowd: a sociological study (1950) of individualism
and the masses in contemporary society, written by David Riesman
and his research associates.

quasi-science: seemingly but not actually a science.

Ed Howe: Edgar Watson Howe (1853–1937), author of *The
Story of a Country Town.*

heroic couplet: two lines of rhymed verse, each line containing
five iambic feet.

phrase, and since to tell well is the special province of humane letters, they are no doubt responsible for more seemingly immortal lies than erroneous science ever has been. On the other hand, it is the great body of these same humane letters that have kept alive many supremely important concepts like those of "honor," "love," "duty," "the good life," et cetera, which science dismisses or at least ignores just because it has no means of dealing with them. A scientist may be and often is also a humanist, but he can be such only insofar as he recognizes the legitimacy of problems with which he cannot, as a scientist, deal. Accept science as the only legitimate concern of the human mind, and you must cease to concern yourself with anything that cannot be measured or experimented with. And a world that disregards everything thus excluded would be a world in which the human being as we know him would cease to exist.

18 The humanist cannot claim any success in his enterprise comparable to that which the scientist boasts of in his. He is compelled, generation after generation, to begin all over again. It is not certain that he has made any progress since the time of Plato and Aristotle or the times of Homer and Shakespeare. He may even find himself carrying less and less conviction to others, perhaps even being less and less sure himself. He never has, and he probably never will have, a method that produces results as the method of science does. But that is not because he is less intelligent and less competent. It is because the human being is more complicated than the physical world—more complicated even than the atom. But it is also at least as important to all of us; and as long as we continue to ask questions, even unanswered questions, we at least continue to recognize the reality of what the scientist tends to regard as nonexistent or unimportant just because he does not know how to deal with it. Perhaps the best defense of the humanities was made by Justice Holmes ° when he said that science teaches us a great deal about things that are not really very

Justice Holmes: Oliver Wendell Holmes, Jr. (1841–1935), famous jurist and son of the celebrated physician and author.

important, philosophy a very little bit about those that are supremely so.

ANALYSIS

The first six paragraphs of this essay are wisely devoted to stating the problem. Though Krutch tries to be objective, he shows his bias in paragraph 3 when he calls himself "an unregenerate humanist," but we must keep in mind that he is modest about his knowledge of scientific disciplines, that he is anything but ignorant of the enormously complex problems science faces as he writes. But rather than conclude his essay with a vague question mark, he takes sides. If the humanist and the scientist are to "coexist," we must answer the real question: "On whose terms?" Not on the scientist's terms, he argues, because science can give "no guidance in the making of an ethical decision." These are broad generalizations, and Krutch knows it. He also knows that by the time he has written paragraph 6 he has a good many of his readers protesting. The remainder of his essay tries to meet those protests and convince the pro-scientists that humanism—the study of philosophy, metaphysics, religion, and poetry—not only will but must save the world.

To support his "case for the humanities" he clarifies the distinctions between science and the humanities (paragraphs 7–9). If science "deals with whatever is measurable and subject to experimental verification," the humanities must treat all that is left over, for example, "the question of contentment, happiness, and joy." We can see the hackles rise on the scientists when Krutch, in paragraph 11, puts "a monstrous assumption" in the mouth of science. If this assumption is not clear, reread this paragraph. It is a vital part of the main argument.

Beginning with paragraph 12, Krutch asks "what methods does the humanist rely on" if he can neither measure nor experiment. Without specifying these methods, he judges their success by "the extent to which [the humanist] can carry conviction." Belief rather than proof is the test.

Krutch leans heavily (paragraphs 13–16) on this word "belief," and it leads him to a less common but more pregnant phrase, "the shock of recognition." We will want to understand thoroughly what he means by it since he uses it to bring such famous scientists as Sigmund Freud and David Riesman into the humanists' camp. We will also want to question the validity of this assumption before reading the last two paragraphs of the essay. Are you certain, for example, that Freud did not establish a science, that sociology is only a quasi-science, that since C. P. Snow cited no hard statistics he speaks "as a humanist, not as a scientist"? In so short a space as this brief essay, we cannot expect Krutch to support his arguments at length. He must anticipate objections, however, and the attentive reader is likely to make them.

Certainly the scientist has doubts, as the last paragraphs admit, but Krutch is ready to override them. It is true humane letters are "responsible for more seemingly immortal lies than erroneous science has ever been," but the humanities have also kept alive "supremely important concepts" such as honor, love, duty, and the good life without which we would cease to exist. The measure of human nature is infinitely more demanding than science recognizes, infinitely more complex than the atom. The sooner we recognize that only philosophy and religion and poetry can teach us to know ourselves, the sooner we will see the humanities in their proper sphere. Science discovers facts; it teaches special knowledge; it tests and proves. A study of the humanities shows us how to live.

Questions on Content

1. C. P. Snow argues that there is more good will among scientists, a larger common ground on which to operate. How does Krutch counter this statement?
2. What are the two attitudes Krutch is trying to define through the phrases "better-red-than-dead" and "He who loseth his life shall gain it"?
3. Why does the scientist tend to brush aside the question of happiness?

4. Why did *The Lonely Crowd* not actually "prove" anything?

Add to Your Vocabulary

coexistence, unregenerate, alienation, incompatible, pernicious.

Questions on Technique

1. Krutch expends the first third of his essay on introduction. Do you feel he wastes valuable space? Why? ·
2. The opening sentence of paragraph 2 makes two risky assumptions, that every reader knows C. P. Snow and, further, that we are acquainted with "his case." Is this gesture intelligent of Krutch? Why?
3. If, in paragraph 6, Krutch is backing himself into a corner with the *tu quoque* argument, why admit it at all? Why not cut this paragraph from the essay?
4. In paragraph 12, Krutch mentions one general example of the humanist at work, drawing a picture of a happy person and telling a story that seems to account for that person's happiness. Wouldn't it have been wise for Krutch to illustrate this example with specific references to literature? The phrase two sentences later—"the extent to which he can carry conviction"—might then have meant more to his readers. Do you agree?
5. Would you have enlarged his discussion of *The Lonely Crowd* with some discussion of what David Riesman was trying to do in this book? What details are lacking here?

Techniques to Imitate

Definition of important terms

Early in his article Krutch uses effectively a technique important in most writing but especially important in argumentative writing. This technique is the practice of defining clearly the terms the writer is using. Unless both sides in a debate mean the same thing by the words they use in common, misunderstanding is bound to result. Unless a writer makes sure that the reader knows what is meant by such a general term as "science" or "humanities," misunderstanding is inevitable.

For this reason, Krutch decides that he must, first of all, clarify his subject by defining the terms about which he is writing. He takes several paragraphs for this purpose (paragraphs 7–10). In paragraph 7 he says, "What seems to me necessary (and lacking) to clarify any general discussion of the 'case for the humanities' is some clear definition of science on the one hand and, on the other, of the subject matter that the humanist believes he alone can deal with and of the methods he uses." In paragraph 9, he gives his definitions: "Suppose we say that science . . . deals with whatever is measurable and subject to experimental verification. . . . The subject matter of the humanities is whatever cannot be measured or verified experimentally."

Definitions are themselves made clear by examples, and Krutch proceeds in paragraphs 10 and 11 to supply examples of the kind of subject with which the humanities can and science cannot deal.

In your own argumentative or persuasive writing, imitate Krutch's technique by defining any important terms that you think might otherwise cause confusion. If, for example, you are writing in defense of such abstractions as democracy, socialism, liberal, conservative, or universal education, you should define the term early in your essay.

Suggestions for Writing

1. Taking Krutch's word "coexistence" as a starting point, write a 500-word essay explaining why you feel science and the humanities *can* work together.
2. If you feel strong objections to Krutch's position, outline an answer to his most blatant anti-science statements. In 500 words, write an essay titled "Humane Science" or "Progress in a Scientific World."
3. Do some research. Read C. P. Snow's little book called *The Two Cultures and the Scientific Revolution* and devote a 600-word paper to a discussion of his "case."

4. Educational curricula are constantly undergoing revisions. Discuss your own school's courses in both science and the humanities and what improvements you think they need to prepare educated citizens for understanding the world we live in.

5. Krutch's article is a *defense* of the humanities. Choose another subject that you think needs defense and write a 500-word essay in defense of it. Model your essay after the Krutch essay; that is, devote the first part to explaining the two sides and making clear which side you are defending. Then answer the claims of those who take the opposite view—the attackers rather than the defenders. Conclude your essay with your strongest arguments. Possible subjects are:

   In Defense of Democracy
   In Defense of Socialism
   In Defense of Federal Aid to Education
   In Defense of Television
   In Defense of Baseball
   In Defense of High School Dropouts

RICHARD L. NEUBERGER
and HARLEY B. MARKHAM

Outdoor Advertising:
Two Points of View

We mentioned earlier in this book that argument and
persuasion are closely allied. As the Schrank and the
New Yorker pieces demonstrate, argument tries to make
us believe what the author believes, to share an opinion,
to feel the same enthusiasm or outrage. Persuasion does
all of this, and proposes a certain action or actions as
well. We have all heard debaters raise their voices to
convince us that we must give up smoking or enlist in the
drive against slums or fight the construction of a new
highway. We hear politicians persuade listeners to vote
the liberal or the conservative ticket. The mails are full
of letters and brochures which urge one to buy more insurance, to subscribe to a new book club, to assist the
Community Players in a benefit performance. All of these
''arguments plus'' are persuasion.

As a member of the Senate Public Works Committee,
Senator Richard L. Neuberger proposed a bill ''to pro-
vide Federal assistance in the control of signboards
along the 41,000 miles of our new Interstate Highway.''
In 1957 the proposal was defeated. That same year the
Saturday Review invited the Senator from Oregon to de-

bate the issue, in their pages, with Harley B. Markham, who had served as chairman of the Outdoor Advertising Association of America. You will discover very quickly, in reading these essays, that Neuberger and Markham hold diametrically different points of view. You are asked to take sides. Notice also that you are being persuaded here by a heightened style. These are emotional appeals. Neuberger and Markham are moved by their own "oratory." They use more than reason to convince us.

RICHARD L. NEUBERGER

What Is America For?

1   **W**hen I was a schoolboy in
my native state of Oregon, my favorite song was "America
the Beautiful." At the age of forty-four it was my unhappy
lot, however, to sit at a green-felt conference table while my
colleagues of the Senate Public Works Committee voted
down my bill to provide Federal assistance in the control
of signboards along the 41,000 miles of our new Interstate
Highway system. "America the Beautiful" did not fare very
well that afternoon in the Senate Office Building. A well-
organized billboard lobby had licked it. The vote in committee was seven to six.
2 The greatest advertising bonanza in history has thus
come to the men who dominate the signboard industry.
The publishers of a newspaper or magazine, as well as the
operators of TV and radio stations, must risk heavy in-
vestments to give their media some value to advertisers.
They must buy tons of costly paper, purchase or lease huge
printing presses, erect elaborate studios and transmitting
equipment, hire editors and photographers and entertainers,
and finally often distribute their product from door to door
or through the mails. No such burden falls on what is
euphemistically ° known as the "outdoor advertising in-

euphemistically: substituting a mild word for a harsh or blunt
one.

dustry." It will have its media ready-made, after the American motoring public spends $33 billion to construct a vast network of roads linking every major metropolitan area in the land.

3 Furthermore, the signboard proprietors hold enslaved a captive audience. Readers can avoid the advertisements in this issue of the *Saturday Review*. I need not read the displays in the *Washington Post* or *Pendleton East-Oregonian*. But the motorist must look at the signboards along U. S. 30 or else prepare to meet his Maker. Indeed, among the relatively modest expenses of the billboard industry lurks the pay of skilled road engineers, who craftily locate the sprawling twenty-four foot sheets where the driver's eye cannot possibly shun these signs as he wheels his sedan around a curve or over the crest of a hill. They are purposely situated to be within his normal sweep of vision.

4 The threadbare case for outdoor advertising is exposed by the flimsy arguments advanced in support of allowing our roadsides to be defaced for private profit. In testimony before the Senate Public Works Committee these arguments fitted into three principal categories:

1. State's rights
2. Highway safety
3. Free enterprise

5 My wife and I know how hollow and hypocritical is the trite shibboleth ° of "state's rights" with respect to this particular issue. As members of the Oregon State Legislature, we tried to secure anti-billboard legislation at the state level. There we were told that such matters were more properly the concern of cities, counties, and local zoning authorities. We also were advised, of course, that keeping highways free of billboards by law would be a first step in "Sovietizing" America. Although the signboard operators raised the cry of "state's rights" to defeat my bill in the U. S. Senate, there is no record of the industry ever having

shibboleth: a phrase that is distinctive of a particular group; a slogan or catchword.

supported effective regulation or control in any of the forty-eight states.°

6   Then, in its presentation before our committee, the outdoor advertising colossus * claimed that its gaudy picket fence of signs would keep motorists from falling asleep at the wheel. The insult implicit in his claim is that the senses of the average American have been so deadened by raucous * sales messages that he needs the stimulus of whiskey, gasoline, and soft-drink ads in order to break the monotony of rivers, fields, and groves of evergreen or alder trees! Two main roads connect the teeming Washington and Baltimore citadels of population—U. S. 1 and the Washington-Baltimore Freeway. U. S. 1 is a verdant * billboard jungle. Signs sprout along it like undergrowth in the Matto Grosso.° The Freeway has been protected—thus far—from mutilation. It is my understanding that the Freeway, in addition to affording an infinitely more pleasant pilgrimage between the two cities, actually is safer than its sign-plastered sister route. Certainly, no statistics uphold the thesis of the companies that the billboards flanking U. S. 1 are a safe contrast to the dangerous monotony of the Freeway.

7   The free-enterprise argument of the signboard companies implies that they have an inherent right under our Constitution to plaster with signs any road built with public funds. If this is an inalienable American privilege, why should not other advertisers set up their material at the Government Printing Office or hang posters from Federal courthouses? And what of the right of Conrad Hilton ° to install a guest wing at the Pentagon Building?

8   One of the most effective claims of the outdoor advertisers was that rigid control of signs would work a grim hardship on small business along the roads—motels, hotels, garages, restaurants. Ex-Senator Scott Lucas, one of the leading spokesmen for the advertisers, even referred ominously to an adverse impact on the entire U. S. economy

forty-eight states: Alaska and Hawaii became states in 1959.
Matto Grosso: a state in Brazil, also spelled Mato Grosso.
Conrad Hilton: prominent international hotel owner.

because of the $25 billion spent by families touring our
highways. This, of course, implies that people traveling a
sign-free road will not buy fuel for their cars, food for their
stomachs, or seek shelter at night! I have always thought
the warning voiced by Mr. Lucas was exactly contrary to
facts. For example, there are three places in the world
where tourist expenditures comprise a major source of income—Switzerland, Hawaii, and Alaska. All these realms
are virtually free of billboards. Indeed, such protection of
the alpine and tropical countrysides actually may stimulate
the flow of wayfarers' dollars, pounds, or francs.

9 One of our most authoritative witnesses was Bertram
D. Tallamy, appointed recently by President Eisenhower
to be Federal Highway Administrator. He will have charge
of the great new interstate road program. In his home state
of New York, Mr. Tallamy supervised the 432-mile Thruway from New York City to Buffalo. Signs on the Thruway
are restricted to neat, standardized panels which indicate
the distance to a general "Service Area" or the fact that a
gas station and coffee shop are one mile away. These signs
are in precisely the same pattern as those which herald
distance, speed limits, directions, or curves. Actual commercial or brand advertising, as such, is forbidden. Two or
three times I asked Mr. Tallamy if roadside business had
suffered as a result of these controls on signs and billboards.
He always answered in the negative.

10 Despite so categorical a reply from a famous highway
engineer with actual experience in this domain, the outdoor
advertising companies insisted—right up to the hour that
my bill was narrowly defeated in committee—that restrictions on billboards would seal the fate of small entrepreneurs ° pumping gas, serving food, or patting down
beds beside the roads. Yet, if our highways are made more
attractive to the eye, will not a larger number of nomads
set out upon them with their families—and will not these
people need all the commodities and services offered along
the way?

entrepreneurs: owners or managers of a business, as Neuberger
uses the word.

11 With one breath the outdoor advertisers try to hide behind the backs of small, locally owned roadside facilities by mourning that these places will suffer in patronage if signs are controlled. But with their next gasp the advertising firms insist that the ugly signs are not those erected in the interest of the mighty national brand-name corporations but, rather, the on-the-premises signs heralding restaurants, motels, etc.

12 Regardless of the equity of this claim, it is academic. The new interstate highways are, by law, to be breached by only limited-access conduits of travel for reasons of safety. Motels and filling stations cannot hem in the interstate roads because such direct intrusion would be illegal. These accommodations will be clustered principally around the interchanges—near the widely scattered clover-leaf turnoffs. My bill, for co-operative Federal-state regulation of signs, would allow a limited number of signs at the interchanges but—to all practical purposes—not in the open countryside.

13 Such concessions have never budged the big outdoor advertisers. Their appetite for plastering our nation's roadsides is insatiable.* What if Mount Hood is shut off or a thicket of lush cedars barricaded? Who cares? The so-called self-policing imposed by the industry is largely confined to areas where signs do not have a high media value, anyway. The tiger vows not to eat carrots!

14 Said ex-Senator Lucas: "This country was built on economics, not beauty." Perhaps this explains why, only 150 years after Lewis and Clark ° were first to span what is now our nation, we have made such awesome depredations * upon so many of our natural resources.

15 The tremendous hardwood forests of the Lake States are all but gone. We wiped out 60 million bison so fast that President Theodore Roosevelt had trouble finding a few hundred to save as museum and zoo pieces. Countless passenger pigeons were slaughtered to the last bird. In my home state of Oregon, greatest of the timber states, one

Lewis and Clark: Meriwether Lewis and William Clark were joint commanders of an expedition to the Northwest in 1804–06.

sawmill community after another has cut itself out of logs. "Only God can grow a tree," wrote John Muir,° "but only Uncle Sam can save a tree." But what if Uncle Sam gets into the hands of people who are indifferent to the pollution of rivers, to the wholesale shooting for sport of herds of elk and caribou, to the systematic destruction of the few grizzlies left in the Rockies and Bitterroots,° to the draining of marshes where migratory waterfowl must find sanctuary, to the choking off of Chinook salmon ° runs which seek the remote headwaters to spawn, to the commercializing of the last handful of upland wilderness solitudes—yes, and callous, too, to the need for preserving the scenic majesty along our $33 billion investment in interstate highways? *16* Is that what we want in America?

John Muir: United States naturalist, explorer, and writer (1838–1914).

Bitterroots: a range of the Rocky Mountains on the boundary between Idaho and Montana.

Chinook salmon: largest of the Pacific salmon, also called king or quinnat salmon.

HARLEY B. MARKHAM

What's All the
Shouting About?

1　　　　　　　　The current attack on "bill-
boards" is intensely emotional in origin and is being waged
with complete disregard of facts, logic, and economics.
Satirical cartoons and poems, biting editorials, clarion *
Senatorial orations, and other militant speeches make lively
reading and listening. They have all but drowned out the
voices of outdoor advertising men and advertisers as they
ask: "Where are these 'billboard canyons' you say blot out
your views of mountains, fields, and rivers?"

2　The truth is that they don't exist. Actually, standardized outdoor advertising—call them "billboards" if you
will—is a socially conscious, legitimate, and useful business which makes substantial contributions to the economic
and social welfare of our country.

3　I am proud to be in the outdoor advertising business,
and so are all my colleagues. For generations outdoor advertising has been a medium of proved effectiveness, an
integral part of a growing America. Standardized outdoor
advertising displays have a colorful heritage as part of
Americana.° As a popular art form they have won recog-

　Americana: books, documents, maps and so forth relating to the
history and development of America. Markham uses the term
loosely.

nition by museums and other art authorities throughout the country. They are just as much a part of the American scene as baseball or the neighborhood drugstore—and they have just as much right to exist. Most important of all, they have helped build many great names of American industry: Coca-Cola, General Motors, Wrigley, Standard Oil, Ford, and many others.

4 Standardized outdoor advertising is represented by the Outdoor Advertising Association of America, Inc., which had its origin more than sixty-five years ago. There are 776 member companies in the Association, doing business in more than 15,000 communities. Their annual volume is about $200 million, which is more than 90 per cent of the total volume of standardized outdoor advertising. These member companies operate standardized poster panels and painted bulletins on land which they own or lease for the purpose, as distinguished from miscellaneous signs.

5 This distinction is important. Nine times out of ten, when our critics charge that "billboards deface the country-side," we have found that they are not talking about our standardized displays at all, but about other kinds of signs for which our industry is in no way responsible.

6 Like all good citizens and good neighbors, we recognize and accept our public and social responsibilities. Our policies are in the public interest. Our Association members voluntarily pledge adherence to a strict code of practices imposing high ethical standards upon our industry. For instance, this code says: *"We share the public interest in natural scenic beauty, parks, and historical monuments. We do not erect our advertising displays in such areas."*

7 That is plain enough and it means just what it says. We want to keep America beautiful, too. Here are other provisions of our self-imposed code to insure operations in the public interest: *"We believe in and support zoning based on sound community planning."*

8 Many communities have adopted zoning standards and restrictions for such purposes as to distinguish between business and commercial areas and those which are residential in character. We agree that reasonable restrictions affecting business and commercial practices are desirable in any well-planned community. We, therefore, pledge full support of sound zoning, and are willing to be treated under zoning just like any other business. *"We place outdoor advertising displays only upon property we own or lease for that purpose."*

9 Critics who would legislate us out of business either don't know or ignore the issue of proper and lawful land use—the fact that private property rights are involved because our displays are always located on private land owned or leased by us—never on highway rights of way. And these same critics who scream that "billboards" are despoiling scenic beauty also conveniently ignore the fact that more than 85 per cent of all standardized outdoor displays are in strictly urban areas zoned for business.

10 *"We locate our structures with discretion and good taste with respect to frequency and concentration."*

11 Again playing fast and loose with the facts, some critics would have the public believe that "billboards" are placed indiscriminately * along virtually every inch of highway, thus creating so-called "billboard canyons" or "ribbon slums." Nothing could be further from the truth. As businessmen we are deeply interested in the orderly growth of the communities where we operate. We recognize the need for discretion and good taste in developing business and industrial areas. Accordingly, we locate outdoor displays in a manner which will promote the business interests of the community, and at the same time preserve attractive features.

12 The term "ribbon slums" has been used to describe heavy concentrations of business and the signs of varied size and shape advertising them. They are for the most part "on premise" signs advertising goods and services available on the premises. They may not be pleasing to some people, but from another viewpoint they represent one way of doing business in a highly competitive area. Thus, "ribbon slums" exist because the people in the area permit them. If a remedy is needed or desired, it lies in proper zoning at the local level.

13   "We only display outdoor advertising which is truth-ful in every respect, and in accordance with high moral standards."

14   Our medium has been praised by objective authorities as the "cleanest" of all advertising media with respect to accuracy, truthfulness, and good taste. We intend to keep it that way.

15   "We actively and continuously support worthy pub-lic causes through our contributions of outdoor advertising displays."

16   For generations the standardized outdoor advertising industry has *every month* contributed a substantial portion of its facilities as a public service in support of worthy causes for the good of the community, state, and nation. These contributions average about $1.7 million worth of outdoor advertising space annually. Typical of the many causes supported by our Association members are Com-munity Chests, Red Cross, Cancer Society, Religion in American Life, March of Dimes, Mental Health, Traffic Safety, and many others.

17   We are proud of our record. It is shocking to have misinformed or malicious critics slander us with the charge that outdoor advertising displays create a traffic safety hazard and are a factor in causing accidents. But we are glad to note, however, that even some of the most reckless and irresponsible of critics are dropping that line, because when challenged they have been unable to muster a single fact to support the charge, not from insurance companies, traffic authorities, or anybody else. On the contrary, a scientific test conducted at Iowa State College said in part: "Numerous signs in the driver's field of vision in no way influenced efficiency at the wheel adversely, and in fact seemed beneficial by about 10 per cent."

18   Much of the argument against outdoor advertising is on esthetic * grounds: "Outdoor advertising is ugly, a highway blight, marring beautiful scenery." We admit that it's not easy to win an argument solely on esthetics. That's because art and esthetics are subjective: opinions, not facts, and not always informed opinions at that. It's all a matter of personal viewpoint and taste. The picture that hangs proudly in the Louvre as a great work of art is just a blob of paint to some people.

19 As for our poster panels and painted bulletins—well, we try to make them as attractive as we can. They are simple and functional. A few years ago we retained Raymond Loewy, the noted industrial designer, to develop a new standard panel. More than half of the panels being rebuilt each year are now Loewy designed.

20 Prize-winning artists such as Howard Scott, Raymond Savinac, and Norman Rockwell illustrate our advertising copy. Their work is judged annually in national competition by leading art authorities. Outdoor advertising art has been praised for its simplicity of design, directness, and symbolism.

21 These are some of the facts about our business, as distinguished from fancy. We don't pretend to be perfect. Like any other business, we have our problems and we make mistakes. But on the whole we think we have a pretty good record. We ask for no special treatment. All we ask is the same fair treatment accorded any other legitimate business. We regard our outdoor advertising structures as business installations, just as much so as the garage or store.

22 The charge has been made that a so-called "billboard lobby," working against the public interest, was responsible for the defeat of proposed federal legislation which would have discriminated against outdoor advertising. That charge is ridiculous. As citizens and businessmen we did present the honest facts of our case, a right granted to every American citizen. Even Senator Neuberger, sponsor of the bill against our medium, recognized at the Senate Subcommittee hearings that our industry representatives had every right to protect their business.

23 With respect to all the punitive legislation proposed against us, we'd like to make one point clear. We have no intention or desire of exploiting the Interstate Highway system in rural areas. In keeping with the policies set forth in our code, the only place we want to be, or have any right to be, is in business or industrial areas or where business is appropriate. We are a business. We create business. We belong with business.

24 Americans are a fair-minded people. We have every confidence that when they have the facts—all the facts—they will join us in demanding: What's all the shouting about?

ANALYSIS

Neuberger is angry. He asks what America is for. His question needs interpretation as well as answering. At first glance, it asks what America is in favor of, what it supports. But his title also poses the questions: What is happening to our countryside? What will be the fate of our roads and hills? Shall our greenery go the way of our bison? Is America for the people or for private profit? Having lost his fight to pass a bill in the Senate, Neuberger is understandably irritated, and he concludes his article with a woefully pessimistic diagnosis. How does he reach his last question: "Is that what we want in America?"

He devotes most of his essay to "exploring the flimsy arguments" of his opponents. For our convenience, he lists them in paragraph 4. Paragraphs 5–11 try to demolish them. While you are judging for yourself the efficiency of his attack, do not fail to note the emotionally charged words and phrases he uses to sway our feelings: "the threadbare case," "hollow and hypocritical," "the outdoor advertising colossus," "gaudy picket fence of signs," "raucous sales messages," "greatest advertising bonanza in history," and others. This heightened language aims at inciting us to write our senators to protest this defacement of public highways.

Paragraph 15 uses analogies ° to emphasize further what dangerous precedents we have set in the past, what foolish waste he sees us now contemplating. Ex-Senator

analogies: See Glossary.

Lucas says, "This country was built on economics, not beauty." Neuberger argues that hardwood forests, marshes, streams, shorelines are both economic *and* esthetic concerns. The body of this essay attacks the economic interests of a billboard lobby. Neuberger's positive arguments are conservation of beauty and natural resources. We *must,* he says, preserve our public lands.

Harley B. Markham takes the defensive in this debate. His opening sentence disapproves of emotional arguments. By the end of the second paragraph we know we are listening to a man who will defend a "socially conscious, legitimate, and useful business" in a business-like way. He centers his essay on six excerpts from the code of the Outdoor Advertising Association of America. He elaborates his defense in terms of these excerpts. For the most part it is a well-reasoned defense, assuming that we understand at the outset that esthetic matters—the preservation of beauty—are not of first importance. In paragraph 22, Markham bluntly states "our industry representatives [have] every right to protect their business."

But if Neuberger is generous with his emotionally-charged words and phrases, so is Markham with his emotional reasoning. Experienced debaters will call some of his sentences *non sequiturs,* by which they mean inferences or conclusions not necessarily derived from the premise or original argument. Consider just a few:

Paragraph 3: [Billboards] are just as much a part of the American scene as baseball or the neighborhood drugstore—and they have just as much right to exist."

Paragraph 14: "Our medium has been praised by objective authorities as the 'cleanest' of all advertising media with respect to accuracy, truthfulness, and good taste."

Paragraph 18: "The picture that hangs proudly in the Louvre as a great work of art is just a blob of paint to some people."

Paragraph 19: "A few years ago we retained Raymond Loewy, the noted industrial designer, to develop a new standard panel."

Paragraph 20: "Prize-winning artists such as Howard Scott, Raymond Savinac, and Norman Rockwell illustrate our advertising copy."

Paragraph 21: "We don't pretend to be perfect. Like any other business, we have our problems and we make mistakes."

Paragraph 24: "Americans are a fair-minded people. We have every confidence that when they have the facts—all the facts—they will join us in demanding: What's all the shouting about?"

Persuasion frequently uses this argument-by-association technique. Markham combines his reasonable point of view—a business has a right to defend its existence—with people and things he doubtless feels most of his readers recognize, understand, and approve of: baseball, the corner drugstore, the "cleanest," Raymond Loewy, prize-winning artists, business problems, fair-minded Americans. The whole of paragraph 16 is argument-by-association. Like Neuberger, Markham hopes you will answer his final question as he wishes you to.

What is your choice?

Questions on Content

1. Why does Neuberger call the veto of his bill the "greatest advertising bonanza in history"?

2. How does Neuberger attack the argument of "free enterprise"? Why does he use Switzerland, Alaska, and Hawaii as examples?

3. Why was Bertram D. Tallamy an "authoritative witness"?

4. In what way does the code of practices, as Markham excerpts it, prevent the abuses Neuberger claims are being made? Does Markham offer proof?

5. What are "ribbon slums"? How does Markham distinguish between "standardized outdoor advertising" and "on premise signs"? Is this distinction vital to the argument?

Add to Your Vocabulary

euphemistically, shibboleth, colossus, raucous, verdant, insatiable, depredations, clarion, indiscriminately, esthetic. What is a "categorical reply" (Neuberger, paragraph 10)? What is "punitive legislation" (Markham, paragraph 23)?

Questions on Technique

1. Neuberger cites the song "America the Beautiful" in his first paragraph. How does he use it as a theme throughout his essay?
2. What is your opinion of the argument in this sentence in paragraph 7 of Neuberger's essay: "And what of the right of Conrad Hilton to install a guest wing at the Pentagon Building?"
3. What does Neuberger mean by this phrase (paragraph 13): "The tiger vows not to eat carrots!"? How else might he have expressed the same idea?
4. Is this statement of Markham's (paragraph 11) self-contradictory: ". . . we locate outdoor displays in a manner which will promote the business interests of a community, and at the same time preserve attractive features"? Why?
5. Why should Markham want to use the figures he employs in paragraph 4 or the names of companies he cites in paragraph 3?

Techniques to Imitate

The framework of a composition

After you have gathered the materials for an essay, you must turn your attention to organization. You ask yourself, "What is the best way to approach this subject? What is the clearest way to present these materials to the reader?" This overall plan for an essay may be thought of as a framework on which the ideas, facts, evidence, and so on are to be placed. Making the framework precedes the more detailed task of preparing an outline.

In both the Neuberger and Markham essays, the framework shows clearly. For his attack on billboard advertising, Neuberger chose to refute each of the three main arguments put forth by the outdoor advertisers: (1) state's rights, (2) highway safety, and (3) free enterprise. He has thus a three-part framework for his article, and it serves him well as a structure on which to hang his own arguments in his attack on outdoor advertising. Markham takes, for his framework, the code of practices followed by the Outdoor Advertising Association of America. He discusses these in order, explaining each briefly as a means of countering charges brought against the members of the Association.

Both authors might have chosen to present their materials on some other framework; the point is that they obviously took time to consider various ways and chose what they believed to be the most effective way for their purposes. Your own essays will be more convincing and easier to follow if they are built on a clearly apparent framework.

Suggestions for Writing

1. Select what you think are the strongest and weakest arguments from either Neuberger's or Markham's essay and write a 300-word essay on why you think as you do in the light of their primary subject: "Outdoor Advertising on Our Interstate Highways."
2. Write an essay of 600 words on the subject "Outdoor Advertising in My Home Town."
3. Prepare one side of a debate on a current school issue. Outline your arguments. Plan a persuasive conclusion which will move your listeners to action. Now write, in 300–400 words, a summary of what you want to say.
4. How well can you write argument or persuasion?

    a. Answer your best friend on an argument which you oppose and he or she favors.

    b. Answer an editorial in a recent newspaper. Do it as a letter to the editor.

    c. Write a letter to your U.S. Senator, member of

Congress, or state representative, explaining why you are in favor of or opposed to a current piece of legislation. Try to persuade the legislator to vote in accordance with your opinion. Muster arguments (ideas, facts, evidence) to support your position and plan a framework and outline for your letter before you begin to write. If you wish to, tell which part of the legislator's constituency you are identified with (the 18-year-old voters, or other "minority" groups).

d. Defend yourself against an accusation.

e. Attack a new regulation of which you disapprove.

CLARK C. VAN FLEET

Invisible Death

The debate on outdoor advertising which precedes this essay by Clark C. Van Fleet was carried on in the pages of the *Saturday Review*. Our popular journals are ideal platforms for debating national issues; they share with radio and television a huge audience, eager for news and entertainment but also eager to be informed of problems that touch every one of us. Van Fleet, a native Californian, a sportsman and conservationist, had published *Steelhead to a Fly* in 1954. That book was full of his warm affection for West Coast waterways and the thrills of fishing in the Northwest. His essay "Invisible Death" has other intentions.

The readers of the *Atlantic Monthly* were first exposed to Van Fleet's wrath when they read his spirited defense of Rachel Carson following chemical company attacks on her book *Silent Spring* (1962). Carson, who was a competent scientist and remarkably fine stylist, had contended that pesticides and insecticides were being used so indiscriminately that they constituted a growing danger to all wild life. Here, in an essay published in the *Atlantic Monthly* three months after Carson's death, Van Fleet gives further evidence that pollution is a growing menace that affects our own survival, that the dangers are to human life as well as wildlife. Van Fleet is emotionally aroused and spares no one's feelings as

he tries to spell out the dangers, describe the causes,
and propose suitable action. Some anti-pollution policies have been legislated since 1964, but—we might
ask—are they enough?

1   **I**f you were to go to a drugstore and attempt to buy a bottle of strychnine or arsenic,
or any other radical poison, you would have to have a
doctor's prescription and sign the poison register. Today
you can patronize any supermarket, corner gasoline station, or many variety stores, make your choice of pesticide
or insecticide, pay for it at the counter, and walk off with
it. Just three drops of some of these radicals in a glass
of water would be enough to kill you. Left carelessly where
children could reach them, they could maim, burn, or kill,
depending on the character of each. You have to read the
fine print to discover that they are deadly poison.

2   An agriculturist, his representative, or his farmhand
can buy these same potions by the barrel or by the hun-
dred-barrel lot (fifty gallons to the barrel) at any supply
station, with either cash or credit. He can then mix his
own formula, apply it to his orchard or row crop at his
own determined time, windy or still, drench his own trees
or land, lightly or heavily, at his own will.

3   Rachel Carson's death in April [1964] was a real blow
to science. Her predictions in *Silent Spring* are proving,
despite the scoffing of her critics, all too true. In fact, as
the truth develops, her warnings of danger were entirely
too modest. Accumulations of chlorinated hydrocarbons
in some areas of the country, particularly in lakes and in
the deltas of many of our rivers, have already reached
dread proportions. The volume of fish kills and the decimation * of crustaceans ° and other marine life are frightening. Unfortunately, if we can read the signs aright, the
losses and the ultimate danger to humans are just at the
threshold of panic possibilities.

crustaceans: lobsters, shrimp, crabs, and other aquatic shelled
arthropods.

4 In my own state of California the crab fishery on the ocean side of San Francisco Bay has heretofore flourished for years. The crab is one of the sea's scavengers.* Dead carcasses of fish from the Sacramento River and the San Joaquin Delta floating down with each tide maintained a constant source of food for the crustaceans on the ocean floor fronting the bay. In the heyday of the fishery, when millions of salmonoid fish spawned and died in the tributaries of these great rivers, millions of crabs battened ° and grew fat on the float from these streams year after year. In 1957–1958 nineteen million pounds of crab were taken off these banks. Since then the crab fishery has declined with appalling suddenness. In 1962 the catch was about 1.2 million pounds. In spite of prognostications * of improvement, the 1963–1964 season has proved to ·be another disappointment, and the catch will be considerably less, disastrously so. The price of crabs in the San Francisco markets has risen above that for caviar and even pâté de foie gras,° but the fishermen who formerly flourished in opulence now are on the verge of bankruptcy. Day after day the pots are brought up with no crabs in them. Hundreds of men will lose their livelihood.

5 Richard Poole, marine biologist in charge of the California Fish and Game crab laboratory at Menlo Park, answered the question as to what had happened to the crab crop with a blunt "I don't know." He then went on to expatiate * on the possibility of a crab Shangri-la somewhere far out in the ocean, undisturbed by man, where millions upon millions of these crustaceans elude us. My own guess is that for the last five years there has been a decided increase in the float of bodies from our inland waters freighted with a deadly load. Thousands, possibly millions, of fish have been killed by pesticide residues where waste waters have been dumped into the river and the delta from rice fields, beet fields, and cotton fields, as well as from the orchards and row crops bordering upon our waterways. Each spraying program is conducted from

battened: fed gluttonously.
pâté de foie gras: a paste of fat goose liver.

early spring until well into the summer. The polluted bodies reach the banks of San Francisco Bay in greater or lesser numbers with every turn of the tide. The crabs feeding on these carcasses die from the poisons contained in the bodies. It is as simple as that.

6   Young crabs are born as free-swimming larvae of rather minute size. In appearance they are something like attenuated * shrimp. They are also extremely vulnerable at this stage. Poison-contaminated water at the mouth of the bay, where the young crabs seek warmer-than-ocean currents, can easily account for serious losses among these creatures.

7   I am reminded of the river of my youth, as it was fifty years ago and as it has now become in my old age. Fifty years ago the Russian River was a scene of constant rustic beauty. There were deep pools, with sparkling riffles pellucid and gin-clear in the summertime, where the minnows sported in the shallows. Game fish boiled in the deep runs, where a sack of crawfish could be captured by the judicious use of a small net and a piece of fresh liver any evening, and where smallmouth bass could be lured from the deeper water with a popper ° or a fly.

8   As one walked along the gravel banks that sloped toward the water, a cloud of frogs, varying in size from the diameter of a nickel to a silver dollar, would jump across the path and plop into the stream to seek safety. Every turn of the river brought the rattle of a kingfisher, the lumbering flight of a heron with his startled croak, the plunge of an osprey as he centered on some unwary prey. In the spring the air was filled with birdsong, the tinkle of robins, the happy warble of chats, the whistle of blackbirds, the insectlike trill of numerous warblers. The world was alive with movement, color, and song. The Russian River had a run of steelhead that was second to none in our coastal streams during the fall and winter, as their progeny * filled the river and its tributaries with summer trout. It is only a small stream as rivers go, probably 175 miles in

   popper: in fishing, a plug that rests on the surface of the water and pops when retrieved; also called a chugger.

length. It drains but a part of Sonoma and Mendocino counties.

9   Today, from Ukiah down, about one half of its length, it is a biological desert. Along its gravel shores one never sees a frog, the crawfish are practically wiped out, bass are very scarce, minnows are in short supply, and rarely does one spot a kingfisher. The heron rookery on the east slope of a steep hill opposite the Wohler Bridge is practically deserted, singing birds are few and far between, ospreys are to be found only along the lower river hard by the sea. The fishing has gone down, down, down. Only by the most strenuous efforts of the Fish and Game Commission in planting salmon and steelhead has some paltry semblance of the runs of former years been maintained. And what a travesty * of its former beauty remains.

10   Winter or summer, the river is never clear. Solids of one kind or another are constantly being carried slowly downstream to reach the ocean eventually. In many respects the river is but an open sewer. At times it stinks. The many deep holes that formerly graced its bed are, for the most part, gone. From the gougings of the dozen or more gravel companies that work its length comes a constant outpouring of wash water to keep the water turbid, while the fines ° and sand fill the holes during every freshet.

11   The condition of the water is utterly deplorable. Open sewers, outfall from inadequate treatment plants, unremoved detergents (their foam looking from a distance like snow), waste water from food processing plants, pesticide and insecticide residue from the orchards that line both sides of the river for miles, all contribute to this sink of evil that once went by the name of a river. Invisible death to all its inhabitants in the name of progress.

12   Thousands of streams from coast to coast are in the same predicament as is the Russian River. Every trickle, runnel, or brook that runs through our arable * land carries its load of poison ineradicable, unbroken down, fatal to all life, from its source to the main rivers. The landlocked salmon of Lake Sebago and other glacial lakes of

fines: finely crushed or powdered material.

the north have been found to contain in their fatty tissues such a high content of DDT ° that they have been banned as food and declared inedible. In some places lake trout are diminishing alarmingly because propagation has stopped. New York State is deeply concerned about the trout in Lake George. There have been reports of heavy fish kill in Lakes Superior and Michigan.

13 Senator Ribicoff ° has made the condition of the delta of the Mississippi the subject of a speech in Congress as well as of an interrogation of members of the fisheries research department and the surgeon general's office. Ten million fish are reported to have been killed in the Mississippi Delta in the past five years, and each year the fatalities are mounting enormously. The shrimp beds off and in the mouths of the river are being seriously damaged, some completely destroyed. Eventually the venom is quite likely to affect the fishery of the Gulf itself. Chesapeake Bay reports infection which if not sharply curtailed will destroy the magnificent oyster beds. From every direction similar reports are being brought in.

14 The President has declared war on poverty in round terms. The citadel of democracy shall end this blight on one fifth of its people. But what of the legacy we of today are about to leave our citizens? Are we to continue to flout and ignore the tenets * of sound health practice so that a few commercial interests can fill their pockets and spew their wastes and poisons into our rivers and streams to the detriment of all?

15 So far Secretaries Freeman and Udall ° have dragged their feet in their own departments. No effort has been made in the field to stop or curtail the use of dangerous or damaging pesticides or insecticides. The Forest Service

DDT: dichloro-diphenyl-trichloroethane; odorless, colorless crystals or powder used as an insecticide; banned in 1972.

Senator Ribicoff: Abraham A. Ribicoff (1910–   ), Secretary of Health, Education, and Welfare, 1961–1962; member of the United States Senate from Connecticut since 1962.

Secretaries Freeman and Udall: Orville Lothrop Freeman (1918–   ), Secretary of Agriculture, 1961–1969; Stewart Lee Udall (1920–   ), Secretary of the Interior, 1961–1969.

goes merrily on with DDD,° DDT, and heptachlor ° spraying programs in spite of the evident dangers involved. Farm advisers still link their recommendations to formulas containing endrin,° aldrin,° and dieldrin,° though they must be aware of the dangerous toxicity of these insecticides. The same may truly be said of state and county agents in the field. All seem to take their cues from the salesmen for the spray chemical companies and the commercial agents in their respective fields.

16 I hold no brief for the managers and officials of the major oil companies, the chemical manufacturers, or their aides and abettors, who foisted on the agriculturist these dreadful combinations of dangerous poisons when they knew full well their nature and deadly properties. Even if they claim they did not, it relieves them of no responsibility whatsoever. If the tests were not made for a sufficient time to determine the true properties of the insecticides or pesticides, their sale and distribution were all the more reprehensible. If they knew and went ahead with sales anyway, it was a dastardly deed.

17 Secretary Celebrezze ° and the Department of Health, Education, and Welfare have now completely boxed the compass ° in their attitude on the dangers of pesticide contamination. The indifference of last year has changed to a demand for immediate and urgent reforms. They now request that steps be taken to control the use of pest poisons on farmlands. But the dangers to human life are still being played down. Dr. James Hundley, assistant sur-

DDD: dichloro-diphenyl-dichloroethane; less toxic than DDT.

heptachlor: a white, waxy, water-insoluble solid ($C_{10}H_5Cl_7$), used as an insecticide.

endrin: a white crystalline poisonous isomer of dieldrin ($C_{12}H_8OCl_6$).

aldrin: a brown poisonous solid containing more than 95% of the chlorinated hydrocarbon $C_{12}H_8Cl_6$.

dieldrin: a light tan poisonous solid ($C_{12}H_8OCl_6$).

Secretary Celebrezze: Anthony J. Celebrezze (1910–   ), Secretary of Health, Education, and Welfare, 1962–1965.

boxed the compass: literally, recited all the points of the compass in clockwise order. Van Fleet means they have completely reversed their attitude or direction.

geon general, told the subcommittee of which Senator
Ribicoff is temporary chairman that he would have no
hesitation about drinking the New Orleans water or eating
shrimp from the Gulf. He admitted, however, that if he
had an alternative, he would not eat catfish caught in
the Mississippi River. But there are people living in the
delta to whom eating catfish is almost a daily event.

18 The danger is now and immediate. The evidence of
a rapid buildup of virulent * poisons in our streams, lakes,
and rivers is mounting every day. The spraying season has
already begun in California. Pears, apples, prunes, apri-
cots, and peaches have all been sprayed for psylla,°
blight, codling moth, scale, and so forth. Some orchards
have received two or three doses. Nearly every agent, co-
operative, and supplier has laid in his full supply of
insecticides, enough to last him well into the fall. In California this supply runs into hundreds of tons. Soon the
airplanes will be flying their loads over cotton, sugar beets,
and rice fields. The season is rapidly getting into full swing.
Later will come aphis, stinkbug, red and two-spot spider,
and so on, until harvesttime. Each application will drench
the trees and saturate the ground. Then the autumn rains
will come, and every trickle, rivulet, and ditch will carry
a deadly load of poisons into our streams and rivers again.
This war will not be won by inaction. The time to act is
now.

19 It is my feeling that many of the spray formulas
(there are now some sixteen hundred registered in the
state of California) have not been sufficiently tested by
the manufacturers or the state departments charged with
the testing and the issuance of the licenses. I believe all
licenses for chlorinated hydrocarbons, derivatives thereof,
or mixtures with other chemicals should be canceled as
of October 1, and that no further licenses should be issued
until the substances under discussion have been tested and
passed by competent federal authorities. Then there should
be strict regulations for their use.

20 It should be the duty of the Department of Agri-

psylla: a genus of jumping plant lice.

culture alone to issue licenses for the manufacture and sale of any of these substances, formulas, derivatives, or mixtures. The states should recognize the federal licenses and forbid the use of any such formula unless a license can be shown at the person's, corporation's, or partnership's place of use or sale. The corporations manufacturing these substances at present will cry to high heaven, but they have only themselves to blame.

ANALYSIS

Van Fleet has one object in view in writing this essay and he pursues it relentlessly: to convince his readers that "the time to act is now." This is his last sentence in paragraph 18, a climax he reaches after detailed argument. His last two paragraphs propose exactly what action he has in mind—note that he is *not* opening this matter for debate—and his reader is left with the implication that the author has made these decisions after much hard thought. In short, the essay is a model of persuasive writing, beautifully organized to introduce us to the subject, arouse us emotionally, pique us intellectually, and move us to action. But what makes Van Fleet's writing more effective than many of the polemics ° we read in magazines is his personal involvement and his determination to involve every reader. Through local details he speaks nationally; through personal experience he speaks for all of us. It will pay us to look closely at his prose to learn just how he builds an argument and at the same time addresses us, as it were, face to face.

Introduction (paragraphs 1–3): The technique here is obvious, from the first sentence onward: "If you were to go to a drugstore and attempt to buy a bottle of strychnine or arsenic . . ." We instinctively react by saying to ourselves "Why should I want to poison anyone?" and Van Fleet picks up the reaction immediately. Visit any supermarket and you can buy deadly poison, he tells us, with emphasis on the pronoun. The farmer can buy "these same

polemics: attacks or disputes.

potions" by the barrel and drench the countryside with them. Rachel Carson warned us in *Silent Spring,* but we did not heed her warning. Now "the losses and the ultimate danger to humans are just at the threshold of panic possibilities." Van Fleet fires both barrels in this brief introduction.

Demonstration I (paragraphs 4–6): Prepared for our saying "Prove it," Van Fleet gets down to bold facts. Statistics alone will not serve, so he mixes them with visual images ("a crab Shangri-la somewhere far out in the ocean"), economic pressures ("the price of crabs . . . has risen above that of caviar and even pâté de foie gras"), personal losses ("hundreds of men will lose their livelihood"), and emotional language ("the float of bodies from our inland waters freighted with a deadly load"). He does not need to linger on these details.

Demonstration II (paragraphs 7–8): In prose that is just short of sentimental, Van Fleet recalls the Russian River in the halcyon days of his youth. These, too, are emotional arguments, and he does not hesitate to play on the heartstrings with reminiscences of clouds of frogs, the happy warble of chats, and the lumbering flights of herons. He is setting up his next demonstration, of course, by making the past sound idyllic.

Demonstration III (paragraphs 9–11): What is the Russian River today? Rather than lean on statistics, Van Fleet simply describes the devastation. Note the increasing emphasis on adjectives (like *deserted, deplorable, inadequate, paltry*) and on absolutes (the river is never clear; the fishing has gone down, down, down; this sink of evil that once went by the name of a river). The essay is gathering our emotional involvement.

Demonstration IV (paragraphs 12–13): Is only California affected? We expect, and the essay needs, this brief extension into Maine, Mississippi, the Great Lakes, and the Chesapeake Bay.

Accusation (paragraphs 14–17): At last Van Fleet raises the important questions: Who is to blame? What can we do? With admirable directness, he names names:

the President's cabinet officials, the Forest Service, the assistant surgeon general, congressional subcommittees. Suddenly Van Fleet's prose becomes spare and concise without losing its personal involvements.

Reiteration (paragraph 18): More details heighten the urgency of the problem as Van Fleet describes what is happening now, at the very moment we are reading his essay. And as we said earlier, the paragraph rises to its climax with a call to action, unequivocal in its demands.

Proposals (paragraphs 19–20): Van Fleet minces no words. He suggests we cancel, as of October 1, 1964, all licenses for the manufacture and sale of chlorinated hydrocarbons, their derivatives, or their mixtures; and thereafter test every spray formula before permitting its use. He has put the problem into a proposal and handed the proposal to the reader.

Questions on Content

1. What happened to the crab fishery on the ocean side of San Francisco Bay and what is Van Fleet's explanation of the cause?
2. What evidence does Van Fleet supply for calling the Russian River an open sewer?
3. What kind of pollution, specifically, has occurred elsewhere in the United States?
4. Were Secretaries Freeman, Udall, and Celebrezze responsible for the crisis? How? Who else is to blame?

Add to Your Vocabulary

decimation, scavengers, prognostications, expatiate, attenuated, progeny, travesty, arable, tenets, virulent.

Questions on Technique

1. Van Fleet opens his essay with direct address: "If you were to go . . ." He might well have begun with an anecdote, with a newspaper clipping, or with a recapit-

ulation of past history. Do you think he has chosen wisely? Why?

2. Would paragraph 3 have been improved by a more thorough discussion of Rachel Carson's book? Why?

3. In paragraph 4 Van Fleet includes more than statistics in his description of the decline of crab fishery. Why do you suppose he chose to do so?

4. Do you feel Van Fleet's conclusions (paragraphs 19–20) are treated too briefly? Should he have devoted at least the last third of his essay to positive proposals?

5. Paragraphs 14–17 and 19–20 point the finger at those responsible and state what Van Fleet thinks should be done—a logical progression. Why then did he choose to reiterate in paragraph 18 the arguments and facts he used earlier?

Techniques to Imitate

Types of evidence

The strength of an argument depends on the quantity and quality of evidence that can be gathered in support of it and the soundness of the reasoning behind the argument. In very general terms, there are two kinds of evidence: facts and testimonials (statements by authorities). Van Fleet uses both kinds. He also reasons logically about them.

After stating his case in paragraph 3, he devotes paragraph 4 to giving facts about the sudden decline in the crab fishery on the ocean side of San Francisco Bay. This decline he is using as an example of the dangers of chemical farming. He follows his facts by discussing a probable cause of this decline. His reasoning is roughly as follows: Crabs feed on carcasses of fish brought down from inland waters. In the areas drained by the inland waters pesticides are widely used. Washed from the fields into the rivers, pesticide residues are killing millions of fish. The crabs that eat these poisoned fish are, in turn, killed by the poisons. Van Fleet refers to this idea as a guess, but it is an informed guess, as he shows throughout his essay by giving facts concerning other areas of the country where similar things have happened. To conclude his reasoning: since similar things are happening elsewhere under conditions like those in California, the crabs in California are also dying as a result of the pesticide. Thus, by means of a guess—a hypothesis—supported by facts, he tries to convince the reader that the conclusion to which his reasoning has led is a sound one: Indiscriminate spreading of deadly chemicals for agricultural purposes is destroying the crab fishery. Thus we see that Van Fleet gives many facts and engages in sound reasoning about them.

In paragraph 13 he also uses somewhat indirectly the second kind of evidence—the testimonial. He refers to Senator Ribicoff who, when he was Secretary of Health, Education, and Welfare, conducted an investigation of the condition of the delta of the Mississippi. Senator Ribicoff's investigation made him an authority on the subject and his testimony, therefore, is valuable.

As you plan an argumentative essay, you will undoubtedly present these kinds of evidence. Relevant facts, of course, are most important, and the more you can give, the stronger your case will be. Your reasoning must be logical, as Van Fleet's is. Testimonials, of course, are effective only when given by persons who are truly authorities.

Suggestions for Writing

1. Van Fleet argues, indirectly, that pollution of water, air, and natural resources is a national problem. Consult your own Chamber of Commerce for facts; research your home town newspapers; talk with local officials. Find out whether any of these problems exist in your community. If they do, write a 500-word paper on the subject, telling your reader what must be done to alleviate the local problem.

2. Taking paragraphs 9–11 as a cue, write an essay describing a blighted area of your town. Or better still, compare one section of town with another to show

how rehabilitation can beautify the environment we live in.

3. Take Rachel Carson's book *Silent Spring* from your library, read it carefully, then condense her arguments into a 700-word essay. Make certain that your reader understands that her arguments are scientific as well as socio-political.

4. As a scientist, you may be interested in investigating chlorinated hydrocarbons and their derivatives. Have Van Fleet's arguments been supported in recent years? Do some reading in current magazines, chemical journals, or science yearbooks. Then either support his accusations with additional evidence or counter his arguments with evidence to the contrary. Or, if you wish, check the *Reader's Guide to Periodical Literature* for articles on conservation and pollution. Give your impressions of the pro and con arguments.

PART FOUR

NARRATION

The urge to hear a story is strong within all of us. Our ears perk up at an anecdote just as quickly as our eyes are attracted to a picture.

Narration is that kind of discourse which answers the question: "What happened?" It is concerned with action, with events in motion. Other kinds of writing—description and exposition, for example—are employed in telling a story. But *what* happened and *when*—that is, in what sequence—are the storyteller's major concerns. They make the story.

Narration, then, is concerned with time. A series of events moves through time, and what connects these events is a plot or sequence: a beginning, a middle, and an end.

Is *time* the narrator's only concern? Once the plot is worked out and the selected events are in motion does the writer face no more problems? Hardly. Let us look at the opening sentences of three well-known novels:

> I have just returned from a visit to my landlord—the solitary neighbor that I shall be troubled with. This is certainly a beautiful country! In all England, I do not believe that I could have fixed on a situation so completely removed from the stir of society.
>
> EMILY BRONTË, *Wuthering Heights*

> An unassuming young man was traveling, in midsummer, from his native city of Hamburg to Davos-Platz in the Canton of the Grisons, on a three weeks' visit.
>
> THOMAS MANN, *The Magic Mountain*

> Strether's first question, when he reached the hotel, was about his friend; yet on learning that Waymarsh was apparently not to arrive till evening he was not wholly disconcerted. A telegram from him bespeaking

a room "only if not noisy," with the answer paid, was produced for the inquirer at the office, so that the understanding that they should meet at Chester rather than Liverpool remained to that extent sound.

HENRY JAMES, *The Ambassadors*

You will notice that all three excerpts place us at once in *time*. All three likewise tell us something about *setting,* that is, the physical background or atmosphere, and about *point of view,* that is, who is telling the story. Let us look briefly at these two additional aspects of narration.

Setting is handled in many different ways. In some stories it controls, almost dominates, the action. We feel sometimes that *place* is almost a character in the story, its influence is so strong. Such is the case with Emily Brontë's *Wuthering Heights.* The Yorkshire moors are very much removed from "the stir of society," as Mr. Lockwood, the narrator, will discover. Their isolation is overpowering. Wuthering Heights is the name of Heathcliff's dwelling. Why it is so called is part of the fascination of this first chapter. The title of Thomas Mann's novel also suggests immediately the importance of place. This story is set in a tuberculosis sanitarium in the Swiss Alps, near Davos-Platz. From the first sentence the hero is headed there. The "three weeks' visit" turns into a seven years' stay. Henry James is concerned with the influence of all of Europe on his character Strether, not just the influence of a house or a hospital. The novel opens in England (as the names "Chester" and "Liverpool" indicate) but moves eventually to Paris. James expends great effort in describing the atmosphere of that beguiling city. Not all stories weigh the setting so heavily in determining action, but setting is one way of bringing coherence to narration.

Point of view is equally vital in achieving coherence. When we use this term in discussing narratives, we mean "who is telling the story?" and "what is that person's relation to the action?" Emily Brontë narrates her novel in the first person. Mr. Lockwood is the new tenant at Thrushcross Grange and, as he tells us, he is curious about Heathcliff, the master of Wuthering Heights. His curiosity leads us directly into the story. But Heathcliff, not Lockwood, is the main character. We call Brontë's method first-person point of view, the narrator's relation to the action in this case being that of observer. If Heathcliff were to tell his own story—as do Huck Finn and Robinson Crusoe—we would still call the technique first-person point of view, but the narrator's relation to the action would be that of the main character or protagonist. And what a difference the shift would make.

It is important to note that whether the story is told by Mr. Lockwood or by Heathcliff, we would learn only what is going on in the mind of the narrator, only what the narrator perceives and is aware of. If a story is told by one person involved in the action (as observer, participant, or main character), there is no way we can be sure of what is going on in the other characters' minds—although the narrator may offer guesses. A story so told—from one person's point of view—is said, appropriately enough, to be written from the personal point of view.

Mann tells his story in the third person. He uses what is called the omniscient point of view. He roams wherever he wishes, into any character's mind, into any conversation, interpreting behavior if he so desires, commenting on action, telling us what all his characters think and feel. He knows all.

In *The Ambassadors,* James also tells his story in the third person, but he tells it from the viewpoint of *one* character in the story. James looks at all the events through Strether's eyes. He interprets Strether for us, but no other characters; he never leaves Strether's elbow. We see only what Strether and James see. We are given no knowledge of what other characters think and feel except as Strether knows these things. So, although the story is written in the third person, it, like Brontë's, is said to be written from the personal point of view. Quite obviously, these different ways of writing—from the personal point of view, from the omniscient point of view, in the first person, in the third person— produce totally different kinds of stories.

All, however, are the author's way of establishing coherence in narration.

Time, place, point of view are three important aspects of narration to watch for. Another aspect of narration deserves mention. Let us call it *point of emphasis*. What is the author's motive in telling the story? All stories are made from characters in action (even when they are animals we call them characters). But some narratives stress character, some stress action (we call it "plot"), and some stress theme (the "point" or "meaning" of the story). In reading the five narratives that follow you will want to observe many things: who tells the story, what is happening, when, where—and after you have finished reading perhaps you will ask yourself "What was the author's major intention, the *point of emphasis?*"

One final point: the narratives included here all happen to be fiction. The narrative form is, of course, not limited to fictional stories. Any account of events or happenings that occur in time is "narrative." Nonfictional narratives abound—in history books, biographies, memoirs, and also as parts of exposition (see the "Techniques to Imitate" in the Eiseley selection, page 308).

10

SIMPLE NARRATIVE, FIRST PERSON

JAMES JOYCE

Araby

"Araby" is included in a collection of short stories called *Dubliners,* which was published by Irish writer James Joyce in 1916. "I always write about Dublin," Joyce once said, "—because if I can get to the heart of Dublin I can get to the heart of all the cities of the world." The story's title, "Araby," is the name of an oriental bazaar that used to be held in Dublin. The word *Araby* is a corruption of *Arabia,* a name that would have called forth exotic fantasies for Dubliners of the time, or in fact for any people living in a city that was often bleak, in a country that was poverty-stricken, and in a society that was often repressive. This story is not about Arabia, of course; it is about a boy who has romantic fantasies but who lives in a world that is all-too-real.

1   **N**orth Richmond Street, being blind,° was a quiet street except at the hour when the Christian Brothers' School set the boys free. An uninhabited house of two stories stood at the blind end, detached from its neighbors in a square ground. The other houses of the street, conscious of decent lives within them, gazed at one another with brown imperturable faces.

blind: dead-end.

2 The former tenant of our house, a priest, had died in the back drawing room. Air, musty from having been long enclosed, hung in all the rooms, and the waste room behind the kitchen was littered with old useless papers. Among these I found a few paper-covered books, the pages of which were curled and damp: *The Abbot,* by Walter Scott, *The Devout Communicant* and *The Memoirs of Vidocq.* I liked the last best because its leaves were yellow. The wild garden behind the house contained a central apple tree and a few straggling bushes under one of which I found the late tenant's rusty bicycle pump. He had been a very charitable priest; in his will he had left all his money to institutions and the furniture of his house to his sister.

3 When the short days of winter came dusk fell before we had well eaten our dinners. When we met in the street the houses had grown somber. The space of sky above us was the color of ever-changing violet and towards it the lamps of the street lifted their feeble lanterns. The cold air stung us and we played till our bodies glowed. Our shouts echoed in the silent street. The career of our play brought us through the dark muddy lanes behind the houses where we ran the gauntlet of the rough tribes from the cottages, to the back doors of the dark dripping gardens where odors arose from the ashpits, to the dark odorous stables where a coachman smoothed and combed the horse or shook music from the buckled harness. When we returned to the street light from the kitchen windows had filled the areas. If my uncle was seen turning the corner we hid in the shadow until we had seen him safely housed. Or if Mangan's sister came out on the doorstep to call her brother in to his tea we watched her from our shadow peer up and down the street. We waited to see whether she would remain or go in and, if she remained, we left our shadow and walked up to Mangan's steps resignedly. She was waiting for us, her figure defined by the light from the half-opened door. Her brother always teased her before he obeyed and I stood by the railings looking at her. Her dress swung as she moved her body and the soft rope of her hair tossed from side to side.

4　Every morning I lay on the floor in the front parlor watching her door. The blind was pulled down to within an inch of the sash so that I could not be seen. When she came out on the doorstep my heart leaped. I ran to the hall, seized my books and followed her. I kept her brown figure always in my eye and, when we came near the point at which our ways diverged, I quickened my pace and passed her. This happened morning after morning. I had never spoken to her, except for a few casual words, and yet her name was like a summons to all my foolish blood.

5　Her image accompanied me even in places the most hostile to romance. On Saturday evenings when my aunt went marketing I had to go to carry some of the parcels. We walked through the flaring streets, jostled by drunken men and bargaining women, amid the curses of laborers, the shrill litanies of shop boys who stood on guard by the barrels of pigs' cheeks, the nasal chanting of street singers, who sang a *come-all-you* about O'Donovan Rossa,° or a ballad about the troubles in our native land. These noises converged in a single sensation of life for me: I imagined that I bore my chalice safely through a throng of foes. Her name sprang to my lips at moments in strange prayers and praises which I myself did not understand. My eyes were often full of tears (I could not tell why) and at times a flood from my heart seemed to pour itself out into my bosom. I thought little of the future. I did not know whether I would ever speak to her or not or, if I spoke to her, how I could tell her of my confused adoration. But my body was like a harp and her words and gestures were like fingers running upon the wires.

6　One evening I went into the back drawing room in which the priest had died. It was a dark rainy evening and there was no sound in the house. Through one of the broken panes I heard the rain impinge upon the earth, the fine incessant needles of water playing in the sodden beds.

　　come-all-you about O'Donovan Rossa: a ballad about Rossa, an Irish hero. "Come-all-you" refers to the words that open most such ballads.

Some distant lamp or lighted window gleamed below me. I was thankful that I could see so little. All my senses seemed to desire to veil themselves and, feeling that I was about to slip from them, I pressed the palms of my hands together until they trembled, murmuring: *"O love! O love!"* many times.

7 At last she spoke to me. When she addressed the first words to me I was so confused that I did not know what to answer. She asked me was I going to *Araby*. I forgot whether I answered yes or no. It would be a splendid bazaar, she said she would love to go.

8 "And why can't you?" I asked.

9 While she spoke she turned a silver bracelet round and round her wrist. She could not go, she said, because there would be a retreat that week in her convent. Her brother and two other boys were fighting for their caps and I was alone at the railings. She held one of the spikes, bowing her head towards me. The light from the lamp opposite our door caught the white curve of her neck, lit up her hair that rested there and, falling, lit up the hand upon the railing. It fell over one side of her dress and caught the white border of a petticoat, just visible as she stood at ease.

10 "It's well for you," she said.

11 "If I go," I said, "I will bring you something."

12 What innumerable follies laid waste my waking and sleeping thoughts after that evening! I wished to annihilate the tedious intervening days. I chafed against the work of school. At night in my bedroom and by day in the class-room her image came between me and the page I strove to read. The syllables of the word *Araby* were called to me through the silence in which my soul luxuriated and cast an Eastern enchantment over me. I asked for leave to go to the bazaar on Saturday night. My aunt was surprised and hoped it was not some Freemason ° affair. I answered few questions in class. I watched my master's face pass from amiability to sternness; he hoped I was not beginning

Freemason: a secret fraternal society which Roman Catholics were forbidden to join.

to idle. I could not call my wandering thoughts together. I had hardly any patience with the serious work of life which, now that it stood between me and my desire, seemed to me child's play, ugly monotonous child's play.

13 On Saturday morning I reminded my uncle that I wished to go to the bazaar in the evening. He was fussing at the hallstand, looking for the hat brush, and answered me curtly:

14 "Yes, boy, I know."

15 As he was in the hall I could not go into the front parlor and lie at the window. I left the house in bad humor and walked slowly towards the school. The air was pitilessly raw and already my heart misgave me.

16 When I came home to dinner my uncle had not yet been home. Still it was early. I sat staring at the clock for some time and, when its ticking began to irritate me, I left the room. I mounted the staircase and gained the upper part of the house. The high cold empty gloomy rooms liberated me and I went from room to room singing. From the front window I saw my companions playing below in the street. Their cries reached me weakened and indistinct and, leaning my forehead against the cool glass, I looked over at the dark house where she lived. I may have stood there for an hour, seeing nothing but the brown-clad figure cast by my imagination, touched discreetly by the lamplight at the curved neck, at the hand upon the railings and at the border below the dress.

17 When I came downstairs again I found Mrs. Mercer sitting at the fire. She was an old garrulous ° woman, a pawnbroker's widow, who collected used stamps for some pious purpose. I had to endure the gossip of the tea table. The meal was prolonged beyond an hour and still my uncle did not come. Mrs. Mercer stood up to go: she was sorry she couldn't wait any longer, but it was after eight o'clock and she did not like to be out late, as the night air was bad for her. When she had gone I began to walk up and down the room, clenching my fists. My aunt said:

garrulous: talkative.

18 "I'm afraid you may put off your bazaar for this night of Our Lord."

19 At nine o'clock I heard my uncle's latchkey in the halldoor. I heard him talking to himself and heard the hall-stand rocking when it had received the weight of his over-coat. I could interpret these signs. When he was midway through his dinner I asked him to give me the money to go to the bazaar. He had forgotten.

20 "The people are in bed and after their first sleep now," he said.

21 I did not smile. My aunt said to him energetically:

22 "Can't you give him the money and let him go? You've kept him late enough as it is."

23 My uncle said he was very sorry he had forgotten. He said he believed in the old saying: "All work and no play makes Jack a dull boy." He asked me where I was going and, when I had told him a second time he asked me did I know *The Arab's Farewell to his Steed.*° When I left the kitchen he was about to recite the opening lines of the piece to my aunt.

24 I held a florin tightly in my hand as I strode down Buckingham Street towards the station. The sight of the streets thronged with buyers and glaring with gas recalled to me the purpose of my journey. I took my seat in a third-class carriage of a deserted train. After an intolerable delay the train moved out of the station slowly. It crept onward among ruinous houses and over the twinkling river. At Westland Row Station a crowd of people pressed to the carriage doors; but the porters moved them back, saying that it was a special train for the bazaar. I remained alone in the bare carriage. In a few minutes the train drew up beside an improvised wooden platform. I passed out on to the road and saw by the lighted dial of a clock that it was ten minutes to ten. In front of me was a large building which displayed the magical name.

25 I could not find any sixpenny entrance and, fearing that the bazaar would be closed, I passed in quickly through

The Arab's Farewell to his Steed: a popular sentimental poem.

a turnstile, handing a shilling to a weary-looking man. I found myself in a big hall girdled at half its height by a gallery. Nearly all the stalls were closed and the greater part of the hall was in darkness. I recognized a silence like that which pervades a church after a service. I walked into the center of the bazaar timidly. A few people were gathered about the stalls which were still open. Before a curtain, over which the words *Café Chantant* were written in colored lamps, two men were counting money on a salver.° I listened to the fall of the coins.

26   Remembering with difficulty why I had come I went over to one of the stalls and examined porcelain vases and flowered tea sets. At the door of the stall a young lady was talking and laughing with two young gentlemen. I remarked their English accents and listened vaguely to their conversation.

27   "O, I never said such a thing!"

28   "O, but you did!"

29   "O, but I didn't!"

30   "Didn't she say that?"

31   "Yes. I heard her."

32   "O, there's a . . . fib!"

33   Observing me the young lady came over and asked me did I wish to buy anything. The tone of her voice was not enouraging; she seemed to have spoken to me out of a sense of duty. I looked humbly at the great jars that stood like eastern guards at either side of the dark entrance to the stall and murmured:

34   "No, thank you."

35   The young lady changed the position of one of the vases and went back to the two young men. They began to talk of the same subject. Once or twice the young lady glanced at me over her shoulder.

36   I lingered before her stall, though I knew my stay was useless, to make my interest in her wares seem the more real. Then I turned away slowly and walked down the middle of the bazaar. I allowed the two pennies to fall

salver: plate.

against the sixpence in my pocket. I heard a voice call from one end of the gallery that the light was out. The upper part of the hall was now completely dark.

37   Gazing up into the darkness I saw myself as a creature driven and derided ° by vanity; and my eyes burned with anguish and anger.

ANALYSIS

Critics Cleanth Brooks and Robert Penn Warren analyze this story on page 383 of this book.

Add to Your Vocabulary

garrulous, derided.

Techniques to Imitate

Using description in a narrative

In this first-person account of an experience of early adolescence, Joyce's main interest is in showing how the experience affected the narrator. Telling the story as an adult looking back, the narrator is shown to be aware of all the factors that influenced his feelings at the time: the house, the neighborhood, the people. Joyce must describe these things so that his readers will share and understand the narrator's sense of isolation, his feeling that he was different from others and that he was misunderstood, and finally his emotions when he concludes: ". . . I saw myself as a creature driven and derided by vanity; and my eyes burned with anguish and anger."

Description, which is an important part of all stories, becomes especially important here. Joyce, as you have undoubtedly noticed, is a master of description. He opens his story not with action but with a picture of North Richmond Street, its houses, the boy's own house, the area around the house where the boys played. His story, in the most limited sense of story, does not begin until the end of the third paragraph, where he introduces the girl.

derided: ridiculed.

If asked to do so, you could easily pick out from this story a dozen examples of Joyce's descriptive power. His descriptions are always imaginative. Note how he uses sensory impressions in all his descriptions, and how often his language is metaphorical. ° Remember too that these descriptions are expressed by the narrator of the story, by the man who, as a boy, made this trip to *Araby*. The descriptions, as well as the actions, reveal the adult to us.

The houses: "The other houses of the street, conscious of decent lives within them, gazed at one another with brown imperturbable faces." (paragraph 1)

His house: "Air, musty from having been long enclosed, hung in all the rooms, and the waste room behind the kitchen was littered with old useless papers." (paragraph 2)

The boys' play and the area around the house: "When we met in the street the houses had grown somber. The space of sky above us was the color of ever-changing violet and towards it the lamps of the street lifted their feeble lanterns. The cold air stung us and we played till our bodies glowed. Our shouts echoed in the silent street. The career of our play brought us through the dark muddy lanes behind the houses where we ran the gauntlet of the rough tribes from the cottages, to the back doors of the dark dripping gardens where odors arose from the ashpits, to the dark odorous stables where a coachman smoothed and combed the horse or shook music from the buckled harness." (paragraph 3)

The emotions of first love: "My eyes were often full of tears (I could not tell why) and at times a flood from my heart seemed to pour itself out into my bosom. . . . my body was like a harp and her words and gestures were like fingers running upon the wires." (paragraph 5)

"From the front window I saw my companions playing below in the street. Their cries reached me weakened and indistinct and, leaning my forehead against the cool glass, I looked over at the dark house where she lived. I may have stood there for an hour, seeing nothing but the brown-clad figure cast by my imagination, touched discreetly by the lamplight at the curved neck, at the hand upon the railings and at the border below the dress." (paragraph 16)

metaphorical: See Glossary.

In your own writing, you will do well to emulate Joyce in describing scenes and feelings so clearly that your reader can share the complete experience.

Suggestions for Writing

1. Joyce has tried to "get at the heart of Dublin," and by doing this, to get at the heart of every other city in the world. Write a short description, from a first-person point of view, of a place that you know very well. This description could be the basis for a short story, or it could remain as pure description. You might use Joyce's paragraphs 1–3 as models. You could also refer back to pages 20, 31, and 47 of this book for techniques to imitate.

2. Paragraph 3 of "Araby" could be used as a model of narration. It tells about certain events in the narrator's day, as the sun sets and the day begins to close. Narrate, from the first-person point of view, what happens during late winter days in your neighborhood or area. You might also open with the words: "When the short days of winter came . . ." If you prefer, use another season.

3. Paragraphs 24–37 tell what happens after the narrator leaves his home and makes his journey to *Araby*. Write three or four paragraphs in which you narrate what happens as a young person makes a journey to a particular place. Write in the first person, even though this character and his or her journey might be entirely imaginary.

4. Write a sequel to these events in "Araby." What might have happened to the boy when he arrived home? Does he return empty-handed? What does he tell Mangan's sister? Does he tell the truth or does he create an illusion?

5. The events of this story follow a common pattern. A young person undergoes some kind of trial or ordeal. After the trial or ordeal, the person is changed in some way. Often he or she has become more experienced in

the ways of the world. (This theme is also suggested in Sancton's recollection called "The Silver Horn"; see his comment on page 45.) Write a story on this theme; it does not have to be autobiographical but you should write about people and a place you know well. (Joyce might never have had this particular experience, but he tells about a kind of boy he would have known well and sets the story in a place he knew intimately.) Tell the story from the point of view of the adult looking back on some event in his or her childhood. Use either the first person or the third person, but keep to a personal point of view (see pages 528–29). What innocent dream or hope did the person lose? What new knowledge did the person gain? Try to make your descriptions reveal the person's attitude toward the setting and the other people involved.

11

SIMPLE NARRATIVE, THIRD PERSON

EUDORA WELTY

A Worn Path

Eudora Welty has lived nearly all of her life in Jackson, Mississippi, where she was born in 1909. There she grew up and there she was educated, and educated well. After studying at the University of Wisconsin and Columbia University in New York City, she returned to Jackson, where she lives among old friends and makes her living by writing. While many writers have felt that they had to "leave home" to gain worldly experience, Eudora Welty has received sufficient nourishment as a writer from her hometown.

All her stories are set in the South, but none of them are strictly autobiographical. She has always written objectively. In "A Worn Path," her method of narration is simple and direct, but the theme of the story is anything but simple.

1　　　　　　　　It was December—a bright frozen day in the early morning. Far out in the country there was an old Negro woman with her head tied in a red rag, coming along a path through the pinewoods. Her name was Phoenix Jackson. She was very old and small and she walked slowly in the dark pine shadows, moving a little from side to side in her steps, with the balanced heaviness and lightness of a pendulum in a grandfather clock. She carried a thin, small cane made from an umbrella, and with this she kept tapping the frozen earth in front of her. This made a grave and persistent noise in the still air, that seemed meditative like the chirping of a solitary little bird.

2 She wore a dark striped dress reaching down to her shoe tops, and an equally long apron of bleached sugar sacks, with a full pocket: all neat and tidy, but every time she took a step she might have fallen over her shoelaces, which dragged from her unlaced shoes. She looked straight ahead. Her eyes were blue with age. Her skin had a pattern all its own of numberless branching wrinkles and as though a whole little tree stood in the middle of her forehead, but a golden color ran underneath, and the two knobs of her cheeks were illumined by a yellow burning under the dark. Under the red rag her hair came down on her neck in the frailest of ringlets, still black, and with an odor like copper.

3 Now and then there was a quivering in the thicket. Old Phoenix said, "Out of my way, all you foxes, owls, beetles, jack rabbits, coons and wild animals! . . . Keep out from under these feet, little bob-whites. . . . Keep the big wild hogs out of my path. Don't let none of those come running my direction. I got a long way." Under her small black-freckled hand her cane, limber as a buggy whip, would switch at the brush as if to rouse up any hiding things.

4 On she went. The woods were deep and still. The sun made the pine needles almost too bright to look at, up where the wind rocked. The cones dropped as light as feathers. Down in the hollow was the mourning dove—it was not too late for him.

5 The path ran up a hill. "Seem like there is chains about my feet, time I get this far," she said, in the voice of argument old people keep to use with themselves. "Something always take a hold of me on this hill—pleads I should stay."

6 After she got to the top she turned and gave a full,

severe look behind her where she had come. "Up through pines," she said at length. "Now down through oaks."

7 Her eyes opened their widest, and she started down gently. But before she got to the bottom of the hill a bush caught her dress.

8 Her fingers were busy and intent, but her skirts were full and long, so that before she could pull them free in one place they were caught in another. It was not possible to allow the dress to tear. "I in the thorny bush," she said. "Thorns, you doing your appointed work. Never want to let folks pass, no sir. Old eyes thought you was a pretty little *green* bush."

9 Finally, trembling all over, she stood free, and after a moment dared to stoop for her cane.

10 "Sun so high!" she cried, leaning back and looking, while the thick tears went over her eyes. "The time getting all gone here."

11 At the foot of this hill was a place where a log was laid across the creek.

12 "Now comes the trial," said Phoenix.

13 Putting her right foot out, she mounted the log and shut her eyes. Lifting her skirt, leveling her cane fiercely before her, like a festival figure in some parade, she began to march across. Then she opened her eyes and she was safe on the other side.

14 "I wasn't as old as I thought," she said.

15 But she sat down to rest. She spread her skirts on the bank around her and folded her hands over her knees. Up above her was a tree in a pearly cloud of mistletoe. She did not dare to close her eyes, and when a little boy brought her a plate with a slice of marble-cake on it she spoke to him. "That would be acceptable," she said. But when she went to take it there was just her own hand in the air.

16 So she left that tree, and had to go through a barbed-wire fence. There she had to creep and crawl, spreading her knees and stretching her fingers like a baby trying to climb the steps. But she talked loudly to herself: she could not let her dress be torn now, so late in the day, and she

could not pay for having her arm or her leg sawed off if she got caught fast where she was.

17 At last she was safe through the fence and risen up out in the clearing. Big dead trees, like black men with one arm, were standing in the purple stalks of the withered cotton field. There sat a buzzard.

18 "Who you watching?"

19 In the furrow she made her way along.

20 "Glad this not the season for bulls," she said, looking sideways, "and the good Lord made his snakes to curl up and sleep in the winter. A pleasure I don't see no two-headed snake coming around that tree, where it come once. It took a while to get by him, back in the summer."

21 She passed through the old cotton and went into a field of dead corn. It whispered and shook and was taller than her head. "Through the maze now," she said, for there was no path.

22 Then there was something tall, black, and skinny there, moving before her.

23 At first she took it for a man. It could have been a man dancing in the field. But she stood still and listened, and it did not make a sound. It was as silent as a ghost.

24 "Ghost," she said sharply, "who be you the ghost of? For I have heard of nary death close by."

25 But there was no answer—only the ragged dancing in the wind.

26 She shut her eyes, reached out her hand, and touched a sleeve. She found a coat and inside that an emptiness, cold as ice.

27 "You scarecrow," she said. Her face lighted. "I ought to be shut up for good," she said with laughter. "My senses is gone. I too old. I the oldest people I ever know. Dance, old scarecrow," she said, "while I dancing with you."

28 She kicked her foot over the furrow, and with mouth drawn down, shook her head once or twice in a little strutting way. Some husks blew down and whirled in streamers about her skirts.

29 Then she went on, parting her way from side to side

with the cane, through the whispering field. At last she came to the end, to a wagon track where the silver grass blew between the red ruts. The quail were walking around like pullets, seeming all dainty and unseen.

30   "Walk pretty," she said. "This the easy place. This the easy going."

31   She followed the track, swaying through the quiet bare fields, through the little strings of trees silver in their dead leaves, past cabins silver from weather, with the doors and windows boarded shut, all like old women under a spell sitting there. "I walking in their sleep," she said, nodding her head vigorously.

32   In a ravine she went where a spring was silently flowing through a hollow log. Old Phoenix bent and drank. "Sweet-gum makes the water sweet," she said, and drank more. "Nobody know who made this well, for it was here when I was born."

33   The track crossed a swampy part where the moss hung as white as lace from every limb. "Sleep on, alligators, and blow your bubbles." Then the track went into the road.

34   Deep, deep the road went down between the high green-colored banks. Overhead the live-oaks met, and it was as dark as a cave.

35   A black dog with a lolling tongue came up out of the weeds by the ditch. She was meditating, and not ready, and when he came at her she only hit him a little with her cane. Over she went in the ditch, like a little puff of milkweed.

36   Down there, her senses drifted away. A dream visited her, and she reached her hand up, but nothing reached down and gave her a pull. So she lay there and presently went to talking. "Old woman," she said to herself, "that black dog come up out of the weeds to stall you off, and now there he sitting on his fine tail, smiling at you."

37   A white man finally came along and found her—a hunter, a young man, with his dog on a chain.

38   "Well, Granny!" he laughed. "What are you doing there?"

39 "Lying on my back like a June-bug waiting to be turned over, mister," she said, reaching up her hand.

40 He lifted her up, gave her a swing in the air, and set her down. "Anything broken, Granny?"

41 "No sir, them old dead weeds is springy enough," said Phoenix, when she had got her breath. "I thank you for your trouble."

42 "Where do you live, Granny?" he asked, while the two dogs growled at each other.

43 "Away back yonder, sir, behind the ridge. You can't even see it from here."

44 "On your way home?"

45 "No sir, I going to town."

46 "Why, that's too far! That's as far as I walk when I come out myself, and I get something for my trouble." He patted the stuffed bag he carried, and there hung down a little closed claw. It was one of the bob-whites, with its beak hooked bitterly to show it was dead. "Now you go on home, Granny!"

47 "I bound to go to town, mister," said Phoenix. "The time come around."

48 He gave another laugh, filling the whole landscape. "I know you old colored people! Wouldn't miss going to town to see Santa Claus!"

49 But something held old Phoenix very still. The deep lines in her face went into a fierce and different radiation. Without warning, she had seen with her own eyes a flashing nickel fall out of the man's pocket onto the ground.

50 "How old are you, Granny?" he was saying.

51 "There is no telling, mister," she said, "no telling."

52 Then she gave a little cry and clapped her hands and said, "Git on away from here, dog! Look! Look at that dog!" She laughed as if in admiration. "He ain't scared of nobody. He a big black dog." She whispered, "Sic him!"

53 "Watch me get rid of that cur," said the man. "Sic him, Pete, Sic him!"

54 Phoenix heard the dogs fighting, and heard the man running and throwing sticks. She even heard a gunshot. But she was slowly bending forward by that time, further and further forward, the lids stretched down over her eyes, as if she were doing this in her sleep. Her chin was lowered almost to her knees. The yellow palm of her hand came out from the fold of her apron. Her fingers slid down and along the ground under the piece of money with the grace and care they would have in lifting an egg from under a setting hen. Then she slowly straightened up, she stood erect, and the nickel was in her apron pocket. A bird flew by. Her lips moved. "God watching me the whole time. I come to stealing."

55   The man came back, and his own dog panted about them. "Well, I scared him off that time," he said, and then he laughed and lifted his gun and pointed it at Phoenix.

56   She stood straight and faced him.

57   "Doesn't the gun scare you?" he said, still pointing it.

58   "No, sir, I seen plenty go off closer by, in my day, and for less than what I done," she said, holding utterly still.

59   He smiled, and shouldered the gun. "Well, Granny," he said, "you must be a hundred years old, and scared of nothing. I'd give you a dime if I had any money with me. But you take my advice and stay home, and nothing will happen to you."

60   "I bound to go on my way, mister," said Phoenix. She inclined her head in the red rag. Then they went in different directions, but she could hear the gun shooting again and again over the hill.

61   She walked on. The shadows hung from the oak trees to the road like curtains. Then she smelled wood-smoke, and smelled the river, and she saw a steeple and the cabins on their steep steps. Dozens of little black children whirled around her. There ahead was Natchez shining. Bells were ringing. She walked on.

62   In the paved city it was Christmas time. There were red and green electric lights strung and crisscrossed everywhere, and all turned on in the daytime. Old Phoenix would have been lost if she had not distrusted her eyesight and depended on her feet to know where to take her.

63 She paused quietly on the sidewalk where people were passing by. A lady came along in the crowd, carrying an armful of red-, green- and silver-wrapped presents; she gave off perfume like the red roses in hot summer, and Phoenix stopped her.

64 "Please, missy, will you lace up my shoe?" She held up her foot.

65 "What do you want, Grandma?"

66 "See my shoe," said Phoenix. "Do all right for out in the country, but wouldn't look right to go in a big building."

67 "Stand still then, Grandma," said the lady. She put her packages down on the sidewalk beside her and laced and tied both shoes tightly.

68 "Can't lace 'em with a cane," said Phoenix. "Thank you, missy. I doesn't mind asking a nice lady to tie up my shoe, when I gets out on the street."

69 Moving slowly and from side to side, she went into the big building, and into a tower of steps, where she walked up and around and around until her feet knew to stop.

70 She entered a door, and there she saw nailed up on the wall the document that had been stamped with the gold seal and framed in the gold frame, which matched the dream that was hung up in her head.

71 "Here I be," she said. There was a fixed and ceremonial stiffness over her body.

72 "A charity case, I suppose," said an attendant who sat at the desk before her.

73 But Phoenix only looked above her head. There was sweat on her face, the wrinkles in her skin shone like a bright net.

74 "Speak up, Grandma," the woman said. "What's your name? We must have your history, you know. Have you been here before? What seems to be the trouble with you?"

75 Old Phoenix only gave a twitch to her face as if a fly were bothering her.

76 "Are you deaf?" cried the attendant.

77 But then the nurse came in.

78   "Oh, that's just old Aunt Phoenix," she said. "She doesn't come for herself—she has a little grandson. She makes these trips just as regular as clockwork. She lives away back off the Old Natchez Trace." She bent down. "Well, Aunt Phoenix, why don't you just take a seat? We won't keep you standing after your long trip." She pointed.

79   The old woman sat down, bolt upright in the chair.

80   "Now, how is the boy?" asked the nurse.

81   Old Phoenix did not speak.

82   "I said, how is the boy?"

83   But Phoenix only waited and stared straight ahead, her face very solemn and withdrawn into rigidity.

84   "Is his throat any better?" asked the nurse. "Aunt Phoenix, don't you hear me? Is your grandson's throat any better since the last time you came for the medicine?"

85   With her hands on her knees, the old woman waited, silent, erect and motionless, just as if she were in armor.

86   "You mustn't take up our time this way, Aunt Phoenix," the nurse said. "Tell us quickly about your grandson, and get it over. He isn't dead, is he?"

87   At last there came a flicker and then a flame of comprehension across her face, and she spoke.

88   "My grandson. It was my memory had left me. There I sat and forgot why I made my long trip."

89   "Forgot?" The nurse frowned. "After you came so far?"

90   Then Phoenix was like an old woman begging a dignified forgiveness for waking up frightened in the night. "I never did go to school, I was too old at the Surrender," she said in a soft voice. "I'm an old woman without an education. It was my memory fail me. My little grandson, he is just the same, and I forgot it in the coming."

91   "Throat never heals, does it?" said the nurse, speaking in a loud, sure voice to old Phoenix. By now she had a card with something written on it, a little list. "Yes. Swallowed lye. When was it?—January—two-three years ago—"

92   Phoenix spoke unasked now. "No, missy, he not dead, he just the same. Every little while his throat begin to close up again, and he not able to swallow. He not get his breath. He not able to help himself. So the time come around, and I go on another trip for the soothing medicine."

93 "All right. The doctor said as long as you came to get it, you could have it," said the nurse. "But it's an obstinate case."

94 "My little grandson, he sit up there in the house all wrapped up, waiting by himself," Phoenix went on. "We is the only two left in the world. He suffer and it don't seem to put him back at all. He got a sweet look. He going to last. He wear a little patch quilt and peep out holding his mouth open like a little bird. I remembers so plain now. I not going to forget him again, no, the whole enduring time. I could tell him from all the others in creation."

95 "All right." The nurse was trying to hush her now. She brought her a bottle of medicine. "Charity," she said, making a check mark in a book.

96 Old Phoenix held the bottle close to her eyes, and then carefully put it into her pocket.

97 "I thank you," she said.

98 "It's Christmas time, Grandma," said the attendant. "Could I give you a few pennies out of my purse?"

99 "Five pennies is a nickel," said Phoenix stiffly.

100 "Here's a nickel," said the attendant.

101 Phoenix rose carefully and held out her hand. She received the nickel and then fished the other nickel out of her pocket and laid it beside the new one. She stared at her palm closely, with her head on one side.

102 Then she gave a tap with her cane on the floor.

103 "This is what come to me to do," she said. "I going to the store and buy my child a little windmill they sells, made out of paper. He going to find it hard to believe there such a thing in the world. I'll march myself back where he waiting, holding it straight up in this hand."

104 She lifted her free hand, gave a little nod, turned around, and walked out of the doctor's office. Then her slow step began on the stairs, going down.

ANALYSIS

Phoenix and her journey in the near-dead of winter call forth deep human responses in most readers. They seem to remind us of other people and other journeys.

One interesting way of looking at "The Worn Path" is to look at Phoenix and her journey as having mythological overtones. In Egyptian mythology the phoenix is a lone bird which is supposed to live for several hundred years and then to consume itself on a fiery nest. From its ashes a new phoenix is born, and the cycle of birth, death, and rebirth is then repeated. Phoenix, like her mythical namesake, is also very very old. ("I the oldest people I ever know," she says to herself.) Like the ancient bird, she also periodically suffers: she takes the worn path to bring the life-giving medicine to her little grandson, who, in paragraph 94, is compared to a tiny peeping bird. In fact, the sound of Phoenix's umbrella-cane is also compared, in paragraph 1, to the chirping of a solitary little bird.

Another way of looking at this story is to consider the possibility that it contains religious symbolism. Phoenix's journey occurs in December. On Decmber 21 the winter solstice occurs, with the longest night of the year. After this comes Christmas, when, with lights and song, the birth of Jesus Christ is celebrated. According to Christian tradition, Jesus, like Aunt Phoenix and like the mythical bird, also sacrificed his life so that others could live.

The worn path: it leads "a long way," it invites Phoenix to give up (something "pleads I should stay"), it contains many perils: mazes, ghosts, darkness, caves, threatening animals, and deathtraps. But at the path's end is "Natchez shining," and bells ringing—like the heavenly city waiting for the pilgrim at the end of life's journey. Ironically, however, Phoenix finds in this shining city not divine help and eternity, but doctor's attendants who are anxious about time.

Questions on Content

1. What do you think is the point or theme of the story?

That is, why did the writer want to tell this story?
2. What does the hunter suppose is Phoenix's purpose in going to town? How does this contrast with her real purpose?

Questions on Technique

1. Why do you suppose Welty keeps the reason for Phoenix's journey a secret until nearly the end of the story?
2. The story could have been written without the hunter. What does the scene with the hunter contribute? What do we learn about Phoenix during this scene?
3. Why do you suppose the writer does not give more information about the tragic situation of the grandson?

Techniques to Imitate

Characterization: "Show, don't tell."

Welty is well aware of one of the important axioms of narrative writing—show, don't tell. This means that a writer should *show* characters in action, not simply tell us about them as though writing an essay. Welty reveals Phoenix Jackson by showing her in action and by revealing the old woman's thoughts. Nowhere, for example, does she say outright that Phoenix is poor, that her eyesight is failing, that her mind is showing the effects of senility, or that she is courageous and fearless. Welty *shows* us what Phoenix does and says and leaves it to us to gather these characteristics from her story. She does not simply announce them.

Note how she does this.

We learn that Phoenix is poor, not because we are told she is poor in so many words, but rather because her apron is made "of bleached sugar sacks," because her cane is made from an umbrella, because she is eager to retrieve the nickel that fell from the man's pocket, because she is a charity case at the doctor's office.

Welty does not announce the failing eyesight; she shows

it by describing the old woman's use of the cane to guide herself on the path. She shows it by what the woman says: "Thorns, you doing your appointed work. Never want to let folks pass, no sir. Old eyes thought you was a pretty little *green* bush." The woman is confused by the scarecrow because she could not immediately see what it was. She finds out by touching it.

We are not told that Phoenix Jackson's mind is showing signs of senility, but we learn this fact from her actions and her thoughts. Her mind is clear at times, as when she quickly manufactures a ruse to divert the man's attention while she picks up the nickel, but at other times her mind is shown to be tired and confused. There is the hallucination that comes to her when, relieved but exhausted after crossing the log above the stream, she sits down to rest, "and when a little boy brought her a plate with a slice of marble-cake on it" she spoke to him. "That would be acceptable," she said politely, but "when she went to take it there was just her own hand in the air." When she lay on her back after her fall, "A dream visited her, and she reached her hand up, but nothing reached down and gave her a pull." In a moment of clarity after her experience with the scarecrow, she mutters, "I ought to be shut up for good. My senses is gone. I too old." And finally, after her long and strenuous journey ends in the doctor's office, she cannot, for a moment, even remember why she made the journey. "It was my memory had left me. There I sat and forgot why I made my long trip."

The entire story points to Phoenix's courage and fearlessness, but Welty does not tell us she was courageous and fearless. She has the man sum it up: "Well, Granny," he said, "you must be a hundred years old, and scared of nothing."

In your own story writing, do not merely tell your readers what they should think of your characters; do not merely summarize what they do. Make sure that you *show* what your characters are like. Portray their actions and let them speak. In doing this, you will be demonstrating an important technique of narrative writing.

Suggestions for Writing

1. This story ends with a beginning: Phoenix is starting another journey along the worn path—the journey home with the medicine and the paper windmill. Imagine what this homeward journey is like. What are its perils? Whom does she meet? Is her journey successful? Write a story about this return journey, using the third-person point of view as Welty does.

2. Narrate the incidents in the doctor's office from the first-person point of view, either that of the doctor's attendant or the nurse.

3. Narrate from the hunter's point of view the part of the story in which he appears. What is he thinking? Where is he going? Why did he tell Phoenix he had no money with him? (Show, don't tell.)

4. Often no one knows where a writer gets ideas for stories —whether they come from experience or from imagination. Eudora Welty seems to have drawn her characters and settings from the Southern region she is so familiar with. But she also obviously drew a great deal of this story from her creative imagination. Some ideas for a story might come to you if you concentrate on the place and the people you are most familiar with. Write your story from the third-person point of view; feel free to show your readers what your main character is thinking and feeling. If the idea appeals to you, you could also use a journey as a framework for your story.

5. The setting is important in this narrative, as it is in Joyce's story "Araby." You might write a story about a journey in which the setting is equally important in establishing a mood and in providing some kind of symbolism. Choose your season and time of day carefully. Where will the journey take the character? What perils will the setting provide? How will the character feel about the setting?

6. Paragraphs 1–3 describe Phoenix. Write a description of a character from the point of view of an all-knowing narrator, modeling your description on Welty's description of Phoenix. (See techniques discussed on page 20.)

JUANITA PLATERO and SIYOWIN MILLER

Chee's Daughter

It is not often that we find a short story that is a successful result of a collaboration. But Juanita Platero and Siyowin Miller have produced in "Chee's Daughter" a carefully structured short story, a tale of Navaho life in which love outwits greed. Platero herself is a Navaho and lived at one time on a reservation in New Mexico, which is the setting for this story.

The two authors do not participate as characters in this story at all. They tell their story from the third person point of view, though the events are related almost entirely from the perspective of Chee, a young Navaho man.

1   The hat told the story, the big, black, drooping Stetson. It was not at the proper angle, the proper rakish angle for so young a Navaho. There was no song, and that was not in keeping either. There should have been at least a humming, a faint, all-to-himself "he he he heya," for it was a good horse he was riding, a slender-legged, high-stepping buckskin that would race the wind with light knee-urging. This was a day for singing, a warm winter day, when the touch of the sun upon the back belied the snow high on distant mountains.

2   Wind warmed by the sun touched his high-boned cheeks
like flicker feathers, and still he rode on silently, deeper
into Little Canyon, until the red rock walls rose straight
upward from the stream bed and only a narrow piece of
blue sky hung above. Abruptly the sky widened where the
canyon walls were pushed back to make a wide place, as
though in ancient times an angry stream had tried to go all
ways at once.

3   This was home—this wide place in the canyon—levels
of jagged rock and levels of rich red earth. This was home
to Chee, the rider of the buckskin, as it had been to many
generations before him.

4   He stopped his horse at the stream and sat looking
across the narrow ribbon of water to the bare-branched
peach trees. He was seeing them each springtime with their
age-gnarled limbs transfigured beneath veils of blossom
pink; he was seeing them in autumn laden with their yellow
fruit, small and sweet. Then his eyes searched out the indistinct furrows of the fields beside the stream, where each
year the corn and beans and squash drank thirstily of the
overflow from summer rains. Chee was trying to outweigh
today's bitter betrayal of hope by gathering to himself these
reminders of the integrity of the land. Land did not cheat!
His mind lingered deliberately on all the days spent here
in the sun caring for the young plants, his songs to the
earth and to the life springing from it— ". . . In the middle
of the wide field . . . Yellow Corn Boy . . . He has started
both ways . . . ," then the harvest and repayment in full
measure. Here was the old feeling of wholeness and of
oneness with the sun and earth and growing things.

5   Chee urged the buckskin toward the family compound
where, secure in a recess of overhanging rock, was his
mother's dome-shaped hogan,° red rock and red adobe
like the ground on which it nestled. Not far from the hogan
was the half-circle of brush like a dark shadow against the
canyon wall—corral for sheep and goats. Farther from the

hogan: a Navaho dwelling, constructed of earth and branches and
covered with mud or sod.

hogan, in full circle, stood the horse corral made of heavy cedar branches sternly interlocked. Chee's long thin lips curved into a smile as he passed his daughter's tiny hogan squatted like a round Pueblo oven beside the corral. He remembered the summer day when together they sat back on their heels and plastered wet adobe all about the circling wall of rock and the woven dome of piñon twigs. How his family laughed when the Little One herded the bewildered chickens into her tiny hogan as the first snow fell.

6 Then the smile faded from Chee's lips and his eyes darkened as he tied his horse to a corral post and turned to the strangely empty compound. "Someone has told them," he thought, "and they are inside weeping." He passed his mother's deserted loom on the south side of the hogan and pulled the rude wooden door toward him, bowing his head, hunching his shoulders to get inside.

7 His mother sat sideways by the center fire, her feet drawn up under her full skirts. Her hands were busy kneading dough in the chipped white basin. With her head down, her voice was muffled when she said, "The meal will soon be ready, son."

8 Chee passed his father sitting against the wall, hat over his eyes as though asleep. He passed his older sister who sat turning mutton ribs on a crude wire grill over the coals, noticed tears dropping on her hands. "She cared more for my wife than I realized," he thought.

9 Then because something must be said sometime, he tossed the black Stetson upon a bulging sack of wool and said, "You have heard, then." He could not shut from his mind how confidently he had set the handsome new hat on his head that very morning, slanting the wide brim over one eye: he was going to see his wife and today he would ask the doctors about bringing her home; last week she had looked so much better.

10 His sister nodded but did not speak. His mother sniffed and passed her velveteen sleeve beneath her nose. Chee sat down, leaning against the wall. "I suppose I was a fool for hoping all the time. I should have expected this.

Few of our people get well from the coughing sickness.°
But *she* seemed to be getting better."

11 His mother was crying aloud now and blowing her
nose noisily on her skirt. His father sat up, speaking gently
to her.

12 Chee shifted his position and started a cigarette. His
mind turned back to the Little One. At least she was too
small to understand what had happened, the Little One who
had been born three years before in the sanitarium where
his wife was being treated for the coughing sickness, the
Little One he had brought home to his mother's hogan to
be nursed by his sister whose baby was a few months older.
As she grew fat-cheeked and sturdy-legged, she followed
him about like a shadow; somehow her baby mind had
grasped that of all those at the hogan who cared for her
and played with her, he—Chee—belonged most to her.
She sat cross-legged at his elbow when he worked silver at
the forge; she rode before him in the saddle when he drove
the horses to water; often she lay wakeful on her sheep-
pelts until he stretched out for the night in the darkened
hogan and she could snuggle warm against him.

13 Chee blew smoke slowly and some of the sadness left
his dark eyes as he said, "It is not as bad as it might be. It
is not as though we are left with nothing."

14 Chee's sister arose, sobs catching in her throat, and
rushed past him out the doorway. Chee sat upright, a terrible fear possessing him. For a moment his mouth could
make no sound. Then: "The Little One! Mother, where is
she?"

15 His mother turned her stricken face to him: "Your
wife's people came after her this morning. They heard
yesterday of their daughter's death through the trader at
Red Sands."

16 Chee started to protest but his mother shook her head
slowly. "I didn't expect they would want the Little One
either. But there is nothing you can do. She is a girl child
and belongs to her mother's people; it is custom."

coughing sickness: tuberculosis.

17   Frowning, Chee got to his feet, grinding his cigarette into the dirt floor. "Custom! When did my wife's parents begin thinking about custom? Why, the hogan where they live doesn't even face the east!" He started toward the door. "Perhaps I can overtake them. Perhaps they don't realize how much we want her here with us. I'll ask them to give my daughter back to me. Surely, they won't refuse."

18   His mother stopped him gently with her outstretched hand. "You couldn't overtake them now. They were in the trader's car. Eat and rest, and think more about this."

19   "Have you forgotten how things have always been between you and your wife's people?" his father said.

20   That night, Chee's thoughts were troubled—half-forgotten incidents became disturbingly vivid—but early the next morning he saddled the buckskin and set out for the settlement of Red Sands. Even though his father-in-law, Old Man Fat, might laugh, Chee knew that he must talk to him. There were some things to which Old Man Fat might listen.

21   Chee rode the first part of the fifteen miles to Red Sands expectantly. The sight of sandstone buttes near Cottonwood Spring reddening in the morning sun brought a song almost to his lips. He twirled his reins in salute to the small boy herding sheep toward many-colored Butterfly Mountain, watched with pleasure the feathers of smoke rising against tree-darkened western mesas from the hogans sheltered there. But as he approached the familiar settlement sprawled in mushroom growth along the highway, he began to feel as though a scene from a bad dream was becoming real.

22   Several cars were parked around the trading store which was built like two log hogans side by side, with red gas pumps in front and a sign across the tarpaper roofs: *Red Sands Trading Post—Groceries Gasoline Cold Drinks Sandwiches Indian Curios*. Back of the trading post an unpainted frame house and outbuildings squatted on the drab, treeless land. Chee and the Little One's mother had lived there when they stayed with his wife's people. That was according to custom—living with one's wife's people

—but Chee had never been convinced that it was custom alone which prompted Old Man Fat and his wife to insist that their daughter bring her husband to live at the trading post.

23   Beside the Post was a large hogan of logs, with brightly painted pseudo-Navaho designs on the roof—a hogan with smoke-smudged windows and a garish blue door which faced north to the highway. Old Man Fat had offered Chee a hogan like this one. The trader would build it if he and his wife would live there and Chee would work at his forge making silver jewelry where tourists could watch him. But Chee had asked instead for a piece of land for a cornfield and help in building a hogan far back from the highway and a corral for the sheep he had brought to this marriage.

24   A cold wind blowing down from the mountains began to whistle about Chee's ears. It flapped the gaudy Navaho rugs which were hung in one long bright line to attract tourists. It swayed the sign *Navaho Weaver at Work* beside the loom where Old Man Fat's Wife sat hunched in her striped blanket, patting the colored thread of a design into place with a wooden comb. Tourists stood watching the weaver. More tourists stood in a knot before the hogan where the sign said: *See Inside a Real Navaho Home 25¢.*

25   Then the knot seemed to unravel as a few people returned to their cars; some had cameras; and there against the blue door Chee saw the Little One standing uncertainly. The wind was plucking at her new purple blouse and wide green skirt; it freed truant strands of soft dark hair from the meager queue into which it had been tied with white yarn.

26   "Isn't she cunning!" one of the women tourists was saying as she turned away.

27   Chee's lips tightened as he began to look around for Old Man Fat. Finally he saw him passing among the tourists collecting coins.

28   Then the Little One saw Chee. The uncertainty left her face and she darted through the crowd as her father

swung down from his horse. Chee lifted her in his arms, hugging her tight. While he listened to her breathless chatter, he watched Old Man Fat bearing down on them, scowling.

29 As his father-in-law walked heavily across the gravelled lot, Chee was reminded of a statement his mother sometimes made: "When you see a fat Navaho, you see one who hasn't worked for what he has."

30 Old Man Fat was fattest in the middle. There was indolence * in his walk even though he seemed to hurry, indolence in his cheeks so plump they made his eyes squint, eyes now smoldering with anger.

31 Some of the tourists were getting into their cars and driving away. The old man said belligerently to Chee, "Why do you come here? To spoil our business? To drive people away?"

32 "I came to talk with you," Chee answered, trying to keep his voice steady as he faced the old man.

33 "We have nothing to talk about," Old Man Fat blustered and did not offer to touch Chee's extended hand.

34 "It's about the Little One." Chee settled his daughter more comfortably against his hip as he weighed carefully all the words he had planned to say. "We are going to miss her very much. It wouldn't be so bad if we knew that *part* of each year she could be with us. That might help you too. You and your wife are no longer young people and you have no young ones here to depend upon." Chee chose his next words remembering the thriftlessness of his wife's parents, and their greed. "Perhaps we could share the care of this little one. Things are good with us. So much snow this year will make lots of grass for the sheep. We have good land for corn and melons."

35 Chee's words did not have the expected effect. Old Man Fat was enraged. "Farmers, all of you! Long-haired farmers! Do you think everyone must bend his back over the short-handled hoe in order to have food to eat?" His tone changed as he began to brag a little. "We not only have all the things from cans at the trader's, but when the Pueblos come past here on their way to town we buy their salty jerked ° mutton, young corn for roasting, dried sweet peaches."

36   Chee's dark eyes surveyed the land along the highway as the old man continued to brag about being "progressive." *He* no longer was tied to the land. He and his wife made money easily and could *buy* all the things they wanted. Chee realized too late that he had stumbled into the old argument between himself and his wife's parents. They had never understood his feeling about the land— that a man took care of his land and it in turn took care of him. Old Man Fat and his wife scoffed at him, called him a Pueblo farmer, all during that summer when he planted and weeded and harvested. Yet they ate the green corn in their mutton stews, and the chili paste from the fresh ripe chilis, and the tortillas from the cornmeal his wife ground. None of this working and sweating in the sun for Old Man Fat, who talked proudly of his easy way of living—collecting money from the trader who rented this strip of land beside the highway, collecting money from the tourists.

37   Yet Chee had once won that argument. His wife had shared his belief in the integrity of the earth, that jobs and people might fail one but the earth never would. After that first year she had turned from her own people and gone with Chee to Little Canyon.

38   Old Man Fat was reaching for the Little One. "Don't be coming here with plans for my daughter's daughter," he warned. "If you try to make trouble, I'll take the case to the government man in town."

39   The impulse was strong in Chee to turn and ride off while he still had the Little One in his arms. But he knew his time of victory would be short. His own family would uphold the old custom of children, especially girl children, belonging to the mother's people. He would have to give his daughter up if the case were brought before the Headman of Little Canyon, and certainly he would have no better chance before a strange white man in town.

---

jerked: preserved by being cut in strips and dried in the sun.

40 He handed the bewildered Little One to her grand-father who stood watching every movement suspiciously. Chee asked, "If I brought you a few things for the Little One, would that be making trouble? Some velvet for a blouse, or some of the jerky she likes so well . . . this summer's melon?"

41 Old Man Fat backed away from him. "Well," he hesi-tated, as some of the anger disappeared from his face and beads of greed shone in his eyes. "Well," he repeated. Then as the Little One began to squirm in his arms and cry, he said, "No! No! Stay away from here, you and all your family."

42 The sense of his failure deepened as Chee rode back to Little Canyon. But it was not until he sat with his family that evening in the hogan, while the familiar bustle of meal preparing went on about him, that he began to doubt the wisdom of the things he'd always believed. He smelled the coffee boiling and the oily fragrance of chili powder dusted into the bubbling pot of stew; he watched his mother turn-ing round crusty fried bread in the small black skillet. All around him was plenty—a half of mutton hanging near the door, bright strings of chili drying, corn hanging by the braided husks, cloth bags of dried peaches. Yet in his heart was nothing.

43 He heard the familiar sounds of the sheep outside the hogan, the splash of water as his father filled the long drinking trough from the water barrel. When his father came in, Chee could not bring himself to tell a second time of the day's happenings. He watched his wiry, soft-spoken father while his mother told the story, saw his father's queue of graying hair quiver as he nodded his head with sympathetic exclamations.

44 Chee's doubting, acrid ° thoughts kept forming: Was it wisdom his father had passed on to him or was his in-heritance only the stubbornness of a long-haired Navaho resisting change? Take care of the land and it will take care of you. True, the land had always given him food, but

acrid: stinging, irritating.

now food was not enough. Perhaps if he had gone to school he would have learned a different kind of wisdom, something to help him now. A schoolboy might even be able to speak convincingly to this government man whom Old Man Fat threatened to call, instead of sitting here like a clod of earth itself—Pueblo farmer indeed. What had the land to give that would restore his daughter?

45 In the days that followed, Chee herded sheep. He got up in the half-light, drank the hot coffee his mother had ready, then started the flock moving. It was necessary to drive the sheep a long way from the hogan to find good winter forage. Sometimes Chee met friends or relatives who were on their way to town or to the road camp where they hoped to get work; then there was friendly banter and an exchange of news. But most of the days seemed endless; he could not walk far enough or fast enough from his memories of the Little One or from his bitter thoughts. Sometimes it seemed his daughter trudged beside him, so real he could almost hear her footsteps—the muffled pad-pad of little feet clad in deerhide. In the glare of a snow bank he would see her vivid face, brown eyes sparkling. Mingling with the tinkle of sheep bells would be her laughter.

46 When, weary of following the small sharp hoof marks that crossed and recrossed in the snow, he sat down in the shelter of a rock, it was only to be reminded that in his thoughts he had forsaken his brotherhood with the earth and sun and growing things. If he remembered times when he had flung himself against the earth to rest, to lie there in the sun until he could no longer feel where he left off and the earth began, it was to remember also that now he sat like an alien against the same earth; the belonging-together was gone. The earth was one thing and he was another.

47 It was during the days when he herded sheep that Chee decided he must leave Little Canyon. Perhaps he would take a job silversmithing for one of the traders in town. Perhaps, even though he spoke little English, he could get a job at the road camp with his cousins; he would ask them about it.

48 Springtime transformed the mesas. The peach trees in the canyon were shedding fragrance and pink blossoms on the gentled wind. The sheep no longer foraged for the yellow seeds of chamiso but ranged near the hogan with the long-legged new lambs, eating tender young grass.

49 Chee was near the hogan on the day his cousins rode up with the message for which he waited. He had been watching with mixed emotions while his father and his sister's husband cleared the fields beside the stream.

50 "The boss at the camp says he needs an extra hand, but he wants to know if you'll be willing to go with the camp when they move it to the other side of the town." The tall cousin shifted his weight in the saddle.

51 The other cousin took up the explanation. "The work near here will last only until the new cut-off beyond Red Sands is finished. After that, the work will be too far away for you to get back here often."

52 That was what Chee had wanted—to get away from Little Canyon—yet he found himself not so interested in the job beyond town as in this new cut-off which was almost finished. He pulled a blade of grass, split it thoughtfully down the center as he asked questions of his cousins. Finally he said: "I need to think more about this. If I decide on this job I'll ride over."

53 Before his cousins were out of sight down the canyon Chee was walking toward the fields, a bold plan shaping in his mind. As the plan began to flourish, wild and hardy as young tumbleweed, Chee added his own voice softly to the song his father was singing: ". . . In the middle of the wide field . . . Yellow Corn Boy . . . I wish to put in."

54 Chee walked slowly around the field, the rich red earth yielding to his footsteps. His plan depended upon this land and upon the things he remembered most about his wife's people.

55 Through planting time Chee worked zealously and

tirelessly. He spoke little of the large new field he was planting because he felt so strongly that just now this was something between himself and the land. The first days he was ever stooping, piercing the ground with the pointed stick, placing the corn kernels there, walking around the field and through it, singing, ". . . His track leads into the ground . . . Yellow Corn Boy . . . his track leads into the ground." After that, each day Chee walked through his field watching for the tips of green to break through; first a few spikes in the center and then more and more until the corn in all parts of the field was above ground. Surely, Chee thought, if he sang the proper songs, if he cared for this land faithfully, it would not forsake him now, even though through the lonely days of winter he had betrayed the goodness of the earth in his thoughts.

56   Through the summer Chee worked long days, the sun hot upon his back, pulling weeds from around young corn plants; he planted squash and pumpkin; he terraced a small piece of land near his mother's hogan and planted carrots and onions and the moisture-loving chili. He was increasingly restless. Finally he told his family what he hoped the harvest from this land would bring him. Then the whole family waited with him, watching the corn: the slender graceful plants that waved green arms and bent to embrace each other as young winds wandered through the field, the maturing plants flaunting ° their pollen-laden tassels in the sun, the tall and sturdy parent corn with new-formed ears and a froth of purple, red and yellow corn-beards against the dusty emerald of broad leaves.

57   Summer was almost over when Chee slung the bulging packs across two pack ponies. His mother helped him tie the heavy rolled pack behind the saddle of the buckskin. Chee knotted the new yellow kerchief about his neck a little tighter, gave the broad black hat brim an extra tug, but these were only gestures of assurance and he knew it. The land had not failed him. That part was done. But this he was riding into? Who could tell?

flaunting: displaying.

58   When Chee arrived at Red Sands, it was as he had expected to find it—no cars on the highway. His cousins had told him that even the Pueblo farmers were using the new cut-off to town. The barren gravel around the Red Sands Trading Post was deserted. A sign banged against the dismantled gas pumps *Closed until further notice.*

59   Old Man Fat came from the crude summer shelter built beside the log hogan from a few branches of scrub cedar and the sides of wooden crates. He seemed almost friendly when he saw Chee.

60   "Get down, my son," he said, eyeing the bulging packs. There was no bluster in his voice today and his face sagged, looking somewhat saddened; perhaps because his cheeks were no longer quite full enough to push his eyes upward at the corners. "You are going on a journey?"

61   Chee shook his head. "Our fields gave us so much this year, I thought to sell or trade this to the trader. I didn't know he was no longer here."

62   Old Man Fat sighed, his voice dropping to an injured tone. "He says he and his wife are going to rest this winter; then after that he'll build a place up on the new highway."

63   Chee moved as though to be traveling on, then jerked his head toward the pack ponies. "Anything you need?"

64   "I'll ask my wife," Old Man Fat said as he led the way to the shelter. "Maybe she has a little money. Things have not been too good with us since the trader closed. Only a few tourists come this way." He shrugged his shoulders. "And with the trade gone—no credit."

65   Chee was not deceived by his father-in-law's unexpected confidences. He recognized them as a hopeful bid for sympathy and, if possible, something for nothing. Chee made no answer. He was thinking that so far he had been right about his wife's parents: their thriftlessness had left them with no resources to last until Old Man Fat found another easy way of making a living.

66   Old Man Fat's Wife was in the shelter working at her loom. She turned rather wearily when her husband asked with noticeable deference if she would give him money to buy supplies. Chee surmised that the only income here was from his mother-in-law's weaving.

67   She peered around the corner of the shelter at the laden ponies, and then she looked at Chee. "What do you have there, my son?"

68   Chee smiled to himself as he turned to pull the pack from one of the ponies, dragged it to the shelter where he untied the ropes. Pumpkins and hardshelled squash tumbled out, and the ears of corn—pale yellow husks fitting firmly over plump ripe kernels, blue corn, red corn, yellow corn, many-colored corn, ears and ears of it—tumbled into every corner of the shelter.

69   "Yooooh," Old Man Fat's Wife exclaimed as she took some of the ears in her hands. Then she glanced up at her son-in-law. "But we have no money for all this. We have sold almost everything we own—even the brass bed that stood in the hogan."

70   Old Man Fat's brass bed. Chee concealed his amusement as he started back for another pack. That must have been a hard parting. Then he stopped, for, coming from the cool darkness of the hogan was the Little One, rubbing her eyes as though she had been asleep. She stood for a moment in the doorway and Chee saw that she was dirty, barefoot, her hair uncombed, her little blouse shorn of all its silver buttons. Then she ran toward Chee, her arms outstretched. Heedless of Old Man Fat and his wife, her father caught her in his arms, her hair falling in a dark cloud across his face, the sweetness of her laughter warm against his shoulder.

71   It was the haste within him to get this slow waiting game played through to the finish that made Chee speak unwisely. It was the desire to swing her before him in the saddle and ride fast to Little Canyon that prompted his words. "The money doesn't matter. You still have something. . . ."

72   Chee knew immediately that he had overspoken. The old woman looked from him to the corn spread before her. Unfriendliness began to harden in his father-in-law's face. All the old arguments between himself and his wife's people came pushing and crowding in between them now.

73   Old Man Fat began kicking the ears of corn back onto the canvas as he eyed Chee angrily. "And you rode all the way over here thinking that for a little food we would give up our daughter's daughter?"

74   Chee did not wait for the old man to reach for the Little One. He walked dazedly to the shelter, rubbing his cheek against her soft dark hair and put her gently into her grandmother's lap. Then he turned back to the horses. He had failed. By his own haste he had failed. He swung into the saddle, his hand touching the roll behind it. Should he ride on into town?

75   Then he dismounted, scarcely glancing at Old Man Fat, who stood uncertainly at the corner of the shelter, listening to his wife. "Give me a hand with this other pack of corn, Grandfather," Chee said, carefully keeping the small bit of hope from his voice.

76   Puzzled, but willing, Old Man Fat helped carry the other pack to the shelter, opening it to find more corn as well as carrots and round pale yellow onions. Chee went back for the roll behind the buckskin's saddle and carried it to the entrance of the shelter where he cut the ropes and gave the canvas a nudge with his toe. Tins of coffee rolled out, small plump cloth bags; jerked meat from several butcherings spilled from a flour sack, and bright red chilis splashed like flames against the dust.

77   "I will leave all this anyhow," Chee told them. "I would not want my daughter nor even you old people to go hungry."

78   Old Man Fat picked up a shiny tin of coffee, then put it down. With trembling hands he began to untie one of the cloth bags—dried sweet peaches.

79   The Little One had wriggled from her grandmother's lap, unheeded, and was on her knees, digging her hands into the jerked meat.

80   "There is almost enough food here to last all winter." Old Man Fat's Wife sought the eyes of her husband.

81   Chee said, "I meant it to be enough. But that was

when I thought you might send the Little One back with me." He looked down at his daughter noisily sucking jerky. Her mouth, both fists, were full of it. "I am sorry that you feel you cannot bear to part with her."

82 Old Man Fat's Wife brushed a straggly wisp of gray hair from her forehead as she turned to look at the Little One. Old Man Fat was looking too. And it was not a thing to see. For in that moment the Little One ceased to be their daughter's daughter and became just another mouth to feed.

83 "And why not?" the old woman asked wearily.

84 Chee was settled in the saddle, the barefooted Little One before him. He urged the buckskin faster, and his daughter clutched his shirtfront. The purpling mesas flung back the echo: ". . . My corn embrace each other. In the middle of the wide field . . . Yellow Corn Boy embrace each other."

ANALYSIS

Eudora Welty's and James Joyce's stories (pages 541 and 530) describe the interior life of a character. Platero and Miller, on the other hand, are more interested in plot ° and in the solution to a conflict. They tell us much about Chee's thoughts and emotional reactions, but our major interest is in the outcome of the plot: we want to know what is going to happen to Chee's daughter.

That plot will be important is revealed immediately with the opening words: "The hat told the *story* . . ." By the time we've finished paragraph 12, we know part of the "story" that is revealed by the "drooping Stetson."

The story assumes more tragic proportions in paragraphs 13–15 when Chee realizes that his daughter is gone. The dimensions of the conflict are extended when Chee speaks in paragraph 17: "Custom! When did my wife's parents begin thinking about custom?" To the personal conflict (Chee versus his wife's parents for custody of Little One) is added a cultural clash: Navaho custom versus the "new ways."

plot: See Glossary.

The conflict deepens even more when (paragraph 46) Chee becomes aware that he is separated not only from his child, but also from his land ("the belonging-together was gone. The earth was one thing and he was another.").

The rest of the story tells how these conflicts are resolved. The narrators don't tell us everything at once. They create suspense, making us wonder if this plot will end tragically or happily. A hint of change in Chee comes as winter turns to spring. In paragraph 52 something important happens. In a sentence we might skip if we were going too fast, we read: ". . . he found himself not so interested in the job . . . as in this new cut-off . . ."

By the story's end, readers might feel like rejoicing themselves, a reaction often produced by stories that have a happy ending after we feared a tragic one. Chee is with his daughter. His corn flourishes and "embraces," just as Chee embraces Little One. Even Old Man Fat and his wife are not excluded from the general happiness, as they are left with a feast that will carry them through the next winter.

Questions on Content

1. What kind of man is Chee's father-in-law?
2. What reason does Old Man Fat give for taking Little One? What is his real reason? (Hinted at in paragraph 25)
3. Why did Chee's first attempt to recover Little One fail?
4. Why was Chee interested in the new cut-off of the road beyond the Red Sands?
5. How did Chee succeed in his second attempt?
6. How does the land also triumph over "trade" or "business" at the end of this story?

Add to Your Vocabulary

indolence, acrid, flaunt.

Questions on Technique

1. "Land did not cheat!" Chee thinks this as the story

opens. Why did the authors add this and other details relating to the earth and its products? In other words, how do these details function as part of the plot?

2. We do not know why Chee is sad until paragraph 8. How does this narrative technique affect your interest in the story?

3. In what other ways could the narrators have organized this material?

4. The narrators devote some paragraphs to a description of where Chee lives, and in paragraphs 21–24 they describe the Trading Post. How do the two descriptions contrast? Which place do they want you, as reader, to feel is a more desirable home? Explain.

5. Chee is amused at the thought of Old Man Fat's brass bed, though we are not told explicitly why. How does this detail relate to one of the conflicts in the story?

Techniques to Imitate

Including small details that give reality to a story

Competent writers of narrative give reality to a story by including a great many small details. Through these details readers get a clear idea of the setting, the characters, and the action. For example, when Chee enters the hogan early in the story, the authors might have written just, "Chee entered the hogan." But, while this bald statement of a fact tells us what happened, it does not give us any details to help us fully experience the happening. What the authors actually wrote is, "He passed his mother's deserted loom on the south side of the hogan and *pulled the rude wooden door toward him, bowing his head, hunching his shoulders to get inside.*" By means of the italicized details, the authors tell us that the hogan is a crudely built structure ("rude wooden door"), that its doorway is low and probably narrow. Chee had to "hunch" his shoulders.

The smooth inclusion of small details in this way is a different technique from the writing of long passages of description which most stories also contain. It is a technique worth imitating in your own narrative writing.

Here are some other examples. Instead of telling us simply that the wind was plucking at Little One's blouse and skirt, the authors tell us that it was a "*new purple* blouse and *wide green* skirt." Instead of saying, "Old Man Fat walked across the lot," they say, he "walked *heavily* across the *gravelled* lot."

In the following sentences taken from the story, the details are italicized.

"Chee walked slowly around the field, *the rich red earth yielding to his footsteps*."

"Through the summer Chee worked long days, *the sun hot upon his back*, pulling weeds from around young corn plants..."

"Chee knotted the *new yellow* kerchief about his neck a little tighter, gave the *broad black* hat brim an extra tug..."

"Old Man Fat came from the *crude* summer shelter built beside the log hogan *from a few branches of scrub cedar and the sides of wooden crates*."

Suggestions for Writing

1. Write a narrative about a series of events that revolve around one character. Narrate these events from a third person point of view. Choose a limited period of time. A possibility would be to follow one character around your town, or locale, for a single typical morning. If you think it would add to the effect you want to create, you could also reveal your character's thoughts, just as these authors reveal Chee's thoughts.

2. These authors use small but effective descriptive details as they narrate what Chee does from the time he appears in the story (paragraph 1) to the time he enters his hogan (paragraph 6). In 200 words narrate what you do on your way *to* your home and on your way *into* your home. Use descriptive details to add reality to the narration. Write the narrative from the third person point of view.

3. This story is told almost exclusively from the perspective of Chee, although the third person point of view is

used. Narrate the scene at the Trading Post (paragraphs 24–41) from Little One's point of view. Use small details as you describe the setting and narrate what happens, but tell everything as though it is seen through the child's eyes. Use the third person pronoun.

12

NARRATIVE AND CHARACTERIZATION

KATHERINE MANSFIELD

Miss Brill

Katherine Mansfield Beauchamp was born in New Zealand but went to Queen's College, London, for her education. With John Middleton Murry, whom she married in 1913, and the novelist D. H. Lawrence, she founded a literary review. Success with her own writing came slowly. Not until 1920, three years before her death, did a volume called *Bliss and Other Stories* bring her the acclaim that was her due. *The Garden Party* (1922) and *The Doves' Nest* (1923) established her reputation as one of the most important short-story writers of the twentieth century.

In discussing types of fiction, we frequently speak of a "*New Yorker* story," meaning a brief sketch with ordinary but sensitive characters, perceptive dialogue, and understated theme, and without strong plot or climax.° Three authors might be said to be the models for this kind of fiction: Anton Chekhov, the nineteenth-century Russian doctor who wrote of frustrated middle-class lives in the Russian provinces; James Joyce, the Irish exile who wrote all his life about middle-class Dubliners; and Katherine Mansfield. Irony and pathos are terms that recur in criticism of their work. By "irony" we mean, here, a

theme, plot, climax: See Glossary.

result that is the opposite of what is expected or considered appropriate. By "pathos" we mean simply the
sense of pity. You will want to consider whether either
applies to "Miss Brill."

1   Although it was so bril-
liantly fine—the blue sky powdered with gold and great
spots of light like white wine splashed over the Jardins
Publiques °—Miss Brill was glad that she had decided on
her fur. The air was motionless, but when you opened your
mouth there was just a faint chill, like a chill from a glass
of iced water before you sip, and now and again a leaf
came drifting—from nowhere, from the sky. Miss Brill put
up her hand and touched her fur. Dear little thing! It was
nice to feel it again. She had taken it out of its box that
afternoon, shaken out the moth powder, given it a good
brush, and rubbed the life back into the dim little eyes.
"What has been happening to me?" said the sad little eyes.
Oh, how sweet it was to see them snap at her again from
the red eiderdown! ° . . . But the nose, which was of
some black composition, wasn't at all firm. It must have
had a knock, somehow. Never mind—a little dab of black
sealing wax when the time came—when it was absolutely
necessary. . . . Little rogue! Yes, she really felt like that
about it. Little rogue biting its tail just by her left ear. She
could have taken it off and laid it on her lap and stroked
it. She felt a tingling in her hands and arms, but that came
from walking, she supposed. And when she breathed, something light and sad—no, not sad, exactly—something gentle
seemed to move in her bosom.

2   There were a number of people out this afternoon, far
more than last Sunday. And the band sounded louder and
gayer. That was because the Season had begun. For although the band played all the year round on Sundays, out
of season it was never the same. It was like some one playing with only the family to listen; it didn't care how it played

Jardins Publiques: public gardens.
eiderdown: a quilt filled with duck feathers.

if there weren't any strangers present. Wasn't the conductor wearing a new coat, too? She was sure it was new. He scraped with his foot and flapped his arms like a rooster about to crow, and the bandsmen sitting in the green rotunda blew out their cheeks and glared at the music. Now there came a little "flutey" bit—very pretty!—a little chain of bright drops. She was sure it would be repeated. It was; she lifted her head and smiled.

3 Only two people shared her "special" seat: a fine old man in a velvet coat, his hands clasped over a huge carved walking-stick, and a big old woman, sitting upright, with a roll of knitting on her embroidered apron. They did not speak. This was disappointing, for Miss Brill always looked forward to the conversation. She had become really quite expert, she thought, at listening as though she didn't listen, at sitting in other people's lives just for a minute while they talked round her.

4 She glanced, sideways, at the old couple. Perhaps they would go soon. Last Sunday, too, hadn't been as interesting as usual. An Englishman and his wife, he wearing a dreadful Panama hat and she button boots. And she'd gone on the whole time about how she ought to wear spectacles; she knew she needed them; but that it was no good getting any; they'd be sure to break and they'd never keep on. And he'd been so patient. He'd suggested everything—gold rims, the kind that curved round your ears, little pads inside the bridge. No, nothing would please her. "They'll always be sliding down my nose!" Miss Brill had wanted to shake her.

5 The old people sat on the bench, still as statues. Never mind, there was always the crowd to watch. To and fro, in front of the flowerbeds and the band rotunda, the couples and groups paraded, stopped to talk, to greet, to buy a handful of flowers from the old beggar who had his tray fixed to the railings. Little children ran among them, swooping and laughing; little boys with big white silk bows under their chins, little girls, little French dolls, dressed up in velvet and lace. And sometimes a tiny staggerer came suddenly rocking into the open from under the trees, stopped, stared, as suddenly sat down "flop," until its small

high-stepping mother, like a young hen, rushed scolding to its rescue. Other people sat on the benches and green chairs, but they were nearly always the same, Sunday after Sunday, and—Miss Brill had often noticed—there was something funny about nearly all of them. They were odd, silent, nearly all old, and from the way they stared they looked as though they'd just come from dark little rooms or even—even cupboards!

6   Behind the rotunda the slender trees with yellow leaves down drooping, and through them just a line of sea, and beyond the blue sky with gold-veined clouds.

7   Tum-tum-tum tiddle-um! tiddle-um! tum tiddley-um tum ta! blew the band.

8   Two young girls in red came by and two young soldiers in blue met them, and they laughed and paired and went off arm-in-arm. Two peasant women with funny straw hats passed, gravely, leading beautiful smoke-colored donkeys. A cold, pale nun hurried by. A beautiful woman came along and dropped her bunch of violets, and a little boy ran after to hand them to her, and she took them and threw them away as if they'd been poisoned. Dear me! Miss Brill didn't know whether to admire that or not! And now an ermine toque ° and a gentleman in grey met just in front of her. He was tall, stiff, dignified, and she was wearing the ermine toque she'd bought when her hair was yellow. Now everything, her hair, her face, even her eyes, was the same color as the shabby ermine, and her hand, in its cleaned glove, lifted to dab her lips, was a tiny yellowish paw. Oh, she was so pleased to see him—delighted! She rather thought they were going to meet that afternoon. She described where she'd been—everywhere, here, there, along by the sea. The day was so charming—didn't he agree? And wouldn't he, perhaps? . . . But he shook his head, lighted a cigarette, slowly breathed a great deep puff into her face, and even while she was still talking and laughing, flicked the match away and walked on. The ermine toque was alone; she smiled more brightly than ever. But even the band seemed to know what she was feeling and played

toque: a brimless, close-fitting hat.

more softly, played tenderly, and the drum beat, "The Brute! The Brute!" over and over. What would she do? What was going to happen now? But as Miss Brill wondered, the ermine toque turned, raised her hand as though she'd seen some one else, much nicer, just over there, and pattered away. And the band changed again and played more quickly, more gaily than ever, and the old couple on Miss Brill's seat got up and marched away, and such a funny old man with long whiskers hobbled along in time to the music and was nearly knocked over by four girls walking abreast.

9   Oh, how fascinating it was! How she enjoyed it! How she loved sitting here, watching it all! It was like a play. It was exactly like a play. Who could believe the sky at the back wasn't painted? But it wasn't till a little brown dog trotted on solemn and then slowly trotted off, like a little "theater" dog, a little dog that had been drugged, that Miss Brill discovered what it was that made it so exciting. They were all on the stage. They weren't only the audience, not only looking on; they were acting. Even she had a part and came every Sunday. No doubt somebody would have noticed if she hadn't been there; she was part of the performance after all. How strange she'd never thought of it like that before! And yet it explained why she made such a point of starting from home at just the same time each week—so as not to be late for the performance—and it also explained why she had quite a queer, shy feeling at telling her English pupils how she spent her Sunday afternoons. No wonder! Miss Brill nearly laughed out loud. She was on the stage. She thought of the old invalid gentleman to whom she read the newspaper four afternoons a week while he slept in the garden. She had got quite used to the frail head on the cotton pillow, the hollowed eyes, the open mouth and the high pinched nose. If he'd been dead she mightn't have noticed for weeks; she wouldn't have minded. But suddenly he knew he was having the paper read to him by an actress! "An actress!" The old head lifted; two points of light quivered in the old eyes. "An actress—are ye?" And Miss Brill smoothed the newspaper as though it were

the manuscript of her part and said gently: "Yes, I have been an actress for a long time."

10   The band had been having a rest. Now they started again. And what they played was warm, sunny, yet there was just a faint chill—a something, what was it?—not sadness—no, not sadness—a something that made you want to sing. The tune lifted, lifted, the light shone; and it seemed to Miss Brill that in another moment all of them, all the whole company, would begin singing. The young ones, the laughing ones who were moving together, they would begin, and the men's voices, very resolute and brave, would join them. And then she too, she too, and the others on the benches—they would come in with a kind of accompaniment—something low, that scarcely rose or fell, something so beautiful—moving. . . . And Miss Brill's eyes filled with tears and she looked smiling at all the other members of the company. Yes, we understand, we understand, she thought—though what they understood she didn't know.

11   Just at that moment a boy and a girl came and sat down where the old couple had been. They were beautifully dressed; they were in love. The hero and heroine, of course, just arrived from his father's yacht. And still soundlessly singing, still with that trembling smile, Miss Brill prepared to listen.

12   "No, not now," said the girl. "Not here, I can't."

13   "But why? Because of that stupid old thing at the end there?" asked the boy. "Why does she come here at all—who wants her? Why doesn't she keep her silly old mug at home?"

14   "It's her fu-fur which is so funny," giggled the girl. "It's exactly like a fried whiting." °

15   "Ah, be off with you!" said the boy in an angry whisper. Then: "Tell me, ma petite chère——" °

16   "No, not here," said the girl. "Not *yet*."

.   .   .   .   .   .

17   On her way home she usually bought a slice of honey

whiting: a European fish of the cod family.
ma petite chère——: my little dear.

cake at the baker's. It was her Sunday treat. Sometimes there was an almond in her slice, sometimes not. It made a great difference. If there was an almond it was like carrying home a tiny present—a surprise—something that might very well not have been there. She hurried on the almond Sundays and struck the match for the kettle in quite a dashing way.

18   But today she passed the baker's by, climbed the stairs, went into the little dark room—her room like a cupboard—and sat down on the red eiderdown. She sat there for a long time. The box that the fur came out of was on the bed. She unclasped the necklet quickly; quickly, without looking, laid it inside. But when she put the lid on she thought she heard something crying.

ANALYSIS

Though her method is subtle, Mansfield's story is easy reading. She uses many sensitive strokes in this portrait, and the play of light on them illuminates every detail. The climax, if we can call it that, is so openly and deftly arrived at that it wants nothing more than careful reading. Let us look chiefly at her diction, that is, her choice of words. In this way we can watch an artist at work.

Rather than tell us *about* Miss Brill, she puts her into action. She *shows* us this woman on a Sunday afternoon in the park. "Jardins Publiques" at once suggests France; Miss Brill is a stranger here. There is a "faint chill" in the air and (we are still in paragraph 1) "something light and sad—no, not sad, exactly—something gentle" moves her. Keep these words "chill" and "sad" in mind. By the end of the story we might want to say that something cold and ungentle and decidedly sad happens to this lady. But we anticipate. We read, in paragraph 1, a description of the fur, the "dear little thing," with its "dim little eyes" and ·a nose that "must have had a knock, somehow." Will the fur have something to do with the action, we might ask.

Paragraph 2 tells us the "Season" has begun. This is a kind of "first Sunday" in her weekly ritual, not "opening

night" but "opening matinee." Everything is gay and bright.
The flute notes are "a little chain of bright drops." The
band seems to be playing for her. Paragraphs 3 and 4 plant
the idea that Miss Brill is accustomed to hearing all the conversations around her, "listening as though she didn't
listen." Eavesdropping is her vicarious pleasure, her substitute for the real thing. Paragraph 5 suggests that she also
judges her park companions. The young mother is "like a
young hen." The "other people" are "odd, silent, nearly all
old." They look "as though they'd just come from dark
little rooms or even—even cupboards!" "Cupboards" is
another planted word. Mansfield will use it again.

Paragraph 8 introduces what, with hindsight, we could
call a "parallel" character. She has no name. Mansfield
calls her "the ermine toque" and notes that the hat was
bought "when her hair was yellow." She and her hat are
old. Her hand is a "paw" dabbing her lips. Her friend is
rude to her. He breathes slowly (the adverb makes it ruder)
"a great deep puff [of smoke] into her face." The "ermine
toque" smiles at the offense. But does "smiled more brightly
than ever" suggest the alternative to crying? What would
Miss Brill have done? We will have a chance to hear when
a "parallel" action happens to her. The overheard conversation (paragraphs 12–16) will come like a "puff of
smoke" in her face.

Paragraph 9 uses a natural simile: ° sitting in the park
is like playing a role on stage. "Yes," Miss Brill hears herself saying to her invalid friend, "I have been an actress for
a long time." Paragraph 10 extends the simile. It seems as
though they would all sing together, they would all understand. But a "something, what [is] it?" creeps in. Again
the "faint chill" appears. And later she has more doubts:
"Yes, we understand, we understand, she thought—though
what they understood she didn't know."

With paragraph 11 the "hero and heroine" come on
stage. They are no hero and heroine, of course. Calling
them that is part of Miss Brill's make-believe world.

simile: See Glossary.

Reality, when it appears, comes crashing in: "her silly old mug," "fu-fur which is so funny," "like a fried whiting." Mansfield has chosen these words carefully. They are cruel but apt. They are words that come naturally to a young boy and girl. And Miss Brill, who (as paragraph 3 told us) "had become really quite expert at listening," hears every one.

What next? Taking these cues, reread paragraphs 17 and 18; then finish the analysis. Is Miss Brill on stage now? Can she accept her role or is life *not* a play? What has honey cake to do with sorrow? You will want to raise and answer several other questions.

Questions on Content

1. Why does Mansfield not tell us exactly in what city or country this story occurs? Does it matter that Miss Brill is a stranger here?
2. What makes where Miss Brill sits in the park her "special" seat?
3. What details (and how far along in the story) do we hear about Miss Brill's occupation?

Questions on Technique

1. Mansfield has Miss Brill talk *about* conversation she hears, but she does not record any before paragraph 12. Why do you suppose she waits so long?
2. How does Mansfield employ the band and its music throughout the story?
3. In how much detail are the other visitors to the park described? What details do you find especially effective?
4. Between paragraphs 16 and 17, Mansfield makes a decided break in the narrative. Why is it necessary to get Miss Brill back to her room?

Techniques to Imitate

Revealing a character through his or her thoughts

Note, to begin with, that Mansfield follows carefully the primary rule of narrative writing that we discussed in connection with Welty's story: Show, don't tell. Instead of using an essay technique and *telling about* Miss Brill's position in life, her personality, her interests, and her attitude toward the life around her, Mansfield *shows* her to us. By detailing for us her actions and thoughts for an hour on Sunday afternoon, Mansfield lets us see for ourselves what kind of person Miss Brill is. Instead of *telling* us that Miss Brill lives the tragically barren life of a lonely and aging person, she conveys the idea by *showing* her living a brief moment of that life. She does not *tell* us that Miss Brill rather pathetically tries to compensate for the barrenness of her existence by sharing imaginatively the lives of others and by romanticizing her own drab role; she *shows* her doing these things. We will remember Miss Brill much better for having watched her for an afternoon than we would remember her if we had only heard about her.

A second narrative technique Mansfield demonstrates here is a skillful method of letting the reader share a character's thoughts. She uses the method so skillfully, in fact, that we are never aware of when the story shifts from the author's description to Miss Brill's own thoughts. We simply know that we are readng her thoughts most of the time. A few examples will make this clear, showing how at one point Mansfield may be looking on from the outside and then at the next moment giving Miss Brill's thoughts from the inside, so to speak. We have italicized the thoughts. "Miss Brill put up her hand and touched her fur. *Dear little thing. It was nice to feel it again. . . .*"

"They did not speak. This was disappointing, for Miss Brill always looked forward to the conversation. *She had become really quite expert,* she thought, *at listening as though she didn't listen, at sitting in other people's lives just for a minute while they talked round her.*"

"She glanced sideways at the old couple. *Perhaps they would go soon.*"

"Other people sat on the benches and green chairs, but

they were nearly always the same Sunday after Sunday, and—Miss Brill had often noticed—*there was something funny about nearly all of them. They were odd, silent, nearly all old, and from the way they stared they looked as though they'd just come from dark little rooms or even— even cupboards!*"

The technique is subtle, hardly noticeable, as it should be. Sometimes she says, parenthetically, "she thought" or "Miss Brill had often noticed," but far more often she shifts easily and directly from her objective statements as a storyteller to the subjective thoughts in the mind of her character.

In your narrative writing you should, like Welty and Mansfield, *show* actions and characters instead of merely *telling about* them. You may wish also to try Mansfield's technique for revealing a character through the character's thoughts.

Suggestions for Writing

1. Rewrite this story making it an American park and making the main character a young girl or boy who is lonely or unhappy or worried with indecision.
2. Narrate an imaginary incident involving an overheard telephone conversation. You can hear, however, only one half of the conversation. As author, you will have to have your main character imagining the rest.
3. From your own experience, narrate an incident that involved one or more of the following: mistaken identity, eavesdropping, sudden change of mood, a meeting in a park or on the boardwalk, a quarrel between two people observed at a distance. Keep the story in the third person.
4. Write a short story emphasizing one emotion—fear, happiness, hate, pleasure.

13

NARRATIVE AND THEME

WALTER VAN TILBURG CLARK

The Portable Phonograph

We come now to one of the most disturbing short stories of the last few decades. In 1941, Walter Van Tilburg Clark was so moved by newspaper headlines full of war and destruction that, in order to dispel his emotions, he began writing this story. It was published that fall. In 1945, the world witnessed the first military use of an atomic bomb, over Hiroshima and Nagasaki. The destruction was so enormous that we faced for the first time, in what is now called the Atomic Age, the possibility of wiping ourselves off the face of the earth. The apprehension that Clark says he had felt in 1941 had multiplied tenfold.

Clark published *The Ox-Bow Incident* in 1940 and two other novels before his death in 1971. He knew that if he wanted to capture a universality of apprehension for other generations to ponder over he would have to project it through human beings in action, through a meaningful incident. It would not suffice to talk about the end of the world. "One cannot afford," he wrote later, "to speak seriously of the end of the world." One could *suggest* it, however, pictorially, in a fiction that would lie close to truth. "I just began to write," he says. "I can't remember exactly what set me off. . . . In this case

it was the prairie, the vast, desolated backdrop of the dugout, which first appeared, accompanied by a feeling that such a scene implied in itself all that one could afford to say directly about a final war." His theme °
is the human fight for survival. His method is narration. Watch how he slowly develops one through the other.

1   The red sunset, with narrow, black cloud strips like threats across it, lay on the curved horizon of the prairie. The air was still and cold, and in it settled the mute darkness and greater cold of night. High in the air there was wind, for through the veil of the dusk the clouds could be seen gliding rapidly south and changing shapes. A queer sensation of torment, of two-sided, unpredictable nature, arose from the stillness of the earth air beneath the violence of the upper air. Out of the sunset, through the dead, matted grass and isolated weed stalks of the prairie, crept the narrow and deeply rutted remains of a road. In the road, in places, there were crusts of shallow, brittle ice. There were little islands of an old oiled pavement in the road too, but most of it was mud, now frozen rigid. The frozen mud still bore the toothed impress of great tanks, and a wanderer on the neighboring undulations ° might have stumbled, in this light, into large, partially filled-in and weed-grown cavities, their banks channelled and beginning to spread into badlands. These pits were such as might have been made by falling meteors, but they were not. They were the scars of gigantic bombs, their rawness already made a little natural by rain, seed, and time. Along the road, there were rakish * remnants of fence. There was also, just visible, one portion of tangled and multiple barbed wire still erect, behind which was a shelving ditch with small caves, now very quiet and empty, at intervals in its back wall. Otherwise there was no structure or remnant of a structure visible over the dome of the darkling earth, but only, in sheltered hollows, the darker shadows of young trees trying again.

theme: See Glossary.
undulations: wavelike curves or elevations.

2   Under the wuthering ° arch of the high wind a V of
wild geese fled south. The rush of their pinions ° sounded
briefly, and the faint, plaintive notes of their expeditionary
talk. Then they left a still greater vacancy. There was the
smell and expectation of snow, as there is likely to be when
the wild geese fly south. From the remote distance, toward
the red sky, came faintly the protracted howl and quick
yap-yap of a prairie wolf.

3   North of the road, perhaps a hundred yards, lay the
parallel and deeply intrenched course of a small creek,
lined with leafless alders ° and willows. The creek was
already silent under ice. Into the bank above it was dug a
sort of cell, with a single opening, like the mouth of a mine
tunnel. Within the cell there was a little red of fire, which
showed dully through the opening, like a reflection or a
deception of the imagination. The light came from the
chary burning of four blocks of poorly aged peat,° which
gave off a petty warmth and much acrid ° smoke. But the
precious remnants of wood, old fence posts and timbers
from the long-deserted dugouts, had to be saved for the
real cold, for the time when a man's breath blew white,
the moisture in his nostrils stiffened at once when he
stepped out, and the expansive blizzards paraded for days
over the vast open, swirling and settling and thickening,
till the dawn of the cleared day when the sky was thin blue-
green and the terrible cold, in which a man could not live
for three hours unwarmed, lay over the uniformly drifted
swell of the plain.

4   Around the smoldering peat, four men were seated
cross-legged. Behind them, traversed by their shadows, was
the earth bench, with two old and dirty army blankets,

wuthering: a provincial adjective from Yorkshire, England, meaning hostile, fierce, tumultuous.

pinions: terminal sections of a bird's wings.

alders: shrubs or trees similar to the birch, of the family *Betu-
laceae,* genus *Alnus.*

peat: a soil of partially decomposed vegetable matter which is
drained, cultivated, cut, and then dried for fuel.

acrid: stinging, irritating.

where the owner of the cell slept. In a niche in the opposite wall were a few tin utensils which caught the glint of the coals. The host was rewrapping in a piece of daubed °burlap four fine, leather-bound books. He worked slowly and very carefully, and at last tied the bundle securely with a piece of grass-woven cord. The other three looked intently upon the process, as if a great significance lay in it. As the host tied the cord, he spoke. He was an old man, his long, matted beard and hair gray to nearly white. The shadows made his brows and cheekbones appear gnarled, his eyes and cheeks deeply sunken. His big hands, rough with frost and swollen by rheumatism, were awkward but gentle at their task. He was like a prehistoric priest performing a fateful ceremonial rite. Also his voice had in it a suitable quality of deep, reverent despair, yet perhaps at the moment, a sharpness of selfish satisfaction.

5   "When I perceived what was happening," he said, "I told myself, 'It is the end. I cannot take much; I will take these.'

6   "Perhaps I was impractical," he continued. "But for myself, I do not regret, and what do we know of those who will come after us? We are the doddering remnant of a race of mechanical fools. I have saved what I love; the soul of what was good in us is here; perhaps the new ones will make a strong enough beginning not to fall behind when they become clever."

7   He rose with slow pain and placed the wrapped volumes in the niche with his utensils. The others watched him with the same ritualistic gaze.

8   "Shakespeare, the Bible, *Moby-Dick,*° the *Divine Comedy,*" ° one of them said softly. "You might have done worse, much worse."

---

daubed: covered over with mud or paste.

Moby-Dick: an American novel (1851) written by Herman Melville. Moby Dick is an elusive white whale.

Divine Comedy: an epic poem by Dante Alighieri, divided into three parts: *Inferno* (1300), *Purgatory* (1308), and *Paradise* (1311).

9 "You will have a little soul left until you die," said another harshly. "That is more than is true of us. My brain becomes thick, like my hands." He held the big, battered hands, with their black nails, in the glow to be seen.

10 "I want paper to write on," he said. "And there is none."

11 The fourth man said nothing. He sat in the shadow farthest from the fire, and sometimes his body jerked in its rags from the cold. Although he was still young, he was sick and coughed often. Writing implied a greater future than he now felt able to consider.

12 The old man seated himself laboriously, and reached out, groaning at the movement, to put another block of peat on the fire. With bowed heads and averted eyes, his three guests acknowledged his magnanimity.

13 "We thank you, Doctor Jenkins, for the reading," said the man who had named the books.

14 They seemed then to be waiting for something. Doctor Jenkins understood, but was loath to comply. In an ordinary moment he would have said nothing. But the words of *The Tempest,*° which he had been reading, and the religious attention of the three made this an unusual occasion.

15 "You wish to hear the phonograph," he said grudgingly.

16 The two middle-aged men stared into the fire, unable to formulate and expose the enormity of their desire.

17 The young man, however, said anxiously, between suppressed coughs, "Oh, please," like an excited child.

18 The old man rose again in his difficult way, and went to the back of the cell. He returned and placed tenderly upon the packed floor, where the firelight might fall upon it, an old portable phonograph in a black case. He smoothed the top with his hand, and then opened it. The lovely green-felt-covered disk became visible.

19 "I have been using thorns as needles," he said. "But tonight, because we have a musician among us"—he bent

The Tempest: Shakespeare's last comedy (1611). It takes place on an island.

his head to the young man, almost invisible in the shadow —"I will use a steel needle. There are only three left."

20 The two middle-aged men stared at him in speechless adoration. The one with the big hands, who wanted to write, moved his lips, but the whisper was not audible.

21 "Oh, don't!" cried the young man, as if he were hurt. "The thorns will do beautifully."

22 "No," the old man said. "I have become accustomed to the thorns, but they are not really good. For you, my young friend, we will have good music tonight.

23 "After all," he added generously, and beginning to wind the phonograph, which creaked, "they can't last forever."

24 "No, nor we," the man who needed to write said harshly. "The needle, by all means."

25 "Oh, thanks," said the young man. "Thanks," he said again in a low, excited voice, and then stifled his coughing with a bowed head.

26 "The records, though," said the old man when he had finished winding, "are a different matter. Already they are very worn. I do not play them more than once a week. One, once a week, that is what I allow myself.

27 "More than a week I cannot stand it; not to hear them," he apologized.

28 "No, how could you?" cried the young man. "And with them here like this."

29 "A man can stand anything," said the man who wanted to write, in his harsh, antagonistic voice.

30 "Please, the music," said the young man.

31 "Only the one," said the old man. "In the long run, we will remember more that way."

32 He had a dozen records with luxuriant gold and red seals. Even in that light the others could see that the threads of the records were becoming worn. Slowly he read out the titles and the tremendous, dead names of the composers and the artists and the orchestras. The three worked upon the names in their minds, carefully. It was difficult to select from such a wealth what they would at once most

like to remember. Finally, the man who wanted to write named Gershwin's "New York." °

33 "Oh, no," cried the sick young man, and then could say nothing more because he had to cough. The others understood him, and the harsh man withdrew his selection and waited for the musician to choose.

34 The musician begged Doctor Jenkins to read the titles again, very slowly, so that he could remember the sounds. While they were read, he lay back against the wall, his eyes closed, his thin, horny hand pulling at his light beard, and listened to the voices and the orchestras and the single instruments in his mind.

35 When the reading was done he spoke despairingly. "I have forgotten," he complained; "I cannot hear them clearly.

36 "There are things missing," he explained.

37 "I know," said Doctor Jenkins. "I thought that I knew all of Shelley ° by heart. I should have brought Shelley."

38 "That's more soul than we can use," said the harsh man. "*Moby-Dick* is better.

39 "We can understand that," he emphasized.

40 The Doctor nodded.

41 "Still," said the man who had admired the books, "we need the absolute if we are to keep a grasp on anything.

42 "Anything but these sticks and peat clods and rabbit snares," he said bitterly.

43 "Shelley desired an ultimate absolute," said the harsh man. "It's too much," he said. "It's no good; no earthly good."

Gershwin's "New York": George Gershwin (1898–1937), American composer, played his "Second Rhapsody for Orchestra with Piano" for the first time in 1932, with the Boston Symphony Orchestra. While being composed it was often referred to as the "New York Rhapsody" or the "Manhattan Rhapsody."

Shelley: Percy Bysshe Shelley (1792–1822), English poet of the Romantic period.

44 The musician selected a Debussy ° nocturne. The others considered and approved. They rose to their knees to watch the Doctor prepare for the playing, so that they appeared to be actually in an attitude of worship. The peat glow showed the thinness of their bearded faces, and the deep lines in them, and revealed the condition of their garments. The other two continued to kneel as the old man carefully lowered the needle onto the spinning disk, but the musician suddenly drew back against the wall again, with his knees up, and buried his face in his hands.

45 At the first notes of the piano the listeners were startled. They stared at each other. Even the musician lifted his head in amazement, but then quickly bowed it again, strainingly, as if he were suffering from a pain he might not be able to endure. They were all listening deeply, without movement. The wet, blue-green notes tinkled forth from the old machine, and were individual, delectable * presences in the cell. The individual, delectable presences swept into a sudden tide of unbearably beautiful disso-nance,* and then continued fully the swelling and ebbing of that tide, the dissonant inpourings, and the resolutions, and the diminishments, and the little, quiet wavelets of interlude lapping between. Every sound was piercing and ˙ singularly sweet. In all the men except the musician, there occurred rapid sequences of tragically heightened recol-lection. He heard nothing but what was there. At the final, whispering disappearance, but moving quietly so that the others would not hear him and look at him, he let his head fall back in agony, as if it were drawn there by the hair, and clenched the fingers of one hand over his teeth. He sat that way while the others were silent, and until they began to breathe again normally. His drawn-up legs were trembling violently.

46 Quickly Doctor Jenkins lifted the needle off, to save it and not to spoil the recollection with scraping. When he

Debussy: Claude Debussy (1862–1918), French impressionist composer.

had stopped the whirling of the sacred disk, he courteously left the phonograph open and by the fire, in sight.

47 The others, however, understood. The musician rose last, but then abruptly, and went quickly out at the door without saying anything. The others stopped at the door and gave their thanks in low voices. The Doctor nodded magnificently.

48 "Come again," he invited, "in a week. We will have the 'New York.' "

49 When the two had gone together, out toward the rimed ° road, he stood in the entrance, peering and listening. At first, there was only the resonant * boom of the wind overhead, and then far over the dome of the dead, dark plain, the wolf cry lamenting. In the rifts of clouds the Doctor saw four stars flying. It impressed the Doctor that one of them had just been obscured by the beginning of a flying cloud at the very moment he heard what he had been listening for, a sound of suppressed coughing. It was not near-by, however. He believed that down against the pale alders he could see the moving shadow.

50 With nervous hands he lowered the pieces of canvas which served as his door, and pegged it at the bottom. Then quickly and quietly, looking at the piece of canvas frequently, he slipped the records into the case, snapped the lid shut, and carried the phonograph to his couch. There, pausing often to stare at the canvas and listen, he dug earth from the wall and disclosed a piece of board. Behind this there was a deep hole in the wall, into which he put the phonograph. After a moment's consideration, he went over and reached down his bundle of books and inserted it also. Then, guardedly, he once more sealed up the hole with the board and the earth. He also changed his blankets, and the grass-stuffed sack which served as a pillow, so that he could lie facing the entrance. After carefully placing two more blocks of peat upon the fire, he stood for a long time watching the stretched canvas, but it seemed to billow naturally with the first gusts of a lowering

rimed: covered with a rough, white ice, formed not by frost but by fog.

wind. At last he prayed, and got in under his blankets, and closed his smoke-smarting eyes. On the inside of the bed, next the wall, he could feel with his hand the comfortable piece of lead pipe.

ANALYSIS

Not every storyteller will want to begin with so over-powering a sense of *setting,* particulary when it is to be nameless. But the method Clark uses works beautifully for the theme he wants to expound. In a long, full opening paragraph we learn that "there was no structure or rem-nant of a structure visible over the dome of the darkling earth." The time is sunset, in autumn, and the cold night and a colder winter are approaching. How right that end of day and end of growing season should be the *time* of the story. The only sound is the rush of geese overhead and the howl of a prairie wolf. The only color is "a little red of fire" in "a sort of cell." The air smells of "poorly aged peat" making "acrid smoke." It is paragraph 4 before we meet living human beings.

Clark has set his stage meticulously. In fact, the story begins as though a curtain were rising slowly on a mam-moth, desolate stage and the audience were invited to contemplate empty shadows before hearing a man's voice. When the voice finally comes, it too is anonymous. We know him as "the host" at first. Later he is called Doctor Jenkins, the professor. He has been reading Shakespeare to "the other three." And who are they? In time we meet them as the writer, the musician, and the man with the unknown past. That is all we need to know. Clearly the story is about survival, not about these four men. The *point of emphasis* °is the theme or underlying meaning.

Clark works his theme into the action; he does not superimpose it on an incredible series of events. How believable it is that the professor should save the great works of human imagination (Dante, Shakespeare, Mel-

point of emphasis: See Glossary.

ville), that the phonograph should be portable (this idea was a happy invention on Clark's part), that the records should be played only once a week, that already Jenkins has learned how to substitute thorns for needles, that the musician should select Debussy, not Gershwin. These are homely but important details, and through them Clark is able to make powerful implications about the human spirit. But does he also suggest that the body will, in time, make its demands? And will these demands overpower the longings of the spirit?

Reread his solemn, frightening, last paragraph. We see Jenkins lower "the piece of canvas which served as his door and [peg] it at the bottom." But man can endure cold. What are his greater fears? Jenkins works with "nervous" hands. He "quickly and quietly" slips the records into the case. He pauses to stare and listen. He "guardedly" seals up the hole. He changes his blankets to "lie facing the entrance." For a long time he stands "watching the stretched canvas." Then comes the final sentence, even more effective than Katherine Mansfield's "She thought she heard something crying."

Clark recalls (see his essay in the *Pacific Spectator,* Summer, 1949) that "that sentence plucked the proper closing note, one that might linger for a time with a tenuous but moving reminder of the whole intention. If so, it was so, happily, by means of the very last phrase, and particularly by means of the one word 'comfortable.' Nothing in the phrase was considered, not 'comfortable' any more than the rest, but even as it came, that 'comfortable' tickled me, not so much because of its immediate implication, in which the paradox was clear enough, as for some remote, redoubling connotation.°"

Here we have it all said, and in the author's own words. The last sentence is a "moving reminder of the whole intention"; the theme of the story, *survival,* is summed up in five words. The adjective is a paradox; Jenkins is anything

connotation: See Glossary.

but comfortable, having just closed "his smoke-smarting eyes." But Clark and the careful reader sense "some more remote, redoubling connotation." Clark tells us he borrowed the word, unconsciously, from *Romeo and Juliet:* "Remember how Juliet, waking in the tomb, and not yet aware that Romeo is dead, murmurs drowsily to the gentle Friar Lawrence, 'Oh, comfortable Friar—'?" Most of us will not remember. But our imaginations *will* go to work on why Jenkins finds his lead pipe "comfortable," what connotations surround the word. Survival implies self-preservation. Does self-preservation imply fighting for protection? Against wild animals? Against one's neighbors? But fighting one's neighbors is war, and war has just brought Jenkins to this low state. Will we never learn? Is our fate on this earth not struggle for food or warmth but struggle to master our own destructive passions?

Questions on Content

1. What specific indications of war (now past) does Clark give us in paragraph 1?
2. What book has Jenkins been reading from? Does the choice of the specific play tell us anything about the situation?
3. Does the musician listen to Debussy in the same way as all the other men? What makes him different?
4. Why does Jenkins use a real needle instead of a thorn for the playing of Debussy?

Add to Your Vocabulary

rakish, delectable, dissonance, resonant.

Questions on Technique

1. Clark could have begun his story with Doctor Jenkins's taking out his books in anticipation of the arrival of guests. Why do you think he sets the stage first?
2. In paragraph 4, what effect does Clark wish to achieve with adjectives like "smoldering" peat, "dirty" army

blankets, "tin" utensils, "daubed" burlap, "grass-woven" cord, and the like?

3. In paragraph 10, we learn that there is no paper to write on. How do you react to this simple fact? Does this sentence, like "comfortable lead pipe," also have connotations? Is it connected with using thorns for needles?

4. What irony lies behind the sentence (paragraph 32), "It was difficult to select from such a wealth. . . ."? Are twelve records "wealth"?

5. In paragraph 49, what use does Clark make of "a sound of suppressed coughing" and a "moving shadow"?

Techniques to Imitate

Imagining narrative details

Unless they are describing their own experiences exactly as they happened, writers must draw constantly on their imaginations. In describing places they have not seen, characters they have not met, and actions that never occurred, they must be able to imagine all the details necessary to depict these things convincingly. Supplying narrative details is a major part of the art of story writing.

In writing a story about events that obviously had never happened, Clark shows how expert he is in this aspect of fiction. Some examples will make clear what we mean by imagined narrative details. In his description of the barren landscape after the final war, Clark says, "Out of the sunset, through the dead, matted grass and isolated weed stalks of the prairie, crept the narrow and deeply rutted remains of a road. In the road, in places, there were crusts of shallow, brittle ice. There were little islands of an old oiled pavement in the road too, but most of it was mud, now frozen rigid." Many of us, imagining such a scene, might have envisioned the dead matted grass and weed stalks and the rutted road, but the "little islands of an old oiled pavement" is a masterful detail that we recognize as being just right.

In his description of the men sitting in the cell, Clark

shows his keen eye for detail when he says, "Behind them, traversed by their shadows, was the earth bench." Probably only a writer as skillful as Clark would see these shadows as he imagines the scene. When the old man reaches out to put another block of peat on the fire, Clark has him "groaning at the movement," a detail that suggests clearly his weakened condition. The young man speaks "anxiously between suppressed coughs." To the men, the portable phonograph is an almost miraculous symbol of a lost world, and Clark adds significant details: "He smoothed the top with his hand, and then opened it. The lovely green-felt-covered disk became visible." As the doctor prepares for the playing, Clark imagines the men rising to their knees to watch "so that they appeared to be actually in an attitude of worship."

Not all imagined narrative details are descriptive. For example, note how carefully Clark has imagined the effect of the first notes. "At the first notes of the piano the listeners were startled. They stared at each other. Even the musician lifted his head in amazement. . . ." And when the record is finished, Clark imagines the doctor lifting the needle quickly, "to save it and not to spoil the recollection with scraping." You can find many other examples in this story of perfectly imagined narrative details.

While it is not possible to write any fiction without narrative detail, good fiction contains most carefully, most keenly imagined details. The reader responds in recognition, as though saying, "Yes, that's just the way it would be." In your own narrative writing make sure to give your imagination time to figure out exactly "the way it would be."

Suggestions for Writing

1. Rewrite this story for experience in creating dialogue. Open it with Jenkins talking to the other men. Cut description to a minimum. Try to convey the feeling of desolation through the conversation.
2. From your own experience, build a narrative, in 600 words, around a special place: a cabin in the woods,

a camp site, a beach house, a hotel room, your home. Make the description of *place* the major aspect of the story.

3. Stretch your imagination. *You* have just landed on a distant planet, the first person from Earth to have done so. Describe in the first person all you see, and tell what happens, including narrative details.

4. Many stories are based on the theme of survival after a major catastrophe. Some of these stories end with renewal; some end tragically as Clark's does, with little if any hope in sight. (You might recall the account of Deucalion and the flood in Greek mythology.) Write your own narrative based on the theme of survival. Whether your plot will end with renewal or tragedy is up to you. Perhaps your ideas of what life would be like after a holocaust are different from Clark's. For example, how would the experience of these survivors be different if they were in the ruins of a large city?

GLOSSARY

Analogy. A comparison made between two things (because of some point or points held in common); sometimes called an extended comparison. For example, an analogy is often made between sleep and death because both states exhibit passivity and seeming serenity. Analogies can be made between the heart and a pump, between the eyes of a person and the windows of a house, and so on.

Caricature. A picture or description characterized by gross exaggeration or distortion.

Cliché. A stale, worn-out phrase or idea; for example, "accidents will happen" or "easy come, easy go" or "last but not least."

Climax. The decisive point or culmination of an argument or an action. The term *anticlimax* refers to arguments or actions which are of less importance than the climax which precedes them.

Coherence. The continuity or logical flow from one idea or event to another in a composition; the interrelation of the various parts of a composition and of the ideas within those parts.

Colloquialism. An expression characteristic of informal speech and writing; for example, "He's done a *bang-up* job" or "Early that morning we *hit the road*."

Connotation. The suggestions or associations, often emotional, aroused by a word beyond its dictionary definition. "Politician" connotes someone who is pragmatic, self-interested, and opportunistic. "Statesman" connotes someone who is wise and skilled in the art of government.

Denotation. The primary or dictionary definition of a word, as opposed to its connotations or associated meanings.

Diction. The writer's choice of words or mode of expression.

Emphasis. The arrangement of the various elements of a composition in an order best calculated to make the reader aware of, and sympathetic to, the writer's purpose.

Epithet. A descriptive word or phrase modifying or taking the place of the name of a thing or person. For example, Homer refers to the ocean as the *"wine-dark* sea" and to the dawn as *"rosy-fingered* dawn." A descriptive title like "Catherine *the Great"* is an epithet. Frequently, epithets are negative in their connotation: "egghead" or "big shot."

Figurative language. Language used imaginatively, not in a strict literal sense. Three common figures of speech are *Metaphor, Simile, Hyperbole,* and *Personification.*

Hyperbole. A figure of speech based on exaggeration: "mountainous waves" or "millions of friends."

Idiom. A form of expression or construction peculiar to a language, approved by usage, and sometimes having a meaning other than its grammatical or logical one; for example, "She *carried out* her assignment" or "When you come to town, please *drop in.*"

Imagery. The verbal description of any sense experience; not merely sights, but also sounds, smells, and textures.

Irony. A mode of expression which involves a contrast between what is said or stated and what is suggested or understood. Ironic statements say one thing and imply the opposite. An example is Antony's repeated statement, "Brutus is an honorable man," in his famous oration in *Julius Caesar*. Irony sometimes employs *Understatement* (saying less than the situation warrants, such as describing a hurricane as a small shower) or *Paradox* (saying something that is seemingly contradictory or opposed to common sense but which, on examination, turns out to be true, such as "wasteful efficiency"). A situation is called ironic when an event occurs that turns out to be exactly the opposite of what was expected.

Metaphor. An identification made between essentially unlike things; for example, "His mind is an unweeded garden" or "Jealousy is a green-eyed monster."

Objective. An *objective* treatment of a subject implies a certain detachment on the writer's part. Writers who are objective are not likely to reveal their personal feelings in their writings. A *subjective* treatment, on the contrary, implies that the material is highly colored by the writer's feelings, impressions, memory, opinions. Purely objective or subjective writing is, of course, rare.

Paradox. See *Irony*.

Pathos. A sense of pity or sympathetic sorrow. When a writer tries to elicit pathos from a situation or character that does not legitimately call for this reaction, we call the effect *bathos*.

Personification. Attributing human characteristics to inanimate objects or abstract ideas; for example, "The land shows its ravaged face" or "The streets wander aimlessly about."

Plot. The sequence, plan, or structure which the writer chooses in arranging the events of a narrative.

Point of emphasis. The writer's primary motive for writing; for example, to relate a chain of events, to describe a character or place, to stress a theme, or to propound a moral.

Point of view. The relationship of the narrator to the story being told. The simplest method is *first person,* or personal point of view: the narrator tells his or her own story. This first-person narrator might be the main character of the story or merely an observer of the action. The other point of view is *third person:* a third-person narrator might be omniscient and tell us what all the characters feel and think and interpret all their behavior, or the third-person narrator might choose to tell the story from the point of view of only one character.

Sarcasm. Harsh or taunting remarks, expressing contempt, usually ironical.

Satire. A method of writing in which vices and abuses are held up for ridicule. Satirists generally wish to correct that which they mock. In the course of writing satire, a writer may use *Irony* or *Sarcasm.*

Semantics. The study of the meanings of words, of changes of meanings, and of human responses to meanings.

Setting. The place or locale of a story.

Simile. An explicit comparison made between two essentially unlike things, introduced by *like* or *as;* for example, "Her skin was as soft as a cloud" or "She had a voice like the north wind in January."

Style. A writer's distinctive mode of expression, that which marks a work with individual characteristics. A writer might be known for a terse style (exceedingly clear and concise) or for an ornate style (excessively embellished with figures of speech), and so on.

Subjective. See *Objective.*

Symbol. An object or character which *stands for* something else; a material object representing something immaterial; an emblem, token, or sign. In chemistry, Cl stands for chlorine; in mathematics ∞ stands for infinity. In art and literature, white is often a symbol of purity or innocence; the serpent is often a symbol of evil or Satan or temptation; the lamb is often a symbol of innocence; and so on.

Theme. The main or central point of a composition. The

theme unites a composition, just as the topic sentence unites a paragraph.

Tone. The writer's attitude toward the subject matter. Tone can be conveyed by choice of words and by selection of details. A writer's tone may be flippant, or affectionate, or formal, for example.

Topic sentence. The sentence in the paragraph, often the first, which announces or summarizes the subject of the paragraph.

Understatement. See *Irony*.

Unity. The consistent relationship of all the elements of a composition to its central theme. To achieve unity, a writer must have (1) a clearly defined purpose, and (2) an orderly means of achieving that purpose.

STYLE SHEETS
Capitalization

Mexico City—a city in Mexico
Ocala National Forest—our national forests
Twenty-ninth Street—across the street
the South—a mile south
North America—northern Wisconsin
the Explorers' Club—a club for explorers
Ford Motor Company—an automobile company
Central High School—a new high school
Pomona College—four years in college
the American Revolution—a successful revolution
the Wrigley Building—a Chicago building
the Fourth of July—the fifth of July
the Freshman Class—freshman classes
English, French, Latin—social studies, physics, art
History II—a course in world history
spring, summer, winter, fall
Principal Langley—Mr. Langley, the principal
the President (U.S.)—the president of our club
God made His will known—ancient gods of the Greeks
Don't tell Mother (or mother)—Don't tell my mother
Ivory soap
the Democratic party
a Presbyterian, a Swede
<u>The Last of the Mohicans</u>, the <u>Reader's Digest</u>

Comma

Fran, Harry, and Joe   or   Fran, Harry and Joe
Fran and Harry and Joe
A tall, thin, emaciated man
A tall, thin young man
My sister Elsa, a freshman at Cornell, went . . .
I knew, therefore, that she was right.
I therefore knew that she was right.
Address me at 22 Oak Road, Akron, Ohio 44313, after May 10.
A student who is late must stay after school.
John, who was late, must stay after school.
When the weather is bad, we practice indoors.
We practice indoors when the weather is bad.
Sensing the danger, the dog barked.
They offered to help, but they did not show up.
They offered to help but did not show up.

Semicolon

The football team won all but two games; one of these was a tie.
Each student takes several standardized tests; for example, the DAT, STEP, SAT, and ACE.
The delegates were Carol Woodson, High School of Commerce; Randall Howe, Technical Trade School; and Ellen Glaeser, Classical Senior High School.

Colon

They asked me to bring the following items: flashlight, raincoat, blanket, and matches.

Apostrophe

It's late.	men's clothing
I like its lines.	a girl's coat
The car is hers.	two girls' coats
Let's go!	Ulysses' pen
a man's hat	Hughes' poem or Hughes's poem

Hyphen

dem-on-strate (not demonstr-ate)
com-mand, hap-py
will-ing, at-ten-tion
thirty-three students
a two-thirds majority
two thirds of the students
a second-story room
a room in the second story

Italics and Quotation Marks

(In manuscript form, underlining a word indicates that the word should be in italics.)

A Tale of Two Cities (book)
Newsweek (magazine)
the Evening Bulletin
"Casey at the Bat" (poem)
"The Devil and Daniel Webster" (story)
Mother said, "You may drive."
Mother said I might drive.
"Drive carefully," he warned. "Speed causes accidents."
"Drive carefully," he warned, "because speed causes accidents."
"We won!" Jan shouted. "Did you hear Lyn say, 'We won!' ?"

Correction Symbols

cap	error in capitalization	**k**	awkward sentence
p	error in punctuation	**nc**	not clear
sp	error in spelling	**rs**	run-on sentence
frag	sentence fragment	**gr**	error in grammar
ss	error in sentence	**w**	error in word choice
	structure	**¶**	Begin a new paragraph.
ref	unclear or incorrect	**t**	error in tense
	reference of pronoun	**∧**	Something is omitted.

The errors **sp, ss, k, nc** should be rewritten on a separate correction sheet attached to the composition, or, if there is space, on the final page of the composition. Each error requiring rewriting should be numbered in the margin of the composition and marked with the same number on the correction sheet. Errors which do not require rewriting a whole sentence should be corrected on the composition at the place where the error occurs.

Example of Symbols in Margin of a Composition

p	A repertory company, with it's com-
gr	mand of a number of plays, are quite
sp	different from a cast which preforms
	only one play for a run and then breaks
cap	up. The usual company on broadway con-
	sists of actors brought together to pro-
w, ref	duce one (thing.) If (it) is a success, the
	actors repeat the same roles night after
p	night. A repertory company on the other
r s	hand produces a number of plays, it may
	produce three or four different plays
frag	in the course of one week. Each actor
	thus playing a different role each night.
k	At any time a repertory company is able to revive an old play with as many as twenty-five plays in its repertoire.

nc The parts are all ready and the scenery, properties, and costumes.

Passage Corrected by the Student

p A repertory company, with it's com-

gr mand of a number of plays, ~~are~~ *is* quite

sp different from a cast which ~~preforms~~ *performs*

only one play for a run and then breaks

cap up. The usual company on Broadway con-

sists of actors brought together to pro-

w; ref duce one ~~thing~~ *play* If ~~it~~ *the play* is a success, the

actors repeat the same roles night after

p night. A repertory company, on the other

r s hand, produces a number of plays. *I*t may

produce three or four different plays

in the course of one week, *E*ach actor

frag thus playing a different role each night.

① *k* At any time a repertory company is able to revive an old play with as many as twenty-five plays in its repertoire.

② *nc* The parts are all ready and the scenery, properties, and costumes.

Correction Sheet

① A repertory company, with as many as twenty-five plays in its repertoire, is able to revive an old play at any time.

② The actors are familiar with their parts, and the scenery, properties, and costumes are ready in the company's storeroom.

INDEX

"Aaron Hits 715th, Passes Babe Ruth," 215
Action, 154
Adjectives, 20, 56, 99
Altick, Richard D., 168
Analogy, 343
Analyses, 208
Anecdotes, 408
Angelou, Maya, 60
Answering questions, 389
"Araby," 530
" 'Araby': An Interpretation," 383
ARGUMENT AND PERSUASION, 437
Baldwin, Hanson W., 135
Baldwin, James, 336
"Between Two Extremes," 440
Bias, 263
"Bird and the Machine, The," 297
"Bird of Freedom," 100
Brooks, Cleanth, 383
Campbell, Joseph, 417
Carpenter, Scott, 219
"Celestial Navigation by Birds," 195
Characterization, 552, 575, 581, 583
"Chee's Daughter," 555
Ciardi, John, 357

Circumlocutions, 171
Clarity, 268
Clark, Walter Van Tilburg, 586
Clarke, Arthur C., 270
Clichés, 171
Colloquial language, 29
Colloquial style, 235
Connotation, 371
"Creative Process, The," 336
Critical essay, 310, 345
"Dark of the Moon, The," 311
"Dawn over Zero," 237
Definition, 160
Definition of terms in argument, 489
Denotation, 371
DESCRIPTION, 7
Description in narration, 537
Details, 8, 20, 31, 47, 86, 98, 572, 598
Diction, 581
Dictionary Entries, Two, 161
Digressions, 398, 399
Durso, Joseph, 215
Eiseley, Loren G., 297
Elaboration, 278
Encyclopedia Entry, An, 163
Evidence, 522
Exaggeration, 79, 433
Examples, supporting state-

ments with, 415, 469

Explaining difficult concepts, 281

EXPOSITION, 157

Facing opposing views, 324

Feeling, 47

Figurative language, 69, 133

"First Observations," 89

First-person point of view, 527, 530

Fowler's *Modern English Usage,* An Entry in, 164

Framework, 508

Frost, Robert, 358

"Future of Man, The," 316

"Girls' Liberation," 374

"Great Secret, The," 219

Haley, Alex, 283

Hayakawa, S. I., 250

Honesty, 268

"How to Name a Dog," 392

Humor, 80

"I Know Why the Caged Bird Sings," 60

"I Remember . . .," 410

Incongruous, the, 80

Inferences, 253, 266

Informal essay, 391

Interest, arousing, 281

"Invisible Death," 511

Jargon, 171

Judgments, 256, 260, 266

"Kilimanjaro!," 117

Knowing your subject, 115, 355

Krutch, Joseph Wood, 478

"Language of Reports, The," 250

Laurence, William L., 237

Lee, Laurie, 23

Lists, 415

Literary criticism, 345

Literary style, 248

"Living with the Natives of Melanesia," 181

"Lone Sailor Is Back, Recounts Perils," 210

"Loud Sneer for Our Feathered Friends, A," 49

"*Macbeth:* An Afterword," 346

McKenney, Ruth, 49

Mansfield, Katherine, 575

Markham, Harley B., 492, 500

Matthes, Gerard H., 172

Maynard, Joyce, 410

Mead, Margaret, 181

Metaphor, 69, 133, 333, 358

Miller, Siyowin, 555

"Miss Brill," 575

Mock-seriousness, 433

Mood, 47

"Moon Walk, The," 417

"Mythology Today," 456

NARRATION, 525

Narration in description, 131

Narration in exposition, 308

Neuberger, Richard L., 492, 494

New Yorker, The, 473

"Newspaperese," 168

Non sequiturs, 506

Nouns, 99

Objective experience, 82

Omniscient point of view, 528

Organization, 46, 203, 470, 519

"Outdoor Advertising: Two Points of View," 492

Outline, 370

Overstatement, 80

Personal point of view, 528

PERSUASION, ARGUMENT AND, 437

Phillips, McCandlish, 210

Plain style, 295
Platero, Juanita, 555
Plot, 526, 570
Pogrebin, Letty C., 374
Point of emphasis, 529, 595
Point of view, 527
"Portable Phonograph, The," 586
Priestley, J. B., 346
Process, 180
"Professions for Women," 327
Purr-words, 258, 267
"Quicksand," 172
Quoting other writers, 424
"R.M.S. *Titanic*," 135
"Report in Spring, A," 401
Reports, 208
"Robert Frost: The Way to the Poem," 357
Sancton, Thomas, 34
Satire, 432, 435
Sauer, E. G. F., 195
Schrank, Jeffrey, 456
"Science and the Humanities," 478
"Science Has Spolied My Supper," 444
"Search for an Ancestor," 283
"Secret of the Sun, The," 270
Sensory impressions, 9, 31, 98, 158, 406
Series, 415
Setting, 527, 595
Sevareid, Eric, 311
"Silver Horn, The," 34
Simile, 69, 133, 358
Slanting, 261, 267
Snarl-words, 258, 267
Snow, C. P., 316
Staccato style, 131, 154
Startling fact, the, 281
Steinbeck, John, 82
"Stopping by Woods on a

Snowy Evening," 358
Structure, 314
Style, adapting to purpose, 177
Subjective experience, 12
Supporting evidence, 355, 469
Symbol, 358
Teale, Edwin Way, 100
Tense, 153, 406
Theme, 529, 586, 595
Third-person point of view, 528, 541
"Three Boys," 12
Thurber, James, 70, 392
Tone, 58
Train of thought, 334, 372
Transitions, 205
Turner, Joseph, 440
"Turtle, The," 82
"Two Stories," 473
Ullman, James Ramsey, 117
Understatement, 232
"University Days," 70
Updike, John, 12
Van Fleet, Clark C., 511
van Lawick-Goodall, Jane, 89
Verbs, 20, 56, 99
"Verel Modacrylic and Mr. Inside Floormat," 425
Verifiability, 251, 265
Vigorous style, 454
Warren, Robert Penn, 383
Weak passive, 171
Welty, Eudora, 541
"What Is America For?," 494
"What's All the Shouting About?," 500
White, E. B., 401
"Winter Treat, A," 23
Woolf, Virginia, 327
Word selection, 20, 406
"Worn Path, A," 541
Wylie, Philip, 444
Zinsser, William K., 425

B 7
C 8
D 9
E 0
F 1
G 2
H 3
I 4
J 5